Flight of the Gods

PERSPECTIVES IN CONTINENTAL PHILOSOPHY
John D. Caputo, Series Editor

Flight of the Gods

PHILOSOPHICAL PERSPECTIVES ON NEGATIVE THEOLOGY

Edited by

ILSE N. BULHOF *and* LAURENS TEN KATE

Fordham University Press
New York
2000

This volume is an entirely reworked and augmented edition of Ilse N. Bulhof and
Laurens ten Kate, eds., *Ons ontbreken heilige namen: Negatieve theologic in de
hedendaagse cultuurfilosofie* (Kampen, The Netherlands: Kok Agora, 1992).
Publication was made possible in part by the support of the Catholic
Theological University of Ultrecht, The Netherlands, and of the
Radbond Foundation in The Netherlands.

The authors are grateful to the *Journal of the History of Philosophy* for
the permission to reprint J.-L. Marion's article "Is the Ontological
Argument Ontological?"

Translation by Catherine Vanhoven-Romanik. Translation of
"Zarathustra's Yes and Woe" by Dirk de Schutter.

Perspectives in Continental Philosophy Series, No. 11
ISSN 1089–3938

Library of Congress Cataloging-in-Publication Data

Ons ontbreken heilige namen. English.
    Flight of the gods : philosophical perspectives on negative theology / edited by
Ilse N. Bulhof and Laurens ten Kate.—1st ed.
        p.   cm.—(Perspectives in continental philosophy ; no. 11)
    Rev. papers presented at a conference held in 1990 at the International School
for Philosophy, Leusden-Zuid, Netherlands
    Includes bibliographical references (p.   ) and indexes.
    ISBN 0-8232-2034-6 (hardcover)—ISBN 0-8232-2035-4 (pbk.)
    1. Death of God theology.   2. Theology—History—20th century.   3.
Culture—Philosophy—History—20th century.   I. Bulhof, Ilse Nina.   II. Kate,
Laurens ten, 1958–   . III. Title.   IV. Series.
BT83.5 O5713   2000
231′.042—dc21   00-055151

Printed in the United States of America
00 01 02 03 04 5 4 3 2 1
First Edition

CONTENTS

PREFACE

Ilse N. Bulhof and Laurens ten Kate

> The question concerns neither dogmatics nor any articles
> of faith. The question is simply, whether God has fled
> from us or not, and whether we are still able to experience
> this flight truly and creatively.
>
> Martin Heidegger*

VANTAGE POINT OF THIS BOOK

CONTEMPORARY CONTINENTAL PHILOSOPHY approaches metaphysics
with great reservation. A point of criticism concerns traditional focuses on philosophical speaking about God. Whereas Nietzsche,
with his question "God is dead; who killed Him?," was, in his time,
highly shocking and 'unzeitgemäß,' the twentieth century, in contrast, saw Heidegger's concept of 'onto-theology' quickly become a
famous term. This concept expresses a critical attitude toward the
God of the philosophers who is only to be conceived of according to
the logic of Being. In Heidegger's words, to such a God we can neither pray nor kneel. He did not, however, return to the God of the
Christian faith, but tried to initiate a new philosophical way of
speaking about God—a way that also reveals the limits of philosophical discourse. Thinkers like Derrida, Marion, Bataille, Adorno,
Taubes, and Bakhtin, each in their own way, continue the explora-
tion begun by Nietzsche and Heidegger. It is striking that what once
belonged to the traditional domain of philosophical theology now
finds new life among these contemporary thinkers in the form of
cultural philosophical reflections.

The authors of this book take a fresh look at these developments,

---

* *Mein bisheriger Weg* (1937/38; *Gesamtausgabe* 66, 415. (Editor's translation.)

and try to reach their own view. The 'death of God,' as the editors
note in the Introduction, announces not only the death of the 'old
god'—the god of philosophers, theologians, and believers—but also
the death of the modern god who set himself on his own throne:
autonomous human reason. With the death of this 'new god,' might
a sensitivity reappear for transcendence, for difference, for the sacred, for negation, in short, for religion? Or will religion return to us
on its own terms, whether we want it or not? In listening to the
reactions to this dethronement of autonomous reason, the editors
believe they hear echoes of an experience of embarrassment rooting
partly in an old tradition: negative theology. The editors present this
book as a platform for investigating this embarrassment.

In the first three texts, the history of negative theology in the
Middle Ages and the possible rediscovery of this history in our time
are discussed. Thinkers such as Dionysius the Areopagite, Eckhart,
and John of the Cross, whom the first chapter treats, and Anselm of
Canterbury and Thomas Aquinas, to whom the second and third
chapters are devoted, will be central to this discussion. The following
chapters study the question of whether aspects of this tradition can
be found in modern authors like Kant, Nietzsche, Heidegger, Marion, Levinas, Derrida, Barth, Eco, Bataille, Blanchot, Nancy, Foucault, Adorno, Taubes, and Bakhtin. A short phenomenological
reflection on the specific experience of faith and an Epilogue conclude the book.

THE ARTICLES

The first series starts with a contribution by Bert Blans (Chapter 1).
Blans reviews several well-known names from the tradition of negative theology (Dionysius the Areopagite, Eckhart, John of the Cross).
He shows how their work can have a contemporary meaning by high-
lighting the debate between thinking on unity and thinking on exteriority; Emmanuel Levinas and Jacques Derrida serve as points for
comparison.

Jean-Luc Marion (Chapter 2) focuses on the work of Anselm of
Canterbury and stresses his famous, but equally enigmatic 'proof of
God.' This proof is nearly always seen, especially since Kant's inter-

pretation of it,[1] as Anselm's attempt to think of God as the funda-
ment of Being: God would then be reduced to the abstract concept
of a Highest Being, to "something such that anything greater than it
cannot be thought." Marion, however, shows that Anselm's speaking
about God leans more toward the tradition of negative theology
since it opposes the metaphysical identification of God with a concept of Being. Kant's criticism of the proof of God rests on a misunderstanding, for "God's existence is demonstrated, but without any
claim to having a concept of His essence. . . ."

Jozef Wissink (Chapter 3) describes how elements of negative theology are at work in Thomas Aquinas's systematic works, and how
this encourages a redefinition and revaluation of Thomas's work,
which for centuries has been the basis of the teachings of the Catholic Church. Wissink uses the work of two contemporary theologians[2]
to provide a contrast with and a perspective on Thomas's position.

The ensuing chapters start with a study on Friedrich Nietzsche by
Dirk de Schutter (Chapter 4). As the editors note in their Introduction, the former's philosophy opened the "space" in which the twentieth-century search for a new way to speak about God takes place.
Nietzsche's proclamation of the death of God is an attempt to dis-
mantle theology and morality as it had developed within traditional
nineteenth-century Christianity. In the place of the Christian idea of
meaningful suffering, Nietzsche posits a suffering without a higher
meaning or cause. His Dionysian philosophy affirms in a new way
ancient concepts such as 'good news,' 'creatio ex nihilo,' and 'incarnation.' De Schutter shows how Nietzsche's criticism takes the shape
of a *parody* in which, surprisingly, we hear themes resonate from
Eckhart's negative theology and the lyricism of Paul Celan. The author also draws a line from Nietzsche's parodic thinking to Heidegger's critical analysis of 'onto-theology.'

Among contemporary thinkers influenced by Nietzsche and Heidegger, who in their own way follow in their footsteps, are Derrida,
Jean-Luc Marion, and Georges Bataille.

Marion directly resumes the negative theology developed in the
Christian tradition but lost in modern times. Victor Kal (Chapter 5)
outlines how Marion reaches a theology of *distance*, a distance that

---

[1] Kant rejects Anselm's 'argument' because he believes it is ontological.
[2] Karl Barth and the Dutch theologian/ethicist Harry Kuitert.

must be eternally "walked through" and in which we must abandon all idols and concepts, even our metaphysical-religious images of God. Kal emphasizes Heidegger's influence on Marion's work and brings him into a discussion with two exponents of contemporary French philosophy: Derrida and Levinas.

Although Derrida admits to feeling a certain affinity for negative theology, he, unlike Marion, dissociates himself from its Greek-metaphysical and Christian content. Derrida's intense attempts to deconstruct and rearticulate the inheritance of negative theology result in his playing a central role in this book; three chapters are devoted to his work. Hent de Vries (Chapter 6) shows that Derrida is done an injustice by those who would label him a neostructuralist, and argues that Derrida cannot be completely understood when studied either only against the background of Jewish tradition or only against that of negative theology. De Vries shows how the paths of deconstruction and negative theology cross and where they diverge. Ilse Bulhof (Chapter 7) contrasts negative theology to nominalism as described in Umberto Eco's novel *The Name of the Rose*. In her view Derrida can be better understood against the background of negative theology than that of nominalism. But Derrida's resumption of negative theology bears a totally unique stamp: in his work we find more a performance *of*, rather than a presentation *about*, a transcendence which, like the '*khora*' in Plato's dialogue *Timaeus*, 'is' nothing, has nothing unique, cannot be put into words, and is open to all names without ever coinciding with any. Rico Sneller (Chapter 8) confronts Derrida's treatment of negative theology with the work of the theologian Karl Barth, specifically with his explanation of Paul's Epistle to the Romans. He 'organizes' this discussion by using Derrida's commentaries on Levinas's thinking.

According to Laurens ten Kate (Chapter 9), the French writer, philosopher, and theoretician Georges Bataille points to the impossibility of escaping the questions posed by negative theology; the *problem* of negative theology lies at the heart of modernity: How do we react to the emptiness that God's disappearance, His death, has left behind? Is it possible to speak about God, however negatively? Perhaps in raising these questions and in recognizing their unanswerableness, this speaking has already begun—without the promise of an answer, but as the (always uncertain) answer to the promise. Ten Kate outlines the way in which Bataille's "atheology" uncovers how the experience of the death of God—strangely enough—might be the only *sacred* experience left to modern culture: an "inner experience," as Bataille calls it, that is both our poverty and our "opportunity." He explains Bataille's thinking against the background of two contemporary French thinkers who, critically and from a distant nearness, have continued along his path: Michel Foucault and Jean-Luc Nancy.

Even the title, *Negative Dialectics*, of the last great work by the philosopher Theodor Adorno makes us think of negative theology. Gerrit Steunebrink (Chapter 10) compares the ideas of negative theology with Adorno's thesis on *utopia* as a radical surpassing and denial of what is: the existing unjust world, source of his *"unausdenkbare Verzweiflung* (unthinkable despair)." According to Steunebrink, the expected utopia as Adorno sees it is not the expected Messiah, nor the expected Kingdom of God. Although this utopia is a kingdom without God, a gift without giver, people are nevertheless unable to bring it about by themselves. The author contrasts Adorno's inner conflict beween hope and despair with Kant's trust in God and his belief that history will finally come to a good end.

In a completely different way Marin Terpstra and Theo de Wit (Chapter 11) find echoes of negative theology in the work of a thinker who, like Adorno, is of Jewish origin: Jacob Taubes. Taubes developed a 'negative political theology.' The authors confront Taubes's project with the thought of Carl Schmitt, with whom Taubes maintained an intriguing contact; Schmitt's writings are an emotional plea for a *positive* political theology in which political power is a representative of religious, 'theological' authority. Taubes, in his own political theology, replaces an appropriation of the future (the 'Eschaton') by worldly powers with an attitude of detachment and a refusal to "invest" an ultimately spiritual authority in the political world. This attitude is nourished by a messianic expectation that calls for preparedness for the end, the coming of the Messiah.

In twentieth-century Russia—a country that belongs to Orthodox culture, in which apophatic (negative) theology has played an important role over the centuries—amid the terror of communism, there was an echo of negative theology: the work of the philosopher and literary theoretician Mikhail Bakhtin. Anton Simons (Chapter 12) shows how Bakhtin seeks links with negative theology within the

context of a violent situation: Stalinism. Bakhtin feels himself compelled to articulate an ethic of justice and responsibility, but his
problem is that the need to speak about violence and injustice collides with the impossibility of the 'correct' word. This impasse leads
Bakhtin to his ideas on *dialogue* as an eternal, an unending, *polyph-
ony* that neither can nor may cease and that involves people in the
absence of every "last word." This absence itself is the "last word"
to be heard in modern culture. Bakhtin thus rejects pure silence—
but, as a consequence, his own silence on the situation in which he
works and lives becomes problematic.

The book closes with an existential-phenomenological reflection
by Paul Moyaert (Chapter 13). He presents the experience of embarrassment in negative theology as an experience of faith that may well
belong to our times. Moyaert thinks a form of negative theology may
be the only possible theology left us: a form of reflection in which
faith is maintained *despite knowing better*, a form based on a fundamental attitude of trust for which no reason can be given. We can
no longer, like Dionysius, maintain a negative theology while continuing to hold on to the idea that all of creation witnesses to God. For
modern people, reacting to God's transcendence means *surviving* the
silence He has left behind. We observe a modern 'relationship' to
God when we think of the image of the lover who trusts the beloved
as long as possible, to the extreme, whatever she or he does. This
relationship consists in the absence of every guarantee. A modern
faith can only be a "groundless," empty faith.

Genesis

The research that led to this book arose in the framework of the
Research Program in Cultural Philosophy sponsored by the Depart-
ment of Philosophy and Ethics, at the Catholic Theological Univer-
sity of Utrecht. In 1990 a conference was held, in conjunction with
the then 'Subjectivity, Rationality, and Normativity' Network, at the
International School for Philosophy in Leusden, The Netherlands.
Papers presented at this conference were later published in Ilse N.
Bulhof and Laurens ten Kate, eds., *Ons ontbreken heilige namen*
(Holy names are lacking; Kampen: Kok, 1992). During a visit to The
Netherlands in 1993, Professor John D. Caputo, of the Department

of Philosophy, Villanova University, in Pennsylvania, expressed interest in the book's themes. He proposed an English-language edition. The editors then decided to thoroughly rework the Dutch version for this English edition: new articles were added, a few of the original articles were dropped, and all the other articles were rewritten to a greater or lesser degree. Those who have worked on this new book are honored that Fordham University Press is willing to publish it in its series *Perspectives in Continental Philosophy*. They express their thanks to Professor Caputo for his initiative and mediation, and hope that *Flight of the Gods: Philosophical Perspectives on Negative Theology* will contribute to a fruitful intercontinental exchange of research and ideas.

The editors wish to thank the Catholic Theological University of Utrecht, in particular the Department of Philosophy and Ethics, which offered the intellectual and organizational room that made this project possible. This is especially true of Professor Dr. Peter Jonkers, chairman of the research group. We also want to thank Professor Theo Zweerman for his long involvement with this book's content. Finally, our thanks go to Catherine Vanhove-Romanik, STL, who undertook the not inconsiderable task of translating nearly all the texts.

Flight of the Gods

Echoes of an Embarrassment
PHILOSOPHICAL PERSPECTIVES ON NEGATIVE THEOLOGY—AN INTRODUCTION

Ilse N. Bulhof and Laurens ten Kate

How many know how to be silent!
How many *know* only what being silent is!

Kierkegaard[1]

1. NIETZSCHE'S QUESTION: A PREAMBLE

IN 1882 FRIEDRICH NIETZSCHE published a parable that became famous after his death. He depicts a madman who leaps about the marketplace proclaiming the 'death of God' to astonished onlookers.[2] From the night of modern culture this madman enters the public arena, lights a lamp in full daylight, and calls out "I seek God!" He immediately recognizes the futility of his search and then announces that God is dead and that modern man has killed him. The madman shouts that this murder is the greatest deed ever done, but it puts the doer in a difficult position: "What was holiest and mightiest of all that the world has yet owned has bled to death under our knives: who will wipe this blood off us? . . . Must we ourselves not become gods simply to appear worthy of it?" For Nietzsche, the death of God is not merely the symbol of a historical and cultural

---

[1] Cited from M. Blanchot, *Faux pas* (Paris: Gallimard, 1943), 27 (author's translation; our italics).

[2] F. Nietzsche, *The Gay Science*, trans. W. Kaufmann (New York: Vintage, 1974), fragment 125.

stage at which humanity has finally liberated itself from religious ties, leaving it free to take control of history. The death of God initiates an experience that continues to haunt modernity: "Do we not feel the breath of empty space?" However famous Nietzsche's parable has become and however influential it has been in twentieth-century philosophy, theology, and literature, it by no means confirms a new era of worldwide atheism. Indeed, if it affirms anything, it is an affirmation of a deep embarrassment: Have people taken God's place? If so, how could they do this? According to Nietzsche's analysis, the self-elevation of humanity and of human reason requires that God be sacrificed. But to what? As Nietzsche writes four years later, "Did one not have to sacrifice God himself and, out of cruelty against oneself, worship stone, stupidity, gravity, fate, nothingness? To sacrifice God for nothingness—this paradoxical mystery of the ultimate act of cruelty was reserved for the generation which is even now arising."[3] Can we survive this last cruelty, in which we actually sacrifice *ourselves* "for nothingness"?

Nietzsche's cogent, lamenting question refers to a comprehensive analysis of Western history in which the place of religion, in the broadest sense of the word, had become radically problematical. Since the modern period began, that is, since the end of the Middle Ages, this development has been gaining speed, but it is by no means limited to the modern period. The death of God touches not only the God of the dogmatic theology of its time; not only the God of Descartes and Hegel, supposedly dissolved in a modern metaphysical system; and not only the God of Christian faith, who for nearly two thousand years has been an inalienable factor in personal and public life. The death of God refers to a slowly spreading banishment of the transcendent dimension (for example, the 'sacred' as opposed to the 'profane') that has marked cultures from the time of the earliest human being, and that has found its universal expression in sacrifice. In this oldest of rituals, humanity momentarily surrenders itself to a world it cannot control. Yet, and this is the "paradoxical mystery" of which Nietzsche speaks, it is questionable whether modernity really has excluded transcendence, and whether its remains and traces no longer continue to work. The death of God, as Nietzsche presented

---

[3] F. Nietzsche, *Beyond Good and Evil: Prelude to a Philosophy of the Future*, trans. R. J. Hollingdale (Harmondsworth, U.K.: Penguin, 1975), fragment 55.

it, is still a holy sacrifice, even if it is a sacrifice that seems to make all other sacrifices superfluous because the sacrificer takes the place of the sacrificed. But is this strange exchange of roles possible? That is the difficult question Nietzsche's madman puts to us.

Negative Theology as an Experience of Discomfort

If the force of Nietzsche's dictum "God is dead" is less an observation than an evocation, if these three words do not refer to a fait accompli, a "definitive knowing or stable proposition" (Blanchot),[4] but to an *experience* that guides but also disrupts modernity, what kind of experience is it?

It is the experience in which the word 'God,' however often it may be used or misused, has become a strange, meaningless word. This experience contains the moment in which people hardly know any more what they are doing when they pronounce this word, when they speak about or to God. For many people, the image of God—whether 'God' is associated with the name of a concrete person, with a characteristic or idea (perfection, divinity), or only with a vague higher power—is no longer meaningful; it remains empty and seems to have become superfluous. The discrepancy between modern life and its relationship to God determines this experience.

The obvious conclusion would be that this situation opens the way for an atheistic life, whether this is explained euphorically or tragically/nostalgically. One possible interpretation of the cultural historical analysis present in Nietzsche's parable says that the way Western culture has developed logically leads to a society in which God is no longer needed, in which 'God is dead.' The dominant value that grounds modern Western culture is the rational control of the world. The bearers of this value are the humans with their autonomous subjectivity, *"maistres et possesseurs de la Nature"* (masters and possessors of nature; Descartes[5]), who think of the world as their autonomous creation. In many ways, modern culture can be regarded as the result of a powerful self-affirmation of humanity that produces itself in history, and as an impressive attempt

---

[4] M. Blanchot, "Du côté de Nietzsche," in *La part du feu* (Paris: Gallimard, 1949), 293 (author's translation).

[5] R. Descartes, *Discours de la méthode*, ed. É Gilson (Paris: Vrin, 1976), 6.61–62 (author's translation).

by humanity to manage and control the world rationally. Through scientific and technical progress and the development of institutions that guarantee freedom, security, and self-determination, humanity has largely stripped nature of its frightening forms and has grounded human interaction on freedom and free agreement.

Yet this conclusion would be premature. At the same time, Western modernity and its philosophical reflection contain both latent and open signs of *embarrassment* at this self-made world of self-production. The affirmation of the Western subject and his or her rational project seems to be interrupted regularly by tendencies and voices that express skepticism and that point to an 'outside' the subject and to the limit of rationality. At this limit the question again arises of whether modern humanity is sufficient unto itself, and whether in its claim to be able to live without God and in its desire to exclude every dimension that transcends its existence humanity is wandering into a dead end. The history of this embarrassment is what sparked this book. Its object is to link this history to an ancient tradition whose echoes are still heard: the rich tradition of *negative theology*.

A *Definition of Negative Theology*

Negative theology is indeed an old tradition whose sources, as we will show in this Introduction, reach back to late antiquity and the early Christian period; it reached its first high point in the Neoplatonic philosophy and theology that held sway in the third century A.D. and for long afterward. Its most radical representatives are found among the mystics of the late Middle Ages.

The term 'negative theology' is easily misunderstood. We must think less in terms of a religious current and more in terms of a tradition of reflection on Being, God, humanity, and religion. This 'theology' is concerned with a desired philosophical insight into an ultimate, final Reality: the divine 'Stuff,' Cause, or Source, from which all beings come and from which they derive their meaning. Hence the name 'theology' for a thinking that encompasses the areas of philosophy that traditionally are known as ontology and metaphysics, as well as the area that is now called 'theology,' in which we reflect on God. Negative theology can thus be considered philosophical theology. The relevance of negative theology for modern thinking lies in its breaking through the limits of Greek thought on Being, and this from the point of view of Being.

The tradition is nourished by a fundamental intuition diametrically opposed to the main line of classical Greek philosophy: what human desire seeks, the divine, highest Being, cannot be defined, pronounced, or known because it is radically *transcendent*. This tradition tries to find different ways to approach the ultimate mystery— for example, the way of mysticism. Negative theology rejects Parmenides' dictum that Being and thought are one. Western philosophizing and Western culture have never really been able to escape this motto, this 'fate.' Negative theology's emphasis on the unknowableness, the unutterableness, and the deep darkness of transcendent Being elicits the idea that transcendence is best approached via denials, via what according to earthly concepts *is not*. Hence the name *'negative* theology.' Denying what is given, speaking in contradictions, and using the *'alpha privans'*[6] were means for evoking transcendent or hidden entities.[7]

The Polemical as well as Affirmative Starting Point of Negative Theology from Its Neoplatonic Origin

The starting point of negative theology as a whole can be clarified with a few examples. We will distinguish four *negative* polemical positions, and then three *positive* affirmative positions.

1. Negative theology rejects the *anthropomorphism* of Greek mythology, that is, the 'human, all too human' stories about the gods.
2. It rejects *claims to authority* by those who cast their lot with the

---

[6] Rendered by the English 'un-'/'in-'/'a-' as in 'unthinkable,' 'unnameable,' 'invisible,' 'unspeakable,' 'amoral.'

[7] Here we situate negative theology in the long tradition of *philosophical theology* as described and grounded by Wilhelm Weischedel in his superb study *Der Gott der Philosophen. Grundlegung einer philosophischen Theologie im Zeitalter des Nihilismus* (Darmstadt: Wissenschaftliche Buchgesellschaft, 1983). Weischedel argues that the question of God was the most important topic throughout the history of philosophy. He expressly calls this philosophical theology a subdivision of philosophy (xxi). In The Netherlands, we consider L. Heyde's work, *The Weight of Finitude: On the Philosophical Question of God*, trans. A. Harmsen and W. Desmond (Albany: State University of New York Press, 1999), a step along the way of philosophical theology. Interesting here is how he touches on the key themes in negative theology (specifically the 'absent God'). See also Heyde's *De maat van de mens. Over autonomie, transcendentil en sterfelÿkheid* (Amsterdam: Boom, 2000).

existing religious or political order—be they priests or rulers—and who legitimize their place in society by referring to their initiation into the Truth.

3. Negative theology thus opposes the *dogmatism* that often accompanies such pretensions to truth.

4. It rejects the *hubris of human reason,* the claim that people can know everything, even the divine, and can enclose everything in definitions. It rejects the philosophy that arose in Greek culture, philosophy seen as Aristotelian.

These positions reveal negative theology's subversive character. But they are the converse of what negative theology positively represents:

1. Negative theology affirms that a direct insight into *mystery*—for example, the mystery of love—is possible. This is a *knowledge derived from experience* that is usually called 'mysticism,' a knowledge that cannot be logically proven, but only personally experienced.

2. Negative theology, with its idea of a truth hidden from reason, is linked to tolerance for other opinions and to openness to the possibility of a *polyvalent truth.*

3. Negative theology recognizes that there are *other ways of speaking* about the divine than the clear distinctions in philosophy—for example, evocative, poetical ways.

The philosophical articulation of the negative theological experience of the divine, understood as an 'Ultimate Reality,' is reached not by speaking about Being, but by speaking about *Supra-Being* or *Supra-Essence.* Put differently: because of its supra-essential character that surpasses all being, the 'Ultimate Reality' is inaccessible to human thinking, inexpressible in human language, invisible to human eyes, unimaginable for the human mind. Negative theology witnesses to a wholly unique experience of transcendence, to a unique religious sensitivity, in which silence is the symbol of the divine, the Ultimate, face to face with the Supra-Essence—a 'He,' 'She,' or 'It,' a 'Name' or 'Sign'—left completely open. Thus a negative, denying language about the divine, with its tone marked by feelings of respect and desire, is felt to be the least inadequate.

The Radicalization of Negative Theology in the Late Middle Ages: Symptom and Protest

As we said, the most radical exponents of negative theology lived during the late Middle Ages. They flourished at a time of transition between premodern and modern forms of living and thinking, in the "waning of the Middle Ages," during which, as Huizinga describes it, "the glorious edifice of dependencies willed by God has become a necropolis." In the fourteenth, fifteenth, and sixteenth centuries, the sacred symbols are no longer the "living breath" of culture and "all things" are no longer obvious "in their meaningful connection and can no longer be seen in their relation to the eternal."[8] Authors like Eckhart, Tauler, Dionysius the Carthusian, Nicholas of Cusa, and John of the Cross[9] see themselves in their culture placed before a dilemma that would continue to guide modernity into our century: humanity emancipates itself from its world, but disenchants that world at the same time.[10]

Humanity liberates itself from the old 'meaningful connection,' raises itself above the world, and is no longer a part of it: it becomes the creator of its own existence. The fundamental duality between God and humanity is pushed into the background, ultimately to be obliterated; humanity no longer feels subjected to an order that is profoundly a divine order, but gives its own thinking and speaking an autonomous role and meaning. And in that thinking 'God' is merely one of many names and concepts. But the representatives of negative theology mentioned above question this ineluctable progressing emancipation, and in doing so they join in their own unique, and perhaps unconscious, way the aforementioned signs of embarrassment. Thus, the synonymity of emancipation and real liberation has been a problem since the end of the Middle Ages.

For it is not obvious that an existence that loses its duality (God and humanity) is automatically a liberated existence. As soon as this idea is put in doubt, the experience arises that leads to Nietzsche's phrase. The world above which humanity raises itself, and which it makes its object (of knowledge, of activity), becomes its own prison: a scene without depth, a one-dimensional play. In the expanding modern life there is no place for a limit, for an 'exterior' to which people relate and that plays an active, if mysterious and often fright-

---

[8] J. Huizinga, *Herfsttij der Middeleeuwen* (Groningen: Tjeenk Willink, 1973), 216; the English ed., *The Waning of the Middle Ages* (London: Edwin Arnold, 1976), has omitted this sentence.

[9] Their dates are, respectively, 1260–1327, c. 1300–1361, ?–d. 1471, 1401–1464, and 1542–1591.

[10] We will return to this process of emancipation below.

ening, role in daily experience. It is this exterior in its many possible religious variations throughout the centuries—as prayer, rite and myth, wonder and mystery, polytheism, worship of saints, hatred of witches, fear of Satan, and so on—that is forced into a passive role as modern culture slowly unfolds. This exterior becomes empty, and as a result God can be spoken of only in purely negative, empty words. A belief in the limitless possibilities of human reason—so characteristic of the Enlightenment—leads, strangely enough, to a limiting, a reduction, of existence.

In this sense we may put negative theology and particularly the writings of its medieval proponents in a double context. Their uniqueness consists in their being a first *symptom* of this embarrassment, which would later gnaw on the self-awareness of modernity, and in their being a *protest* against the systematic denial of this embarrassment, a denial that will prove to be so characteristic and necessary for the self-affirmation of modern people and their belief in progress.

Thus negative theology as symptom and protest is more than an old tradition; it poses a problem that is very much alive today. Many modern thinkers—theologians, philosophers, historians—defend the position that modernity has gradually met its limit and is now at an end. Some speak of a postmodern period,[11] in which the obviousness of modernity is at greater risk than ever and in which its aporias are displayed. It is surprising, but understandable, that several of these thinkers and writers again examine the heritage of negative theology. We can deduce that, like the negative theology of an earlier period, twentieth-century philosophy is in its "waning" years. It stands on the outer limit, the far end of Western modernity, face to face with the need to cross it; yet it halts at the question of whether this crossing is desirable and how it is possible.

The same kind of protest is characteristic of both forms of "waning," the late medieval and the postmodern. The distrust in modern philosophy and theology for the dominance of scientific rationality finds its parallel in the distrust of late medieval, mystical (negative) theology for rationalistic Scholasticism and skeptical nominalism, from which those oriented toward negative theology expected only an "aged world" and a "great darkness." Yet despite this protest, negative theology realized that it could not escape this darkness, but shared in it.

---

[11] See below, the Epilogue to this Introduction.

But this inability of mine to see is perhaps the effect of the shadow that the great darkness, as it approaches, is casting on the aged world. All I can do now is be silent. . . . Gott ist lauter Nichts, ihn rührt kein Nun noch Her.[12]. . . I shall soon enter this broad desert, perfectly level and boundless, where the truly pious heart succumbs in bliss. I shall sink into the divine shadow, in a dumb silence and an ineffable union.

These words sound mystical to us, they seem to come from days long past. Yet they are the final words of a recent novel, a book that was an immediate success and is one of the most widely read works of recent decades: Umberto Eco's *The Name of the Rose*.[13] It is striking that this best-selling book closes with the language of negative theology, with paraphrases of and quotations from texts by Angelus Silesius and Tauler. In his novel, Eco creates an experience in which the symbolic view of life is abandoned and the difference between word and thing, God and humanity, becomes an object of thought and thus a gnawing problem. He lets this experience result in an "inability to see" and highlights it as the experience of an "approaching darkness" in which "God [becomes] a pure Nothing," His place becomes an empty place. It seems worth the effort to investigate why so many modern readers are fascinated by this experience or even recognize themselves in it. The possible relevancy of this experience is the starting point of this book.

This relevancy expresses itself in the continued distrust of every effort to capture God in human—political, social, ethical— structures. The critical tradition, to which various authors in this book return and of which they see their contribution an echo, tries to avoid integrating God in a thought system or a perspective for action. God always remains the Other, the Invisible, the Foreign, the Far (Marion).[14] It is not a question of finding a concept or proof for God, but of making a protest against the philosophy of Being, of

---

[12] "God is a pure Nothing, the Here and Now does not touch Him"; Angelus Silesius, *Cherubinischer Wandersmann*, 1.25. Silesius (1624–1677), unique in his time, returned to the traditions of radical mysticism and negative theology that had reached their apex two centuries earlier. See, for a contemporary commentary on Silesius, J. Derrida, *Sauf le nom (Post-Scriptum)*, in *On the Name* (Stanford, Calif.: Stanford University Press, 1995), 35–85.

[13] See Umberto Eco, *The Name of the Rose*, trans. W. Weaver (London: Picador, 1983), 501. Ilse Bulhof's chapter in this volume expands on the link between Eco's novel and negative theology.

[14] See the chapter by Victor Kal in this volume.

metaphysical theology, which dominated philosophy and theology, inseparable as they were, into the early modern period. This long history of metaphysical thought about and understanding of God is not univocal. We repeatedly detect doubting, critical, 'negative theological' undercurrents, as the following historical sketch will show. Negative theology rejects all attempts to integrate God into a philosophical construction. It thus opposed late medieval Aristotelian philosophy[15] and Scholasticism that eventually disintegrated into sterile disputes about definitions and distinctions. Similarly, today it sharply opposes Descartes's seventeenth-century rationalism that tried to deduce God as Infinity from the infinite possibilities of finite Reason: a self-elevation of human thinking that gave modernity its philosophical wings.

Instead of a *concept* of God, negative theology, earlier and now, looks to an *experience* of God, in which the duality of God and humanity is often endured as a distance. It thinks that by opening itself to this experience, humanity becomes involved in a transcendence that traditional negative theology represents as divine life and divine light. The primary inspiration for this religious experience and the type of reflection that accompanies it can be found in a work written in the early Middle Ages: the texts of Dionysius the Areopagite, also called Pseudo-Dionysius. Most of the studies gathered here enter into discussion with this 'founder' of negative theology whose existence, ironically, has never been proven;[16] his position, defended in his main works, *The Divine Names* and *Mystical Theology*, that 'People can only speak of God via denials,' will be examined more than once in the following pages.[17]

It is not surprising that the fundamental distrust of every knowledge and appropriation of God by humanity elicits in its turn distrust

---

[15] Thomas Aquinas tried to reconcile Aristotle and negative theology. Jozef Wissink argues in his contribution to this volume that Thomas succeeded.

[16] Dionysius is also called Pseudo-Dionysius because his epithet 'the Areopagite' is a pseudonym, borrowed from an earlier author of whom we know nothing. In choosing this pseudonym, Pseudo-Dionysius forged a link between his theology and the Dionysius who heard Paul's preaching on the unknown God on the Athenian Areopagus, and who then decided to join the Christians. The pseudonym implies a program. The writer of the Pseudo-Dionysian texts was well informed on the discussions that took place in the preceding centuries within the context of non-Christian and Christian negative theology.

[17] On Dionysius, see esp. the chapter in this volume contributed by Bert Blans.

and even hatred and repression. This is particularly true for the second half of the Middle Ages when Scholastic theology dominated the universities and the Church and, supported by a secularized religious power, contested deviant religious attitudes and views. In not seeking an order given by God and maintained by people, but only for a *"lieu pour se perdre"* (De Certeau),[18] negative theology left little or no room for 'acting in God's name' and thus implicitly opened the authority of the clergy to discussion. In convent communities this "place to lose oneself" was partly realized; but they too were more than once subjected to persecution and exclusion.

Echoes . . : Our Thesis

The way in which negative theology has been 'present' and at work in the history of Western culture is like an *echo*—or better, a multifaceted whole of echoes. Above we have given a preliminary introduction to the history of these echoes, one that we now would like to refine and explicate further. This history can be represented schematically in the following *four stages*. Each is marked by being a critical reaction to a specific dominant 'discourse' in the thinking of its period. However much these stages may differ from one another, each is, we believe, the echo of a desire to interact with transcendence in a different, new way.

1. The Neoplatonic origin of negative theology is the first echo of this desire. It reacts polemically against the *Greek philosophy of Being* found in Plato and Aristotle, and thus against the fundamental structures of what Heidegger in the twentieth century called 'ontotheology.'

2. A second stage begins with the thinkers of the eleventh, twelfth, and thirteenth centuries (e.g., Anselm of Canterbury, Bonaventure and, most fully, Thomas Aquinas), who reacted critically or at least with reservations—correctively—to *the rediscovery of Aristotle's philosophy* in this period. They tried to uncover the limits of the unlimited trust in *logic's ability to reason*, a trust that marked this Aristotelian revival.

3. The third stage soon followed: the above-mentioned late medieval

---

[18] Michel de Certeau, *La fable mystique* (Paris: Gallimard, 1982), vol. 1, esp. throughout the first part.

period of radical mysticism. It reacted primarily against the *formal Scholasticism* of its day.

4. Finally, we discern in the modern and 'postmodern' periods a fourth stage that is the most difficult to delineate. It comprises a comprehensive and diffuse spectrum of critical reactions to *Enlightenment thinking*—both latent and more open. The previously mentioned history of the discontent concerning the self-emancipating human subject can summarize this fourth stage; as its axis, we offer Nietzsche's question, as presented at the start of this Introduction. The present resonance of negative theology among cultural philosophers is, we believe, a recent continuance of this stage.

When we look over this history of echoes, we may conclude that in the first three stages there resounds a *maximal* echo of negative theology. We speak of a maximal echo because the criticism or 'negation' (apparent in all three stages) of the ontological reduction of transcendence is accompanied by a positive position: an affirmation of a Being-above-being, a Super-Being. Both positions, negative and positive, are, from Dionysius the Areopagite to John of the Cross, interwoven and subsumed in one another.

The fourth modern stage, in contrast, shows only *minimal* echoes. Here the two positions diverge. Resistance to reason's 'hubris' either cannot or will not be translated into the confirmation of (and devoted respect for) a Supra-Essence. These minimal echoes are radically reserved before every new content for the negative.

Tentative Summary and Further Outline of Our Argument

We believe that these echoes—both maximal and minimal—point to a double *experience*. On one side, this experience is inspired by the discomfort and *embarrassment* we described above. We will show that this embarrassment was initially directed toward reductionism in the thinking on Being that had dominated the West and in which there was no room for a multiplicity of Being, let alone for an 'outside' highest Being. We also show that this discomfort, this 'crisis of onto-theology,' finds its direct result in a critique of modern culture and its history of emancipation and secularization.

On the other side, at the heart of this experience is an appeal, a passion, to go beyond this history and to look for ways toward creat-

ing a new, contemporary way of speaking and thinking about transcendence. Here we especially have in mind the minimal echoes of
negative theology found in the authors studied in this book. We refer
to a thinking about the 'outside' (Blanchot, Foucault), a passion of
'passibility' (Derrida, Nancy, Levinas) in which people are open to
the signs and signals of what presents itself as an exteriority or an
alterity, which the West can neither absorb or integrate, nor exclude
or destroy. These contours, these echoes of the new and unknown,
come to us from the past and the future, and distort our awareness
of time; they hide in the margins of our culture, of our knowledge,
whence they arise only to fade again, like ghosts who are present in
their absence. One of these margins, in our view, is the tradition of
negative theology. Perhaps it has always played the role of an
echo—an echo of the other.

It is this double experience that, as we will show (in Section 4), is
present in Nietzsche's words "God is dead," and which gives these
words their intensity and complex ambivalence. The death of God is
simultaneously a complaint and a perspective: it is the "drama" and
the "myth" of the West that finds its expression in the nineteenth
and twentieth centuries, in literature and in philosophy. The origin
of these words, which Nietzsche was not the first to speak, is unexpectedly not humanistic, not atheistic, but religious:

> In no way can the theme of the Death of God be the expression of a
> definitive knowledge or the design of a stable proposition. Whoever
> wishes to distill a certainty from it, a 'There is no God' in the dogmatic
> sense of a banal atheism, secretly moves this theme to the side of
> reassurance and satisfaction. The dictum 'God is Dead' is an enigma,
> an affirmation that is ambivalent because of its religious origin, its
> dramatic form and the literary myths of which it is the result (that of
> Jean-Paul and of Hölderlin, for example).[19]

We now wish first to present a short history of the classical—that
is, late antique, early Christian, and late medieval—echoes of negative theology (Section 2), and then work toward an evaluation of the
way they resonate in the work of modern (Section 3) and contemporary (Section 4) thinkers (among them those implicitly or explicitly
studied in this book).

---

[19] Blanchot, "Du côté de Nietzsche," 293 (authors' translation).

2. THE BEGINNINGS OF CLASSICAL NEGATIVE THEOLOGY: PHILOSOPHICAL AND HISTORICAL BACKGROUND

When we interpret the tradition of negative theology as a series of echoes of a fundamental experience, the question that arises first is: Where can we find the bottom of the well that produces these echoes? The answer requires a brief examination of negative theology's role in the history of thinking.[20]

Negative Theology in Its Pre-Christian Shape: Greek Neoplatonism

In its Greek and early Christian forms, negative theology is founded on Neoplatonism as developed by Plotinus and others.[21] It thematizes the relationship between the highest transcendent Being and

---

[20] We provide a brief overview of the relevant literature. On Dionysius the Areopagite and negative theology, see John D. O'Meara, *Eriugena* (Oxford: Clarendon Press, 1988), 57–69; O. Semmelroth, "Die Theologia des Pseudo-Dionysius Areopagita," *Scholastik* 27 (1952): 1–343; R. Roques, *L'univers dionysien* (Paris: Aubier, 1954); E. Von Ivánka, *Plato Christianus: Übernahme und Umgestaltung des Platonismus durch die Väter* (Einsiedeln: Johannes Verlag, 1964); A. J. Festugière, *La révélation d'Hermès Trismégiste*, Vol. 4: *Le dieu inconnu et la gnose* (Paris: Gabalda, 1953); J. Hochstaffl, *Negative Theologie: Ein Versuch zur Vermittlung des patristischen Begriffs* (Munich: Kösel-Verlag, 1976); D. Carabine, *The Unknown God: Negative Theology in the Platonic Tradition: from Plato to Eriugena* (Leuven: Peeters Press, 1995); E. Jüngel, "Zur Sagbarkeit Gottes," in *Gott als Geheimnis der Welt* (Tübingen: J. C. B. Mohr [Paul Siebeck], 1977), 307–408; and Raoul Mortley, *From Word to Silence*, Vol. 2: *The Way of Negation: Christian and Greek* (Bonn: Hanstein, 1986). This last study was particularly stimulating for our concept of negative theology. On the apophatic theology of the Orthodox Church, see V. Lossky, *The Mystical Theology of the Eastern Church* (Cambridge: Cambridge University Press, 1957); and Wilhelm Weischedel, *Der Gott der Philosophen* (Darmstadt: Wissenschaftliche Buchgesellschaft, 1983). See, in this work, on Dionysius, 1.92–97; on the tradition of negative theology in the Middle Ages, chap. 3, "Die philosophische Theologie im Mittelalter," 118–64 (among those treated: Bernard of Clairvaux, Bonaventure, Thomas Aquinas, Eriugena, Eckhart, Nicholas of Cusa). We also recommend: F. Copleston, *A History of Philosophy*, Vol. 2, Part 1: *Augustine to Bonaventure*; Vol. 2, Part 2: *Albert the Great to Duns Scotus*; Vol . 3: *Late Medieval and Renaissance Philosophy* (London: Burns, Oates, & Washbourne, 1948); and Julius R. Weinberg, *A Short History of Medieval Philosophy* (Princeton, N.J.: Princeton University Press, 1964), esp. 46–57 (on Dionysius and others). A useful short overview of negative theologians can be found in David R. Law, *Kierkegaard as Negative Theologian* (Oxford: Clarendon Press, 1994), 26–34.

[21] In our culture, negative theology arose as a reaction to the Greek thought on Being. But other cultures know trends that move in the same 'negative' direction—e.g., in Buddhism.

the derived beings and the way in which the transcendence of Being is experienced as absolute. Neoplatonism starts from the desire, *eros*, for what surpasses this world, what is outside humanity, and for what is unknowable to human knowledge. This desire implies a strong awareness of one's own limits and feelings of hesitancy and respect before the Highest. Its goal is worship, kneeling before, abandoning the self, and being included in the Highest—submerging oneself in it and viewing it without words, concepts, or images. It is a goal very close to mysticism. People can advance, by their own power, a certain distance along the way to the Ultimate Reality, but the last insight is something that overcomes them.

Insight into the unthinkableness and the unknowableness of the Ultimate Reality (for Plato, this was the transcendent Idea of the Good on the other side of this world, and also on the other side of the Ideas that people vaguely remember from a former existence) goes back to pre-Socratic philosophical and religious notions. It had to do with a critique of the humanization of the divine. Plato himself speaks in his Seventh Letter[22] of the impossibility of thinking and articulating what is on the other side of reality as we experience it.

Neoplatonism strengthens the moment of transcendence present in Plato's Idea of the Good: the One from which all emanates is absolutely on the other side of what it generates. It is therefore inaccessible to knowledge. This teaching on emanation introduces a dynamic element into Platonic philosophy: beings flow from a transcendent Source, the Origin, the One, and eventually return to it. The deepest desire of all beings is to return to the One. Only people, helped mainly by asceticism, can self-consciously start on the way back, and on rare occasions experience, in an '*unio mystica*,' a oneness with the Highest. As a result of this teaching on emanation, Neoplatonism and negative theology are very hierarchically oriented: the Source is high and superior, the beings that flow from it are in the hierarchically ordered lower regions.

The meaning of *unio mystica* in Neoplatonism as highest fulfillment of the pursuit of wisdom shows its strong link with spirituality. This is connected with the distinction between various levels of in-

---

[22] Plato, *Timaeus, Critias, Cleitophon, Menexenus, Epistles*, with an English translation by R. G. Bury (London: Heinemann/Cambridge, Mass.: Harvard University Press, 1967), 476–565, 541.

sight in knowing the Highest Being. This distinction is centuries' old, and is a mark of all spiritual traditions in the great world religions. A holy life is a precondition for insight into the truth; life and teaching must march along together step by step.[23] In Greek and Christian thinking, the idea of levels of insight was coupled with a spiritual or mystical 'way.'[24] In antiquity and the Middle Ages these levels of insight were linked to levels of being (Plato's doctrine of participation distinguishes between the 'full' Being of the Ideas and the 'weak' being of the phenomenal world that is only a 'shadow' of the world of Ideas). Each of these levels of being has its own form of knowledge that is acceptable on that level. In the Middle Ages, people, following Augustine, believed that those well advanced along the way to personal perfection—typically, members of religious orders—were given a deeper insight than those 'in the world' who did not go into it deeply. In the same way, negative theology also outlined a mystical way: from positive, via symbolic, to negative theology. The phases on the mystical way, the gradation in insight, correspond in negative theology with three ways of speaking about God: (1) positive, or *cataphatic*, speaking; (2) the speaking by creatures who each reflect and 'symbolize' in their existence an aspect of the divine mystery; and (3) negative, or *apophatic*, speaking, resulting in the no-longer-speaking or silence that is the hallmark of mystical unity.

According to Plotinus (205–270) and Proclus (410–485), the transcendence of Ultimate Reality implies that negations say more than affirmations: they reveal a Higher Being, a Source of all being, about which something can be said. Proclus ultimately ends with the negation of all negations (including all language: all negations taken together reveal *nothing* of what, ontologically speaking, the One is). In terms of logic and language, the negative method goes far, but does not reach the very end. To reach that end, language has to be abandoned. Negative language is an instrument that makes itself superfluous. Does this also imply abandoning the terminology of Being and metaphysical thinking about Being? The only one to reach this conclusion was the Neoplatonist Damascius Diadochus, head of the Platonic school in Athens when Emperor Justinian closed it (in A.D. 529).

---

[23] See H. M. Vroom, *Religion and the Truth: Philosophical Reflections and Perspectives*, trans. J.W. Rebel (Grand Rapids, Mich.: Eerdmans, 1989).

[24] See Han de Wit, *Contemplatieve Psychologie* (Kampen: Kok, 1987).

For Damascius, negation is not merely a form of (ultimately) affirmative language. It is "only talking," though a "good" kind of talking. His goal is to reach "hyperignorance." He explains this type of ignorance by using the sun as an example. The closer we move toward the sun, the less we can see it. The eye, completely filled with light, becomes itself light. "We agree that we neither know it, nor are ignorant of it. We are rather in a state of hyperignorance in respect of it, whose proximity obscured even the One."[25] For Damascius, the unknowable that, *logically* speaking, is the opposite of the knowable, is, *ontologically* speaking, even beyond the One: completely invisible. Damascius goes further than Proclus. For Damascius, the gap between human experience and what he called "That Over There" was absolute.

With this, thinking takes an interesting step forward. Philosophical negative theology and the accompanying mysticism abandon the philosophical principle of noncontradiction that had, till then, formed the foundation of philosophy. On one side, God is unutterable, and on the other, God has many names; God is the affirmation of all things, and is *at the same time* the negation of all things. God is omniscience and at the same time ignorance. The Trinity is both one and triple. The logical formula *p is p* and *p is not-p* is applied.

In the framework of pre-Christian—and as we will see, Christian—negative theology, the following questions arise: How can we know what we do not know? How can we speak about what we cannot speak about? And how can language come outside itself? Based on the absolute gap between people and "That Over There," Damascius consciously reinstates ontology in epistemology. Epistemology does not regain its place in logic, but depends on the levels of being on the part of the knowing subject; it is not the knowableness or unknowableness of the object that is important, but the ability or inability of the subject to know. For him, saying something negative about Ultimate Reality is in the end saying something about the limits of mental ability: ignorance describes the state of the speaking subject, indeed *is* this state. Negative language reveals the speaker's state, belongs to the subject; it does not typify the object. Damascius believes that the subjective state in which the subject faces "That Over There" is incorrectly presented as the unknowableness of the

---

[25] Mortley, *From Word to Silence*, 2.122.

object that people want to know. "Hyperignorance" is, paradoxically, a positive state of not-knowing, a positive faculty of not-knowing. Damascius's philosophy focuses on this state.[26] Here he is surprisingly close to Buddhism.[27]

Damascius, however, was an exception. Most negative theologians, despite their problem with thinking about Being, kept the idea of emanation, the idea that the Source presupposes a cause and a goal—a source that may or may not take the shape of a personal, Christian, God. Yet it is striking that in Damascius the tradition of negative theology appears to encompass the possibility of surpassing thinking about Being.[28]

Christian Faith and Neoplatonist Negative Theology

How do Christian faith and Christian thinking, the *philosophia Christiana*, relate to this originally Greek, 'pagan,' negative theology? What could a revelation religion like Christianity have in common with negative theology?[29]

For Christian theologians and philosophers in the period of classical antiquity, the Greek Absolute was the Judeo-Christian God of revelation of which the 'pagan' authors had had a premonition. Those who are not philosophers have an advantage over philosophers: they have not invested so heavily in their own ruminations and can thus more easily accept revelation. In his address on the Areopagus, Paul speaks of the unknown God worshipped there, which now, thanks to Christ, can be known.[30] Non-Christian philosophical negative theology made a deep impression on many early Christian thinkers. In the Greek Orthodox world it still orients belief. Christian Neoplatonists reinterpreted the idea that all people

---

[26] On this basis, we could include Damascius's philosophy among the 'minimal' echoes of negative theology: his way of thinking excludes acceptance of a Super-Being. Yet he tends to attribute a supra-essential status to the *experience* of the absolute unknowing.

[27] And probably close to Derrida when the latter analyzes Plato's concept of 'khôra' (See Ils N. Bulhof's chapter in this volume). J.-F. Lyotard's notion of the "unpresentable" is also reminiscent of Damascius's theme.

[28] See also Sara Rappe, *Reading Neoplatonism: Non-discursive Thinking in the Text of Plotinus, Proclus, and Damascius* (Cambridge, U.K.: Cambridge University Press, 2000).

[29] Von Ivánka, in *Plato Christianus*, addresses primarily the confrontation between Neoplatonist ideas of causality and the Christian idea of creation.

[30] Acts 17.1–34.

know about God by arguing that all people by nature *vaguely* know of God's existence, but that revelation is needed for *real* knowledge of God. The relation between vague and real knowledge is— primarily in the West[31]—explained historically: today we know, thanks to the revelation in Christ, more than was known before.[32] The *topos* of the unknowableness of transcendence, borrowed from Neoplatonism, is interpreted, as we noticed above, by saying that God has two sides: one side turned toward us, God's revealed side (and therefore visible and speakable: cataphatic theology), and one side hidden from us, God as He Himself is (invisible and unspeakable: apophatic theology).

These interpretations have not prevented Western Christianity, over the intervening centuries, from becoming ever further removed from negative theology. It is said to contradict the Christian experience of faith. It is said first that faith legitimates the earthly: God created the world; thus, despite the Fall, it is essentially good and has something to say to us. Moreover, God has sent a mediator (His Son), who showed us through his living and speaking how we must order our earthly humanity in relation to Him. Christianity has always defended the world against gnostic views, traces of which were thought to be found in negative theology. Furthermore, Christianity asserts that faith also legitimates human, 'earthly' language: Christ spoke in human language, and the Holy Scriptures are written in human language, too. In short, it is emphasized that the God of Christian faith did not leave people in total ignorance.[33]

---

[31] In this historical overview, 'West' refers to that part of Europe descended from the Western Roman Empire (centered in Rome); a synonym is 'Latin world.' This 'West' contrasts with the 'East' of the Eastern Roman Empire (centered in Constantinople and, earlier, in Alexandria); this 'East' is also called the 'Greek world.' Of course, this is not the way these terms are used in the general history of culture but the way they are used in a specifically theologically historical context. In 1054 East and West will become definitively separated in a schism.

[32] The view of knowledge in this Western Christian framework could also be strongly colored by logical and scientific knowledge. Hegel stands at the end of this development. For him the goal of Being is complete insight: Being that knows itself "is by itself" and is no longer alienated from itself. Hegel's thinking starts with the confidence that someday God will be completely open, that this is true now for the thinker, and that Being itself will be open to people.

[33] In modern times negative theology has been contested in Western churches, and not only for reasons of systematic theology (see, e.g., Hans Urs von Balthasar's reticence: he thinks negative theology can be fruitful for the Christian faith only after a thorough reinterpretation ["Negative Theologie," in *Theologik* (Einsiedeln: Johannes Verlag, 1985), 2.80–112)]). Mysticism lives from direct experience of the

Negative theology had little appeal for Augustine, for example, the Church Father who exercised the deepest and longest influence on the West. In his thought and faith, the Incarnation is central: the Word, Christ, became flesh, and brings us the gospel message. Revelation in Christ enlightens people whose view of the world was darkened by the Fall. Thanks to the revelation in Christ, an event in time, people can again know God—even though direct knowledge of God face to face in this life is impossible. For Augustine, God's descent to us in material life and in history implies no lessening or degradation of divinity. Nor is language, the audible word, thinking,

---

divine, and therefore tends to withdraw from hierarchically organized authority structures. In the West, church officials have always been ambivalent toward negative theology. The dangers for the church inherent in negative theology could only be exorcized by binding it tightly to its own hierarchy: by positing that contact with God as described by negative theology was possible only via the church, or in the context of strict ecclesiastical life. This limited possibility existed in Roman Catholic circles thanks to the mystical experience that liturgy and sacraments permitted. Even today this mystical experience has been preserved in the Orthodox Church. In Protestant circles mysticism found a home in the different forms of pietism. Protestant thinkers approach negative theology in a completely different way than do the thinkers of the Roman Catholic and Orthodox Churches. They start with the Word of God—Christ—that, through the Holy Scripture, tells of a God that can certainly not be discovered by human reason. We cannot even reason our way to knowing that such a God exists. For, as Jüngel in *Gott als Geheimnis der Welt* says, how are we to separate *that* He is from *what* He is. If we want to make this separation, we must first know *who* the God of Abraham, Isaac, and Jacob is. How do we know that this God is not the impersonal divinity of Greek philosophy, or the many gods of animist religions, or the pervasive divinity of Buddhist thinking? Alone, reason knows nothing about God. But Protestants emphasize that the Word of God, once given to people, can be understood, even though there remains an element of mystery (Jüngel). After Thomas Aquinas's causal view of the sacraments won terrain in the West, the mystical element disappeared for a long time from the Roman Catholic Church. Mysticism lived outside church ties. Jean-Luc Marion's philosophy and theology is a reaction to this. The position Marion takes toward negative theology in a Roman Catholic world may be comparable to Jüngel's in the Protestant world. After Thomas, and more strongly after the development of the philosophy of science in modern times, theology became completely detached from philosophy and science. This made theology's role more marginal. Nominalism and the thinking of the Protestant Reformers supported this reduction philosophically and theologically. In our time, we have seen Karl Barth defend this reduction passionately. He wants to keep theological dogmatics, based on revelation and Scripture, strictly distinct from scientific and philosophical reflections on transcendence. In sum, we can say that the history of Christian faith looks with reservation, if not rejection, toward negative theology and its echoes, since (1) the latter inherently subverts hierarchical religious structures, and (2) opens the door for a (sometimes 'philosophically' qualified) 'superstition' that is not totally submissive to biblical revelation.

degraded. The word does not injure thought. Thanks to this view of the Incarnation, the model of *reading* is important for Augustine: reading as an interpretation of signs that the author uses to say something. Reading involves grasping the true meaning of the signs.[34] For Augustine of Hippo, the whole of creation was a comprehensible and legible body of signs. Christ, the Logos, is also a comprehensible sign, as are, of course, the Scriptures.[35] Mortley concludes that Augustine "appears to have no interest in the kind of experiential growth which, in the Neoplatonic tradition, systematic negation provides."[36] So, what does Christianity as revelation religion have to do with negative theology?

Gregory of Nyssa (d. 394) shows that in the Eastern Church the situation is more complicated. Gregory's texts are an eloquent example of a Christian negative theology. On the one hand, he does not want to play the linguistic game of the Neoplatonic philosophers.[37] But, on the other hand, he recognizes emphatically that there are matters that cannot be put into words. God transcends all language and all thinking. As for language, words have no substance, they disappear; no single word encompasses or 'is' God. Words are only human creations. At best they can point in the right direction. With this view of language as *convention*[38] Gregory turns away from Philo of Alexandria (25 B.C.–A.D. 50), who saw a close tie between names, words, and things.

The high point of the Christian negative theological tradition in the early Christian period is found in Dionysius the Areopagite, whom we have already mentioned. His texts served as the rich layer of humus in which the seeds of negative theology could grow in philosophy and theology. His influence was extensive throughout the Middle Ages in the Greek Orthodox world, and to a lesser extent in the Latin Western world. We can point here to Anselm of Canterbury, Bernard of Clairvaux, Bonaventure, Thomas Aquinas, Eckhart, and—at a later time—Nicholas of Cusa, Ficino, and John of the

---

[34] See H. Blumenberg, *Die Lesbarkeit der Welt* (Frankfurt am Main: Suhrkamp, 1981), 17–57.

[35] Only in Augustine's *De Ordine* (2.16.44) is there a passage that approaches negative theology. See Mortley, *From Word to Silence*, 2.210. Because negative theology is not an important aspect of Augustine's thinking, some authors (e.g., Hochstaffl, *Negative Theologie*, note 20) do not even mention him.

[36] Mortley, *From Word to Silence*, 2.224.

[37] Ibid., 2.143.

[38] Words are only conventions, perishable 'agreements' between people.

Cross.[39] It remains an enigma in the history of thought, how a current—linked to the name Dionysius—that had been so important for so many centuries was eventually all but forgotten in the West. "Why has the West lost its own tradition of trans-linguistic mysticism, so that it turns to Buddhism for what it once possessed as its own," wonders Mortley,[40] who recognizes negative theology as "a cultural undercurrent" when he writes that "the Dionysian tradition has become a cultural undercurrent emerging at times, but which always maintains the capacity to influence and redirect."[41]

Dionysius the Areopagite

Dionysius tried to link the heart of Christian faith, the idea of Incarnation, to Neoplatonism. He wanted to tell the Christian story as a philosophical, that is, nonmythological story. But he wanted more. He sought a link between Christian faith and the religious thinking about and experience of God as absolute transcendence—on the other side of Being and reality. He tried to think beyond Being. Given his goal, we could perhaps say that he tried to liberate God from the philosophy of Being.

Here lies his meaning and his appeal for later generations, even to the present. Certainly, Christ, the Word that was with God from the beginning—on the other side of being—emerged from secrecy, took on, for Dionysius, human form and became visible to us. Yet even after his appearance he remained hidden. What 'really' was said, still remains unsaid. What 'really' was known, remains unknown. Between the hidden and the unhidden being of Christ lies a moment that is 'not of our time,' 'not of our world.' It is a moment in which the hidden and the unhidden exist *side by side.* Dionysius emphasizes the moment of "the sudden," in the sense of a crash in time, an epiphany.

One of the recurring issues, as we saw with Gregory of Nyssa, involves the question of whether names are conventional or 'natural.' In general, proponents of negative theology, including Gregory, support the first view. But Dionysius adopts a more nuanced view, one consistent with his conception of analogy.

---

[39] Their dates are, respectively, 1033–1109, 1090–1153, 1221–1274, 1225–1274, 1260–1327, 1401–1464, 1433–1499, and 1542–1591.

[40] Mortley, *From Word to Silence,* 2.15–16.

[41] Ibid., 2.220.

We read in *The Divine Names* that names are images, in the sense of copies, of an immaterial reality. They are things that flow from Unity. They reflect, as all creatures that flow from the One, a higher principle: their Source. Names *are* and they *mean*. Dionysius posited that divine names had a special meaning. Like all beings, they bear the stamp of spiritual beauty. Divine names are the basis for affirmative speech about God, for a positive, cataphatic theology. These special names are inspired by the Spirit. They have a special effective power: they unify the human spirit with the highest principles. Human intellect moves from nature to the Good—just as all things according to their ability strive toward *analogy* with the Good. Here we see that for Dionysius analogy is a way of being for things, a proportion of beings in relation to one another. This proportion permits knowledge, based on comparisons, and refers to a *via analogiae*: every being has its own relationship to the Good, and a suitable share of knowledge of the Good. Analogy is the way by which creatures participate in God. Creatures are self-expressions of God through and in the various levels of reality. Analogy is expressed in love for, or orientation toward, the Good; it is inseparably linked to the creature's free will, with his or her desire for the Good. Analogy is therefore above all an attitude: a being in harmony, a being 'in tune.' Thus Dionysius is less directed than Damascius toward a complete rejection of all thinking about God and humanity in terms of Being. He is looking for an analogy between the divine Being and beings, an analogy that in his view *emanates*, proceeds 'naturally' (that is, according to the nature of the Names, of the language God Himself created), from divine Being.

In the context of Dionysius's thinking, analogy thus has an ontological aspect. This is in contrast with Thomas's later purely epistemological use of analogy. For Dionysius, God is not an object, and certainly not an object of knowledge. God is on the other side of being and therefore unknowable. There can be no question of a proportionality between God and creatures, for then God would be a being, a thing, an object. God—the hidden—can only be known via participation in His reality.

We must view Dionysius's concept of the effectivity of divine names within the context of this notion of analogy: they help people who are oriented toward the Good to come closer to the Good, to God, and so to become more divine (*"deiformis"*). In this regard

Dionysius is, for a negative theologian, surprisingly positive about language. Names are real, are true; their origin goes back to the True, the Real itself, that is, to God from whom they flow and to whom they can return.

How does this view of language relate to the negative theology that Dionysius represents? We find an explanation of this in his *Mystical Theology*. The negative way reaffirms a nescience; it is a way that ends in "mystical silence" and "not-knowing." This form of knowing, knowing as not-knowing, is a "higher and more original form of knowing,"[42] as in Damascius. For example, Dionysius denies that Christ was human—but this does not mean that Christ was not a person. What he wants to show with this language is that Christ was 'super'-human. God lives in the dark. Through the working of divine darkness, forms that for us in normal reality are oppositions are no longer opposites. For, according to Dionysius, that darkness existed long before these oppositions. Whoever is on the other side of the light, whoever is in divine darkness, sees by not seeing, knows by not knowing. And we must pray to be allowed to see and to know in this way. We can only know what cannot be known in veiled form: through what is knowable to all being. Divine light veils, conceals, shows nothing. Dionysius reverses Plato's images that were so influential in later Greek metaphysical—and even Christian—thinking. By continuing Plotinus's Neoplatonism, Dionysius—like Damascius—reaches a moment when the dualism of light and darkness collapses and light becomes the symbol of darkness.

Did Dionysius, like Damascius, deny the existence of a personified object of love and adoration? Is God in mystical union still an object of faith, a 'something else'? The literature generally maintains that for Dionysius God remained a Person. But the more God's unknowableness is emphasized, the closer people come to the point where God, being a Person, must be thought of in a way totally different from the image normally suggested by 'person.'[43]

Negative Theology in the Latin West: The Rediscovery of Aristotle at Issue

For the time being we can say that early Christian thinking has great affinity with Neoplatonic philosophical negative theology. But this

---

[42] Ibid., 2.231.
[43] We see this also in Eckhart and Nicholas of Cusa.

does not mean that there was no discussion, within Christian faith and Christian philosophy, from the very beginning, about the question of whether the silence with which negative theology ends is the most adequate answer to the revelation of God in Christ. In the world of Greek Orthodoxy the answer was positive: there silence has remained the answer. It has also remained the prevailing answer for mysticism in Greek and Latin Christianity.

Philosophy and theology in the West had greater difficulty with this issue. Besides the influence of Neoplatonism and negative philosophy and theology, there was also the influence of Aristotle, most especially in the use made of logical thinking to clarify faith, to make it, as it were, logically coherent. Increasing familiarity with the 'Corpus Aristotelicum,' from the tenth and eleventh centuries onward, provided the impulse for this effort of clarification. This led to a greater effort to distinguish between the *that* and the *what* of God.

Aristotle's works were reintroduced into Western Europe via Islamic and Jewish philosophy (Averoës, Maimonides) during the period of Islamic Spain. Via Spain, the Aristotelian corpus became known to Christian Europe, but a potentially broad attention to his many-sided work was quickly reduced to a concentration on Aristotle's *logic*. For this reason, the echoes of negative theology in the West consist mainly in a critical assimilation of this Aristotelian influence either by keeping its logical distinctions and definitions at bay (Anselm) or by giving them a heavily nuanced interpretation (Thomas).

Two historical phases in knowing about God had long been distinguished: the vague knowledge of the pre-Christians and the real knowledge of the Christians. This culminated in the distinction between knowledge *that* God is ('that' God exists), a possibility open to pre-Christians, and knowledge of *what* God is ('who' God is), something given only to those with faith. If *what* God is is beyond the reach of natural reason, can God still be the subject of *theology* (literally, 'speaking about God'), of the holy science, or 'sacred doctrine'? John of Damascus (675–750), the Church Father who systematized Christian doctrine for the Greek Orthodox Church, but who also influenced Western Scholasticism, answered this question with a very decisive 'No.' We cannot think or say what is *in* God. It is the 'side' of God that is turned away from us.

This distinction between knowing 'that' God is and knowing 'what' God is reenters the discussion via Aristotle. Anselm of Canterbury and Thomas Aquinas contribute to this distinction in different ways. For Anselm of Canterbury, the 'that' and the 'what' of God were not strictly separated epistemologically and ontologically. Whoever uses the word 'God' knows what the word means. The meaning of that word can remain purely superficial, for example, when we only know the meaning of the word as word, or it can be vague and ill-defined, for example, as is the case with those who have no knowledge from revelation. Or understanding can be refused, for example, when the one hearing the word rejects revelation. But whoever accepts revelation can really understand God and take Him to heart. Anselm introduces the famous formulation that God is *id quod maius cogitari non potest*, God is what extends beyond what people can think. In other words, I know that my thinking falls short. Whoever is fully aware that God is *id quod maius cogitari non potest* comes closer to God, is increasingly filled with happiness—even though God in the last instance remains unknowable and unreachable. Anselm's work is a good example of a coincidence of mysticism and logical thinking.

For Anselm, thanks in part to his definition of what the word 'God' means, the 'that' and the 'what' coincide in the word itself, in the holy name *God*. Human insight in the 'what' of the 'that' and in the 'that' of the 'what' can be deepened by repeatedly saying and reflecting on the word during meditation (the medieval 'rumination'). *Credo*, I know it, I accept it, because I am created by God and am oriented toward Him by nature; *ut intelligam*, this allows me to deepen my insight into God, the world, and myself. Thanks to the specific revelation of Christian faith, people can obtain greater and deeper insight into what they vaguely already know than what is possible from reason alone, be it only the insight that God always surpasses thinking.[44]

For Thomas Aquinas, it is not so evident that the 'that' and the 'what' can be combined as easily as Anselm proposes. Aquinas asks whether it is not possible to 'invent' a theological and philosophical way of speaking that expresses itself in an awareness of its inadequacy. Thomas Aquinas, fascinated as he was by Aristotle, but believing as no other that human reason met its limit in the 'what' of God, tried to give shape to such thinking. He designed his own

---

[44] On Anselm, see also the chapter in this book by Jean-Luc Marion.

method: analogous speaking about God. As we said, his view of analogy differs from Dionysius's view of analogy. For Thomas, it had a different, more Aristotelian, dimension than it had for Dionysius.

Thomas agreed with the Neoplatonic tradition of negative theology and with Anselm that God could not be compressed in a definition, that God could not be 'put into words.' To believe so would be to overestimate human reason and to do an injustice to transcendence. But, Thomas said, we can approximate the heart of the matter, the matter toward which our desire is oriented, God, if we approach the problem from a different angle, that is, if we do not follow Aristotle's search for exact definitions for our speaking about God that would distinguish 'that' dicta from 'what' dicta. Thanks to our reason, we know the effects of God's essence: the order in creation and creatures as it was given once and for all. Reason first recognizes these effects and then names their source—with the words 'prima causa'—for something can only be named when it is known. Thomas substitutes natural reason's recognition of the effects (God's creation) for the Aristotelian definition (or exact proposition) about God's essence and for the Augustinian and Anselmian inner enlightenment through Christ. The knowledge that natural reason, philosophy, gives must be complemented[45] with the knowledge of revelation, theology. Theology is speaking about God, but not about God's essence.

According to Thomas, God's essence is not discussed in theology. Compared to their originals in God's spirit, names are as imperfect as the creatures to which they refer. Yet names say something, for, Thomas says, in their imperfection names, human words and human concepts (such as 'good'), say something about God's much greater perfection. When theology says of God, "God is good," it must recognize that God is not good in the way people are good. The human word remains an analogy. Thomas seems to save the mystery by using the logical method of analogy.[46]

Thomas's doctrine of analogy is often misunderstood. He designed the doctrine to fit Aristotle's thinking into Christian faith. As a correction to Aristotle's thinking, he wanted to keep humanity and God

---

[45] And not the Anselmian deepened.

[46] In his chapter, Joseph Wissink addresses the question of whether Thomas's work on this question contains any resonance of negative theology. His answer is ultimately positive.

separate, to keep them out of a relationship accessible to human reason. At the same time he did not want people to think God could be understood from his creatures. But in later centuries the doctrine of analogy was erroneously used in this sense.[47] Philosophy, with Thomas the first to state it so clearly, studied being (creation, things, people, nature) *and* the Highest Being, in the limited sense of the 'that' of God. Thomas was also the first to separate philosophy and theology so sharply, to keep God beyond the reach of human reason. However, as Aristotle gained influence in Scholastic thinking, confidence in human thinking about creation increased. The distance between theology and philosophy increased, and creation became more univocal. Nominalism affirmed this development by understanding knowledge and speaking instrumentally: as a means that people use to grasp the world. Thanks to the development of nominalism, modern empirical natural sciences could arise.[48]

Summary

Classical negative theology can be summarized as follows: It takes seriously the limits of reason and the importance of emotions such as love and surrender. It focuses on an experience of God in which transcendence is radically analyzed and lived.

Ultimate Reality is far from human experience. This reality, hidden from human rational knowledge, surpasses all philosophy. Therefore, the instruments of philosophy can neither prove nor disprove it. Negative theology disorients thinking and is itself disoriented by the question how it can surpass itself to reach other levels of experience, how it can elevate itself. An important theme in negative theology is this 'self-transcendence' of thought. Negative theology not only rejects—as is customary in philosophy—anthropomorphic language about the Ultimate Reality, but goes much further. Some thinkers reject *all* language. Language and the entire human conceptual and linguistic apparatus is surpassed. Nev-

---

[47] See E. Jüngel, *Gott als Geheimnis der Welt*, 384, 388.

[48] On nominalism, see esp. Meyrick H. Carré, *Realists and Nominalists* (1946; Oxford: Oxford University Press, 1961), Heiko Oberman, *The Harvest of Medieval Theology: Gabriel Biel and Late Medieval Nominalism* (Grand Rapids, Mich.: Eerdmans, 1976), and Louis Dupré, *Passage to Modernity: An Essay in the Hermenuetics of Nature and Culture* (New Haven, Conn.: Yale University Press, 1993).

ertheless, there is an insight, a knowledge, that cannot be logically reasoned.

All forms of negative theology affirm a not-knowing, a silence, that implies the end of philosophy. They lead to a limit behind which philosophy becomes madness. The negative theological path of contradiction encourages abandoning ideas, not wrestling with them. This path is a means to overcome the divisive thinking contained in the desire to delimit exactly what something is, and thus to demarcate exactly what it is not. Negative theology is an inclusive manner of thinking: it permits the espousal of what does not go together, instead of requiring a choice for this or that. This 'ecumenical' effect is seen in Dionysius and Nicholas of Cusa, the latter being not accidentally the last great medieval proponent of unifying the churches of East and West.

3. Echoes of Negative Theology in the Margins of the Modern Period

Modernity, and the development of Western history that made it possible, is a stage in thinking where negative theology disappears into the background. Up to the end of the Middle Ages negative theology accompanied prevailing thought about Being as a—pluriform—critical undercurrent, and this subversive position toward thinking about Being grew during the "waning of the Middle Ages," as we saw, into a radical opposition to the ecclesiastical, Scholastic teaching authority.

In the modern period of human *emancipation* and *secularization*, this double-layered structure in theological and philosophical discourse—main current and undercurrent—seems to have become superfluous. Thinking seems to become one-dimensional once it discovers and focuses on humanity. This kills not only God, but the *borderline* between humanity and God that negative theology wanted to evoke and articulate. Modern thinking bears the stamp of anthropocentrism, despite the doubt and critical reflection that is unexpectedly, sometimes explicitly but more often implicitly and secretly, heard from numerous modern thinkers.

We must pause here to examine more closely this movement toward emancipation and secularization in modernity.

Emancipation: An Ambivalent History

The renewed interest in negative theology within contemporary philosophy of culture flows from a critical reflection on modern Western culture and its history. It is generally observed that this history is a process of emancipation and secularization, but the interpretation and evaluation of this process proceeds in very different directions. We distinguish two below.

First, there is the *positive* interpretation. According to Nietzsche's diagnosis, modern culture has killed God. This diagnosis, which, as we saw, he formulates primarily as a cogent and painful question, receives here a univocal and unproblematical conclusion. The death of God is the obvious result of the emancipation of human reason, which is said to have liberated itself from ecclesiastical authority, imposed in theology, philosophy, and politics. People now sit on the seat from which God directed the world. People have grown up and God has faded into a superfluous fiction. From the seventeenth and eighteenth centuries onward, the Enlightenment's optimism has lent strength and radiance to this self-awareness. The empirical sciences freed themselves from the authority of the church, a church that pretended to be the only legitimate guardian of truth and morality. A sharp, often belligerent separation between church and state was the logical result of this emancipation, a separation whose possibility and desirability was analyzed in early modern political philosophy (Hobbes). The implementation of this separation was the necessary political answer to the disruptive religious wars that held burgeoning modern Europe in their grasp; but it was also an expression of belief in human emancipation from God and church, a belief that modernity has maintained ever since.

Church and theology have had trouble adjusting to the Enlightenment's ideals.[49] Reason was given its own, and the largest, domain: creation, nature. Since the time of Thomas Aquinas, theology agreed with the division of tasks: the terrain of theology (God, religion) was independent of all other areas of life, which were given over to

---

[49] See Ernst-Wolfgang Böckenförde, "Kirche und modernes Bewußtsein," and Hermann Krings, "Zur Modernitätskritik der Kirchen: Kommentar zu Ernst-Wolfgang Böckenförde," both in Peter Koslowski, Robert Spaemann, and Reinhard Low, eds., *Diskussion über Kirche und Moderne: Moderne oder Postmoderne?* (Weinheim: VCH Verlagsgesellschaft, 1986), 103–42.

philosophy, science, art, economics, and politics. Such a division had serious consequences for nature: it was no longer seen as the gift of God's creation, but as an object for reason, which as subject could and must dominate it, order it, and use it—even *re-create* it. The division between faith and reason, between God and humanity, and between church and state is closely related to the division that has determined modern thought since Descartes: the division between subject and object. It is the division between, on one side, free, sovereign, speaking and reasoning humanity, and, on the other side, an unfree, mute nature that is, or should be, subjugated to this humanity. Modern humanity hopes that through this division a better world will arise, a world in which the destructive forces of nature will be shackled by science and the aggressive forces in humanity will be held in check by the creation of humane institutions and discoveries in human sciences.

Second, there is the *critical-negative* interpretation of the process of emancipation and secularization. It rejects the idea that the emancipation described above could lead to a real liberation of humanity and the world. Sometimes this view is clothed in nostalgia and conservatism: people attack the secularization of culture for being a process by which humanity loses contact with God, and they plead for a return to 'lost' authority in which the 'old faith' was the central, binding factor. This nostalgia is not very interesting for contemporary echoes of negative theology, since it immediately translates and resolves the fundamental embarrassment that accompanies modern culture and its history of emancipation and secularization into a desire for a 'way back.' The experience to which negative theology referred as early as the late "waning" Middle Ages is one of aporia, of an unsolvable ambivalence that implies a challenge: the 'way back' is closed, but the future of the emancipation process is also a problem.

Damage to the environment, overpopulation, and the threatened exhaustion of the earth's regenerative abilities; the scientific domination over and commercialization of life; the economic marginalization and isolation of the Third World; the increasingly sharper dichotomy between poor and rich—all create a macabre image of the tentative result of the emancipation process, which seems to be becoming hopelessly tangled. The articulation of this despair, and the attempt to see the 'project' of modernity no longer as a glowing perspective, but as an extremely risky challenge, is characteristic of this critical undercurrent in modern philosophy and literature that, in part, presupposes a creative resumption of the heritage of negative theology.

The despair before the failure of the modern subject that faces objectivity and excludes a sensitivity for the Other, the nonhuman, found expression early in the last century in the poet Hugo von Hofmannsthal: "My condition is, in brief, this: I have completely lost the ability to think or say anything coherent about anything at all." Von Hofmannsthal can no longer see anything with the simplifying glance of normality: "everything fell in pieces, and the pieces in smaller pieces, and nothing permits itself to be enclosed in a concept."[50] Nietzsche has earlier met the limits of language: ". . . We believe that we know something about the things themselves when we speak of trees, colors, snow, and flowers; and yet we possess nothing but metaphors which correspond in no way to the original entities."[51] This inability to name things 'adequately' and the doubt whether that is even possible also undermine the pretensions of twentieth-century science. When von Hofmannsthal and Nietzsche articulate the limits of language, they question and problematize the division of subject and object. Their experience is a symptom of the failure of modernity, an awareness that the historical developments in the last century—the immense butchery of two world wars—has only made stronger. The claims of the dominant subject at best smoulder in our memory, from the crematoria of Auschwitz, from the ruins of Hiroshima, until now. We now look back at a century that, as it seems, simply underwent these terrors before it would inevitably return to the illusion of an undisturbed rest.

Hans Blumenberg analyzed the challenge that accompanies the articulation of this despair.[52] He posits that the development of Western culture is not a linear process of progress or regression. Hu-

---

[50] H. von Hofmannsthal, *The Lord Chandos Letter*, trans. R. Stockman (Vermont: University Press of New England, 1986), 45, 48.

[51] F. Nietzsche, "On Truth and Lies in a Nonmoral Sense," in David Breazeale, ed., *Philosophy and Truth: Selections from Nietzsche's Notebooks of the Early 1870's* (New Brunswick, N.J.: Humanities Press, 1979), 79–197, 82–83.

[52] See esp. his *Die Legitimität der Neuzeit* (1966; Frankfurt am Main: Suhrkamp, 1988), particularly the first part, "Säkularisierung—Kritik einer Kategorie des geschichtlichen Unrechts."

manity is repeatedly challenged to give shape to its humanness.[53] After antiquity and the Middle Ages, modernity marks a new creative stage in which thinking about humanity, God, Being, nature, and art are radically changed. Humanity, during the Renaissance, acted like a *cocreator* of the world, but by the time of the Enlightenment humanity viewed itself as the *only creator* of and source of meaning for culture. This development cannot be explained simply as a deterioration, but is the impressive answer to a deterioration: the disintegration of the medieval synthesis that shaped God, humanity, and the cosmos into a harmonious whole. The shadow side of this secularization does not bring modernity completely into discredit. Blumenberg's question is, How do modern people find ways to resist "evil" when science and reason fail? How can they behave toward religion, science, and technology without raising them to universal criteria for what is true and false, good and evil? Secularized people have as yet not 'liberated' themselves from anything; their emancipation confronts them with the problem of how to live without predetermined frameworks for interpretation.[54]

In our treatment of the unique condition of modernity, the 'space' of the death of God, we have focused particularly on the opposition, the gap, between modern and premodern experience. In a way, we have followed Blumenberg's thesis of the '*Neuzeit*' understood as a singular event, although we have accentuated its 'crisis' much more dramatically than he does. Still, it should be noted that there is an equally fundamental *continuity* between modernity and the era preceding it. One might think here of the 'invention' of the individuality of the human being and of the desire for authenticity[55] that clearly should be located in early Christianity and not only in modern culture; in this way, Karl Löwith's claim that modernity is after

[53] Blumenberg opposes here the so-called secularization thesis that Karl Löwith launched in *Meaning in History: The Theological Implications of the Philosophy of History* (Chicago: University of Chicago Press, 1949), which states that Western culture demonstrates a continuous development from "believing" to "secularized" thinking.

[54] Cf. Louis Dupré's recent *Passage to Modernity*, reviewed in *Tijdschrift voor Filosofie* 56 (1994): 552–55. In his final chapter, Dupré concludes that transcendence must be thought differently from the way it is thought in classical metaphysics.

[55] See also Charles Taylor, *The Sources of the Self: The Making of Modern Identity* (Cambridge, U.K.: Cambridge University Press, 1989), in which he shows that the fundamental traces of the *modern* ideal of an authentic 'self' are, among others, already to be found in Augustine of Hippo's work.

all just a secular variation on Christianity must still be treated seriously. One might also think of Nietzsche's and—in a different discourse—Freud's diagnosis that the death of God is not the event of modernity, but of its presumed enemy, Christianity, that replaced the 'living' gods of the naturalist religions with a distant, abstract, and monotheistic god. A third way to interpret and evaluate modern emancipation and secularization—besides the positive and negative approaches discussed above—probably announces itself here, which would neither be positive nor negative, but simply challenges both ways.

The *discontinuity* of modern and premodern experience should thus be complicated by an analysis of their *continuity*. Although the scope of this Introduction is too limited for such an undertaking, our discussion of premodern negative theology as the expression of an embarrassment and a discomfort that is resumed more radically in the modern experience may already hint at this continuity.

Hidden Echoes of Negative Theology in a Period of Self-Emancipating Thinking?

As in the history of thinking Being became more univocal, there was less room for negative theology. The divine Being that Plato and Aristotle distinguished from all beings, and that Christian philosophers would later interpret as a vague, general indication of what was openly given in a special revelation in Scripture, slowly became something of the same order as human being. It thus became subject to the categories of language and reason. A medieval, heterogeneous, polysemic view of Being, in which divine Being is distant from human 'derived' being, was gradually transformed into a modern, homogeneous, univocal view of Being in which thinking itself, understood as the unlimited ability of reason, became central. In other words, thinking makes itself the master of Being and homogenizes it.

Consistent with Thomas Aquinas's doctrine of analogy, it was thought that different criteria were used to know creation and nature from those used to know God: this latter 'knowledge' was repeatedly recognized as a philosophical problem that revealed the limits of philosophical speaking. In the late Middle Ages Duns Scotus (1266–1308) and Ockham (1300–1350) tended to reject this distinction;

modern philosophy has followed them more radically.[56] Being was seen as univocal, it could be known by using oppositions: either something 'is,' is Being, and the linguistic expression that reflects this Being is true, or it 'is not,' is not Being, so that the reflected expression is false. This view of language and reality is at the core of medieval *nominalism* (discussed above).

In Descartes, true knowledge of Being is thought of only as *certain* knowledge: knowledge that survives the test of systematic, methodical rationality. Descartes's contemporary, Pascal, passionately rejected the god approached in this way, "the god of philosophers," and in reaction only follows "the God of Abraham, Isaac, and Jacob" known from biblical revelation. Pascal's thinking did not gain much of a following in his own time.[57]

The neutralization of the heterogeneous view of Being that bears the mark of a differentiation, a multiplicity in Being, reaches its peak in Hegel's metaphysics. Here absolute Being, abstracted in the Spirit, is the complete unity of thinking and Being, and implicitly of humanity and God. His philosophy can be considered a doctrine of emanation, but without the hiddenness of divine Being favored by Neoplatonism.

Nevertheless, at the beginning of this Introduction we noted a fundamental discomfort with this development that accompanies, disrupts, and haunts modern thinking and the culture in which it has won its place. Strikingly, the relationship between God and Being, between transcendence and rationality, and thus between God and humanity, however hidden, remains one of the great and central problems of modern thinking: a problem with which it wrestles in embarrassment. In the repeated reformulations of this problem we unavoidably hear the critical voice of the tradition of negative theology. We presented the echoes of this voice as a symptom of this embarrassment, and as a protest against the modern denial of it.

---

[56] See J.-L. Marion, *Sur la théologie blanche de Descartes* (Paris: Presses Universitaires de France, 1981). Here we find a convincing reflection of the misunderstanding around Thomas's concept of analogy (24–160), and on the univocal view of being (161–230).

[57] See Blaise Pascal, "Le mémorial," in Pascal, *Oeuvres complètes*, ed. L. Lafuma (Paris: Seuil, 1963), 618. See also Theo de Boer, *De god van de filosofen en de god van Pascal: Op het grensgebied van filosofie en theologie* (Zoetermeer: Meinema, 1989).

Descartes, Kant, and the Crisis of Reason

In the works of René Descartes (1596–1650) and Immanuel Kant (1724–1804), both seen as paradigmatic for modern thinking, we can discover minimal traces of this embarrassment, leading to a 'subcutaneous' opposition to the comprehensive systems they built. But this observation does not mean that their work could 'really' be regarded as a disguised form of negative theology.

Seeking the axioms from which all knowledge can be deduced, Descartes concluded that these will not only be the foundations of a new epistemology, but will also uncover the basis of Being: these basic principles will reveal to the 'Cogito' in a clear way the substances that ancient and medieval metaphysics had so long sought. During this philosophical search human reason discovers that all the certainties it tries to formulate are just as *doubtful*. The senses can deceive, reason can err, the ideas that people maintain are no more than molds, images of reality. Even God and His existence can be doubted. The thinking 'ego,' it appears, can only doubt everything that is. For Descartes, thinking *is* doubting. The only certainty that I have is *that* I doubt, so philosophy must conclude that the first basic principle of reason is doubt, to doubt everything. That reason is able to doubt so comprehensively makes it, for Descartes, the supporting substance of all Being: in doubting it surpasses and grounds the experienced reality (with all its disorder and all its defective 'certainties'). This substance, this certainty-in-doubt, is the pivot of Descartes's system, and marks the turn that philosophy takes here: the ultimate foundation is no longer in Being itself, but in reason. Human reason's autonomy before Being receives here its metaphysical foundation, albeit in a paradoxical way. Descartes breaks with a *static* essentialism—the belief that the ultimate ground, the deepest essence, lies in Being—and rigorously pleads for the first time in the history of Western thinking for a *dynamic* essentialism: the belief that the ultimate ground lies in the *search for* an ultimate ground, and thus in the dynamism of reason.

In this seemingly closed circle, Being seems to have become univocal: there is no question of any differentiation, even though Descartes maintains a dualism between the thinking ego (the '*res cogitans*') and another substance, the reality outside the ego (the '*res extensa*'). But this latter is subjected to reason, is derived from it, and is literally an extension of it. Yet Descartes's wrestling begins with this severe system. He has difficulty with concepts like 'transcendence,' 'infinity,' and 'God,' since he can only think in terms of the faculties of human autonomous reason. The circle is not completely closed, for how can God be both an Idea of reason and precede reason? How can reason's doubt be the only foundation for certainty, and still refer to a higher certainty: God? The problem is that reason cannot support everything all at once, and still ultimately be supported by something else. Descartes's scientific-philosophical passion and his religious passion are in an irresolvable conflict.

The foundation Descartes seeks is a foundation without foundation, such that reason is left with nothing but its own doubt. Reason represses God's alterity by including the Other in itself, and thus eliminates its own limits. Yet in this repression it collides with its own limits, and is left embarrassed. Despite Descartes's ambitions, a discomfort remains amid the certainty of the 'Cogito.'[58]

The reactions to Descartes's rationalism were vehement and polemical, particularly from the English empiricists. John Locke and after him David Hume expressed in the seventeenth and eighteenth centuries a skepticism regarding the way Descartes tried to modernize the old metaphysical tradition by making reason the last metaphysical foundation. Consistent with nominalism, they considered any metaphysical system unreliable because it creates its own axioms and uses them as a basis for endless speculation, and thus alienates itself from empirical reality. For the sciences, metaphysics is more a hindrance than (as Descartes asserts) a foundation. Locke and Hume do not deny *that* there are 'things behind things,'[59] but of these people can know nothing. As soon as they try, they go beyond the limits of existence. Empiricism is thus not only an antirationalist, but also an antimetaphysical tendency. More radically than Descartes, it breaks with premodern philosophy: that is, it says little, and that carefully, about pronouncements about God or the soul and the body. Yet it remains in a way more faithful to premodern life, be-

---

[58] See, on the relation between Cartesian rationalism and doubt, Hannah Arendt, *The Human Condition* (Chicago: University of Chicago Press, 1958), chap. 38, "The Rise of the Cartesian Doubt."

[59] That is, μετά τά φυσικά, "after/behind the physical things"; here we vary the original Aristotelian meaning of 'metaphysics' (i.e., 'the books that come after those on physics').

cause it protests against the limitless self-elevation of reason and respects the distance between people and world, between thinking and Being. Locke and Hume advance the line of the late medieval '*via moderna*,' which denies reason any right to speak about transcendence: transcendence is declared a 'topic' no longer relevant to philosophy.

Descartes's empirical opponents turn against both the ontological attempts to understand God with reason and against mysticism, that tried to bridge the distance between transcendence and immanence with other-than-rational means. We can speak here of an amystical skepticism.

These ambivalences in rationalism and empiricism preoccupied the young Kant. Kant was initially educated in the school of German rationalism (Wolff, Leibnitz), but, by his own witness, in his *Prolegomena*,[60] was awakened by Hume from his "dogmatic slumber." The limits of human reason, with which the rationalism of early modern philosophy unwillingly—and unconsciously—conflicted, were for the first time explicitly and critically investigated and analyzed by Kant.

He restored the multiplicity of Being, but not, as in premodern thinking, by distinguishing between two 'worlds,' a divine and a human, which more or less complemented one another. Kant points to a *break* between the two dimensions of reality that he names in his famous distinction between a "phenomenal" and a "noumenal" reality. On one side the "*Vernunft*" with its faculty of knowing relates to the world of appearances. On the other side, this phenomenal world repeatedly withdraws when our knowledge appears to encompass it in a successful process of knowing and science; on this border there 'appears' a noumenal world that remains unknowable for reason. People can touch this world of the "noumena" by thinking it, representing it, or experiencing it, but people cannot know it. The "noumena," as it were, force their way into every 'successful' relationship between subject and object, always causing people to lose their way in the process of knowing. This noumenal world is the break in the subject–object schema that philosophy and science took as their starting point before Kant. Things can be known insofar as

---

[60] See Kant's "Preface" to this work, ed. K. Vorländer (Hamburg: Meiner, 1993), 260.

they appear to people, but this knowledge remains limited. The things "in themselves" ("*das Ding an sich*") escape knowledge. At the point where the certainty of knowledge is at risk, people touch this hidden world. The unobservable and unthinkable enter human knowledge of reality as soon as people try to penetrate this reality. For this reason an epistemology and a metaphysics that take themselves seriously must not be oriented only toward the possible results of knowledge, but also toward the process of 'knowing' itself and its limitations.

The differentiation in Being that Kant expresses in his way refers immediately to a discontentment with the homogeneous view of Being. Echoes of a radical negative theology are tacitly present in his critical reworking of Enlightenment philosophy. The 'what' of God remains hidden to reason, just as the 'what' of Being (of "das Ding an sich") does. Even the 'that' of God and Being is unknowable on the basis of the appearances in which the world makes itself known to people. Reason is essentially broken, and finds its purpose only in a sensitivity to this break in Being that ruptures its ability to know and that challenges it to halt before its own limits. We could call respect for these limits the "categorical imperative" in Kant's *Kritik der reinen Vernunft*, next to the more famous one in his *Kritik der praktischen Vernunft*. Perhaps this respect is reminiscent of the starting point of negative theology.

After Kant, in the middle of the nineteenth century, Kierkegaard sharpened the protest against any form of thinking about Being. In doing so, he attacked primarily Hegel's metaphysical system. The echoes of negative theology resound more loudly and openly in his writings than in Kant's, since he studied such radical critics as Jacobi (1743–1819) and Hamann (1730–1788). Where Hamann posited that the divine can never coincide with the truth of Being, and can only reveal itself "through reason's lies and contradictions,"[61] Kierkegaard went further by heavily emphasizing that if revelation can be 'thought,' this thinking can only have meaning in a language of absolute irony, paradoxes, and absurdities. God leaves human reason behind in crisis and divisiveness, since in speaking about God it must go further than it can go—and must surrender.

---

[61] J. G. Hamann, "Konxompax," in *Sämtliche Werke*, ed. J. Nadler (Vienna: Herder, 1950), 3.227 (authors' translation).

Kierkegaard starts with the *experience* of this divisiveness, which is completely subjective: this experience is a 'lived' knowledge and a unique, personal-existential truth. To reach God, Kierkegaard thinks people must leave all positive knowledge behind and rely solely and radically on this experience. The religious person cannot come *to* God, but can only stand *before* Him, "in fear and trembling." Kierkegaard, in his own way, links the truth of Christian faith with a philosophical critique of thinking about Being. This makes him an untimely thinker in a period when the separation between theology and philosophy—initiated earlier by Thomas Aquinas—had long been taken for granted.

Thus David Law has good reasons for his thesis that Kierkegaard "was not only a negative theologian, but outdid negative theology." According to Law, he was "more apophatic" than negative theology, since he did not even recognize the mystical way to God.[62] Are the 'minimal' echoes of which we spoke earlier intensified here?

4. PHILOSOPHY AFTER THE DEATH OF GOD: ECHOES OF NEGATIVE THEOLOGY IN THE TWENTIETH CENTURY

How can an old tradition like that of negative theology become relevant again in the twentieth century? Can a period of emancipation and secularization that represents human history as a self-creation, as its own project, appreciate anew and incorporate a tradition that gnaws on its foundations? Or must we see the echoes of negative theology that we have described as a break, an interruption, even an invasion into the history of thought there where modern thinkers try to trace, hear, and perhaps answer these echoes?

This question is not easy to answer; the authors studied in this book pose it repeatedly and differently. We can share negative theology's discomfort as described above, but it remains uncertain whether an echo of its themes and motifs can really be meaningful in modern culture. Contemporary thinkers, such as Adorno, Bakhtin, Bataille, Derrida, Eco, Foucault, Levinas, Marion, Nancy, Taubes, and even Barth, each in his own way feel a certain rapport with negative theology, but they also wrestle with the problem of *inheriting*

---

[62] See D. R. Law, *Kierkegaard as Negative Theologian*, 221.

and adopting a tradition that can no longer be presented as simply a copy of the past. Has not every speaking about God today, even a negative speaking, become a problem? The 'negative' seems to have made itself independent of the speaking, so that even in a reprise of a radical emptying of the concept of God (Eckhart's "God is Nothing") these cultural philosophers detect a last denial and even a betrayal of the deep embarrassment of modern culture. This embarrassment must not be celebrated and praised. This would lead to the trap of "modern nihilism" analyzed and criticized by the Dutch theologian K. H. Miskotte, one that makes "the Nothing itself into the content, the last and emptiest, but *formally 'absolute'* content of our faith."[63]

If we share, perhaps unconsciously and unemphatically, in the inheritance of negative theology, then the purpose of this book is to make a new start in this direction: an analysis of the question as to how we are to receive this inheritance, how we are to do justice to its 'relevancy' once it comes to us.

Nietzsche: The Change in Modernity's Self-Image

The history we have summarized of the embarrassment and discomfort to which negative theology has been linked since its earliest days, and particularly since its late medieval exponents, meets a decisive turn in Nietzsche's analyses of the death of God. We described these analyses at the start of this Introduction as a cogent question addressed to Western culture and its tentative 'end product': modernity. This shows that this is not only a question of an intervention in a philosophical debate, but that Nietzsche's dictum is an answer to and an assimilation of the development modern culture has undergone on the threshold of the twentieth century.

The influence of Nietzsche's "God is dead" thesis on thinking about God, people, and religion in the last century has been enormous. It is important to go into it in greater detail here, because we think all authors treated in this book somehow work in the space

---

[63] K. H. Miskotte, *Als de goden zwijgen* (Amsterdam: Uitgeversmaatschappij Holland, 1956), 23 (author's translation). According to Gerrit Steunebrink (see his chapter in this volume), Adorno adopts a similarly critical position.

Nietzsche opened.[64] We wish particularly to address the plurality of meaning in his analyses, since Nietzsche's pronouncements on this point are sometimes interpreted too one-sidedly and simply, as in the now somewhat dated horizontalist 'God-is-dead' theology of the 1960s.[65]

Nietzsche was one of the first thinkers to transform the philosophical critique of the homogeneous view of Being into a critique of culture. He believed that this conception of Being that reaches its high point in the phenomenon of secularization expresses the views of humanity and the world held by a culture that, unawares, has actively killed God. Since the time of Nietzsche's analyses, a critical position in or regarding metaphysics and philosophy of religion can hardly do without a critical cultural philosophical position. To the extent that philosophy of culture is now developing a new interest in negative theology, it shares in the inheritance of Nietzsche's work.

Here again caution is needed: it would be senseless to decipher in Nietzsche's critique of culture a program for a contemporary negative theology. The most that can be done is to see in elements of his work an unintentional expression of the echoes we are concerned with in this discussion. It would be remarkable, and fascinating, to hear such echoes in a work that so sharply wants to break with the whole Christian theological tradition.

It is very important to realize now that Nietzsche's 'death of God' is not a statement of truth, but refers to an ambivalent experience.[66] How is this experience ambivalent? For Nietzsche, the death of God has two meanings, which, although they flow from one another, offer two different perspectives on the same 'event.'

In the first meaning, the death of God is the deed of a humanity that emancipates itself: this death functions as a liberation—from God—*through* reason. It is the best known and most predictable explanation of Nietzsche's dictum. But in the second meaning the

---

[64] We will mention but one high point in the revival of interest in Nietzsche since the 1960s, a revival we encounter first in France, then in the rest of Europe and America: the two-volume collection *Nietzsche aujourd'hui*, Vol. 1: *Intensités*, Vol. 2: *Passions* (Paris: Union Générale d'Éditions, '10/18', 1973). Alongside contributions by Derrida, Lyotard, Deleuze, and Nancy, there are studies by Eugen Biser and Paul Valadier, in which they present their new interpretation of the death of God.

[65] See, e.g., A. T. Robinson, *Honest to God* (London: SCM Press, 1963), and, with more philosophical depth, Thomas Altizer, ed., *Towards a New Christianity: Readings in the Death of God Theology* (New York: Harcourt, Brace & World, 1967).

[66] See above, Section 1.

death of God marks the end of human self-emancipation. Humanity with its reason has taken God's place since the start of modernity. But this humanity-as-God, will ultimately succumb after the death of the old God, "sacrificed for nothingness."[67] In this meaning, reason as the 'new' God is liberated *from* itself. The nihilism that Nietzsche so announces is also his fear and challenge.

We wish to pause to consider the implications of these two meanings.

In the death of God humanity liberates itself from the old God: this is the first meaning of the thesis. The death of God is the unavoidable result of a long development of secularization started during the modern period; humanism, the emancipation of the arts, the development of the planet, rationalism and the newly dominant position of the sciences, and the birth of humanity as the unique and irreplaceable center of history have made the twentieth century a period without God. The death of God thus consists in a resistance against religion in favor of reason: a resistance against the old God, in both his pre-Christian and Christian forms.

It is a resistance against the god of archaic humanity: the God of whom we no longer know anything, but whose daily proximity people must once have felt. This God was always present in plurality: as the gods to whom humanity sacrificed and to whom humanity related in ever-differing ways, to each God according to his or her divine characteristics as known from the traditions found in myths and narratives. To these Gods the human community related personally, but in a way different from the relationship of two people—indeed, in a certain sense, it must have been a 'nonrelationship.' Only in sacrifice, in the proximity of death, in the feast, in surpassing daily existence could this daily relationship take shape.

It is also a resistance against the Christian God: the God who slowly became a singular, even abstract, power, a spiritual authority that guaranteed the ultimate harmony of existence. This God, protected by the dogmas of the churches, became the unfathomable Figure *behind* existence, lost His personal, daily proximity in distance, and forfeited His function as outside place that elicited fear and ecstasy. Although mystical traditions tried in numerous ways to reappreciate and even reintegrate this God's ecstatic function within

---

[67] Nietzsche, *Beyond Good and Evil*, fragment 55.

the limits of Christian faith, they remained marginal and often sub-versive.

Liberation from the grasp of this twofold old God slowly opens the modern period: the period in which human thinking tries to free itself from God. Jean-Luc Nancy describes this process as follows:

> The death of God is philosophy's *ultimate* image; philosophy posits it as the *end* of religion. It is the image to which the West . . . repeatedly leans. It involves the death of death, the negation of negation, the end of being separated from God, the divinization of humanity, the absolutizing of its knowledge and its history (or the confirmation of its total meaninglessness).[68]

Thus the death of the old God does not mean the end of the gods: one god remains: human reason that subjugates the whole world and instrumentalizes all Being in a movement toward appropriation. This 'ratio' is no longer "separate from God," in Nancy's words, but is itself a new god to be worshiped. Paradoxically, the death of God establishes a new, secular 'religion,' one without exterior, without sacred limits, without transcendence.

But the death of God, in Nietzsche, refers to more than liberation from the old God. In its second meaning, *it is a liberation from the new god, from reason, leaving humanity in an empty space.* In this space, people can no longer rely on God: secularization has made his 'death' irreversible. But humanity is equally unable to rely on 'humankind' and on the unambiguous character of Being, of which it would imagine itself to be the center. The last sacred cruelty that humanity imposes on itself is, as Nietzsche puts it, to sacrifice itself-as-God "for nothingness."

In this interpretation, the death of God is not the description of an event that has made modernity what it is, but is instead a proclamation, a vision in which modern humanity must pay for His 'death,'[69] but in doing so will surpass itself to find a humanity beyond

---

[68] J.-L. Nancy, *Des lieux divins* (Mauvezin: T. E. R., 1987), 23 (authors' translation); English translation, "Of Divine Places," trans. M. Holland, in Nancy, *The Imperative Community*, ed. P. Connor (Minneapolis: University of Minnesota Press, 1991), 110–50.

[69] ". . . who will wipe this blood off us? What water is there for us to clean ourselves? What festivals of atonement, what sacred games shall we have to invent?" *The Gay Science*, fragment 125.

humanity, Nietzsche's "*Übermensch.*"[70] Directly preceding his famous parable of the death of God,[71] Nietzsche points to an "unending horizon," stating: "We have left the land and have embarked.
We have burned our bridges behind us—indeed, we have gone far-
ther and destroyed the land behind us." The openness, the emptiness portrayed here is welcomed elsewhere as a new horizon:
"Indeed, we philosophers and 'free spirits' feel, when we hear the
news that 'the old god is dead,' as if a new dawn shone on us. . . . At
long last the horizon appears free to us again."[72] But will humanity
inhabit this new world? Have the "freie Geister" become new gods?
No, this horizon is empty, and in a certain sense uninhabitable, like
a sea. Nietzsche immediately speaks of "the sea, *our* sea, which opens
its expanses before us." It is as if the emptiness here creates the
opportunity for a new, modern experience of transcendence. The
next fragment in *The Gay Science* bears the title: "How we, too, are
still pious" . . . "And how many new gods are still possible!"[73]

The death of God, understood in its ambivalence (death of the
old God, death of humanity-as-God), implies that humanity is deprived of a goal: it can only feel its way, hesitantly, into an open
space essentially unknown. Understood in this way, the death of God
is by no means a one-time event. On the contrary, it is an element
of what Nietzsche calls the "eternal return," recurring repeatedly. It
is the 'event' to which modern times as a component of Western
history owes its fractured identity. This event[74] breaks open a space
for an experience of transcendence that exists in a relationship to a
God who is dead, without this 'death' being the simple negation of

---

[70] On the death of God as proclamation ('vision') of the end of humanity, see also
the final passages in M. Foucault, *Les mots et les choses* (Paris: Gallimard, 1966)
which discusses the crisis of humanity discovered and exalted by modern human
sciences; and J. Derrida, "Les fins de l'homme," in *Marges—De la philosophie* (Paris:
Minuit, 1968; English translation, *Margins of Philosophy*, trans. A. Bass [Chicago:
University of Chicago Press, 1982]), which analyzes Nietzsche's critique of the modern concept of the subject. We think Charles Taylor in his impressive study *Sources
of the Self* (see above) illuminates the historical stage on which Nietzsche's critique
of culture and his view of modern humanity are presented as "Deicide."

[71] Nietzsche, *The Gay Science*, fragment 125.

[72] Ibid., fragment 343.

[73] Ibid., fragment 344. Followed by *The Will to Power*, trans. W. Kaufmann and
R. J. Hollingdale (New York: Vintage, 1968), 1038.

[74] In the sense of Heidegger's term 'Ereignis': that which *is performed on* history
('despite' this history), instead of flowing from it.

His existence: in His absence this God proves that He is God. Blanchot points out that Nietzsche's parable ends with the complaint of the madman who announced the death of God: "I have come too soon." And it is questionable whether there will ever be a time, says Blanchot, when the madman will not come too soon, when the world will be ready to hear and understand his cries, and when his arrival will coincide with the event of which he speaks.

> In a certain sense the madman will never come at the right time, he will always precede the event; questioned and ostracized, he can only be the mad witness of a deed that always seems further away than the farthest stars, and that nonetheless is present and complete. For this reason Nietzsche's dictum "God is dead" is not effective as knowledge that provides an answer, but as a refusal of an answer, the negation of salvation, a 'no' to the elevated agreement that humanity may rest and unburden itself of itself based on an eternal truth that God exists. "God is dead" is a task, a task without end. History includes the moment that it surpasses. "God is dead, but humanity is such that for millennia grottos may exist in which His shadow is visible. . . . And we . . . we too must see to conquer this shadow." The death of God conceals in itself the sacred and enigmatic character of the sacrifice evoked by his name.[75]

Since the death of God human history bears with it its *own* denial, its own 'death' and 'end.' It had to kill God to reach its autonomous completion; but this completion destroys the movement that history is, and thus its subject, human reason. A history cannot exist without

---

[75] Blanchot, "Du côté de Nietzsche," 294 (authors' translation). See also M. Foucault's essay, "Préface à la transgression," in *Critique* 195–96 (1963): 751–769, 753; later included in *Dits et ecrits* (Paris: Gallimard, 1994), 1.233–250, 235: "What, indeed, is the meaning of the death of God, if not a strange solidarity between the stunning realization of his nonexistence and the act that kills him? But what does it mean to kill God if he does not exist, to kill God *who has never existed*? Perhaps it means: to kill God both because he does not exist and to guarantee that he will not exist—certainly a cause for laughter: to kill God to liberate life from this existence that limits it, but also to bring it back to those limits that are annulled by this limitless existence—as a sacrifice; to kill God to return him to this nothingness he is and to manifest his existence at the center of a light that blazes like a presence—for the ecstasy." English translation, "A Preface to Transgression," trans. D. F. Bouchard and S. Simon, in Foucault, *Language, Counter-Memory, Practice: Selected Essays and Interviews*, ed. D. F. Bouchard (Ithaca, N.Y.: Cornell University Press, 1977), 19–52; 32. (For more on this essay, see the chapter in this volume by Laurens Ten Kate.)

being in a permanent tension with what is 'outside history,'[76] the name-without-name called 'God.' Hegel's "End of History" marks not only the neutralization and the end of religion, but also the end of humanity. As long as modern history continues without reaching its completion—despite Hegel's system—the shadow of God's death pursues this history as a sacred remainder. The death of God must therefore 'return eternally,' will never be completed once and for all: modernity consists in an unceasing 'sacrifice of God,' in the different meanings used here: sacrifice of God, sacrifice of divinized humanity.

The death of God affirms itself as an eternal return—of God and of His death. Nietzsche's Zarathustra takes on the ambivalence of God's death when he resignedly accepts the words of the "old pope."

> "What do I hear" the old pope said at this point, pricking up his ears; "O Zarathustra, you are more pious than you believe, with such an unbelief! Some god in you has converted you to your godlessness. Is it not piety itself that no longer allows you to believe in a god?"[77]

As we will show, Nietzsche opens a series of cultural philosophical reflections closely related to the earlier mentioned embarrassment for which negative theology is partly an articulator. He does this by playing modern culture against its own view of itself: a culture that kills God kills itself as well. He asks whether a culture without an 'outside' is viable, even thinkable. His answer is an unambiguous 'no,' but here his questioning only starts. How can we think of a place for transcendence in a culture that cannot deny its modern, secularized situation? Nietzsche's work gives no answer to this question, but is an attempt to criticize and disrupt all standard answers.

He wraps his speaking about God in contradictions and enigmas, and in so doing tries, we suspect, to do justice to his own 'image' (or rather, a suspicion, a trace?) of God, which touches on that of negative theology, although in a new variation. He emphasizes in God the enigmatic, His unbearable appearance and disappearance, and,

---

[76] Here we are inspired by Jewish-oriented thinking on history, which we find developed primarily in works by Walter Benjamin. See also the chapter by Marin Terpstra and Theo de Wit in this volume.

[77] F. Nietzsche, *Thus spoke Zarathustra: A Book for Everyone and Noone*, trans. R. J. Hollingdale (Harmondsworth, U.K.: Penguin, 1975), part 4; "In Rest," *Kritische Gesamtausgabe*, 6.7.327.

taking this into account, calls it by other names but often by the name 'God.' But as soon as God becomes an answer, His wound healed, His death undone, Nietzsche deconstructs this God as an escape, an illusionary bottom that can become modernity's abyss.[78]

After Nietzsche

The problem of the death of God, this 'space' in our time that Nietzsche wanted to analyze and evoke, marks twentieth-century philosophy of culture and many of the domains allied to it: philosophy of religion, linguistic philosophy, metaphysics, and (political) theology—to mention only the most important. Searching for answers to Nietzsche's question of how we are to think of and react to the death of God, authors try to formulate the question with greater precision. One characteristic of this attempt is the refusal to reject the ambivalence of Nietzsche's words by choosing instead to give them their due and to make them fruitful. This is true of the thinkers studied in this book, some of whom are treated elaborately (Adorno, Bakhtin, Bataille, Derrida, Marion, and Taubes), others of whom are treated more indirectly (among them Barth, Blanchot, Eco, Foucault, Heidegger, Levinas, and Nancy).

In this way, the chapters devoted to twentieth-century thinkers offer a differentiated image of the way contemporary philosophy of culture reacts to the death of God and regains interest in the tradition of negative theology. We would like to touch briefly on a few central themes and lines of thought, before letting the different texts and approaches speak for themselves.

Heidegger's Criticism of Onto-Theology   Many of the above-mentioned authors seek ways to break through the homogeneous view of Being that, according to Nietzsche, ultimately was largely responsible for the death of God. The critique of *onto-theology* is a determining factor in this search.[79] Martin Heidegger's work on this has had a

---

[78] Dirk de Schutter goes more deeply into Nietzsche's theme of the death of God in his chapter in this volume.

[79] Regarding 'onto-theology,' see esp. Heidegger's "Die Onto-theo-logische Verfassung der Metaphysik," in *Identität und Differenz* (Pfullingen: Neske, 1957), 35–73.

decisive influence, one found extensively, for example, in Derrida and Marion.[80]

Heidegger's work in many ways bears the stamp of Nietzsche's analysis of the death of God—for example, his essay "Nietzsches Wort: Gott ist tot."[81] Yet of greater importance than the cultural critical assimilation of Nietzsche's dictum is Heidegger's independent criticism of thinking on Being, which he tried to disentangle and transform from within. He seeks to penetrate the concept, or rather, the word 'Being' ('*Sein*'), in whose enigmatic nature he suspects a resistance to the categories of Being in Western metaphysics and ontology. Where ancient, mainly pre-Socratic and Socratic, philosophy was still open to the fundamental inability to grasp Being, this openness was later stifled in the West.

Heidegger presents the verb 'to be,' the most mundane, unobtrusive, and indispensable in the language, as *the* problem of thinking. This Being is not simply the reality in which we live, which we come to know and 'assimilate': it does not coincide with 'objectivity,' for objectivity needs Being before it can become 'something,' become a being. Being thus in a way precedes reality. This is evident from having to use some form of the verb 'to be' if we want to say anything at all about reality. This word slips unnoticed into our speaking. Neither objectivity nor human existence—thinking and speaking subjectivity—coincide with Being. The subject loses its Being before it can determine and grasp it, for Being precedes all speaking and thinking. In speaking about what is, we 'automatically' forget that the Being of things—of 'beings'—does not arise through this speaking, but is their unthinkable, hidden source.

That Being is something else than the objectivity or the subjectivity of Being is apparent when we think of the phrase 'there is,' or in German, '*es gibt*.' In the anonymity and neutrality of this word '*there*' we see that Being escapes attempts to point to it, to objectivize or subjectivize it. In Heidegger's view, pure Being is an emptiness, it withdraws from every concept of Being, it is indomitable. It cannot be pinned down, it is not static, but functions literally as *verb*, as indicator of action: it moves through language without being re-

---

[80] But in different ways; see the chapters in this volume contributed by Victor Kal and Ilse N. Bulhof.

[81] In *Holzwege* (Frankfurt am Main: Vittorio Klostermann, 1950), 193–247.

duced to it. This 'emptiness of Being' is opened behind or under thinking wherever Being and non-Being flow together. This unbalances every thinking about Being and leaves an experience that Heidegger calls 'fear,' or radical openness: the fear that arises when people open themselves to a form of Being that 'is' not what it is, that withdraws as soon as it is sought.

Heidegger pleads in a new and radical way for a heterogeneous view of Being in which he distinguishes between 'Being' and 'beings.' Being is the indeterminate condition of all beings, but it is also their impenetrable limit. Is the emphasis on this limit an attempt to go beyond *thinking* about Being? Can Heidegger's redefinition of the classical question of Being be fruitful for a new concept of transcendence and a modern way of speaking about and relating to God? Or does his thinking merely mark the end of philosophy, compelling it to recognize that the end of metaphysics that he proclaimed is also the end of philosophical theology?[82]

His critique of onto-theology that thinks of God and Being as one seems to follow the same steps as his critique of an ontology that neglects distinguishing Being and beings. But does his new, critical, and 'negative' definition of Being not secretly coincide with his view of the divine and the sacred, and thus with his images of transcendence? Heidegger's attempts to transform theology into "theiology" and thus to transform a thinking/speaking about God into a thinking/speaking of the divine (*theion*) point in this direction. These questions and presuppositions will be discussed in various chapters in this collection.[83]

Negative Theology in Recent Philosophy of Culture: Two Possible Variations of a Minimal Echo   We said earlier that the history of classical negative theology repeatedly leads to a polemical answer to homogeneous thinking about Being: it repeatedly pleads in various ways for the idea and experience of a *Supra-Essence*, a Highest Being

---

[82] According to Weischedel (see his *Der Gott der Philosophen*), philosophical theology becomes a radical problem in Nietzsche's and Heidegger's thinking. In his view, philosophical theology consists only of posing the (philosophical) question of how, in our time, we can speak about God. It is likely that there remains only this 'path of radical questioning,' as Weischedel says. But we think this does not proclaim the end of philosophical theology in our time; wherever the echoes of negative theology lead to this 'radical questioning,' we must find new links between philosophy and theology.

[83] In this regard, see also R. Kearney and J. S. O'Leary, eds., *Heidegger et la question de Dieu* (Paris: Grasset, 1980), which contains articles by Levinas and Marion.

or Ultimate Reality, with which it wants to do justice to the polyvalency and heterogeneity of Being.[84] We would now like to distinguish two reactions elicited by this 'supra-essentialism': two conflicting reactions prominent in contemporary philosophy of culture as it is presented in this book. Both echoes betray their modern and 'postmodern' character by being minimal and by questioning the affirmation of a Supra-Being, so characteristic of premodern negative theology.[85] Beyond this point their ways diverge.

The *first reaction* indicates the need for *faith:* faith in a revelation coming from beyond, a self-communication of the divine. Philosophers of religion and theologians end with new ideas on revelation, in which they try to translate and rephrase the core of the experience of a Supra-Essence in modern terms, and to link it to Christian notions. We think Marion's work is one example. In his work he tries to reach an *active* resumption and revaluation of negative theology: God surpasses our thinking and imagination. The emphasis on revelation leads to an emphasis on revelation's authority. Because God Himself is the *author* of His 'self-communication,' revelation is the only *authority*. Because of this authority, people must accept and obey it, and because it comes from God, it must be believed. God is transcendent, as we understand Marion, and is not accessible for philosophical thinking: He is *"sans l'être."*[86] But the God of Christian faith is Trinitarian: Christ is the *icon* in which God communicates Himself lovingly to humanity. Faith in other forms of knowledge too easily tempts humanity to idolatry, to the worship of human creations. Through the bishops, the Church has the task of guarding this gift from God which—as icon—is the Truth itself and to proclaim it to humanity. In its subtle, free, and creative but nevertheless very positive affirmation of Christian doctrine, Marion's position may be compared to that of the philosopher Jean-Louis Chrétien.[87] In theologians like Barth we meet this radical thinking on revelation as well, but with different results for a 'dogmatics of the Church.'[88]

---

[84] See above, Section 1.

[85] On our explanation of this 'minimal' see above, Section 1.

[86] See the title of Marion's book, *Dieu sans l'être. Hors-texte* (Paris: Fayard/Communio, 1982); English translation, *God without Being: Hors-texte*, trans. T. A. Carlson (Chicago : University of Chicago Press, 1991).

[87] See J.-L. Chrétien, *Lueur de secret* (Paris: L'Herne, 1985), esp. chap. 1, "Théocryptique de la révélation," and chap. 4, "Dieu caché et théologie de la croix dans la pensée de Luther"; and *L'appel et la réponse* (Paris: Minuit, 1992).

[88] On Barth's 'dialectical theology,' see Jozef Wissink's chapter in this volume, as well as Rico Sneller's.

Others, including most of the contemporary authors treated in this book, agree in principle with Marion's critical reflection on the question of what the Supra-Essence could be. Is it, as divine Being, a *more*-being, an intensification or expansion of Being, and is it for this reason impossible for finite beings to understand? Or is this Supra-Essence something *on the other side of* Being, something different from Being, no longer even 'facing' it? But this *second reaction* does not attempt an active resumption or even rehabilitation of negative theology, as Marion, however cautiously, seems to undertake; nor does this second reaction wish to revitalize Christian doctrine, as an ultimate tradition of reference. It's rapport with negative theology, far from being 'anti-Christian' (if this is a meaningful expression anyway), is very reticent and *passive*, 'entering' the tradition of negative theology at exceptional moments and exceptional places. We may remember the time bomb that Damascius[89] put under all forms of the philosophy of Being. Well then, it is the 'echos' of negative theology, heard, for example, in Derrida, that sets the timer on this bomb. Derrida's thesis is that the return to this concept of a Highest Being, withdrawn from human knowledge, is not possible. He tries to deconstruct every thinking about Being. He rejects every *investment* of a Highest Being in an authoritative revelation incarnated hierarchically in a Church (or in any institution). Here he closely approaches a political theologian like Taubes, but also Bataille, Bakhtin, and Adorno, and differs from Marion.[90] Derrida does not seek to revitalize negative theology, but he is interested in the relevance of

---

[89] See above, Section 2.

[90] See J. Derrida, "Comment ne pas parler? Dénégations," in *Psyché: Inventions de l'autre* (Paris: Galilée, 1986), 553–54n1; English translation, "How to Avoid Speaking: Denials" (see next note), 134n9. Here, Derrida discusses Marion's "model of Hierarchy," which is not "political" but "has to do with mystery," as Derrida resumes Marion's words in *L'idole et la distance* (Paris: Grasset, 1977), 217. But, Derrida asks, "How is it possible that 'distance'—in the sense Marion gives to this word and which also makes up the distance between the two hierarchies—can have let itself be overstepped or 'traversed' and *give place to the anological translation of one hierarchy into another* [i.e., the institutional, 'political' one into the mysterious one]?" Derrida then problematizes this "analogy" on behalf of an "unfathomable economy," a "limit," a "noneconomy," or "an anarchy of the gift" between the two hierarchies. "In this regard I feel that Marion's thought is both very close and extremely distant: others might say opposed." See, for a comparison of Derrida and Marion, Rodolphe Gasché, *Inventions of Difference: On Jacques Derrida* (Cambridge, Mass.: Harvard University Press, 1994), 153ff. Graham Ward even resumes Marion's thought as a "conservative postmodern theology"; see his chapter "Post-

the questions, paradoxes, and dilemmas with which negative theology confronts us today.

The critical élan of Nietzsche's 'death of God' and of Heidegger's rejection of an onto-theology is a most important frame of reference for Derrida. His article "Comment ne pas parler. Dénégations" has been particularly influential in this regard.[91] Levinas's attempts, inspired by Jewish thinking, to reach a way to speak about God as the Other ('l'Autre'), as a name that is "*autrement qu'être*" (otherwise than Being),[92] contribute to the philosophical climate in which this second reaction can arise.[93]

When new ways of speaking about God are at stake, this endeavor seems very fruitful, even though the philosophical and theological language for this speaking must still be invented. One of the burning questions is how 'negative' this new language must be if it wants to speak of God in terms other than Being.[94]

---

modern Theology," in *The Modern Theologians: An Introduction to Christian Theology in the 20th Century*, 2nd ed., ed. David F. Ford (Oxford, U.K.: Blackwell, 1997), 585–601, 593ff.

[91] See the chapters in this volume contributed by Hent de Vries, Ilse N. Bulhof, and Rico Sneller. The English translation appeared as 'How to Avoid Speaking: Denials,' in S. Budick and W. Iser, *Languages of the Unsayable: The Play of Negativity in Literary Theory* (New York: Columbia University Press, 1999), 3–70, and in H. Coward and T. Foshay, eds., *Derrida and Negative Theology* (Albany: State University of New York Press, 1992), 25–72. On Derrida's relationship to negative theology, see also David E. Klemm, "Open Secrets: Derrida and Negative Theology," in Robert P. Scharlemann, ed., *Negation and Theology* (Charlottesville/London: University Press of Virginia, 1992), 8–24; John D. Caputo, "Mysticism and Transgression: Derrida and Meister Eckhart," in H. J. Silverman, ed., *Derrida and Deconstruction* (New York/London: Routledge, 1989), 24–39, and Caputo, *The Prayers and Tears of Jacques Derrida: Religion without Religion* (Bloomington/Indianapolis: Indiana University Press, 1997), esp. chap. 7, "The Apophatic"; and finally Hent de Vries, *Philosophy and the Turn to Religion* (Baltimore: Johns Hopkins University Press, 1999), esp. chap 2, "Hypertheology," and chap. 5, "The Kenosis of Discourse."

[92] See Derrida's study of Levinas, "Violence et métaphysique," in J. Derrida, *L'écriture et la différence* (Paris: Seuil, 1967); English translation, *Writing and Difference*, trans. A. Bass (Chicago: University of Chicago Press, 1978).

[93] Might this second reaction, or echo, in which the influence of Derrida and Levinas seems to be pivotal, lead us to a 'new theology,' a 'theology of difference'? See for a treatment of this question L. ten Kate, "Randgänge der Theologie: Prolegomena einer 'Theologie der Differenz' im Ausgang von Derrida und Barth," in *Zeitschrift für dialektische Theologie* 14–1 (1998), 9–31.

[94] Weischedel, in *Der Gott der Philosophen*, suggests a new name for God "Wovonher." "Wovonher" expresses the only available truth about the word 'God'. He refers here to the tradition of negative theology: "die . . . immer wieder Gott und die göttlichen Dinge unter das Sein als Geheimnis ausgelegt hat" (217). He notes

This language will have to articulate a new sensitivity for the 'exterior' of Western culture. Does this exterior, Damascius's "That Over There," give itself to whomever is receptive to it? But how is one 'receptive,' how do we listen to these echoes? These questions repeatedly seem to withdraw from a straightforward answer. But they point toward the critical awareness that we—if this is possible—must look beyond the borders of the Western foundation of Being to meet the unknown.

5. EPILOGUE

How do we speak about God? Does the crisis of modernity lead to the failure of this 'about'? Even when we cannot speak, we are still not freed from God, nor can we shake ourselves free of modernity and its crisis.[95]

We are pursued by the emptiness that vanished Highest Being has

---

that this philosophical theological "Whence" is by no means identical with the Christian concept of God (242). This does not mean that the God of Christian faith is a 'mistake'; rather that Christian theology gives the shape of an 'accessible, speakable' God to what in philosophical theology—as Weischedel describes it in the second part of his study—is experienced as unspeakable (245).

[95] Insofar as the present interest among philosophers for negative theology comes from a critical reflection on modernity, it is natural to include the authors studied in this book among the so-called postmodern writers. Especially an author like Derrida is often seen as an exponent of this tendency. On the other side, authors like Nietzsche, Heidegger, Bataille, Bakhtin, and Adorno are considered their precursors. A neutral description of this postmodernism in continental philosophy over the last decades would be satisfied with just showing the refusal of these authors to formulate comprehensive, declarative theories. They no longer pretend to be able to put the truth or reality into words, but 'deconstruct' concepts as 'truly' and 'really'. Frequently such descriptions do not stop here, but associate this 'postmodernism' with an extreme relativism. Here, it is said, we would detect a decadent and principled attitude to life marked by radical doubt and indifference. Of course, the intense interest among these thinkers regarding ethical and theological questions belies this association.

Given this stigmatization, it is apparently impossible for some philosophers, publicists and critics to show interest in the tactile, seeking, unfixed character of this philosophical direction. The lack of appreciation sometimes turns into real fear, followed by an attempt to deflect 'postmodernism' as a danger and to pare it with a new knife of Ockham. They see 'postmodernism' as a game of accusations leveled against reason. Yet 'postmodern' authors are characterized less by accusations than by a continual self-analysis derived from the traditions of modernity and its dilemmas: 'postmodern' thinkers question the foundations of Western philosophy and left behind. We feel God's 'death' as a wound in modern culture that will not heal. His absence haunts us. A contemporary contact with negative theology can only lead to what Michel de Certeau calls a "theology of the phantom," a theology that is no longer aware that it can speak, nor that it must speak.

The One God is no longer there. "They have taken him away," say so many mystical songs that proclaim the history of His return by telling

---

seek the limits of philosophical knowledge and speech.

According to Jean-François Lyotard, the unfortunate inventor of the term, 'post-modernism' has nothing to do with a stylish view of life. He sees it as an attitude in modern thinking that tries to take into account the situation to which thinking has come. This attitude does not oppose modernity, but is its hidden ground: a ground that can no longer function as foundation, a "Letztbegründung" (Apel), but as a source of embarrassment, dilemmas, and critical reflection that also bring forth the seeds of a sensitivity to the 'new' and the 'unknown'" (See J.-F. Lyotard, La condition postmoderne [Paris: Minuit, 1979]). For Lyotard, 'postmodern' does not mean the end of modernity, but another relationship to modernity.

The connecting element between 'postmodernists' lies not in a relativism but in the recognition of the factual crisis of modernity—in this sense they can all be called 'philosophers of culture.' But this 'postmodern' thinking can hardly be called postmodern, since it questions the tacit hope to undo or leave behind the failure of modernity, and thus questions every notion of 'post-.' It asks whether the desire to soar above modernity is not itself a modern desire.

In her 'Huizinga Lecture' (Tradities van het nieuwe, of: Moeten wij modern zijn? [Amsterdam: Bert Bakker, 1990]; original lecture in English, Traditions of the New or: Must We Be Modern?), Susan Sontag similarly discussed the distinction 'modern/postmodern.' She notes that "for the moment it is in style to posit that it is our duty to be ready to go beyond modernity, indeed, to say that we have already done so, willingly or not," and she continues with the critical observation that this 'post-modern' "does not soar above the logic of the modern" (47–48; author's translation).

According to Sontag, "the dictum that we live in a 'postmodern' culture pushes the axiom of freedom, implicit in modern consciousness, to its extreme consequences. It is a construction with as goal to allow humanity to do as it will. . . . But we cannot do what we will, and that is a lesson we must learn. Postmodernism is only a variation on, an expansion of, the modern. And the dilemmas of the modern are far from being solved, and are very dangerous" (45).

Given this, the description 'postmodern' is utterly problematic. Insofar as we can use it, it refers to a thinking that puts central the experience of limit: the limits of language, of philosophical speaking, and of Western subjectivity that is constituted in its urge for truth. The awareness of time—oriented toward domination that is characteristic of this subjectivity, in which the present is continually subjected to what precedes and follows it, to a 'pre-' and a 'post-'—reels. The limit confronts this modern awareness of time sometimes in an oppressive and sometimes playful way with 'the destruction its seriousness has caused" (Sontag). At this limit we lose our grasp on everything and stare into emptiness. But perhaps this emptiness will (again? for the first time?) teach us to be, will bare us to the world, and teach it to the story of His disappearance, repeatedly, elsewhere and differently, along paths that are the result, rather than the denial, of His absence. Although He is no longer the Living One, let this 'dead One' leave in peace our city that was built without Him. He haunts our places.[96]

Strangely, this experience refers us to a language, to texts handed down from a past that lies thousands of years further away than the tradition of negative theology. On the eve of Western civilization the difficulty of speaking about God was put into words in a language to which we, perhaps, feel more bound than ever: the language of prayer, of supplication, as articulated in the Psalms:

> The Heavens are telling the glory of God
> and the firmament proclaims his handiwork
> Day to day pours forth speech,
> and night to night declares knowledge.
> There is no speech, nor are there words;
> their voice is not heard;
> yet their voice goes out through all the earth,
> and their words to the end of the world.[97]

The language perceived in Psalm 19 is no longer (or not yet) a speaking *about*. It speaks *to* an unknown and nameless God, to four letters, YHWH, and extols His invisible 'handiwork.' This old language faces the emptiness of being unable to speak: "no speech," "no words," "their voice is not heard.". . . Yet this 'negating' language is not one of isolation and despair, but expects that the empty space is the

---

bear its fruit. We think this tacit wish lies hidden in the present interest in negative theology.

> A man cannot know where he is on earth
> except in relation to the moon or a star.
> Astronomy comes first; maps flow from them.
> Just the opposite of what you would expect.
> If you think about it long enough,
> your brain turns inside-out.
> A here exists only in relation to a there, not the reverse.
> There's this only because there's that;
> if we do not look up, we will never know what is down.
> Think of it, boy.
> We only find ourselves by looking down at what we are not.

(Paul Auster, *Moon Palace* [London/Boston: Faber & Faber, 1987], 153–54).

[96] M. de Certeau, *La fable mystique*, 10 (authors' translation).

[97] Ps. 19.1–4; trans., *The Holy Bible: Revised Standard Version, An Ecumenical Edition* (New York: Collins, 1973), 481–82.

trace of 'another' space, like a tacit sign. It is a place from which we are given language and speech: "the Heavens," the place of God and the limitation of the earth. Understood thus, the Psalms express a prayer spoken from more than emptiness and despair. They are odes to the space of heaven.[98] This space is really no space, but a non place, an *atopy*, known to us only as limit, as "firmament" that—from the first words of creation in Genesis—divides the heaven from the earth. The heaven is an ever-moving borderline and functions as an open "end" to our "world"; its "voice" warns us not to take our existence into our own hands, not to lead it as if it were our creation, our product.

Negative theology: a speaking to . . .? A prayer, not to the gods/the God, but to their neverending flight into "the Heavens," only to 'come back' and haunt us and our prayers again? Although the texts you have in hand do not intend to give a new, 'postmodern' form to such a prayer, they study the need for, the possibility or the untenability of, this speaking: a task that, for the moment, is large enough.[99]

---

[98] The Hebrew title of the Old Testament Book of Psalms is *Tehillim*, which means 'songs of praise.'

[99] Among other relevant literature not referred to so far, we mention: Kevin Hart, *The Trespass of the Sign: Deconstruction, Theology, and Philosophy* (Cambridge: Cambridge University Press, 1989); Walter Lowe, *Theology and Difference: The Wound of Reason* (Bloomington: Indiana University Press, 1993); Charles E. Winquist, *Epiphanies of Darkness: Deconstruction and Theology* (Chicago: University of Chicago Press, 1986); Philippa Berry and Andrew Wernick, eds., *Shadow of Spirit: Postmodernism and Religion* (London: Routledge, 1992); R. Scharlemann, ed., with T. J. Altizer, M. C. Taylor, C. E. Winquist, and R. P. Scharlemann, *Theology at the End of the Century: A Dialogue on the Postmodern* (Charlottesville: University of Virginia Press, 1989); Michael A. Sells, *Mystical Languages of Unsaying* (Chicago/London: University of Chicago Press, 1994); Mark C. Taylor, *Deconstructing Theology* (New York: Crossroad, 1982), *Erring: A Postmodern A/theology* (Chicago: University of Chicago Press, 1984), and *Nots* (Chicago: University of Chicago Press, 1993); Graham Ward, *Barth, Derrida, and the Language of Theology* (Cambridge, U.K.: Cambridge University Press, 1995); Edith Wyschogrod, *Saints and Postmodernism: Revisioning Moral Philosophy* (Chicago: University of Chicago Press, 1990); David R. Griffin, *God or Religion in the Modern World: Essays in Postmodern Theology* (Albany: State University of New York Press, 1989); and Ernest Gellner, *Postmodernism, Reason, and Religion* (New York: Routledge, 1992). Fine overviews are presented in Graham Ward, ed., *The Postmodern God: A Theological Reader* (Oxford, U.K.: Blackwell, 1997), and in Pierre Gisel and Patrick Evrard, eds., *La théologie en postmodernité* (Geneva: Labor et Fides, 1996). Finally we refer the reader to *Literature and Theology: An International Journal of Theory, Criticism, and Culture* 9, no. 1 (1995): 99–103, where Marius Buning reviews recent publications on negative theology and philosophy.

Chapter 1

Cloud of Unknowing

AN ORIENTATION IN NEGATIVE THEOLOGY FROM DIONYSIUS THE AREOPAGITE, ECKHART, AND JOHN OF THE CROSS TO MODERNITY

Bert Blans

HERE I TREAT three names from the tradition of classic negative theology that still hold an exceptional place in that tradition. The first to be treated is Dionysius the Areopagite (Section 1). His texts bring us directly to the two roots of negative theology: the Greek and the Jewish (Section 2). After a brief discussion of the language of mysticism (Section 3), I will present two figures who have been of decisive importance for the development of negative theology: Eckhart (Section 4) and John of the Cross (Section 5). After examining their thinking, I will pose the question of how we are to understand the relevancy of these three figures (Section 6): What contribution do they, given negative theology's double root, provide to the philosophical and ethical debate on *unity* as opposed to *exteriority*? In other words, is a modern recapturing of mysticism concerned with rethinking a unity that takes precedence above all duality and multiplicity, or with a revaluation of the radical 'other' with whom we can never become one?

1. DIONYSIUS THE AREOPAGITE: MYSTICISM AND NEGATIVE THEOLOGY

Such be my prayer; and thee, dear Timothy, I counsel that, in the earnest exercise of mystic contemplation, thou leave the senses and the activities of the intellect and all things that the senses or the intellect can perceive, and all things in this world of nothingness, or in that world of being, and that, thine understanding being laid to rest, thou strain (so far as thou mayest) towards an union with Him whom neither being nor understanding can contain. For, by the unceasing and absolute renunciation of thyself and all things, thou shalt in pureness cast all things aside, and be released from all, and so shalt be led upwards to the Ray of that divine Darkness which exceedeth all existence.[1]

The expressions 'negative theology' and 'mystical theology' most likely derive from the baffling figure who named himself after the Dionysius of whom Paul speaks in Acts 17.34, but who must have lived in Syria around A.D. 500: Dionysius the Areopagite.[2] The two terms, 'mystical theology' and 'negative theology,' are closely related. 'Mysticism' is derived from '*muoo*,' which means 'to close oneself,' applied primarily to the eyes and mouth; even before Dionysius the word was used when people spoke of the mystical dimension, that is, the hidden sense in the reading of Scripture and in liturgy. The mystical sense is hidden in words and gestures, such that people had to focus on it and become one with it. As Origin said, "No one can understand Scripture without first becoming deeply one with the reality of which it speaks."[3] Similarly, liturgy is a transforming *celebration*, a being absorbed in an invisible world (which comes to us in liturgy, in Scripture, and in God's incarnation).

We can say of Dionysius that he has a multitude of theologies. For him, theology is first of all God's speaking. Thus the Holy Scriptures are "theology." When he calls the inspired writers "theologians," it is because God speaks through them. In the same sense the angels are also "theologians," and Christ is the greatest theologian, the living Word of God. God himself is the "primeval theologian." Because God speaks in different ways, there are different

---

[1] Dionysius the Areopagite, *The Divine Names and the Mystical Theology*, trans. C. E. Rolt (London: SPCK, 1977), *Mystical Theology* I, 1 (= migne, *Patrologia Graeca* [Paris: Garnier, 1844–1864, vol. 3, 997B]).

[2] On Dionysius see, among others, J. Vanneste, *Le mystère de Dieu: Essai sur la structure rationnelle de la doctrine mystique du pseudo-Denys l'Areopagite* (Paris: Desclée de Brouwer, 1959).

[3] See Origen, "In Exodus XIII, 13," in Migne, *Patrologia Graeca*, vol. 12, col. 391a/b, and "Commentarium in Matthaeum, 05," ibid., vol. 13, col. 1734a/b (author's translation).

theologies. These are not distinct disciplines, courses, or fields of study, but different ways in which God speaks, and in which I, trusting in that speaking, can understand Him.

According to Dionysius, real speaking about God is a speaking that strikes human language dumb: that before which every imagery is powerless. Where 'theology' no longer finds help in images and parables (symbolic theology) nor is practiced via concepts and ideas is where we find real 'mystical theology': there God reveals himself in His silence.[4]

'Mystical theology' is thus essentially *mystagogia*, 'initiation in the secret.' The person with all that she or he is is immediately involved. It is not the study of a phenomenon outside ourselves, but a change in the nature of the person. To express this unity of reflection and experience, we can best speak of a 'path.'

Besides *positive* theology, in which it is said that God is good and is love, Dionysius also speaks of a *negative* theology. This is a theology in which it must be denied that He is good in the way people are good, or that He is father in a way a man is a father. It means that God's secret is preserved. We cannot articulate it, we cannot even know it. Not only has no one ever seen God, but He is removed from visibility: it is a principle that He cannot be seen or known. "Cloud" and "darkness" symbolize the impossibility of exhausting the object considered. In addition, negative theology can be explained as the revelation of God's own darkness or night.

Mystical theology is moving along a path that leads to the silent entrance into the divine secret; this is well expressed in the brevity and the dark ending of *The Mystical Theology*. (In Dionysius's method of negative theology the path that is followed has ever fewer words available, becomes increasingly speechless, as God's own dark silence comes nearer.)

The Three Paths

In *On the Heavenly Hierarchy* Dionysius says that "God's nature is absolutely pure, without any admixture, full eternal light and so perfect that it excludes every flaw. No, even more, it is pure, light, perfect above everything what is pure, light and perfect."[5] To share in

---

[4] It is open to discussion whether God also reveals Himself *as* silence.
[5] In Migne, *Patrologia Graeca*, vol. 3, III, 3 (author's translation).

this we must enter the path of *purification, enlightenment,* and *unification*. Plotinus (A.D. 204–c. 244) used these three terms, but for him they indicated three successive stages through which the soul must pass to free itself from the material and attain unity with the One. Dionysius does not use these three terms chronologically. They are no longer successive moments, but more-or-less simultaneous dimensions. Later writers equated these phases with initiation, advancement, and perfection. The neophyte would be on the way to perfection, with the special characteristics of avoiding sins, restraining passions, acquiring virtues, and using prayer as a meditation exercise. The more advanced would be on the path of enlightenment in which they no longer train themselves but allow themselves to be led by the light. Prayer changes in character, causing one to become more contemplative. Finally, there are the perfect, those who follow the path of unification. As "prayer of rest" this is also the phase of a return to carrying on normally, but totally in the light of the Infinite and thus of unity in love.

The advantage of Dionysius's representation of the simultaneous dimensions is that the neophyte freely chooses for purification, exercise, and asceticism because he or she already is partly aware of enlightenment and unification. He or she does not differentiate self from the advanced and the perfect in applying different means or different faculties, but by a more elementary or imperfect use of the same means and faculties. Enlightenment and unification are necessary for purification, and purification is always necessary for reaching a deeper knowledge and a greater inner union. As John of the Cross said, "A unification of the soul with God, although it be but brief, enlightens more and purifies more in the soul than many years spent in the active exercise of spiritual prayer and mortification."[6]

For Dionysius, it is especially true that the highest stage (like purification) is marked by "releasing renunciation," surrender to the "darkness" or the "unnameable." As was said to Timothy in the prayer cited at the start of this chapter, leaving sense perceptions and intellectual labors behind occurs through and in the presence of transcendence. The transcendence itself is first the request for

---

[6] Cited from John of the Cross, *Mystieke Werken* (Ghent: Carmelitana, 1980), 72 (author's translation).

purification, and later it is that which realizes it. This is probably the most significant difference between Dionysius's negative theology and Plotinus's Neoplatonism; what Dionysius did take over from Plotinus is the concept of knowledge as "a turning toward."

Knowledge as "Turning Toward"

For Dionysius, like the Neoplatonists, knowledge is a "turning toward."[7] This means that knowledge is not merely 'learning something about something,' but is a way of becoming one with the object of our orientation so that we may know it better. This turning toward shares knowledge with all forms of life and being. It is its highest form. All beings proceeded from the One or the Good, and return to it in a 'reversal' or turning toward. As long as knowledge is confined in a multiplicity of reasonings and objects, it has not reached the One. Even when it, as spirit, contemplates the Ideas, concentration on a particular Idea still implies the exclusion of the other Ideas, and there is still the duality of the contemplator and the contemplated. How, then, can the One be known as it really is? This is only possible through a "suspension," a "renunciation," a "setting aside" of all activity, by ignoring everything that could distract or imprison attention. "Pure presence," "openness," and "pure attention" are ways of referring to this state. It requires (as it does for Plotinus) an "elimination," a "suspension of the duality" between knower and known, and a willingness to receptivity. It is a question of a path into the indeterminable and unnameable, and perhaps even beyond. Dionysius explains this by speaking of what lies beyond thinking and speaking.

In Dionysius's mysticism there is the remarkable ambiguity that—although this is impossible—it tries to explain God's secret as well as it can. In this explanatory unfolding God's elevation is so absolute that it becomes darkness for the created spirit. The Stoic prescription "Divest yourself from everything," the goal of which was to guarantee inner peace, returns here in a Christian form in the command, imposed on the contemplating soul, seek God above all in *denial.*

Dionysius illustrates this *via negativa* with an image he borrows

---

[7] This is the central idea of *The Mystical Theology.*

from the story of the divine revelation to Moses. Here is spoken of the *gnophos*, the darkness that, just like the cloud that surrounded Sinai, envelopes God's essence. The idea that God's characteristics are unknowable to reason, to thinking, and to speaking has become common property to nearly all Christian mystics and mystical schools. Above all, we must follow the path of *experience* through negation, renunciation, and purification.[8]

2. NEGATIVE THEOLOGY: GREEK PHILOSOPHICAL OR JEWISH BIBLICAL ORIGINS?

Negative theology owes its origin to both Greek philosophy and the Jewish Bible.

Ancient Israel spoke of the 'Holiness' of YHWH, of God. This 'Majesty' is so lofty and inviolable that seeing or touching it is fatal. This is expressed in the prohibition against worshiping foreign gods and the prohibition against graven images. The 'having no other gods before me,' as the Decalogue put it, says that the God who liberated the people from Egypt is one and unique and will tolerate no other gods beside Him. This is confirmed by the prohibition against making an image of YHWH: "You shall not make for yourself a graven image, or any likeness of anything that is in heaven above, of that is in the earth beneath, or that is in the water under the earth." The prohibition against misusing the divine name is also very strong. This has led to the custom that wherever the letters YHWH stand, people speak in formulas such as 'the Holy One, blessed be His Name.' This raises the question of how to refer to something that may not be named. These commandments and prohibitions have also received an allegorical or symbolic reading. The Most Holy One cannot be named and must therefore be *assumed* to be 'behind' or in the text, or there where the text is silent.

---

[8] It must be said of the relationship between mysticism and negative theology that the two do not overlap completely. A form of mysticism is possible that is not completely subsumed in negative theology. But every negative theology is probably linked to one or another type of mysticism. It is certainly linked to the effective following or 'exercising' a spiritual path, from which it is inseparable. After thought and will are reversed, initiative is taken over by a force that cannot be named or thought.

A criticism of religious speaking also lies at the basis of the second origin of negative theology: Greek philosophy. As we know, the origin of philosophy can be described as the rise of *logos* (reason) from *mythos* (the mythical story). When myths no longer reflect a view of the world that is taken for granted, but are organized in a mythology, people will feel disturbed by the *anthropomorphic* character of the gods and will search for a more rational explanation for the cosmos. Parmenides (c. 540–c. 475 B.C.) tried to recommend the only way to the truth and to advise against the path of "un-being" of appearances with his thesis that "being is and un-being is not." It is as if the whole history of philosophy has disagreed with him and has tried to think un-being and to give a place to becoming, change, multiplicity, and nothingness. Here we find a parallel for negative theology: an approach to the undisclosed and the forbidden. Socrates' (469–399 B.C.) irony, his 'knowing the unknowing,' is certainly a valid precursor of negative theology. He criticized his contemporaries, the Sophists, who posited that truth is relative and justice dependent on power. For them, attention to negativity is meaningless. But when we seek the basis for Socrates' criticism, we find that it is not explicitated as such. He wanders about to gain insight but must repeatedly conclude "This is not it, this is not the truth." He knows more than those with whom he discusses because he knows that he does not know, while they think that they do. Socrates also allows himself to be led by a *daimon* (similar to our conscience) who in the end only hinders his desire for knowledge by saying nothing positive.

Plato (427–347 B.C.) speaks of a highest knowledge, against which all other knowledge can be judged and is valuable: the knowledge of the Idea of the Good. This knowledge can only be spoken of in images (e.g., 'light' and 'sun') and he says of it that it is ἐπέκεινα τῆς οὐσίας, "on the other side of being." What 'surpasses' all cannot be spoken.

This explains something of the development from Plotinus to Dionysius. In our time Jacques Derrida contemplates the inexpressible of what is on the other side (*"au-delà"*): matter, the indeterminate.

3. On the Language of Mysticism

The Dutch poet Leo Vroman said when he started the second part of his poem *God en Godin* (God and goddess), "I reread the first part. It is a magnificent poem if you think away the words."[9] A blank page is not a poem. A poem is built of words; we cannot think them away without the poem's ceasing to be a poem. And yet the poem is more than words. We must be open to what is said *beyond* the mass of letters and obvious meanings. Poetry and mysticism increase sensitivity to the limits of language. On one side, language is a creative use of sense and meaning; on the other side, it is always too limited and falls short. When we stop with the first meaning, we are superficial and ignore the rich possibilities of language. If we are only attentive to the life of the world beyond the words, we land in the amorphous and everything evaporates. Real penetrating vision comes by reading *through* to the other side of language and words. Mystical speech is paradoxical in structure. This had already been the case for one of the first representatives of negative theology: Gregory of Nazianzus (c. A.D. 329–390). He wrote (I cite a fragment):

> You are one.
> You are everything.
> You are no one.
> You are not one.
> You are not everything.
> O, You who bear all names,
> what shall I call You?
> You Unique Unnameable,
> You Surpassor of All.[10]

Paradoxical speaking can be expressed in several ways: by denial, by superlatives, by incongruous imagery and confusing parables, by witty proverbs and eloquent silence.

Paradoxical speaking is grounded in the tension unique to mystical experience. Bernard of Clairvaux (1091–1153) expressed this tension in a passage in which he speaks of "the word that entered into him." He said, "When I looked outside, it seemed beyond all what was furthest from me. When I looked inside, then the word was more inner than my most inner self. And I understood how true it was what I had read, 'In Him we live, we move, and we are.' "[11]

---

[9] L. Vroman, *God en Godin* (Amsterdam: Querido, 1967), 33 (author's translation).

[10] Gregory of Nazianzus, in Migne, *Patrologia Graeca*, vol. 37, 507–8 (author's translation).

[11] Bernard of Clairvaux, "Sermonis super cantica," in Migne, *Patrologia Latina*, vol. 183, sermon 74 (author's translation).

Standing in this tension the mystic knows that no language can express what he or she has to say, and at the same time he or she feels, like an overflowing well, that the unpronounceable must be spoken. The essence of mystical language lies not in what is said, but in the way something is said; not in the content, but in the form of the speaking. The apparent contradiction and the confusing imagery work like a rip or slit, through which they point to an 'I-don't-know-what.'

4. Meister Eckhart (1260–1327)

Now we will take a closer look at two Christian mystics from the classic tradition because their work expresses negative theology very pregnantly: Eckhart and John of the Cross. I choose from their work the aspects most directly related to negative theology. For Eckhart, these are *separateness*, *purity*, and *letting-be*.

Separateness

By 'separateness' Eckhart means a letting go, a disengagement, a stepping outside the self and becoming empty. These are all variations of Jesus' expression that whoever loses his life, will regain it (Mark 8.35).

What must be lost or let loose? To start with the most important: first of all, God. We must abandon the picture we have of God. Every speaking, every image, every concept is insufficient. That is why Eckhart uses terms like "Nothing," "Emptiness," "Giving space," and "Poverty." He writes, for example, "So we say that a man should be so poor that he neither is nor has any place for God to work in. To preserve a place is to preserve distinction. Therefore I pray to God to make me free of God."[12] We must make room for God and then God turns out to be absolute Emptiness and Poverty.

Because God can be an object of possessiveness, we must separate from Him. All types of religious practices and pious exercises or good works can be detrimental. Thus, according to Eckhart, do many good

---

[12] M. Eckhart, Sermon Eighty-Seven, in *Sermons and Treatises*, ed. and trans. M. O. C. Walsh (Longmead: Element, 1989), 2.274.

people hinder themselves because they are so attached to remorse and penance, and because they stay with the signs and do not do their best to reach the pure truth. Thus do they hinder themselves because they all too eagerly run after the holy sacrament. They dispense an abundance of external eagerness on what is only preparation and do not prepare themselves for the truth.[13] When people are too attached to these practices, they lose their freedom. Eckhart also says people should stop seeking their own interests and desiring reward. When they do something in order to gain eternal life, they are secretly working for themselves and their own salvation. Even the image of God could become a hindrance: "for if you love God as He is God, as He is spirit, as He is person and as He is image—all that must go!—'Well, how should I love Him *then?*'—You should love Him as He is: a non-God, a non-spirit, a non-person, a non-image."[14] And not only images of God, but also religious feelings: Eckhart judges severely when people lose themselves or wallow in religious feelings. The place where God is worshiped should be equally unimportant: "Indeed, if a man thinks he will get more of God by meditation, by devotion, by ecstasies or by special infusion of grace than by the fireside or in the stable—that is nothing but taking God, wrapping a cloak round His head and shoving Him under a bench."[15] By this Eckhart means that one place is no better than another for worshiping God, whether at the market or in a barn, in a church or wherever one happens to be. Those who have attained a freedom of Spirit know this and are "separate."

Purification

This separateness as renunciation and liberation also has results for theological and philosophical thinking. "A man should not have, or be satisfied with, an imagined God, for then, when the idea vanishes, God vanishes! Rather, one should have an essential God, who far transcends the thought of man and all creatures."[16] Experience surpasses its theological and philosophical expression. Whoever under-

[13] On this topic, see Eckhart's "Talks of Instruction," in Walsh, ed., *Sermons*, 3.30–31.

[14] M. Eckhart, Sermon Ninety-Six, in Walsh, *Sermons*, 2.335.

[15] M. Eckhart, Sermon Thirteen (b), in Walsh, *Sermons*, 1.117.

[16] M. Eckhart, "The Tasks of Instruction," § 6, in Walsh, *Sermons*, 3.18.

goes it will change his or her attitude toward theology and philosophy. He or she is fed from a new source and has a new starting point, just as someone who has 'tasted' tea will describe it differently than someone who has never 'tasted' it. Eckhart pushes this very far. He will, for example, see in the Trinity a revelation of the "pure Divinity." "The soul then comes on the track of the pure Divinity, of whom the Trinity is only a revelation. The soul is completely beatific when it hurls itself in the desert of the Divinity, in which neither work nor image exists, and beyond the eagerness of the hurling it will so lose itself that it is destroyed as 'I'; it is so little interested in all things, it will be as if these things did not exist. With this the soul is as such through—and lives in—God."[17]

The soul is as unspeakable as is God, and negative theology is absorbed in it too: there are no words for it. Eckhart speaks of "something in the soul," a force, comparable to the force of the work of God himself, a "spark" or "fortress," full of contradictions and retractions. For God is hidden in the "innermost recesses of the spirit, and *this* is the inner world. Here God's ground is my ground and my ground is God's ground."[18] The soul can touch God's unutterableness; for this reason Eckhart uses ever different concepts and images and does not avoid paradoxes.

God is more deeply present in me than I am in myself and at the same time is higher than, more foreign to, me. The well-known divisions 'interior'/'exterior,' 'inner'/ 'outer,' 'high'/'low,' 'foreign'/'familiar,' 'movement'/'rest' no longer apply. To give but one example: "God and I are one in this operation: He works, and I come into being."[19] And while it sounds logical to distinguish rest and movement, the liberated person sees rest and movement together. "And in truth, if you were truly one, then you would even remain one in difference, and difference would be one to you, and then nothing could hinder you."[20]

The core of Eckhart's preaching and writing is the *"Durchbruch,"* the *"Gottesgeburt in der Seele"*(God-birth in the soul): "for this breaking-through [*Durchbruch*] guarantees to me that I and God are one. *Then* I am what I was, then I neither wax nor wane, for

---

[17] See M. Eckhart, Sermon Eighty-Seven, in Walsh, *Sermons*, 2.269–87.
[18] See M. Eckhart, Sermon Thirteen (b), in Walsh, *Sermons*, 2.117.
[19] See M. Eckhart, Sermon Sixty-Five, in Walsh, *Sermons*, 2.137.
[20] M. Echkart, "The Nobleman," in Walsh, *Sermons*, 3.110.

then I am an unmoved cause that moves all things. Here, God finds no place *in* man, for man by his poverty wins for himself what he has eternally been and shall eternally remain."[21] For the understanding of negative theology it is important to note that unity with God in the soul implies an infinite breadth and depth: "It is free of all names and void of all forms, entirely exempt and free, as God is exempt and free in Himself. It is as completely one and simple as God is one and simple."[22] "So one and simple is this citadel in the soul, elevated above all modes, of which I speak and which I mean, that that noble power I mentioned is not worthy even for an instant to cast a single glance into this citadel; nor is that other power I spoke of, in which God burns and glows with all His riches and all His joy, able to cast a single glance inside; so truly one and simple is this citadel, so mode- and power-transcending is this solitary One, that neither power nor mode can gaze into it, nor even God Himself!"[23] God's entrance into the essence of a person unveils a transcendence that is nameless and selfless, stripped of every singularity.

Practically speaking, separateness and purification can be rendered as something 'without a why' or *letting-be*.

Letting-Be

"Now pay earnest attention to this! I have often said, and eminent authorities say it too, that a man should be so free of all things and all works, both inward and outward, that he may be a proper abode for God where God can work."[24] This does not mean that mystical experience and contemplation is a second type of consciousness beside the normal one. The illuminated state must coincide with normal consciousness. There is no longer any separation between sacred and secular, between active and passive or contemplative. Everything is sacred. Or—for those who prefer to put it differently—nothing is sacred. Angelus Silesius (1624–1677) transmits this thought by saying, "Himself God acts in saints, performs their actions here: He

---

[21] M. Eckhart, Sermon Eighty-Seven, in Walsh, *Sermons*, 2.275–76.

[22] M. Eckhart, Sermon Eight, in Walsh, *Sermons*, 1.76.

[23] Ibid., 1.76–77.

[24] M. Eckhart, Sermon Eighty-Seven, in Walsh, *Sermons*, 2.273–74.

walks, stands, lies, sleeps, wakes, eats drinks, is of good cheer."[25] Eckhart puts it this way: "A man may go into the fields and say his
prayers and know God, or he may go to church and know God: but
if he is more aware of God because he is in a quiet place, as is usual,
that comes from his imperfection and not from God: for God is
equally in all things and in all places."[26]

Against this background we can understand Eckhart's strange explanation of the Gospel story of Martha and Mary (Luke 10.38–42).
The normal interpretation is that the laboring Martha, who asks why
Mary stays sitting with Jesus, is told that Mary has chosen the better
part. Eckhart wants to show that Martha is more advanced than Mary
who still needs contemplation. "Martha feared that her sister would
stay dallying with joy and sweetness, and wished her to be like herself."[27] Martha is free to devote herself to ordinary things, while Mary
could during exalted contemplation remain stuck half way in this
experience. The decisive factor in mysticism is not rapture, but being
able to do day-to-day things uninhibitedly. That is what is meant by
'letting-be.'

Letting-be is no resignation and not so much an acceptance as it
is an attitude of being able to let go: an emptying in which people
shake off all their attachments to reach a correct (more pure) surrender. Letting-be also implies a 'setting free,' a 'letting loose,' a dis-
banding in the sense of untying. Abstinence is also positive and
means making place for something, letting people be.

If we wonder how people can *will* letting-be, two simultaneous answers are possible. First we can think of letting-be as an act of the will.
We could also choose not to will it. Letting-be is then initiated by the
will in the sense of 'letting go' and then adopting a purely waiting
attitude. But a second form of letting-be is the one that no longer
belongs to the domain of the will. The will cannot reach or perfect it.
There something happens for which we must be grateful, which is
received. We meet this second form of letting-be in John of the Cross's
"passive night." This is the second figure in the tradition of negative
theology whom I would like to present and discuss briefly. Like no
other he gave this tradition a poetic and imposing articulation.

---

[25] Angelus Silesius, *The Cherubinic Wanderer*, trans. M. Shrady (New York: Paulist
Press, 1986), Book V (no. 174), 113.

[26] M. Eckhart, Sermon Sixty-Nine, in Walsh, *Sermons*, 2.167.

[27] M. Eckhart, Sermon Nine, in Walsh, *Sermons*, 1.86.

5. John of the Cross (1542–1591)

Upon a darksome night,
Kindling with love in flame of yearning keen
—O moment of delight!—
I went by all unseen,
New-hush'd to rest the house where I had been.
Safe sped I through that night,
By the secret stair, disguisèd and unseen,
—O moment of delight!—
Wrapt in that night serene,
New-hush'd to rest the house where I had been.
O happy night and blest!
Secretely speeding, screen'd from mortal gaze,
Unseeing on I prest
Lit by no earthly rays,
Nay, only by heart's inmost fire ablaze.
'Twas that light guided me,
More surely than the noonday's brightest glare,
To the place where none would be
Save one that waited there—
Well knew I whom or ere I forth did fare.
O night more winsome than the rising sun!
O night that madest us,
Lover and lov'd, as one,
Lover transform'd in lov'd, love's journey done!
Upon my flowering breast,
His only, as no man but he might prove,
There, slumbering, did he rest,
'Neath my caressing love,
Fann'd by the cedars swaying high above.
When from the turret's height,
Scattering his locks, the breezes lay'd around,
With touch serene and light
He dealt me love's sweet wound,
And with the joyful pain thereof I swoon'd.

Forgetful, rapt, I lay,
My face reclining on my lov'd one fair.
All things for me that day
ceas'd as I slumber'd there,
Amid the lilies drowning all my care.

John of the Cross provided two commentaries on this poem, the first in "The Ascent of Mount Carmel" (or "The Ascent") and the second in "The Dark Night."[28] John wrote the poem while he sat in prison in miserable circumstances. The two commentaries were added to it later.

To understand traditional negative theology, it is important that the "active night" be distinguished from the "passive night." "The Ascent of Mount Carmel" sees the night as the moment of *going forth*, through personal effort: actively. "The Dark Night" discusses the same poem and the same subject, but as *something undergone*, a being met by the Lover: hence a passive night. Thus the first text is a report of the difficult movement upward (Ascent), and the second speaks of what happens to people, what arouses their fear, and how love finds them. Both treat the difficult parting from familiar and obvious certainties. What is left behind? The senses ("active night of the senses") and the intellect ("active night of reason, will and memory"). This, briefly, is the content of "The Ascent." Neither the senses, nor knowing or willing, nor memory are sufficient. And John lets us feel how shattered people become: they are in complete darkness and night. All levels are pervaded by an anxiety-provoking darkness now that natural light no longer shines. People cannot themselves complete what they have so nobly started. In "The Dark Night" we meet the same theme, but now as "passive night of the senses" and "passive night of the spirit," [29] in which to reason, will, and memory are added faith, love, and hope: the morning glow of the meeting with God.

John of the Cross takes seriously the awareness of "being abandoned by God," even to the point of making it a condition for meeting God. The night of abandonment is a 'happy' night, not because abandonment makes one happy—certainly not—but because it purifies people thoroughly from all that could hinder unity with God. All the certainties of the senses and reason, but also all conceptions of God, truths of the faith, and other human projections on which be-

---

[28] Saint John of the Cross, *The Complete Works of Saint John of the Cross, Doctor of the Church* (hereafter cited as *Works*), eds. P. Silverio de Santa Teresa and E. Allison Pers (London: Burns Oates, 1943), 2.441–42. See also "The Ascent," 1.11, and "Dark Night," 2.347, where this poem also occurs.

[29] John of the Cross's reflection on the first night is found in book 1 of "Dark Night"; his reflection on the second night is found in book 2.

lievers depend, must first be eliminated. According to John, this purification can be worked on, but more often it overcomes people, and
they become lost in it. And then it remains to be seen if they can
love God as He 'is.' For all this human dependence on 'having,' on
possession, must disappear.

In the poem, it is striking that John identifies himself with the
feminine figure. In this sense we could call him a feminine mystic, if
it is true that femininity and passivity belong together. John is passive and lets the Lover overcome him. At the heart of John's mysticism we meet love. And there, too, negative theology plays a role, in
the sense that love strives toward unification, but through the secret
of emptying, setting free, and making room. No sticky, possessive
love is this, but one that is disinterested and that in a pure way keeps
desire alive!

John's style is 'all or nothing.' This severity and exactingness
frightens some people away. But he believes that the choice for love
demands *everything* and that there is nothing except love that cannot
be abandoned for God. "Thus he that will love some other thing
together with God of a certainty makes little account of God."[30] As
we have seen, asceticism is a giving up of all human thoughts and
fantasies, as well as private desires, in which, as it were, the passive
night becomes both sides of the medal; the result is *dispossession*.
Supports are gone; there are no certainties; only then can people
again receive; only when they stand completely naked, can they be
dressed. An impressive articulation of this theme can be found in
what could be called the 'canticle of negative theology,' a text that
John wrote on a drawing of the "Mount of Perfection." He wrote and
drew thirteen copies for Carmelite nuns to keep in their breviaries
as a souvenir of a conference he had given. The text is also found in
the first book of "The Ascent of Mount Carmel."[31]

> In order to arrive at having pleasure in everything, desire to have
>   pleasure in nothing.
> In order to arrive at possessing everything, desire to possess nothing.
> In order to arrive at being everything, desire to be nothing.
> In order to arrive at knowing everything, desire to know nothing.

---

[30] "Ascent," book 1, chap. 5, § 4, in de Santa Teresa and Pers, *Works*, 1.31.
[31] Ibid., book 1, chap. 13, § 11–12. in de Santa Teresa and Pers, *Works*, 1.62–63.

In order to arrive at that wherein thou hast no pleasure, thou must
go by a way wherein thou hast no pleasure.
In order to arrive at that which thou knowest not, thou must go by a
way that thou knowest not.
In order to arrive at that which thou possessest not, thou must go by
a way that thou possessest not.
In order to arrive at that which thou are not, thou must go through
that which thou art not.
If you pause near something—you do not enter with full heart into
the All.
When thou thinkest upon anything, thou ceasest to cast thyself upon
the All.
For, in order to pass from the all to the All, thou hast to deny thyself
wholly in all.
And, when thou comest to possess it wholly, thou must possess it
without desiring anything.
For, if thou wilt have anything in all, thou hast not thy treasure purely
in God.

6. UNITY VERSUS EXTERIORITY? A MODERN DISCUSSION

Plotinus, Dionysius, Eckhart, and Heidegger seem to stand in a tradition of thinking about a Unity that surpasses unity, a Being that
precedes all being, an Origin before the origin. But there is another
tradition of radical negative theology, reminded of by contemporary
thinkers, that rejects this unity, this totality. This other tradition
involves a thinking about the *other* that escapes from this unity; it
involves a philosophy of *exteriority*. I think here of Franz Rosenzweig
(1886–1929) and Emmanuel Levinas (1906–1995). This brings a different evaluation and interpretation of 'mysticism.' Levinas writes,
for example, "It is certainly a great honor for the Creator to have
created a being capable of atheism."[32] For Levinas, atheism is synon-
ymous with separation and independence, and expresses a relationship that exists before the affirmation or negation of God. It is a
prerequisite for a relationship with God. Atheism is necessary because Levinas wants to free the relationship with God, the 'Other,'

---

[32] E. Levinas, *Totalité et infini. Essai sur l'extériorité"* (The Hague: Nijhoff, 1961),
52 (author's translation); English trans., *Totality and Infinity: An Essay on Exteriority*
(Pittsburgh: Dusquesne University Press, 1969).

from mythical detritus, from participation in a mystical unity, and from sacred powers. We could call this rejection of unity a typically Jewish rejection.

The difference between a Greek-oriented mysticism of unity and a Jewish-oriented silence about God, based on separation, reaches back to the double origin of negative theology. Are there two different traditions of negative theology, one Jewish-biblical and another Greek-philosophical? We find the two original traditions inseparably conjoined in Jacques Derrida's work, as they were, as we saw, in that of Dionysius the Areopagite.

It is true that Rosenzweig and Levinas, in the first instance, want nothing to do with the totalitarian character of the 'One' and reject most forms of mysticism. But is it possible to avoid unity language and thinking altogether? On the one hand, we can think so broadly of the One that it permits everything: the many, time, being other, and our existence as it really is (Eckhart). On the other hand, motivated by interest in what the 'Other' really is and by openness to the foreign, we can refuse ultimately every unity: a rejection of totality (Levinas). But with Derrida we could posit that we cannot escape the violence of the language of the *one*, yet that we must escape it. Always when we speak of God this speaking seems to be forbidden by the many languages and the problem of translation. For Derrida, a Jew born in Algeria, this speaking is nearly an autobiographical necessity. In a footnote to his essay "How to Avoid Speaking: Denials" Derrida says that he "never has yet been able to speak of what my birth, as one says, should have made closest to me, the Jew, the Arab," and notes that he is compelled to express himself via several languages: "French, English, German, Greek, Latin, the philosophic, metaphilosophic, Christian, etc."[33]

Ethical Implications: The Language of the Other

For some time, French philosophy was under the influence of structuralism; its philosophy was antihumanistic.[34] In reaction to existen-

---

[33] J. Derrida, "How to Avoid Speaking: Denials," in H. Coward and T. Foshay, eds., *Derrida and Negative Theology* (New York: State University of New York Press, 1992), 135n13.

[34] For a critical consideration of structuralism and neostructuralism sparked by Derrida's thinking, see the chapter contributed by Hent de Vries in this volume.

tialist humanism, it was thought that the human subject no longer needed to hold the central place. There was talk of a decentralization of this subject. Derrida appeared similarly to oppose humanism. But closer examination, and the appearance of more of Derrida's texts, showed that the center of Derrida's thinking was singularity, uniqueness. One theme that came ever more strongly to the fore was the theme of *responsibility*, the responsibility in which people feel addressed, but also are aware that there is a moment of irresolution. When someone makes a decision, Derrida asks attention for irresolution. Against the ideal of complete control, complete calculability, where everything is transparent, manipulated, and can be controlled, Derrida wants to show that there is a continually operative heteronomy, a moment that escapes us. In this sense the subject is indeed decentralized. At the same time, with the themes of singularity, alterity, and heteronomy, we reach the limits, the margins of philosophy. Philosophy bears in it the drive to master and to think in concepts and so to possess and occupy. By contrast, deconstruction as Derrida practices it tries to show that there is always a latitude, that there are always transgressions. How does Derrida reach a discussion of human subjectivity? He does not speak of a free and autonomous subject who is its own origin or that is completely transparent for itself, for there is a more deep-lying heteronomy. A person is addressed by another who makes claims on his or her freedom and autonomy, who invites or sometimes challenges.

One possible interpretation of Derrida accentuates the Jewish background to his thinking. One could posit that deconstruction shares several aspects with Jewish thinking. An example is the attention to detail and to the unique and singular within the generality of language. That characteristic of Jewish thinking is also present in Derrida's work. Deconstruction works with texts, as does the rabbinic tradition; it provides commentary on a commentary, and this commentary is written in the margins and is commented upon in still smaller margins. Never is there a definitive answer; instead answers multiply. This does not mean that Derrida is as 'at home' in Jewish writings and Talmudic commentary, as is Levinas. Here is it important to note briefly the relationship between Levinas and Derrida. Levinas philosophizes explicitly against the background of the Holocaust and the terrors of World War II. He asks what went wrong with the teachers with whom he studied, Husserl and Heidegger, and what went wrong with Western thinking—in particular, how such insufficient resistance could have been offered against this terror. Levinas's answer is that Western thinkers did not give a central enough place to ethics, and gave too little attention to the other. Thought is in principle totalitarian and violent when it does not start with the other and does not think of responsibility for the other. In his commentary on Levinas,[35] Derrida also works deconstructively. He wonders whether it is possible to put the other into words. Would this not do him or her an injustice? Levinas is part of a strong patriarchal tradition. Derrida wonders how the feminine is present or absent in his work. In these texts he plays with Emmanuel Levinas's initials, E.L., which in French sound like *'elle,'* 'she' or 'her.' When Derrida cites Levinas we continually see 'E.L.'/'elle.' He also notes that when Levinas speaks of the divine it is pervaded by feminine notions such as mercy (in Hebrew linked to the womb), bearing, being secure. It is a feminine voice that can be heard speaking then. In this complex relationship between Derrida and Levinas, who each speak of one another with great respect, deconstruction asks whether the other and the Other come under discussion, whether every speaking is not totalitarian and violent insofar as it does not do justice to the otherness of the this other/Other.

In posing these questions modern philosophers of culture who dig into the most radical aspects of negative theology, and the representatives of classic medieval negative theology whom I have discussed in this chapter, meet each other—in a meeting that creates a sensitivity for what escapes us and what we, thinking, writing, and speaking, cannot grasp.

> . . . but everything which was so dear
> that I have lost,
> has, only since I have lost it,
> really become mine.[36]

---

[35] J. Derrida, "En ce moment même dans cet ouvrage me voici," in *Psyché* (Paris: Galilée, 1987), 159–203. For an English translation, see J. Derrida, "At This Very Moment in This Work Here I Am," trans. R. Berezdivin in *Re-reading Levinas*, eds. R. Bernasconi and S. Critchley (Bloomington and Indianapolis: Indiana University Press, 1991), 11–48.

[36] Jean-Pierre Rawie, "Bezit" (fragment), in *Woelig stof* (Amsterdam: Bert Bakker, 1989), 38 (author's translation).

Chapter 2

Is the Ontological Argument Ontological?

THE ARGUMENT ACCORDING TO ANSELM AND ITS METAPHYSICAL INTERPRETATION ACCORDING TO KANT

Jean-Luc Marion

1

FOR A LONG TIME the so-called ontological argument was not called ontological at all.[1] Saint Anselm and even Descartes both introduce it as "meum argumentum"—my argument.[2] Leibniz speaks only of

---

[1] An earlier discussion of this subject, "L'argument relève-t-il de l'ontologie?," was published in the *Archivio di Filosofia* (Rome, 1990) as the record of a paper delivered at the Colloque international: L'argument ontologique (Istituto di Studi Filosofici 'Enrico Castelli'/Catedra di Filosofia della Religione, Università degli Studi di Roma 'La Sapienza'), held in Rome, January 3–6, 1990. This English version differs from the French one on some important points, mainly in the evaluation of the results of my demonstration. I would like to thank Professor Marco M. Olivetti for inviting me to debate this fascinating but very difficult topic, and Professors Gary Hatfield and Richard A. Watson for giving me the opportunity to debate my thesis with the Departments of Philosophy, respectively, of the University of Pennsylvania and of Washington University. I am grateful to Ian Bourgeot and to Professor Richard A. Watson for revising and improving as far as possible my first English draft. The present English text appeared first in *Journal of the History of Philosophy* 30, no. 2 (1992): 201–218.

[2] Anselm, *Proslogion*, ed. F. S. Schmitt, vols. 1–3 of Anselm of Canterbury, *Opera omnia*, ed. F. S. Schmitt (Edinburgh and Rome: Thomas Nelson, 1938–1961), vol. 1, 95, lg.6. When I quote Anselm in translation, I often use Anselm of Canterbury, *Works*, vol. 1, edited and translated by Jasper Hopkins and Herbert Richardson (To-

an "argumentum dudum inter Scolasticos celebre et a Cartesio reno-vatum"—a most celebrated argument among Scholastics, now re-newed by Descartes.[3] Kant, who, we should add, sometimes calls it "Cartesian,"[4] was probably the first one to describe it as an "ontolog-ical proof."[5] Therefore we cannot avoid asking a very obvious ques-tion: Why did the 'ontological argument' attain so late the explicit qualification of 'ontological'? At the very least, this latency period reveals, although it does not explain why, that the 'ontological argu-ment' could perfectly well have continued *without* becoming onto-logical, for it managed to be born and then reborn without this qualification. But could Anselm (and even Descartes) have devel-oped the 'ontological argument' without using the very concept of ontology? From a historical point of view, this question is all the weightier since the term 'ontology' first appears six hundred years

---

ronto and New York: Edwin Mellen, 1974). I give first the page and lines of the Latin text, then the standard English translation. See also ". . . vulgaribus argumentis . . . ," *Monologion*, Prologue, ibid., 7, 9; and ". . . connexionem hujus meae argumentis . . . ," *Quod ad haec respondent editor ipsius libelli* [= *Responsio*], 3.133.9. Descartes, *Oeuvres*, ed. Adam-Tannery, rev. P. Costabel and B. Rochot (Paris: J. Vrin, 1966–), 7.115.22; see 65, 20. On this point, I agree with the statement of Alexandre Koyré, to whom the argument of Anselm no longer seems "une preuve ontologique au sens exact du terme" (*L'idée de Dieu dans la philosophie de Saint Anselme* [1923; reprint, Paris: J. Vrin, 1984], 193).

[3] *Meditationes de cognitione, veritate, et ideis*, in *Die philosophischen Schriften*, ed. C. J. Gerhardt (Hildesheim: Olms, 1978), 4.425.

[4] ". . . argumento Cartesiano . . . ," in *Principiorum primorum cognitionis meta-physicae nova dilucidatio*, II. 7. Akademie-Ausgabe I, 395: or ". . . cartesianischer (Beweisgrund) . . . ," in *Der einzig mögliche Beweisgrund zu einer Demonstration des Daseins Gottes*, III, 5, Akademie-Ausgabe II, 162; and also ". . . dem so berühmten ontologischen cartesianischen Beweis . . . ," in *Critique of Pure Reason*, A602/B630.

[5] *Der einzig mögliche Beweisgrund zu einer Demonstration des Daseins Gottes*, III, 4, Akademie-Ausgabe II, 161, and *Critique of Pure Reason*, A592/B620. Henceforth the formula "ontological argument" is established. Hegel uses it to define both Descartes ("Das ist also die Einheit des Denkens und Seins und der ontologische Beweis vom Dasein Gottes"; *Vorlesungen über die Geschichte der Philosophie*, vol. 20 of *Werke von 1832–35*, eds. E. Moldenhauer and K. Markus Michel [Frankfurt am Main: Suhrkamp, 1971], 138) and even Anselm (". . . den sogennanten ontologi-schen Beweis vom Dasein Gottes"; *Vorlesungen über die Geschichte der Philosophie*, eds. P. Garniron and W. Jaeschke, vol. 6g of *Vorlesungen. Ausgewälte Nachschriften und Manuskripte* [Hamburg: Meiner, 1983–], 33–34). Schelling sometimes places side by side, on the same, page, the old formula (". . . cartesianischen Beweis . . .") and the new one (". . . durch die Ausstellung des ontologischen Beweises ist Carte-sius für die ganze Folge der neueren Philosophie bestimend geworden"; *Zur Gesch-ichte der neueren Philosophie*, vol. 10 of *Sämmtliche Werke* [Stuttgart and Hamburg: Cotta, 1856–1869], 14).

after Anselm—when, in the days of Descartes, Goclenius, Clauberg, and others progressively imposed it.[6] Thus, the original argument raised by Anselm was perfectly acceptable for a very long time as a demonstration without any help from ontology: that is a plain fact in the history of concepts.

Thus, the obvious question arises: Does Anselm's argument appear, without any reservation or exception, in the realm of the question of being, that is, is it within the limits of the history of metaphysics (understood according to the precise acceptation suggested by Heidegger)? Or, on the contrary, was the original argument capable of succeeding without any appeal to 'ontology' as it is defined by metaphysics—that is, outside the horizon of being? In philosophy, questions of rights matter more than facts; it is therefore clear that no purely historical result will provide an answer sufficient to our question. To outline something like an answer, one would have to analyze what Kant meant when he first called the argument an "ontological" one. Let us proceed in three steps: (a) determine the characteristics of such an 'ontological' argument according to Kant; (b) check if and how some thinkers in the history of metaphysics prepare or fulfill these characteristics; and (c) decide whether Anselm's argument (and perhaps, to some extent, Descartes's) agrees or disagrees with these characteristics and, as a consequence, with any 'ontological argument' in the proper Kantian sense.

2

When Kant discovered and imposed the syntagm 'ontological argument,' he gave it an accurate definition: this ontological argument infers "gänzlich a priori aus blossen Begriffen auf das Dasein einer höchsten Ursache"—the existence of a Supreme Cause absolutely a

---

[6] On that point, see the studies of P. Petersen, *Geschichte der aristotelischen Philosophie im protestantischen Deutschland* (1921; reprint, Stuttgart: Friedrich Fromann, 1962); M. Wundt, *Die deutsche Schulmetaphysik des 17. Jahrhunderts* (Tübingen: J. C. B. Mohr [Siebeck], 1939); E. Vollrath, "Die Gliederung der Metaphysik in eine *Metaphysica generalis* und eine *Metaphysica specialis*," *Zeitschrift für philosophische Forschung* 16, no. 2 (1962); my own essay, *Sur le prisme métaphysique de Descartes* (Paris: Presses Universitaires de France, 1986), chap. 1; and Jean.-François Courtine, *Suarez et le système de la métaphysique* (Paris: Presses Universitaires de France, 1990).

priori from mere concepts—that is, establishes the "Dasein eines höchsten Wesens aus Begriffen"—the existence of a Supreme Essence (Being) from concepts.[7]

Therefore, the argument deserves to be called 'ontological' when it reaches the existence of a Supreme or Privileged Being by means of pure concepts. However, a difficulty appears: if the ontological argument deserves its qualification only because it leads, through mere concepts, to existence, then all the other proofs of God's existence in rational theology would deserve this qualification of 'ontological' as well. Don't they reach the conclusion of an existence, too? In fact, Kant meant something entirely different: the argument becomes 'ontological' because it leads to the existence of a Supreme and Privileged Being by relying not merely on concepts, but also on the concept of the essence of this Being, that is, the "Begriff eines höchsten Wesens," or the "Begriff des allerrealsten Wesens."[8] 'Ontological' does not indicate the simple attainment of Being as existence, but rather the quite extraordinary fact that this Being attains existence solely by means of its pure essence. The ontological argument becomes really 'ontological' only insofar as it proves existence (as other proofs do) under two exceptional conditions (quite apart from all other proofs): (a) by starting from a pure concept; and (b) by starting from the pure concept of an essence. In identifying these two conditions of the genuine 'ontological argument,' Kant merely explicated some decisions already made by his predecessors. Let us recall them briefly.

That a proof of God's existence becomes an 'ontological proof' only by relying on a concept of God was already clearly assumed by Descartes (though he avoided the word 'ontological'). The a priori demonstration of God's existence in *Meditatio* V derives in fact from a 'cogitatio de Deo'; this 'thought' claims the status of a true idea ("ejus ideam tanquam ex mentis meae thesauro depromere"—the idea of Him I bring out, as it were, from the treasury of my mind); that is, it claims to be at the same level of intelligibility as any other idea—for instance, a mathematical idea ("non minus apud me invenio quam ideam cujusvis figurae aut numeri"—I find [this idea of Him] no less in me than the idea of some figure or number). The

---

[7] *Critique of Pure Reason*, A590/B616, A602/B630.
[8] Ibid., A601/B629, A596/B624.

idea of God thus belongs to the class of innate ideas, of which it presents a very peculiar but not an irregular case: with the idea of God, we are still dealing with one of the "ideae verae mihi ingenitae, quarum prima et praecipua est idea Dei"—the true and innate ideas in me, of which the first and principal is that of God.[9] The common epistemic claims weigh so much upon this idea of God that Descartes finally admits—in spite of his insistence on preserving God's incomprehensibility—a "Dei conceptus," that is, a "divinae naturae conceptus" or a "conceptus entis summe perfecti"—a concept [understanding] of God, of the divine nature, of the most perfect Being.[10] So a decisive step is taken: from now on, the 'ontological' argument relies on the (first) presupposition that a concept—whatsoever it may be—can match the divine essence, or that a concept can reach God within the limits of an essence—whatsoever it may be. All subsequent discussions, whether they deal with the determination of this essence (Spinoza, Malebranche, Leibniz) or with the transition from the concept of an essence to its existence beyond the concept (Gassendi, Locke, Hume, Kant, Hegel, Schelling, etc.), will henceforth admit and use a certain concept of God—in short, will agree that it may be possible and correct to identify God with a concept.

We are now able to proceed to the second characteristic of the 'ontological' argument and ask for a definition of this essence of God, which is supposed to make it accessible by a concept. The philosophers did not answer this second question as swiftly as they did the first. They needed to go through several stages.

(i) Descartes restricts himself to a definition of God as the Supreme or Supremely Perfect Being: "cogitare Deum (hoc est ens summe perfectum)"—to think God (that is the most perfect being), "ens primum"—first Being, or "summum ens, sive perfectum"—highest and perfect Being.[11] But this conceptual determination of the essence of God did not obviously open an unbridged gap between essence and existence; the word "perfection" emphasizes the gap even more than it succeeds in filling it: God does not yet exist by an immediate effect either of His concept or of His essence, but

---

[9] *Meditationes de prima philosophia*, in Oeuvres, vol. 7, 67, 21–23; 65, 22–23; 68, 8–10.

[10] Ibid., 167, 1; 151, 6; 166, 18.

[11] Ibid., 66, 12–13 (= 67, 9–10 or 54, 13–14).

only through the mediation of a third operator—the "supreme perfection," which includes, among many others, the perfection of existing. In order to reach the existence directly by means of pure
essence, that is, to think of God as "id cujus essentia involvit exis-
tentiam," that whose essence includes existence (as Spinoza says
without any proof at all[12]), metaphysics has to go one step further.

(ii) Malebranche takes this step by repeating the Cartesian argument not merely from the concept of "Dieu ou l'être infiniment
parfait"—God or the Infinitely Perfect Being—but also through the
absolute identity, in the concept of God, of the essence and being as
such. So "l'idée de Dieu, ou de l'être en général, sans restriction, de
l'être infini"—the idea of God, or of being in general, of being without any restriction, of infinite being[13]—is squarely opposed to the
idea of such and such finite being, in the sense that only in God
could the essence be one with the whole being, so that God could
reach nothing but Himself as He achieves His existence. The 'ontological' argument means, for Malebranche, only that God uses all the
manifold meanings of being according to Aristotle: the argument
proceeds from being as essence (possibility) to being as existence
(substance, act) through being as concept (categories and truth). It
would be advisable indeed to dwell, at this point, upon the fundamental ambiguity of Malebranche's understanding of the very term
'being,' since the opposition between "l'être en général"—being in
general—and "tel être"—such a being (or "tels êtres"—such beings)—may lead to two opposed interpretations: on the one hand,
to the ontic difference between being as Absolute Being—ὄντως
ὄν—and finite, lapsing, derivative beings; on the other hand, to a
quasi-ontological difference between all beings and Being itself, universal and abstract. Malebranche never confronts directly the essential and obvious ambiguity of his concept of 'being'; but, insofar as
the incapacity of thinking out the ontological difference as such
seems to be the main feature of metaphysics—as Heidegger says—
this very failure makes Malebranche a very distinguished metaphysi-
cian indeed. In any case, for our purposes this failure does not matter
that much; the decisive point remains that, in stating that "l'être

---

[12] *Ethica*, I. Def. I (= § 11, Dem. 1).

[13] *Recherche de la vérité*, IV, 11, §§1 and 2, in *Oeuvres complètes*, ed. André Robinet, vol. 2 by Geneviève Rodis-Lewis (Paris: J. Vrin, 1972), 93, 95.

sans restriction, en un mot l'Être, c'est l'idée de Dieu"—the being
without restriction, in a word the Being, is the idea of God[14]—
Malebranche abolishes any further mediation between God's essence
and God's existence to the point that he reestablishes, at least tentatively, the Thomistic identity of the divine essence with Being as
such, that is, *in actu.* God exists by the immediate consequence of
His essence, which amounts solely to Being. In this formulation, the
Cartesian argument appears to deserve, for the first time, the title
(if not yet the word) 'ontological.'

(iii) Leibniz, however, is to be credited with the perfection of the
so-called ontological argument: he identifies the divine essence not
only with the concept of being in general, but also definitively with
the concept of the Necessary Being: "l'Existence de l'Être nécessaire,
dans lequel l'Essence renferme l'Existence, ou dans lequel il suffit
d'être possible pour être actuel"—the existence of the Necessary
Being, in whom essence encloses existence, or for whom to be possible is enough to be actual.[15] Indeed, the formulation by Malebranche
(and that by Descartes) does not make clear *why,* in the core of
the manifold meanings of being, essence could amount to existence.
Leibniz makes this transition by establishing the equivalence, at
least in the one concept of God, of possibility and necessity, beyond
effectivity itself as mere (extra)position: "Si l'Être nécessaire est possible, il existe. Car l'Être nécessaire et l'Être par son Essence ne sont
qu'une même chose"—if the Necessary Being is possible, He exists.
For the Necessary Being and Being by His essence are one and the
same thing.[16] To become perfectly 'ontological,' the argument had to
make sure that the concept of divine essence fully coincides with
Necessary Being—God is as the Necessary Being, with the minimal
condition that He be possible. This formulation brings the former
merely 'Cartesian' argument to its full ontological dignity. Even
though they intend to criticize it, Kant and Schelling still refer to
its Leibnizian expression: God *is* by His mere concept of necessary
existence, provided that this concept be possible. However, we must
notice that Descartes himself has at least once anticipated such an

---

[14] *Entretiens sur la métaphysique et la religion,* II, §4, vol. 12 of *Oeuvres complètes,*
ed. André Robinet (Paris: J. Vrin, 1965), 53.

[15] *Monadologie* §14, ed. André Robinet (Paris: J. Vrin, 1954; repr. 1986), 95.

[16] *Meditationes de cognitione, veritate, et ideis, Die philosophischen Schriften,* vol.
4, 406.

outcome; in his pedagogical exposition of the a priori proof, he re-formulates the argument previously developed from the point of view of perfection within the horizon of possibility and necessity: "nempe continetur existentia possibilis sive contingens in conceptu rei limitatae, sed necessaria et perfecta in conceptu entis summe perfecti"—possible or contingent existence is contained in the concept of a limited thing, whereas necessary and perfect existence is contained in the concept of a supremely perfect being.[17] This means that, to some extent, Descartes has already reached the ontological status of the argument, even though he lacked the word. When Schelling argues against Descartes that the latter's demonstration confuses the concept of a necessary Being with the concept of a Being existing by necessity—"dass Gott nicht bloss das notwendige Seiende, sondern notwendig das notwendige Seiende ist; dies ist aber ein bedeutender Unterschied" (God is not only the necessary Being, but necessarily the necessary Being; this is an important distinction)[18]—he admits at least that there is evidence that Descartes was fully aware that the core of the argument lies in the connection of necessity and possibility; this means that Descartes was already developing a genuine ontological argument—without the right name.

3

We are now at the point where it is possible to formulate our second question: If the argument proposed by Anselm deserves to be called 'ontological,' it has to fulfill the two requirements set by its later metaphysical interpretation, namely, (a) to reach existence through a concept of God's essence; and (b) to interpret this essence as Being as such, universal and without restriction. Does Anselm's argument fulfill both those requirements?

Let us start with the first one: Does the original argument rely on any concept of the divine essence? A totally negative answer is imperative, for several matching motives.

---

[17] *Meditationes de prima philosophia*, 166, 16–18.

[18] *Philosophie der Offenbarung*, I, 8, vol. 13 of *Sämtliche Werke*, 159. On this point, see X. Tilliette, "Argument ontologique et ontothéologie. Notes conjointes. Schelling et l'argument ontologique," *Archives de Philosophie* 26, no. 1 (1963); reprinted in *L'absolu et la philosophie: Essais sur Schelling* (Paris: Presses Universitaires de France, 1987), chap. 9.

We notice first that the starting point of the argument is explicitly a matter of faith, not of conceptual obviousness: the two mottos "fides quaerens intellectum" and "exemplum de ratione fidei"— 'faith seeking insight,' and 'an example of the rationality of faith'— inaugurate, respectively, the *Proslogion* and the *Monologion;* in both cases, the point is only to rationalize what faith has already given us to think about. Faith here does not simply provide reason with a mere neutral *datum,* which it could later appropriate from faith as its own property; rather, faith leads reason and rationality all along the speculative way: "Neque enim quaero intelligere ut credam, sed credo ut intelligam. Nam et hoc credo: quia 'nisi credidero, non intelligam' "—For I do not seek to understand in order to believe, but I believe in order to understand. For I believe even this: that I shall not understand unless I believe (*Proslogion* I/100, 18–19/93).[19] Intelligence proceeds from faith, because rationality consists mainly in recognizing in faith the permanent and radical condition of the possibility of thinking; in that sense, intelligence needs not merely faith, but explicitly specified faith—belief in exactly this: that reason has to believe in order to achieve understanding. As Hegel admits later, Anselm recognizes faith as the first condition of speculation, but, contrary to Hegel, he also admits faith as the last horizon of understanding. (By the way, no concept—no matter which—ever plays the central and original role in speculation.)

The final point of the argument also escapes from the concept, because its ultimate goal is to reach the God who lives in a "lux inaccessibilis" (an inaccessible light; 1 Tim. 6.16). The fact that God dwells in this unreachable light defines not only the starting point of the argument (as it does in *Proslogion* I/98, passim), but also its final result (*Proslogion* XVI/112, 18ff.): knowledge never abolishes faith or

---

[19] The motto "fides quaerens intellectum" comes from Isaiah 7.9 (according to the Septuagint). "Nisi credideritis, non intelligetis," through Augustine: "Intelligere vis? Crede. Deus enim per prophetam dixit: 'Nisi credideritis, non intelligetis.' . . . . Si non intellexisti, inquam, crede. In tellectus enim merces est difei, ergo noli quaerere intelligere ut credas, sed crede ut intelligas" (*In Johannis Evangelium,* XIX, 6, Corpus Christianorum 36, p. 287; see also XLV, 7; XV, 24; XXVII 7; LXIX, 2; ibid., pp. 273, 391, and 500–501). Augustine chooses the version of the Septuagint, but reconciles it with the translation from the Hebrew: "Nisi credideritis, non permanebis" (*De doctrina christiana,* 2.12, 17; PL 34, col. 43. See F. Thonnard,"Caractères augustiniens de la méthode philosophique de Saint Anselme," in *Spicilegium Beccense* I [Paris: J. Vrin, 1959]).

God's inaccessibility; it makes the mind recognize this inaccessibility as a definitive feature of God. Anselm's argument proves quite unable either to exhibit any concept of God or to hope for one. What is more, this argument never implies any such concept,[20] because it relies precisely on the impossibility of any adequate concept of God whatsoever. The root of the argument is not reliance on the concept, but reliance on a nonconcept, acknowledged as such.

This nonconceptual starting point is obviously expressed by the keynote formula of the *Proslogion:* "id quo majus cogitari nequit," or "aliquid quo nihil majus cogitari possit"—something such that anything greater than it cannot be thought. One must stress this point: God, if there is such a being, can be thought of only as something that we *cannot* conceive. As a concept, God admits only His very transcendence of any conceivable concept at all. As long as anything can be conceived within fixed limits, this item does not reach God in any way. Inversely, thought opens itself to the question of God only insofar as it reaches the utmost limits of its own field. The only evidence that thought might really deal with the question of God and His supposed essence consists in this: it can transcend all conceivable concepts, and, more, it can experience the limits of its conceiving power. God can be met by thought only insofar as, first, thought experiences the maximum of the conceivable—something like an "id quo majus cogitari *potest*" (something such that anything greater *can* be thought—though Anselm never uses this formula)— and, then, in a further step, it faces up to what this same finite thought *cannot* surpass, conquer, or rule—something like an "id quo major cogitari *nequit.*" As long as our thought can still think in concepts, no God appears; God appears only as soon as thought cannot go further; God begins exactly where and when the concept stops

---

[20] Nor a divine name, as Etienne Gilson emphasized against Karl Barth (*Fides quaerens intellectum: Anselms Beweis der Existenz Gottes* [Munich: Kaiser, 1931]): "Or il n'est pas besoin d'être grand exégète pour savoir que jamais l'Écriture n'a donné à Dieu nom semblable; les théologiens du Moyen Age les ont colligés et commentés, à la suite de Denys, dans leurs *De divinis nominibus,* ils n'y ont jamais trouvé celui-là" ("Sens et nature de l'argument de Saint Anselme," *Archives d'Histoire doctrinale et littéraire du Moyen Age* 9 [1934]: 26ff., reprinted in *Études médiévales* [Paris: J. Vrin, 1983], 74ff.). We fully agree with Gilson's thesis, against the recent reinforcement of Barth's position by M. Corbin ("Cela dont plus grand ne puisse être pensé," *Anselm Studies* 1, 1983; and the "Introduction" to the *Proslogion* in his *L'oeuvre de Anselme de Cantorbéry* [Paris: Cerf, 1986], 1.210, 214, 216, 220–21).

short. The fascination raised straightaway by the *nonontological* argument of Anselm—notwithstanding any question about its validity—comes clearly from this genuinely critical aspect. In fact, the syntagm "id quo majus cogitari nequit" claims neither to define God by a concept, even in a negative way, nor to give access to any transcendental item or being. It only indicates the limits felt by all possible efforts toward any conception of God, that is, all efforts to think beyond the limits of our power of thinking. This syntagm deals more with our finitude than with the conception of God. More precisely, it deals with the impossibility of any conception of God, as it reveals the essential finitude of our thoughts, whatever progress they may indefinitely achieve.

If, according to Kant, the word 'transcendental' means "niemals eine Beziehung unserer Erkenntnis auf Dinge, sondern nur aufs Erkenntnisvermögen"—never a relation of thought with things, but only with our power [or faculty] of thinking[21]—then we must conclude paradoxically that Anselm's argument aims at a *transcendent* but inaccessible item only through the *transcendental* test of our *cogitatio.* Any critical evaluation of this argument that would begin by ignoring its obvious critical status in order to disqualify it in an easier way—as it happens in most cases—would prove immediately self-defeating; and, in fact, the majority of these refutations do refute their own attempts, though by no means Anselm's proof. The dogmatic bias appears in most discussions on the side of the opponent (who does not understand the critical argument), not on the side of Anselm. And it is not in the least paradoxical that Kant was the first to miss the point and to criticize Anselm as if he had not been as 'critical'—in Kant's very sense—as Kant himself was supposed to be. This can also be confirmed by referring to the other

---

[21] *Prolegomena,* §13, Akademie-Ausgabe, 293, "third remark." This comparison was suggested by P. Naulin: "Le paradoxe du *Proslogion* est de développer une argumentation proprement dogmatique dans une perspective qui, par sa référence à la conscience de soi, est déjà critique" ("Réflexions sur la portée de la preuve ontologique chez Anselme de Cantorbéry," *Revue de Métaphysique et de Morale,* 74–1 [1969], 19). See also C.-E. Viola: "C'est à tort qu'on identifie souvent l'argument d'Anselme avec la preuve cartésienne ou leibnizienne, qui part de l'*idée* de Dieu conçu comme *ens perfectissimum,* l'idée du plus parfait. . . . En effet, chez Anselme, il ne s'agit pas de l'analyse d'un *concept* comme chez la plupart des partisans de l'argument ontologique," but rather "d'une analyse de notre manière de comprendre Dieu que celle d'un simple concept" ("Journées internationales anselmiennes," *Archives de Philosophie* 35 [1972]: 153).

famous opponent of Anselm's argument, Thomas Aquinas. The whole burden of the Thomistic refutation rests upon the fact that God is not obviously known by us ("per se notum quoad nos"), so that we are deprived of any concept of Him; therefore Thomas first strongly confirms our interpretation of Anselm's argument, as relying on the impossibility of conceiving God, but then, second, interprets this lack of any concept of God as a failure of Anselm's, although it is precisely the core of Anselm's argument. Thus, Thomas gives the utmost evidence that he did not understand at all the powerful paradox of his opponent. Third, he confesses plainly (but unwillingly) that he himself endeavors to construct his own *viae* (ways) upon noncritical, dogmatic, and quasi-empirical concepts of the essence of God, and he obviously does so by assuming Aristotelian starting points. The real issue between Anselm and Thomas Aquinas does not consist, as traditional critics insist too exclusively, in the use of a priori versus a posteriori concepts of God's essence, but primarily in whether to use any concept at all. Far from precluding the demonstration of the existence of God (as Thomas implicitly suggests), the impossibility of any concept of God's essence proves to be, for Anselm, the core of all proof supposed to remain critical and transcendental (in Kant's sense). Far in advance of his critics, Anselm frees himself from the presuppositions of the metaphysical conception.[22]

The solidity of this nonconcept of God is further confirmed by the three steps of the demonstration based upon it. Let us repeat them.

---

[22] This transcendental interpretation of the *cogitatio* is precisely laid out in the reply to Gaunilo: "Sed et si verum esset non posse cogitari vel intelligi illud quo majus nequit cogitari, non tamen falsum esset 'quo majus cogitari nequit' cogitari posse et intelligi. Sicut enim nihil prohibet dici 'ineffabile,' licet illud dici non possit quod 'ineffabile' dicitur; et quemadmodum cogitari possit 'non cogitabile,' quamvis illud cogitari non possit cui convenit 'non cogitabile' dici: ita cum dicitur 'quo nihil majus cogitari' valet, procul dubio quod auditur cogitari vel intelligi potest, etiam si res illa cogitari non valeat aut intelligi, qua majus cogitari nequit" (*Responsio*, IX /138, 4–11). In his first academic essay (still unpublished), F. Alquié perfectly put the stress on this critical and transcendental character of thought as applied to God: "Saint Anselme ne veut pas définir Dieu dans la pensée, mais hors de la pensée. . . . Dieu est défini non dans la pensée, mais par rapport à elle. Il est défini comme extérieur à la pensée, ou du moins comme constituant pour elle une limite infranchissable," as "un obstacle à la pensée, quelque chose que la pensée sentira comme une limite, à laquelle elle se heurtera, qui l'empéchera d'aller plus loin" (*L'argument ontologique chez Saint Anselme: Les critiques de Gaunilon et Saint Thomas d'Aquin*, Diplôme d'Études supérieures directed by Étienne Gilson, and defended before É. Gilson, P. Fauconnet, and L. Brunschvicg, in May 1929, pp. 17, 18.

(i) It is impossible to deny the critical nonconcept of the "id quo majus cogitari nequit." For whoever refuses it on the pretext of not being able to understand its meaning (i.e., cannot conceive it "in intellectu") contradicts self: to reject this point, one must first understand it ("audit hoc ipsum quod dico"); so whoever understands the nonconcept enough to refute it must admit to this much understanding. According to the very definition of the nonconcept, the maximum of the thinkable must not be completely conceived; moreover, it must not be conceived in the strictest sense of a concept. To object on the basis of this impossibility of conceiving it is not to dismiss it, but to acknowledge it as it must be. The deeper misunderstanding of the "id quo majus cogitari nequit" consists in objecting to it on the basis of common rules of meaning, to which it has to be an exception.[23]

---

[23] *Responsio* VIII to Gaunilo claims to need only a "conjecture" (*conjicere*) in order to argue, not a concept; see 137, 14, 18, and 27). Étienne Gilson underlined this point: "Saint Anselme a simplement dit que la vue des choses suffisait à permettre de 'conjecturer' le 'quo majus cogitari nequit,' et qu'à partir de cette notion, même conjecturale, la preuve pouvait se développer complètement" (*Études médiévales*, p. 9 or p. 56). Alexandre Koyré, too, has admitted that the proof "part d'un concept indirect et n'exprimant pas l'essence de Dieu," and remains a "démonstration indirecte" (*L'idée de Dieu dans la philosophie de Saint Anselme*, 201, 202). See J. Paliard, "Prière et dialectique: Méditation sur le Proslogion de Saint Anselme," *Dieu vivant* 6 (1946); H. Bouillard, "Le preuve de Dieu dans le *Proslogion* et son interprétation par K. Barth," in *Spicilegium Beccense*, I, 196; Hans Urs von Balthasar, *Herrlichkeit*. II. *Fächer der Style* (Einsiedeln: Johannes Verlag, 1962); M. Kohlenberger, *Similitudo und Ratio: Überlegungen zur Methode bei Anselm von Canterbury* (Bonn: Grundman and Bouvier, 1972); and I. U. Dalferth, who says: "weder ein Gottesbegriff noch ein Name Gottes, sondern eine Regel, eine Anweisung, wie man *denken* muss, wenn man Gott denken Will," in "Fides quaerens intellectum: Theologie als Kunst der Argumentation in Anselms *Proslogion*," *Zeitschrift für Theologie und Kirche* 81 (1984): 78ff. It is, on the contrary, a bias of J. Vuillemin's study, yet a very clever one, to presuppose that Anselm intended to use a genuine concept of God (*Le Dieu d'Anselme et les apparences de la raison* [Paris: Aubier Montaigne, 1971], 54). We also rely here on the demonstrations of Henri de Lubac, in "Sur le chapitre XIV du *Proslogion*," *Spicilegium Beccense* I, 300, and in " 'Seigneur, je cherche ton visage': Sur le chapitre XIVe du *Proslogion* de Saint Anselme," *Archives de Philosophie* 39, no. 2 (1976). With this thesis, Anselm follows a tradition that includes, among many others, Gregory of Nyssa (*Vita Moysis*, §163, *Patrologia Graeca*, vol. 44, 377A = ed. Jean Daniélou, Sources Chrétiennes 1 *bis* [Paris: Cerf, 1987], 210); Dionysius (*Mystical Theology* II, *Patrologia Graeca*, vol. 3, 1025A); Augustine (*Sermo CXVII*, 3, *Patrologia Latina*, vol. 38, col. 663, and *De Trinitate* XV, 2, 2); Nicholas of Cusa (*De Visione Dei*, XVI, *Philosophisch-Theologische Schriften* III, ed. L. Gabriel [Vienna: Herder, 1967], 166), and even Descartes (*Meditationes de prima philosophia*, 368, 2–4).

(ii) A second step (God cannot be only in understanding, but must be "in re"—that is, in the order of things) follows from the first (the nonconcept of God is "in intellectu"): "Et certe id quo majus cogitari nequit, non potest esse in solo intellectu"—surely, that than which a greater cannot be thought cannot be only in the understanding (*Proslogion* II/101, 15ff./94). But this plain conclusion of the logic of the maximum has to be corrected in the case of God, where a nonconcept is at issue. The maximum of what can be thought about requires not only that, in a transcendental way, the *cogitatio* (thought) can reach the limits of its thinking power, but also that it recognize the transcendence of the *majus*. The *cogitatio* has to admit its inability to think (*cogitare nequit*) some item that transcends the transcendental limits.

(iii) This implies a third step in the argument: to recognize that such a transcendent item as God stretches far beyond the field of understanding. How, then, to name this item beyond understanding (*intellectus*), if not under the title of the *res*, if not by conceding its existence outside the understanding—"esse et in re"?

Indeed, an objection may immediately be raised: Why should that which is no longer completely and plainly in the understanding (transcendental) notwithstanding be in reality (transcendent)? Why should the unthinkable be thought at the second degree as though it were a real entity? Should not the conclusion be, on the contrary, that the item which no longer is according to the lowest degree of being (i.e., being in understanding) has that much less reason to be according to the highest degree of being (i.e., being in reality)? Although this objection looks obvious, it collapses as soon as it is raised. For, at least in Anselm's intention, there is no question here of interpreting the "id quo majus cogitari nequit" as a minimum; it must be interpreted rather as a maximum; and this claim to a maximum turns the hierarchy of the degrees of being back against the previous objection, by distinguishing three different levels. First, there is being in the understanding only and not in reality (e.g., the painter who has in understanding a pattern of that which does not yet exist outside, on his or her canvas). Then, there is the being of that which is in understanding and also in reality ("in intellectu et in re"). And, finally, the last moment is when something is in reality, without being in understanding ("in re et non in intellectu"). This last degree of the hierarchy of being often escapes attention, because most *Proslogion* readers do not press the analysis further than Chapter 4—but Anselm does. In Chapter 15, the theme of the highest possible thought attains its final determination: "Ergo, Domine, non solum es quo majus cogitari nequit, sed es quiddam majus quam cogitari possit"—O Lord, not only are You that than which a greater cannot be thought, but You are also something greater than can be thought (112, 1–15/104). That is: if God is to be thought only insofar as our thought reaches its transcendental limits, God remains beyond the power of thought, that is, is transcendent to it, surpasses it, and, in sum, is not in our understanding. To think about God does not mean only to admit that He exists, but to admit precisely that He remains beyond and outside our understanding. Therefore, God exists *in re* in a very special way—not because He is in understanding, but despite the fact that He is not. Further, He is in reality *because* He is not in understanding. And this is the last and highest degree of being.

Another confirmation for this paradox can be taken from the casual statement that God "utique sic vere est, ut nec cogitari possit non esse." This text does not mean that God so truly is that He could not not be. That translation might suggest that our finite power of thinking is or could be capable of thinking about the infinite; and this makes no sense to Anselm and contradicts his transcendental (critical) method. In fact, the quotation requires and imposes a completely different reading: it is not a question of understanding in a direct and dogmatic way that God exists, as if our thought could surpass its own limits; it is a question of "our not being able to think that God is not." According to the transcendental method, our thought admits its limits and, so to speak, rebounds from them to think in the second degree that it cannot deny that the transcendent item that escapes any concept *in intellectu* must be *in re*. Therefore, Anselm's argument infers God's existence from the very impossibility of producing any concept of God or His essence, according to a critical and transcendental examination of the limits of our power of thinking. God is known as existent inasmuch as He remains unknown through the concept of His essence. Anselm's argument not only does not satisfy the first characteristic of its metaphysical interpretation as an 'ontological argument,' but actually contradicts this interpretation in advance. Thus, the first rupture between Anselm's argument and its metaphysical interpretation appears.

4

It remains to be seen if Anselm's argument also breaks with the second characteristic of its metaphysical interpretation as an 'ontological argument.' The question can be stated thus: Is God's supposed essence to be identified with "essence par excellence"? In brief, does the "id quo majus cogitari nequit" admit to being interpreted (even negatively or in a remote way) in terms of essence, that is, in terms of the question of being or οὐσία?

We noticed a first rupture: the formula "id quo majus cogitari nequit" contradicts the legitimacy of any concept of God. We must now record a new rupture, accomplished through a second formula, "[id] quo nihil melius cogitari potest" (*Proslogion* XIV/111, 9/102–3). This formula, defining something such that nothing better than it can be thought, differs from the first by substituting *melius* for *majus*, that is, the principle of the best for that of the greatest possible quantity. What we have reckoned as a logic of the (undetermined) maximum now takes shape as a logic of a maximum of good, therefore of a sovereign good. But before interpreting it, we have to establish the textual evidence for it. In the *Proslogion*, the first occurrence of this substitution occurs as early as Chapter 3, which, to justify the *majus*, warns: "Si enim aliqua mens posset cogitare aliquid melius te, ascenderet creatura super creatorem, et judicaret de creatore; quod valde est absurdum"—For, if any mind could conceive something better than you, the creature would rise above the Creator and would sit in judgment over the Creator: an utterly preposterous consequence (103, 4–6/94–95). Therefore, *melius* does not contradict *majus*, but rather justifies it by specifying it. The confirmation is to be found in Chapter 5, which states as a rule that God is "quidquid melius est esse quam non esse"—whatever it is better to be than not to be.[24] The principle of the *majus* first becomes

---

[24] *Proslogion*, V.104, 9. See "Si ergo vere es . . . quidquid melius est esse quam non esses" (XI, 110, 1–3); and also "Quis enim verbi gratia vel hoc cogitare non potest, etiam si non credat in re esse quod cogitat, scilicet si bonum est aliquid quod initium et finem habet, multo melius esse bonum, quod licet incipiat non tamen desinit; et sicut istud illo melius est, ita isto esse melius illud quod nec finem habet nec initium" (*Responsio*, VIII, 137, 18–22); or "Credimus namque de divina substantia quidquid absolute cogitari potest melius esse quam non esse. Verbi gratia: melius est esse aeternum quam non aeternum, bonum quam non bonum, imo bonitatem ipsam quam non ipsam bonitatem" (*Responsio*, X, 139, 3–6). Hence, we

operative when it is ruled by the principle of the *melius:* to be greater means to be better; the greatest has to be understood as having a qualitative, not a quantitative, meaning. In order to decide if a determination suits God or not, it is enough to test whether it adds a good to (or subtracts one from) the sovereign good. "Quaerebas Deum, et invenisti eum esse quiddam summum omnium, quo nihil melius cogitari potest"—You were seeking God, and you have found that He is something such that nothing better can be thought (*Proslogion* XIV/111, 8ff./102–93).[25] The claim to a maximum of the *cogitatio* would have remained ineffective and empty without this interpretation.[26] This means that above and beyond the concept of any essence, the good defined as ἐπέκεινα τῆς οὐσίας (beyond being) in Plato's sense (*Republic* 509b) gives the criterion for the "id quo majus cogitari nequit." The good appears as the dominant feature of any radical definition of God, because it exceeds the essence by the same leap by which it gets rid of the concept. The good can be

---

have to be cautious if we speak of a "mouvement de la pensée vers un *optimum et maximum* posé comme l'Absolu" (P. Vignaux, "Structure et sens du *Monologion*," *Revue des sciences philosophiques et théologiques* 31 [1947]: 211), or an *Ens perfectissimum*, as Alexandre Koyré did (*L'idée de Dieu dans la philosophie de Saint Anselme*, 41, 43–44, 46–47); for neither *summe perfectum* nor *perfectissimum* ever appear in Anselm's works, according to G. R. Evans, *A Concordance to the Works of St. Anselm* (Millwood, N.Y.: Kraus, 1984), vol. 3, 1032, and to *Index generalis personarum et rerum*, vol. 6 of *Opera omnia*, ed. F. S. Schmitt, 275.

[25] *Proslogion* XIV, 111, 8–9. The same reduction is to be found in other texts: "Deum vero summum bonum esse nullus negat, quia quidquid aliquo minus est, nullatenus Deus est, et quidquid summum bonum non est, minus est aliquo, quia minus est summo bono" (*Epistula de incarnatione verbi*, VIII, *Opera omnia*, vol. 2, pp. 22, 24–26); and: "Nempe sicut a summo bono non est nisi bonum, et omne bonum est a summo bono: ita a summa essentia non est nisi essentia, et omnis essentia est a summa essentia. Unde quoniam summum bonum est summa essentia, consequens est ut omne bonum sit essentia, et omnis essentia bonum" (*De casu diaboli*, I, *Opera omnia*, vol. 1, 234, 29–235, 3). Here *minus/majus* explicitly refer to *summum*, and the *summum* itself to the *bonum*.

[26] How far the "id quo majus cogitari nequit" taken alone may be deceiving becomes clear with Gaunilo's confusion between the right formula and the mere "majus omnibus" (*Responsio*, V, 134, 24f.). On the contrary, the principle "Deo nihil majus aut melius" (*Cur Deus homo*, I, 13, *Opera omnia*, vol. 2, 71, 13 = "nec major nec justior cogitari possit [misericordia Dei]," II, 20, 131, 29) may be applied to each particular attribute of God; e.g., to justice: "te sic esse justum, ut justior nequeas cogitari" (*Proslogion*, XI, 109, 11); or to mercy: "Benigne, plus es clemens quam possim cogitare" (*Oratio*, XIV, *Opera omnia*, vol. 3, p. 56, 29–30); and: "Nam, cum Deus . . . sit benignus, ut nihil benignius cogitari queat" (*Cur Deus homo*, I, 12, 70, 7).

thought only as it is given—without any measure or concept. God, as a maximum, can be aimed at, but only as a sovereign good.

These two ruptures can be linked together by the relation between the two syntagms that characterize their respective operations. The first rupture (between the original argument and any concept of God) admits a transcendental limit, comes up against it, and marks it as a comparative of simple superiority: *nihil majus cogitari potest, quod majus cogitari nequit*. Indeed, we need only a comparison when our thought faces only one item, its limit. But the second rupture (from *majus* to *melius*) reaches a transcendental ideal, which transcends the transcendental limit of our power of knowing. Therefore, it cannot be expressed by a mere comparative, but requires an absolute superlative, a *summum bonum*. The *summum bonum* indicates more than a limit; it means the crossing of the limit. As a consequence, the indeterminate and unidentified comparative has to be—if I may say so—colored by the light shed from the absolute *summum*, which is now identified as a *bonum*. Thus: "O immensa bonitas, quae sic omne intellectum excedis!"—O goodness without limits, which surpasses every understanding! (*Proslogion* IX/107, 26–27). Absolute transcendence leads to goodness, as the superlative of the *summum bonum*; the transcendental limit leads back to thought, as a mere comparative of οὐσία.

This second rupture, which is even more fundamental than the first and justifies it retrospectively, structures the whole of Anselm's undertaking. Beginning with it, the entire *Proslogion* sets only one goal for its argument: to demonstrate that God is "summum bonum nullo alio indigens, et quo omnia indigent ut sint et bene sint"—the highest good that needs nothing and that everything needs in order to be and to be good (*Prooemium*, 93, 6–9). If the first syntagm "id quo majus cogitari nequit" plays the leading role in Chapters 1–3, it is supplanted by the second, because it is in the end "cogitare aliquid melius te"—to think something better than You (*Proslogion* III/103, 5)—which proves impossible, and leads to the recognition of God's existence as and through a maximum: "summum omnium solus existens"—the one existing maximum of all; according to the principle that "deus sit quidquid melius est esse quam non esse"—God is whatever it is better to be than not to be (104, 9 = 104, 16). Moreover, both the deduction of the divine attributes (Chapter 12), and the theoretization of the definitive incomprehensibility of God's essence, which follows immediately (Chapters 13–23), obey the principle of the *melius*,[27] leading to the *summum bonum*.[28] Therefore, the conclusion leads quite logically from the motto of the maximum to the motto of the best: "cogita quantum potes, quale et quantum sit illud bonum"—think over, as far as you can, which good this is and how good it is (*Proslogion* XXIV/117, 25–26). To reach the limit of our power to understand (according to the maximum) amounts to aiming at the best by loving it ("tantum amabunt, quantum cognoscent"). Love goes further than understanding, because love can desire that which remains unknown, while knowledge cannot reach that which remains unknown or unknowable: "Desidera simplex bonum, quod est omne bonum"—Let us long for the simple good, which is the entire good.[29] If it is a matter of knowing God as the *melius*, that is, as the sovereign good, our thought must not and cannot rely on the (impossible) concept of an inaccessible essence, but must use its own desire, with no other help than its infinite power to love.

By substituting at the end the *melius* for the *majus*, the good for the ὐσία, Anselm extracts—in advance of Kant and for the second time—his argument from any metaphysical, that is, ontological, interpretation. Therefore, it is all the more surprising that the best interpreters have never (at least to my knowledge) pointed out this radical decision. Still more puzzling, the sources that scholars have sometimes tried to assign to the motto "id quo majus cogitari nequit"[30] confirm, on the contrary, that Anselm had recourse to the

---

[27] See chap. VI, 104, 20; chap. IX, 107, 10 and 108, 12; chap. XIV, 119, 9 ("summum omnium, quo melius cogitari nequit"); chap. XVIII, 114, 21. The principle appears one more time as such in chap. XI, 110, 2. All occurrences of *melius* are given in Evans, *Concordance to the Works of St. Anselm*, vol. 2, 852ff.; of *majus*, 2.819ff.

[28] *Summe bonus*: chap IX, 107, 20 and chap X, 109, 5. *Summum bonum* in chap. XXII, 117, 1 and XXIII, 117, 5 (expressed as "omne et totum et solum bonum").

[29] See chap. XXIV, 117, 25–26; chap. XXVI, 121, 9–10; and chap. XXV, 118, 17.

[30] Strangely, F. S. Schmitt (*Index generalis*, 102n) cites, for the *majus*, *Monologion*, LXXX, 86, 19–21, which does not mention it and *Monologion*, XV, 29, 17–211, which uses only *melius* and *melior*, exactly as Augustine and Boethius do! The one text, among those quoted by Schmitt, that used the *majus* comes from a non-Christian, Seneca: "Quid est Deus? Mens universi, quod vides totum et quod non vides totum. Si demum magnitudo sua redditur, qua nihil majus excogitari potest, si solus est omnia, opus suum et intra et extra tenet" (*Naturales Quaestiones*, I, *Praefatio*). When a non-believer uses *melius*, it still qualifies the world: "nihil omnium rerum melius est mundo, nihil praestabilius, nihil pulchriorius" (Cicero, *De*

melius only with the authority of Augustine himself; Boethius, too, might have provided some examples to Anselm.[31] Thus, the second thesis of our nonontological interpretation of Anselm's argument lacks neither speculative articulation nor support in the patristic tradition. It is neither a matter of detail in the formulation nor of originality devoid of consequences. It is a question of the possibility of going back to a strict identification of the argument, far removed from its later metaphysical interpretation. God's existence *is* demonstrated, but without any claim to having a concept of His essence or to submitting this supposed "essence" to the jurisdiction of the οὐσία, that is, of the *Seinsfrage*. If God is to be known, it can only be within the horizon of the good.

5

We have now come far enough to answer the third question: At least one form of the so-called ontological argument—the first one, given

---

natura deorum, II, 7, 18). On the use of *melius*, see A. Daniels, "Quellenbeiträge und Untersuchungen zur Geschichte der Gottesbeweise im dreizehnten Jahrhundert, mit besonderer Berücksichtigung des Arguments im *Prologion* des heiligen Anselm," *Beiträge zur Geschichte der Philosophie des Mittelalters* 8, nos. 1–2 (Münster, 1909)d J. Chatillon, "De Guillaume d'Auxerre à Saint Thomas d'Aquin: L'argument de Saint Anselme chez les premiers scolastiques du XIIIème siècle," in *Spicilegium Beccense* 1). See also N. Malcolm, *The Ontological Argument: From Anselm to Contemporary Philosophers*, ed. Alvin Plantinga (Garden City, N.Y.: Anchor, 1965), 142.

[31] E.g., Augustine: "Sic enim nitebar invenire caetera, ut jam melius inveneram melius esse incorruptibile quam corruptibile, et ideo te, quidquid esses, esse incorruptibilem confitebar. Neque enim ulla anima unquam potuit poteritve cogitare aliquid quod sit te melius, qui summum et optimum es. Cum autem verissime atque certissime incorruptibile corruptibili praeponatur, sicut ego jam praeponebam, poteram jam cogitatione aliquid attingere, quod esset melius Deo meo, nisi tu esses incorruptibilis" (*Confessiones*, VII, 4, 6, *Patrologia Latina*, vol. 32, col. 735 = CSEL XXXII, p. 145 = *Oeuvres de Saint Augustine* [Paris: Desclée de Brouwer, 1962], 588, quoted by Schmitt, *Proslogion* I). "Nam cum ille unus cogitatur deorum Deus, ab his qui alios et suspicantur et vocant et colunt deos sive in coelo et terra, ita cogitatur, ut aliquid quo nihil melius sit atque sublimius illa cogitatio conetur attingere" (*De doctrina christiana*, I, 7, *Patrologia Latina*, vol. 34, col. 22 [quoted by Schmitt, *Index* generalis, I, and by Vuillemin, *Le Dieu d'Anselme et les apparences de la raison*, 93]). "Summum bonum omnino et quo esse aut cogitari melius nihil possit, aut intelligendus, aut credendus Deus est, si blasphemiis carere cogitamus" (*De moribus Manichaeorum*, II, 11, 25, *Patrologia Latina*, vol. 32, col. 1355). See *De duabus animabus contra Manichaeos*, VIII, 10, *Patrologia Latina*, vol. 42, col. 101; and *De natura boni contra Manichaeos*, I, *Patrologia Latina*, vol. 42, col. 551. Boe-

by Anselm—does not fulfill the two distinctive requirements of the metaphysical interpretation of the argument. Therefore, Anselm's argument does not belong to ontology, that is, is not an 'ontological argument' at all.

As surprising as this conclusion may seem, it is backed by numerous and strong reasons.

(i) The independence of Anselm's argument from the question of being and ontology in general does not sentence it to irrationality and 'mysticism.' It means only that God's most characteristic features escape the grasp of finite concepts, that God's transcendence has to be termed a transcendence of the good and not a mere maximum of entities. God transcends by the preeminence of the sovereign good: in other words, only the good deserves the qualification of infinite, as if Anselm were convinced (in advance of Kant and Heidegger) that being as such is always finite. The two theoretical decisions on which the argument relies prove to be one: God escapes any concept (or theoretical reason) insofar as He remains open to love (or practical reason). "Id enim summum est, quod sic supereminet aliis, ut nec par habeat, nec praestantius. Sed quod est summe bonum, est etiam summe magnum"—This is the highest good, which transcends everything else such that it has neither equal nor more excellent. But that which is the highest good is therefore also the greatest (*Monologion* I/15, 9–11).

(ii) By attributing transcendence to the good, and depriving being of it, Anselm stands on firm ground: two major authorities support his attempt. First, Plato, who has placed the good far above entities (οὐκ οὐσίας ὄντος τοῦ ἀγαθοῦ, ἀλλ' ἔτι ἐπεκείνα τῆς οὐσίας— the good being not a being, but beyond being), has also acknowledged the hyperbolic transcendence of good ("Απολλον, ἔφη, δαιμονίας ὑπερβολῆς—miraculously transcendent; *Republic* 509b/ c). This doctrine gives to Anselm's position not only a strong legitimacy, but, more, an indisputable right to be termed a pure philosophical doctrine. Second, in a quite different tradition, Paul's Epistle to the Ephesians (3.10) gives another standard meaning for understanding the transcendence of the divine good according to

---

thius appears as the probable link between Augustine and Anselm: "Deum rerum omnium principem bonum esse communis humanorum conceptio probat animorum. Nam cum nihil Deo melius excogitari quaet, id quo melius est bonum esse quis dubitet?" (*Philosophiae Consolatio*, III, 10).

Anselm: γνῶναι τε τὴν ὑπερσάλλουσαν γνῶσες ἀγάπην τοῦ Χρισ-τοῦ—to know the hyperbolic charity of Christ, which surpasses any knowledge. We remark that the translation of this text in the Vulgate—"scire etiam *supereminentem* scientiae charitatem Christi"—fits exactly Anselm's own words: "summum est, quod sic *supereminet*." But, on the other hand, we must concede that Anselm's use of the *summum bonum* refers neither to Christ nor to *caritas* as such, at least in the *Proslogion*. As a result, the question remains to be answered whether or not Anselm intended to teach as a theologian. Therefore, the question whether Anselm stands closer to Plato or to Paul remains open, too. But the very fact that we waver between those two authorities demonstrates that Anselm's nonontological argument remains within the field of rational and intelligible discussion.

(iii) In fact, the greatest difficulty of our claim that there is a nonontological interpretation of Anselm's argument and a very obvious discrepancy between his argument and its later metaphysical interpretation lies in the possibility (or the impossibility) of arguing beyond or outside the field of metaphysics. Does it make sense to admit conclusive and rational arguments without admitting the primacy of being, that is, of metaphysics and, as a consequence, of logic? How far does logic depend on metaphysics? How could a non-metaphysical argument be valid?

We would suggest that at least one author was convinced that some arguments are not involved in metaphysics—Anselm himself.

Chapter 3

Two Forms of Negative Theology Explained Using Thomas Aquinas

Jozef Wissink

IN THIS CHAPTER I will examine the meaning of the expression '*theologia negativa*,' and in so doing I will distinguish between two types of negative theology: the first motivated by a religious or an epistemological need, and the second by the Christian belief in the Creator (Section 1). Next I will give reasons why theologians would do well to turn to Thomas Aquinas with their questions (Section 2). Then I will show that in Thomas we meet a strictly pursued negative theology of the second type (Section 3). Finally, I will examine whether, given the previous arguments, there are theological criteria that can help answer the question whether and when it is 'theologically meaningful' to speak of negative theology with regard to contemporary philosophers (Section 4).

1. Two Types of Negative Theology

Similar phenomena can be very different according to the contexts in which they function. Some conversions are well characterized when we say that the converted turned 360 degrees. In that case the converted faces the same direction as the unconverted. But they each see from a different point of view: the one has covered a tremendous trajectory, while the other has not moved.

The first type of negative theology relates to a phenomenon found in various religions. It is known in religious science that religions develop in the direction of an increasingly *transcendent* concept of

God. The gods who are originally close (as close as love, fire, struggle, power, the family hearth, etc.) eventually move further away from humanity. They climb continually 'higher' and eventually remove themselves/are removed to heaven. The final phase of this process seems to result in a *Deus otiosus*, a resting God, retired to heaven. Thus the God of deism rested after the act of creation. He explains the creation of our world and at the end of time He will reward the good and punish the evil, but meanwhile He plays no further role in our lives. The future does not look good for such a resting God (or Goddess): He (or She) is close to His (or Her) abolishment. As this process continues, thinkers gradually adopt an *antianthropomorphic* standard that serves an ever more negative theology.[1] I will describe this process in greater detail.

The (Hellenistic and Christian) antianthropomorphic tradition asks about the *'natura deorum'* (nature of the gods) or the *'natura Dei'* (God's nature), only to reject speaking in physical and emotional terms as *'Deo non dignum'* (unworthy of God). The first context of the question about the *'natura deorum'* is polytheism: problems with and contradictions between the various gods and difficulties with the gods' unethical behavior require that the divine sphere be better understood philosophically and better organized politically. Plato's measures in his *Republic* are known: the divine is strictly separated from the (all too) human and the 'theologians' (poets and their myths) are strenuously controlled. The gods must become 'more transcendent.' At the root of this whole procedure is a *predicative concept* of the divine: the divine is a certain aspect of the cosmos, which presents itself as mysterious and superhuman. Thus Ares is another name for (the sacrality of) violence, Aphrodite for (the sacrality of) sexuality, and so on. In this critique, the gods

---

[1] I use the dissertation by H. M. Kuitert, *De mensvormigheid Gods: Een dogmatisch-hermeneutisch studie over de antropomorfismen van de Heilige Schrift* (Kampen: Kok, 1969).

Antianthropomorphism is the tendency that opposes speaking about gods/goddesses in terms of human characteristics, e.g., by attributing to them arms and legs, or by suggesting that they feel despair, anger, and such like. Kuitert's analyses offer an interpretation of the antianthropomorphic tradition within Christianity: he wants to reduce it to its 'foreign' ('pagan') origin and then reject this antianthropomorphic standard in the name of the anthropomorphic language in the Scriptures about a revealing God with human features. I do not share his interpretation of the Scriptures and the theological tradition, but I find Kuitert's observations on several phenomena very useful.

lose their mythic stature, but the original mythical structure of the divine is preserved: the divine is still an added predicate to a cosmic aspect of being.[2] God and divinity are predicates, not subjects: something or someone is God, because He/She/It is divine and not the reverse: something or someone is divine because He/She/It is God.[3] This critique denies the gods' *corporeality, emotions, injustice,* and *change.* This need not coincide with a complete negative theology: in Plato the knowing soul is related to the divine, intelligible world of Ideas. It can thus obtain real knowledge.

It is just a small step beyond this critique of the gods to another positing that the divine is totally unknowable. The predicative concept of God presupposes a transparent cosmos, which allows the divine to shine through. Whoever has eyes to see can see that the cosmos is full of gods (Thales of Miletus). But when the cosmos becomes less transparent, or skepticism about the human ability to understand grows, the concept of transcendence is stretched so far that it includes the gods' unknowability. This occurs in the Hellenistic period. Philo is probably the first to move in this direction. It is an existentially gripping matter: the cosmos keeps silent. God has become foreign, humanity feels lonely, the cosmos no longer offers humanity security. To put it in the words of the Dutch poet Leo Vroman,

> Go ahead, sob,
> For from here to God
> No one, no one
> Sobs over our lot.[4]

We feel the same drama in the gnostic dictum that calls God 'the eternal silence.' We then make a virtue of necessity and formulate a concept of God whose distinction lies in its radical transcendence.[5]

In conclusion we can say that the first type of negative theology in this analysis has as context the predicative concept of the divine, an

---

[2] Ibid., 72.

[3] Ibid., 75. We only become aware of the scope of this dictum when we see that Thomas Aquinas calls God the "subject of theology" (*subjectum theologiae; Summa Theologiae* 1.1.7). In the Christian tradition there is one important exception to the rule that God is not subject but predicate: in speaking about the Trinity, '*theos*' is used as a predicate. The Father is God, the Son is God, and the Holy Spirit is God.

[4] L. Vroman, "De ruinte in," in *262 gedichten* (Amsterdam: Querido, 1974), 168.

[5] Kuitert, *De mensvormigheid Gods,* 103–5.

ever more radical transcendence of the divine, skepticism about human ability to know, and a more profane view of the cosmos that is no longer transparent to the divine. My question now is whether Christian negative theology is only a variant of this more general religious phenomenon or whether it is so unique that we must consider it a phenomenon sui generis.

I find a first indication that the latter may be the case in the theology of Karl Barth (1886–1968). He rejects negative theology as described above, but does recognize a negative theology applicable to the God of Abraham, Isaac, and Jacob. For this last theme we must not seek in those places in his opus where he explicitly speaks of the phenomenon 'negative theology' because he identifies this term with negative theology as it is described above. Rather, we must look in those places where he speaks of 'God's hiddenness'; Barth makes a sharp distinction between God's hiddenness that humanity discovered and conceded after wandering long (what we have described as the first kind of negative theology) and God's hiddenness that is made known in God's revelation, and is not diminished by God's revelation, because God remains God.[6]

Barth sharply contrasts *natural theology* and *revelation theology*. Natural theology involves humanity's looking for and finding the divine without God. Revelation theology presupposes that God can be known only by God (in the Son, through the work of the Holy Spirit) and that people participate in this knowledge when the gift of faith is given to them, and with it an insight into the mystery of Jesus Christ, God's preeminent revelation. In this revelation, God is revealed precisely as the Hidden One, whom humanity can never have at its disposition. The knowledge of faith given in revelation is critical to all that humanity had previously 'learned' about the divine, even when the result of this search was a resigned admission of God's unknowability.

Barth notes explicitly that he reached this theological position guided by Scripture and not by any epistemology. A negative estimate of the (religious) ability of human reason need not lead to Barth's position: we could also decide to just stop speaking about God. Conversely, were Scripture to tell us that human intelligence made an independent contribution to human knowledge about God

---

[6] See Karl Barth, *Kirchliche Dogmatik* (Zurich: EVZ-Verlag, 1940), 2.1.52–54.

and that natural theology is thus required, then in a 'negative' epistemology the contribution of natural theology could still be to convince people, on philosophical grounds, that one should abstain from
a philosophical theology.[7] Barth also explicitly delimits his theological approach from what he calls the "Religionsphilosophie der Autorität." This philosophical method implies that people who seek God
are led to skepticism and doubt, after which, in Kierkegaardian style,
they are advised to leap out of doubt and into faith: "If your head
bothers you, cut it off, for it is better to find rest without a head than
to wander about with a head between gods who give no rest." In that
case people in doubt try to lift themselves from the morass of doubt.
Barth's reply is that if we do not begin with the Word, we will not
end with it.[8]

Thanks to Barth we meet a second type of negative theology. Before I further develop this Christian negative theology, I must point
out that although the two types are separated by a chasm, the one
type can use the reflections and dicta of the other. Philo (c. 13 B.C.–
A.D. 45 or 50), Basilius (c. A.D. 330–379), and Pseudo-Dionysius (c.
A.D. 500) were probably motivated by the Jewish or the Christian
faith to adopt a predominantly negative way of speaking about God,
but in doing so used Middle Platonic and Neoplatonic thinking. The
opposite can also happen.

For a more precise analysis of the motives and foundations of the
second type of negative theology I turn to Robert Sokolowski. His
analyses prepare us well for reading Thomas Aquinas.[9]

Sokolowski shows that the Judeo-Christian faith confesses God as
the Creator, Preserver, and Ruler of heaven and earth (= 'everything'), and that it therefore distinguishes between God and 'everything' in a way not found in any other religion or philosophy of life.
Greek religion and philosophy did not know this distinction because
there the gods or the divine could always be seen as (the highest)

---

[7] See Ibid., 47. See J. Wissink, *De inzet van de theologie: Een onderzoek naar de motieven en de geldigheid van Karl Barths strijd tegen de natuurlijke theologie* (Amersfoort: Horstink, 1983), 88.

[8] Barth, *Kirchliche Dogmatik*, 2.1.7 (author's translation). See Wissink, *De inzet van de theologie*, 39–41.

[9] R. Sokolowski, *The God of Faith and Reason: Foundations of Christian Theology* (Notre Dame, Ind./London: University of Notre Dame Press, 1982).

part of the one cosmos.[10] For this reason Sokolowski speaks of the
distinction between Creator and 'everything' as "the Christian distinction." This distinction between God and creatures is different
from any distinction between individual creatures.[11] In the context
of 'everything' the one is distinguished from the other by not being
the other from which it is distinguished. The 'being' of the one distinguished consists partly in its being 'other' and depends on its
being distinct from the other.[12] Christian faith in creation denies
this relationship between the terms of the distinction God–
'everything.' For God would be and remain the same God, even if
there were no world.[13] The distinction between God and creatures is
unique *in that* the distinction *is only there* thanks to one of the terms
of the distinction: God, who Himself permits the distinction to
arise.[14] God is 'differently different.' That means that God's creation
cannot be understood in terms of any creaturely activity or any creaturely relationship. And here we find ourselves in the middle of the
'theologia negativa': we do not know what the word 'created' means
in the sentence 'God created heaven and earth.' We know what it

---

[10] Ibid., 12–20.

[11] I found a good description of this 'different difference' in John D. Caputo,
Heidegger and Aquinas: An Essay on Overcoming Metaphysics (New York: Fordham
University Press, 1982), 145: "Now, God and creatures do not differ as one being
and another do. For the creature is distinct from God as the likeness is distinct from
the original, as the participated from the unparticipated. There is no simple 'ontical'
difference between God and creatures, but an ontological difference. . . ."

[12] Sokolowski, *The God of Faith*, 32: "When we turn away from the world or from
the whole and turn toward God, toward the other term of the distinction that comes
to light in Christian belief, we begin to appreciate the strangeness of the distinction
itself. In the distinctions that occur normally within the setting of the world, each
term distinguished is what it is precisely by not being that which it is distinguishable
from. Its being is established partially by its otherness, and therefore its being depends on its distinction from others."

[13] Sokolowski shows that this is an implication of Anselm's formula which states
that God is "id quo nihil maius cogitari possit" (that than which nothing greater
can be thought). We could formulate this implication as follows: (God plus the
world, the creatures) is not 'greater' than God alone. Or: (God plus the world, the
creatures) cannot be understood as greater than God alone. The contingency and
gratuity of the being of creatures cannot be formulated more sharply; of God it says
that He is "nullo alio indigens" (in need of no one or nothing else) and that He
must be "benevolens" (benevolent) because He created without needing to do so
(*The God of Faith*, 6–10). On Anselm's formula, see esp. J.-L. Marion's chapter in
this book.

[14] Ibid., 33.

does not mean. 'To make' and 'to flow from' are only images for God's creating.[15]

It is important to realize that Sokolowski speaks of a God whom we know (and also do not know) in our faith. For him, the 'Christian distinction' had been lived for centuries before it was explicitly put into a concept. He shows extensively and convincingly that the Church knew of this distinction in its disputes on Christological dogma[16] and rejected every blurring of this distinction as heretical. When, in thinking of the Incarnation, we forget the specific distinction between God and 'everything' and think of God as a (highest and closing) part of the cosmos, there arises a competition between 'natura Dei' (God's nature) and 'natura humana' (human nature). Thus the chief Greek god Zeus can hide in human form, but cannot become human. God can do this.[17]

It is obvious that the 'Christian distinction' on the one side offers us little information on God's nature and on the other side will penetrate all our speaking about God. It will cause a negation line to pass through all positive dicta about God. He (She? It?) is doubtless present, but differently from how creatures are present. God is doubtless absent, but differently from how creatures are absent.

---

[15] This is occasionally forgotten in some philosophical circles, where 'creatio' is understood exclusively as a form of (remarkable) causality. One example is M. Heidegger. See Caputo, *Heidegger and Aquinas*, 64–96. The author unfortunately adopts this critique without correction.

[16] I refer here to the theological reflection and struggle that led to the dogma of Chalcedon (A.D. 451), which said of Christ that He was one (divine) hypostasis in two natures, so that He must be called truly God and truly human. This was formulated with greater precision in the reflection and struggle of the following centuries, until the third council of Constantinople (681) decided that there were two 'wills' and two 'energies' in Christ: Christ also willed and acted as human.

[17] One has to be very precise in formulating this distinction. In lectures I have summarized belief in creation as "God is noncreature and the creature is non-God." Strictly speaking, this does not reflect the uniqueness of the distinction between God and creation: the danger is still present that the infinite is understood as a simple opposite to the finite. Thomas warns against this in his commentary on *De Divinis Nominibus* (*The Divine Names*) by Pseudo-Dionysius (Rome: Marietti, 1950), § 661: "His being is not limited through a nature determined by a genus or species, so that we could say 'He is this' and 'He is not that,' as the spiritual substances are determined" (Non enim esse suum est finitum per aliquam naturam determinatam ad genus vel speciem, ut possit dici quod est hoc et non est illud, ut sunt determinatae etiam substantiae spirituales; author's translation). A theological consequence is that the proposition 'God became human' contains no contradiction! See Sokolowski, *God of Faith*, 42 and 47n1.

Often it must be said that customary religious language about God is used metaphorically. The theologian wants to *think* about God and he or she does not want to be limited to increasing the number of metaphors. On the other hand, the theologian has no other access to God's secrets beyond what 'normal' believers have. But what he or she can do is indicate the 'logical space' within which the metaphors move, show why the object of faith *requires* metaphors, negations, and linguistic transformations.[18]

In conclusion we can say of the second type of negative theology that it does not presuppose a skeptical epistemology. Further, that the theologian allows a negative line to pass through all (positive *and* negative) speaking about God out of respect for God's being God, because of the unicity of the 'Christian distinction.' Finally, it is striking that speech about God's hiddenness is not ruled by the opposition between *transcendent* and *immanent*. Of the God close to us in Jesus Christ it is said that He remains God and thus the Hidden One in His completely confirmed presence.

2. WHY CONSULT THOMAS AQUINAS?

Since the 1950s we have lost the habit of theologically consulting Thomas Aquinas. Everyone agrees he was a great theologian and had something to say about nearly everything, so that we find in many thematic studies at least some brief reference to his work. But today someone who is known as a 'Thomist' is soon suspected of being a restorative, conservative thinker.

Several motives could be mentioned for this attitude. First, there is the general image of Scholasticism itself, which is accused of having too great a trust in rationality. This image also communicates a view of Scholastics being lost in distinctions and concepts that make their thinking irrelevant to reality. Second, Thomas has been labeled a systematic thinker who nailed Aristotelian philosophy and Chris-

---

[18] Ibid., 3–4. It seems to me necessary for a theologian to be aware of language in speaking about God: what 'grammar' or 'logic' holds sway? That this attention does not diminish the attention given to God will by now be clear. There is thus no contradiction between thinking about God and being attentive to the rules of speaking about God. The second functions pragmatically as a beneficial break, to prevent our forgetting that it is God we are speaking about.

tian faith together in one metaphysical construction. Third, Thomas is accused of enclosing Christian faith in a great, philosophical ontology that leaves practical salvation history buried under an avalanche of general concepts.

When we recall that in our culture rationality is under pressure, that postmodernism has made us extrasensitive to how reality is filtered away in systems, and, finally, that in our culture Christian faith is best accessed in short narratives, not in the 'Grand Narratives' of the world and of life, it is clear that such a Thomas can play only a minor role.

Then why Thomas? For many philosophers, the revival of interest in Thomas is situated in the framework of their interest in premodern thinkers: now that the aspirations of modernity (with Hegel as figurehead) have run aground, new inspiration is sought in the old sources provided by masters from the 'Vorzeit' (to use a term from the neo-Thomist Kleutgen).[19] Furthermore, studies by Marie-Dominique Chénu, Yves de Lubac, Henri Congar, and others have caused a rift in the image people have had of Thomas. Thomas's 'rationalism' appears to be of a completely different kind than the rationalism of post-Cartesian thought. In the Middle Ages, 'ratio' is not yet the judge before whose bench all must acquit themselves, but strongly connotes receptivity. 'Ratio' must bow before the data of reality. The great interest in distinctions and concepts appears to coincide with an equally great interest in the language of tradition and for the implications of the 'grammar' of human language. This has led Anglo-Saxon philosophy to develop a renewed interest for this side of Thomas. Wittgenstein and Thomas are relatives. In addition, a closer look at Thomas shows that he is not the great system builder he is reputed to be. His works reflect a lifelong search in which old or new questions lead to the weighing of possible answers and their pros and cons. The answer reached in this way has the character of 'the best answer to be reached so far':[20] a renewed study can lead to a different formulation, it can be corrected by new data. Corbin's major study shows convincingly that Thomas elected to start over several times in his life.[21] The question of the relationship of salva-

---

[19] Cf. the way Thomas and neo-Thomism are appreciated in A. MacIntyre, *Three Rival Versions of Moral Enquiry* (London: Duckworth, 1990).

[20] See MacIntyre, *Three Rival Versions*, 124.

[21] M. Corbin, *Le chemin de la théologie chez Thomas d'Aquin* (Paris: Beauchesne, 1974).

tion history and 'ontology' is also not as simple as suggested above. Thomas is more a Scripture 'exegete' than has been supposed[22] and the so-called ontology involves more an in-depth search for presuppositions and consequences of scriptural witnesses (with the help of Aristotle, but also of Neoplatonism, Dionysius, Augustine, etc.) than their insertion into a prefabricated Aristotelian system.

At the University of Utrecht a group of theologians, philosophers, historians, and lawyers have devoted their time for the last fifteen years to Thomas research, to making Thomas's 'legacy' fruitful for present-day theological discussion. In this group Thomas is read primarily as theologian: the expositor of the 'Sacra Pagina,' the interpreter of the Christian tradition in the context of his time. If we put aside the commentaries on Aristotle, we could say that all the philosophical parts of his work serve the mission of the 'Magister in Sacra Pagina.' Attentive reading supported by unceasing attention for his 'linguistic moves' shows that his theology is a consistent negative theology: we do *not* know what God is. This 'discovery' is certainly not new,[23] but it must be constantly repeated. This negative 'doctrine of God' belongs, for me, to Thomas's legacy and we would do well to include it in the present postmodern debate.

3. Thomas's Negative Theology

We are now ready to sketch Thomas Aquinas's position and methodology.[24] I read Thomas Aquinas (c. 1225–1274) as a theologian who

---

[22] See esp. W. Valkenberg, *Did Not Our Heart Burn? Place and Function of Holy Scripture in the Theology of St. Thomas Aquinas* (Utrecht: Thomas Institute, 1990).

[23] As an example I mention only K. Rahner, "Fragen zur Unbegreiflichkeit Gottes nach Thomas von Aquin," in *Schriften zur Theologie* (Zurich/Einsiedeln/Cologne: Benziger Verlag, 1975), 12.306–19.

[24] I make no claim to originality in this section. The hypotheses first, on the predominantly theological character of Thomas's work; second, on his attention to language; and third, on the negative character of all his dicta on God arose, as I noted, in the context of the KTU (Catholic Theological University, Utrecht, The Netherlands) research program on the theology of Thomas Aquinas with particular attention to its sources and influence on later theology. Of fundamental importance for the first hypothesis is the work mentioned above by Corbin (note 20). For the second and third hypotheses, see D. Burrell, *Aquinas: God and Action* (London: Routledge & Kegan Paul, 1979), and *Knowing the Unknowable God: Ibn-Sina, Maimonides, Aquinas* (Notre Dame, Ind.: University of Notre Dame Press, 1986). See also H. Rikhof, "Negative Theology," in J. Wissink, ed., *(Dis)continuity and (De)-*

represents the second type of negative theology. This reading is not without controversy: since the Renaissance many have read parts of his *theological* work as *philosophical* reflection. They think its goal is to create room for a positive doctrine on God. Taking part in this discussion, I wish to sketch Thomas's position by using two questions:

1. If it is true that Thomas in his doctrine on God speaks primarily negatively about God, is he doing so on the basis of a 'Christian distinction' or of a skepticism regarding human ability to know? Thus I first examine the theological character of Thomas's work.
2. Does Thomas really speak negatively? Can he not be interpreted as someone who presents a developed positive 'doctrine on God'?

Thomas as Theologian

No one denies that by profession Thomas was a theologian ('Magister in Sacra Pagina'). Yet for the last two centuries attention paid to Thomas came primarily from philosophers.[25] An important factor is that since the appearance of Leo XIII's encyclical *Aeterni Patris*, Thomistic philosophy was the official philosophy of the Roman Catholic Church. People read Thomas as one who provided a philosophical system. This 'odium' has followed him to this day. It would make little sense in this chapter to resurrect the battle between theologians and philosophers on whether philosophers are correct in reserving a place for Thomas on their bookshelves. *Everyone* can learn from him. Thomas doubtless also wrote strictly philosophically (for example, in his commentaries on Aristotle). It is also obvious that he integrated much philosophical thinking into his theological reflections. Yet a specifically theological reading has the advantage that we read from the same attitude that Thomas had, from an orientation toward acquiring an *'intellectus fidei'* (understanding of the faith).

The most vehement dispute on Thomistic interpretation involves the *Summa Contra Gentiles* (or better, considering its original title,

---

construction: *Reflections on the Meaning of the Past in Crisis Situations* (Kampen: Kok, 1995), 154–71.

[25] See J. v.d. Eijnden, "Sacris sollemniis: inleidende beschouwingen," in J. van den Eijnden, ed., *De gelovige Thomas: Beschouwingen over de Hymna Sacris Sollemniis van Thomas van Aquino* (Baarn: Ambo, 1986), 13 and 23n5.

On the Truth of the Catholic Church[26]) and large parts of the *Summa Theologiae*. I would, therefore, like to describe briefly the theological alloy of these two works.

The *Summa Contra Gentiles* is usually presented as an apologetic work directed against Muslim thinkers or as a theological handbook to help Dominican missionaries who wanted to preach the gospel to the Muslims. This latter view relies on a few lost pages from the chronicle of the little-known Peter Marsilio on the deeds of James I of Aragon.[27] This tradition does not seem all that reliable; moreover, the resulting work does not coincide with the content of the task that Raymond of Peñaforte, according to Peter, assigned Thomas.

A more weighty argument is that Thomas, in his *Summa Contra Gentiles*, placed first the truths about God "that natural reason can also reach"[28] and only in the fourth book turned to the truths "that exceed the ability of human reason."[29] Yet I think that this argument contributes little to proving that Thomas wanted to be a philosopher in the first three books, only to change profession in the fourth. This would be to underestimate the influence of the fourth book. Corbin illuminated the purpose of the *Summa Contra Gentiles* by situating it in the development of Thomas's thought. He thinks that the so-called third entrance of Aristotle in the thirteenth century confronted theology with the task of finding a new relationship to philosophy. It was not merely the question of borrowing methods from Aristotle's philosophical work: theology was now confronted by a complete (and completely different) view of the world. For Thomas, the problem was urgent because he agreed with much of what Aristotle said and became involved via the Averroist interpretation in a 'conflict of the faculties.'[30] According to Corbin, the introductory

---

[26] *Summa de Veritate Catholicae Fidei.*

[27] In this work Peter Marsilio also devoted a few pages to Raymond of Peñaforte (1180–1275). Peter Marsilio wanted to show that Raymond had done something good for all people. Peter had no difficulty finding good deeds directed toward the popes, doctors, canonists, pastors (= bishops), and other believers, the heretics, the Jews and Moors, for there was enough material to be found in Raymond's life. To show that Raymond had also thought of the (other) "*infideles*" (unbelievers), Peter mentions that Raymond asked Brother Thomas to write a *Summa* against their errors. See Corbin, *Le chemin de la théologie*, 477–86.

[28] Ad quae etiam ratio naturalis pertingere potest. . . .

[29] Quae omnem facultatem humanae rationis excedunt.

[30] Because of the interpretation given by the Muslim philosopher Averoes (1126–1198) to Aristotle, namely, to his thinking on the "*intellectus agens*" (active intel-

questions[31] of Thomas's first work, the *Scriptum Super Libros Senten-
tiarum Magistri Petri Lombardi*, avoid methodological problems and
are still satisfied with the traditional answers regarding the task and
specificity of theology. Then in the *Summa Contra Gentiles* Thomas
tried to organize matters by treating successively what could be
known of Christian faith through natural reason and what exceeded
human reason. But, according to Corbin, he abandoned this procedure in the *Summa Theologiae*.[32] According to this view, the plan of
the *Summa Contra Gentiles* is the result of a search for the shape
that theology must take when it wanted to address the challenge
posed by Aristotle's thinking.

In the *Summa Theologiae*[33] the dispute on the interpretation of
the theological content is sharpest for the Questions 2–16 of the
'First Part' (Prima pars). This part has been read as a philosophical
doctrine on God in which quotations from the Scriptures and the
Church Fathers would be more ornamental than essential. If we consider the 'quaestio style' a mere literary device and read only the
responses (in some editions even summarized in a thesis preceding
Thomas's text), we can get this impression. But when we study the
objections (the *sed contra*, on the contrary) or the responses, and the
answers to the objections, the real purpose of an article proves each
time to be directly or indirectly theological. This is so evident that I
will select only a few examples from the texts where neo-Scholastic

---

lect), in which one "intellectus agens" was ascribed to the whole of humanity,
Christian thinkers' faith in a *personal preservation* after death was endangered. Because the 'artes' faculty (we would say philosophy department) accepted this Averroist reading of Aristotle, it came in conflict with the theologians.

[31] Thomas's systematic works are built of '*quaestiones*' (questions on a given
theme). The *quaestio* consists of one or more '*articuli.*' An *articulus* treats one question. The structure is as follows: first arguments (from authority or reason) are posited that support one answer to the question (or for several possible answers); then
in the '*sed contra*' (on the contrary, on the other hand) one or more arguments are
put forth for the opposite idea. In the '*responsio*' (response), which begins with the
words "I answer that it must be said that . . ." (Respondeo dicendum quod . . .),
Thomas gives his own answer. Then the arguments are discussed insofar as they
refute, or seem to refute, Thomas's answer. In this procedure a question is approached from the maximum number of angles: each 'articulus' is a whole journey
of thought!

[32] Corbin, *Le chemin de la théologie*, 643–80.

[33] I use the Blackfriars edition: St. Thomas Aquinas, *Summa Theologiae*, 60 vols.
(London: Blackfriars in conjunction with Eyre & Spottisville/New York: McGraw-
Hill, 1964–1975). Hereafter cited in the text parenthetically as *STh*.

authors ignored the theological sentences or where the theological interest is not immediately obvious.

From the famous article on the question whether God *is* (*STh* 1.2.3) everyone knows the five ways (the so-called proofs of God). But it is striking how often people skip over the objection: "On the other hand, the book of Exodus represents God as saying, I am who I am."[34]

When Thomas in *STh* 1.3.4. introduces as first objection against the identity of 'being' (*esse*) and 'essence' (*essentia*) that in this case divine being adds nothing to divine nature and that being means here the shared being or being in communication common to all creatures (*esse commune*) he cites Wisdom 14.21, "Because they . . . invested stocks and stones with the incommunicable name." The 'Christian distinction' appears to be at risk!

When Thomas speaks of the divine Ideas (*STh* 1.15) it is not only because of a Platonic inheritance, but because it is critical for Christian thinking. When God is the Creator and 'everything' is contingent, does that mean that this 'everything' becomes arbitrary? Or is the '*quidditas*' ('whatness,' essence) of things something that exists apart from God? Is the only foundation for the goodness of, for example, children's respect for their parents, that God has commanded it? Or has God commanded it because it is good? The dilemma seems to be that either every form of 'necessity' in things, every rational consistency, disappears or that the essences become independent of God. But in his teaching on the divine ideas, Thomas escapes from this dilemma. When the question is examined, the words in *STh* 1.15.1c are striking: "In all things that are not generated by chance . . ."[35]; our world is not a chance occurrence when God created it.[36]

After the question on the Ideas, there are two questions on truth and untruth that resemble a philosophical intermezzo.[37] But when

---

[34] Thomas refers to Exodus 3.14: Sed contra est quod dicitur Exodi 3 ex persona Dei, Ego sum qui sum.

[35] In omnibus enim quae *non a casu* generantur. . . .

[36] For the theological content of *STh* 1.22–24, see my "Providentie, predestinatie en praktijk," in *De praktische Thomas: Thomas van Aquino; de consequenties van zijn theologie voor hedendaags gedrag*, vol. 10 of the KTUU series *Theologie en samenleving* (Hilversum: Gooi en Sticht, 1987), 74–87.

[37] And they are read as such by R. te Velde, trans. and annotator, *Over waarheid en onwaarheid* (Kampen: Kok, 1988).

Thomas 'consults' Anselm and Augustine on the question whether there is only one truth (the divine) or many truths (*STh* 1.16.6), he turns, to support the existence of many truths, to a *theological* examination of twelfth-century naturalism, which argued for a causality of its own for earthly reality. In this theological examination, it is not only a question of defending Aristotle, but one of properly understanding faith in the Creator and of distinguishing between Creator and creature. In the question whether created truth is eternal, the objection states decisively "that only God is eternal"[38] (*STh* 1.16.7).

My thesis is thus that Thomas in his *Summa Theologiae* is above all a theologian and that from the very start the Trinity is the subject of his thinking (*STh* 1.1.7). The 'Christian distinction' between God and 'everything' dominates the whole doctrine of God even though Thomas only comes to speak thematically about creation in *STh* 1.44. This does not deny that he incorporated elements from the religious and philosophical tradition of thinking about God.

Thomas as Negative Theologian

In the introductions to the first questions of the *Summa Theologiae* Thomas shows clearly that he does not plan to give a positive description of God's essence. It starts with Question 2: "First must be treated whether there is a God, secondly what manner of being He is, or better, what manner of being He is *not*."[39] This is explicitly developed in the introduction to Question 3: "Having recognized that a certain thing exists, we have still to investigate the way in which it exists, that we may come to understand what it is, that exists. Now we cannot know what God is, but only what He is *not*."[40] Earlier Thomas had stated as a first objection against the thesis that God is the subject of theology that since a science must presuppose the 'what' ("quid est") of its subject and John of Damascus said, "It is impossible to say what God is,"[41] that God can thus not be the

---

[38] Quod solus Deus est aeternus.

[39] Primo considerandum est: an Deus sit; secundo quomodo sit, vel potius quomodo non sit.

[40] Cognito de aliquo an sit, inquirendum restat, quomodo sit, ut sciatur de eo quid sit. Sed quia de Deo scire non possumus quid sit, sed quid non sit, non possumus considerare de Deo quomodo sit, sed potius quomodo non sit.

[41] In Deo quid est dicere impossibile est.

subject of theology. Thomas answered, "Though we cannot know what God is, nevertheless this teaching employs an effect of his, of nature or of grace, in place of a definition and by this means discusses truths about him"[42] (*STh*, 1.1.7.ad 1).

After answering the question whether God *is*, Thomas begins his discussion of how God is *not* with an analysis of 'God's simpleness' (*simplicitas Dei*). In the introduction to the question he tells what he plans to do: "The ways in which God does not exist will become apparent if we rule out from Him everything inappropriate, such as compositeness, change, and the like. Let us inquire then first about God's simpleness, thus ruling out compositeness."[43] Next he 'removes' several forms of compositeness: that of physical divisibility, of form and matter, of subject and nature, of essence and being, of genus and species, of substance and accident. The temptation is great to select an element, for example, the identity of essence and being, and to interpret it as a positive 'description.' But what exactly is meant by the identity of essence and being is difficult to make clear in another way than by saying that in creatures we can distinguish essence from being and that we must not do that for God. We can easily show why we as thinking believers must *say* of God that His being and His essence coincide, but *what* exactly we are saying is difficult to grasp positively. Likewise the temptation is great to think at the end of the question that after all this 'removal' of composite qualities we are left with a positive result, that God is "completely one" (*omnino simplex*). At first sight this also seems to be the function of the last article of Question 3 (*STh* 1.3.7). But in this article Thomas denies especially implications of forms of compositeness. He does not give arguments for simplicity, but rather arguments against compositeness. What is said about God in Question 3.11 does not so much produce God's attributes or characteristics as provide warning signs that must be remembered when speaking about God and that put a negative accent on this speaking.[44]

---

[42] Licet de Deo non possumus scire quid est, utimur tamen ejus effectu, in hac doctrina, vel naturae vel gratiae, loco definitionis ad ea quae de Deo in hac doctrina considerantur. . . .

[43] Potest autem ostendi de Deo quomodo *non* sit, removendo ab eo ea quae ei non conveniunt, utpote compositionem, motum et alia huiusmodi. Primo ergo inquiratur de simplicitate ipsius, per quam removetur ab eo compositio.

[44] Burrell (in *Aquinas: God and Action*) compares the so-called attributes with 'formal features.' Rikhof gives the following explanation in his *Over God spreken*.

Thomas continues his introduction to Question 3 with, "And then, because in the material world simpleness implies imperfection and incompleteness, let us ask secondly [that is, after investigating simpleness] about God's perfection."[45] This reveals another negation: Thomas does not speak negatively about God because he speaks about an emptiness, but because he speaks of an overabundant *fullness*. Among creatures, the most simple is the least. In the theory of evolution, the greater complexity represents a higher and later phase of development. If applied to God, this concept of simplicity might lead to a misunderstanding: for God is simple but not low. Theologians speak of the Trinity that brings our salvation and that can thus not be 'lower' than what He creates and redeems.

But does this negative character also apply to those places where Thomas speaks positively of God's knowledge (*"scientia"*), will (*"voluntas"*), and ability or power (*"potentia"*)? This is indeed the case. My study of Thomas's speaking about God's knowledge, will, and power[46] confirms the hypothesis of the negative theological character of Thomas's speaking when applied to the questions in *STh* 1.14–26, especially if we are attentive to more than the explicit negations present there, but also to the way he undermines models for God's knowledge, will, and power.[47] Moreover, we must keep in mind that Thomas always refuses to look at a question 'from God's point of view.' In treating the question whether God knows "contingent future events" (*STh* 1.14.a13), the answers to the objections are at first

---

Een tekst van Thomas van Aquino uit de Summa Theologiae (translation, introduction, and annotation; Delft: Meinema, 1988): "Wittgenstein uses 'formal features' to express the facticity of a fact or the givenness of a given, and to show the difference in level between a fact and the facticity of a fact. With our language we can describe facts, but the facticity of facts cannot be separately described: it is apparent from our speaking" (38–39n21).

[45] Et quia simplicia in rebus corporalibus sunt imperfecta et partes, secundo inquiretur de perfectione ipsius.

[46] J. Wissink, "Aquinas: The Theologian of Negative Theology. A Reading of *STh*. I, Questions 14–26," in *Jaarboek van het Thomas-Instituut te Utrecht* 13 (1993): 15–83.

[47] E.g., in *STh* 1, Question 14, a.1, on the question whether God has "knowledge," the model of *"scientia"* is developed in the objections: knowledge is a disposition (*"habitus"*), it concerns conclusions deduced from principles, and treats either universals or particulars. In the answers to the objections, all these traits of *scientia* are denied for God. When we read the article we realize why we must attribute knowledge to God, but also that we do not know how we must imagine such divine knowledge.

sight unsatisfactory[48] until the reader discovers that he or she keeps
wanting to reason 'from God's point of view'[49] and to apply univo-
cally our model of knowledge and causality. When we see that
Thomas steadfastly refuses to do these two things, we understand
the article's development. This 'style' witnesses to a theological 'pru-
dence,' which may yet be a more convincing proof of Thomas's perseverance in his negative theology than are his express statements.

Nothing in Thomas's teaching on *analogy* contradicts this. Rikhof
correctly points out that analogy is not a third way of speaking beside
"univocal" (*univoce*) and "equivocal" (*aequivoce*) speaking—
although Thomas calls analogy a middle way between univocal and
purely equivocal speaking. There are apparently gradations in equivocal speaking.[50] Thomas does say that we can use perfection words
such as "true," "good," "beautiful," "knowledge," and "will" "in
their proper sense" (*proprie*) for God (*STh* 1.13.3c), but then he
uses a distinction from grammar between "way of signifying" (*modus
significandi*) and the "thing signified" (*res significata*). Here again
we lose our grasp on God. In terms of what these perfection words
mean, they can be spoken "properly" of God, but in terms of their

---

[48] The first objection states that a necessary result flows from a necessary cause.
Since God's knowledge is the cause of the things known and God's knowledge is
necessary, the things known are also necessary. The response is that a highest cause
can be necessary and yet the effect contingent because of a more proximate contingent cause. Thus the sun is the first cause of the sprouting of plants, but this sprouting can be hindered by poor soil. My first reaction as reader is that the answer is
insufficient because the sun is only a limited cause, so that the nature of the soil
lies outside its causality, while this cannot be said of God. Thomas's point is in fact
that he wants to distinguish between treating the question of divine causality and
will and that of God's knowledge.

[49] In the definition of "contingent future events," Thomas maintains that it concerns things that are not determined by their most proximate cause, and that therefore are unknowable *for us*. "In the second place, a contingent event can be
considered as it is in its cause. Thus it is taken as going to happen, as a contingent
event not yet determined to one effect; because a contingent cause is indifferent to
opposite effects. . . . Therefore anyone who knows a contingent effect in its cause
only has no more than a conjectural knowledge" (Alio modo potest considerari
contingens ut sit in sua causa. Et sic consideratur ut futurum et ut contingens
nondum determinatum ad unum, quia causa contingens se habet ad opposita. . . .
Unde quicumque cognoscit effectum contingentem in causa sua tantum, non habet
de eo nisi conjecturalem cognitionem). But the reader continually wonders, Does
God also see the world as contingent? Thomas systematically avoids this question:
he stands firmly rooted in the creature's place and steadfastly refuses to stand behind God, as it were, and look over His shoulder.

[50] Rikhof, "Negative Theology," 74.

way of meaning they cannot in a real sense be 'said' of God, for they have a way of meaning fitting to creatures. The suggestion is that to speak of God we only have to strip off our "modus significandi," but that 'only' is rather drastic: we only have to remove the 'our' from 'our speaking.'

If the interpretation presented here is correct, we recognize in Thomas the characteristics that we noted in the Christian form of negative theology. His negative theology finds its context in the thoughtful orientation toward the secret of the present, known, and familiar God. This secret causes no fear; that we can in no way grasp God in our concepts and words is not conceded grudgingly, it is joyfully affirmed. God is continually new, always richer. Finally, this negative theology does not presuppose a skeptical epistemology or a negative experience of the world. Thomas has a positive view of our knowledge of the world and takes every truth, even when it comes from 'pagan' philosophers, as one of God's many gifts.

4. Philosophers as Negative Theologians?

In the question whether we can or must interpret the work of certain modern philosophers (Derrida, Foucault, Nietzsche, etc.) as negative theology, it is important that we agree about the content of the qualification 'negative theology.' Earlier in this chapter I developed two meanings or forms.

Both forms have in common that people speak explicitly about God and/or the gods: on one side the gods that disappear and on another the God who is near us, but remains God. When we want to describe philosophical thinking as 'negative theology' we must question the intentionality of that thinking. Does the thinker want to eliminate the gods or God to make room for the true secret of reality? Has something of the secret that we call 'God' been shown to the thinker and does his or her thinking circle around it? If so, the rejection of closed systems is positively motivated by the desire to keep reality open to what transcends it. Or does this imply a thinking for which the cosmos has become less transparent and the gods thus unthinkable, but that still hopes to catch a glance of another side?

The question whether the thinker explicitly names God or the gods and whether she or he calls herself or himself a 'theist' or an 'atheist' is secondary. Of course when we interpret atheistic thinkers in the direction of negative theology we open ourselves to the accusation of *annexing* thinkers, similar to the accusation leveled at Rahner and Röper when they introduced the idea of 'anonymous Christianity.'[51] But such an accusation need not be feared when we honestly try to discover and respect the intention behind a work.

More important than the question of whether we can speak of negative theology in a thinker who calls himself or herself an atheist is the question to which type of 'negative theology' we should assign the thinker; in other words, is it a question of 'anonymous paganism' or 'anonymous Christianity'? For example, when *postmodernism* speaks on the basis of hermeneutics gone off the rails, I would hesitate to give it the qualification 'negative theology'; and when it could be given, then it would be more in the direction of '(anonymous) paganism' than of '(anonymous) Christian negative theology.'

Does it make much difference for theologians whether a thinker can be interpreted in the direction of negative theology? I note for myself that it does not make much difference at first sight. If the thinker has *truth* to tell, something can always be learned, even if the truth is profane. From Bonhoeffer I learned to be cautious when it is a question of linking theological thinking to *crisis thinking* (and postmodernism is sometimes interpreted in this way).[52] When we want to theologically join up with crisis thinking, we risk making God a "*Lückenbüßer.*"[53] I mean that theologically 'using' a crisis in

---

[51] Rahner and his student Anita Röper assumed that God desires the salvation of all people and that humanity is essentially open on a transcendental level to God and His gracious presence. On a categorical level people only know of God's gracious salvation in Christ when the gospel is proclaimed to them. When people cannot articulate their transcendental orientation to God and His grace in categorical Christian terms, e.g., because they have never heard of Jesus Christ or have heard of Him in such a way that the preaching of the gospel could not be experienced as salvation, but when they live such honest lives that we can recognize in their lives an honest search for the ultimate Secret, then Rahner and Röper speak of an 'anonymous Christianity.' They then recognize the religious life of 'pagans' as "faith" (*fides*) in the sense in which Paul used it, even if the name Jesus Christ has not yet been spoken. Both authors have always denied that they speak in this way from a desire to annex people; they call their view a protest against a Christian underestimation of the 'pagans.'

[52] By George Steiner, *Real Presences: Is There Anything in What We Say?* (London/Boston: Faber & Faber, 1989), esp. in the second part "The Broken Contract," 53–134.

[53] A 'stopgap'; the term is used by Bonhoeffer.

culture bears the danger of the above-mentioned form of "Religions-philosophie der Autorität," criticized by Barth. Reacting in despair to, for example, Foucault, people surrender to a pope, guru, sect leader, or dictator. My distinction between two types of negative theology intends to post a warning against this "Religionsphiloso-phie der Autorität."[54]

On the other hand, when a theologian recognizes in a thinker something of the search by which he or she is also driven, when the theologian must recognize a philosopher as a 'negative theologian' of the second type (however anonymously, perhaps), then the matter is less noncommittal. Such a philosopher then functions as one of the 'signs of the times' of which the Second Vatican Council spoke in the constitution on the Church and the world, *Gaudium et Spes*.[55] These signs should be accepted with gratitude and a desire to learn. For the exercise of theology it produces an enrichment in that we are offered new data and new articulations to help *re*think the faith in terms of modern culture. This had always occupied the theologian whenever he or she exercised the profession responsibly, but now it can occur in a dialogue that allows new articulation of the faith be-cause the thinker has thought about the same problem without the whole conceptual baggage that the theologian inherited from tradi-tion. For this reason, dialogue with such a thinker is even mandatory.

---

[54] R. Houdijk sees thinkers like Koslowski and Spaemann go in this direction. See his "De mens onttroond? Het postmoderne denken en de theologie," *Tijdschrift voor Theologie* 30 (1990): 276–96, esp. 282–84. I cannot judge whether his represen-tation of these two authors is fair, and I do not plan to enter the dispute here, regardless of who is correct, but Houdijk's question is valid.

[55] GS, no. 4.

Chapter 4

Zarathustra's Yes and Woe

NIETZSCHE, CELAN, AND ECKHART ON THE DEATH OF GOD

Dirk de Schutter

1. Some Introductory Remarks

"I should believe only in a God who understood how to dance." This sublime statement belongs to Zarathustra's discourse "Of Reading and Writing," in which the teacher of the *Übermensch* declares that he prefers texts that elate the reader and encourage laughter. Zarathustra likes aphorisms, "Sprüche," because they carry the reader away and oblige him or her to leap from rock to rock as if on a mountain excursion. Aphorisms carry the reader into the sublime and lofty, away from the land of earnestness and gravity and onto the peaks where elation reigns. In the highlands the heart learns the excitement of holy laughter and the bliss of dancing. These are the glad tidings of the prophet Zarathustra, who sets on his head this rose-wreath crown of laughter and calls himself the laughing prophet, "der Wahr-lacher" (Z, "Of the Higher Man," 18).

---

[1] All references to Nietzsche are inserted in the text by means of abbreviations: Z—*Thus Spoke Zarathustra: A Book for Everyone and Noone*, trans. R. J. Hollingdale (Harmondsworth, U.K.: Penguin, 1975); HH—*Human, All Too Human: A Book for Free Spirits*, trans. M. Faber (Lincoln: University of Nebraska Press, 1984); D— *Daybreak*, trans. R. J. Hollingdale (Cambridge: Cambridge University Press, 1982); GS—*The Gay Science*, trans. W. Kaufmann (New York: Vintage Books, 1974); BGE—*Beyond Good and Evil: Prelude to a Philosophy of the Future*, trans. R. J. Hollingdale (Harmondsworth, U.K.: Penguin, 1975); TI—*Twilight of the Idols*, trans. R. J. Hollingdale (in one edition with *The Anti-Christ*) (Harmondsworth, U.K.: Penguin, 1972); A—*The Anti-Christ* (see above); EH—*Ecce Homo*, trans. R. J. Hollingdale (Harmondsworth, U.K.: Penguin, 1980); WP—*The Will to Power*, trans. W. Kaufmann and R. J. Hollingdale (New York: Vintage Books, 1968).

More than any other philosopher Nietzsche compels us to reflect on style, to opt for a specific way of thinking and writing. How does one write about Nietzsche without systematizing, taming, and actualizing him? How does one do justice to his fragmentary, wild, and provocative writings? Nietzsche's rejection of systematic philosophy is unconditional: "I mistrust all systematizers and avoid them. The will to a system is a lack of integrity" (*TI*, "Maxims and Arrows"). Twentieth-century philosophy has been known to waver between a systematic interpretation that categorizes Nietzsche in the tradition of Western, logocentric metaphysics, and a critical reading that does not try to obliterate or argue away the impertinent contradictions, the disturbing flaws, and the offensive exaggerations, but stays tuned in to what is essentially incomplete, experimental, and challenging in Nietzsche's writings.[2] Which reading is most faithful to Nietzsche and what it means to be faithful to an author like Nietzsche remains, however, a matter of uncertainty. A pious imitation of Nietzsche is altogether a mistake, unless one is content—despite all possible warnings—to be a slave, a nobody. As Nietzsche himself puts it with his typical caustic sarcasm, nobodies or noughts hang about in the company of leaders who want to increase: "What? you are seeking? you want to multiply yourself by ten, by a hundred? you are seeking followers?—Seek *noughts!*" (*TI*, "Maxims and Arrows").

That is why the topic "Nietzsche and Negative Theology" looks like an appropriate line of approach, precisely because it seems to run counter to the drift of Nietzsche's philosophy. Few things disgusted him more than "theologian blood"; nothing was assailed by him in a harsher way than "this theologian instinct traces of which he has found everywhere" (A, 9). Both parts of the word '*theo-logy*' have roused his suspicion: what about the *logos*, the logic, as the standard of speaking and writing? Is the logos adapted for a discourse on God? Or is it only right to talk to God, to address God? The ancient conviction that considers the Logos to be the place of truth is addressed and finished with in a posthumous fragment: "Parmenides said, 'one cannot think of what is not';—we are at the other

---

[2] The first way to interpret Nietzsche is represented by, e.g., Martin Heidegger, Karl Jaspers, Eugen Fink, Karl Löwith, Jean Granier, Michel Haar, and Walter Kaufmann; the second is typified by Jacques Derrida, Philippe Lacoue-Labarthe, and Bernd Magnus.

extreme, and say 'what can be thought of must certainly be a fiction'" (WP, 539).[3] This aphorism does not proclaim the unity of thinking and being as acknowledged by Parmenides, but *mundus fabula*—the world is a fable. This immediately raises the question of what the repercussions are for God and the godly in this generalized fabling. Nietzsche was particularly exasperated by the monotony and one-dimensionality of monotheism. Time and again he pleads in favor of polytheism: "And how many new gods are still possible!" (WP, 1038). Only a profusion of tales meets the polymorphous, abundant generosity of the divine.

"Have I been understood?—*Dionysus against the Crucified.*" With this malediction of Christianity Nietzsche concludes his last book, *Ecce Homo*, which was published posthumously like a testament. The handwritten copy he sent to Otto von Bismarck at the beginning of December 1888 included in an accompanying letter a declaration of war, signed "The Antichrist." And a few days later, in the first days of 1889, when he collapsed mentally and physically, the friends of yore, Erwin Rohde, Jakob Burckhardt, Peter Gast, Franz Overbeck, and Cosima Wagner, were mailed postcards signed with the name "Dionysus" or with the epithet "The Crucified."

How is it possible for Nietzsche to call himself at the same time the Antichrist and the Crucified? What do these names with which he introduces himself to the world mean: immoralist, monster ("Untier")? Shall we make do with these names, or ascribe them to a slowly spreading insanity? Or shall we take into consideration a suggestion made by Heidegger in his *Rectoral Address* (1933), in which Nietzsche is described as "a passionate seeker of God"?[4] No matter how, Nietzsche remains ambiguous: he proclaims the death of God and confesses his belief that a new type of gods is possible. He blames the West for having put up with the God of Christianity, with the miserable "monotono-theism," and then sighs: "Almost two millennia and not a single new God!" (A, 19).

---

[3] This aphorism has drawn the attention of Philippe Lacoue-Labarthe; see "La fable," in *Le sujet de la philosophie* (Paris: Aubier-Flammarion, 1979), 7–30.

[4] As will become evident in what follows, I do not intend to fully interpret Heidegger's *Rectoral Address* (*Die Selbstbehauptung der deutschen Universität* [Frankfurt am Main: Klostermann, 1983]). I take Heidegger's suggestion, as it were, out of context.

2. By Way of Parody

Nietzsche's lifelong obsession with Jesus and Paul, with the Jew and the priest, gradually developed into a parody of the Jewish-Christian tradition. With Zarathustra he inaugurated the era of parody: the *Incipit Zarathustra* from *Twilight of the Idols* is accompanied in *The Gay Science* by an *Incipit tragoedia* and an *Incipit parodia*. Right away it is certain that Nietzsche's parody has nothing to do with a haughty, ironical distance, but that contrariwise it leads to a tragic embrace: parody lives on a loving respect for, an almost physical proximity with, what has been parodied. Even when Nietzsche stands apart from Christianity, he does not take the secure place of the neutral observer: deep down he knows with a visceral understanding that he aims the tarnishing arrows at himself, at his own body and mind, at his own life and death.[5] The parodist does not target a stranger, but applies the axe of sacrilege to self: the parodist laughs not because he or she sees through and nullifies the truth of what has been parodied, but because he or she has been struck by the futility of the momentous and realizes that only the momentous is laughed at. Not *what* we take seriously makes Nietzsche laugh, but that we take it *seriously* and that it is part of human fate to take things seriously. The parodist does not get rid of what is parodied: every parody remains an ode, a form of praise. That is why parody blurs the boundaries between defilement and deference, between imitation and alienation, between betrayal and loyalty.

Nothing less is at stake in Nietzsche's two last books, *The Anti-Christ* and *Ecce Homo*[6]: the words with which Pilatus—whose skepticism Nietzsche admired—hands the tortured Christ over to the Jewish crowd are quoted in order to celebrate the coming of the Antichrist, but the polemical pamphlet of the same name, which Nietzsche presents in his letters as the first part of the *Transvaluation of All Values*, curses Christianity in its Pauline shape and praises Jesus, who died on the cross like a thief. "Behold the man": the words cast doubt on the regality and divinity of Christ, and emphasize the holiness of humanity's suffering and death. It may sound

---

[5] A similar attitude is found in the Nietzsche-inspired work of Peter Sloterdijk, *Critique of Cynical Reason* (London: Verso, 1988).

[6] For a detailed discussion, I refer the reader to Sarah Kofman's *Explosion* (Paris: Galilée, 1993).

paradoxical, but in parody the themes and topoi of negative theology and mysticism are broached.

Nietzsche himself verbalizes his parodist program in his habitual lapidary way: "*Historia in nuce.*—The most serious parody I have ever heard is the following: 'in the beginning was the madness [der Unsinn], and the madness *was*, by God!, and God (divine) was the madness'" (*HH*, "Assorted Opinions and Maxims"). This saying, which according to Nietzsche renders the history of humankind in a nutshell, caricatures the first sentence from the Gospel According to John. In Nietzsche's version the Word that according to John constituted the beginning and origin of every single thing has been defigured into the monstrosity of meaningless, nonsensical madness. Nietzsche does not really doubt the originality of the Word, but he does reject the logic and the rationality attributed to the divine Word. The history of humankind and god is not a meaningful story: what has been, what really is and was, is meaningless nonsense, the absurdity of humankind's efforts, the groundlessness of what has been achieved, the insolence of neglect, the incomprehensibility of forgetfulness, the inanity of endeavor, the irrationality of God's presence and absence. Not the true, the logical, the comprehensible, and the spiritual have been realized—as the onto-theological tradition up to Hegel wanted it—but the nonsensical, and apparently God has hardly been able to remedy this. "By God!" Nietzsche curses, and with the commas before and after this oath he syncopates in a striking way the caricature of John. The swearword accentuates his indignation about the catastrophical history: honest to God, it is, God-awfully, true that nonsense reigns. As John reflects on the fundamental coexistence of God and Logos, Nietzsche fumes about the absurdity of what is called world history and jokes about Christianity's frantic attempts to conceal this fearsome story. Above all his suspicion is directed toward "the theistic gratification" (*BGE*, 53): he suspects theism of wishing to secure a life insurance policy from God and to hire him like a Mr. Clean, who removes the insensible evil and the foolish dirt from the world.

According to Nietzsche, the madness ("der Unsinn") does not give one permission to withdraw from the world. On the contrary, he blames Christianity for having damned the irrationality and incomprehensibility of the world and for having assumed that the world's absurdity becomes understandable in the light of God's providential logic: it is the belief that whatever remains incomprehensible for humankind on earth will become sensible and wholly meaningful *sub specie aeternitatis*. The same holds true for the *stultitia crucis:* the cross would only be a folly according to the short-sighted logic of the world; calculated with the measures of eternal life, the cross would all of a sudden become a wise, sensible, and prudent choice. This double-faced morality, coupled with a two-worlds theory, is what eventually caused God's death.

3. God's Death

"God is dead! And we have killed him" shouts "the madman"—one more emissary of nonsense and madness (GS, 125). The distressed madman not only parodies the gospels' story about how the Jewish crowd gave freedom to Barabbas and sentenced Jesus to death, he vituperates against the belief that God stands for eternal life and that his existence is beyond any doubt. Whereas in the Christian tradition Jesus' death is followed and dialectically superseded by his Resurrection, the madman's story confirms the irrevocability of God's death.

The madman wonders how we have been able to kill God, possibly answering the question while formulating it: "What were we doing when we unchained this earth from its sun? Whither is it moving now? Whither are we moving? Away from all suns? Are we not plunging continually? Backward, sideward, forward, in all directions? Is there still any up or down? Are we not straying as through an infinite nothing? Do we not feel the breath of empty space?" God's death is here connected with the scientific insights of Copernicus and Kepler: the collapse of the Ptolemaic worldview that put the earth at the center of the created universe has dealt a fatal blow to belief in the privileged relation between God and humankind. Later Freud will describe heliocentrism as the first wound inflicted on humankind's narcissism. As soon as the earth is reduced to one unsightly planet in the vast universe, the conviction that God elected this clod and made the human being part of a messianic history ending in salvation gets lost. Creationism crumbles and is replaced by representationism. God is no longer thought of as the creator of heaven and earth, but as the guarantor of humankind's thoughts or *cogitationes;*

the totality of beings no longer manifests itself as God's creation, but as an object and representation of the human subject that in its objectifying enterprise takes the measurements of God's rationality.[7] God has been turned into a *ratio sufficiens*, into a sufficient ground founding humanity's calculations, into an origin, or *archē*, enabling the predictability of the seemingly anarchic, chaotic universe, into a principle keeping the purportedly aleatory movements of subatomic particles within the orbit of computation. In my opinion, Nietzsche would have gladly signed Heidegger's analysis in "The Onto-Theo-Logical Constitution of Metaphysics": "*Causa sui* is the right name for the god of philosophy. Man can neither pray nor sacrifice to this god. Before the *causa sui*, man can neither fall to his knees in awe nor can he play music and dance before this god. The god-less thinking which must abandon the god of philosophy, god as *causa sui*, is thus perhaps closer to the divine God."[8] God's glory has been stabbed to death by "*messieurs* the metaphysicians": these "conceptual albinos" stained and dulled the God of heaven and earth. God has been drained in their web of pallid concepts; he has not become flesh, but an ideal—a perverted transfiguration for which there is no cure: "thenceforward he transformed himself into something ever paler and less substantial, became an 'ideal,' became 'pure spirit,' became '*absolutum*,' became 'thing in itself' . . . *Decay of a God*: God became 'thing in itself' . . ." (A, 17).

This scientistic attitude, which instead of singing songs to God proves his existence, does not pay attention to the madman's story. He is mocked by the philosophers of scientism who on the one hand do not believe in God, but who on the other hand cling to the total comprehensibility and computability of Being. God is not their truth, but the truth is their god—and this truth remains unassailable for them, because scientifically calculable. That is why the theory of relativity is in perfect harmony with Einstein's relieved conclusion that God does not play with dice. Though they have lost every con-

---

[7] The transition from creationism to representationism is the subject of Martin Heidegger's text "Die Zeit des Weltbildes" (The age of the world view), in *Holzwege* (Frankfurt am Main: Klostermann, 1950), and also of his *The Principle of Reason* (Bloomington: Indiana University Press, 1991), and of Michel Foucault's *The Order of Things* (1966; New York: Vintage, 1994).

[8] M. Heidegger, *Identity and Difference*, trans. J. Stambaugh (New York: Harper & Row, 1974), 72.

tact with the God of Abraham and Jesus and are therefore accomplices to the assassination of God, they stick to their theological understanding: the scientific nature of the truth, the meaningfulness of life, the purposefulness of history, the chosenness of humankind. Marxists, humanists, scientists, process theologians—all will discuss the interpretation of these principles, but none will discuss their value.

But this 'theologian blood' is throbbing in the veins of moralists as well. Just as the scientist proves God's existence, so the moralist calculates God's goodness. God is taken up in the statistics of good and evil: he is a judge who rewards and punishes.

Nietzsche's diagnosis does not mince matters: the classical interpretation of Christian ethics produces a *slave morality*. This is the case for various reasons. First, Christian morality involves a defense of the weak and the sick, the decrepit and the pusillanimous, the cheerless and the unfree, and turns against any movement that affirms the sensuality of life. Slave morality takes revenge on life, on the transitoriness of life. "This, yes, this alone is *revenge* itself: the will's antipathy towards time and time's 'It was,' " warns Zarathustra (Z, "Of Redemption"). The revenge of slave morality is driven by a negative or reactive will; it acts out of aversion, "Widerwille," a will turned awry: it is not directed at what is coming, but instead wants to undo the passing of time. It acts in aversion and repugnance, as it abhors the temporary for its transitoriness. Confronted with the wry awareness that human actions achieve little that is permanent and that good deeds are enacted without effect or are quickly forgotten, slave morality revenges itself by claiming for itself an eternal remembrance. The slave wants to be rewarded: she or he cannot bear her or his virtues to pass inconspicuously and postulates a reward unaffected by time and space.[9] The saying "Let not thy left hand know what thy right hand doeth" is wasted on the slave: he or she is not generous, not disinterested, counting and calculating and investing in an otherworldly capital. Zarathustra flays these 'accountants of goodness': "You want to be paid as well, you virtuous! Do you want reward for virtue and heaven for earth and eternity for your today?

---

[9] Nietzsche's opposition between the ones who are giving and those who are giving back, between the ones who are acting and those who are reacting, is the starting point of *Nietzsche and Philosophy* (London: Athlone, 1986) by Gilles Deleuze.

You love your virtue as the mother her child; but when was it heard of a mother wanting to be paid for her love?" (Z, "Of the Virtuous").

With these words Nietzsche retrieves a powerful theme from the mystical writings of Meister Eckhart. In the latter's sermon on justice we can read: "The just does not seek anything with his deeds. For those who have something in mind with these deeds are slaves and mercenaries, people who act in the name of a *why*; even if it is for the sake of beatitude or of eternal life or of the kingdom of heaven or anything else in time or eternity. All these people are not *just*. But justice consists in acting without a *why*. Yes, if I dared to say it, and I shall say it anyhow: even if it were *God* you had in mind, the deeds you do with that intention, I shall say it truthfully, they are dead, they are nothing! And not only that, but that way you corrupt *good deeds* as well." Eckhart hesitates, because he is aware of the unconventional in his statements, but he urges himself on and moves from the reserved aside "if I dared to say it" to the bold "I shall say it."[10]

Slave morality is dominated by the words 'reward' and 'punishment,' 'retribution' and 'compensation.' Christianity uses these terms even when it thinks about God—and this is the second reason why Nietzsche imputes to it a slave morality. If Christianity wants to bring a message of true love, it should renounce its doctrine of (the last) judgment: "a judge, even a merciful judge, is no object of love" (GS, 140). Especially the conditions binding God's love damage the true meaning of the word 'love.' "What? A god who loves men, provided only that they believe in him, and who casts an evil eye and threats upon anyone who does not believe in this love? What? A love encapsulated in if-clauses attributed to an almighty god? A love that has not even mastered the feelings of honor and vindictiveness?" (GS, 141). As is well known, Nietzsche considers this view that determines the love for and of God by contract to be the Jewish remnant in the Bible. "Jesus said to his Jews: 'The law was made for servants—love God as I love him, as his son! What have we sons of God to do with morality!' " (BGE, 164).

The calculations of slave morality culminate in the so-called theodicy, which sits in judgment upon God. The Creator is subpoenaed, because being almighty He does not prevent the world from being

---

[10] "Justi antem in perpetuum": sermon 65 in *Sermons and Treatises*, trans. and ed. M. O'C. Walsh (Longmead: Element, 1989), vol. 2, 269–77. Translation modified by author.

scourged by evil and injustice, by suffering and calamities. Still, God is always acquitted with the argument that this is the best of all possible worlds. So, the theodicy (for example, Leibniz's version) as well tries to explain away history's nonsensical events by entering them in the almighty calculations of God's goodness.

Slave morality is a reverse alchemy. By putting a stress on the sole sanctifying virtue and on the justice of retribution, the gold of the good deed that gives itself away is altered into the lead of calculated profit. It was Eckhart who already drew attention to the corruption of well-reasoned virtue: whoever is just with a certain intention—and this intention can be extremely noble, for example, the amelioration of mankind's condition—*corrupts justice*. Thus morality defaults and overshoots precisely because of its ulterior motives, which is why Nietzsche sees more good in an interdiction of morality. Referring to Eckhart, he writes: "Hasn't the time come to say of morality what Meister Eckhart said: 'I ask God to rid me of God' " (GS, 292). Eckhart makes a similar statement in the sermon "Beati pauperes," which interprets the well-known saying "Blessed are the poor in spirit." In this sermon Eckhart says that the poor will nothing, know nothing, and have nothing. What it means to will nothing is made clear by the following explanation: "What I willed, I was, and what I was, that I willed." In the poor, who will nothing, willing and being coincide: this makes the poor relatives of the Nietzschean Übermensch, who also wills what (she/he) is. Whereas the slave, who never is able to forget self, cleaves deed and doer and assumes that the doer always does something with a certain intention, the Übermensch is granted the possibility to be nothing but the place where willing occurs and the deed is done. Eckhart continues: "So long as a person has this particular wish to fulfill the ever-beloved will of God, then this person does not yet possess the poverty of which we want to speak. . . . Therefore we beg God to rid us of God. . . . Thus we say that mankind shall keep itself rid and void so that it neither understands nor knows that God works in it. Only so can mankind possess poverty."[11]

4. THE GOD OF DEATH

Like Eckhart centuries earlier, Nietzsche, time and again, stands up for a justice that acts for the sake of the just itself, for the sake of

---

[11] Sermon 87, *Sermons and Treatises* vol. 2, 269–77. Translation modified by author.

love, and not because it is under an obligation or wants to accuse.[12] The just, the poor in spirit, the Übermensch are free because they have freed themselves from a guilt-ridden morality. According to Nietzsche, the Jewish component of morality should be dropped. Similar conclusions are arrived at by Paul Celan, who reflects in his poetry about what it means to be a Jew after Auschwitz. In the poem "Treckschutenzeit," from the volume *Lichtzwang*,[13] someone who is called "der Enthöhte" (The Dis-heightened) says the following words: "Todes quitt, Gottes quitt" (rid of death, rid of God). The radical nature of these words is not only due to the identification of God and death; above all it is due to the idea that we, the people from Auschwitz and Birkenau, have nothing to lose or to gain, that we have nothing to lose since everything has been lost. We are quits, we have settled our debts to God, after Auschwitz we are no longer indebted to God and death, "der Meister aus Deutschland," has nothing to demand.[14]

We know now what it means to suffer and to die, to lose our sons and daughters, to be lonely, expelled, and betrayed. The cup did not pass from us. Our body, too, has been lacerated; our blood, too, has been drunk. Is it then audacious to think that the words of Jesus on the cross are addressed to us, to us mortals, like the poem "Tenebrae" (Shadows, darkness) suggests?

> Bete, Herr,
> bete zu uns,
> wir sind nah.

> [Pray, Lord,
> pray to us,
> we are near.][15]

In this unbelief that refuses to praise the god of death *another covenant* may grow. Bewildered by the horrors of Auschwitz that were

---

[12] An ontology of the pure gift is at stake in Heidegger's "Zeit und Sein" (Time and Being), in *Zur Sache des Denkens* (Tubingen: Niemeyer, 1969), 1–25. Its "anthropological" and "economical" consequences are worked out by Jacques Derrida in *Given Time* (Chicago: University of Chicago Press, 1992) and *Specters of Marx* (New York: Routledge, 1994).

[13] P. Celan, Lichtzwang (1970; Frankfurt a.M.: Suhrkamp, 1997).

[14] P. Celan, "Todesfuge," in *Gesammelte Werke*, vol. 1 (Frankfurt a.M.: Suhrkamp, 1986), 42.

[15] Ibid., 163.

known and willed by God, mortals lose every word to address God. They are left nothing but the memory of the dead they bury. But while digging, while toiling in the earth, a relationship comes to be, a movement toward something that is hardly anything or anybody and yet leaves traces on the gravedigger: a smudge of earth, a callus founding a bond. In the opening poem of *Die Niemandsrose*[16] it says:

> There was earth in them, and
> they dug.
> They dug and dug, so went
> their day, their night. And they did not praise God,
> who, so they heard, willed all this,
> who, so they heard, knew all this.
> They dug and heard nothing more;
> they did not get wise, found no song,
> thought up no speech.
> They dug.
> [. . .]
> O one, o none, o no one, o you:
> Where did it go, when it went nowhere?
> O you dig and I dig, and I dig myself to you,
> and at the finger awakens us the ring.

These words break with every religious sacrifice and every sacrificial religion. An adieu resounds: farewell to the god who sacrifices his son, farewell to the god who sacrifices his chosen people. After Auschwitz the daunting truth dawns that a sacrifice does not achieve anything. For centuries religion has fed on the illusion that sacrifices would bring about a reconciliation, that atonement would fill up the crack in the world, that expiation would heal whatever has fallen apart.[17] The idea that someone could bring unity into the world or restore a broken unity by sacrificing self turns out to be a delusion, precisely because the world is forever chaos, because it is forever marked by chaos, by a gap or crack: being itself is finite, afflicted by an uncanny failing impossible to cancel, by a fault impossible to rectify.

Slave morality will not and cannot accept the meaninglessness of

---

[16] "Es war Erde in ihnen." In P. Celan, *Die Niemandsrose* (1963; Frankfurt a.M.: Suhrkamp, 1996). (Author's translation.)

[17] 'Overcoming an ethics of sacrifice' is a very important theme in the works of Georges Bataille and Jean-Luc Nancy.

suffering: it adores a lamb of God that is sacrificed but that takes away all the sins of the world with its death. The fact that suffering and death do not affect the world, that life runs its usual course, is the radical evil slave morality tries to gloss over. The sufferer is met with the doubtful honor of understanding that pain has been meaningless and has brought no redemption. In an aphorism not by chance called "On the knowledge acquired through suffering" we can read the following: "the bitterest of all exclamations 'my God, why has thou forsaken me!' contains, in its ultimate significance, evidence of a general disappointment and enlightenment over the delusion of his life" (D, 114).

In a note from 1888 Nietzsche's view of God's death is once more summarized: "You call it the decomposition of God: but it is only His peeling—He peels away His moral skin! And soon you will see Him again, beyond good and evil." In another note, also written down in 1888, the end of *Ecce Homo* is anticipated: "Dionysus versus the 'Crucified': there you have the antithesis. One will see that the problem is that of the meaning of suffering: whether a Christian meaning or a tragic meaning. In the former case, it is supposed to be the path to a holy existence; in the latter case, being is counted as *holy enough* to justify even a monstrous amount of suffering" (WP, 1052).

5. GLAD TIDINGS

From the very beginning Christianity has displayed a disconcerting incomprehension of the love Jesus lived by and testified to even in his death agony. Due to Paul, the most nonevangelical of emotions, resentment or vengeance, has gained the upper hand. Immediately after the sorrow of Golgotha the question about the culprits was raised, and Jesus' life on earth was connected with his return as divine judge at the end of times. But the criminal on the cross had a better view of things: "When even the criminal undergoing a painful death declares: 'the way this Jesus suffers and dies, without rebelling, without enmity, graciously, resignedly, is the only right way,' he has affirmed the gospel: and with that he is in Paradise" (WP, 162). On the cross Jesus shows what he has preached during his life: whoever accepts and loves life unto death may be called a son of God. This does not mean that after his death he will be taken up into heaven, but that it is godly and sublime to live and die that way, to fully affirm life.

Jesus does not condemn life, but blesses it. In the eyes of Nietzsche this attitude of a fundamental life acceptance distinguishes the Christian religion. Not faith, but a specific practice characterizes Christ's life. This practice, this way of doing that is above all an exercise in love of one's own destiny, is not a way to get into heaven, but a *manner of being-in-the-world that itself is godly*. Paradise and God's realm do not belong in the hereafter, they have nothing to do with a reward that awaits humankind after death. God's realm is a condition of the heart: whoever affirms life unto death, like Jesus did, has been taken up in God's realm, has entered paradise. "This 'bringer of glad tidings' died as he lived, as he *taught*—*not* to 'redeem mankind' but to demonstrate how one ought to live. What he bequeathed to mankind is his *practice*: his bearing before the judges, before the guards, before the accusers and every kind of calumny and mockery—his bearing on the *Cross*. . . . *Not* to defend oneself, *not* to grow angry, *not* to make responsible. . . . But not to resist the evil man—to *love* him. . . . The life of the redeemer was nothing else than *this* practice—his death too was nothing else. . . . He has settled his accounts with the whole Jewish penance-and-reconciliation doctrine; he knows that it is through the *practice* of one's life that one feels 'divine,' 'blessed,' 'evangelic,' at all times a 'child of God.' It is *not* 'penance,' *not* 'prayer for forgiveness' which leads to God: *evangelic practice alone* leads to God, it *is* God!" (A, 33–35).

The *amor fati* that is here testified to makes clear why "Christ on the Cross remains the most sublime symbol." Jesus accomplished what Nietzsche resolves to do at the beginning of the fourth book of *The Gay Science*, which is in the sign of "Sanctus Januarius," of a new beginning: "*Amor fati:* let that be my love henceforth! I do not want to wage war against what is ugly. I do not want to accuse; I do not even want to accuse those who accuse. And all in all and on the whole: some day I wish to be only a Yes-sayer" (GS, 276). Zarathustra as well incarnates "the vast and boundless declaration of Yes and Amen": "into all abysses do I carry my consecrating declaration Yes" (Z, "Before Sunrise").

To bless, to say yes, to love—all belong together like the unconditional embrace of everything that is. Suffering and death, evil and injustice, atrocities and barbarism are not used as an argument against life. The most striking formulation of this Dionysian pathos Nietzsche confesses to can be found in a poem by Lou Salomé entitled "Lebensgebet" (Life prayer). The first stanzas run as follows:

> Sure, thus a friend loves a friend,
> Like I love you, enigma life—
> Whether I shouted in you, or cried,
> Whether you gave me happiness or grief.
> I *love* you together with your harm;
> And should you destroy me,
> I withdraw from your arm
> Like a friend withdraws from a friend's chest.[18]

And the poem ends with the following verses that are quoted by Nietzsche in *Ecce Homo*:

> Have you no more happiness to give me,
> Well then! still do you have your pain.

Sorrow does not count as a reproach of life, nor is it covered up or obfuscated. Sorrow is affirmed and accepted as an inextricable part of life.

6. Zarathustra's Yes and Woe

Has Nietzsche ever known that the yes-saying is exercised by no less a person than Paul whom he despised so much? In 2 Corinthians 1.20 we read: "for with him there was always yes." This yes precedes any and every contrast, it is presupposed by every affirming and negating proposition. It is the pure performative that unconditionally welcomes whatever will happen. Whereas the normal performative speech act only functions in a well-defined ritual and whereas it states its dependence from certain circumstances, the yes and amen Paul ascribes to Christ and Zarathustra to Dionysus has an unlimited validity: it is not determined, not bound by circumstances, facts, or objects. With an appeal to Eckhart we could state that only the poor in spirit, who will nothing and have nothing, are given the possibility to lose themselves in this yes. Indeed, only subjects who do not

---

[18] L. Salomé, *Lebens Rückblick* (Frankfurt am Main: Insel, 1968; orig. 1932).

hold on to themselves in any way, only subjects who are poor because they forgets themselves, only subjects who are poor and who therefore open themselves up without any reserve, are given the possibility to exist in this yes and to sustain the boundless rapture of this yes.

"In the beginning was the Word," "in the beginning was nonsense," "in the beginning was the Yea." The yes is the origin, founded in nothing and therefore groundless, without reason, and nonsensical. The yes is the absolute a priori not bound by time and space, because it itself is the condition of time and space. The yes is the act of creation par excellence. "God only and always says Yes," writes Angelus Silesius in his *Cherubinic Wanderer,* and he beseeches people to commend themselves to this "Ja" (of Yahweh): "Man, entrust thyself to God, hide thyself in His light; I swear to Yes, the devil does not see thee."

The Jewish mystic and philosopher Franz Rosenzweig puts similar insights into words: "In the beginning is the Yea. . . . An infinity is affirmed: God's infinite essence, his infinite actuality, his Physis. Such is the power of the Yea that it adheres everywhere, that it contains unlimited possibilities of reality. It is the arch-word of language, one of those which first make possible, not sentences, but any kind of sentence-forming words at all, words as parts of the sentence. Yea is not part of a sentence, but neither is it a shorthand symbol for a sentence, although it can be employed as such. Rather it is the silent accompanist of all parts of a sentence, the confirmation, the 'sic!,' the 'Amen' behind every word. It gives every word in the sentence its right to exist, it supplies the seat on which it may take its place, it 'posits.' The first Yea in God establishes the divine essence for all infinity. And this first Yea is 'in the beginning.' "[19]

The divine, Dionysian yes should not be confused with the braying of asses: "The ass, however, brayed 'Ye-a' " (Z, "The Awakening"). Zarathustra lodges a loud protest when he finds out that people see in the ass an incarnation of his doctrine of affirmation. He pleads in favor of a light-footed, gay, dancing yes that affirms the *innocence of becoming*: the ass, however, gasps out a yes that is torn by the burden of a heavy responsibility and a biting sense of guilt. The ass is a beast of burden: it looks behind itself, neglecting the future and losing the

---

[19] F. Rosenzweig, *The Star of Redemption* (London: Routledge & Kegan Paul, 1970), 26–27.

knack of laughter. The real yes is uttered by children in whose innocent, useless play the divine manifests itself. "I have been driven
from fatherlands and motherlands. So now I love only my *children's
land*, the undiscovered land in the furthest sea: I bid my sails seek it
and seek it" (Z, "Of the Land of Culture").

The divine, childlike yes does not take possession of the future,
anticipates nothing. It blesses what happens, what befalls. Zarathustra's yes is so radical that it delivers itself to oblivion; it accepts the
risk of being obliterated. And so Zarathustra does not ask his disciples to commemorate him: instead, he commands them to get rid of
him. "Now I bid you lose me and find yourselves; and only when you
have all denied me will I return to you" (Z, "Of the Bestowing Virtue"). With this statement Nietzsche not only caricatures Christ's
desire expressed at the Last Supper, but also Peter's disavowal that
is considered to be a deadly sin. In 1889, besieged by madness in the
streets of Turin, he wrote a postcard to Georg Brandes, the first to
have lectured on "Nietzsche's aristocratic radicalism": "After you
had discovered me, it was no trick to find me: the difficulty now is
to lose me. . . ."

Right away we are confronted with the enormous difficulty, not to
say impossibility, of Nietzsche's endeavor. The Dionysian yes is the
absolute a priori, it is the transcendental condition of possibility of
everything that occurs and thus precedes every propositional affirmation and/or negation. But at the same time it is said that a distinction must be made between this yes and the asinine ye-a. On the one
hand, Nietzsche cannot but acknowledge that the ye-a is affirmed by
the yes as well; on the other hand, he wants to distinguish between
the two. Nietzsche tries to keep the yes pure; he is anxious for every
contamination by the reactionary, but fully understands that the yes
has accepted to expose itself to this contamination. The same problem presents itself elsewhere. Nietzsche orders his disciples to lose
him and to deny him, but at the same time he does not cease asking
whether he has been understood. "Have I been understood?" are the
final words of *Ecce Homo*, which moreover opens with the appeal
"Hear me! for I am such and such a person. Above all, do not mistake
me for someone else!" The twentieth century assigned Nietzsche to
the right: he has been put down as a nihilist, an atheist, an anti-
Semite, and a protofascist. Yet we must ask how Nietzsche can defend himself against these interpretations the moment he orders to

be disavowed. Are there good and bad disavowals? Is there an ethics of disavowing? Apart from that, the question remains concerning what it means to give someone the order to disavow (or to disobey): the commandment "deny me" is a double bind, and in some respects seems to be the most violent attempt to control every disavowal.

The foregoing sheds light on the strange position Nietzsche's critique takes. Nietzsche resists slave morality because it is reactive and preoccupied by its own mediocrity and because it only says no. He makes a stand for a morality of the Dionysian pathos, which is active, spontaneous, and magnanimous. But this yes, which is designated as origin, can only be heard and read after a critical parody. Western civilization has lost this yes and buried it beneath a contemptible morality. But the fact that history has bashed the yes of the origin beyond all recognition becomes evident only in a parody that itself is a phenomenon of the second degree. The yes of the origin that is expressed to be the preeminently spontaneous and active is only revealed in a parodying reaction that in its turn denounces any reactive attitude. Or put differently, in a parodying reaction to the reactive civilization any reactive attitude and performance is unmasked as decadent and the active yes is lauded.

But no matter how correct these objections may be, they at the same time cut no ice, because they presuppose that Nietzsche's philosophy sticks to the rules of rationality. Nietzsche, however, breaks with the logical and the hierarchical and affirms a general mimesis. Indeed, the original yes is no origin at all: it does not lay any foundations, no thing originates from it. Above all, it is the tragical acceptance of the groundlessness of events. The yes emphasizes and adds a new meaning to one of the most conspicuous notions of Christianity: the *creatio ex nihilo*. Out of nothing, just like that, in a gratuitous nonsensical way, the world with which humanity's fate is linked manifests itself. Whoever succeeds in affirming this blesses what occurs in a spontaneous act, that is, in an act of loyalty and allegiance to the future.

Nietzsche thinks the impossible because he thinks the other and the future. As long as one thinks and projects what is possible or what belongs to the realm of possibilities, one worries about the probable and is taken in by what can be predicted and expected. Nietzsche, however, is after the radically different, which lies beyond the human-all-too-human and can therefore only present itself in the uncanny shape of a monster. The unpresentable withdraws from the prescriptions laid down by an economy of the possible that views the future as an extension of the present. But whoever invents the future relates to the impossible; one is connected with nothing in a radical suspension of the tradition in order to meditate on the meaning of invention. Only where inventing itself is invented, a different human being can come to be—someone who maybe will take on the figure of the Übermensch. Such a *radical invention* belongs to no one, befalls no one, except maybe the poor in spirit who knows nothing and has nothing, the free spirit who wills nothing but the yes and amen of the future and of chance.[20]

7. *"Unschuld ist das Kind und Vergessen"*[21]

The authentic future is the chancy, which befalls us, the unpredictable, which happens to us and thwarts our plans. Wherever our plans are stymied, another time comes our way, not the time of appointments and of useful occupations controlled by the managers of economical time, but the time that summons and claims us, the time of adventure. We are given the latter when and where a child is born, a book grabs us, a friend dies. Chance is a gift and a task, a risk and an adventure. Summoned by the time of chance we acknowledge our mortality, accepting the truth that life's offerings far exceed the limits of our own abilities and that life is fulfilled when it is taken off our hands. The love for life's coincidences affirms the innocence that beats the rhythm of coming into being and decaying: "Loving and perishing: these have gone together from eternity. Will to love: that means to be willing to die, too" (Z, "Of Immaculate Perception"). As is often the case, Nietzsche's words set forth a discussion with Heraclitus, for whom Dionysian life never entails a denial of finitude: "ὡὐτὸς δὲ Ἀίδης καὶ Διόνυσος" (but Hades and Dionysos are the same).[22]

---

[20] J. Derrida writes: "Deconstruction is inventive or it is nothing at all"; see his *Psyché: Inventions de l'autre* (Paris: Galilée, 1987), 35. (Author's translation.)

[21] "The child is innocence and forgetting."

[22] Heraclites, in *The Presocratic Philosophers*, ed. G. S. Kirk and J. E. Raven (Cambridge: Cambridge University Press, 1980; orig. 1957) fragment 15, 211.

Wherever life appears under the sign of chance, it is liberated from every guilt: the question why such and such occurs becomes irrelevant, the question what such and such is for becomes a trifle. What remains is the "that," the givenness, the peculiar and over- whelming event that the world is. "Truly, it is a blessing and not a blasphemy when I teach: 'Above all things stands the heaven of chance, the heaven of innocence, the heaven of accident' " (Z, "Be- fore Sunrise"). Chance is ennobled: while slaves count and cannot live without reasons or culprits, the aristocrat lives without why, in the aimlessness of "so be it." Chance is raised to the peerage: " 'Lord Chance'—he is the world's oldest nobility, which I have given back to all things; I have released them from the servitude under pur- pose."

The openness for chance characterizes the player: he has "la vo- lonté de chance," as Bataille calls it.[23] The player is divine because he has removed himself from the guardianship of purpose and use. Heraclitus's description of time as "παῖς παίζων" (a child playing) is applied by Nietzsche to God (WP, 797), but whereas Heraclitus sees time playing checkers, Nietzsche—like Mallarmé—sticks to dic- ing. "O sky above me, you pure, lofty sky! This is now your purity to me, that you are to me a gods' table for divine dice and dicers!" (Z, "Before Sunrise").

The sky is not just a gambling table, but a dance floor as well. The dancer has overcome revenge and reconciled himself with passing time. "O my soul, I taught you to say 'today' as well as 'once' and 'formerly' and to dance your dance over every Here and There and Over-there" (Z, "Of the Great Longing").

Play and dance cannot do without laughter. Zarathustra decrees by law what the tradition rejected as frivolous. Whereas Christianity for centuries has tried to prove that Jesus never laughed and that laughing is diabolical, Zarathustra suspects every doctrine that is in- capable of laughing. "And let that day be lost to us on which we did not dance once! And let that wisdom be false to us that brought no laughter with it!" (Z, "Of Old and New Law-Tables"). Ultimately,

---

[23] "Volonté de chance" (will to chance) is the subtitle of Bataille's book *On Nie- tzsche* (New York: Paragon, 1994; 1992). On the affinity between the two thinkers, see F. Warin, *Nietzsche et Bataille* (Paris: P.U.F., 1994).

play, dance, and laughter are the total, undaunted acceptance of the nonsensical.

In laughter and dance the subject abandons its unsurpassed autonomy and self-consciousness. The subject joins a rhythm it has been offered, and lets itself be carried away in an incomprehensible ecstasy. What W. B. Yeats says about the dance in "The Tower" is equally true for laughter: "How can we know the dancer from the dance?" Like the dancer who disappears in the dance, so the laugher is lost in the frenzy of laughter.

To laugh, to dance, to play, to sing: it all happens for the sake of itself. These are pure acts, aimless, pointless; they do not found anything, they do not leave anything behind, but disappear in the innocence of a mad time. Through this sovereignty that abandons itself to the vicissitudes of time and does not care a straw for the demands of use and efficiency, the divine manifests itself in the purity of an *unconditional promise*.

In the novel *See under: Love*, a title that could be translated as *Ecce Amor*, the Jewish author David Grossman tries to settle the traumatic memories of the extermination camps. The impossible task of coming to terms with the Holocaust is overcome in the ritual of humor: to die of laughter looks like an alternative for the inhuman liquidation in the camps. One of the characters narrates:

> According to Shimon Zalmanson humor is not just a disposition or mental faculty but the only true religion. "If you were God and you wanted to reveal the potential of creation to your believers, all the coincidences and paradoxes, all the joy and reason, the ambiguity and deception your divine powers spilled out into the world every minute, and if, let us say, you wanted to be worshipped as befitting a deity, that is, without sentimentality and flattering hymns but with a clear and lucid mind instead, what method would you choose, eh?" Zalmanson said humor was the sole means to understand God and His Creation in all its mystery, and to go on worshipping Him in gladness. . . . Laughter itself was the spontaneous ritual of his religion. "Every time I laugh," he explained, "my deity, who doesn't exist, of course, knows I cleave to Him, knows I have understood Him profoundly, if only for an instant. Because the good Lord created the world out of nothingness, out of chaos, and He took His blueprint and building materials from chaos. . . .' "According to Zalmanson, jokes were

touchingly primitive offerings to this God. . . . Most people laugh in a voice unlike their speaking voices. It would seem that the vocal qualities used for laughter cannot be used for—how shall I put it—"secular purposes."[24]

Only in laughter is the subject given the chance to fully forget himself and to give himself away. In this unreserved abandonment that does not recoil from what appears out of nowhere and that embraces the groundlessness of the soul the divinity of action manifests itself. *Each gift is divine.* To give oneself away is the highest virtue (Z, "Of the Bestowing Virtue"). Only the soul that lets itself be overwhelmed by the madness of laughter is granted the gay spontaneity to empty itself out. The subject that disappears in its actions like the dancer and the laugher does not seek itself. The true friend is up to this: "May the friend be to you a festival of the earth and a foretaste of the Übermensch. I teach you the friend and his overflowing heart—the creative friend, who always has a complete world to bestow" (Z, "Of Love of One's Neighbor")

The dancer does not dance in honor of God, the laugher does not laugh in honor of God, the gift is not given in honor of God. Rather it is the case that whenever there is dancing, laughing, and giving, the divine becomes manifest in all its glory. Divine is what leaves behind the human-all-too-human, and divine is the place where room is made free for what withdraws from every presentation. Giving and laughing open up a domain beyond every control where the limits of what can be presented are crossed and the utopia of an originary affirmation delivers itself to a jubilation of joy. This occurrence is known to no one, it is dedicated to "the nameless one for whom only future songs will find a name" (Z, "Of the Great Longing").

Only nature is capable of such selflessness. Only the sun is so exuberant, only the earth is so fertile that they can give us their gifts without attracting any attention. Their generosity is nameless, remains without a face: their magnanimity is so inexhaustible that even a thanksgiving occurs without shame and turns into a sublime feast (D, 464). People are granted this sublimity when they bring themselves to approaching nature without any anthropomorphic expectations and to abandoning themselves to the great silence (D,

---

[24] D. Grossman, *See under: Love* (London: Picador, 1991), 330.

423). As soon as they have learned to stop being human, they are given the nonhuman ability to say thanks and to express this in the meaningless madness of laughter.

Not the spiritual gravity of prayers, but the gay corporality of the dance reveals what is divine. "Ledig allen gebets," Celan writes in *Lichtzwang*, "empty of all prayers." A prayer begs, laughter blesses and jubilates. But laughter manifests as well the extreme connection between the divine and the material. We lack prayers and rituals, songs and gestures, but laughter and dance remind us of the unbelievable, yet wonderful event that the divine never turns away from the material and always pledges its fate to the most relative of things. The divine has never been anything but the naked presence of a letter, the insistence of a melody, the enchantment of a color, the silence of a building. Dionysian humanity welcomes it in the unforgettable yet never understood elation of laughter. "Instead of prayers we should be blessers!" (WP, 32).

Chapter 5

Being Unable to Speak, Seen As a Period

DIFFERENCE AND DISTANCE IN JEAN-LUC MARION

Victor Kal

"What cannot be put into words should not be suppressed."[1]

1. INTRODUCTION

JEAN-LUC MARION is a well-known figure among living French philosophers. He is respected as a Descartes specialist; he is a prominent phenomenologist, and as such the author of several important studies on Husserl and Heidegger; finally, he is a thinker driven by his commitment to Christianity to pursue several very specifically colored, quasi-theological philosophical investigations.[2] When we add to this Marion's work as editor-in-chief (of the important collection

---

[1] J.-L. Marion, *L'idole et la distance. Cinq études* (hereafter cited as *ID*; Paris: Grasset, 1977), 232: "Ce qui ne peut pas être dit, ne doit pas être tu"; cf. 242.

[2] J.-L. Marion (b. 1946) studied at the École Normale Supérieure and is currently professor of theology at the Université de Paris X/Nanterre. His most important works include: *Sur l'ontologie grise de Descartes* (Paris: Vrin, 1975, 1981²); *L'idole et la distance. Cinq études* (hereafter cited as *ID*; Paris: Grasset, 1977)—English translation forthcoming from Fordham University Press; *Sur la théologie blanche de Descartes* (Paris: P.U.F., 1981); *Dieu sans l'être. Hors-texte* (Paris: Fayard, 1982)—English translation, *God without Being: Hors-texte*, trans. T. A. Carlson, Preface by D. Tracy (hereafter cited as *GB*; Chicago: University of Chicago Press, 1991); *Sur le prisme métaphysique de Descartes. Constitution et limites de l'onto-théologie dans la pensée cartésienne* (Paris: P.U.F., 1986)—English translation, *On Descartes' Metaphysical Prism: The Constitution and the Limits of Onto-Theo-Logy in Cartesian*

'Epiméthée' published by the Presses Universitaires Françaises) and publisher of a periodical (*Communio*), we need not be surprised that he is considered to be an influential French thinker.

Marion is easily placed in the large and broadly subdivided family of French 'différence thinkers.' To this family belong well-known names such as Jacques Derrida and Emmanuel Levinas. Différence thinking says, in brief, that the human subject does not merely dominate and dispose of the world, or rule over itself; this subject must tolerate something else outside itself over which it has no say and which it cannot grasp. This 'other' shatters the illusion of complete autonomy in which the subject possibly lives, and puts the subject in the relationship it had always already served. 'Différence'[3] refers to the *difference* between this other and this relationship, on the one hand, and, on the other hand, being as it is presented readymade by us to be observed and manipulated in our quasi-autonomy.

But for Marion, as for Levinas, the difference is linked to the *Different*, the *Other*, or the very Distant. In Marion *God* is always the point. But we should be aware of a possible misunderstanding. In Marion's view, God is not primarily *a* being, not even the highest Being (*GB*, 2–3). Moreover, Marion follows Heidegger in rejecting the way metaphysics turns God into the highest Being and the capstone of ontology. Heidegger accuses theology of having been mostly an 'onto-theo-logy.' But Marion differs from Heidegger in incorporating more than just an *ontological* difference, that is, that we have not yet given a meaning to 'Being' when we list available beings; Marion also focuses on a *difference with God*. He uses the term 'distance' to refer to this type of difference. With Heidegger he recog-

---

Thought, trans. J.-L. Kosky (Chicago: University of Chicago Press, 1999); *Prolégomènes à la charité* (Paris: Éd. de la Différence, 1986); *Réduction et donation. Recherches sur Husserl, Heidegger et la phénoménologie* (Paris: P.U.F., 1989)—English translation, *Reduction and Givenness: Investigations of Husserl, Heidegger, and Phenomenology*, trans. T. A. Carlson (Evanston, Ill.: Northwestern University Press, 1998); *Questions cartésiennes. Méthode et métaphysique* (Paris, P.U.F., 1991)—English translation, *Cartesian Questions: Method and Metaphysics* (Chicago: University of Chicago Press, 1999); *Questions cartésiennes*, Vol. 2: *L'ego et Dieu* (Paris: P.U.F., 1996). The *Revue de Métaphysique et de Morale* 91, no. 1 (1991) is devoted entirely to this work.

In this limited and specifically accentuated study of Marion, I ignore his works on Descartes and only touch upon his Heidegger research. Among Marion's recent works are *Le croisée du visible* (Paris: P.U.F., 1996) and the key work *Étant donné. Essai d'une phénoménologie de la donation* (Paris: P.U.F., 1997).

[3] 'Différence' is a cognate to the English 'difference.'

nizes that it is blasphemy to want to demonstrate that God exists and is a being, taking into consideration that such terminology ('exists,' 'being') has the meaning that our times give them (GB, 37). Marion's philosophical project is oriented toward speaking about God without committing this blasphemy.

One of his main themes is how the subject of God can be raised in human existence. 'Be raised' in this context is a term that leaves open the decision whether we can speak *about* God, the far Distant, and put Him into words, characterize Him, or whether we can only to some degree become receptive to the word that, coming from the other side, resounds within us. In this latter case, we could then utter that word when it resounds within us. Moreover, we could try to describe what receptivity is, how the word comes to us, and perhaps even how one can listen better to hear it. But this would not be saying anything about God Himself.

Marion holds strictly to God's unutterableness. He excludes the possibility that any intention on our part could ever touch this unutterable. To this extent he joins the ranks of negative theologians. He not only posits that no predicate can be attributed to God, he also believes that it is impossible to *deny* God any predicate. Nevertheless, he thinks that such a radical negative theology should not be given the last word. God's unutterableness should rather be considered *a period*, a passing pause as a circumambulation, a period that is necessary and that should be spent actively. Marion thus chooses the side of a more mystically tinted negative theology, especially that of Pseudo-Dionysius. He speaks of a *received* word that like an icon makes the invisible visible.

When Marion situates his thinking about God, seen as the very Distant and as the Sought, in the framework of contemporary philosophy, Heidegger is his most important interlocutor. Derrida and Levinas also play a role. I will therefore start (in Section 2) with an attempt to show how Marion tries to forge a link with Heidegger's ontological difference while recognizing that on this point Heidegger's discussion lacks something. Next (in Section 3) I will offer a three-part presentation of the way Marion envisages a way of speaking about God in which ultimately a word from the other side might resound. Finally (in Section 4), I interrogate Marion's views about the nature of the activity in which people approach God, the very Distant, and about the possible result of this activity.

2. The Conversation: Heidegger, Levinas, Derrida, and Marion

The Ontological Difference and Distance: Heidegger

Marion's most important theme is the 'distance' (*la distance*) or 'being at a distance' (*l'écart*). The two elements that lie far apart here are people and God, but also the Son and the Father. The accent on the distance between people and God camouflages the point that most concerns Marion: people's *nearness* to God. In brief, his thesis is that the more this distance is taken seriously, the greater the chance for this nearness to be achieved. As illustration Marion refers to the story of Jacob's struggle with God at the Jabbok ford (Genesis 32); according to Marion, it is not accidental that before Jacob received the blessing there was a conflict with, and increased distance from, God (*ID*, 256). We will return to this idea later.

Marion is interested in the possibility of a philosophical theology. But he wants to avoid situating this (philosophical) theology in metaphysics and onto-theology as Heidegger sees them. He considers them overly limited insofar as they ignore the ontological difference. The theology Marion seeks must keep in mind the ontological difference, the difference between Being and a being (*Sein und Seiendes*).[4]

Now that we have situated Marion's project externally, our first question is: What is this *distinction* between ontological difference and 'distance'/'being at a distance,' given that Marion's God is no more a being than is Heidegger's 'Being.' Marion explains the distinction as follows (*ID*, 258ff.). This difference is continually forgotten. This being forgotten is inherent to the difference. A being has always been our possession while Being has always escaped our grasp. This forgetfulness leads us to construct a metaphysics and an onto-theology; here one being provides the foundation or ground for the other beings, ending with a highest Being that is its own cause. Only when, startled, we ask whether the whole structure is not just hanging in midair; only when, without justifiable ground, we feel embarrassed about this highest Being, and the notion of Being in general; only when we feel our own foundations—as 'beings'—begin to shake, only then are we concerned again about Being. Only the thinking that then may possibly arise pays attention to Being *as* Being and lets Being *be* without prematurely appropriating it.

---

[4] See, e.g., *ID*, 279, 292ff.

The difference between a being and Being is forgotten time and time again, and thus Being itself is forgotten. The difference is always already over with; a being (ein Seiendes) seems simply there. The difference is not recognized, but it is there, even when it is not recognized. Even in this lack of recognition difference is active. Only when we look back at it is difference not forgotten.

The distance Marion has in mind, by contrast, is only there when it *is* recognized. When there is no person who *maintains* this distance from God, it is not there. Without that maintained distance, God is taken to be someone who is either present as a being or simply absent. In this lack of recognition of distance, distance is not active. Here difference and distance diverge. Yet the agreement between the two is still more impressive. For just as speech of any kind lives in the difference, without, however, our being able to thematize this difference, the word from the other side lives in the distance, again without our being able to thematize this distance as object. In both cases human intentions, with good cause, feel passed by.

But difference and distance differ in yet another way. Difference seems indifferent to whether attention is given to Being or not. We have just seen that difference may possibly even contain a theory of a highest Being that is its own cause, the perfect capstone of all that is. Difference does not exclude such an idol that takes away attention from Being. Distance, on the contrary, the distance between people and God, between Son and Father, forbids *every* idol, however great its attraction. The One maintaining the distance cannot remain indifferent on this point, whereas the difference does permit such indifference.

This dissimilarity between difference and distance rests on still another distinction. Heidegger thinks of God *within* the difference between a being and Being, and against the background of the question of Being. Distance, in contrast, or the person who maintains that distance, wants to think of God without situating Him somehow, somewhere as Being, however exclusive, or within whatever variant of difference. Seen from the distance, God is on the other side of all this; God is the very Distant. Marion rejects Heidegger's linking of 'God's' meaningfulness to a possible *location* for God.[5]

---

[5] *ID*, 268ff. Cf. M. Heidegger, "Brief über den 'Humanismus,'" in *Wegmarken*, 2nd ed. (Frankfurt am main: Klostermann, 1978), 347ff., and, against Heidegger, E. Levinas, *Totalité et infini* (The Hague: Nijhoff, 1971), 15ff., 39ff. Could it not be

Marion thinks that a God bound by our human conditions can be nothing other than an idol. Distance forbids such idols. Only a thinking without any postulates, a thinking that avoids thinking about God from the perspective of Being, a thinking, therefore, that moves toward the unthinkable—only such a thinking may possibly reach God. A negative theology is thus necessary.

Having reached this point, I will interrupt my presentation of Marion's thinking. Not only because this abstract discussion cannot be maintained for long; not only because Marion goes on to discuss Jesus, which might deter readers who expect philosophy; but especially because before continuing with Marion's discussion of God, some translation might be helpful. This chapter, however, will provide only a sketch without referring each time to links between Heidegger and Marion. I will translate into a language that the philosopher knows, but that in doing philosophy he or she seems to have forgotten his or her mother tongue.

Let us focus on two terms: 'creation' and 'revelation.' I define creation philosophically as 'arising from a destination,' thus as a destination-caused event or teleology. Creation takes place where a child plays a game. The child just plays and plays, with ever-new inspiration and intuition. In other words, the child is continually given something to do. She lives from destination. Destination continually comes toward her. She does not turn away from it. The child plays without frustration and without boredom. She lives as creation. The child *is* an event that can be called 'creation.' In the child's play destination becomes what *is*.

A child plays seriously with gleaming eyes and a smile. But a serious child does not *laugh*. Her play is not ridiculous. The child does not know that what she does is 'only a game.' She always forgets this. God creates, the child discovers her game; this finding is the Being of this being. But in playing no thought is given to this. The child simply learns what has to be done in her game; the child is not bored. Being is always hidden behind what the child is given to do and what the child takes in hand.

---

said, against Marion and Levinas, that God's 'appearance' occurs in an empty space, the *Sabbat, within* creation, thus in an open space that *people* keep open? See Heidegger, *Beiträge zur Philosophie*, Gesamtausgabe 3 (Frankfurt am Main: Klostermann, 1989), 65.417.

Now the child builds a tower, being driven to create. She feels inspired to build a tower as high as that table over there. She is fixated on this plan. She throws herself into her task. Imperceptibly the game is no longer a game. 'Creation' gets bogged down. The child is now more like an adult: her gravity becomes frenetic, she plays without play. The child is drawn to build a 'Tower of Babel,' a metaphysics, as high as the table over there, as high as the presupposed end of the world. But her ambitions are too much for the child, she does not know what language to speak. While being driven to create, she risks being cut off from creating.

Nothing more is heard of *destination*. The child can no longer reach unity; she becomes dissatisfied, until this child, perhaps still a child, gets up, laughs, laughs for the first time, and asks rhetorically, "Should I knock it all down?" The tower collapses, and now there is room for a new game. The child has withdrawn from the metaphysics that frustrated her creative activity. Although itself inspired by the event of difference, metaphysics almost eliminated the difference.

Perhaps this is one of the ways a child learns to laugh, to laugh at her own life that at that moment seemed a joke, that is, interrupted creation, frustrated play, a sudden awareness that gravity and frenetic activity are indications that only laughter makes room for new creation.

When people are only functionaries within a system, creation necessarily becomes a marginal affair. Creation or difference is not only forgotten, but people cut themselves off from creation, making it henceforth unlikely that anything of destination will approach them. Nothing occurs but the routine of the system. Under such circumstances, no longer thinking about creation could become disastrous. In a life where frenzy is turned into a system, there is not only no room for play—which cannot even be seen as a joke—there is nothing to laugh about. When frenzy is turned into a system, the *gravity* of difference is excluded.

In this situation, 'revelation' becomes urgent. I define revelation philosophically as a specific type of inspiration. This inspiration differs from more general inspiration and from the being aware of destination as described above. As I see it, revelation as inspiration is an expectation or even a conviction that says that creation is always possible, or that it is always possible to step back from a game that has become derailed. 'Back' means back to creation, back to being aware of destination. Revelation thus leads to a commemoration of creation. It encourages keeping open the space in which creation and difference occur. This leads, even in play, to attention and vigilance. Revelation sees to it that play does not lose its gravity and so degenerates into wantonness, rut, or system.

A child does not experience such revelation. She does not need it. She just plays without knowing that she plays. She is always forgetting this. The child has no time for creation, for Being. Or, she has incipient attention, but is fully integrated in the game and not as a separate revelation. She has a specific presence of mind, one that allows her to be a tireless child.

Revelation can take on the special form that implies the *awareness* that all that occurs in creation is still endlessly far away from a comprehensive destination that, when it comes to us in the creation of Being, confers on this creation or Being an *absolute, definitive* tenable allure. This revelation and awareness makes *every* game a joke, *long before* there is any question of reaching the intended destination. But when this awareness is taken seriously, it can prevent—at least theoretically—play from degenerating and creation from being forgotten. Revelation forbids turning play into an idol and remaining rooted in it. The thought of the far-removed destination, completely unknown, motivates the child to clean up the uprooted, God-forgotten creation to make it a place where destination can be heard and received.

I have defined revelation as becoming aware of and involved in a very distant destination. Revelation thus implies distance, a nearly infinite distance. This implied distance between what Marion calls people and God—or Son and Father—performs its motivating task only where people are aware of this distance as implied by revelation. When this aspect of the distance is forgotten, it does not work. Then there is nothing that leads to the expectation of a destination, in contradiction to dry facts. Then these dry facts are not shaped in a way that offers any perspective on the as-yet-unknown destination. On this point there is an important difference between creation and revelation. I believe, as I said earlier, that this difference is phrased by Marion as the major difference between Heidegger's ontological 'difference' and Marion's 'distance.'

With one more point relating to distance I close my attempt to put Marion's rigorous and abstract conversation with Heidegger in a different language. This distance is the distance from God, the far Distant, the completely Unknown. The unthinkability of God, however, implies the opposite, His exceptional nearness. For a word can come from God without *our* first having to find the words to define his exclusive location. God will be closer when people do not look toward Him with such idolatrous intentions and encompassing pretensions. An awareness of nearness is only real when people cease making a graven image of what is near and what, perhaps, will reveal itself in its nearness.

The Ontological Difference and the Other: Levinas

I briefly noted that Marion turns against Heidegger when the latter does not do justice to God's radical otherness, giving Him a place *within* his outline of Being and beings. Marion considers this a reduction of God, a neutralizing. Here he sees Levinas as an ally (ID, 275ff.). Levinas speaks of a distant Other. For Levinas, this relation of distance between God and beings precedes all ontology. The ethical call that constitutes Levinas's 'metaphysical' relationship of distance moves the concern for Being and the ontological difference to a second plane.

Marion notes that in Levinas a being, the other, moves toward Being and is decisive for what *is*. Levinas has, in a way, reversed the ontological difference. But, says Marion, in this way one does not really avoid the ontological difference. One even risks confirming its exclusivity, for again the perspective of a being and Being dominates the perspective of the destination I am given to reach.

Marion situates the relationship of my distance to the far Distant elsewhere, beyond the ontological difference. He therefore feels no need to reverse or eliminate the ontological difference. Put differently, in the terms we used above, the far Distant, with whom I have a relation through revelation, cannot be situated *within* the creation event. However attractive the child's play may be, however much she plays carefully, attentively, or responsibly toward others, the distance to *that* destination that encompasses all that will ever be given to this child to do has not yet been brought under discussion. With this distance we move onto another plane.

The Ontological Difference and Différance: Derrida

Marion adopts another position toward Derrida (ID, 280ff.). Marion thinks that Derrida's 'différance' (Derrida's variant of the concept 'difference'[6]), seen as event, is completely indifferent to the content of this event. There is no *archē* (beginning) nor *telos* (end) active in this event. There is thus neither truth nor untruth. The trace left by the 'différance' is anonymous. The 'différance' crystallizes without there being anything that is crystallized. The Heideggerian ontological difference in which a being belongs to Being and in which belonging it is what it is, is only an arbitrary variant of this 'différance.' The hope or feeling of belonging somewhere, which Derrida thinks Heidegger did not abandon, becomes, in Marion's view, itself indifferent in the 'différance.'[7]

Marion, however, is not convinced. He thinks that an indifferent difference cannot be forgotten, nor can it leave a trace. One cannot even speak of it in terms of 'crystallizing' or 'leaving a trace.' When in creation, a being has no destination coming toward it, or when awareness of the destination has no support, the buoyancy of a child's play becomes incomprehensible. This leads to the question of why awareness of destination has not ended in chaos. The child, however, plays against the background of an overabundance of order so that she need not be worried. But Derrida, according to Marion, *takes advantage*, with his concept of 'différance,' of several characteristics of difference. He keeps speaking of a trace even though it makes no sense to do so outside the difference of a being and Being. Marion concludes that Derrida's 'différance' is as unsuccessful in escaping the ontological difference as is Levinas's 'Other.'

Marion does not find in Derrida what he calls 'the distance.' Levinas does discuss something similar, and even uses the word. But, in Marion's view, Levinas can only think of this by usurping the ontological difference. Yet, for Marion, Heidegger and Derrida stand together facing Levinas. While Levinas believes that there is an 'Other' who rules its (reversed) difference, Heidegger and Derrida believe

---

[6] On Derrida and 'différance,' see Hent de Vries's chapter in this volume.

[7] Marion does not mention that Derrida feels indebted to this 'différance.' Derrida speaks of a "having to" (*il faut*) and a "necessity" (*nécessité*) and writes "While I focus on that orientation point, I write and try to think." See F. Guibal, "L'altérité de l'autre—autrement sur les traces de Jacques Derrida," in *Altérités: J. Derrida et Pierre-Jean Labarrière* (Paris: Osiris, 1986), 92. In Levinas, too, the 'social relationship' is without *archē* and without *telos* in the 'I.' On Derrida's relationship to Marion, see further J. Derrida, "How to Avoid Speaking: Denials," in H. Coward and T. Foshay, eds., *Derrida and Negative Theology* (Albany: State University of New York Press, 1992), 73–142.

such a 'fatherly figure' is absent. With a view to eliminating radically the place where this figure can be thought, Derrida in the end eliminates the ontological difference. Both Heidegger and Derrida leave no room for the notion that a distant God can intervene in what is. Heidegger's idolatrous condition, as Marion puts it, that God must be subject to the claims of Being, loses its meaning in Derrida. For Derrida, *every* theology is onto-theo-logy.

Here Marion joins with Derrida in opposing Heidegger and Levinas. This is strange and paradoxical, since Marion seeks a (philosophical) theology, while Derrida reaches a view in which nothing is left of God but an *empty space*; here Derrida goes a step further than any proponent of negative theology. According to Marion (*ID*, 293), the remnant of positive idolatry that we find in Levinas (God occupies an eminent place, be it that this place is beyond the reach of our activity; we only *sense* God) is abandoned in Derrida's purely negative idolatry (the place where God could have been is empty; we sense, but only in indifference). Marion adopts Derrida's insight radically. For, according to him, it becomes clear in Derrida that the theology being sought can only be found *on the far side of the onto-logical difference*. This theology situates its subject on the far side of the sense of destination and of the play that takes place in difference, experienced indifferently or not. It does not help to think of this difference as *pure* attention (Heidegger), as *radical* substitution (Levinas), or even as *complete* indifference (Derrida), for each puts God in the context of human hearing. It is true that a person can only hear *within* and *in the context of* this Being, this creation or, even, this indifference, but, says Marion, this exactly indicates that God Himself is distant. Nothing is learned of Him. He is *still further* away.

We live only within Being, and not also somewhere else. Yet we find ourselves elsewhere, but without this elsewhere implying a 'somewhere' or a form of Being or of a being. Put differently, we live in creation and we have nothing else available than the game we are given to play; yet to the extent that, in the sense defined above, there is a *revelation*, we have an awareness that the game in which we are included—and, to repeat, we are included in nothing else—is not very serious.

The Ontological Difference As Icon of Distance

We see that Marion wants to take the ontological difference very seriously. He tries to use this difference to reach something other than difference, namely, something above it. On this last point, he discovers that Levinas and Derrida bring him no further. He thus decides to return to Heidegger (*ID*, 280ff.).

I anticipated matters somewhat when discussing 'creation' and 'revelation.' I defined 'revelation' as a being involved in a very far removed destination. This involvement, or dedication, was the motive for seeing creation as a possible place where we can again discover destination, meaning, or sense. After the revelation, which comes across as a specific form of creation, people become motivated to return in dedication to the origin of creation and revelation. In this dedication (Marion speaks of 'charité': love, beneficence), an inspiration, that of revelation, is 'put into practice.' This practice, like the discovery of this inspiration, has a specific character. Now the game being played is directed toward another game still to be reached. This other game is craved, but it is still unknown and distant. But the game that we play here and now continues to be played until a new meaning reveals itself in it. At that moment the game is transformed into what Marion calls an *icon* of the distance, that is, nearness; in that proximate distance a word from the far side opens up. I will return extensively below to this notion of 'icon.'

Marion understands *the ontological difference* as *the icon* of distance. On the one hand, this is preposterous, for no God or Father is at work in this difference. Moreover, for Marion, God is the far Distant, on the other side of beings and Being, and is Himself nothing of the sort. Yet, the difference is always more than it is. It never loses itself completely in the game it inspires. Marion thus draws a parallel between difference and distance: one pole of the distance withdraws so far that one is tempted indeed to consider it anonymous, meaningless, or even absent. Here we find a precarious interpretation of Heidegger; it nearly presupposes a deferring (*différant*) Subject behind the difference. Given the way Marion incorporated Derrida's insights, we must say that *if* there were a God or Father active in the difference, He would be active in a completely indifferent way.

It is here, therefore, that Marion introduces a *doubling* of the distance. He keeps the Distant at a distance from difference. Difference can become an icon of Distance, but first, inspired by dedication, the difference must be taken so seriously as difference that the distance to the Distant can be walked through. So, first, one comes in the position of distance to God and only then can one, in greatest proximity, be receptive to hearing a word coming from that side. In dedication, difference can become a place where the distance to God Himself is 'received'; with this it becomes possible to hear a word coming from the far side. Thus, the negative theology that is linked to the ontological difference and that Derrida pushes to its extreme becomes in Marion an active *period* or phase, pointing beyond itself. Marion thinks that it is possible in this way to return to a modern variant of negative theology similar to that of Pseudo-Dionysius.

Having reached the end of this section, I will try to put this unusual conversation between Heidegger, Derrida, Levinas, and Marion in less abstract terms. The child played and played. She lived from what gave itself as destination, and had no further concern for this destination, nor did she realize that she lived from it. Yet she lived with an obvious concentration and attention, always intent on the attracting possibility that might come. Later her life became slower, and sometimes she had to face defeat. Soon the child became aware that she is dependent on whatever was given as destination. She wondered whether the game held any promise, and whether it made any sense to be concerned with the game at all. Would it really make any difference? Suppose that the child, somewhat embarrassed by her own life, is touched by the thought of a life with allure, a brilliant life. Then she begins to suffer. For such a life is far distant. The distance is immeasurable; one cannot even know in what direction to look. The only possibility is to vary the game that is available, to play it and replay it, listening whether, somehow, another destination makes itself known. Perhaps the child, now an adult and dedicated to this far brilliance, trying to put her life in order and to live conscientiously, can cover part of the distance. She may reach the *open space* where the unexpected occurs. There she may hear something of that brilliant life: close up, because it can be heard, and at the same time, for the first time now, very far away. Only now is it quite clear that that brilliance, which is so close, and so far, only *passes by* and is ungraspable.

3. WALKING THROUGH THE DISTANCE

Idol and Icon

The concepts 'idol' and 'icon' are perhaps the most important aspects of Marion's approach to his theme, the distance and proximity of God in a 'non-onto-theological' theology. His theory of the icon is a theory of the way the invisible shows itself. Marion discusses the icon by contrasting it to the *idol*.[8]

The difference between icon and idol is not a difference between two types of being. The same being can be both icon and idol. A single thing can be one moment icon and another moment idol by using its being a visible *sign* in specific ways. Both the icon and the idol make the divine visible.

A being becomes an idol when the glance directed toward it allows itself to be filled by this visible being. The glance, filled by this being, is under its spell. The intention of the one looking is absorbed in the sight of the idol. This means that intention and glance allow themselves to be fixed on a given visible shape. The glance, with its intention, does not allow itself to be transcended. This intention and what is seen function as the divine. Intention and glance do not *see through* the visible; there is no intention and glance that *go further* than the visible. Intention and glance are enraptured with the visible. This is possible not because the being that is the idol is so special, but because it becomes an ideal and merely reflects the fixed intention of a bemused seeing. But the one seeing in this way does not realize this; the mirror remains invisible. Seeing with this intention and with this glance, the viewer lives in the illusion of seeing something divine.

The glance that is filled by the idol no longer recognizes what is *not* intended. The content of the glance's intention is exhaustively preset on the idol. The mirror of which it is unaware does not allow any 'beyond.' The beyond, the 'on the other side,' is here per se not intended. This means that *everything* is visible. The idolatrous glance rules out any intention that could reach further than the idol that is openly visible before me. The divine is, thus, encompassed in the measure of the human glance. This 'primary visible,' to use Marion's words, receives material shape in an image. The thing that the idol represents becomes the object of religious veneration. Confronted with an object so laden, the worshiper falls to the ground, in the thrall of the glance.

---

[8] For Marion on 'Idol' and 'Icon,' see *ID*, esp. 311ff.; 'Fragments sur l'idole et l'icone," *Revue de Métaphysique et de Morale* 84 (1979); *GB*, passim; and "La double idolâtrie. Remarques sur la différence ontologique et la pensée de Dieu," in R. Kearney and J. S. O'Leary, eds., *Heidegger et la question de Dieu* (Paris: Grasset, 1980).

Marion believes that *concepts* can also serve as idols—for example, a concept that is believed to encompass God. In this case, too, the measure used to gauge the concept that supposedly represents 'God' is the product of human thought, instead of arising 'from the other side.'

The *icon*, however, is not produced by the human glance. On the contrary, the icon summons a glance. The being, functioning as idol, is a mirror in which the glance sees only *itself*. But the being that serves as icon gradually shows something of the real divine. Here the invisible is not excluded. It appears in the visible, but without being trapped in it. Marion believes that the icon makes the invisible visible *as invisible*. In other words, the icon, the visible object, refers beyond itself to the invisible. This visible reference is the visible dynamism that, when noticed by the glance, permanently holds forth the invisible to the glance. The icon here is by no means a *reflection* of the invisible. The icon does not make the invisible *tangibly* present. The icon makes the invisible *as invisible* present for the glance. In this way the glance, with all its intentions, no longer has any rest. Instead of being fixed on an object, the glance can now only focus on infinity; it must constantly surpass itself.[9]

The icon can be seen and refers beyond itself. Whoever sees a being as icon looks further than the visible. The icon's intention, oriented toward the invisible, draws along our glance to the invisible and confronts our glance with it. The icon's face is thus never, as external shape, the outer limit of our vision; on the contrary, it is the beginning of a vision that reaches further. This presupposes that this face has a fathomless depth, a dedication without reservation, an immaculate piety.[10] Looking at the icon means going to the furthest depth in the visible icon. This is a 'reading along' with the intention that the icon divulges, in the hope of hearing from this intention the intended unknown and distant. Marion does not explicate how this process proceeds, nor does he speak of the demands that may be made.

Just as the idol can take on the shape of a concept, so too can the icon function in the form of a 'concept.' It would be a 'concept' that

---

[9] Marion does not speak of the folly that threatens the glance so constituted.

[10] Marion does not speak of the danger of an unindividualized and even empty devotion, nor of the problem that a modern glance toward the icon may seek nothing but these.

must reach its own depth before it can say what it wants to say. Marion suggests that the idea of the *infinite* in Descartes may be such a concept.

Should it happen that something is observed of the brilliance one seeks, this does not decrease the distance to this brilliance. Rather, this distance is now more than ever present, for now a profound respect for the brilliance is for the first time truly felt. There is an awareness that this brilliance is not something that can be drawn like an object into one's own sphere of life. The experience of presence and nearness is simultaneous to that of distance.

The brilliance comes to me. It is therefore a *gift*. In Marion's view, one can only surrender to such a gift. This surrender implies that intention or will becomes love (*charité, amour*). Such an intention or will is not aimed at acquiring or safeguarding possessions. It is only the readiness to be drawn along through this distance, so that the nearness that accompanies this distance, like the distance itself, becomes reality and something that people actually experience.[11]

Marion's considerations on the icon are without doubt consistent. But they remain very abstract. It is questionable whether I, in this section on the question of how the ontological difference can be thought as icon, have provided any greater clarity on the matter. It seems that for Marion hearing of the destination can be so transformed that the hearing itself refers beyond itself to a more brilliant hearing of destination. Thus the ontological difference would serve as the icon of distance. This transformation seems to be borne by dedication.

I do not believe that in presenting the thought of the difficult Marion I should supplement this thinking too swiftly. I have not yet reached the end of his train of thought. At first, the next step seems only to deepen our difficulties.

The Expression 'Jesus Is Lord'

According to Marion, the *best example of an icon* is the figure of Jesus. Marion calls him 'Jesus Christ,' that is, Jesus the Messiah (the

[11] See "De connaître à aimer. L'éblouissement," *Communio* 3 (1978): 25 (= "L'évidence et l'éblouissement," in *Prolégomènes à la charité*); "Intimität durch Abstand. Grundgesetz christlichen Betens," *Communio* 1 (1975): 224.

Anointed)—Jesus as Christians know Him. Jesus points, without digression and to the very end, to the invisible. He is permanently filled with God, but He also *endures* the distance to God and suffers this distance in the extreme. Whoever is receptive to this icon, who feels inspired, feels the inspiration, or is even drawn to make a choice, saying 'Jesus is Lord.' But how is it possible to say such a thing, and how can one make such a choice?[12]

Marion thinks that the utterance 'Jesus is Lord' is only acceptable when one strictly follows the *logic of love*. Love alone legitimates this confession of faith. An empirical verification and an empirical referent are beyond reach; the utterance 'Jesus is Lord' shows characteristics of a highly personal language. But when we ground the legitimacy of this utterance in the speaker, in his or her inviolable authority or mere personal conviction that what he or she says is true, then we fall into absolute caprice, confirming the self-opinionated dominance of a speaker over his or her words. Marion seeks an escape from this problem by referring to the phenomenon of the *performative use of language*, in which what is said becomes true in the speaking. In Marion's example, someone says, "In the name of the law, you are under arrest." The example shows that the performative utterance can only be spoken by a qualified person, in this case, a police officer. The question to be posed now is: What qualification must one have to utter the performative expression 'Jesus is Lord'? How does one obtain such qualification?

An 'I' that can utter this expression on the level required must have authority on the same level as the 'Lord' in the example. It may be helpful to clarify this by referring, in a way somewhat different from Marion's, to the love that, in his view, lies at the basis of this expression. We could say that the one who says 'You are all (for me)' can only do so when his or her heart is already so spacious and so radiant that the 'all' in this utterance does indeed have the requisite content and allure. This is also true of Jesus. He received from God the necessary qualification, as the lover receives it from the beloved; through the beloved, the lover's heart has become spacious and has

---

[12] See "De la 'mort de Dieu' aux noms divins. L'itinéraire théologique de la métaphysique," in *L'être et Dieu* (Paris: Cerf, 1986), 118; "Die Strenge der Liebe," in B. Casper, ed., *Gott nennen. Phänomenologische Zugänge* (Freiburg/Munich: Alber, 1981), 166 and passim.

begun to radiate. In this way the utterance is possible for the 'Son' and for us as 'adopted sons and daughters.'

But how do we *know* whether we are qualified to say such a thing? Again a shift occurs; not from what is said toward the speaker, but from the speaker to the utterance. In saying 'Jesus is Lord,' the speaker is assumed to allow himself or herself to be moved along by the existing rules of this kind of speech and to allow himself or herself to be transformed by it. In doing so the speaker moves from autonomous, willful speaking to 'ecstatic' speaking. He or she is no longer concerned with performative speaking in the usual sense. The *formal* expression 'Jesus is Lord' is said and repeated *until* the 'I' is so transformed that he or she speaks the utterance as a true utterance.

Similarly, and by way of supplementary illustration, the utterance 'You are all for me' can only be a true utterance after the 'I' walks through the infinite distance between it and that 'all.' Walking through the distance is a form of *katharsis* (purification). Drawn to this far-removed brilliance, and motivated by my involvement with it, I 'utter' the words available to turn it into an utterance that voices something that I cannot control. This, it seems to me, is Marion's 'logic of love.'

In Marion's view, Jesus is someone who performed this *katharsis* fully. Jesus therefore *in and of Himself* refers to the 'Lord,' to God. He *is* the Lord, the Eternal. He *is* the preeminent icon, that is, something visible that refers beyond itself to something else; in this icon, Jesus, there is no idolatrous intention. Surrender to this pure icon,[13] to Jesus, or to the beloved, is expressed in covering the distance to the love that earlier, be it only fleetingly and brilliantly, made claims

---

[13] The icon, here, is not *pure* by being an unabridged *reflection* of the very Distant or by being a 'duplicate' of God; the icon is not a copy of God. The icon is pure by serenely suffering the *distance* to God, in complete surrender and without any petty preoccupation. When one views the icon *without* taking this distance and utterly active suffering into account, and thus imagines that one really learns of God, there are two possibilities: either one worships a graven image, or one ends up with a diffuse and meaningless relationship to 'something mysterious.' The Son's *distance* from the Father is what displays the divinity, the all-comprehensive depth, of this person. When the Father's begetting the Son is treated solely within Trinitarian speculation, *nothing* remains visible of Jesus' humanity, nor of the divinity of this humanity. See, as an example of such a speculation, Thomas Aquinas in *Summa Contra Gentiles*, 4.11, and the treatment of this passage in B. Vedder, "De metafoor van de vruchtbaarheid," in J. A. Aertsen, ed., *Vruchtbaar woord* (Leuven: Leuven University Press, 1990).

on the lover. Yet it remains true that the nearness to the beloved that may thus be gained only accentuates the distance; less than ever is nearness a question of possessing or of ever being able to possess.

Praise (The 'Discours de Louange')

According to Marion, it is impossible to *predicate,* say something about, God. But this does not imply, in his opinion, that we should only be silent about God. Being unable to speak is only a pause, a temporary period. Ultimately, it is quite possible to say something relating to God, even to utter a word we find 'fitting for God.' Something true can be said when it is *'made true,'* namely, in performative speaking. But the 'performance,' the action that makes the speaking true, is not the speaker's accomplishment; it is a *gift* from the other side. Truth, concerning God, *resounds* in me.

Meanwhile, the unspeakability of God is not, in a negative sense, *'merely* a period.' Being unable to speak implies distance. For Marion, thinking of and being in this distance are *positive,* the starting point from which the desired nearness to God can be sought. The period of being unable to speak indicates a meaningful and indispensable detour. It is so important because the unspeakable, in being unspeakable and unthinkable, is named and intended *as* the Unspeakable or, as God in an absolute sense.[14] Without this period the *katharsis* would lack a motivation. And without this motivation (the involvement with the very Distant), we cannot argue that our cathartic intentionality and activity are a preparation for what is expected from the other side.

A last attempt to characterize speaking during the period of inability to speak leads us to *praise;* for Marion, this is the heart of the speaking he has in mind.[15] 'Blessed art Thou, O Eternal,' it is said. Here God is addressed and praised, and He is called 'the Eternal.' Whether what is said and done here is correct and true cannot be determined from external evidence. When I take this utterance as

---

[14] This point is particularly important with regard to Levinas; see his "À l'image de Dieu, d'après rabbi Haim Voloziner," in *L'au-delà du verset* (Paris: Minuit, 1982), § 3, and "Dieu et la philosophie," in *De Dieu qui vient à l'idée* (Paris: Vrin, 1982), § 4 ("Divine comédie"). See also my "Deernis en toewijding. Ethiek en religieuze cultuur bij Emmanuel Levinas," in *De Uil van Minerva* 7 (Spring 1991).

[15] *ID,* 227ff.; cf. 309; "Die Strenge der Liebe," 183ff.

just one expression among many others, it may be no more than a tautology or even an empty expression that provides no information. The utterance does not immediately abrogate the addressee's anonymity. That it is a rote formula that at first may have no meaning for me confronts me with the distance that exists between me and the addressee.

Yet I say this formula, repeatedly. According to tradition, it should even be *sung*. When it is sung, the formula is heard. In hearing, I can *listen* to what I hear. This can be continued until we begin to hear in what we hear something that cannot be heard. My own intention, which gave its content to the word 'eternal,' makes room for or is transformed into a content that gives a meaning to this rote formula that does not come from me. Here my heart becomes aware of a truth that may be called 'God,' and my heart is transformed. Knowledge *about* God is not reached. Calling upon and blessing God is calling God *over oneself*.

Having reached this point, I could recall my excursus on the child at play. The seriously playing child 'listens' attentively to her own game. This is probably how the child incessantly learns what she has to do. Adults sometimes try by listening to use 'revelation,' understood as defined above, to reach the same thing. An awareness of distance moves them to this listening. A listening 'experience' of the difference could be construed similarly. In this case there would be a movement motivated by an awareness of distance, an attempt to walk through the distance, and so a possible experience of distance and nearness. We would then need to develop the distinction that might exist between an untroubled child's play and adults' religious activity.

At a certain point Marion's thinking can be presented no more clearly than what I have tried to do in the preceding argument. I may perhaps have wandered too far along the path of the free paraphrase. In Marion, it is not always clear whether the pious soul that succeeds in walking through the distance returns to earth with something specific. Does Marion's enterprise not end in a diffuse participation in a mystery?

4. The Possibility of Religious Activity

Marion concludes his study entitled "L'intentionnalité de l'amour" (The intentionality of love) with the comment that love needs faith (*foi*).[16] A surprising result, for in what precedes this statement he showed, more or less in line with Levinas, that love is *not* a form of intentionality; love implies a certain accent of 'passivity'(*IA*, 233ff.). The *ratio* of this closing statement that is not developed further lies, it would seem, in the idea that the glance of another person—a glance that *reaches further* than what is objectively in front of me—will escape me when I do not bind myself to a space, or a distance, in which that *reaching* can take place. How can I, without this (intentional) dedication, be receptive to someone's glance?!

Here the main lines of Marion's thinking are repeated. In contrast to a one-sided accent on the difference, the reversed difference or the différance, seen as variants of a given event or of a given dynamism, Marion maintains that something else is possible, something beyond this. In the case of love, it even seems that this something else, namely, the dedication, provides access to the phenomenon in question. In stressing this 'something else' Marion differs radically from Levinas who seems to need no 'faith,' covenant, or the like.[17]

I have referred several times to a relation of 'access' with regard to the relationship between difference and distance, between creation and revelation. In the case of love, this interpretation of what Marion says is not difficult to defend. In the other cases, matters are less clear. Praise is thought to end in some indefinable intimacy with God, but Marion does not describe the results of this intimacy. Does Marion recognize that difference and Being are the permanent media of our activity, or does he turn this intimacy into a world apart in which we, after crossing a particular border, would find ourselves in an area of mystery? In Marion, too, the distance seems occasionally to be at risk.

It is important, in this context, to investigate more closely what the relationship is between on the one hand the link Marion seeks with the far Distant—a link that moves us to a praise that opens up the difference and the idol, stuck in fixation as they are—and on the other, the self-recollection of which Heidegger speaks—a self-recollec-

---

[16] "L'intentionnalité de l'amour" (hereafter cited as *IA*), in *Les cahiers de la nuit surveillée*, vol. 3: *Emmanuel Levinas* (Paris: Verdier, 1984); also included in *Prolégomènes à la charité*.

[17] Levinas often identifies faith with a purely *theoretical* position; cf. "Pensée et prédication," in A.-T. Tymieniecka, ed., *The Self and the Other* (Dordrecht: s.n., 1977).

tion that arises from an involvement, if we may interpret it as such, with an awareness of poverty.[18] Are not both Marion and Heidegger concerned with keeping a particular kind of openness open?[19] When, and if, this openness is reached, it provides no 'knowledge of God,' or any special knowledge or extraordinary insight at all. It is no more than a renewed observation of destination. Put differently, revelation provides an access to creation, not to something on the other side of creation. On this point Marion is not very explicit.

What is prominent in Marion's undertaking, it seems to me, lies in his drawing forward and emphasizing elements that belong to this 'keeping open.' First is, of course, *distance,* distance from what is on the far side of the factually occurring difference. In Marion's view, this distance is an indispensable motivating factor. Second, the way Marion treats this distance demonstrates clearly that the activity to which this distance leads, for example, praise, is not an everyday activity. It is a *religious* activity. It does not fulfill any need, nor does it express a moral responsibility. Finally, Marion shows that people, in 'walking through the distance,' *actively* bring about a specific result, or at least pursue a path that they hope will lead to that result. Marion does not explain what exactly happens in praising and in trying 'to see an icon,' or whether its core is always a *katharsis,* or what the results are of these preparations. Perhaps we should seek 'intimacy with God' or 'walking with God' less in a *having walked through* the distance, than in the act of walking through it, and especially in the accompanying *awareness of distance.* For only in this activity do we feel a promise and the need of a covenant.

The activity in which the adult, at play, *is* this activity without being a functionary and without methodically or instrumentally applying himself or herself to the activity, while carefully uttering the rote praise, can be concrete and prosaic. He or she removes obstacles, becomes receptive and open, passing along all the places mentioned in the praise, moved by a passion for the very Distant. Knowledge *of* this latter, or even a confirmation of its existence, adds nothing to this passion. The only thing that counts is keeping the distance.

---

[18] See M. Heidegger, *Sein und Zeit* (Tübingen: Niemeyer, 1927), § 31, 144; § 40, 189; § 53, 264; § 60, 299; § 65, 326–28 ("Sich zurückholen aus dem Verfallen"), and *Wegmarken,* 308, 338, 348, 360 ("Die Armut der Ek-sistenz").

[19] Cf. M. Heidegger, *Sein und Zeit,* § 53, 265; § 62, 307, 308. This same 'keeping openness open' is also found in Levinas; see *Autrement qu'être ou au-delà de l'essence* (The Hague: Nijhoff, 1974), 182.

Chapter 6

The Theology of the Sign and the Sign of Theology:

THE APOPHATICS OF DECONSTRUCTION

Hent de Vries

"The sign and divinity have the same place and time of birth. The age of the sign is essentially theological."[1]

IT HAS BECOME COMMON to introduce Derrida's thinking by paraphrasing its supposedly 'neo- (if not 'post-) structuralist' character. Manfred Frank's *Was ist Neostrukturalismus?* (What is neostructuralism?) is the best-known example of this trend.[2] The classification 'neostructuralist' suggests that Derrida's work is immediately linked to the classical structuralism of Ferdinand de Saussure, Claude Lévi-Strauss, and others and preserves, as Frank asserts, an *"inner* continuity" with them: "Put differently, neostructuralism is not only—as the title 'post-structuralist' suggests—a line of thinking that appears *after* structuralism; it is also one that is critically linked to structuralism without which its origin cannot be understood."[3] Whereas classical structuralism had been understood as a consequent continuation of a renewing *linguistic* method in the human sciences, spe-

---

[1] Jacques Derrida, *Of Grammatology,* trans. Gayatri Chakravorty Spivak (Baltimore and London: Johns Hopkins University Press, 1974), 14.

[2] Manfred Frank, *Was ist Neostrukturalismus?* (Frankfurt am Main: Suhrkamp, 1984). In his equally critical book, *Logics of Disintegration: Post-structuralist Thought and the Claims of Critical Theory* (London/New York: Verso, 1987), Peter Dews chose the adjective "post-structuralist."

[3] Frank, *Was ist Neostrukturalismus,* 31–32.

cifically ethnology, political economy, and literary criticism, neostructuralism, according to Frank, must be understood as a *philosophically* inspired revolution in the history of reception. The novelty of neostructuralism, so Frank's argument goes, consists first of all in the fact that its transformation of the structuralist method is inspired by Nietzsche, but also by Freud, Heidegger, Bataille, and Levinas.

1. NEOSTRUCTURALISM?

The attempt to understand Derrida's work against the background of the "structuralist controversy"[4] easily results in a warped image. This widespread interpretation, I would claim, is disputable not only because it overlooks the structuralist insight that the arbitrary character or differentiality of the sign is merely one of the many possible entries for clarifying the 'point' of deconstruction—supposing that there is one or just one. What is particularly striking in this reduction of Derrida's writings to a variant of neostructuralism is that *it neutralizes beforehand* the ethical effort and implications of deconstructive practice. The very circumstance that the term 'structuralism' has become a well-known term has undoubtedly contributed to the association of the term 'deconstruction' with a 'negative' operation: the dismantling or destruction of structures. If we disregard terminological details and skip over subtle reinterpretations of the Heideggerian notions of *"Destruktion"* (destruction) and *"Abbau"* (dismantling), we can easily forget that deconstruction involves in the first place an *affirmative* act. To demonstrate this we must do more than follow the line of argument in Derrida's texts, particularly his much-discussed analyses of de Saussure and Lévi-Strauss; equally important are the diverse occasional references to the appeal of the *"Viens!"* (Come!), to the original, even preoriginal, *gift* and to the

---

[4] The term 'structuralist controversy' is the (revised) title of the acts of the famous symposium held at Johns Hopkins University in Baltimore in 1966, which initiated the reception of Derrida's work in the United States. See R. Macksey and E. Donato, eds., *The Structuralist Controversy: The Languages of Criticism and the Sciences of Man* (Baltimore and London: Johns Hopkins University Press, 1972). Derrida delivered the lecture entitled "La structure, le signe et le jeu dans le discours des sciences humaines," later included in *Writing and Difference* (see below).

response of the *"oui, oui"* (yes, yes), in short, to the motives that
have little in common with a prolongation of so-called structuralism
nor with its suppposed Nietzschean or Heideggerian transformations.

Why does Frank's *Was ist Neostrukturalismus?*—one of the most
frequently cited works on recent French philosophy—repeatedly lose
sight of this complexity? What is it that makes him link the criticism
of 'logocentrism,' which Derrida, Lyotard, and Deleuze have used,
with nothing less than that of Bäumler's, Spengler's, and Klages's
"prefascism"?[5] Is this comparison a 'slip of the pen'? Or is it a symptom of a widespread inability *to read* what is written, combined with
total inattention to the most elementary premises of academic ethics? To answer this question we must turn to several—ostensibly abstract—problems of interpretation. That much is at risk here should
be obvious by now.

We noted that, according to Frank, Derrida's thinking on writing
and difference must first of all be understood as a critical analysis
and further development of the *differential interpretation of the sign*
in Ferdinand de Saussure's semiology (*'semeion'* is the Greek word
for sign) most pregnantly formulated in his *Cours de linguistique
générale.*[6] Derrida is said to have found in this theoretical matrix of
later structuralism the argumentation that is central to his own
thinking on the *différance* and that shows that every linguistic sign
is *essentially arbitrary.* What does this mean?

De Saussure's use of the term 'arbitrary' reflects a simple, yet stag-
gering, insight into how language and meaning work that he summarizes in three closely connected propositions:

1. Neither the linguistic sign (the signifier, the *signifiant*) nor the concept or notion that it represents, and to which it refers (the signified, the *signifié*), are ever given 'positively,' that is, endowed with
   intrinsic 'meaning.'
2. There is no natural, that is, immediately evident, link between written signs (graphemes) and acoustic signs (phonemes) and the concepts to which they refer.

[5] Manfred Frank, "Kleiner (Tübinger) Programmentwurf," *Frankfurter Rundschau*, March 5, 1988.

[6] Ferdinand de Saussure, *Course in General Linguistics*, eds. Charles Bally and
Albert Sechehaye with the collaboration of Albert Riedlinger, trans. Roy Harris (La
Salle, Ind.: Open Court, 1986).

3. Linguistic signs derive their meaning solely from the endlessly expanded tissue or network of mutual references or differential relations.

Regarding this last point, Derrida writes: "In language there are only differences without positive terms. Whether we take the signified or the signifier, language has no ideas nor sounds that existed before the linguistic system, but only different conceptual and phonic differences that have issued from the system. The idea or phonic substance that a sign contains is of less importance than the other signs that surround it."[7]

Derrida notes that this differential, structuralist semiotics breaks *to a certain extent* with traditional (and modern) semantics. De Saussure shows clearly that the signified is inseparably bound to the signifier and is incomprehensible without it. They are two sides of the same coin, of the same effort to "produce" meaning.[8] Linguistic signs are never a purely sensible reflection of an intelligible meaning 'beyond meaning,' nor are they the ultimate expression of any preceding inner (psychic, intentional) process.

If there is no 'meaning' or 'idea' that can exist *independently of* the linguistic signifier or differential articulation of this meaning or idea, then this implies that a *transcendental signified* is from the start, that is, structurally or a priori, impossible. A 'first cause,' 'idea,' or 'purpose' in any metaphysical sense that is not itself a link in an endless chain of finite mutual references, but instead *grounds, orients,* or *terminates* this chain, would not only be unthinkable and unspeakable, but would remain without any physical, semantic, practical, or historico-political 'effect.' The "effects" of linguistic differences are effects in an unusual sense of the word: "Since language . . . has not fallen from the sky, its differences have been produced, are produced effects, but they are effects which do not find their cause in a subject or a substance, in a thing in general, a Being that is somewhere present, thereby eluding the play of *différance*."[9] Metaphysics stands or falls with the postulation of such a *transcendent* and *transcendental* Being. It is borne by the conviction that the world

---

[7] De Saussure cited by Derrida, in *Margins of Philosophy*, trans. Alan Bass (Chicago: University of Chicago Press, 1982), 11.

[8] Jacques Derrida, *Positions*, trans. Alan Bass (London: Athlone Press, 1981), 18; cited hereafter as *Positions*.

[9] Derrida, *Margins of Philosophy*, 11.

of transitory phenomena is a more-or-less accurate reflection of a
deeper, more original, unchangeable, and permanent Reality. Derrida points out that we could understand the history of Western
thinking as a sequence of different names for this meaning-confer-
ring foundation, center, and goal that pretend to be unique and that
must guarantee the cohesion of reality: "*eidos, archē, telos, energeia,
ousia* (essence, existence, substance, subject), *aletheia*, transcenden-
tality, consciousness, God, man, and so forth"; their common
denominator, Derrida assures us, following Heidegger, is "the definition of Being as *presence.*"[10]

It is in reducing the 'structural character' of all experience to a
'something' of which it is claimed that it is not part of any 'structure,' that metaphysics both constitutes and effaces itself. It puts
itself *out of bounds*, literally and figuratively. For if metaphysics
claims to be meaningful, then its concepts must be defined to a
certain extent. But, as de Saussure shows, every sign in a spoken or a
written discourse—every phoneme and grapheme—always refers to
something other than itself. It can only be understood, thought,
read, spoken, and discussed insofar as it is delimited from other linguistic elements. The centrality the sign claims is thus an 'illusion.'
No metaphysical postulate can be proclaimed or claim validity without betraying itself, without becoming something else than it means
or pretends to mean. Nothing has meaning and sense *in, of, or as
itself*. There is no meaning without context, that is to say, without
difference.

Derrida notes that even the very theoretical-systematic distinction
between signifier and signified remains in debt to the binary opposition of the intelligible and the sensible that it had made it its purpose to complicate and undercut. Nor does de Saussure fully escape
the Stoic and Scholastic distinction between the so-called *signans*
and the *signatum*. Although he concedes that signifier and signified
can never de facto act separately, he nonetheless believes that they
differ de jure. But if every signifier, in its turn, takes on the role of
signified, then this analytical distinction, Derrida notes, loses from
the outset its very foundation.

Yet this conclusion should not lead to forsaking the distinction

---

[10] Jacques Derrida, *Writing and Difference*, trans. Alan Bass (Chicago: University
of Chicago Press, 1978), 279–80.

between signifier and signified altogether. Use of this opposition is even, within certain limits, unavoidable. As Derrida rightly observes:

> For example, no translation would be possible without it. In effect, the theme of a transcendental signified took shape within the horizon of an absolutely pure, transparent, and unequivocal translatability. . . . But if this is never pure, no more so is translation, and for the notion of translation we would have to substitute a notion of *transformation*.[11]

Translation can thus no longer be thought of as if it were a 'transportation' of pure meaning between two languages or linguistic systems in which the 'vehicle' is irrelevant. Similarly, *communication* is no longer imaginable as the transposition of a content in or by a neutral homogeneous medium that does not change the shape of the message sent.

According to Derrida, the doctrine of the differentiality of meaning and sense has repercussions for the *concept of system* used by classical structuralism. The metaphysical-critical potential of the (re)discovery of the sign's arbitrary character itself returns to a certain degree to semiotics! De Saussure distinguished between the actual usage of language (*la parole*) and the abstract system of language (*le système de la langue*). The latter—though never tangibly present—is a prerequisite for every linguistic utterance that is identifiable and thereby understable or iterable. Without the presupposition of this deeper structure, every use of language, all ability to understand and communicate, would be inexplicable. This does not mean that the use of language is merely a derivative, or a realization, of the linguistic system. Each presupposes or implies the other. For although no *parole*, no *repetition* of meaning, is imaginable without accepting the silent basis of the *système de la langue*, the reverse is equally true: the linguistic system is present only in reiterated linguistic usage. Put more forcefully, "historically the fact of speech always comes first."[12]

Derrida does not reject without further ado that the linguistic system is the—quasi-, simili-, or cryptotranscendental—condition of possibility of any linguistic utterance. But he leaves no doubt that a consequent reflection on the differentiality of all meaning is hardly

---

[11] Derrida, *Positions*, 20.
[12] Cited after Derrida, *Margins of Philosophy*, 12.

compatible with the assumption of synchronicity, taxonomics, and the supposed ahistoricity of the concept of the structure or of the system of language. This does not mean that the principle of differentiality is astructural.[13] It should be described as a 'moving structure' to which we can scarcely apply the customary contrasts used to define concepts like 'movement,' for example, dynamic and static, present and absent. The 'structural character' at risk here *precedes and destabilizes* every system, every real or virtual structure of *langue* or *parole*, even the constitution and the structure of all experience, and is thus in a certain way their 'foundation.' This preceding should not be understood in a logical or chronological sense. Furthermore, the principle of differentiality is *nowhere else* a separate— intelligible—area of Being. Nor is it Being proper. It is only 'revealed' in the meaning it effects. Alone it 'is nothing,' and not even that: it withdraws not only from the Hegelian dialectical logic of negativity, but also from the movement Heidegger attributes to the *Nichts*. This differentiality meshes only with the more complex working of the *sans* (without) and the *pas* (not) that play such an important role in the writings of Maurice Blanchot,[14] and that also permeate the tradition of *negative theology* (In "How to Avoid Speaking: Denials," Derrida cites Eckhart who in turn cites Augustine: "God is wise without being wise, good without being good," etc). I will return to this.

Interestingly, the *circular* relationship or mutual implication that de Saussure ascribes to *langue* and *parole* resurfaces in Derrida on another plane and, I would claim, in a far more differentiated way.[15] De Saussure thought that when we pause at one of these two necessary postulates of (linguistic) communication, we can never explain how meaning is created or transmitted. Only their interaction makes them comprehensible. Compared to this interaction, linguistic system and usage are, in a certain sense, secondary and abstract. "In a certain sense" because the aforementioned principle of differentiation is located nowhere as such. It differs from the start from 'itself.' Moreover, that *système* and *parole* are secondary to both this interplay and to their 'own' interaction must not be taken in any logical or chronological sense. The interplay of differentiation 'marks' the

---

[13] Derrida, *Positions*, 27–28, cf. 9.
[14] See Derrida's essay "Pas," in *Parages* (Paris: Galilée, 1986), 109–16.
[15] Derrida, *Positions*, 28.

paroles in language, and the relationship of these *paroles* to language. It is the 'detour' we have to take if we are to speak, but then again it is also "*the silent promise* [or pledge; *gage silencieux*] *I must make.*"[16]

In his early writings Derrida calls this differentiality "*Différence*"[17] (with a capital 'D') while in his later work he speaks of "difference in general"[18] and finally "*différance.*" This neologism—or better, "neographism"[19]—is, like so many of Derrida's key terms, untranslatable because it is neither a word nor a concept. But the inability to translate it by no means excludes precision and rigor in describing it. More than once Derrida typifies *différance* as "the production of a system of differences,"[20] "the movement . . . in which the linguistic system, *like every code, every system of references,* is 'historically' constituted as a tissue of differences."[21] Seen in this way *différance* stands for another 'order' (a 'law,' necessity, fate, or fatality, but also an 'order,' command, or imperative) than the one delimited by our traditional ontological or deontological concepts. This explains why Derrida puts immediately after the sentence cited above the warning: " 'Is constituted,' 'is produced,' 'is created,' 'movement,' 'historically,' etc., necessarily being understood beyond the metaphysical language in which they are retained, along with all their implications."[22] The customary distinction between a diachronical-generative and a synchronic-structuralist reflection is no longer applicable to the differential movement or production of *différance* 'as such.' *Différance* is "no more static than dynamic, no more structural than historical. But also no less." Put differently, "the differend, the *différence,* between Dionysius and Apollo, between ardor and structure, cannot be erased in history, for it is not in history. It too, in an unexpected sense, is an original structure: the opening of history, historicity itself. Difference does not simply belong either to history or to structure."[23] It is certainly no preoriginal "cause" or (supreme) Being whose purely "phenomenal" reality gives only signals.[24]

---

[16] Derrida, *Margins of Philosophy*, 15.
[17] See Edmund Husserl, *L'origine de la géometrie*, trans. J. Derrida (1962; Paris: P.U.F., 1974), 171.
[18] Derrida, *Of Grammatology*, 18.
[19] Derrida, *Margins of Philosophy*, 3.
[20] Derrida, *Positions*, 28.
[21] Derrida, *Margins of Philosophy*, 37; my italics.
[22] Ibid., 12.
[23] Derrida, *Writing and Difference*, 28.
[24] Derrida, *Positions*, 107, n42.

The introduction of the silent but legible *a* in the French word for difference—with an unmistakable reference to the active connotations of the present participle of *différer* (that is, *différant*)—not only draws attention to the 'production' and movement of temporal and spatial displacement, it marks the 'conflict' side of this process. Long before the publication of Lyotard's *Le différend* and anticipating the interpretation of Heidegger's "Herakleitos" lecture, this *différence*, *différante*, and *différend* evoke the connotation of controversy, conflict, and *polemos*.[25]

We can now bring together several lines in our argument against this background. Derrida uses the motif of the "arbitrary sign" and that of the "differential structure" to refer indirectly to a "production" or "movement" that permits meaning (without itself having any meaning, strictly speaking). The concepts 'sign' and 'structure' are not simply adopted or rejected, but are grafted onto 'something else': on the 'otherness,' the difference par excellence, the *grammè* (or better, the *marque*), or, in still other words, on *différance*. The latter figure, if that's the right word, is a *grapheme*, not a word, concept, idea, substance, or material. It represents a "configuration,"[26] a bundling, or 'graph' of various transformational and transgressional motifs. The semiological formulation of the principle of differentiation is only one of these, and absolutely not the most *striking*. Certainly, Derrida leaves no doubt that writing (about) the *différance* "develops the most legitimate, principled exigencies of 'structuralism.' "[27] But it should be noted that this does not turn *différance* into, say, a neostructuralist motif.

In *Margins of Philosophy* Derrida therefore explains that a relentless reflection on the "structural nature" of the linguistic experience "consists neither (a) in restoring the classical motif of the system, which can always be shown to be ordered by *telos, aletheia,* and *ousia,* all of which are values reassembled in the concepts of 'essence' or of 'meaning'; nor (b) in erasing or destroying meaning. Rather, it is a question of determining the possibility of meaning on the basis of a 'formal' organization which in itself has no meaning, which does not

---

[25] In *Positions*, 8, Derrida speaks of the (silent) "graphic and grammatical aggression" of the *a* in *différance*.

[26] Derrida, *Positions*, 8.

[27] Ibid., 28.

mean that it is either non-sense or anguishing absurdity which haunt metaphysical humanism."[28]

As a 'formal' organization, the interplay of differences is stripped of every specific content; as the prerequisite for the functioning of every sign, and thus of all meaning, it is itself 'silent.' It remains noncommittal and "exceeds the order of truth at a certain precise point, but without dissimulating itself as something, as a mysterious Being, in the occult of a non-knowledge or in a hole with indeterminable borders (for example, in a topology of castration)."[29] This means, again, that *différance* goes beyond the psychoanalytical frame of mind (from, say, Freud to Lacan). Nor can it be envisioned simply as the hidden object of a negative theology, even though Derrida recognizes that various formulations could very well lead us to this conclusion. The *différance* is neither this nor that, no essence or existence, and while it is nothing specific, it is therefore not merely 'nothing.' All this, then, would allow us to conclude only that it is sufficient to remember that *insofar as* psychoanalysis or negative theology rest on the—intolerable—premise that Ultimate Reality must be pictured as self-satisfied Being present to itself or felt only as a lack or absence, it is not immune to deconstructive reservations. Nothing more and nothing less is claimed here.[30]

Metaphysics stands or falls with the misjudgment of the 'principle of difference' that states that no single linguistic or other element of meaning can function—or have 'meaning'—without referring to others, without invoking something other than itself. What does this mean? Metaphysically speaking, every attempt to snatch a privileged concept away from the differential chain in which everything refers to something else is to be avoided: "Every time people pretend to cut free or isolate an area or layer of pure meaning or pure signified [in the play of signifiers], they make the same gesture. . . . And every time that a region or layer of pure meaning or a pure signified is alledgedly rigorously delineated or isolated this gesture is repeated."[31]

In this critique of the supremacy of meaning above the sign and

[28] Derrida, *Margins of Philosophy*, 134.

[29] Ibid., 6.

[30] For a more elaborate discussion of these restrictions, see my *Philosophy and the Turn to Religion* (Baltimore: Johns Hopkins University Press, 1999), chap. 1.

[31] Derrida, *Positions*, 32.

of the conceptual unity of the sign above the play of *marques*, we find the deconstruction of an at-bottom theological motif: "The sign and divinity have the same place and time of birth. The age of the sign is essentially theological."[32] The deconstruction of the sign ipso facto disrupts the onto-theological presuppositions and ramifications linked to the Western logos. And while this theology of the sign may never *end*, it has already demarcated the historical *limit* of onto-theology.

It would be incorrect to think, however, we could just abandon the metaphysical gesture of wanting to reach beyond differentiality. The metaphysical hypostasis of a single signifier is a *transcendental illusion* or a *longing of reason*, to use Kant's terms, that is given with thinking, speaking, and judging or acting "as such."[33] When we read in the essay on Lévi-Strauss found in *Writing and Difference* that "even today the notion of a structure lacking any center represents the unthinkable itself,"[34] the reason is not so much an empirical-psychological secondary *condition humaine* (the desire for firm footing or the cherishing of a presupposed certainty that makes fear of the unmanageable manageable). What Derrida means is that we cannot simply put behind us the structural distortion of reality in the light of some supposedly Archimedean vantage point. Western metaphysics is only the best-known and most dominant expression of this need to posit a foundation. If 'postmetaphysical' thinking were possible, indeed, it would still have to obey this very same 'law.' And deconstruction is no exception to this rule, which explains, perhaps, why traditional ethical and theological images and motifs continue to play a crucial role in Derrida's analyses. We cannot simply push aside this heritage (and the accompanying concept pairs of spirit and letter, 'pneumatology' and 'Scripture,' symbol and allegory) as if a totally other, more adequate—nonmetaphysical—conceptual apparatus were available somewhere. Without concepts, Derrida insists, no less than Kant, thought is impossible.

If we deduce from the arbitrary character of the sign that *everything is merely a signifier* and that every theoretical initiative is based solely on a random collection of arbitrary perspectives, then every

---

[32] Derrida, *Of Grammatology*, 14.
[33] Derrida, *Positions*, 33; also see 22, 60.
[34] Derrida, *Writing and Difference*, 279.

attribution of meaning becomes obsolete indeed and thinking loses its *critical* potential. At the risk of returning to a 'regressive' stage, we must therefore try to set traditional concepts in motion to the point where they begin to betray their own internal and external limits. Through this narrow opening in language, Derrida writes, we can, perhaps, perceive the "yet unnameable glimmer"[35] of otherness.

The repetition of 'the same,' for example, of the inherited fundamental structure of metaphysics, is thus never a repetition in the strict or even in the Heideggerian and Kierkegaardian sense of the word. It always causes a certain, minimal, yet critical, shift, and thereby displaces the borders of possible experience.

Seen against this backdrop, a certain indelible distance with regard to linguistic structuralism seems to dominate Derrida's reading of de Saussure within the 'theoretical matrix' of his own work, that is, in the first part of *Of Grammatology*, in *Margins of Philosophy*, notably "La différance," and in the opening interviews of *Positions*. What is more, de Saussure's text is only presented as a "privileged example"[36] of the question of the sign—no more and no less. There is no question of any affinity in content or method, let alone of a natural alliance between deconstruction and semiotics or semiology. Derrida's exposition of the differentiality of the sign fits with Saussure's linguistics because the latter is the backbone of the "dominant discourse,"[37] one, moreover, that in truth prolongs metaphysics although it pretended to have superseded it once and for all. Derrida's assertion that he draws only extreme consequences from the legitimate—metaphysical-critical—aspiration of structuralism does not contradict this conclusion.[38] De Saussure's linguistics and the structuralist sciences that espouse his methodological principles have reminded[39] us again of the arbitrary character of the sign, but deconstruction does not halt at this insight. It aims at nothing less than "the transformation of general semiology into grammatology."[40] The term 'grammatology' also falls short as a description of the effort and process of deconstruction. Its concern cannot be en-

---

[35] Derrida, *Of Grammatology*, 14.
[36] Ibid., 29; cf. *Positions*, 18: "only one example."
[37] Derrida, *Of Grammatology*, 99, and *Positions*, 82.
[38] Cf. Derrida, *Positions*, 18, 36.
[39] Ibid., 9.
[40] Derrida, *Margins of Philosophy*, 15.

capsulated in any term ending in '-*ology*', and does not even coincide with the '*gramma-*', the written sign, that easily leads to misunderstanding, for example, as a limited interpretation of the *written* text.

Deconstructions rather obey, and witness to, a paradoxical "*pas d'écriture*" (step of [not] writing)—a 'step' and also a crossing out—that can probably best be expressed as a "practice" (*pratique*[41]), at least insofar as this term is removed from the traditional Aristotelian opposition between *theoria* and *praxis* as well as from the Hegelian, dialectical (i.e., 'negative') "labor of the concept."

The argumentative pattern in which Derrida approaches de Saussure—playing the text's letter against the spirit, exposing the "tension between gesture and statement"[42]—differs in no way in effort and result from that of the accompanying deconstructive readings of Hegel, Freud, Heidegger, Levinas, or, for that matter, anyone else. The same ambiguity uncovered in de Saussure is also found in Hegel's semiology, in Freud's psychoanalysis, in Heidegger's fundamental ontology, and in Levinas's thinking on the Other. Yet one would hesitate to call these deconstructive readings neo-Hegelian, neo-Freudian, neo-Heideggerian, or neo-Levinasian. Why, then, insist on the adjective 'neostructuralist'?

Frank's assertion that Derrida both "radicalizes" and "refutes"[43] de Saussure's theory of signs and system of concepts—from a Nietzschean perspective or, rather, perspectivism—can only with great difficulty be seen as an adequate response to this question. Neither the repertory of radicalization, nor that of radical refutation, nor of the decisive break—of a "*coupure épistémologique*," to use Althusser's terminology—are characteristic of the gesture or practice called 'deconstruction.' All the characterizations of deconstruction in terms of some iconoclasm are of little help in clarifying its '*pointe*'—if there is one (or only one). They put Derrida's enterprise in a certain—suspect, adventuresome, and at bottom irresponsible—light.

Derrida and the Jewish Tradition: Habermas's Critique

If Derrida's notions of scripture and trace should be understood as neither neostructuralist, nor as Heideggerian, Nietzschean, or Freud-

---

[41] Derrida, *Positions*, 89.
[42] Derrida, *Of Grammatology*, 30.
[43] Frank, *Was ist Neostrukturalismus?*, 32.

ian, or even Levinasian, against what background should they be understood? Is it useful and justifiable to carry them back to a Jewish or to a negative theological and mystical heritage? Or does this hermeneutical search for the most appropriate context neutralize the purpose of Derrida's work in the first place? In other words, does such a maneuver block the ability to observe his particular use of, for example, religious idiom?

In a cultural climate in which 'deconstructive' thinking is often accused of 'indifferentism,' its surprising links with the religious-theological tradition can offer an important counterweight. Yet here, too, care should be taken. We meet here a theme in Derrida's work that, until recently, has appeared marginal in several respects. Except for one crucial lecture devoted to his preoccupation with negative theology, the theme announced itself mainly in marginal notes to texts by Kafka, Benjamin, Celan, Jabès, Blanchot, and Levinas in which ethical-religious motifs were traced and varied. The undeniable involvement of these and other writings with the Jewish heritage can only with difficulty, if at all, be traced back to their sources (Tenach, Talmud, Cabala) and is only obliquely observable in a continuous process of translation and reinscription. Yet, at the same time, it seems to involve no more than occasionally inserted *quotations*.

But a quotation is never 'merely' a quotation: it summons, shakes awake, spurs on,[44] even (or especially) where it is cited out of context. This does not deny that for deconstruction all supposedly 'original' motifs are always already subject to a ceaseless process of shifting meanings. The 'origin' that Derrida's text more-or-less expressly 're-flects' and to which it reacts was in a certain sense never there in its integrity or as such.

It does not help to remind Derrida of the—unconscious or un-planned—Jewish signature of his own work.[45] Although he signed the final essay in *Writing and Difference* "Reb Dérissa,"[46] Derrida reacts with unconcealed irony to the suggestion that he may be under the latent influence of the Jewish tradition of commentary and midrash. In an interview he admitted that he regretted being unfamiliar with

---

[44] A quotation, says Derrida, referring to the Latin connotation of the term, is an "incitement," a "solicitation"; see his *Parages*, "Introduction," 10.

[45] See F. Laruelle, *Les philosophies de la différence. Introduction critique.* (Paris: P.U.F., 1986), 125.

[46] Derrida, *Writing and Difference*, 300.

the Talmud. The supposed echo of Jewish themes in his writings cannot be explained by a thorough familiarity with Hebrew or by religious education. The most that could be suspected, he suggests, was that the Talmud, in some puzzling way, knows *him*—or perhaps *itself in him*.[47]

To further analyze the scope of Derrida's use of religious tradition, we may perhaps best turn to the equally intriguing as moot interpretation that Habermas has given of his work. In his polemical treatment of several alleged characteristics of Derrida's thinking, in his *Philosophical Discourse of Modernity*,[48] Habermas defended two—apparently contradictory—theses. First, he asserts that, all things considered, Derrida has been unable to free himself from the so-called subject-philosophical premises in Heidegger's "temporalized philosophy of origins." Second, he stresses that the *tenor* of these thinkers' writings nevertheless show a remarkable difference. Certainly, Derrida's work, like Heidegger's, is obsessed by the—as it were, exponentially—increasing volatility of meaning in the modern epoch. Both would agree that this 'withdrawal' of what was once unified in the True, Good, and Beautiful, is no longer comprehensible in classic, metaphysical, or substantialist terms. What we are left with is no longer the feeble silhouette of an original divine revelation and the reason reflected in and on it.

Yet Derrida is supposed here to (want to) give a more radically different turn to this diagnosis than does Heidegger. This other orientation finds its foundation, according to Habermas, in the numerous *themes* or quotations taken from Jewish messianism and from mysticism. But various characteristics of rabbinical and cabalistic *hermeneutics* are also said to have left their traces in Derrida's reading. His rehabilitation of scripture is to have drawn on religious sources without being theological in the customary sense. What is more, according to Habermas, Derrida owes to this thematic and methodological heritage his resistance to the political-moral insensitivity of the "paganism purified by Hölderlin,"[49] that, Habermas

---

[47] See Christian Delacampagne's introduction to "Philosophies" in *Entretiens avec Le Monde I* (Paris: Éditions de la Découverte, 1984), 78–90, 80–81.

[48] Malden, Mass. and Oxford, U.K.: Blackwell, 1988. I will refer to the original German edition (see below).

[49] Jürgen Habermas, *Der philosophische Diskurs der Moderne* (Frankfurt am Main: Suhrkamp, 1985), 197.

believes, ultimately characterizes Heidegger's work. Unlike Heidegger, he is said to have been on his guard against discovering a diffuse ontological "fluid"[50] in what withdraws in or from modern experience. A *labyrinthine* mirror of texts is thus found to have replaced the epochal history of Being. These texts—and the commentary attached to them—refer to a primeval scripture that as such can never be discovered by any text, concept, or poetic word.

Yet Habermas thinks that, in the final analysis, this different *tone* leaves a fundamental agreement between the two authors intact. And that is ultimately his point. Both Heidegger and Derrida are thought to abandon the task of critical reflection, preferring to invoke an *indefinable* authority. To be sure, Derrida is said no longer to fixate on a thought of "Being that lacks being," but rather turns to deciphering a "no longer holy Scripture, wandering in exile, alienated from its own meaning and witnessing to the absence of the Holy Testament."[51] Undermining the hierarchy of living word and dead writing, of spirit and letter, as well as the contrast between pneumatology and grammatology, Derrida's texts reveal in essence a radically transformed rabbinical hermeneutic.[52] It is no longer the reflection on the unique incarnation of a divine act of will, creation, or recreation, for from now on only an interminable process of revelation that takes place in the indefatigable interpretation of texts is deemed to bring about the redemption of humanity and the world. Even the most secular translation of the holy continues this revelation.[53] Derrida drastically modifies the traditional way of commenting on texts because he includes nonreligiously inspired texts in his considerations and gives no text absolute authority. But this procedure nonetheless guarantees him a place in the tradition of what is called the *heretical* hermeneutic, which Gershom Sholem's historical studies on Jewish mysticism, especially on Cabala, have recalled from oblivion. Derrida's work is said to return to orthodox tradition via a "heretical" way of thinking.[54] His Kafkaesque vision of the documen-

---

[50] Ibid., 196.

[51] Ibid., 214.

[52] See Susan Handelman, "Jacques Derrida and the Heretic Hermeneutic," in *Displacement: Derrida and After*, ed. Mark Krupnick (Bloomington: University of Indiana Press, 1983), 98–129, 111, 113.

[53] Ibid., 104, 120.

[54] Ibid., 119.

tary value of modern experience is said to renew a Jewish tradition
that, in contrast to Christian teaching, cannot be incorporated in
the one Book that seals the canon, but seeks traces where totality or
ultimate meaning no longer shines through. For this same reason his
work is said to show no archaic or fatalistic traits. On the contrary,
the bent toward subversive, anarchistic revolt dominates.[55]

According to Habermas, this difference in intention is linked to a
difference in frame of reference. Not Hölderlin and the romantic
Dionysus reception, but monotheistic tradition ultimately determines the horizon of deconstruction. While Heidegger turns against
the onto-theological heritage, even against all of modernity, Derrida—"luckily,"[56] that is to say, less radically than Heidegger—falls
back to the critical point where monotheism and mysticism turned
into Enlightenment. Seen in this way, the main point of Derrida's
work is not so much the destruction of all traditional dogmatic content, but the renewal of a 'discourse with God,' albeit this time under
postmetaphysical and, perhaps, postmodern conditions.[57] What
makes Derrida's undertaking more responsible but—philosophically
speaking—no less problematic in Habermas's opinion, is a melody
whose timbre, while not excluding certain perilous dissonances,
does, in the end, also *drown them out*.

How are we to understand this minimal but crucial and indelible
distinction between Heidegger and Derrida? Must we examine biographical and historical elements, *data*, in the emphatic sense Derrida gives to these notions, in the wake of Paul Celan?[58] Or does a
more meticulous reading provide us with additional information on
the undeniable differences between Heidegger and Derrida? Does
not Habermas's polemical essay unwittingly provide the best proof
of Derrida's thesis that the decisive difference between philosophical
discussions ultimately lies in their different *tonality*? What is decisive seems thus not an argumentative, reconstructible difference in
the way thought is structured, but a distinction in tact and judg-

---

[55] See Habermas, *Der philosophische Diskurs*, 214.
[56] Ibid., 216.
[57] Ibid., 218.
[58] See Hent de Vries, "Le schibboleth de l'éthique. Derrida avec Celan," in Jean-
Michel Rabaté and Michael Wetzel, eds., *L'éthique du don. Jacques Derrida et la
pensée du don*, Colloque de Royaumont, décembre 1990 (Paris: Métailié-Transition,
1992), 212–38.

ment. The so-called thinking of Being, or *Andenken,* unlike deconstructive thinking, responds to an indefinable sending of Being, or
Seinsgeschick. Nevertheless, Habermas suspects, even in the subversive Derridian thinking on difference, there is a merely formal pattern of thought that is poor in concrete political content, a pattern
that can only be filled in, as the historical-social situation requires,
in an arbitrary and therefore ultimately *decisionist* manner.[59] Need-
less to say, this is not Derrida's own view.

Derrida notes somewhere that his thinking is marked by

> what is more at home in literature than in philosophy, . . . an *idiomatic*
> writing . . . , a character that you cannot appropriate [because] it char-
> acterizes you without belonging to you. You never notice it, only oth-
> ers do, except in fits of madness that fuse life and death. It is ruinous
> to dream of creating a language or song that would be yours—not, as
> the attributes of an 'ego,' but rather the accented timbre, I mean, the
> musical timbre of your own most illegible history . . . ; not a *style* but
> an intersection of singularities, life styles, voices, writing, the baggage
> you carry with you and cannot leave behind.[60]

In this sense, there is in Derrida a certain participation in a manner
in which a community—the Jewish—deciphers its forcefully uprooted existence in writings and, in this way, lives out its restless-
ness.[61]

It is not in any religious *content* or *substance* that we should seek
the common element that links deconstruction to the Jewish hermeneutical tradition. Habermas again shows this in a comment as involuntary as it is apt. He refers to Scholem's analysis of a cabalistic
tradition,[62] according to which only the *aleph* (as first letter of all
commandments) really belongs to revelation in the strict sense of
the word. This revelation would then become a mystical concept
that "while itself being infinitely filled with meaning is yet without
specific meaning. It is something that—to ground religious authority—would have to be translated into human languages. . . . Every

[59] Habermas, *Der philosophische Diskurs,* 168–69.
[60] "An Interview with Derrida," in David Wood and Robert Bernasconi, eds., *Derrida and Différance* (Evanston, Ill.: Northwestern University Press, 1988), 71–82, 73.
[61] Didier Cahen, "Entretien avec Jacques Derrida," *Digraphe* 42 (1987): 14–27; see esp. 20–21.
[62] Gershom Scholem, *Zur Kabbala und ihrer Symbolik* (Frankfurt am Main: Suhrkamp, 1973), 47.

utterance that grounds authority [in this way], however valid and eminent it may be, is still a human interpretation of something that transcends this explanation."[63]

In this cabalistic, mystical concept of a revelation that precedes every articulation of content, being its prerequisite without being its possession, Habermas sees an analogy with the '*a*' of Derrida's *différance*. Is this analogy plausible? Does it bring us any further? My closing considerations center on the inevitability and limited value of such a parallelism.

3. DERRIDA AND NEGATIVE THEOLOGY

There is a good deal of confusion about the ethical-theological pur-port of Derrida's work. Some authors accuse Derrida of a suspect revival of mysticism and negative theology; others do just the reverse, accusing him of being insensitive to religious questions. At the basis of both interpretations lies a widespread incomprehension that I would like to try to clarify here. My working hypothesis is treacher-ously simple, almost trivial. I wish to show that Derrida neither writes off the core questions of negative theology nor naively repeats them. His position is best summarized with an early quotation from *Of Grammatology*: "The 'theological' is a determined moment in the total movement of the trace."[64] What does 'the theological' mean here? In what sense is it a 'well-determined,' *inevitable*, and even perhaps *constitutive* "moment within the total movement of the trace"?

Peter Kemp has noted that there is a deep abyss between decon-structive thinking and eighteenth- and nineteenth-century human-ism and materialism. The latter, in his view, only reverse the hierarchy of metaphysical oppositions, specifically theology and an-thropology, without putting them in question as deconstruction does. But, Kemp continues, the deconstruction of these oppositions also overshoots its goal because it loses sight of the *ethical impetus* of modern religious criticism. By contrast, Kemp concludes, Derri-

---

[63] Habermas, *Der philosophische Diskurs*, 216.
[64] Derrida, *Of Grammatology*, 47.

da's work, all things considered, leads to the defense of an *amoral atheism.*[65]

Various motifs in Derrida's post-1972 work—after the so-called turn or *Kehre* apparent in the publication of *Dissemination* (Kemp refers to *Glas* and *Spurs*)—contradict this interpretation on virtually each and every page. They are all linked to the notion of a *gift* that is said to precede Being and its truth (and, it should be added, also the very figure of the *es gibt* in Heidegger), and is thus no longer thinkable or utterable in ontological terms. But even this new timbre in Derrida's later work does not, in Kemp's opinion, undo the ethical *gap.*

At the other end of the interpretation spectrum, Mikel Dufrenne contends that Derrida's work should not so much be understood as amoral or atheistic, but rather as a resumption of the very tradition of theology—especially negative theology—from which it seeks to set itself apart. [66] In negative theology we encounter the secret core of truth of *every* theology that says that above all we must avoid giving names to God that do not do Him justice. Since every determination (*determinatio*) of the divine essence is at once a *negation* (a denial of other determinations, i.e., other negations), only a permanent 'negating' of all feasible negations can guarantee respect for the name called. Only in traversing the *via negationis* can the idolatry of anthropomorphism be put aside indefinitely. Or so it seems.

Dufrenne believes we find a similar idea in the thought of *différance.* Like negative theology, deconstructive reading affirms the effectiveness of a 'nonpresence.' It endorses the absence of the origin, the 'originary' supplementarity, of all meaning. And such a notion is incompatible with affirmation of a highest Being, an absolute telos, or, for that matter, a creatio ex nihilo. If anything, we are dealing here with a *"nihil* that creates, a determining indeterminateness."[67] In Derrida's analyses of the differential play that precedes Being and beings (and both permits and precludes them) Dufrenne thus sees

---

[65] Peter Kemp, "L'éthique au lendemain des victoires des athéismes: Réflexions sur la philosophie de Jacques Derrida," *Revue de théologie et de philosophie* 111 (1979): 105–21, esp. 112–13.

[66] In "Pour une philosophie non-théologique," the introduction to his *Le Poétique* (Paris: P.U.F., 1973), 4–57.

[67] Ibid., 20.

"a sort of pre-God," meaning "not the negation of God, but the negative of a God."[68]

I see at least two different argumentative strategies in Derrida's work that require a more nuanced analysis of the relationship between deconstruction and negative theology than Kemp and Dufrenne give it. I will analyze them more closely using two texts, one from Derrida's early period, one from his later: the programmatic "La différance" and the Jerusalem lecture "How to Avoid Speaking: Denials." Both texts contain a subtle resumption of the destruction of onto-theology in the line of (and in discussion with) Heidegger.

In his first essay, Derrida emphasizes that the *différance* is preeminently the 'inexpressible.' But as the interplay of temporal and spatial differences, as the "production" of difference, it 'is' in no way "the primary prescription or the prophetic annunciation of an imminent and as yet unheard-of nomination."[69] It includes no "*ineffable Being which no name* could approach: *God, for example.*"[70] *Différance* cannot be classified in any category of Being and must not only be distinguished from a religious doctrine and imperative but also be withdrawn from the jurisdiction of any ontology or any other semantic system:

> Yet aspects which are thereby delineated are not theological, not even in the order of the most negative of negative theologies, which are always concerned with disengaging a superessentiality beyond the finite categories of essence and existence, that is, of presence, and always hastening to recall that God is refused the predicate of existence, only in order to acknowledge his superior, inconceivable, and ineffable mode of Being.[71]

In "How to Avoid Speaking," Derrida's goal is to demonstrate this proposition by using citations from Pseudo-Dionysius the Areopagite and Meister Eckhart, while his recent *Sauf le nom* (originally published as the "Post-Script" to a book entitled *Derrida and Negative Theology*[72]) further explicates this analysis in a few ostensibly freestanding comments to the work of Angelus Silesius.

---

[68] Ibid.

[69] Derrida, *Margins of Philosophy*, 27.

[70] Ibid., 26.

[71] Ibid., 6.

[72] *Sauf le nom (Post-Scriptum)*, in J. Derrida, *On the Name*, trans. J. Leavey (Stanford, Calif.: Stanford University Press, 1995).

Certainly, some mystics withhold every ontic characteristic, some-times even the predicate 'existence' from the Superior, Divine, Exist-ing. Speaking about God's 'perfection' amounts to referring to a reality on the far side of Being, or even to *more* than all that. Derrida tellingly typifies this condition. He writes that in the tradition of negative theology, the *hyper-* of the *hyperousios* attributed to God indicates both "no more being" and "being more than Being," that is, a "being more" beyond all negative and positive predication. The prefix *hyper-* refers to more than a removal in a spacial or temporal sense. It evokes more than a reality that precedes space and time, that surpasses, encompasses, or permeates them. The *hyper* also evokes a notion of hierarchy. Derrida summarizes this pluriform meaning in the expression *"plus d'être"* ("no more being and being more than Being"[73]). Negative theology's hyperbolic imagery thus doubly outdoes the thought of presence. Its project stands or falls with this strategy. For however much it succeeds with a given form of presence, the *deus absconditus*, the *theos agnostos*, about whom it is said that He surpasses all intellectual, discursive knowledge, *is not Himself nothing*. The antithesis between theism and atheism and the question of God's *existence* has lost most of its relevance here. But this does not deny that the *"plus d'être"* of His essence not only includes a negation but above all a superlative modifying Being. Even more, the most negative theology 'is' a *super-ontology*.[74]

The negative theological thinking that Derrida studies here and that to a certain extent is retraveled by him is marked by an "unusual alliance," a *double bind* of "two powers" and "two voices": first, the *"hypercritique"* that leaves nothing intact and, all things considered, undermines every philosophy, every theology, every science, and *common sense*; and, second, an affirmation that withdraws from every discussion and every critique and that sometimes can adopt an ex-tremely dogmatic tone in the tradition.

---

[73] Jacques Derrida, "How to Avoid Speaking: Denials," trans. Ken Frieden, in San-ford Budick and Wolfgang Iser, eds., *Languages of the Unsayable: The Play of Nega-tivity in Literature and Literary Theory* (New York: Columbia University Press, 1989), 3–70, 20.

[74] Also Levinas makes no secret of this hyperbolic *double bind*. In his deployment of the *via eminentiae* the *plus* has above all the meaning of being *better than Being*. But this does not deny that the way of the superlative consists less in the devalua-tion of ontology than in the attempt to outdo it: the "other-than-Being" (*autrement qu'être*) is more ontological than ontology.

By way of clarification Derrida cites Meister Eckhart's sermon "Quasi stella matutina" (Like a morning star).[75] There Eckhart states that the assertion that God proceeds "above Being" (*über Wesen*) in no way implies that He should be denied all Being. The expression stresses that Being is "heightened" (*gehöhet*). Thus the negative predications that Eckhart adopts from Augustine—"God is wise without wisdom, good without goodness, powerful without power"—are, all things considered, *denials without negativity*. Formulations in the pattern of "God is X without X" liberate God not only from all generalities, they are *hyperaffirmative*. They shed light on the "grammatical anthropomorphism"[76] inherent in the vernacular that can only express an inner-worldly—finite—negativity. Above all, they evoke a transcendent instance that, as Derrida suggests in "How to Avoid Speaking," is at once "nothing other" and "wholly other" than whatever it is that is transcended.[77] It is this process of *reiteration without strict or simple repetition* (without mimesis, analogy, or speculative reflection) that permits negative theology to augment finite language 'ad infinitum.' Thus, according to Eckhart, all Being can be considered a "gateway" to the divine space ("temple"),[78] or put differently, as a threshold that must be crossed on the way to God's *atopia*,[79] but one that also separates us from it. And, according to Pseudo-Dionysius, all anthropomorphic words and images can assume the function of 'holy allegories' if they are used and taught in the right way.[80]

The *hyperbole* of the X is above/beyond what witnesses to this transcendence and announces it. It does this in more than one sense: it not only displays it as one possibility, it also evokes it. It 'provokes' and 'produces' the structure that it describes: it is a postscript and an introduction simultaneously.

---

[75] "How to Avoid Speaking," 8. Derrida refers here to *Meister Eckharts Predigten*, ed. J. Quint (Stuttgart: Kohlhammer, 1936), 1.145–46; also available in *Sermons and Treatises*, trans. and ed. M. O.'C. Walsh (Longmead: Element, 1989), Sermon 67, in 2.149–56.

[76] "How to Avoid Speaking," 9.

[77] Ibid., 44.

[78] "Quasi stella matutina," *Predigten* 1.102. Derrida quotes this in "How to Avoid Speaking," 52.

[79] "How to Avoid Speaking," 26.

[80] Ibid., 23. The same logic of our denial also explains why, according to Derrida, mystical theology is, in a certain sense, *coextensive* with the symbolical.

Derrida's deconstruction of theology is therefore aimed against both its classical and its nonclassical concept. 'Theology' here means the hard core of the thought concerning *presence* (i.e., of the *parousia*, the logocentrism at the heart of every onto-theology) as well as the ontologizing or hypostasizing of an *absence* or lack. Every theology continues to be borne by the biblical assurance of a "someday we will see in the light." On closer analysis, this eschato-apocalyptic prospect of removing the veil in a divine manifestation makes of every theology a 'positive' argument, even when it is presented as *via negativa* or mysticism. Where one has no conceivable prospect of *a visio dei*, one has forsaken the realm of theology.

Measured against such a conception of theology, deconstruction can only be called *atheological*. It calls in question every postulation of a center that gives meaning—although it does not disclaim the desire for one—and so it examines classical and modern variants of the *via analogiae, via negationis,* and *via eminentiae* against the light of a more original 'event': a differential 'interplay' without beginning or end that literally thwarts the *existence* of every spiritual secret through its writing—through the *grammē* or, more precisely still, the series of marks.

This 'event' has an unmistakably *negative* aspect. Deconstruction brings about a certain corrosion of the authority of tradition and more: it disrupts the theological specter as well as the emotional charge of *every* sign! If it is correct that "the sign" and "the divinity," as Derrida writes, have "the same time and place of birth," if the "epoch of the sign" is "essentially theological," there ensues an unavoidable conclusion. Deconstruction of the linguistic sign shakes the foundations of nothing less than the central theological premise of Western logos—"even when it professes to be atheistic."[81] Outside 'writing' there is no question of a theological notion and 'within it,' or better, *as* 'writing,' it becomes extremely problematical.

But does this say everything? Is this the only, or even the most decisive, moment in Derrida's argument? Does the "epoch of the sign" really locate itself on the other side of the line that demarcates the religious and isolates the profane? Does Derrida's analysis describe theological difference only with an extreme asceticism, without involving himself any further, or does his analysis bear a certain

---

[81] Derrida, *Of Grammatology*, 323n3.

stamp of this theological difference as well? Is it perhaps possible to read this analysis as a revival of the discursive strategy and as an inscription of the central motif of negative theology?

In the previously cited lecture delivered in Jerusalem in 1986 under the ambiguous title "How to Avoid Speaking: Denials," this question is not answered with a mere denial. This extremely difficult and subtle text promises a more detailed development of what Derrida admits is thus far a brief, elliptical answer to the problem of how the paths of deconstruction and negative theology cross only to diverge again. "How to Avoid Speaking" nuances the delimiting line drawn in "La différance": insofar as negative theology postulates, or at least accepts as possible, a hyperessentiality and an intuitive assessment prepared by the *via negativa*, it rests on premises that can be deconstructed.

This does not deny that Derrida warns his readers to be careful. Is it so easy to speak of *the* tradition of negative theology, as if we knew what that means? Supposing, furthermore, that this negative theology can be identified as a more-or-less homogeneous corpus of texts with its own theme and rhetoric, how is one to speak of it? Is not the *via negativa* the only suitable approach to negative theology? In other words, "Is there ever anything other than a 'negative theology' of 'negative theology'?"[82] If this be the case, the intention to enumerate the agreements and differences between deconstruction and negative theology once and for all is a *promise* that can never be fulfilled. Derrida's intention, expressed in Jerusalem, to take up this subject without further delay sets up an almost impossible task. Perhaps, he suggests, this circumstance is the sought-for 'answer' to the fact that one "can never decide whether deferring, as such, brings about precisely that which it defers and alters."[83]

"How to Avoid Speaking" is a text that 'keeps' an old promise and has itself the character of a promise. There is more to be said on the complex structure of this "*Versprechen*," already analyzed by Heidegger and Paul de Man.[84] It will suffice here to note that Derrida's lecture not only, or not primarily, tries to offer a theoretical essay *about* negative theology. Rather, it consciously adopts—as always—

---

[82] Derrida, "How to Avoid Speaking," 13.
[83] Ibid.
[84] See Derrida's *Memoires: For Paul de Man* (New York: Columbia University Press, 1986).

the contours of what it describes. But this 'performative interpretation' is, in all seriousness, also a parody. Derrida does not speak of a
"fable" without reason.[85]

"How to Avoid Speaking" is, in Derrida's own words, the most
"autobiographical" text he has written thus far[86] (except, perhaps,
for the recent "Circonfession"). Yet, here, Derrida does not directly
pursue what we would expect. There is no explanation of a Jewish
(and Arabic) heritage. These resound only indirectly. That this lecture lets the way of arguing—the *via negativa*—speak for itself, has
repercussions for the contours that this text's 'author' adopts: this
'autobiographical' lecture follows or performs the figure it describes.
The question "How to Avoid Speaking?" touches more than theology, it touches the author, the self in question. How is one to avoid
speaking of oneself? How can one, in an explanation of oneself, be it
arbitrary or not, also find or discover the other?

Thus in the present text Derrida speaks about himself *in obliquo*,
in the nearly casual reference to a negative theological or quasi-mystical category of thought that is neither Greek nor Christian, but
rather Jewish or Arabic. As he says himself, he constructs his reading
of the three different paradigms that he borrows successively from
Plato, Christian mystics (particularly Pseudo-Dionysius and Eckhart), and finally Heidegger, into an open space—an emptiness or
desert, the most consistent apophasis—in which the vague echo of
this other quasi-mystical category can resonate.[87]

What permits Derrida to link his indirectly discussed 'heritage' to
the tradition of negative theology? He gives the following reason.
Wherever (philosophical, ethical-political, or literary) assertions or
presentations appear in a negative guise—and deconstructive reading is also compelled to use a similar mode of speaking and writing—a first step on the path of negative theology has already been
taken and the argument is in a certain sense 'theological.' "Every
time I say: X is neither this nor that, neither the contrary of this nor
of that, neither the simple neutralization of this nor of that with
which it has *nothing in common*, being absolutely heterogeneous to
or incommensurable with them, I would start to speak of God, under

---

[85] "How to Avoid Speaking," 30.
[86] Ibid., 31n13.
[87] Ibid., 31, 53.

this name or another."[88] The name (not the concept) of God, seen this way, represents all what cannot be named directly: " 'God' would name *that without which* one would not know to account for any negativity."[89] Even in denying or suspending God's existence, a certain *respect* can be heard, a "respect for a divine cause which does not even need to 'be.' "[90] According to Derrida, it is here that those who want to brand deconstruction a symptom of (post)modern nihilism (or, on the contrary, of the last convulsions of faith) find their primary argument. Nothing forbids such a reading. One can always with reason assert that the hyperessence of which negative theology speaks has 'the same' referent as the term *différance*, that it expresses an 'event' that does not use the terminology of Being (that is, something present or absent). It is true that such a theological annexation of deconstruction backfires and is only successful when the theological reading empties itself and the name 'God' from every proposition and reference and thereby becomes divided against itself. But this does not deny that this explanation always remains possible, even inevitable. It always remains the "opportunity" (and the risk) of an "incomparable" structure of "limitless ability to translate" that has nothing to do with a "universal language," with an "ecumenism" or a "consensus," but with a future-oriented speaking and writing that in a much more radical sense can be shared and on the basis of which the Greek, Christian, and European *apophasis* permits, or requires, numerous other translations.[91] The real question then becomes: How not to speak, now that theological speaking has become unavoidable and silence impossible?

For these reasons alone, Derrida believes that the well-known last sentence in Wittgenstein's *Tractatus-Logico-Philosophicus*—"Whereof one cannot speak, thereof one must be silent"—cannot be the last word. Derrida turns this logical inference from 'transcendental lingualism' upside down: whereof one cannot speak, thereof one *must* speak. There can, therefore, be no question of God's death *in language*. In Derrida, this 'obligation' to speak of (or from) 'God' is

---

[88] Ibid., 6.

[89] Ibid., 7.

[90] Ibid.

[91] J. Derrida, "Post-Scriptum: Aporias, Ways, and Voices," in *Derrida and Negative Theology*, eds. H. Coward and T. Foshay (Albany: State University of New York Press, 1992), 293.

not a moral obligation. It is, as with Wittgenstein, a *must*, not (or not primarily) an *ought*. Every moral obligation that one adopts with regard to this having to 'name what cannot be named' is always borne by a special structure that makes this injunction a troublesome necessity. For Derrida, this necessity differs from the necessity to keep silent that Wittgenstein analyzes in his *Tractatus*: it has less to do with the propositional structure of language than with the unavoidable risk of a *defilement* (or *contamination*) of every mark.

This structure fares poorly with the express affirmation that, not accidentally, is the converse of Wittgenstein's well-known dictum just quoted: "There are, indeed, things that cannot be put into words [Es gibt allerdings Unaussprechliches]. They make themselves manifest. They are what is mystical."(*Tractatus*, 6.522). According to Derrida, this assurance should make clear that Wittgenstein's radical imperative to be silent, like the circumscribing movement of negative theology, prepares the manifestation of an emphatic (or apophatic) reality. By contrast, this is a promise that the thought of the trace can never keep. Can a totally other 'discourse,' an articulation that precedes every enunciation of speaking and writing, possibly respect the alterity of this trace?

Sometimes it seems as if Derrida sees this respect guaranteed in prepredicative *prayer*. But a closer analysis shows that when negative theologies begin or end with prayer, this does not turn them into a *purely* performative genre. They are never protected from the accusation of secretly postulating or implying metaphysical or ontological truths. Although prayer may be antepredicative in the way it addresses the Other, Derrida leaves no doubt that it owes its very existence to a possible contamination. Praise is never purely performative (or never simply "neither true nor untrue," to use Aristotle's words). It always contains a—however implicit—constitutive component. If prayer did not contain the risk of being lost (in predication, citation, mechanical repetition, Scripture, code, or parody) and thus of missing its mark, no theology, positive or negative, would be necessary or, for that matter, possible. In a certain sense it is only the prayer's failure that calls theology into existence. Yet this 'negativity' also presupposes an indelible 'affirmation' lest the trace's lapse become inexperienceable "as such."

This appeal to the other (or others, or Other) which, says Derrida, "always already preceded the speech to which it has never been present a first time, announces itself in advance as a *recall* [*rappel,* a reminder and warning].... Prior to every proposition and even before all discourse in general—whether a promise, prayer, praise, celebration. The most negative discourse, even beyond all nihilisms and negative dialectics, preserves a trace of the other."[92] As Derrida remarks elsewhere, with the original affirmation given with (and through) the introduction of language, we are linked by a faith that cannot be eliminated by any erasure in any discourse and narrative. A text in which an erasure would be complete would be a "figure of evil" (*figure du mal*).[93]

---

[92] Derrida, "How to Avoid Speaking," 28.
[93] Jacques Derrida, *Of Spirit: Heidegger and the Question,* trans. Geoffrey Bennington and Rachel Bowlby (Chicago: University of Chicago Press, 1989), 134n.

Chapter 7

Being Open As a Form of Negative Theology

ON NOMINALISM, NEGATIVE THEOLOGY, AND DERRIDA'S PERFORMATIVE INTERPRETATION OF KHÔRA

Ilse N. Bulhof

SOME AUTHORS link Derrida's philosophy with nominalism. We may think here of Umberto Eco. In the latter's novel *The Name of the Rose* (1980) Derrida is not mentioned by name, but, as I will show in Section 1 of this chapter, he hovers in the background. It seems to me, however, that Derrida has at least as much affinity with what is known in the history of philosophy as 'negative theology' as he does with nominalism, the topic of Section 2. My purpose in tracing these affinities is not to ascertain historical lines, but to obtain a better view of what moves a postmodern thinker like Derrida.

Nominalism rejects the hopeful thought that we humans may have any direct insight into and experience of the Ultimate Reality that is God and of His creation, the reality of which we are a part. Any concepts we may make up or any names we may give do not reflect or express what is; they are merely constructs of our own making. The bond connecting things and names is a matter of convention.

Eco's *The Name of the Rose* can be read as a sketch of the nominalist climate that in many ways dominates our culture. This book is a philosophical diagnosis of our culture with some suggestions for a therapy. According to this diagnosis, our world has become 'cold' in

the wake of late medieval nominalism. In the book, nominalism is
incarnated in the person of the protagonist, William of Baskerville.
This William frees himself from the metaphysical yoke of the one
and only truth. In his student, Adso, this liberation that frees one to
seek many possible truths leads to a cold emptiness.

Eco thus leads his readers to the threshold of a new experience of
truth. It is a thinking about truth in which the need for an honest
faith in 'nice stories' (truths) is accepted in an awareness that many
truths (many nice stories) are possible, but also unavoidable: because
with our limited human understanding we have no access to the one
truth from which, in a metaphysical schema, all other truths are
derived. But although this experience of truth is present in Derrida's
work, I would like to show that Derrida adds something essential to
it. In *Khôra*,[1] an article written in a period when he worked on the
better known "How to Avoid Speaking: Denials,"[2] Derrida sketches
in Socrates a figure who does not know what truth is, who is open to
all possible truths he may meet, and who not only speaks about
openness to all possible truths but is himself open. Derrida's Socrates
exemplifies an attitude of being open. This openness is not mere
cold emptiness. Is it negative theology? No, if we mean the tradition
of *Christian* negative theology. Yes, if we mean that negative theologies—in their Greek and their Christian forms—could be an echo, a
sign of an Outside that allows itself to be experienced by those receptive to it while withdrawing from human knowledge and naming.

1. Umberto Eco on Nominalism in *The Name of the Rose*

In Eco's *The Name of the Rose* I distinguish three voices: that of
William of Baskerville, the protagonist; that of his student, Adso;

---

[1] This article appeared originally in *Poikilia: Études offertes à Jean-Pierre Vernant*
(Paris: Éditions de l'École des Hautes Études en Sciences Sociales, 1989), 265–96.
It was then published separately as *Khôra* (Paris: Éditions Galilée, 1993). It was
published in an English translation by I. McLeod in a volume of related essays by
Derrida: Thomas Dutoit, ed., *On the Name* (Stanford, Calif.: Stanford University
Press, 1995), 89–127. Hereafter the Dutoit *Khôra* will be cited in the text as K.
[2] Appeared in *Psyché. Inventions de l'autre* (Paris: Galilée, 1987), 535–94. This
text was published in Ken Frieden's English translation as *How to Avoid Speaking:
Denials*, in Sanford Budick and Wolfgang Iser, eds., *Languages of the Unsayable*
(New York: Columbia University Press, 1989), 117–39. It was reissued in Harold

and that of the author as known from the text (the implied author). In my reading, William presents nominalism to Adso and to us. Adso is its recipient. His interpretation represents (exemplifies) in its turn the way nominalism was received by modern people. The implied author uses Adso to let readers feel between the lines that nominalism works out negatively. In the background, perhaps as a double figure for the author, is Derrida, who may point the way to another answer to nominalism's question: How do we speak about that toward which our deepest desires reach—the mystery, the last divine reality, God—when it always remains above and outside all language and all understanding?

William of Baskerville (a sly reference to Sherlock Holmes? But the 'Hound of the Baskervilles' was an animal) is a logically thinking detective. "Here is the point," says William, "we must find *from the outside,* a way of describing the Aedificium as it is inside" (215).[3] With these words he does away with intuition and Aristotelian a priori thinking as a way to truth, to knowledge.[4] The knowledge that William seeks is knowledge that can be used for something, in this case to enter the heart of a building. The building was designed by a human brain using mathematics. To gather knowledge about the inside of the building, William uses a new method: he compares "our mathematical propositions with the propositions of the builder, and from this comparison science can be produced, because it is a science of terms upon terms" (215). But what of revelation? Is knowledge based on revelation not knowledge received from outside? Yes, but revelation says nothing about the created world. Nominalism shunts aside Plato's Greek doctrine about Ideas—baptized in the meantime to become a doctrine of Christ as *Logos* (Word) in whom and for whom everything is created and who, therefore, must be known if we want to understand anything about creation. Nominalism calls

---

Coward and Toby Foshay, eds., *Derrida and Negative Theology, with a Conclusion by Jacques Derrida* (Albany: State University of New York Press, 1992), 73–142. Hereafter the Coward and Foshey text will be cited in this text as HTAS.

[3] My italics. The numbers in the text refer to Umberto Eco, *The Name of the Rose,* trans W. Weaver (London: Picador, 1983).

[4] On nominalism, see Meyrick H. Carré, *Realists and Nominalists* (Oxford: Oxford University Press, 1946); Heiko Augustinus Obermann, *Gabriel Biel and Late Medieval Nominalism* (Grand Rapids, Mich.: Eerdmans, 1967); and Julius R. Weinberg, A *Short History of Medieval Philosophy* (Princeton, N.J.: Princeton University Press, 1964), 235–65. See also the Introduction to this volume.

this doctrine idle speculation. The world may well have been created by God's Word, but the Word does not impose its stamp on the world. Instead of knowledge, mediated by revelation in Christ, William introduces knowledge gained through the modern association of mathematics and experiment. Why mathematics? Only mathematics is useful in gathering trustworthy information. Only in mathematics "are the things known to us identified with the things known absolutely [that is, as God knows them]"(215). Absolute or certain knowledge is only thought to be possible about things people have made or designed themselves. Mathematical axioms are a prime example. So are hypotheses. Why experiments? Because experiments must help determine whether the mathematical model accurately reflects reality, whether the hypothesis may pass from hypothesis to thesis. Monological mathematical thinking combined with experimentation allows the knowing spirit to gather knowledge independently—that is, in medieval terms, without the help of revelation.

Nominalism starts from the humble awareness that profound knowledge about God and His work, creation, is impossible. This awareness is a jolt. It disenchants people enamored by their illusions, who believe in fairy tales. Adso, William's helper, thought in his naive innocence that the world was beautiful—especially when he was young and in love, linked in a web of love with a poor and simple girl. When looking at oxen, for example, he saw them "as they were and are, symbols of friendship and goodness, because every ox at his work turns to seek his companion at the plow; if by chance the partner is absent at that moment, the ox calls him with affectionate lowing" (282–83). Lowing is natural for an ox. Its lowing means that the ox is never alone, that he is linked by desire with other oxen. Being in love, Adso was moved "by the spiritual sweetness toward the Creator and the rule of his world, and with joyous veneration [he] admired the greatness and the stability of creation" (284). But Adso's love for the girl has no future. A young monk may not lose himself in earthly passions, and the girl (she meets her unfortunate fate later) is but a wench not to be taken seriously. This hapless creature is the only woman in this story about a world in which women did not count. When love has passed—an event that parallels the effects of William's teaching—Adso's illusions about the world disappear with it. Love's bonds to the world are cut. There is

no more anthropomorphic thinking, no more projecting of his subjective feelings onto nature.

You have to know something about God if you want to recognize
Him in His creatures. But the 'modern' way of philosophy (in the
Middle Ages they spoke of nominalism as the *via moderna*) knows
nothing a priori: it must investigate everything itself and, to the extent that it is philosophy, does not know the story of God and the
world. Because nominalism makes stories—for example, the Christian story—impossible as sources of truth, it also makes symbolism
impossible as well as negative theologies such as that of Dionysius
the Areopagite that were developed partly on the basis of that story.
It thus contributed to the devaluation of the earth.

Are doing mathematics, on the one hand, and trusting in God's
revelation, on the other, the only ways of gathering knowledge?
What about reading human books and human words? Are books
not places where people tell of their experience, where knowledge is
preserved? Yes. But that leads to the question of whether everything
that is written down is really true. A library does not necessarily represent a treasury of truth. It is a "place of a long, centuries-old mur-
muring, an imperceptible dialogue between one parchment and
another, a living thing, a receptacle of powers not to be ruled by a
human mind, a treasure of secrets emanated by many minds, surviving the death of those who had produced them or had been their
conveyors" (*scripta manent*). Is a library, then, an instrument "not
for distributing truth, but for delaying its appearance?" Adso asks
dumbfounded (286). Indeed a library *can* be, William answers. But
it does not have to be so; a library's texts are not certain or true in
advance. Humanists could say that a feeling for nuances and a sense
of contextuality are necessary for making distinctions if we are to tell
in texts the true from the false. These are abilities that are acquired
in the process of learning to read texts. But William has a completely
different way of distinguishing true from false: the modern combination of logical thinking and the formulation and testing of hypotheses—a method William uses with success in his search for the
murderer in the monastery. William thinks in binary schemes: yes/
no, either/or. He does not distinguish, he separates and then eliminates. In binary either/or thinking, a feeling for nuances is not essential: it only has meaning in the area between extremes—the area
where the two are mixed together.

Texts present problems of interpretation that do not use mathematics for their solution: they could be interpreted via many ways,
on various levels (literal, moral, mystical). Thus the question of the
texts' truth includes the question of who has the *authority* to determine what the texts handed down say: the pope, or the people of
God who, via their theologians, demand the right to interpret Scripture themselves (313)? Now we understand: by fleeing into mathematics as the best way to truth, William—when it comes to the
crunch, still a man of the Church—avoids choosing between the
pope and the people of God.

The new way of gathering truth, true knowledge of the world, is
therefore the creation of mathematical models and the empirical
testing of these self-developed possible truths or hypotheses; examining with our own eyes whether they are correct; testing whether
what is said really corresponds to reality, and can function as a thesis.
William contrasts this way of finding truth with the proud Greek—
Aristotelian—way: logically reasoning from first principles in which
human reason, as it were, appropriates the way of knowing of divine
reason, sits in God's chair—as if people had created the world and
thus knew thoroughly what they had created (313).

But mathematics does justice to only one aspect of reality: the
measurable aspect. For the rest, nominalism insists that human
knowledge can never go beyond the stage of faith, can never be absolutely certain. What is proudly said about reality always misses the
point, is always in error. But it unfortunately happens that people
forget the insufficiency of their reason, that they feel certain of what
is essentially faith (errors). It happens that they, as if they were God
Himself, claim truth for their own insights—that is, they make *idols*
of their insights. In the novel, this occurs particularly in "Paris," at
the "University" where the Christian philosopher Aristotle is accepted on faith. A nominalist believer dissociates himself from this
"Parisian" and "University" idolatry of homemade concepts and
harebrained schemes. He respects in faith the God unknowable to
and unreachable by reason: a God who eternally transcends all that
people say.

A parenthetical remark: William ignores the possibilities of mysticism, of mystical or negative theology, for example, undoubtedly because he thinks it another type of pride—the type where people
believe they can know God directly (intuitively, 'intueri' in Latin)

and thus believe that in one way or another they know what He is. Nominalism, obsessed by the pride of those who believe they can know God by using their own reason, wants to have nothing to do with it; it ignores a priori thinking as well as mysticism.

Truth is one and unchangeable, but is not knowable. A one and knowable truth leads to *tyranny*, because it permits but two possibilities: *either* to accept the truth as truth, thus belief, *or* not to accept it, and thus unbelief. If the (one) truth were knowable, it would leave people with no authentic options. A one knowable truth becomes a yoke to which people must submit; it leads to inhuman situations; it claims the whole person. It has dominion, its word is law, it has authority, and brings with it power, enforcement, and inquisition. As the institutions where the knowledge of truth and the power that accompanies it are concentrated, Pope and Church (or State) are the obedient executors of what this one powerful truth commands people to be and do. Can this subjugation be the message of Christian revelation? No. This one knowable truth must be a human fabrication, an idol. We are left with the conclusion that the 'real' (true) truth unknowable to reason is a matter of faith alone, faith in revelation.

William frees himself from the one knowable truth, and he "had to venture some hypotheses. [He] had to venture many" (305). In the place of the one truth he puts several (incorrect?) guesses. As he says, "but instead of conceiving only one [i.e., truth or 'guess'] I imagine many, so I become the slave of none" (306). The nominalist mentality is incarnated in William's emphasis on *freedom*. Nominalism freed from authority those people who were aware that all knowledge consists of guesses. Thanks to the liberation from the one knowable truth, people could decide for themselves which guesses deserve to be taken seriously and be maintained. Instead of the pole of the one truth, William puts another pole, that of many guesses, one of which could be true.

What kind of faith does a nominalist have? A faith tempered by *skepticism*, a faith that is the opposite of dogmatic belief. Old Jorge, with all his piety, is a human monster, a very devil. The devil is born "from piety itself, from excessive love of God or of the truth, as the heretic is born from the saint and the possessed from the seer. Fear prophets, Adso, and those prepared to die for the truth" (491). According to William, total and undissociated (mystical?) faith is devilry. A total faith forbids inquiry. Whoever disagrees with authority must be eliminated. Without skepticism, not to say doubt, faith becomes inhuman.

A text hidden by Jorge and sought by William and Adso teaches (like a hidden gospel, a hidden, liberating good news) how not to become "the slaves of our ghosts" (491). "The only truth lies in learning to free ourselves from insane passion for the truth." May there yet be a single truth?

William explains that there is a "literal" and a "higher" truth (315). Since the time of Philo the Jew (A.D. 25–50) people have agreed that Scripture has many layers of meaning. Very simple passages have a deep hidden meaning, such as the story of the Exodus from Egypt which also and primarily narrates the ascension of the soul to God. Historical or *literal* truth is the report of what happened or of what is, for example, the story of Jesus, or the stories about the chosen people. But when William mentions stories with hidden meanings, Adso thinks of a completely different kind of story: stories from profane literature about unicorns. What is presented in profane texts as literal truth can and must be tested for truth: otherwise we cannot know whether what is told is true or not. In the context of distinguishing and testing newly discovered truth, verification takes the place of logical reasoning and reliance on authorities. In the process, the 'higher' truth (moral, allegorical, mystical), which is the really important truth, the truth that the author 'really' means to say, becomes separated from the 'lower.' Adso quickly realizes where this radical separation of higher and lower can lead when applied to Scripture: the higher truth of Scripture can be correct, while the lower literal truth is not, is illogical, is untrue, or lies. To give an example that anticipates history: figuratively speaking, according to Scripture, people are at the center of the cosmos. But this is not literally true. It can also be the reverse: the verifiable literal truth can speak truly, be true (in the seventeenth century people thought this of nature), while the higher truth (e.g., the symbolic character of the 'book of nature' or God's authorship of nature considered as a book) is a product of imagination, nonsense.

As William gradually learns, a text lay at the basis of the murders perpetrated in the monastery: not Scripture, of course, but a text by Aristotle about *laughter* long thought lost. The old monk Jorge, whom I mentioned earlier, a Benedictine (unlike William, who belonged to the much younger Franciscan order), tried to keep the book away from unauthorized readers. Jorge believed that fear was essential to leading a good life, and for the maintenance of social order (good, since given by God). Without fear of hell and damnation there is no reason for doing good.[5] For Jorge, laughter was mundane and a prime means (opium!) for simple people to cope with their lot. Among simple people laughter can do no harm, is even useful. But laughter becomes dangerous when philosophers and theologians discover it as a weapon against fear and even cultivate it as such. The carnavalesque reversal in which a drunken farmer drinks away one day of the year, a reversal that liberates him for a short time from the fear of God, threatens to become permanent if philosophers and theologians, those at the top of the social pyramid, discover the power of laughter. Jorge fears that then laughter "would be defined as the new art, unknown even to Prometheus, for canceling fear" (475). Indeed, laughter liberates, it has a *democratizing effect*: it turns slavish farmers into autonomous people, kings. How does one organize a population consisting only of kings? In other words, How is democracy possible? This question never occurred to William. His problem is the power of the pope. Laughter (comedy, satire, mimicry)—denigrating, revealing laughter in the form of ridicule and ironic or comic repetition—becomes the new miracle drug against the sickness caused by oppressive faith in the one truth and the authority of those who pretend to know the truth. Laughter purifies emotions by holding up to view faults, shortcomings, and weaknesses (think of Erasmus's *In Praise of Folly*[6])by pulling down the mighty.

The medicine of laughter can lead scholars "to redeem the lofty" by "the acceptance of the base," by accepting, for example, eating and drinking and mundane pleasure (sex?). If laughter were to become the medicine of the future and if the lower pleasures were to be taken seriously, asks Jorge, "would it not prompt the idea that man can *wish* to have on earth . . . the abundance of the land of Cockaigne?" (475). Without fear of hell and damnation, personal

---

[5] A few centuries later Descartes will also emphasize the importance of fear in the letter with which he offered his *Méditations* to the theologians of the Sorbonne.

[6] Erasmus of Rotterdam, *In Praise of Folly*, trans. R. H. Hudson (Princeton, N.J.: Princeton University Press, 1941). For praise of this book, see J. Huizinga, "Erasmus," in *Verzamelde Werken* (Haarlem: Tjeenk Willink, 1950), 6.66–74.

gain, one's own ego, will, body, stomach, and so on, will be given free rein.

William says: "It is hard to accept the idea that there cannot be an order in the universe because it would offend the free will of God and His omnipotence" (492–93). Why *can* there be no order? Is it impossible in the sense of "for us unthinkable"? Or in the sense of "ontologically impossible"? In other words, is it necessarily the case that in a contingent world created by a free God there can be no order, that there is only *chaos*? Indeed, "the freedom of God" becomes our condemnation, or at least the condemnation of our pride (493). God becomes a Being "totally polluted with the possible," a Being without essence (e.g., being good, being love), without 'Being.'[7] Adso concludes that God is something like "primogenital chaos" (493), that God is not, as he writes later before his death, "the God of glory, . . . or of joy, perhaps not even of piety"—the God he was taught about in his youth. God becomes "lauter Nichts," "broad desert perfectly level and boundless," "divine shadow," "dumb silence." Adso worries that "[a]ll equality and all inequality shall be lost," that "no one finds his proper place." He sees his approaching death as a falling "into the silent and uninhabited divinity where there is no work and no image" (501).

These last words echo remarkably the words of Meister Eckhart and Angelus Silesius, representatives of Dionysius's negative theology. What are these allusions doing in Eco's text? Apart from the quotations from Eckhart, this last short paragraph from *The Name of the Rose* does not at all recall negative theology.[8] In the context of William's nominalism, the quotations mean something entirely different than in Eckhart. The book's closing passages begin with words that recall Nietzsche's fragment *Der tolle Mensch*[9] in which

---

[7] Cf. J.-L. Marion, *Dieu sans l'être—Hors-texte* (Paris: Fayard, 1982); English translation, *God without Being: Hors Texte* (Chicago: University of Chicago Press, 1991). See also Victor Kal's chapter in this book.

[8] In his essay "Teken, waarheid, macht," in *De intersubjectiviteit van het zijn* (Kampen: Kok, 1988), T. van Velthoven notes that Eco in *The Name of the Rose* skillfully articulates the nominalistic experience of reality. But in his interpretation of the novel's close he places an accent that differs from mine: he reads in it a negative theology and interprets the quotations from Eckhart and Angelus Silesius as expressions of Adso's mystical interest. He even speaks of the novel's "mystical conclusion."

[9] F. Nietzsche, *The Gay Science*, fragment 125.

the death of God is proclaimed: "it is cold in the scriptorium . . ." (502). Included in a nominalist exposition and read and understood through a nominalistic lens, the rich darkness of mysticism and the superessential Being that is Nothing (Eckhart) leaves behind only a modern, bare emptiness.[10] The highest Being as Super-Being that is central to Dionysius's theological-philosophical exposition is not present in nominalism's pared-down philosophical exposition.

For Adso, a child of his time, made a student of nominalism by time and circumstances, there is no rehabilitation in *The Name of the Rose* for narratives as places of possible truth. They are places of *elimination* of narrative. He loses his confidence in the old stories and in language. The end of the book shows this loss when Adso feels cold and sees the return to God as a disappearance into silent nothing.

Effects of Nominalism in the Present Cultural Context

Not much has become of nominalism's liberation. While nominalism emphasized human freedom, it also stressed the contingency of the world. It thus contributed to the formation of new forms of subjugation: in the world of faith, a subjugation to a hard, loveless God the Father who did not make the world for His children; in the world of thought, a subjugation to 'reality.'[11]

William discovered that the universe is not ordered, and he considered this "the only truth." But even this assertion could, in the framework of his own thinking, be nothing other than an 'error'—an opinion, a conviction, and thus one of the many possible (partial?) truths or stories. In viewing human opinions as hypotheses, we get the impression (even now) that after testing hypotheses, *one* (and that is *the*) truth remains. If it is assumed the universe is without

---

[10] The modern emptiness is the emptiness of the empty fullness of the economic cycle; cf. E. Berns, "Derrida's huishouding," *Algemeen Nederlands Tijdschrift voor Wijsbegeerte* (1990): 269–81.

[11] Ilse N. Bulhof, *The Language of Science: A Study of the Relationship between Literature and Science in the Perspective of a Hermeneutical Ontology, with a Case Study of Darwin's "The Origin of Species"* (Leiden: Brill, 1992), 129–48. Modern empirical natural sciences helped replace the authority of texts (Holy Scripture, Church Fathers, Aristotle) with another authority: nature itself. The question 'true or false?' was, from then on, tested against 'reality,' as it is known to the sciences that perform experimental research.

order, truth might still be seen as a temporary or local truth, as a
truth that is good and satisfactory for a time in a specific situation—
but it would definitely not be the last word always and everywhere.
But William does not reach this view of the truth.[12] William's confidence in mathematics witnesses to the same pride that he attributed to the followers of Aristotle. But neither he nor Adso saw that.
They were too deeply under the impression of the new methods of
finding truth and the discoveries that solved the murders, which
brought that truth to light—even though it was at the cost of the
library, that is, of humanism and humanity.

We could state that the ideal of divine omniscience degrades
human knowledge to 'mere' opinions, half truths, lies. What can be
the validity of human knowledge when absolute knowledge, God's
kind of knowledge, is presumed to be the only real knowledge?

Summarizing my reading of *The Name of the Rose*, I would say
that William and Adso exemplify the form that the inability to speak
about what people really want to know (truth, God) has taken in the
West. It is a form in which there is no place for love, desire, Platonic
Eros, for wisdom or Christian love of God, or put differently, for
being fascinated or called by mystery. All the ties of love that bound,
and could again bind, have been severed. Despite all the good intentions of philosophers and theologians to liberate people, and of people to liberate themselves, nominalism ultimately became one cause
of the 'entrapment' of Western culture in nihilism. *The Name of
the Rose* shows how the perspicacious and independent William's
nominalism led to emptiness, to a purely formal and naked freedom,
and to a desert of nihilism in his student Adso.

But this development, this interpretation of Being's transcendence, was not inevitable. There were and are other ways beside
nominalism for avoiding a totalizing faith or a totalizing science.
Could Derrida's deconstruction be one?

In *The Name of the Rose* there are frequent allusions to Derrida.
We see Derrida, for example, in the distinction between lower (literal) and higher (figurative) truth. Derrida would take the following
step: that the higher truth can be nonsense while the lower truth is

---

[12] Cf. T. Adorno on nominalism in his *Negative Dialectics* (New York: Seabury
Press, 1973), 49–57: "A genuinely critical philosophy's relation to nominalism is not
invariant; it changes historically with the function of scepticism" (49n1).

true invalidates the whole idea of a distinction between a higher and a lower truth. When it comes to the crunch, what is literal truth? In a text, it is a report of an experience, a more-or-less exact eyewitness report. But over time anything can be made of this report in repeating and copying it, once it can no longer be verified. Anything we receive, any book we have before us, contains only traces of the original report. According to Derrida, a sign of the thing is an image, and the image is a sign of a sign. The 'original' of which the text tells, what is called the 'literal truth,' has disappeared from sight.[13]

In speaking of the role of laughter, which Jorge so opposes, we also meet Derrida, the Derrida who with his deconstruction strategy surprisingly undermines the authority of all the texts that theology, philosophy, and modern culture consider sacred. We meet him again in a comment such as "when what had been marginal would leap to the center and every trace of the center [here we can think of the old center, God] would be wiped out" (475).

Again we meet Derrida when we read of William's new way of gaining knowledge which opens visions of "a different truth" than what Aristotle understood, "a different image of the truth," truth as deceit: "deceit is necessary and to surprise in deceit, . . . to say one thing and to mean another" (284). To say the one and mean the other—is this using metaphors?[14] Is this irony? Ridiculing the truth? Or art?

But, I would like to ask, is a multiplicity of possible truths in itself liberating? Is pluralism alone sufficient? And is the idea of pluralism all that Derrida has to offer us? Is not something essential missing from this view of Derrida: his sensitivity for an Outside that can never be encapsulated in language and thought?

Through the occurrence of signs in the text that link Derrida with nominalism, nominalism becomes the atrium to deconstructionist

---

[13] Cf. Derrida in *De la grammatologie* (Paris: Éditions du Minuit, 1967), English translation by Gayatri Chakravorty Spivak, *Of Grammatology* (Baltimore and London: Johns Hopkins University Press, 1976), 36: "Representation mingles with what it represents. . . . There is no longer a simple origin. . . . The reflection, the imagine, the double splits what it doubles. The origin of the speculation becomes a difference."

[14] Cf. Derrida, "La mythologie blanche," in *Marges— de la philosophie* (Paris: Éditions du Minuit, 1972), English translation by Alan Bass, as "White Mythology," in *Margins of Philosophy* (Chicago: University of Chicago Press, 1982).

thinking; and conversely, the latter is given nominalism as prehistory, it is put in this history.

But I believe that Derrida's thinking can be seen differently: as a criticism of nominalism's repercussions in our time, and as an effect of what remains outside philosophical exposition and outside the horizon of nominalism and has been hinted at by many theological and philosophical names.

2. DERRIDA AND NEGATIVE THEOLOGY

In "How to Avoid Speaking: Denials" Derrida states that negative theology is anything but a clearly delimited and defined phenomenon. Even Dionysius speaks in the plural of negative *theologies*. Negative theology has different paradigms, we could say, different examples, occasions, resumptions, versions. For example, in Meister Eckhart and Dionysius, both considered representatives of negative theology, we find very different expositions of the superessential divinity of God, a divinity that cannot be fully manifested in words.[15]

But the negative theological style of thinking and writing is not limited to Christian writers; there are also non-Christian versions or paradigms such as the work of 'post-Christians' like Heidegger and of a 'pre-Christian' like Plato. In the following section I discuss Derrida's reflection on possible contacts between Heidegger's thinking and negative theology.

Did Heidegger Write Negative Theology?

According to Derrida, Heidegger's paradigm of negative theology has a completely unique character: it is neither Greek nor Christian. The theme's development is scattered throughout Heidegger's writings.

Derrida points to Heidegger's reinterpretation of negativity expressed in a highly unusual way of writing. Heidegger crosses out the

---

[15] For an interesting view of the relationship between Derrida and Eckhart, see John D. Caputo, "Mysticism and Transgression: Derrida and Meister Eckhart," in J. Silverman, ed., *Derrida and Deconstruction* (New York and London: Routledge, 1989), 24–39. See also Caputo, *The Prayers and Tears of Jacques Derrida: Religion without Religion* (Bloomington: Indiana University Press, 1997), part 1, "The Apophatic."

word 'Being' in his text: he puts a cross (X) through it. The word is there, you can still see it, yet it is not there, it is crossed out. This implies that for Heidegger Being is not a normal word to be represented in a normal way of writing and printing, like the word 'God' is always written with an initial capital. The crossed-out word 'Being' shows it "celebrated": gathered together, put in the center of the cross of four lines (heaven, earth, mortals, and gods) and as a point, the tip of a dagger (HTAS, 126). The place of the Nothing? This must also be crossed out. For Heidegger, Being is not God and not nothing.

Another unusual practice Heidegger uses to show that Being is something unusual is his avoiding using the word 'Being,' not writing it at all, not letting it appear in or touch the text (HTAS, 126). During a lecture[16] Heidegger orally explained this strange way of (non-)writing by linking it to a project that he wanted someday to complete: to the writing of a theology. "If I ever write a theology (and I would like to) the word 'Being' would not be used in it." Heidegger does not *use* the word 'Being,' he only *mentions* it, and such a mention need not be crossed out. When Heidegger crosses out or avoids the word, is he, Derrida asks, practicing negative theology? Has he not always wanted to write a negative theology? Is not that what he had always been doing? With a reference to Luther, Heidegger says later that "Faith does not need the notion of Being." Being is neither the foundation nor the essence of God. The experience of God, the experience of revelation, nevertheless occurs in the dimension of Being (or arrives in this dimension). Heidegger's view of revelation is clearly not the Christian view, although it is striking that he still uses the word. Derrida notes that by 'revelation' Heidegger understands the *possibility* of revelation in religions—for example, the Christian—a possibility, we could say, that the various religions can define further. For Heidegger, the experience of God is the opening, the empty *openness* for the revelation of religions. The dimension of Being (not a hierarchy, not a voice in us, not our common or philosophical understanding) opens for Heidegger the breach to the arrival of (or the meeting with) God-who-is-not. The frighten-

---

[16] Heidegger met with some students in Zurich in 1951 and responded to their questions. A transcript of this discussion was published in French by F. Fédier and D. Saatdjian in *Poésie*, 13 (1980).

ing experience of emptiness, openness, or 'nothing' gives access to (or opens) Being, gives access to God—the God for whom Being is neither essence nor foundation. Derrida highlights the notion that in this lecture Heidegger denies any link between God and Being—but in doing so, indicates a sort of proximity. How does Derrida think we should represent Heidegger's relation to theology?

Heidegger distinguishes on one side onto-theology, which is no real theology, for it is a *theiology*: a speaking about the highest being, the foundation, the *causa sui* in his divinity; and on the other side real *theology*: Christian knowledge, a knowledge based on faith and revelation (the divine Word). Derrida asks whether what Heidegger said during this lecture was *theiology* or *theology* (and then whether a negative theiology or a negative theology)? Does Heidegger join the tradition of negative theology or does he deny it? Heidegger does not speak of negative theology, except for once, briefly, in a footnote in *Sein und Zeit* (1927),[17] and then in relation to the question of how we are to speak of God's eternity.

In "How to Avoid Speaking: Denials" Derrida does not go further into what Heidegger may have thought of the latter's relation to negative theology. But he thinks that Heidegger in this lecture and in his further work wrote *theology* "with and without the word God, with and without God."

One side of Dionysius's negative theological use of language fascinates Derrida endlessly: that it is *more* than a language of failure, more than an abandoning of knowledge, conceptual determination, and analysis. Dionysius's exposition is a *prayer* to a Thou, the superessential Trinity. That prayer takes the form of praise, the way of speaking that best agrees with the essence of the Christian Trinitarian God, the form that this God provokes, elicits. The exposition of Dionysius's negative theology is a thoroughly religious exposition: it is not *about* God (it is not theology as we usually think of it) but a *speaking to* God.

Derrida distinguishes two types of prayer: one 'minimal' form as the act of turning to another as other, for example, in the form of asking and supplicating, especially making a supplication for a prom-

---

[17] This note can be found in *Sein und Zeit* (Tübingen: Niemeyer, 1927). This work has been reprinted often. The reference (in chap. 6, toward the end of para. 81) is to the 1963 edition, p. 427, note 1. Cf. D. Scheltens, "Middeleeuwse illuminatieleer en het denken van Heidegger," *Tijdschrift voor Filosofie* 21 (1969): 416–40, 429.

ise of presence; and a 'maximal' prayer as praise and celebration. We find this last form in Dionysius, but not in Heidegger. Does Derrida find the first form in Heidegger?

At first glance, no. Heidegger pronounces no Thou, neither to God, nor to students, nor to readers. But what does this mean? That there is, after all, no negative theology in Heidegger? Perhaps there are more possibilities in his texts. Derrida suggests two.

The first is the most obvious: Heidegger did not write a *theology* (as distinct from *theio*logy) (we must remember that Derrida began in "How to Avoid Speaking: Denials" by saying that what he, Derrida, does is not negative theology). For Heidegger says that faith has nothing to do with thinking. Thinking cannot help faith and grace. Faith and thought are two very different matters. You could thus posit that faith does not think, does not have thinking as task. Because Heidegger's texts are written in an indicative mood and not in the style of prayer, they represent thinking.

A second possibility is that Heidegger's writing witnesses to a deep respect for prayer. Must a prayer be written down, quoted? Does it have a place in an agogic exposition? Does this not offend the nature of, even pervert, a prayer? Does not Heidegger's not writing it down show the deepest respect for the Thou that cannot be captured in texts and words? Indeed, we could wonder whether Heidegger's 'preparatory thinking' and thinking as "Andenken" (recollection) is not a form of the second kind of prayer: supplication for a sign.

On the other side we may also wonder whether we have the right to think that a prayer may never be alienated from its present by noting it down or quoting it or multiplying it. This, in its turn, raises the question of whether we have the right to think that a prayer is a one-time event (HTAS, 130)?

Taken all together, Derrida sticks to his own conclusion that Heidegger wrote a theology—with or without God.

But what of Derrida himself? Does Derrida's interpretation of Dionysius, Eckhart, and Heidegger say something about his own philosophizing and his own relationship to negative theology? We can find an answer to this question in the second article, *Khôra*.

Derrida and Negative Theology in Khôra

The article *Khôra* is about the way the word 'khôra' should be interpreted in Plato's dialogue *Timaeus*. Because khôra is a little-known and difficult-to-understand phenomenon, I will first say something about it.

A Greek-vernacular dictionary gives several possible translations: place, spot, space, ground, and residence. The English translation of *Timaeus* renders the word with *'receptacle.'* In *Timaeus* Plato says of khôra that it is "a third kind" or "class," between model and copy, the two known elements from Plato's philosophy. He describes it as "the receptacle" of all becoming, "as it were the nurse,"[18] "the substance which receives all bodies the same account must be given,"[19] "in no wise does it assume any shape similar to any of the things that enter into it. For it is laid down by nature as a moulding-stuff for everything."[20] Khôra resembles sometimes this, other times that because she/it is changed by what enters she/it. Plato considers this "receiving principle" comparable to "the mother," and notes of khôra, that as that which is to receive all forms she/it should be "itself devoid of all those forms which it is about to receive from any quarter."[21] He concludes his presentation with these words:

> Wherefore, let us not speak of her that is the Mother and Receptacle of this generated world, which is perceptible by sight and all the senses, by the name of earth or air or fire or water, or any aggregates or constituents thereof: rather, if we describe her as a kind invisible and unshaped, all-receptive, and in some most perplexing and most baffling way partaking of the intelligible, we shall describe her truly.[22]

Derrida speaks in *Khôra* of a *"réceptacle"* cognate with the English *"receptacle,"* a gathering or storage place; and of *"réceptivité"* cognate with English *"receptivity,"* a sensitivity for impressions and influences.

Like Heidegger's, Plato's speaking about khôra is not a negative theology—if that term refers exclusively to Dionysius's type of thinking. In *Timaeus* there is no question of a gift, a promise, an event. Khôra has nothing of the superessential Trinity of Christian negative

---

[18] Plato, *Timaeus, Critas, Cleitophon, Menexenus, Epistles*, Loeb Classical Library 7, trans. R. G. Bury (Cambridge, Mass., and London: Harvard University Press/ Heinemann, 1942). On khôra and related topics, see chaps. 49–53, 112–27, esp. 113.

[19] Ibid., 117.

[20] Ibid.

[21] Ibid., 119. I. McLeod translates 'her,' Plato uses the neuter form. I will refer to khôra as 'she/it' or 'her/it' as Derrida does.

[22] Ibid.

theology. Khôra does not invite to prayer, celebration, or praise; Khôra is not a Thou; khôra is not a triple whole. Yet, to the extent that Derrida shows us, we find in *Timaeus* (and even more in Derrida's interpretation of khôra in *Timaeus*) the same kind of negative language. Khôra is something totally different, not even transcendent; it is removed or near. Khôra is on one side mother and nurturer, and on the other side virgin. She/It is not a link to the father. She/It has no descendants, children. She/It is not fertile, or overflowing with goodness.

Interpretations fixate what is open in what is to be interpreted. This is also true of the interpretation of khôra. The many interpretations given the word fixate her/it in our expositions (K, 94). Interpretations are like a seal that leaves an impression on or gives shape to wax. But in the interpretation of khôra as given in *Timaeus* matters are essentially different than with wax: in fixating the meaning, *she/it itself* is not touched. She/It is never exhausted (used up) by such impressions. Khôra remains formless, amorphic, 'virgin,' it "seems *to receive* the impressions and *give them a place*" (K, 95). But the form that khôra receives is not eidos (*eidos* = idea), she/it becomes no image of a shape. She/It is thus not something that can be known or recognized, she/it does not belong to that order. This not-being can only announce herself/itself; she/it cannot let herself/itself be grasped, or enclosed in concepts—thus not in anthropomorphic schemas of receiving and giving a place. Derrida goes further to explain that this giving a place is not really a giving; and that to 'receive a place' is also a question (K, 95).

In his text Derrida speaks only of khôra (e.g., "this is also true of khôra," "in interpretations of khôra") not of *the* khôra: this would be to limit khôra. Nor does he speak of the *word* 'khôra': a word is not in this way to be separated from the thing it names (as word as concept is separable from the thing, or the meaning is separable from the reference). This is certainly true of the word 'khôra.' Distinctions between word and thing imply on one side a specific thing that is different from others, for example, a book or a pen, and on another side linguistic acts that name this thing.

Is khôra, then, a proper name, is it a person, a woman (e.g., a mother, nurse)? No. For Plato only *compares* khôra with a woman. Khôra is thus not 'really' a woman named 'Khôra.' Derrida emphasizes the theme that through such a comparison, certainly in the

Greek culture of the period, the author and the reader associated the
receptacle with the feminine element. In the Greek context that
means with passive, virginal material, as we know the concept from
Aristotle (material, Greek: *hyle*). From other texts we know that Derrida, unlike Plato, does not care for metaphors as comparisons between different matters. Here that is important because by not
comparing khôra to a woman he prevents us from viewing khôra in
an Aristotelian way. But even though Derrida does not make comparisons, he rejects interpreting khôra as a personal name. She/It is
unique, one-of-a-kind, but however unique she/it may be, the referent of the name does not exist: the reference, he says, points "to
something that is not a thing, that insists on its mysterious unicity,
that lets itself be (or has itself be) called without answering, without
letting itself be seen, without showing itself, without letting itself
be grasped or determined." This something—this khôra—is thus an
'excursus.'

This 'something' is an 'X' that itself has nothing, nothing of 'its
own,' owns nothing; in Derrida's text, there follows a whole ritual of
denials, a ritual met repeatedly. It reminds us of prayer formulas.

In our culture of ownership, something without possessions like
khôra is almost an "impropriety."[23] But it is true that having nothing
of its own, no possession that khôra must keep (*garder*), is precisely
what "must be *kept for it*, what *we* must keep for it" (K, 97) (*qu'il
faut lui garder*—Derrida's italics). Not having anything of its own
also means not having any individual characteristics, not even any
feminine characteristics (motherly, nurturing). But to say that khôra
has no feminine characteristics does not mean that words like
'mother' or 'nurse' are 'merely' rhetorical in the sense of language
that says nothing. Apparently the reader must be shaped by the language used by Plato/Derrida in this article.

How are we to 'let' khôra have no characteristics? By realizing that
khôra does not receive for herself/itself, that she/it only loans herself/
itself (*se prête*, the same expression Derrida uses of God in his reflections on Dionysius) to those characteristics she/it receives. That
is what 'receiving' is for khôra. We could say that real receiving is

---

[23] The French *'impropre'* means 'unsuitable,' hence 'incorrect'; khôra's 'impro-
priété' thus implies both having nothing *of its own* and that it is unsuitable, incorrect, even unseemly.

being and remaining open. Can she/it receive just anything at all? Yes—Plato's only restriction is that she/it always be approached in the same way, always be spoken of with the same language, always be named with the same language (K, 98). Is this way that must remain the same unique in the sense of only being valid in these passages in *Timaeus*? Or are these passages in *Timaeus* an example of the way something, an X, khôra, must always be approached? According to Derrida, it is not so much the name but the appellation (*appellation*) that remains the same and can in this way be translated, moved. This approach indicates, I would say, a single attitude. An attitude of prayer?

The many interpretations produced new objects in khôra (children? How can we avoid such an association in our culture?); they left behind other sediments (semen); innumerable exegeses have been given, to Plato's text and to khôra itself, to that X. Once khôra has been spoken of as Plato speaks of her/it in the *Timaeus*, this way of speaking, this exposition, sets the tone for the future, for other ways of speaking about her/it. It becomes dominant. Put generally, Plato's discourse is a speaking that brings to the fore the visible, the demonstrable, in *Timaeus*: the cosmos as living, visible heaven, the sensible God, who is unique, the only one of its kind, the highest Being. The Platonic discourse did not know what to do with khôra. The 'metaphysical tradition' that gives preferred place to the visible, the demonstrable (demonstrative method!), begins with Plato. Does it end with Derrida who writes about khôra? Or with Heidegger who, although he never used the word 'khôra,' speaks of the *Lichtung*, the open place in the forest, and who said in so many words that he wants to think 'postmetaphysically'?[24]

Whatever the case, khôra receives all interpretations or 'determinations' and gives them a place, but possesses none of them for herself/itself. She/It does not own them (K, 99), she/it is not the present support (subject) on which all these interpretations rest. This not-being-a-support, this "absence of support provokes *and* resists any binary and dialectectical determination" (K, 100). That is to say, it provokes every kind of philosophical speech, while resisting the same. Philosophical speaking is defied and thus receives new force.

---

[24] As was argued in the Introduction to this book, philosophical theology as metaphysical tradition ends with Nietzsche.

Plato compares khôra with a nurse and mother, the demiurge who shapes the cosmos after the Ideas with a father, and the invisible, concrete world (copies of the Ideas: nature, humans, etc.) with a child. In this comparison khôra/mother does not form a couple with the father. And the becoming, the tactile, the nature between the two as a magnificent cosmos is seen more as a son than as a daughter. The 'mother' is separate, is thus no mother, no nurse, no woman. Yet khôra, the third class, the third form, is no form: she/it is unique, a unique individual. The third form is dissimilar to everything 'in her/it,' 'beside her/it,' or 'with her/it,' to anything that seems to form a pair with her/it. Khôra is a strange mother that gives place without bearing children, that is no origin, that is preoriginal, before and outside all generation—'before' not in a temporal sense.

Do we find in Derrida's references to a khôra that is everywhere, that gives itself everywhere, something of what in "How to Avoid Speaking: Denials" in a footnote directed against Marion he calls the "anarchy of the gift" (anarchie du don) and the " 'an-economy' of the gift" (an-économie du don)? (HTAS, 91n9). This seems to be the case. Khôra, as Derrida interprets her/it—as an empty place that summons people to emptiness, receptivity, motherliness, nurture—is anarchy, she/it is the opposite of the authority at the top, of full, fatherly, and patriarchal Being. If this is negative theology, it is far removed from that of Dionysius.

A thinking that—as in the Platonic and Neoplatonic/Christian metaphysical tradition—proceeds from the idea of the presence of full Being, and thus desires direct contact with it (unio mystica), is dangerous. It encourages, or so Derrida seems to suggest, the illusion of full knowledge, the knowledge of the real truth, and the illusion that, at least for some people, the initiated who have experienced the unio mystica, language and symbols are superfluous. This makes the language and symbols that ordinary people need something inferior.

In "How to Avoid Speaking: Denials" Derrida wondered whether there is no pure prayer without our vaguely seeing (entrevoir) the threat or contamination of writing, the code, and thus the threat of repetition (mimesis), analogy, imitations, petrification, or fixation of what was once a living experience. But, Derrida notes, however dangerous, we need those "supplements" that help living prayer by helping us remember it. Without these supplements, neither theology nor theology would be possible, human speaking could not continue. If a pure experience of prayer (a direct conversation with God) were possible—if ever, at the end of time—we would no longer need religions and theologies, affirmative or negative, as interpretation of revelation. But who could exist in that light (or that darkness) at the end of time? Let us therefore try to rejoice that we do not know with certainty, that there are various possibilities, that we live in a time of (divine?) twilight.

Meanwhile, the reader has probably already noticed that Derrida's text on khôra is richly abstract, and that whatever Derrida says of it, it comes across as very philosophical. Yet this text involves more. Derrida writes in *Khôra* that interpretations give shape to what is interpreted, that they impose one or more specific meanings from the rainbow of possible meanings to which what is interpreted is open. But according to rhetorical tradition, interpreting is a form of *mimesis*,[25] imitation, copying, but in the sense of resuming.[26] This resumption takes place on one's own responsibility. (Faithfulness to the original—the original or basic text—is one of many possible ways of assimilating a text, comparable with historically interpreting music with old instruments.) *Khôra* is more than a commentary on a text by Plato or a scientific disquisition on one of Plato's terms: it is a creative resumption of an existing text comparable to performing a musical work. We have Derrida's performance in writing before us, it is fixed, as occurs these days with most musical compositions.[27] That the article *Khôra* is first of all Derrida's performance of and only in the second place (or not at all) his scientific commentary on a text by Plato is tangible in Derrida's interpretation of Socrates as a paradigm (but Derrida does not use that term in his text) or, as I would put it, a performance, an exemplification or resumption of khôra.

Timaeus starts with the recollection of a conversation on the best kind of government for a state. There khôra is briefly mentioned as the place where the most promising children are gathered and where each child receives his or her assigned place.

Socrates feels nothing for the kind of state portrayed in that dis-

---

[25] See Samuel IJsseling, *Mimesis: Over schijn en zijn* (Baarn: Ambo, 1990).

[26] See Ilse N. Bulhof, *Van inhoud naar houding: Een nieuwe visie op filosoferen in een pluralistische cultuur* (Kampen: Kok, 1995), 50–72.

[27] In the West, jazz and minimal music are exceptions.

cussion. He compares himself with a group of people, poets and copyists not occupied with acting and speaking, thus not with politics. He is more like an actor or like painters or sculptors who make images—people not occupied with anything serious—and he compares himself to sophists, people who have no place of their own, no home (K, 107), who wander about, in obvious contrast with people with a fixed address and property who fill serious positions in the state or during war. Whoever is not tied down (committed) by possessions goes no further than talking. Having one's own place implies gravity, attachment, commitment, a shared concern with others who also have their own place. One's own place is also the locus where one feels at home, familiar, at ease (e.g., by having a spouse and children there). That having one's own place is a motive for responsible behavior is a widespread belief; only those who have a home are supposed to have something to lose. Socrates, however, has something more important to lose, as he states in his *Apology*: his soul.

Socrates, like the poets and sophists, works from a nonplace; he pretends to belong to those who pretend: he is no philosopher (no speaker of the truth) and no politician (someone who acts seriously). But his discussion partners do have their own places, and therefore they can speak and act seriously (philosophically). Owning their own place lends authority to the truth of their word (*logos*) and thus to its political effectiveness. It guarantees the effective relation between exposition and execution (*pragma*).

Because Socrates cannot claim such a place, he lets his discussion partners speak, they who have a right to speak.[28] He gives them the floor. He makes them speak and becomes the *recipient of their words*. For this reason Socrates seems to exemplify khôra.[29] Yet Socrates does not identify himself with these people who have no place of their own: he *is* not like them, he only *resembles* them. He is somewhere

---

[28] In the leaflet "Prière d'insérer" added to *Khôra*, Derrida writes about Socrates as he is presented in the article: "And see, he comes to resemble it, her, Khôra. . . ."

[29] I have to confess at this point that I wonder about those others with still less right to speak than artists and sophists: women, slaves, and foreigners? Their place, a nonplace, inside or outside the state could be very different from that of artists and sophists who can at least enjoy their work. It could be a place where joy rules but also where there is resentment and rancor and animosity. See Nietzsche on the 'slave mentality' and Eco on heretics. How does Socrates' khôra relate to these outsiders? Socrates is no Jesus. But is Jesus khôra? These are questions I cannot answer here.

in a third place: a place separate from trivial artists and sophists, and separate from politicians and philosophers. It is a neutral place, a place without place; it is *everywhere*, unlocalized, invisible. At this nonplace, Socrates/Khôra receives the word from his partners, he "effaces" himself, becoming a receptive address for all they want to say. He is well prepared for this receiving—a notion that recalls the Greek words 'cosmos' and 'gathering place' (*endechomenon*).

(Cosmos as mother and nurse? That seems strange. Mother and nurse call up images of nature, *physis*. But women and the feminine are not mentioned in *Timaeus* or in Derrida's text "How to Avoid Speaking: Denials." How are we to relate the virginal khôra with khôra as mother and nurse?)

Philosophizing as Performing Khôra?

Derrida's presentation of Socrates as khôra strikes home. It makes me wonder whether Derrida feels *he* is a(n analogy of) Socrates in our time—an exemplification or performance of khôra.

The theme of the Wandering Jew, the person without a place, is well known. Derrida is of Jewish extraction: he reminds us of this in "How to Avoid Speaking: Denials," a text he read to a congress in Jerusalem. Having no place of one's own is both a role and a lot, is both noble and burdensome—Jews have not chosen it freely. Where else do we find such exemplifications of having no place of one's own? In Socrates? In Jesus? In Francis of Assisi? Perhaps in more people that we would at first think possible?

There are more agreements between Derrida and Socrates than their having no place of their own. Like Socrates, Derrida does not purport to proclaim the truth. Derrida also disturbs his contemporaries with his subversive questions; for both of them the act of questioning and speaking seems more important than the results of this act. What mimetic tie links them? What does it mean to philosophize *like* Socrates, *like* khôra? What might philosophy be exemplifying?

Derrida is not Socrates, nor will he become him, however much he tries to imitate him, however faithfully he may follow his model. But he need not resemble Socrates in everything—it is enough if his approach, his attitude, remains the same. Derrida can exemplify

khôra, repeat it, resume it, quote it in his way, as fits his/our times—
for example, in a more motherly or nurselike manner.

Derrida's exposition in *Khôra* is the written result of his performing, his resumption of negative theology. It is a *personal matter*, a
personal activity, like *playing music*, or playing a game. In resuming,
the purpose does not lie outside the doing as it does with construct-
ing a building that at a given moment is finished. Doing is the goal,
not progress. Resumption recalls the playing of a flautist, Aristotle's
illustration of Being as *energeia*.[30]

Besides being something personal, philosophizing as performance
of khôra also means that one no longer speaks (speaks about something) from a distance—a distance that originated in metaphysics
and was radicalized by nominalism. It means that one is oriented
toward that about which one speaks without actually saying it, that
one allows oneself to be led by khôra and even *live* it, that one performs khôra, that one is khôra.

Does exemplifying khôra represent a new version of the Platonic
participation in Being? In Derrida does resuming khôra, an acting
under one's own responsibility, replace the Platonic participation/
imitation of Being from a distance, from the circling of the spirit
that according to Plato in *Timaeus* imitates the circling heavenly
bodies, and whose motion in its turn approximates the being of
Being? For Plato, participating was a relationship in which there was
no preferred or freely chosen personal style because he considered
Being logical. The Ideas must be imitated exactly. For Derrida, performing as imitating an attitude (empty of content) could replace
imitating content (without attitude). Could then resuming, or living, this attitude replace the Platonic-metaphysical imitation of a
Being that imposes its norms from above?

In replacing philosophizing as 'speaking about' by philosophizing
as 'resumption of a previously given text or example,' in assuming
and incarnating a role like an actor, or in devoting himself to performing a philosophical work like a musician, Derrida steps outside
academic scientific exposition (speaking about) as we know it in
modern times and as it was prepared in classical metaphysics.

---

[30] 'Being' as *energeia* (Greek *ergon* = work; *energeia* = to be at work) contrasts
with *dynamis*, working with a view to *later*, which indicates what potential something has, what something can *become*. The Latin translation of *energeia* is *in actu
esse*, of *dynamis* is *potentia*.

The 'normal' academic scientific exposition is, in the tradition of the Cartesian metaphor, contributing bricks to the growing structure of knowledge. The cooperative efforts of many generations will go into this building, making an enormous structure. Every bit of knowledge is a brick in this building. In Cartesian discourse, transferable knowledge is central, knowledge that belongs, in principle, to everyone, that is open to the public. This remains external knowledge, it requires no resumption. (Only Kierkegaard rejected this.) This Cartesian modern model of knowledge was inspired by inventions that can pass from hand to hand, from head to head.

I would like to suggest that it is meaningful to experiment with another concept of knowledge and ultimately with another epistemology and 'metaphysics': a 'knowledge' that one must put into practice, an 'epistemology' of knowing and learning by doing, a 'metaphysics' relying on a performative view of truth.

Do the different and unexpectedly appearing exemplifications of the concept 'khôra' that so embarrasses Plato (Derrida gives even more examples from *Timaeus* in *Khôra*) point to a 'hidden program' in the dialogue and in Plato's thinking, to a different logic than that of philosophy? This is, it seems to me, what Derrida suggests. There is a reason why *Khôra* appeared in a collection presented to a mythologist, Jean-Pierre Vernant, who spoke of the unique "logic" of the myth. Could we think here of a logic that is not compulsive as is the logic of Parmenidian either-or thinking, a logic that does not articulate a compelling Parmenidian Being? A logic that exemplifies a generous openness/khôra, that leaves people free to think as they will, free to act on their own responsibility?

In short, in philosophizing as performing, attention could be directed toward another type of freedom than freedom from authority, freedom as autonomy, which the nominalist William of Baskerville attained in *The Name of the Rose*. It is freedom as generous (vulnerable) and responsible openness to whatever comes. An openness that recalls Heidegger's and Eckhart's "*Gelassenheit*," but—and this is a crucial difference—to which the dimension of responsibility has been added.

Did Derrida write negative theology—with or without God, as he says of Heidegger? He notes that khôra plays for the philosophical *text* the same role that khôra itself plays for the *content* of the philosophical text. It is only possible to write about khôra indirectly using the writing techniques that recall negative theology. But the content of the philosophical text can be written about directly and clearly—in Plato this was the visible cosmos, with its clear and definable outlines, and the invisible Ideas of ever greater clarity (K, 126). Clear writing *is* philosophy. For Derrida, khôra plays in *Timaeus* and in philosophical exposition as a whole the role of an Outside—a radical otherness—that cannot be articulated in that type of exposition. Khôra's role does indeed recall (or echo) the role of God in Dionysius's negative theological exposition. But as difficult to localize as she/it is, she/it is never an other, let alone a Thou. Her/Its role is therefore completely different from God's in Christian negative theology or of the Supra-Essence in Greek Neoplatonism.

Perhaps this Derridian form of negative theology, with that of Eckhart and Heidegger, is in its turn an echo (or trace) of that Outside that can only be conjectured but never known, and that therefore can take on many forms in our human languages and experiences.

Chapter 8

Crisis in Our Speaking about God

DERRIDA AND BARTH'S *EPISTLE TO THE ROMANS*

Rico Sneller

1. INTRODUCTION

HOW ARE WE to speak about God? This apparently innocent question, put in passing, conceals a history. It conceals the exhaustion of a certain way of philosophizing. It is, perhaps, the result of a kind of thinking that in itself tries to find its own anchor. This type of thinking, which accompanies modernity and the Enlightenment, is repeatedly and with ever shorter intervals confronted with its limit.

While apophatic traditions long ago referred to God's ultimate unspeakableness ('regarding the divine denials are true, assertions insufficient'), this call seems to have been repeated early in the twentieth century and from an unsuspected quarter. Karl Barth, who repeatedly stated that he did not wish to delve into mystical experiences, and who stepped back from every *Deus definiri nequit* (God cannot be defined) in the sense of Dionysius the Areopagite, at least since the publication of his *Epistle to the Romans* (second edition, 1922) believes it impossible to speak about God. He studies anew this ancient theme of being unable to speak. But Barth does not intend to draw the Dionysian line further. In his *Church Dogmatics*, for example, he writes:

> Taken in this way, as in Pseudo-Dionysius the Areopagite and all his disciples, the *Deus definiri nequit* is not understood radically enough. Again, we cannot flee from the hiddenness of God into the possibility

of a negative comprehensibility, as if this were less our own human comprehensibility than a positive, and not just as incapable. . . . The misunderstandings of the *Deus definiri nequit* which we have mentioned—they are the misunderstandings of different varieties of mystical theology—are all of them attempts to evade this task, which means, to evade the true God in His hiddenness. It is advisable not to take part in these attempts.[1]

It is this "true God in His hiddenness" that Barth seeks to trace anew. The theological tradition of his time offered him little help, perhaps even less than the negative tradition mentioned above. For this nineteenth-century tradition of 'liberal theology,' which had sought contact with culture and science, was based on the optimistic attitude of the Enlightenment. If so desired, we could see Barth's opposition to this foundation—and its imitation in the last century—as one of the signs of its agony.

The consequences of opposing a thinking ('negative' or 'positive') that, self-satisfied, locates its own purported foundation, are great. God, for Barth, is by no means an extension of humanity or of any human faculty. That is why our speaking about Him always falls short. Barth, echoing Kierkegaard, says that there is an infinite qualitative difference between God and humanity.

For Barth, the eruption of World War I and the support many prominent theologians gave to the German declaration of war unmasked the tradition of his own time. The war was a divine 'judgment' on human culture and behavior, and a 'crisis' in theological speaking.[2] In his commentary on Paul's Epistle to the Romans, Barth tried to discard certain pretensions of human speaking about God. He delimited what would later be called 'dialectical theology' and spoke about God as the 'wholly Other,' who made Himself known 'vertically from above' ('senkrecht von oben'). His message is at right angles with this world. Revelation in His son Jesus Christ, says Barth, is not of the order of this world. It is given ever anew, but always remains *beyond* our reach.

In our time Barth's resistance to every form of appropriating thinking—and the distant echo of this resistance in apophatic tradi-

---

[1] *Church Dogmatics*, eds. G. W. Bromily and T. F. Torrance (Edinburgh: Clark, 1936ff.), 2.1.193; German text, *Kirchliche Dogmatik*, 2.1: *Die Erkenntnis Gottes* (1940; Zürich: EVZ Verlag, 1986), 216–17.

[2] κρίσις comes from κρίνω, which means, among other things, 'to judge.'

tions—seems to be enjoying a kind of revival. Certainly, there are serious differences in the background and formulation of this resistance. Yet there is a strong similarity between the motor moving the theologian Barth and certain intuitions within contemporary philosophy. The latter also call attention to absolute 'alterity,' to 'the other,' and so on. Critical of the same tradition that Barth attacks, contemporary philosophy tries to discuss something that cannot be captured in words. Emmanuel Levinas, for example, speaks of the radical alterity that we meet in the face of the other human. Using this theme of the other, Levinas guides an important contemporary philosophical debate. Jacques Derrida, whose work can be clarified by this debate, also puts the 'wholly other' central. His thinking starts with an impressive essay on Levinas's oeuvre.[3] In this essay Derrida recognizes the need for the question Levinas developed. Derrida, too, rejects everything, even in Levinas, that resembles a definition or localization of the 'other.' With Levinas, he argues for accepting the 'otherness' of all that refuses to be swallowed by thought. But Derrida seems to argue more stringently in the name of the 'other' that radically escapes every attempt at absorption.

The horizon against which this limitless protection of an untouchable alterity (*noli me tangere*—do not touch me) must be understood is a particular negative tradition that confronts Western thought with a certain rhetorical weakness.

Even if Derrida's criticism of Levinas should agree with the latter's deepest motives, as they are presented they bring the issue of speaking about God to the utter limits. Derrida goes to an extreme in radically defying the possibility of an absolute presence. We may ask how this criticism relates to Barth's *Epistle to the Romans*. Like Levinas, Barth seems to give thinking a certain ('positive') orientation. This orientation must prevent our hope and expectation from being defeated by an absolute openness and indeterminacy. But how far does this lead Barth to draw the *orientation point* into the sphere of the ambivalent and the unsure? This question is, from the Derridian perspective, particularly pressing.

---

[3] "Violence and Metaphysics: An Essay on the Thought of Emmanuel Levinas," in *Writing and Difference*, trans. Alan Bass (London: Routledge & Kegan Paul, 1978), 79–153; French original, "Violence et métaphysique. Essai sur la pensée d'Emmanuel Levinas," in *L'Écriture et la différence* (Paris: Seuil, 1967). This essay was first published in 1964. It thus relates to work Levinas had written prior to that date.

A confrontation between the *Epistle to the Romans* and Derrida's thinking, as put forth in his commentary on Levinas, could prove enlightening. If Derrida's criticism of Levinas is correct, theology's right to exist is put at risk. If all speaking about 'above' comes from 'below,' what could this speaking protect or ensure? What could it remove from the domain of ambiguity or doubt? Does Barth really do justice to the "infinite qualitative difference between God and humanity," to use an expression from his *Epistle to the Romans?* Or does his design give in to Derrida's criticism of metaphysics? I will try to answer these questions in the present chapter.

We should keep in mind that the voices in the contemporary debate about (God's) otherness refer to but are not necessarily direct representations of Dionysius the Areopagite, Meister Eckhart, and Angelus Silesius. On the contrary, Barth, Levinas, and Derrida sometimes, each in his own way, step back from apophatic silence and mystical vision. Levinas, for example, who is critical of any provision for mystical union *beyond* the ability of our linguistic expression, says in *Totality and Infinity,*

> This relation [i.e., with a reality infinitely distant from my own reality] does not become an implantation in the other and a confusion with him, does not effect the very identity of the same, its ipseity, does not silence the *apology*, does not become apostasy and ecstasy. It would be false to qualify [this metaphysical relation] as theological. It is prior to negative or affirmative proposition; it first institutes language, where neither the no nor the yes is the first word.[4]

Better known are Derrida's (often cited) words in "Differance":

> Thus, the detours, phrases and syntax that I shall often have to resort to will resemble—will sometimes be practically indiscernible from— those of negative theology. Already we had to note *that* differance *is not,* does not exist, and is not any sort of being-present [τό όν]. . . . and yet what is thus denoted as différance is not theological, not even in the most negative order of negative theology. The latter, as we know, is always occupied with letting a supra-essential reality go beyond the finite categories of essence and existence, that is, of presence, and always hastens to remind us that, if we deny the predicate

---

[4] *Totality and Infinity: An Essay on Exteriority,* trans. Alphonso Lingis (Pittsburgh: Duquesne University Press, 1969), 41ff.; French original, *Totalité et infini. Essai sur l'extériorité* (1961; The Hague: Martinus Nijhoff, 1984), 12 and passim.

of existence to God, it is in order to recognize him as a superior, inconceivable, and ineffable mode of being.[5]

This refusal to flee into what we call 'negative theology' does not alter the fact that a discussion about alterity cannot be sufficiently grounded without express reference to it. Using denials when speaking about the divine has resulted in a paradigm that forms one of the hermeneutical horizons of our culture. The pattern of constantly repeated denials seems to be an effective historical means for contemporary thinkers to step back from every totalizing knowledge and its striving for absoluteness.

2. Barth's *Epistle to the Romans*: Revelation, Negative Theology, and Crisis of Representation

The "Wholly Other"

Compared with his later *Church Dogmatics*, Barth's *Epistle to the Romans*[6] goes much further in positing God's beings wholly other. On nearly every other page we find apophatic terms such as God's 'unknownness,' our 'ignorance' about Him, His 'unapproachableness' and 'distance,' and so on. God's word "intersects . . . vertically from above," without leaving behind any trace of God as result.

God's message, says Barth, is *God's* message, not human imaginings, suspicions, or ideas. His message intersects, but we cannot grasp it: we must hear it repeatedly and wait. It does not answer our expectations or feelings. It encompasses its own credibility and is not dependent on our evaluation.

Of what does God's message consist? It is the historical, human figure Jesus of Nazareth, who is *simultaneously* the Christ (the

---

[5] "Differance," in *Speech and Phenomena, and Other Essays on Husserl's Theory of Signs*, trans. David B. Allison (Evanston, Ill.: Northwestern University Press, 1973), 134; French original, *Marges—de la philosophie* (Paris: Minuit, 1972), 6. The translation of 'différance' (with an *a* rather than an *e*) was modified by this author. Regarding this *a/e* distinction, see Chapter 6, this volume, by Hent de Vries, esp. section 1.

[6] The English quotations here are taken from *Epistle to the Romans*, translated from the 6th German edition by Edwyn C. Hoskins (London: Oxford University Press, 1968); hereafter cited in the text as *E*. The German version, *Der Römerbrief* (Munich: Kaiser, 1924), is cited in the text as *R*. The first edition of this work was published in 1919; Barth completely rewrote the second edition, published in 1922.

'Anointed'), that is, the locus of God's revelation. In Him our human
world and history is limited and delimited. These are not the totality
of what is. There is more than this vale of tears. But that this should
occur in Jesus of Nazareth, that in Him "two planes intersect, the
one known, the other unknown," is only evident after his *resurrection*. The resurrection is the unique framework that opens our eyes
to the "point [*Bruchstelle*] where the unknown world cuts the known
world" (E, 29; R, 5–6).

It is intriguing that, according to Barth, God, in His revelation,
gives us a view of the other world *without* becoming mixed in our
world. His 'world' touches us without touching us, "as a tangent
touches a circle. . . . And, precisely because it does not touch it, it
touches it as its frontier—as the new world" (*E*, 30; *R*, 6). According
to Barth, Jesus, as person, is not the bearer of revelation. His humanity is subject to all possible ambiguities and doubts. The point is that
God reveals *through* the man Jesus. In the resurrected Jesus God
shows us that there is more than this world and this life. But we can
never own this knowledge. It is as if we have glimpsed a blinding
light that only makes us dizzy and anesthetizes us for an intangible
moment. We still do not know what it is we have grasped. We have
nothing in hand, and thus have grasped . . . nothing. Or have we?

God's invasion of our world puts in question this world and all the
good, the important, and so on that is in it. As 'signal' (*Alarmruf*)
and 'fire alarm' (*Feuerzeichen*) of the coming new world, it rejects
totally our world as it now operates. To use Barth's terminology,
Jesus' resurrection displays God's 'no' to this operation. The Resurrection highlights human mortality and finality. It shows us that *this*
life cannot endure eternity.

But this rejection is not the last. It implies a deeper truth, an
ultimate 'yes.' This is what Barth calls 'grace.' If God shows us
through the Resurrection that this world is not as He wants it to be
and can only be crowned with death, He gives us a prospect and a
hope for something else. "Precisely because the 'No' of God is all-
embracing, it is also His 'Yes' " (*Gerade weil Gottes Nein! ganz ist,
ist es auch sein Ja!*; *E*, 38; *R*, 13). In the 'event' that took place early
on Easter morning a promising, messianic sign canceled our sinful
and thus finite world.

At this one point of contact with the Resurrection everything
comes together: our bounded world, God's 'no' to this boundary,

and His ultimate 'yes,' His acceptance of our world, enclosed and protected in His rejection. His total rejection means that He has something totally different in mind. Since Jesus' resurrection we can want and desire this 'something else.'

The boundary of this world, God's 'no' to it enclosed in a hidden 'yes'—all this is expressed in Jesus of Nazareth. But why there? Do not many people, outside and inside Christianity, feel an urge to resist Jesus' exclusivity?

Barth notes that it is not now, and never will be, at all self-evident that God should reveal Himself in Jesus. Nothing, no quest into our unconscious, no mystical immersion in prayer, or whatever else can bring this awareness to us. That our faith is in *Him* is a question of God's trust. Barth often translates the Pauline πίστις with 'faithfulness' (*Treue*).[7] By this he means that the initiative in the act of faith lies with God, namely, when He reveals Himself. It does not start with humans. God cannot—to refer to eighteenth-century deistic notions—be known by natural means. One illustration of this is that faith, in practice, has never accepted a *proven* or *derivative* God. By this, however, I do not mean to say that for Barth practice is the measure of all things.

Faith in God, that is, faith that corresponds (*Gegentreue*) to God's preceding faithfulness, implies a leap in the dark. The one who dares to make this leap, the one who concurs that Jesus's resurrection means a sudden change for the world, but who concurs that God, in this Resurrection, condemns the way this world operates—this person is a believer. It is not a question of being convinced, for there are no reasons for 'choosing' this (corresponding) faith in God. It is a question of a *confrontation that leaves us no alternative*, a confrontation with an absurdity (i.e., God's 'yes' hidden in His 'no') that makes denying it an absurdity, an impossible possibility. Whoever is really touched by the message from the other side can hardly do anything else but assent. But this assent remains without foundation. As assent it is equivalent to a leap in the dark. Because God hides Himself in His revelation, disguises Himself, the man Jesus becomes for us a 'vast chasm' (*klaffender Abgrund*). "In Jesus, God becomes veritably a secret: He is made known as the Unknown, speaking in eternal silence" (*E*, 98; *R*, 73). In other words, we can

---

[7] In Rom. 1.17: ὁ δὲ δίκαιος ἐκ πίστεως ζήσεται.

find in Jesus an experience that is not an experience, because, strictly speaking, nothing happens. A puzzle is unveiled, a puzzling condemnation of what is known and familiar.[8]

Further on, in his commentary on Paul's comparison of Adam and Christ (Rom. 5.12–21), in which 'Adam' stands for the old (restricted) world and 'Christ' for the new (announced) world, Barth speaks of a 'dialectical dualism.' This contrasts with a 'metaphysical dualism' in which the one is simply the complete opposite of the other. Dialectical dualism, on the other hand, involves a contrast in which the one alternative elevates, and has always elevated, the other. In other words, the earthly, our vale of tears, has been defeated from the start. The earthly is *not* related to that of which God has given us a prospect.

---

[8] The duality hiddenness-unveiling is an apophatic theme. Barth puts it in a completely different framework. Yet there remains a certain parallel between Barth and apophatic thinking, a parallel highlighted in the ambiguous role that Christ's humanity plays. This ambiguity is easy to illustrate.

Authors like Dionysius the Areopagite, Meister Eckhart, and Angelus Silesius put a hidden, primeval divine essence (divinity) beside or opposite God's externalization of self-unveiling. This self-unveiling comes down to a self-denial because God presents himself as a figure *with which He does not coincide*. This is the figure of the creation that flows from Him. Jesus Christ seems to be the *model* of this creation. As person, he depicts the divine self-surpassment, *but then in a superior, divine way*. But the question that then arises is, What is the meaning of Christ's humanity, and by extension, the meaning of his human presence? not only for Dionysius, Meister Eckhart, and Angelus Silesius, but also for Barth. Compare the following:

Dionysius the Areopagite: Jesus Christ "was not a human; it is not so that he was human, it is so that He, [born of] humans, was on the far side of humanity and that He, being above humanity, became truly human" (οὐδὲ ἄνθρωος ἦν, οὐχ ὡς μὴ ἄνθρωπος, ἀλλ' ὡς ἐξ ἀνθρώπων ἐπέκεινα καὶ ὑπὲρ ἄνθρωπον ἀληθῶς ἄνθρωπος γεγονώς. See Epistola IV, in Migne, *Patrologia Graeca*, vol. 3, 7071; see also the unusual § II, 10 of *The Divine Names*).

Meister Eckhart: "It would have little meaning for me that the Word became flesh for humanity in Christ differing from me in form [*supposito illo a me distincto*], when [He] did not (become so) in me personally, so that I would be a son of God." *Die lateinischen Werke*, 3.101, J. Quint, ed. (Zurich: Diogenes Verlag, 1979).

Angelus Silesius: "Wird Christus tausendmahl zu Bethlehem gebohrn / Und nicht in dir; du bleibst noch Ewiglich verlohrn" (This verse has been omitted from Maria Shrady's translation, *The Cherubinic Wanderer* [New York: Paulist Press, 1986], Book 1, no. 61) "Were Christ to be born a thousand times in Bethlehem / And not in you, you would remain eternally lost."

Karl Barth: "Within history, Jesus as the Christ can be understood only as Problem *or* Myth. As the Christ, he brings the World of the Father. But we who stand in this concrete world know nothing, and are incapable of knowing anything of that

The Problem of Language

What ramifications does this have for theological speech about God? How can we speak of Him, if He is totally different from us, if He withdraws Himself from our ability to conceptualize? Does not every attempt to speak about God stumble under the 'crisis,' under the judgment He passed on our being human? Would we not do better to keep silent?

Barth is well aware of this problem and will keep it under consideration throughout his theological thinking. His dialectical theology uses a 'method,' that is, its dicta go back and forth. In this sense, we could say, it combines and includes dogmatics (positive theology) and criticism (negative theology). According to Barth, dogmatics runs the risk of becoming too abstract, while criticism risks forgetting or neglecting all the positive that lies behind our denials.[9] All positive utterances about God should be intermixed with negative ones. Our speaking must remain paradoxical, that is, in agreement with the vast paradox of God's revelation in Jesus, His veiling in His unveiling, His 'yes' in His 'no.' Our speech can only try to refer to a truth that lies on the other side of our human dimension.

Thus, within dialectical theology, speaking has another function than in the apophatic tradition. The latter has all positive speech stop at denials and, ultimately, at a silent contemplation or submerging. The (strikingly) extensive second and third paragraphs of the third chapter of Pseudo-Dionysius's *Divine Names* witness to the incompatibility of God's unspeakableness and the task of making Him known to people. All assertions about God, says Dionysius, have a pedagogical purpose. But they are, and will always remain, insufficient. The tradition of negative theology rests on the presupposition that God's word must be spread among humans with the only means that are available, however insufficient. True speech (i.e., silence) is reserved for the theological elite.

Opposite this is dialectical speaking. This does not view itself as a necessary evil, but as a hazardous undertaking. Speaking is impossi-

---

other world. . . . 'If Christ be very God, He must be unknown.' (Kierkegaard)" (*E*, 30, 38; *R*, 6, 14).

[9] On how to distinguish these methods, see C. van der Kooi, *De denkweg van de jonge Karl Barth: Een analyse van de ontwikkeling van zijn theologie in de jaren 1909–1927 in het licht van de vraag naar de geloofsverantwoording* (Amsterdam: V. U. Press, 1985), 122ff.

ble *but is still required!* Barth holds firmly to the hope that failure,
sometimes beyond our willing, is followed by new attempts to succeed.

In his book *Barth, Derrida, and the Language of Theology*, Graham
Ward observes that Barthian thinking seems in some places to resemble but not to coincide with the apophatic. The negative, he
says, is only one moment in Barth's thinking, albeit an important
one. He notes that "the question arises, then, as to why Barth combines a positivist rhetoric and a transcendental epistemology for an
apophatic end. The answer . . . lies in the fact that this negative
moment becomes a positive one."[10] Yet it is not correct, Ward continues, that the negative of the dialectic and the positive of the dogmatic should be kept too far apart as if they represented two separate
theological stadia in Barth. Both should be understood together on
the basis of what Barth would later call the *analogia fidei* (our speaking about God can only be upwardly reevaluated to truth in and
through *faith*): "Too many critics have drawn a sharp distinction
between Barth's dialectical and dogmatic thinking, emphasizing the
negativity of dialectics and the positive theology that issues from the
analogia fidei. But in *The Göttingen Dogmatics* Barth draws together
and demonstrates the complicity of dialogical, dialectical and dogmatic thinking."[11]

While Barth does not distinguish the 'methods' mentioned above
(dogmatic, critical, and dialectic) in his *Epistle to the Romans*, he
does employ dialectical speaking. In the chapter entitled "The New
Man" (on Rom. 5.1–2) he describes the impossible situation in
which we stand in our time, and in which Paul stood in his. "He
[Paul] stands in a most remarkable situation. For he has to speak the
unspeakable [*reden zu müssen von dem, wovon man doch nicht reden
kann*] and to bear witness to that of which God is the only witness"
(*E*, 152; *R*, 128). This is the opposite of what Wittgenstein had written a few years earlier in an Italian prisoner-of-war camp at the end
of his *Tractatus Logico-Philosophicus*: "Whereof one cannot speak,
thereof one must be silent".

Of particular importance here is what Barth says about religion.

---

[10] Graham Ward, *Barth, Derrida, and the Language of Theology* (Cambridge, U.K.:
Cambridge University Press, 1995), 24.
   [11] Ibid., 96.

All forms of religious expression—including theological speaking—could be compared with the fallout that follows the bomb of revelation. This includes the marginal phenomena, the human reactions, that belong to the *human, worldly* sphere. These come under the crisis that revelation as such means for people and the world.

Yet Barth thinks that religion is the highest human possibility. Belonging to the earthly, the human, it is a limited possibility. But in referring to something new, something higher that "bears witness to, and is embraced by, the promise of a new and higher order by which it is itself severely limited," it is encompassed by a special promise. In religion, people are drawn, as it were, as close as possible to the limit. Religious people approach a narrow area where contrasts are sharp. The higher one rises, the deeper one can fall! The religious person, says Barth, is "at once positive, in that he bears noble witness to the relation which exists between God and man; and negative, in that in him human nature is confronted by the reality of God." But the religious person never goes beyond the limit, never reaches God on his or her own power either in intuition, feeling, or knowledge. Human speech, human references, are the furthest we can go toward approaching the limit. They can never make God *present.*

Further on Barth comes close to a 'representationist' conception of religion and religious speaking. Religion is described in terms of a copy or model. From the human world, it bears witness to the divine. Barth writes, "Placed outside the region of divinity, religion, nevertheless, represents [*vertritt*] divinity as its delegate or impress or negative" (E, 254; R, 236).

Barth's *Epistle to the Romans* is here on the verge of a more classic approach to thinking about representation. The expression "placed outside the region of divinity" is striking. Apparently there is a break between the divine and the human, between the exterior and the inner. The immediate relation is lost. Religion bears witness to this break. It guards the borders of our existence. "There is no human advance beyond the possibility of religion, for religion is the last step in human progress. Standing as it does within humanity but outside divinity, it bears witness [*weist hin*] to that which is within divinity [*das göttliche Innerhalb*], but outside humanity [*das Außerhalb der Humanität*]" (E, 254; R, 237).

In this way our human speaking about God does refer to the other side. But we never know with certitude whether it is about Him, or

whether it is just words without referent. For this very reason, because of this referring, it is desirable that we all be religious people:
people who honor, respect, and apply ourselves, people who keep
religion alive by continually 'revolutionizing' (*revolutionieren*) it (*E*,
254; *R*, 237). Religion puts people in an impossible situation: when
we stand on the borderline, all that we hold valuable seems to be
crushed. In this extreme situation, we end up standing there empty-
handed.

In the chapter in the *Epistle to the Romans* entitled "The God of
Jacob" (on Rom. 9.6–13), Barth extends the question of speaking
about God to cover the echoing of God's word: by people, in the
church. But ultimately, this echoing comes down to speaking about
God; it is a speaking that in one way or another makes God the point
of discussion, draws attention to Him. It is an echoing that wants to
be a speaking about. Nevertheless, Barth continually calls upon the
dialectic of God's word and human utterances, underpinning this
dialectic with numerous italics that regrettably have disappeared in
the translation. His argument is charged and passionate. Compare:

> [on Rom. 9.13] The Theme of the Church is the Very Word of God—
> the Word of Beginning and End, of the Creator and Redeemer, of
> Judgement and Righteousness: but the Theme is proclaimed by
> human lips and received by human ears. The Church is the fellowship
> of MEN who proclaim the Word of God and hear it. It follows from
> this situation that, when confronted by the adequacy of the Word of
> God, human lips and ears must display their inadequacy [*versagen
> gegenüber*]; that, though men are bound to receive and proclaim the
> Truth as it is with God, as soon as they do receive it and do proclaim
> it it ceases to be the Truth; that, however true the Theme of the
> Church may be, as the theme of the Church it is untrue. *This is at
> once the miracle* [my italics] and the tribulation of the Church, for the
> Church is condemned by that which establishes it, and is broken in
> pieces upon its foundations [*daß also das* Thema *der Kirche so wahr
> ist, das es als Thema der* Kirche nie *wahr sein kann*—es geschehe denn
> das Wunder!—*das ist ihre eigentliche Not*]. (*E*, 341; *R*, 325ff)

God's word and human utterances: the one infallible, the other
continually failing. Both remain separate. Paul, Barth says, knows
God's word as something absolute, as something "independent" of
the human. Were this not so, he continues, Paul would have known
God's word as one word among many others; then he would have

complained that "the word of God hath come to nought" (cf. Rom. 9.6); then he would have "set to work to consider how he may best repair the breach." But this is not necessary. God helps His own word, He is its guarantee.

One inconspicuous phrase that I have highlighted from the quotation above deserves special attention (although here the English version is hardly exact). God's word is *never* inadequate, while human speech *always* is, *unless a miracle occurs!*—a miracle that arouses the human word, that inspires it, that gives it wings. A few lines further on, Barth clarifies the notion 'miracle.' He distinguishes between the church of Jacob and that of Esau. The latter is the external, visible church, the organization among other organizations, with all the faults and failures inherent in such an organization. It is the church in which the miracle does not take place. The former is the invisible church, in which the miracle does take place. In the church of Esau nothing else is to be expected but that all human speaking about God comes from liars. In the church of Jacob there is a "miracle, and . . . consequently, the Truth appears above the deceit of men."

Barth returns to the miracle again on the same page as something that we can expect. By 'miracle' he means here the divine acceptance of humanity and of human speech. The miracle can reveal to us whether human speech about God can surpass the doom of forever revolving within itself and being a lie. In Barth's terms, it can reveal to us whether we have a place solely in the church of Esau or also one in the church of Jacob. "What choice do we have except to let this question work on us and 'await the miracle'—as those say who have no hope—to listen to the gospel and to stutter over what is grounded for eternity in the church of Jacob" (R, 326ff).[12]

Toward the end of the *Epistle to the Romans* we meet the 'miracle' again in regard to speaking about God. Our speaking about God (in church and lectures), God's word on human tongues, can only mean that the *hidden* God has revealed Himself. Our speaking can only

---

[12] Translation modified by author. Hoskins's English translation is wrong here. He reverses Barth's rhetorical question. Cf.: "Was bleibt uns übrig, als diese Frage ihr Werk an uns tun zu lassen und 'auf das Wunder zu warten', wie die Fragen, die keine Hoffnung haben, zu lauschen auf das Evangelium und zu stammeln von ihm, das die Kirche Jakobs ewig begründet?," which Hoskins translates with: "Must we merely leave this problem as a problem and—'await a miracle'—as they say who have no hope? Must we listen for the gospel, and whisper stammeringly that the Church of Jacob is established in eternity? Assuredly not . . ." (E, 342).

demonstrate that this revelation has given us no ownership or power
of discretion over knowledge about God. Theological speaking is representative when it is not representative (a paradox that also marks
the apophatic tradition). It can only be representative when it does
not want to represent, but rather stresses God's otherness as made
known in the Resurrection. Conversely, people can neither say nor
write that the hidden God has *revealed* Himself. We can only, like
Barth, presuppose revelation. Only then do we become aware of
God's hiddenness. When revelation is complete, that is, when people become aware that God ultimately says 'yes' to them, intends
them good, then God is acting and speaking, and "[this] is the moment of the miracle" (*E*, 422; *R*, 408).

The miracle stands for God's accepting people. Like John the Bap-
tist on Grünewald's Isenheimer altar, people can only point "to God
and to his miracle." God Himself must put the muscle behind this
pointing. 'Revelation' cannot be read in any book and cannot be
adequately reflected. It is a question of waiting for a presentation
without which any (attempt at) representation is no real representation.

In one of the last chapters of the *Epistle to the Romans* ("The
Great Disturbance: The Problem of Ethics"), Barth discusses the
character of conversation about God. This can never be an abstract
or disinterested conversation. The world around us and everyday
events remind us of this. Conversation about God takes place "for
the sake of His will." Just as the thought of God disturbs our whole
human situation, "the problem of ethics" must disturb every conversation about God. In daily life a call (*Anspruch*) goes out to us that
will not allow us to continue reasoning about God undisturbed.
When Paul rebukes his correspondents (Rom. 12.1), Barth adds,

> [on Rom. 12.1–3] Break off—all ye who follow my thoughts, worship
> with me, and are pilgrims with me—break off your thinking that it
> may be a thinking of God; break off your dialectic, that it may be
> indeed dialectic; break off your knowledge of God, that it may be
> what, in fact, it is [*bedeutet*], the wholesome disturbance and interrup-
> tion which God in Christ prepares, in order that He may call men
> home to the peace of His Kingdom. (*E*, 426; *R*, 412)

Since no representation suffices, since God can only present Himself,
our human thinking and speaking about God must always be ready

for interruption from (the thought of) God, whose will stands at right angles to our efforts.

3. CONFRONTATION: DERRIDA AND BARTH: SILENCE AND SPEAKING

As I mentioned in the introduction to this chapter, contemporary authors such as Levinas and Derrida try, like Barth, to take into account the 'wholly other.' Levinas wants to use it to refer to a transcendence that unavoidably penetrates our attention and enters our thinking and our language. The other's face, says Levinas, is the place where God has left His trace and in which He speaks to me. "The Other resembles God," writes Levinas in *Totality and Infinity* and "[we are] in the trace of God."

Levinas's whole project, like Barth's, *formally* creates numerous reminiscences of negative theology. Derrida was one of the first to indicate this resemblance. In "Violence and Metaphysics" Derrida says that Levinas joins the Platonic tradition of believing in the Good beyond Being. Speaking of the other, "always in the form of negative theology," says Derrida, Levinas frequently uses denials and superlatives. These are intended to prevent daily predicates from being applied to the other without modification. These reminiscences of negative theology do not mean—and Derrida is the last to suggest this—that Levinas's affinity with certain apophatic motives or expressions implies a similar thought pattern. The 'manifestation' of the other of which Levinas speaks coincides with an ethical summons, with a compelling appeal. This summons, says Levinas, comes "from the other side of Being" or "from beyond the order of the same." It is not an extension of our customary and familiar language. The summons from beyond arising from the other interrupts the monologue that dominates Western European tradition.

It is not impossible that the numerous surprising agreements between Levinas and Barth run along the lines of the apophatic reverberation in their works. These agreements smooth the way for our attempt to distinguish Barth's thinking, later, from Derrida's.

Of course, we may not ignore in all this the differences between Levinas's philosophy and Barth's theology. Neither knew much about the other's work. Barth stood in a predominantly Christian-theological tradition, Levinas in a Jewish-philosophical one. It is true that both Levinas and Barth show us an absolute transcendence of highest importance for life here and now. They use all possible means to preserve this transcendence from any form of unity or alliance with the earthly (Levinas: 'the order of the same'). But, according to Levinas, we cannot meet transcendence except in the (an)other (fellow)human, while Barth puts the *one* God-man Jesus Christ central, with the understanding that Jesus' *humanity*, as ambiguous and doubtful as anything, falls away before the *content* of revelation. This point, "the Other is to be found in the trace of the other person" and "the Other is to be found in the trace of Jesus Christ," is crucial and forms a significant difference.

There is another area in which Barth's and Levinas's paths diverge. Each attributes another meaning to the world or to the 'I' that faces the other. As we have seen, the *Epistle to the Romans* sketches how God's revelation overwhelms and elevates our world. To be heard, the world and the 'I' raise themselves above themselves. Revelation is accompanied by its own light, it is not dependent on any illumination from outside. Levinas, by contrast, maintains, in one way or another, the 'I' before the face of the other. For him, it has an indispensable *status*. Admittedly, the uncompromising compulsion with which the unapproachable and self-satisfied 'I' is confronted, the unnerving insistence it faces, is essential for both Barth and Levinas.[13]

This is not the place to go extensively into the further differences

---

[13] Certainly, Levinas's 'other' is accompanied, to a certain extent, by its own light: the face is 'expression,' it speaks for itself and needs no content. But for Levinas, at least in *Totality and Infinity*, the other remains, however paradoxically, linked to the 'I.' The other overwhelms the 'I' and in so doing distinguishes itself from the world (the 'order of the same'). This paradox is apparent from the first sentences of *Totality and Infinity*: " 'The true life is absent.' *But we are in the world*. Metaphysics arises and is maintained in this alibi" (33, my italics; *Totalité et infini*, 3). A few pages later we read, "Alterity is possible only in starting from [*à partir de*] me" (40; French ed., 10). Much further on Levinas adds, "But the transcendance of the face is not enacted outside of the world. . . . The 'vision' of the face as face [*La 'vision' du visage comme visage*] is a certain mode of sojourning in a home, or . . . a certain form of economic life. No human or interhuman relationship can be enacted outside of economy; no face can be approached [*abordé*] with empty hands and closed home. Recollection [*recueillement*] in a home open to the Other [*ouverte à Autrui*]— hospitality— . . . coincides with the Desire for the Other that is absolutely transcendent [*le Désir d'Autrui absolument transcendant*]" (172; French ed., 147).

and similarities between Barth and Levinas.[14] Here we are particularly interested in noting that both take seriously the loss of the
Other God. As I mentioned in the introduction to this chapter, they
accuse the apophatic tradition of having contributed to this loss.

In what follows I would like to emphasize the agreements between
Levinas and Barth. On the basis of these agreements we will be able
to further the line of criticism that Derrida addresses to types of
'separation thinking' similar to that of Levinas. We can, *mutatis mutandis*, confront Barth's *Epistle to the Romans* with Derrida's criticism of Levinas. Does Barth, who also focuses on the paradoxical
manifestation of the 'wholly Other' really do justice to this Other's
otherness? Or does he still go too far in linking this Other to our
world, to what Levinas calls "the order of the same"? Derrida's criticism of Levinas is formulated with a similar concern with allowing
the 'other' to be other. Could this provide us with an entry point for
considering the *Epistle to the Romans* from the stance of a contemporary 'philosophy of alterity'?

What is at issue in Derrida's—if we may use the term—
'philosophy of alterity'? It is for him, too, a radical otherness, an
'outside' that withdraws from our thinking. This 'other,' which the
Western tradition has always provided with a label and a content,
does not, in Derrida's opinion, allow itself to be approached in any
direct way whatsoever. The 'images' he uses (writing, trace, *différance*, text, supplement, etc.) always refer to two dimensions: the
outer and the inner, the other and the same. They point to the divid-
ing line between our thinking and what permits this thinking while
escaping it.

The two dimensions belong together. Our thinking is comprised
in one circling body of cross-references that, as such, refers to the

---

[14] See the thesis by J. F. Goud, *Levinas en Barth. Een godsdienstwijsgerige en
ethische vergelijking* (Amsterdam: Rodopi, 1984). See also G. Ward, *Barth, Derrida,
and the Language of Theology*, chap. 7, "Barth's Theology of the Word and Levinas's
Philosophy of Saying." Here Ward notes: "What is being investigated by each is a
phenomenon—not the otherness of God, but a revelation, an unveiling of a Logos
which remains veiled and hidden within logocentrism. Both analyse how that revelation can be, already has been, significant for human beings; how human beings have
been addressed by it." A bit further on Ward daringly posits that a 'theological'
moment is not totally unknown to Levinas: "There is in the logic of signification,
both suggest, a moment which is ineluctably theological" (170).

completely indeterminable space that first establishes these references. The cross-references are like letters that only become legible
against the white background of a piece of paper. The letters contain
no message about or description of the *nature* of this white background. Each description or reference is a betrayal of it. Denying and
reticent speech have a purpose in Derrida's texts; it has led many
critics to accuse Derrida of trying to reinstate the time-honored negative theology.

The danger of betrayal that every form of reference or localization
implies for the 'other' could well be the most important theme of
"Violence and Metaphysics" (1964), Derrida's extensive essay on
what Levinas had published to that date. Correctly, Derrida notes
here, Levinas calls attention to the alterity or transcendence continually repressed in Western thinking. But to what degree does Levinas
remain faithful to his own project? To what degree does he avoid
contradicting himself?

In his essay Derrida raises numerous points. It would lead us too
far astray to treat all of them. One assertion, though, is central: Levinas's work is thought to contain an ambiguity that could be his un-
doing, an ambiguity that tends to determine the content of the
indeterminable. This tendency is seen in expressions such as "the
Other resembles God" and "[we are] in the trace of God." What
does this mean? Derrida wonders. The conclusion that the world or
body of cross-references is permeated by a trace of, a reference to, an
alterity that is *other* than this world, *other* than the order of the
same, seems unavoidable. But the suggestion that this alterity should
coincide with a (positive) Infinity ('God'), who is totally *independent*
of every connection, absolute in Itself, contradicts the idea of an
alterity. Alterity means 'other than . . .' and implies involvement with
the same.

Thus, according to Derrida, Levinas tries to unite two things that
cannot be united: complete alterity and 'positive Infinity,' but an
independence that is completely independent, has meaning only in
itself, and refers to nothing outside itself (which is more than merely
the radical opposite of all finiteness). Derrida writes:

> The positive Infinity (God)—if these words are meaningful—cannot
> be infinitely Other [*infiniment Autre*]. If one thinks, as Levinas does,
> that positive Infinity tolerates, or even requires, infinite alterity, then

one must renounce all language, and first of all the words *infinite* and *other*. Infinity cannot be understood as Other except in the form of the in-finite. As soon as one attempts to think Infinity as a positive plenitude (one pole of Levinas's nonnegative transcendence), the Other becomes unthinkable, impossible, unutterable. Perhaps Levinas calls us to this unthinkable-impossible-unutterable beyond (tradition's) Being and Logos. But it must not be possible either to think or to state this call.[15]

Derrida asks if it is not true that the other's otherness can be respected only when this otherness remains linked to what we know and find familiar. Derrida suggests that Levinas wants more. According to Derrida, Levinas tries to combine this infinity that cannot be separated from finiteness with a 'positive' Infinity, an infinity with content. This attempt is doomed to failure. The other can only be infinitely other as finite and mortal substance, at least when it is subjected to language (as in Levinas).[16] Only an alterity that exists outside language—but how could we envision such a thing?—could perhaps be preserved from finiteness, says Derrida. This is not the case for Levinas's other. In Levinas, thinking does not precede language: both remain involved with one another from the start. This is an element in Levinas's thinking that Derrida will continually recall.

If the other is present in language, if alterity is made manifest there by interrupting the great 'monologue' of Western European tradition, then this implies that there is a certain inevitability in language. The other, who interrupts language, becomes involved in the eternal linguistic game. It becomes entangled in an inextricable jumble of references, making its divine origin uncertain. The infinite Other that breaks through the finite order of the same becomes itself contaminated by the finiteness of what it breaks. So thinks Derrida, who wishes to bring radically under discussion every representation of an absolute Presence or positive Infinity *outside* the body of cross-references.

---

[15] *Writing and Difference*, 114 (French ed., 168).

[16] For Levinas, this does not mean that the other's transcendence can be proven or deduced, let alone described by ontological language. Certainly, Levinas expressly calls attention to a repressed transcendence and does so in philosophical language. What he discusses in this language (originally Greek) is both the disappearance of every form of transcendence in Western, ontological thinking, and the way this transcendence infringes and continually interrupts this. The other's transcendence is manifested in the ruptures in such an ontological language.

Elsewhere, Derrida uses an (implicit) reference to God's revealing his name to Moses (Ex. 3) to describe the Other's entanglement this way: "as a linguistic statement [*en tant que langage*] 'I am he who am' is the admission [*aveu*] of a mortal."[17] Of course, here the Other (God) is the one speaking. But who knows whether or not He was *given* these words? Is not the translation of the infinite in finite terms the worm of doubt in the root faith?

Elsewhere Derrida links the name of God to the Babylonian confusion of languages in which it is heard. He says, "God's own name is already so divided over language that it confusedly signifies 'confusion.' And the war that he declares [against humanity in the story of the Tower of Babel in Genesis 11] first raged in his name: divided, split, ambivalent, polysemic: *God deconstructs*."[18] Thus, for Derrida, the name of 'God' is taken up in (finite) language and is clothed with the same ambiguity as other words.

When we draw up a tentative balance sheet, it seems that Levinas, when compared to Barth, has added the dimension of language to alterity. Both maintain that direct and responsible speaking about the Other, about God, is impossible. But Levinas illustrates this via and in *language*: the Other infringes on the language of the same, a language that identifies and classifies, but that makes no room for the Other. Barth seems to dispute God's dependence on a world totally different from Him. His revelation, rather, implies an elevation of this world beyond its boundary and limitation.

The break that Levinas depicts occurs as *experience*. It resembles what Barth says about the explosion of revelation in humanity. We may perhaps link the other's *interruption* in Levinas with the *Störung* (disturbance) of God's revelation in Barth. For this reason I turn now to another of Derrida's works on Levinas, one entitled, "At This Very Moment in This Work Here I Am."[19]

---

[17] *Speech and Phenomena*, 54; French edition, *La voix et le phénomène* (Paris: PUF, 1967), 61.

[18] See "Des tours de Babel," in *Psyché: Inventions de l'autre* (Paris: Galilée, 1987), 207 and passim. The original reads: "le nom propre de Dieu se divise assez dans la langue, déjà, pour signifier aussi, confusément, 'confusion.' Et la guerre qu'il déclare, elle a d'abord fait rage au-dedans de son nom: divisé, bifide, ambivalent, polysémique: *Dieu déconstruit*."

[19] Originally in *Psyché. Inventions de l'autre*. Translated in R. Bernasconi and S. Critchley, eds., *Re-reading Levinas* (Bloomington and Indianapolis: Indiana University Press, 1991).

Here Derrida goes deeper into the Other's infringement on our safe, familiar world and into the "tear" (*déchirure*) the Other makes in it. While Levinas (like Barth) wants to show how the Other stands at right angles to our world, Derrida points to a "hooking back" (*échancrure*) of its manifestation in this world and with it to its contamination with the world's virus. This tearing is only possible when something *is torn*, the infringement when something *is fractured*, and the interruption when something *is interrupted*.[20] In addition to this, one interruption is insufficient. It would be immediately integrated, just as the one exception *confirms* the rule. Compare:

> The hiatus must insist, whence the necessity of the *series*, of the series of knots [i.e., in the chain of interruptions]. The absolute paradox (of the ab-solute) is that *this series*, incommensurable with any other, series out-of-series, does not tie up threads [*fils*] but the interruptions between threads, traces of intervals which the knot should only re-mark, give to be remarked. . . . And in order to distinguish itself, for instance, from the discontinuous as a symptom within the discourse of the State or of the book, it can break its resemblance only by being *not just any* interruption, and thus also by determining itself within the element of the same.[21]

In other words, if we want to maintain the idea of an interruption of our world by an absolute transcendence, there must at least be several interruptions. To use a fairy-tale image, the 'dragon' named interruption must grow a new head for each one ontology cuts off. And further, the series of interruptions thus created must be distinguishable from other kinds of (finite) interruptions . . . and thus *relate* and *bind itself* to our finite world. Not only the Other's once-only interruption, but the series of interruptions becomes "contaminated" with the immanence of the same (Levinas) or with the world of Adam (Barth).

In his criticism of separation thinking, such as Levinas's, we come to see Derrida's own position. 'Transcendence' and 'immanence,' outer and inner, the other and the same are inextricably linked to one another. A completely transcendent sphere of a wholly Other (God) *without any contact with our reality* would, Derrida believes, be as meaningless as Epicurus's pantheon. But a transcendence or

---

20 Ibid., 26.
21 Ibid., 28.

an alterity linked to immanence or the same, one that is in a certain sense familiar, is as finite as we are.[22] Put differently, a God who speaks our language and can make Himself understood comes from our world. Such a God is clothed in the ambiguity and relativity of this world, in which many voices resound and many gods are worshiped. He must have made His entrance via language where words, sentences, sounds, and the like can take on various meanings according to their context.

In Derrida's discussion with Husserl in *Speech and Phenomena*, he emphasizes the idea that language is constituted by an indeterminate representation structure. To communicate we use (linguistic) signs. As *signs* they have a certain recognizability (a 'formal identity'), but one that can be inserted in varied contexts. The identity of the signs, Derrida says, is ideal, abstract: it is thought. As such this identity implies 'representation.' First is the *signification* of the identity in our thinking. Second is the (possible) *re-present-ation* or *repetition* of signs in general. Third is the effective *representation* or *application* of every sign in our communication. "Since this representative structure is signification itself, I cannot enter into an 'effective' discourse without being from the start involved in unlimited [*indéfinie*] representation."[23]

By emphasizing the representative character of linguistic signs, in all meanings of the word, Derrida tries to show that these signs can be understood *qualitate qua* in divergent and inconceivable ways: their 'representativity' is 'undetermined.' How, then, could an exception be made for the story (the combination of written, fixed linguistic signs) about a Jewish man who, during the Roman domination of Palestine, is supposed to have arisen from the dead and who is thought to have had a very special relationship with God? For an answer, let us return to Barth:

> [on Rom. 3.21–26] This creative word [being discussed here] is spoken—through the redemption that is in Christ Jesus. What is there, then, in Christ Jesus? There is that which horrifies [*Entsetzenerregende*]: the dissolution [*Aufhebung*] of history in history, the destruction of the structure of events within their known structure, the end

---

[22] "The appearing of the infinite *différance* is itself finite"; *Speech and Phenomena*, 102; French ed., 114.

[23] Ibid., 50; French ed., 56.

of time in the order of time. . . . Jesus of Nazareth, *Christ after the flesh*, is one amongst other possibilities of history; but he is *the* possibility which possesses all the marks of impossibility. His life is a history within the framework of history, a concrete [*dinglich*] event in the midst of other concrete events, an occasion in time and limited by the boundaries of time; it belongs to the texture of human life. But it is history pregnant with meaning; it is concreteness [*Dinglichkeit*] which displays the Beginning and the Ending; it is time awakened to the memory of Eternity; it is humanity filled with the voice of God [*redender Gottheit*]. In this fragment of the world [*Weltlichkeit*] there is detached from the world—before the very eyes of men and in their actual hearing!—something which gleams in the darkness and gives to the world a new brilliance. (*E*, 103ff.; *R*, 78)

But again, how do we know, how does Barth know, that *here* we receive a message from the other side, from the wholly other God? How do we know that *here* we have a text that abrogates all texts, a word that is self-sufficient, that can itself help words that speak about this word?

Is this not a question of *experience?* Not of just any experience but of *the* preeminent 'experience': the gracious confrontation with the inescapable Other? "He who knows the world to be bounded by a truth that contradicts it; he who knows himself to be bounded by a will that contradicts him; he who, knowing too well that he must be satisfied to live with this contradiction and not attempt to escape from it, finds it hard *to kick against the pricks* [*wider den Stacheln zu löcken*] . . . ; he is it that believes" (*E*, 39; *R*, 14; my italics).[24]

But is Barth here not fighting against the category 'experience' ("*Also nicht Erlebnisse, Erfahrungen und Empfindungen* . . . ," "not an event, nor an experience, nor an emotion . . ."; *R*, 4; *E*, 28)? Experience does have a place in the *Epistle to the Romans*, and in religion: "Nor must we divorce grace from the experience [*Erlebnis*] of grace which takes form and shape in religion and in morality, in dogma and in ecclesiasticism" (*E*, 230; *R*, 212). Experience, event, and the like always belong on *this* side, in the ambiguous human

---

[24] The German text puts even more strongly the inescapableness of the choice and the impossible possibility of a human 'no': "Wer die Begrenzung der Welt durch eine widersprechende Wahrheit, die Begrenzung seiner selbst durch einen widersprechenden Willen erkennt, wem es schwer wird, wieder den Stacheln zu löcken, weil er zu viel weiß von diesem Widerspruch, als daß er ihm entrinnen könnte, sondern sich damit abfinden muß, damit zu leben. . . ." (*R*, 14).

sphere. But our being given grace, God's ultimately accepting us despite our human shortcomings, raises us out of the ambiguity of the human and the worldly. God's 'yes' to us puts us and all we have and are in the divine sphere where *everything* human is foreign. As accepted and wanted people we have no experiences, and conversely we do not experience that we are accepted and wanted. "But 'our' being under grace is not an experience, not one type of human behaviour, not a particular condition [*Verfassung*] of human activity" (*E*, 237; *R*, 219).

Derrida's criticism of Levinas and of the notion 'experience,' found on the last page of "Violence and Metaphysics," reads as follows:

> But the true name of this inclination of thought to the Other, of this resigned acceptance of incoherent incoherence, inspired by a truth more profound than the 'logic' of philosophical discourse, the true name of this renunciation of the concept, of the a prioris and transcendental horizons of language, is *empiricism*. For the latter, at bottom, has ever committed but one fault: the fault of presenting itself as a philosophy.[25] And the profundity of the empiricist intention must be recognized beneath the naivety of certain of its historical expressions. It is the *dream* of a purely *heterological* thought at its source. . . . We say *dream* because it must vanish *at daybreak*, as soon as language awakens. But perhaps one will object that it is language which is sleeping.[26] Doubtless, but then one must, in a certain way, become classical once more, and again find other grounds for the divorce between speech [*la parole*] and thought [*la pensée*].[27]

Can we separate speech from thought? Can we imagine an inspiration that, by definition, cannot be articulated? According to Derrida, Levinas believed it impossible to think of something that does not also—in whatever paradoxical way—occur in *language*: the idea of the infinite leaves its traces in language, according to Levinas.

If Levinas wants to maintain the idea of an absolute alterity, he would then have to explain where thinking and language divorce (and not where language is 'only' interrupted). Then he would have

---

[25] Barth expressly does not do this. In his Preface he says that he "never presented anything but *theology*" (*E*, 4; *R*, viii).

[26] Would Barth do this? In any case he maintains in principle the unsuitability of language for doing justice to God's revelation.

[27] *Writing and Difference*, 151; French ed., 224.

to show how an infinite idea can occur to me without its being in any way expressible in language, an idea that surpasses language (and what is such an idea except a kind of experience?). And he must do this to keep this 'notion' from forging links with a contaminated finite language that would make it ambivalent.

Derrida's whole work shows that he, too, struggles with this question. He accepts the consequences of the aporia in which he saw Levinas end: the aporia that will ultimately force Levinas to put alterity as he sees it totally, and that means totally, *outside* language. The insurmountableness before which Derrida stands requires that he bind alterity to language as its reverse, if not as its condition of possibility. For, suppose that there is already a point where thinking and language divorce, it would then be impossible to hide this break from language, which casts doubt on this break a posteriori![28]

For Derrida, every speaking is an insurmountable and unceasing betrayal of an 'idea' or 'experience' that never lets itself be spoken or thought, *but that is echoed in language.* Our language stands in an aura of infinity, of something we can never say, but only betray; but it is something that makes itself felt *in* our perfidy and *in* our betrayal. It is that which *permits* language and the game of references in which we are subsumed.[29] Perhaps Derrida's work is an attempt to strengthen the resonance of the unspeakable in our language.

From Derrida's perspective, the Barthian presentation of revelation would be an attempt to go beyond the divorce between speech and thought. Thought is confronted in Barth with an experience that is not an 'experience' in the strict sense and that surpasses thinking without implying any mystical unification. The quasi-experience

---

[28] Note the ambiguity in the following citation from "Violence and Metaphysics": ". . . that the positive plenitude of classical infinity [*infini classique*] is translated into language only by betraying itself in a negative word (in-finite), *perhaps* situates, in the most profound way, the point where thought breaks with language. A break which afterward *will but resonate throughout all language*" (*Writing and Difference*, 114, my italics; French ed., 168ff.).

[29] See "How to Avoid Speaking: Denials," where we meet the following example: "From the moment I open my mouth, I have already promised; or rather [*plutôt*], and sooner [*plus tôt*], the promise has seized the *I* which promises to speak to the other, to say something, to affirm or to confirm by speech [*par la parole*] at least this: that it is necessary to be silent; and to be silent concerning that about which one cannot speak" (in Harold Coward and Toby Foshay, eds., *Derrida and Negative Theology* [Albany: State University of New York Press, 1992], 84; "Comment ne pas parler. Dénégations," in *Psyché. Inventions de l'autre*, 547).

that overcomes our thought can withdraw from language and thought, from all immanence, because it does not lie in human hands. The *Epistle to the Romans* tells us not only that both the good news and its acceptance are offered to us, but that this message always remains beyond our grasp. It does not depend on our judgment or comparison, it expresses itself immediately and speaks for itself. Revelation creates its own means of reception without seeking contact with any human receptivity, not even in a "desire for the infinite" (Levinas).

Revelation is presented as a flash. This flash is the revelatory moment that withdraws from every present or every presence and that we can interpret in the light of the Resurrection. It is an event that sets in motion numerous (in themselves worthless) human reactions, apophatic and mystical if need be, an event that must renew itself daily if it is to preserve the faith.

Is revelation an 'interruption' in Levinas's sense? Does it become entangled in our world or contaminated by the virus of our finiteness? How can we distinguish the series of God's explosions from any other series of wondrous (artistic, emotional, etc.) experiences?

After confronting Barth and Derrida I would like to risk saying that revelation leaves us uncertain, but with a *recollection* of certainty. Essentially, we always remain empty-handed and can never boast of the Other's gift. We are borne through time by an uncertain memory of a sure promise given us once, *outside* time, by an always past promise I can never grasp, and by an unsure promise, *in* time, of a recollection of certainty. Our impotence before a gruesome world faces a certain 'no' in our uncertain memory. A certain 'yes' answers to our indeterminate desire for another world, but this too is in our uncertain memory. Perhaps we still vaguely know from an unremembered past that this world is limited; maybe we can even deduce this limitedness from the fact that this world *seems* to point to intactness and fulfillment, for example, in virgin nature or in the unknown human possibilities for justice.

Revelation cannot be dated; our uncertainty, our empty hands, can. Human speech about God, especially when self-assured, can perhaps be (psychoanalytically) examined for uncertainty. But our speaking about God is honest when it tries, despite this uncertainty, to testify to a promise, a 'yes' in a 'no,' that hides in an uncertain memory. This testimony only knows paradoxes that express the re-calcitrance of the promise toward our words and our world.

When Heidegger said to Barth's friend and proponent Thurneysen that the language of theology consists in seeking a word capable of arousing and preserving faith, he seemed to doubt whether theology were possible. And Barth agreed with him.[30] Theology as speech about God, as speaking the unspeakable, is in itself impossible. It can only progress when at completely unexpected, never ante- or postdatable moments—that may perhaps not be moments at all—it is borne and inspired from above and when it takes into account the absurdity of its subject. Negation in theology was an attempt in this direction, and not the least skillful. But its self-satisfaction ('denials about the divine are *true*') was for Barth a reason for still greater radicalness.[31]

---

[30] See H.-G. Gadamer, "Martin Heidegger und die Marburger Theologie," in O. Pöggeler, ed., *Heidegger. Perspektiven zur Deutung seines Werkes* (Königstein: Athenäum Verlag, 1984), 169. Gadamer, who recalls this dictum, says that it was seen in its time as a doubt whether theology were possible at all.

[31] An interesting new work on Barth and Derrida is Isolde Andrews, *Deconstructing Barth: A Study of the Complementary Methods in Karl Barth and Jacques Derrida* (Frankfurt: Lang, 1996). In his article "Sporen van Derrida bij Noordamerikaanse theologen," *Tijdschrift voor Theologie* 30 (1990): 173–83, F. P. M. Jespers discusses several Anglo-Saxon theologians whom Derrida is supposed to have influenced (M. Lafargue, D. Tracy, T. Altizer, C. A. Raschke, C. E. Winquist, R. P. Scharlemann, M. A. Myers, K. Hart, and M. C. Taylor). Despite his several blunders, Jespers concludes his article with an intelligent comment that I would like to cite here: "North American theologians . . . except for Tracy, are limited to a kind of philosophy of religion in which they uncritically and arbitrarily arrogate ideas from Derrida as if he were the new prophet of the unspeakable and of the wholly Other. This may be stylish, but it is not fertile. Just at the point where they give up, on the metaphysical level, lie the chances for an in-depth dialogue on God's otherness, on the relationship between God and being and on the reference point of religious and theological thought and speech" (183). I think that it is not so much meaningful *to imitate Derrida* in thinking and speaking about God as it is to *confront* theological traditions with his thinking. It is true that it is stylish to cite Derrida, but at present it is equally indispensable to confront a thinking that we have hardly been able to surpass. This chapter is a humble attempt at such a confrontation.

Chapter 9

The Gift of Loss

A STUDY OF THE FUGITIVE GOD IN BATAILLE'S ATHEOLOGY, WITH REFERENCES TO JEAN-LUC NANCY[1]

Laurens ten Kate

1. INTRODUCTION: MYSTICISM AND PHILOSOPHY, A PRECARIOUS RELATIONSHIP

"I AM NEITHER A MYSTIC, nor a philosopher; perhaps I am a saint, perhaps a fool."[2] Georges Bataille might well have introduced himself with such words were he to participate today in a debate on negative theology. In his unsurveyable and nearly impenetrable writings, he makes no effort to reconcile mystical experience and philosophical truths. He seems—often provokingly—to want to force a confrontation between these two worlds. Moreover, his work is marked by an ever-reformulated interest: an interest in the place where mysticism and philosophy reach their limits and face one another with empty hands. Bataille calls this place, this outer limit, the "sacred," and sometimes the "holy": it is a place such that when we are there, we are nowhere. This is the place where Bataille suspects

---

[1] The Dutch text (1992) that served as the source for this chapter was originally a preparatory work for my (1994) dissertation, *The Empty Place: Revolts against Instrumental Life in Bataille's Atheology* (written in Dutch with a summary in French). This chapter is a thorough reworking of the original text, expanded with themes and analyses from the dissertation, and focusing on the concepts 'experience,' 'communication,' and 'sacrality' in Bataille's *Inner Experience*.

[2] Variation on G. Bataille, *Méthode de méditation* (1947), in OC, 5.217n.

that we may be able to undergo an *experience* that is neither mystical nor philosophical (neither state can encompass it, neither can appropriate it), but—in a specific meaning—"sacred." It is his committed attention to the sacred—in our time, in our culture—that would lead him to introduce himself as a "saint" or a "fool."

Who is Bataille?[3] He was born in 1897, he had a miserable youth (his father, first blind and later insane from syphilis, died in 1915; his mother committed suicide a few years later). After a short period of piety, he established himself in Paris in the 1920s as an amateur ethnologist (he was fascinated by the study of foreign cultures) and as a philosopher (he read Nietzsche, Hegel, and Heidegger). He entered a love-hate relationship with the surrealist movement. For a few years he was a member of the so-called Democratic Communist Circle; in 1936 he founded Acéphale, his own antifascist group. In the meantime, he published numerous articles. In 1928 his first novel, *Histoire de l'oeil* (*Story of the Eye*), appeared, under a pseudonym.[4] During the war years, while sick, lonely, and withdrawn, Ba-

---

[3] Available works in English by Bataille include: George Bataille, *Essential Writings*, trans. and ed. M. Richardson (London: Sage, 1998); *The Bataille Reader*, eds. F. Botting and S. Wilson (Oxford, U.K.: Blackwell, 1997); *The Accursed Share: An Essay on General Economy*, Vol. 7: *Consumption* (*La part maudite*), Vol. 2: *The History of Eroticism*, and Vol. 3: *Sovereignty*, trans. R. Hurley (New York: Zone Books, 1988–1991); *The Absence of Myth: Writings on Surrealism*, trans. and ed. M. Richardson (New York/London: Verso, 1994); *Eroticism*, trans. M. Dalwood (San Francisco: City Lights Books, 1986); *Guilty*, trans. B. Boone (Venice, Calif.: Lapis Press, 1988); *The Impossible*, trans. R. Hurley (San Francisco: City Lights Books, 1991); *Inner Experience*, trans. L. A. Boldt (Albany: State University of New York Press, 1988); *Literature and Evil*, trans. A. Hamilton (New York: Marion Boyars, 1990); *My Mother, Madame Edwarda, The Dead Man*, trans. A. Wainhouse (New York: Marion Boyars, 1989); *On Nietzsche*, trans. B. Boone (New York: Paragon Books, 1992, 1994); *Theory of Religion*, trans. R. Hurley (New York: Zone Books, 1989); and *Visions of Excess: Selected Writings, 1927–1939*, trans. A. Stoekle, C. R. Lovitt, and D. M. Leslie and ed. Allan Stoekl (Minneapolis: University of Minnesota Press, 1985). I also highly recommend an Stoekl, ed., *Yale French Studies* 78 (1990), a special issue "On Bataille," including Bataille's "Hegel, Death, and Sacrifice" (1955; see *Oeuvres complètes* [hereafter cited as OC] [Paris: Gallimard, 1970–1988], 12.326–45); Carolyn Bailey Gill, ed., *Bataille: Writing the Sacred* (New York/London: Routledge, 1995); and Michel Surya's biography, *Georges Bataille: La mort à l'oeuvre* (Paris: Gallimard, 1992). Gill's book, an attractive "collection gathered around Bataille's concept of a radical, bversive negativity which he called the sacred," contains a bibliography of English works by and about Bataille.

[4] G. Bataille, *Story of the Eye*, trans J. Neugroschal (New York: Marion Boyars, 1979).

taille wrote the texts that would further determine his thinking and which would later be bundled in an *atheological summa*.[5] After World War II, he founded the periodical *Critique*, still one of the leading journals in France, and wrote various theoretical works on religion, on economy and expenditure, on politics and sovereignty, on eroticism, on art and literature. From early in the 1950s he suffered from a muscular disease that led to his death in 1962.

'Atheology' is thus one of the central projects within Bataille's work. But what does this term mean? A-*theology*: a theology without God? A theology of an absent God? Or a theology that leaves God unuttered (*a-logos*)? In the following text I will question the degree to which Bataille's atheology is a new variation in the tradition of negative theology. We can only approach an answer to this question when we *first* examine his analysis of the sacred in modern culture: the sacred that he intuitively understood as something hidden, repressed, but also violently dynamic, a sacred that attacks the rationality of modern life. We will also discuss his view of the 'death of God' and the way he developed concepts of communication.[6] Bataille's analysis—and this is the second point of my presentation—leads to a stubborn attempt to reintroduce the word 'God' in his texts: to speak again about 'God.' His book *Inner Experience*, the first and most programmatic part of his atheological summa, contains the most striking examples.[7]

2. Negative Theology as an Expression of Embarrassment

To make a choice for a negative theology is tempting in a time when theological reflection feels little attraction to the dogmas of ecclesiastical teaching. In the systematic theology of the last century, and even more strongly in the modern philosophy of religion, there is an increasing fascination with negative theology; there resounds a criticism of a 'positive,' 'anthropocentric,' 'authoritarian' concept or image of God. Yet it is not simple to situate Bataille's atheology in this trend toward the negative. Some texts from his summa seem to

---

[5] In *OC*, vols. 5 and 6. Also see Section 6, this chapter.

[6] See Sections 2–5.

[7] See Sections 6ff.

be linked to negative theology, but his reservations concerning such a theology are more frequent. Before examining Bataille's approach more closely, I would like to present a short deconstruction of some central concepts that determine the present reassessment of negative theology: a deconstruction of notions taken for granted in postmodern thinking and writing.

"God is the Other. God is the—absolute—Other." Such short sentences dominate speech about God, from the moment we recognize that we can no longer simply 'believe' in God; that we no longer feel His presence daily; that we sense that His omnipotent Providence and personal intervention in worldly events have become complicated, if not empty, phrases; and that we no longer will rely on the—ill-defined but no less effective—feeling "that something higher must exist." Neither the Christian articles of faith nor any, more vague, religiosity help in speaking about God; people seek another form of speech, a form more mystical, *more negative*. They seek a new negative theology, not because, as in the various medieval traditions of mysticism and negative theology that are winning or regaining their place, they object to confining God within the institutions of church and political power, but, to be honest, simply because they no longer know how to speak about God. To put it more strongly, they do not even know when this 'no longer knowing' started, no longer knowing the moment when God gradually became subsumed in the human negation of Him and took on a negative shape. Some people point to the Enlightenment, or earlier to the Renaissance, or even earlier to the era of expanding Christianity, or as far back as the classical Greco-Roman culture that made the West what it is.

The modern thesis of God's fundamental *alterity*, the dictum "God is the Other," betrays an embarrassment, a problem. We will have to examine this problem before we can describe the 'importance' of a negative theology for modern philosophy.

'God, the Other': a more formal and abstract description can hardly be conceived. It is the last late-modern residue of speaking about Him, now that the Good, the Wrathful, the Almighty, and even the Humble, the Incarnated God, are receding. But is speaking about the Other the same as speaking about God? Perhaps people speak more about themselves, their own 'other,' their alterity, when they confirm God's otherness. They do not speak of God, if this were even possible. People use Him only when they wish to speak of what lies beyond the outer limits of the human. In other words, they do not speak of this Other that He 'is,' but of those *before whom* this Other is 'other': ourselves.[8]

3. THINKERS ON THE DEATH OF GOD: BATAILLE, FOUCAULT, NANCY

Bataille takes as his starting point this modern embarrassment felt at every attempt to speak of God. For him, the God of/as the Other is not an optimistic beginning for a newly designed negative theology; for Bataille, the thesis of God's fundamental alterity refers to an experience: the experience that the 'other' God might well be a dead God.

We can see this *"inner experience"* as the intuition that is the root of Bataille's work, that keeps it in motion, while remaining the object of his study. After Bataille, other thinkers who pursued the same line of thought have further developed this experience of the death of God in cultural historical studies, in genealogies of Western thought and knowledge. I would like to discuss two of them here, insofar as they can clarify, nuance, radicalize, or criticize Bataille's intuition: two voices—Michel Foucault and Jean-Luc Nancy—that express, each in their own way, the experience that is openly decisive for Bataille. Of these modern French philosophers, Foucault explicitly acknowledges deriving inspiration from Bataille, while Nancy carries on a recurrent dialogue with Bataille.

To commemorate Bataille's death in 1962, Foucault described this experience of the death of God, a year later, in a special issue of *Critique* devoted to Bataille's work. His article is entitled "A Preface to Transgression." He posits that the death of God cannot be understood as

> . . . the finally delivered judgment of his nonexistence, but as the now constant space of our experience. By denying us the limit of the Limitless, the death of God leads to an experience in which nothing may again announce the exteriority of being, and consequently to an

---

[8] Cf. Edith Wyschogrod, *Saints and Postmodernism: Revisioning Moral Philosophy* (Chicago: University of Chicago Press, 1990), esp. chap. 8, "Saintliness and Some Aporias of Postmodernism," 254ff.: "Negativity Is Not Transcendence."

experience which is *interior* and *sovereign*. But such an experience, for which the death of God is an explosive reality, discloses as its own secret and clarification, its intrinsic finitude, the limitless reign of the Limit, and the emptiness of those excesses ["transgression"] in which it spends itself and where it is found wanting. In this sense, the inner experience is throughout an experience of the *impossible* (the impossible being both that which we experience and that which constitutes the experience). The death of God is not merely an 'event' that gave shape to contemporary experience as we now know it: it continues tracing indefinitely its great skeletal outline.[9]

This experience is the starting point for an *'a-theo-logy'*: the inability to speak about God (a-logos), as well as the inability to be with God (a-theos). The experience of the death of God is an *inner* experience because it turns people back upon themselves: they remain alone with their 'interiority,' an interiority that cannot be completed, fulfilled, and elevated/eliminated (*"aufgehoben"*) by any exteriority. The inner experience of which Bataille speaks knows a radical immanence. It no longer receives its meaning and purpose from anything outside that could surpass it: from any God. In this experience, thought and speech meet an *outer limit*, but it is not what Foucault calls the "limit of the Limitless," behind which God lives and which serves as a boundary *and* a link with Him, the Limitless, before whose face people affirm the finiteness of their existence; but this limit we meet is instead the "limitless reign of the Limit," the limit that makes all speech about what or who can be found on the other side, all speech about the Other, an empty gesture, an "empty excess." What can we say of God except that He is God? But this is to say nothing or, as Bataille specifies, it is "not-knowing." It has become "impossible" to speak of God or, to put it differently, insofar as speaking about God is concerned, He is dead.

The death of God is not presented here as a historical fact that is to have definitively marked the start of the secular or atheistic age. For Foucault, the death of God is a "constant space of our experience"—it is, as it were, active *now* in deregulating the history of

---

[9] M. Foucault, "Préface à la transgression," *Critique* 195–96 (1963): 751–69, 753; later included in *Dits et écrits* (Paris: Gallimard 1994), 1.233–50, 235; English trans., "A Preface to Transgression," in Derrida, *Language, Counter-Memory, Practice: Selected Essays and Interviews*, trans. D. F. Bouchard and S. Simon, ed. D. F. Bouchard (Ithaca, N.Y.: Cornell University Press, 1977), 29–52, 32.

secularization, that is, of the self-satisfaction of self-producing and self-completing human reason that believes it has rid itself of God. The experience of the death of God is not the mirror image of the experience of living people; it does not confirm their history. Instead, it marks an irreducible *remainder:* the empty space that God (or the gods), according to Bataille, left behind. This remainder turns this "space of our experience" into a broken space where tension dominates: the tension between secular self-satisfaction ('God is *dead*') and an equally secular discomfort ('*God* is dead'), which Bataille portrays as "an ever-present stomachache concealed within us."[10] Bataille is obsessed by this remainder.

This same remainder also interests Jean-Luc Nancy, who presents "our history" in his book *Des lieux divins* as a history "from which the gods have long departed." Among the series of fragments that compose this book and in a context directed less toward an explicit evaluation of Bataille's thought than we just found in Foucault's words—although they bear Bataille's mark in form and content—the following sentences suddenly resound at the end as a confession:

> In the third century before Christ, Cercidas of Megalopolis said, "the gods left us long ago." Our history, therefore, started with their departure or perhaps even after their departure. Or else: when we stopped knowing about their presence. They cannot return in this history—and 'return' only has meaning outside this history.
>
> But there where the gods are—and however they are, and however their existence is present or absent—is the point where our history stops. And the point where our history stops, where it is no longer history, that is, where it is no longer the moment of an act [*une opération*], but the space of an opening [*une ouverture*], is the point where something can happen.[11]

Here, too, we meet the awareness that Western history is intrinsically linked to the disappearance of the gods and find a reference to a remainder, a 'spot' amid this history, where it is *interrupted,* 'suspended,' and confronted with its outer limit, with what is "*outside* history." Nancy goes even further: in this suspension, when history

---

[10] G. Bataille, "Le sacré au vingtième siècle," in *OC*, 8.189 (author's translation).

[11] J.-L. Nancy, *Des lieux divins* (Mauvezin: T.E.R., 1987), 43–44; English trans., "Of Divine Places," trans. M. Holland, in Nancy, *The Inoperative Community*, ed. P. Connor (Minneapolis: University of Minnesota Press, 1991), 110–50. I will use the French edition.

is no longer history, "something can happen." When God's absence demands its place as a constitutive factor of the history of modern culture and this absence fills Foucault's "space of our experience," it becomes necessary for people to seek means and forms to relate to this emptiness, this foreign remainder, instead of repressing it. But such a relationship demands an unconditional openness (*"ouverture"*), and forces people to interrupt and break their process of self-realization (*"opération"*). Only so can "something happen." This "something," this relationship that challenges modern people to surrender to it, is what Bataille wanted to analyze, not as a new type of religiosity, nor as the basis for a new negative theology or mystical philosophy, but as the modern shape of what he calls "the sacred." It is a 'sacrality' without *and* with God, a sacrality whose essence lies in an absence of 'being,' that is, in a lacking, an impasse, an uncrossable outer limit.

Nietzsche was doubtless the first to formulate logically the thesis that the death of God was the foundation of modern history. Nietzsche is even more interesting for Bataille because he thought Nietzsche expressed the view that history would come to ruin on its own foundations. He considers Nietzsche the first to explore the tension that characterizes the "space of our experience." It is thus not surprising that Bataille finds something in common, an intense connection, between himself and Nietzsche.[12] In a conversation near the end of his life he noted, "For Nietzsche, what he called the death of God left a terrible emptiness, something vertiginous, almost unbearable."[13] The trail that Nietzsche, Bataille, Foucault, and Nancy each blaze in their own way in the modern philosophy of culture leads to a new reflection on the death of God.

4.3. THE THINKING OF THE OUTSIDE: THE SACRED AND THE HOLY

What are the characteristics of this trail? In Bataille's case, it focuses on the sacred or the holy: *'le sacré'* in French has a much broader

---

[12] See G. Bataille, *Inner Experience* (hereafter cited as IE), 26–27; see also OC, 5.39.

[13] Bataille in discussion with M. Chapsal, *Les écrivains en personne* (Paris: Union Générale d'Éditions, '10/18,' 1973), 31 (author's translation).

meaning than does its equivalent in other languages. It covers the nuances of 'sacral,' 'sacred,' and 'holy' in English.

Besides the concept 'sacré,' French also has the concept 'saint.' Bataille uses both terms in *Inner Experience*. Although the two concepts do overlap, they by no means coincide. Thus Bataille tries to exploit the tension between the two layers of meaning and calls attention to the *sacrality* of 'le sacré,' whereas most people generally give precedence to its *holiness* ('sainteté'). His atheology is concerned with the *unholy* implications of the sacred.

'Saint' functions primarily in a Christian context: the elect are holy, the Roman Catholic Church sooner or later confers the title 'saint' on the heroes and heroines of faith. Acts can be called 'holy' when they bring blessings or are blessed by God. 'Sacré,' on the contrary, has a place in a broader religious framework and may be translated with 'sacred' or 'sacral.' Levinas plays with this difference in nuance in his study *Du sacré au saint* where he links 'le sacré' to the mythical, including the traditions of magicians and witches, and where he puts 'le saint' in the perspective of the ethical call found in Jewish wisdom.[14]

The nuance between 'sacré' and 'saint' can be examined philologically by studying the Latin origin of the two words. '*Sacer*' and '*sanctus*' are both derived from the same root '*sak-*', three root letters that refer less to an attribute, characteristic, or situation than to a *rapport*. '*Sak-*' refers to all that takes place between people and the gods, to the outer limits of human existence, to a fundamental *separation*. It is not proven that the root '*sak-*' is related to the root '*sek-*', as found in the verb '*secere*', which means 'to cut,' 'to cleave,' and even 'to lacerate' or 'wound.' Yet it is remarkable that the root '*sak-*' originally indicated the demarcated place intended for a divinity. The Greek

---

[14] E. Levinas, *Du sacré au saint* (Paris: Minuit, 1977). See esp. the 'troisième leçon' entitled 'Désacralisation et désensorcellement'' (82–121), which Levinas ends as follows: "tout ce que nous avons appris sur le monde des illusions et de la sorcellerie, sur cette déchéance du sacré où se tient le faux sacré (ou plutôt le sacré tout court), tout cela, il faut le connaître" (120–21). Jewish 'sainteté,' on the other hand, "comes from the living God," as the author says in his final sentence. Levinas's wrestling with the vagueness and paradox of the concept 'sacré' is striking: the decline of the holy, the false or incorrect holy ("déchéance du sacré," "faux sacré") *is* at the same time the essence of the holy, understood as 'le sacré.' Opposing this is the 'real' holy ('le saint') that should liberate people from the ambivalence of 'le sacré': "*Du* sacré *au* saint."

equivalent, the root *'hag-'* (in *'hagios'*, which means 'holy'), is met first in the verb *'hadzomai'*, with the connotations 'to avoid,' 'to fear,' which always refers to a taboo.[15]

The word *'sacer'*, from which the French *'sacré'* is directly derived, is closest in meaning to the root *'sak-'*. It means both 'dedicated to the gods' and 'burdened by indelible disgrace': in both cases the rapport with the gods is central and encompasses positive and negative elements. Festus gives the following definition: "Someone declared *'sacer'* bears a real disgrace, which bans him from the human community: all contact with him is to be avoided. Someone who kills him is not called a murderer."[16] Benveniste writes that a *'homo sacer'* is for people what an *'animal sacrum'* is for the gods: he or she has nothing in common with the human world.[17]

'Sanctus', reflected in the French (and English) *'saint'* is further from the original root *'sak-'*. The word has little to do with the related meanings 'to separate,' 'to violate,' and 'to limit'; it also refers less to a sacral, tense *rapport* than to a *situation*, that is, the condition of being blessed. The blessing consists in a *sanction*: *'sanctus'* describes someone who (or that which) is empowered by some sanction and is therefore preserved from every form of decay or violation. Laws are thus holy, *'sanctae,'* and a *'homo sanctus'* cannot be killed with impunity. It is extraordinary how the concepts *'sacer'* and *'sanctus'* are apparently diametrically opposed and that, coming from the same root *'sak-'*, they have each developed along totally different religious paths.

Bataille reintroduces a primary and radical distinction between *'sacré'* and *'saint'* without a conscious or explicit reference to the philological study of the Latin. Contrary to Levinas, he is more interested in the sacred than in the holy, more interested in the violating relationship than in the inviolable and blessed state. But Bataille is ultimately aware that this distinction cannot be maintained: the act

---

[15] On this, see esp. C. Colpe, ed., *Die Diskussion um das 'Heilige'* (Darmstadt: Wissenschaftliche Buchgesellschaft, 1977). This collection contains (a translation of) classic and famous studies on the sacred (Otto, Benveniste, Caillois), complemented with new texts. I found my data in the articles by W. Kroll, "Heilig" (119–23, p. 123) and É. Benveniste, "Le sacré" (223–54, 232ff.), published earlier in Benveniste's *Vocabulaire des institutions indo-européennes*, Vol. 2: *Pouvoir, droit, religion* (Paris: Minuit, 1969), 179–207.
[16] Cited by É. Benveniste, in "Le sacré," 189.
[17] Ibid.

of sanctifying (e.g., in a sacrifice) is also an act of violation (immolation), to the extent that 'holiness' means that the person/thing is wrenched away from the profane sphere to live, by necessity or choice, 'beyond life.' Seen thus, 'le sacré' is an aspect of 'le saint' and vice versa.[18]

Insofar as atheology is meant to be a modern philosophy of sacrality, it concentrates on this puzzle. How, Bataille asks, can the sacred have this double status, this contradictory effect, and be a "mixture of fear and contact" (Leiris)?[19]

Thus, for Bataille, the sacral does not indicate an area, sphere, or universe but a rapport: the rapport with the 'exterior.' That this exterior may once have been inhabited by the gods, so that the heart (and not the margin) of human societal life was to be found in the direct and daily proximity of the gods—this exterior—does not interest Bataille. Although he is fascinated by the discoveries of the new science of his time, ethnology, and has a sharp ear for its speculations on so-called archaic humanity, he ultimately focuses on the modern situation in which this exterior has become an empty space. God has disappeared, but with this disappearance the sacred has become an even greater problem: how does one relate to an exterior that can be given no name and that cannot be filled with symbols and mythical stories?

This thinking about the exterior tries, as Nancy shows, to take a position beyond the evidence of 'our' history, not referring to human needs but to the 'extreme': ecstasy, sacrifice, expenditure, lunacy. It does not try to interpret the extreme 'from within' as if it were an individual deviation to which some fall victim, but from which most people are normally preserved; on the contrary, the extreme refers to hidden traces of sacrality in a culture and can only be discussed and studied from the experience of an exterior position. Foucault once opined that this experience of the exterior, source, and challenge of a thinking he called "la pensée du Dehors," found its historical start-

---

[18] On this, see also Francis Huxley in *The Way of the Sacred* (London: Bloomsbury Books, 1989), who writes: "The sacred is both, as the French usage implies. The word 'sacré' can be either a title of holiness or an execration. In either sense, it is a pronouncement of doom, for good or bad, and its service is an imposition laid upon men" (13).

[19] M. Leiris, "Le sacré dans la vie quotidienne," lecture given before the Collège de sociologie on 8 January 1938, published in Denis Hollier, ed., *Le collège de sociologie (1937–1939)* (Paris: Gallimard, 1979), 60.

ing point with mysticism and negative theology, but he immediately casts doubts on his words:

> One might assume that it was born of the mystical thinking that has prowled the borders of Christianity since the texts of the Pseudo-Dionysius: perhaps it survived for a millennium or so in the various forms of negative theology. Yet nothing is less certain: although this experience involves going 'outside of oneself,' this is done ultimately in order to find oneself, to wrap and gather oneself in the dazzling interiority of a thought that is rightfully Being and Word, in other words, Discourse, even if it is the silence beyond all language and the nothingness beyond all Being.[20]

The real analysis of sacrality, the analysis of the rapport with the exterior, is not simply the modern successor to negative theology. 'Outside' there waits no new God, in whom people can disappear only to rediscover themselves sublimely. 'Outside' there is nothing. The meeting with the exterior, this crossing, will be an empty crossing: a meaningless, purposeless, nameless act. But this raises the question that haunts Bataille's thought, and of which he is painfully aware: Should not every notion of the sacred be abandoned?

5.3. COMMUNICATION WITHOUT COMMUNICATION

The exterior has become empty. The gods have abandoned this 'place across' from the human community, to take the step that led to their disappearance. This "pas [step] de dieu" led to an "il n'y a pas de dieu," as Nancy says in a play on words. It is not that they no longer exist, but that they are elsewhere, further away—or closer. "No god" ("pas de dieu"): "that could mean that God's place is really wide open, vacant, abandoned, the divine infinitely released

---

[20] M. Foucault, "La pensée du Dehors," *Critique* 229 (1966): 523–46; later included in *Dits et écrits* (Paris: Gallimard, 1994), 1.518–39, 521; English trans., "Maurice Blanchot: The Thought from Outside," trans. B. Massumi, in *Foucault, Blanchot* (New York: Zone Books, 1987), 9–58, 16 (translation modified by the author). See, on the problem concerning the translation of the 'du' (*du* Dehors) in Foucault's title, my *De lege plaats*, chap. 7. Foucault plays with 'from' ('from outside,' 'de dehors'), but it seems clearly wrong to translate the title this way. The French reads 'du Dehors': the capital shows that 'Dehors' is a noun, as does the 'du' (of the). 'The Outside' is the object of a thinking, not its origin!

and dispersed."[21] Yet, according to Bataille, modernity needs to relate to, to *communicate* with, this empty place, and with this disappearance—this ambivalent 'pas.' He does not understand
communication with this emptiness as a static situation, but as a
dynamic event that is continually repeated and that determines our
experience; this strange communication must provide the outline of
a modern sacrality. In formulating and developing this paradoxical
task, Bataille breaks with the pretensions he shared with others in
the 1930s: the establishment of a new, modern, godless religion. Modernity cannot compensate for or eliminate its shortcomings, it can
only live them. Atheology finds its starting point, during the early
World War II years, with the discovery that communication with the
emptiness is only sacral when it rests first of all on the experience
that every communication on this point is impossible.

Here two tendencies collide, reinforcing each other. On one side,
Bataille strives to appreciate this impossible communication as a
holy, even divine, meeting that obtains its meaning in and through
the loss of meaning. On the other side, he continually disrupts this
dialectic with the observation that only the loss counts: this communication is nothing more than staring into a dark night, eye to eye
with an absent God. People must remain behind alone, deprived of
every exteriority—this deprivation is their only exteriority—where
they can repeatedly revisit the outer limits of this empty place and
thus reach the extremes of their possibilities. The experience Bataille
has in mind is a "voyage to the extreme possible,"[22] but this extreme
is only a place of embattlement; 'our' history's self-satisfaction
(Nancy) is sacrally *violated*, insofar as it is the sacred that violates,
ruptures, and interrupts.

Atheology tries to imagine a communication without communication, that is, without the communicators having 'something' in common ('*commun*'); the only thing shared ('*communiqué*') is the rupture
(the inability, the '*pas*') between those who communicate. Bataille's
language wanders in a labyrinth of such contradictions because he
wants to think into existence a communication with God in which
people no longer desire, like mystics of all times did, to become one
with Him and identify themselves in Him. People communicate with

---

[21] J.-L. Nancy, *Des lieux divins*, 33 (author's translation).
[22] G. Bataille, IE, 7; see OC, 5.19.

God's absence so that an abyss may open beneath every possible identity, an abyss in which the only rule is surrender.

> In all periods, religious excitement has led to the development of balanced, or more-or-less balanced, beings, while I sought to introduce in place of these balanced beings the reflection of a disorder, of something missing, and not of something that had to be respected.[23]

Communication thus becomes a surrender, an abandoning, a giving without receiving anything in return, without a result. Bataille continually wants to analyze the sacred character of this communicative giving, as a form of sacrifice, even in a time when ritual sacrifice appears to have long lost its meaning and function.

6.3. BATAILLE'S ATHEOLOGY

Bataille's atheology is doubtless one of the strangest theoretical projects of our time. It is not a systematically unified whole of philosophical reflections and analyses, but consists instead of a scattered variety of texts that shatter against their own subject: that being the experience that wants to derive its meaning and intensity only from its own ambivalent and aporetic character so it can disappear as soon as it has been aroused.

The four texts that display and express[24] this experience were written, as I said earlier, during the war years, between 1939 and 1945, long before Bataille introduced the term 'atheology.' In 1950 Bataille first formulated his plan to collect these four books in one summa, *La somme athéologique*. Thus atheology as such did not exist when Bataille wrote, for instance, *Inner Experience*. Like the other four parts of the summa, this book is a wondrous composite of diary notes, prose fragments, poetry, and philosophical reflections, all

---

[23] G. Bataille, interview with M. Chapsal, 31 (author's translation).

[24] These four books are: *L'expérience intérieure*, written in 1941–1942, published in 1943, in OC, 5.7–189; English trans., *Inner Experience*, trans. L. A. Boldt (Albany: State University of New York Press, 1988);—*Le coupable*, written from 1939 to 1943, published in 1944, in OC, 5.235–92; English trans., *Guilty*, trans. B. Boone (Venice, Calif.: Lapis Press, 1988);—*Sur Nietzsche. Volonté de chance*, written in 1944, published in 1945, in OC, 6.7–205; English trans., *On Nietzsche*, trans. B. Boone (New York: Paragon Books, 1992, 1994);—*Méthode de méditation*, written in 1945, published in 1947, in OC, 5.191–228.

marked by a variety of styles. Yet Bataille always considered this book the initial section of his summa. The writer confirmed this early in the 1950s in a note: "An *atheology*, that is, a thinking fed by the experience of God—even if it becomes exclusively the experience of God's absence—is the philosophy on which this small book is based."[25] The book consists of one central text, the second part, entitled "The Torment": doubtless the most pregnant part of *Inner Experience*. The author wrote it first, before composing the surrounding parts. The first part contains a theoretical introduction that eventually devolves into a series of loosely connected fragments. The fourth and longest part, an appendix, is an attempt to continue this interrupted introduction. The third part is a compilation of texts that Bataille wrote years earlier. They provide the book's 'prehistory.' The brief fifth and last part contains only poems.

How can this strange composition serve as the program for Bataille's atheology? To grasp this question better, I would like to present a short study of how the word 'God' functions in Bataille's exposition of the inner experience.

Bataille considers the experiences he studies uprisings, or revolts, against the *instrumental* dimension of human life. They derive their meaning and purpose solely from their meaninglessness and purposelessness. The forms of communication (see Section 5) on which he focuses are all characterized by their inability to be understood instrumentally. He seeks the appearances of modern sacrality in this uprising against, this break with, instrumentality, where the assumptions of modern life are put at risk and violated: production and progress, labor and usefulness, rationalism and individualism. He examines the moment of the *extreme*, of the exception, of the limit, which causes the instrumental in life to blanche and undergo a crisis. Bataille studies these extremes and the experience they elicit both in their catastrophic and their innocent forms. Thus, in *Inner Experience*, he examines war, poetry, laughter, wasted gifts, and eroticism.

His whole work is devoted to this investigation of the extreme in modern culture, but in the books of his atheological summa he tries to focus this study on the formulation of a "new mystical theology," which he announces early in the fourth part of *Inner Experience*.[26]

---

[25] G. Bataille, OC, 8.667.
[26] G. Bataille, IE, 19; OC, 5.120.

Bataille denotes the "most general"[27] example of the extremes that besiege instrumentality with the word 'God' that dominates nearly every page of his text. Bataille is only interested in war, poetry, laughter, wasted gifts, or eroticism insofar as they are places where he can meet the absent God. Here we encounter both the one-sidedness and the wondrous concentration of his work.

As we saw, Bataille locates the possibilities for a modern sacrality in the place where we meet the absent God. But he goes further, and here we see the decisive, yet problematical, starting point of his atheological project: this presence can only be met in a concrete form, as 'God.' God's absence has a double, negative and positive, status in his texts. The first is seen in the uncompromising analysis of modernity as the period in which the death of God has become the 'space' that is left for people to live in (Foucault). The second is expressed in Bataille's attempt to formulate a new way of speaking about (and ultimately to) God. Put differently, the ambiguity consists in the reflection on God's absence (negative) turning immediately into a reflection on 'God as absent' (positive). A modern philosophy of sacrality must address both fronts: it must be a philosophy of the disappearance of the sacred while becoming a "sacred philosophy," as Bataille calls his philosophy in the third part of *Inner Experience*.[28]

Atheology is thus interested in the subversive effect and meaning of the word 'God.' In this word we discover the outer limits of instrumentality and of a livable life; the one who utters it enters this borderline region, this margin. The word 'God' is only sacred, and its 'content,' God, is only divine insofar as they deny instrumentality and remain meaningless: they refer only to their own emptiness and make absence present. In a manner of speaking, they are good for nothing: they refuse to be reduced to an instrumental relationship, but combine the unacceptable and the unavoidable. "I call *atheology* the discipline . . . that examines the essence of the *divine*: at its apex it speaks of God, who is most *divine* in the form of His denial."[29] For instrumentality, the word 'God' is off limits: it is useless; insofar as the word 'God' only describes these outer limits, it can do nothing

---

[27] G. Bataille, *OC*, 8.665; see citation below.
[28] G. Bataille, *IE*, 80; *OC*, 5.96.
[29] G. Bataille, *OC*, 8.665.

even with itself and, as prohibition and as limit, it continually abolishes itself. It therefore challenges people to contravene the prohibition, to reject their own instrumentality, while they know they are
unable to do this without losing everything. An atheology must be a
plea for the necessity of this 'double bind' in which people see themselves involved in a revolt they did not begin: in which they "see
themselves placed before God's absence." In the resulting experience people are caught between confession and deconfessionaliza-
tion, between belief and atheism; both poles suddenly betray their
vanity and can no longer serve as refuge. But this is the same experience that in its hopelessness also opens a door to hope: in this interval we may again learn to speak of God, not as a word we create and
use to say something, but one we received as the gift of loss[30]: "the
word 'God' is only a means to indicate the most general prohibition
whose removal is not everyday atheism but the absence of God, or
better: people who see themselves placed before God's absence."[31]

7. 'GOD' IN BATAILLE'S *INNER EXPERIENCE*

Is God, then, according to Bataille, the ultimate hypostasis of the
Limit? Maybe, but it seems, however, that this conclusion could be
too easy. In *Guilty*, Bataille remarks strikingly, "God isn't humanity's
limit point, though humanity's limit point is divine."[32] This thesis
contains two statements, the first about God, the second about
human experience, which he calls a "divine" experience. It is divine
insofar as it is sacred, that is, insofar as people are confronted with

---

[30] Schalk van der Merwe gave me the idea for this description.

[31] G. Bataille, *OC*, 8.665.

[32] G. Bataille, *Guilty*, 105; *OC*, 5.350. Bruce Boone's translations (*Guilty*, *On Nietzsche*—where has the subtitle gone in the English edition?) are considerably more free than those of Leslie Anne Boldt (*Inner Experience*), which leads to inaccuracy. For comparison I provide here the original French of this quotation : "Dieu n'est pas la limite de l'homme, mais la limite de l'homme est divine. Autrement dit, l'homme est divin dans l'expérience de ses limites." Everywhere—this is but one example—the translation rounds off and harmonizes Bataille's 'rocky' (Foucault) and stiff style. Indeed, in Boone's English Bataille sometimes grows into a smooth conversationalist. The translation regularly and too easily brightens the heavy, complex themes that Bataille treats and raises—e.g., by changing the French 'mais' ('but') into the English 'though,' the text loses something of its impossible and irritating contradiction.

their inhuman "limit point." We now have an image of this experience and of how it is involved in sacrality as an outer limit, an experience that is the ultimate subject of *Inner Experience*. In the thesis, the first statement functions as an enigmatic prefix because it introduces a divine figure who will withdraw from everything said in the second statement about humanity and its 'being divine.' "God isn't humanity's limit point . . ."—this sentence says something about God negatively and contradicts (". . . though . . .") the second part: for Bataille, God does not coincide with the divine moment that arises in the experience of the sacred outer limit.

To the extent that atheology is a philosophy of sacrality, this God does not fit well in Bataille's project, which starts not with theology but with philosophy of culture. Bataille broaches a teaching of sacred experience in modern culture, not a new theology. Who is this God of whom atheology prefers not to speak, but who is apparently presupposed by the experience on which it concentrates? Who is this absent one, what do these three letters mean, three letters found on nearly every page of *Inner Experience?*[33] I would like to examine more closely the remarkable duality of the cited thesis.

Bataille wrestles with the idea that the formulation of the death of God does not say what it appears to say. God has disappeared, but in this disappearance He *gives* Himself, He 'exists' in and as sacrifice. In the death of God, that emblem of modern history, we find summoned and announced not only 'something divine,' an unexpected reminder of the sacred, as Nietzsche—and sometimes Bataille with him—diagnosed. In the death of God, God is Himself made present. In the final chapter of *Inner Experience* we see Bataille tempted by this thought without his being able to explain it theoretically. He expresses it as a prayer: speaking *about* God changes, even before it is begun, to speaking *to* God. He prays the Lord's Prayer but in a strange perverted version: in this prayer, people not only pray to God but—more importantly—God prays to people:

> I sleep.
> Although mute,
> God addresses himself to me,
> insinuating, as in love,
> in a low voice:

---

[33] The word 'God' appears 180 times in the book, the word 'divine' 32 times.

"O my father, you, on earth, the evil which is in you delivers me.
I am the temptation of which you are the fall.
Insult me as I insult those who love me.
Give me each day my bread of bitterness.
My will is absent in the heavens as on earth.
Impotence binds me.
My name is lackluster."
Hesitant, troubled, I reply:
"So be it."[34]

Who is this God, without will or power, meaningless, who addresses mortals as His "father"? Is this merely a morbid provocation directed toward Christianity, an attack on one of the most central tenets of its faith, the 'prayer of prayers'? Perhaps. But this does not free us of this image of God.

I think a sacred god is speaking here, 'sacred' in Bataille's sense. It is a filthy god who speaks to us as two people speak during an act of love who intertwine the exciting and the filthy in their reciprocal whispers, "insinuating, as in love, in a low voice." It is a violating god, a god of evil—but one who imposes this sacred violation on *Himself*, "the evil . . . delivers me," "the temptation . . . the fall," "insult those who love me," "give me the bread of bitterness." It is as if God offers Himself here, or as if Bataille wants to say that it is not we who have freed ourselves from Him in the death of God, but that the death of God is intrinsically linked with God Himself. God 'exists' as a sacrifice, an unconditional gift of self. He "is nothing," He "says nothing" ("mute"), He is absent, and to this 'being'—who 'is' nothing, encompasses nothing, refers to nothing, is no longer in any way indicative—people can only answer in the subjunctive mood, the mood of wish and desire: "So be it."

Such an answer, "hesitant, troubled," *unites* God and humanity, it is literally a 'conjunctive'; it unites the people who, having come to the outer limits of their possibilities, become 'divine' with the God who, because He just seems to have always come from these outer limits, reveals Himself *from* and *as* the margin, and lowers Himself and becomes human. He lowers Himself not according to the old pattern in which people are low and God is 'Almighty'—no,

---

[34] G. Bataille, *IE*, 131; *OC*, 5.152–52.

now God and humanity *share* the humility, the violated state, the loss of self—here lies their link, their communication.

The death of God thus precedes the *history* of the death of God. The death of God belongs to God, even before the West reached the point of killing God. This means that the last, most radical sacrifice that Nietzsche expressively describes in his famous "ladder of religious cruelty"[35] has already been performed and is continually being performed by a self-sacrificing God, even before people can lay claim to it.

Humanity does not gain by the disappearance of every representation of God, in the meaninglessness of every concept of God; this sacrifice produces neither winner nor victim. But another experience of God awakens in this disappearance, and that seems to be the inaccessible 'foundation' of Bataille's atheology. Nancy describes this foundation as follows: "And the name God refers, among people, only to the absence of sacred names."[36] The God who is merely His own disappearance or lacking comes to the fore—'reports' Himself as it were—as soon as sacrality can be seen as only a rapport with an emptiness, with an absence, as soon as every sacred name loses its antecedent, becoming an empty gesture. Such a God cannot enter an argument in the form of a *concept* of God, not even in Bataille's argument on the death of God nor in his analysis of sacrality, which begins with this death. In *Inner Experience*, Bataille is aware of this: the word 'God' is always a breach of the text, a word that interrupts the text (e.g., in the sudden insertion of a prayer) without being taken up in the rhythm of his sentences or in his world of concepts: "The word *God*, to have used it in order to reach the depth of solitude, but to no longer know, hear His voice. To know nothing of Him. God final word meaning that all words will fail further on."[37]

---

[35] See F. Nietzsche, *Beyond Good and Evil: Prelude to a Philosophy of the Future*, trans. R J. Hollingdale (Harmondsworth, U.K.: Penguin, 1975), fragment 55: "Finally: what was left to be sacrificed? Did one not finally have to sacrifice everything comforting, holy, healing, all hope, all faith in a concealed harmony, in a future bliss and justices? Did not one have to sacrifice God himself and, out of cruelty against oneself, worship stone, stupidity, gravity, fate, nothingness? To sacrifice God for nothingness—the paradoxical mystery of the ultimate act of cruelty was reserved for the generation which is even now arising: we all know something of it already." Bataille cites this passage in *IE*, 131; *OC*, 5.152.

[36] J.-L. Nancy, *Des lieux divins*, 40 (author's translation).

[37] G. Bataille, *IE*, 36; *OC*, 5.49.

The word 'God' is both necessary and impossible. It is an abyss in language, but it is a word that *as* word, as linguistic unit, is also the "negation of the abyss which God is."[38]

Yet Bataille gives this absent one a role in his text. The absent God even speaks to the writer in several places; they are the most intangible passages in his book: "God speaks to me the idiot, face to face: a voice like fire comes from the darkness and speaks—cold flame, burning sadness—to. . . ."[39] We can thus neither speak of nor keep silent about God, because God, in His death, withdraws and becomes present at the same time. Bataille now tries to analyze this 'at the same time.' In this sense he disagrees with the starting point of what in this book are called 'modern echoes of negative theology,' a starting point usually borrowed from Wittgenstein's "Whereof one cannot speak, thereof one must be silent."[40] God is not the unspeakable, the absolute Other: that would be a last, subtle, negative reduction of the absent content. God is, in Bataille's words, "not humanity's limit-point." *Inner Experience* presents a more tangible image of God: God is dead, and as dead God lurks permanently in human existence and human language. Yet God is nonetheless unspeakable: "We cannot, with impunity, add the word *God* to the language because that word surpasses language; as soon as we try, this word that surpasses itself overwhelmingly destroys its limits."[41]

We will examine this 'overwhelming' that the word 'God' is said to initiate in Bataille's book, concentrating on the most important text elements that speak of God. The difficulty here is first that Bataille continually alternates between a criticism of every use of the word 'God' and his own use of it. This contradiction coincides with the tension in the book between the central second part, "The Torment," and the other parts that are intended to provide a theoretical commentary on "The Torment." Put simply, while we meet Bataille's own God in "The Torment" (and in the poems in part 5), the later often interrupted and rewritten texts are dominated by a criticism of the concept of God.[42]

---

[38] G. Bataille, *On Nietzsche*, 132; *OC*, 5.48.

[39] G. Bataille, *IE*, 36; *OC*, 5.48.

[40] L. Wittgenstein, *Tractatus Logico-Philosophicus*, trans. C. K. Ogden (1920; London: Routledge & Kegan Paul, 1955), 189.

[41] G. Bataille, *OC*, 3.12 ("Foreword" to *Madame Edwarda*).

[42] I will only treat parts 1, 4, and 2; the word 'God' does not occur in the third part of *Inner Experience*.

"Do Not Divinize the Unknown": Criticism of Every Concept of God in Part 1

Immediately in the first chapter we find an orienting exposé of how the Christian experience of God contrasts with the inner experience.

> Experience is, in fervor and anguish, the putting into question [to the test] of that which a man knows of being. Should he in this fever have any apprehension whatsoever, he cannot say: "I have seen God, the absolute, or the depths of the universe," he can only say: "that which I have seen eludes understanding," and God, the absolute, the depths of the universe are nothing if they are not categories of understanding.[43]

"What eludes understanding" Bataille calls "the unknown." The experience deals with this unknown, not with God; the "voyage," which this experience is, leads to "the inconceivable unknown—wildly free before me, leaving me wild and free before it" (4)[44] and not to God, who—as concept, as representation—would make this unknown a "dead object." God is "tied to the salvation of the soul"; He represents the "perfect to which I cling," while the experience that Bataille envisions is "distrustfully hostile toward the idea of perfection (servitude itself, the 'must be')" (4). Even the "God without form and without mode" as described by Saint John of the Cross, one of the most empty images in the mystical tradition, is for Bataille no more than "an obstacle [*arrêt*] in the movement which carries us to the more obscure apprehension of the *unknown*: of a presence which is no longer in any way distinct from an absence" (5).

In the extreme experience, which remains on the sacred outer limit, we do not meet God, but the unknown emptiness. Bataille simply opposes identifying God with this unknown: the ideas of night, emptiness, and not knowing (*"non-savoir"*) that belong to this experience go further ("are more obscure") than every representation of God. 'God' is an obsolete category, the remainder of an experience in which "we still can appropriate to ourselves that which exceeds us" so that "we do not die entirely" (5): the experience of Christian faith.

---

[43] G. Bataille, *IE*, 4; *OC*, 5.120.

[44] For convenience sake, I include a reference to the paragraph in *Inner Experience* within parentheses.

Our answer: do not divinize the unknown; we have just begun to know little.

Once more we are seized by a great shudder; but who would feel inclined immediately to deify again after the old manner this monster of an unknown world? And to worship the unknown henceforth as 'the Unknown One'?[45]

Nietzsche's plea "not to deify the unknown" means in Bataille's words that a person "proceeds to the unknown" without "trickery," without (speaking about) God (5). The unknown 'is,' thus, not God, but points toward the sacred space of the exterior: to the outer limit of the known, controllable world. However, we will see that to reflect on and articulate this space philosophically, Bataille decides to speak about God: this space is the *interval between God and people,* in which both are lost. It is the space of sacrifice in the sense that he wishes to give to it: not the space in which two abstractions (imma-nence vs. transcendence) or two worlds (the known vs. the unknown) duel, but in which two very real figures, God and the human person, are involved and in which they come to grief.

Even though it can be distinguished from the experience of the unknown, the experience of God has not become meaningless. This we see in the closing sentence of the first chapter in the first part: "It is the measure of the unknown which lends to the experience of God . . . its great authority. But the unknown demands in the end sovereignty without partition" (5). While the experience of God is classified here as a weak variant of the experience of the unknown, it also has "great authority"—that is, it has this authority when we experience God as "a presence, which is no longer in any way distinct from an absence," when God as the dead God sees us.

Amid the critique, shared by Nietzsche and Bataille, on negative theology and the metaphysical transformation of the concept of God (God 'is' the unknown), God still creeps into Bataille's texts like a thief in the night. If we turn the unknown into a new, abstract God, we do it injustice. But we can also change the perspective of the criticism to understand Nietzsche's plea—as we just quoted it—as a plea for God: if we equate God with the unknown, we do Him an

---

[45] F. Nietzsche, *Kritische Gesamtausgabe,* VII, 1 (New York/Berlin: De Gruyter, 1967–), 249, fragment 6 (25) (author's translation); then *The Gay Science,* fragment 374.

injustice. So far Bataille seems to want to be free of the word 'God' and to want to give a "sovereignty without partition" to the unknown. But he knows this creates a tension with other parts of his book. This partly explains his difficulty in making his theoretical introduction a coherent whole.

Nuancing the Critique: The Fourth Part

The fourth part continues but modifies the critique of the concept of God. If the word 'God' functioned in the first part as ballast that the philosophy of sacrality should eliminate, the fourth part opens with a short chapter entitled "God." Bataille presents his book as a study of the unknown to which experience stands open ("Life will dissolve itself in death, rivers in the sea, and the known in the unknown" [101] is the first sentence in the fourth part). But the study of this "*inconnu*," the "new theology which has only the unknown as object," as the author calls it in the opening fragment in the fourth part, can apparently not avoid the name 'God.'

The writer opens a discussion with mysticism, specifically Eckhart. In this discussion he develops his own way of speaking about God, his own representation—which immediately turns against itself and tries to do justice to God's unknown character. We cannot speak about God because there is nothing we can say about the unknown; but to articulate this problem, Bataille must—in honesty to the trace of mysticism that is the source of his reflections—introduce his own God. "God savors Himself, says Eckhart. This is possible, but what He savors is, it seems to me, the hatred which He has for Himself, to which none, here on Earth, can be compared."[46] God does not function here as the faulty name for the unknown (as in the opening chapter of the first part) but as a necessary paradox. Nor does He function as the God of Descartes and Hegel, with whom Bataille debates in the following chapters: the name 'God' cannot become an attempt "to relate [the unknown] to the known" (108). God can only be 'self-hatred': *God consists of self-hatred*. In this lies His freedom, His sovereignty and authority, here He is sufficient unto Himself and "does He savor Himself."

God is the unknown, but this does not mean that He is, in a

---

[46] G. Bataille, *IE*, 102; *OC*, 5.120.

dialectical movement in which reason would surpass itself, again a category of Being, be it of absolute negativity, of negative Being. Bataille goes a step further: even for Himself, God is an unknown. Contrary to what Descartes and Hegel thought, He does not coincide with the clear knowledge of absolute knowing, inaccessible to the individual, but transparent for God (for God as universal Spirit). The God of atheology rejects every epistemological representation, even one where He appears and disappears as the Unknowable. This God is outside the dynamism of knowing and not-knowing. Only in His self-hatred is God, God; to this self-hatred "none, here on Earth, can be compared"; it is the inhuman 'par excellence.'

> If this hatred was for a single instant absent from God, the world would become logical, intelligible—idiots would explain it away (if God did not hate Himself, He would be what the depressed idiots believe: dejected, imbecile, logical). What, at bottom, deprives man of all possibility of speaking of God, is that, in human thought, God necessarily conforms to man, to the extent that man is weary, famished for sleep and for peace.[47]

This means that Bataille's God is in an impossible position, and *is* this position. He does not know Himself, He opposes Himself, and He is never identical with Himself. He is outside the dualism of knowing and not-knowing and the "sleep and peace" this dualism brings.

But the writer introduces this opposition, this being-outside conceived in the form of a person, a specific figure in his text: 'God.' This is a person who cannot tolerate Himself: He is always insufficient for the text (as soon as the word 'God' is spoken, He is involved in the game of knowing and not-knowing) and always He is too much for the text ('God' is an infraction into discursivity, a continuous disruption between the words). This wondrous, contradictory personage is the addressee of the sacred relationship; in the 'inner experience' people communicate with God's impossible situation, and allow themselves to be violated by it. "À *la limite de l'homme*" Bataille meets God after the death of God: a God that in no way differs from "His dreadful absence." It is an absence that cannot be understood as a pragmatic fact but which Bataille tries to reflect as an

---

[47] G. Bataille, *IE*, 102–3; OC, 5.120–21.

activity, a *working* in us that arouses our "horror." God 'is' this unrest, He 'is' this lack of fulfillment. He 'is' sacrifice.

> God finds rest in nothing and is satisfied in nothing. Every existence is threatened, is already in the Nothingness of His insatiability. And no more than He can appease Himself can God *know* (knowledge is rest). He knows nothing of the extent of His thirst. And just as He *knows nothing*, He knows nothing of Himself. If He were to reveal Himself to Himself, He would have to recognize Himself as God, but He cannot even for an instant concede this. He only has knowledge of His Nothingness, that is why He is atheist, profoundly so. He would cease right away to be God (instead of His dreadful absence there would no longer be anything but an imbecile, stupefied presence if He saw Himself as such).[48]

God between Positivity and Negativity

Given this, we can summarize Bataille's position as follows. Atheology is a critique of the way Western theology is caught between two tendencies. In the one it enters the path of *"positive* theology," which "is founded on the revelation of the Scriptures" (4) and looks upon God as the One who *reveals* Himself. It follows the other tendency when it tries to make up for this positivity by presenting itself as a *negative* theology that, with Eckhart, worships God as Nothing and so turns the unknown into God.

Bataille works through his doubts about these two apparently unavoidable poles in the plan for a theology focused only on the borderline, the limit, between humans and God, without relating the one to the other or allowing the one to disappear in the other. This borderline is the sacred outer limit, since it violates and destroys the poles that keep them apart, revealing nothing but emptiness. The "new mystical theology" that Bataille presents at the start of the fourth part of his book can be qualified as a *theology of the limit*. This theology has, as we saw, "only the unknown as object" (102), that is, the unknown, free of every divinization or humanization. This theology must concentrate on the emptiness between God and humanity where both are ignorant of who they are and both become unknowable even to themselves.

---

[48] G. Bataille, *IE*, 103; OC, 5.121.

This refusal to choose one of the two tendencies is also central to Nancy's work, which I believe tries to develop Bataille's starting points in a reflection that accentuates the limit and the 'in-between' we have been examining. Positive theology qualifies every attempt to withdraw God from a fixed revelation as "superstition" and "paganism," but negative theology identifies God with this withdrawing movement and equates Him with the "shadowy outer limits" of humanity:

> Over and over again there is a double temptation: either to label all shadowy outer limits of experience (of thinking) 'God,' or to call this labeling a metaphor based on superstition. Since the West is what it is, there is probably no way of speaking about God that does not fall for one of the two temptations, or even for both. But God is not 'a way of speaking'—a way of protecting oneself—nor is He humanity's ultimate truth. People are people and gods are gods. This division is primordial, and there can be no intermixture. As inhabitants of the same world, they face one another on opposite sides of a dividing line from which they both withdraw. Together they form the incarnation of this "facing one another," of this "standing eye to eye." . . . The divine gesture consists in hiding on this dividing line before the face of the people. The human gesture consists in turning away from this line where they meet God's face.[49]

In this theology God and humanity share (in and out) their division, in the double meaning of the French '*partager*.'[50] Their communication is the "incarnation" of the borderline ('*partage*'). They are then in the most pure excess where they meet the outer limits of their being and ultimately the outer limits of communication.

Bataille applies his criticism of these ever alternating positive and negative tendencies to more than just Western theology; Western metaphysics is equally susceptible to this double temptation. It only refines and makes this interaction more subtle, it does not do away with it. Seen this way, Western theology and philosophy are in one another's debt which is expressed in an interweaving of the two since the earliest Neoplatonic and neo-Aristotelian traditions. From Dionysius and Aquinas to Descartes and Hegel we see the same scenario

---

[49] J.-L. Nancy, *Des lieux divins*, 40 (author's translation).

[50] Share as share out: 'divide into pieces (and distribute),' and share as share in: 'participate in.'

in different forms, a phenomenon Heidegger called "onto-theology": a philosophical theology in search of a philosophical foundation for the living God, a theological philosophy trying in its reflection on Being to reach a new understanding of the concrete God.

In the fourth part, therefore, Bataille debates with Descartes and Hegel. For him, they are prime examples of a metaphysics that alternates between the two tendencies without showing any interest in the 'place in-between.' Neither Descartes nor Hegel begin with the sacred outer limit between humans and God, but they try to reconcile the two, to harmonize them. In so doing they underestimate the "inner" experience of God, as Bataille presents it, one in which 'God' is an impossible word, one in which He must die again immediately if He is to live. Such an experience of a fundamental break—*between* humans and God, but also *within* humans and God—does not fit in with the *linear* (Descartes) or *dialectic* (Hegel) movement of knowledge so strong in the history of metaphysics.

Descartes deduces his God directly from the possibilities of human reason: God is the highest part of knowledge.

> In a letter of May 1637, Descartes writes on the subject of the fourth part of the *Discourse*—where he affirms, beginning with the *Cogito*, the certainty of God: "In lingering for a long enough time over this meditation, one gradually acquires a very clear and, if I may speak in such a way, intuitive knowledge of intellectual nature in general—the idea of which, when considered without limitation, is what represents God to us, and when limited, is that of an angel or of a human soul."[51]

God is here the high point of "intellectual nature," reason's ultimate approach. While this knowledge may be "intuitive," it leads in a linear way to a dominant final point in which rational knowledge becomes complete. Bataille calls this movement of knowledge a "vital movement" (105): people imagine the unknowable God as the source and goal of knowledge; we cannot know Him as we know other objects, but we can relate to Him, understand Him. Bataille notes that in a person who undergoes the inner experience, "this vital movement dies."

Inner Experience is dominated by the struggle to remove the evocation of God from its dependence on knowledge, on an ontological

---

[51] G. Bataille, *IE*, 105; OC, 5.123–24.

and conceptual process. When Bataille describes a moment in a once-experienced ecstasy, he notes, "divinity had then a mad, deaf presence, illuminating up to intoxication. . . . I write divinity, not wanting to know anything, not knowing anything. At other times, my ignorance was the abyss over which I was suspended" (58). At a time when we know nothing (from intoxication or from fear) God is "present," but this presence is "mad": only an extreme experience can be fulfilled of it as this presence is neither knowable nor unknowable. We are between knowableness and unknowableness, that is, beyond every possibility of appropriation (even unknowing is a claiming qualification). This fleeting "mad presence" can be compared with the situation of someone "suspended above an abyss": his or her "presence" may change any second into absence, and we "know" only that a few minutes later we will know nothing. Bataille's thinking and speaking about God bear the stamp of this delicate moment.

The "vital movement" in metaphysics consists in categorically misunderstanding this moment. Bataille tries to criticize this movement as follows:

> Descartes imagined man having a knowledge of God, predating that which he has of himself (of the infinite before that of the finite). Yet, he was himself so occupied that he could not represent to himself divine existence—for him the most immediately knowable—in its state of complete idleness.[52]

And Bataille tries to unmask this movement as well:

> God is in us at first the movement of Spirit which consists—after having passed from finite knowledge to infinite knowledge—in passing, as if through an extension of limits, to a different, nondiscursive mode of knowledge, in such a way that the illusion arises from a satisfaction—realized beyond us—of the thirst for knowing which exists in us.[53]

According to Bataille, Hegel radicalized Descartes's "movement of the Spirit," his God, by providing it with a necessary dialectical detour. Knowing reason does not lead people directly to God, it must first discover and integrate its own outer limits. It must die to live,

---

[52] G. Bataille, *IE*, 107; *OC*, 5.125.
[53] G. Bataille, *IE*, 108; *OC*, 5.126.

but in this 'living' it reaches a higher step that definitively wipes out this dying: that eliminates the limit. According to Bataille's reflection on Hegel's idea, knowing not linked to discursivity is the knowing of the Absolute Spirit, that surpasses individual knowing. Through this Absolute Knowing, which people reach by first risking their reason and by involving everything (totality) in their thinking (even the irrational, death), they not only come to know God, they simply become God. Knowing obtains a divine status: the "vital movement" prepared by Descartes. The knowing subject thus itself becomes "everything," itself becomes God.

> If I 'mimic' Absolute Knowledge, I am at once, of necessity, God myself (in Hegel's system, there can be no knowledge, even in God, which goes beyond Absolute Knowledge). The thought of this self—of *ipse*—could only make itself absolute by becoming everything. The *Phenomenology of the Spirit* comprises two essential movements completing a circle: it is the completion by degrees of the consciousness of self (of human *ipse*) and the becoming everything (the becoming God) of this *ipse* completing knowledge (and by this means destroying the particularity within it, thus completing the negation of oneself, becoming Absolute Knowledge).[54]

Bataille earlier defined the "Hegelian man" as the fusion of "Being and God" (80), which is realized in the project of dialectics leading to absolute knowledge.

But, according to Bataille, the dialectical inclusion of everything in one system, even everything that breaks through the instrumentality of thinking (immortality, death), puts Hegel before an unsolvable and alarming problem: Is not reason itself dead when it is "completed" in the Absolute Spirit? And does not human history reach its end when it is "completed" and when 'Being' simply coincides with 'God'? This problem, which Descartes's linear movement of knowledge could not analyze, led to what Bataille calls Hegel's madness—a theme to which he returns several times in *Inner Experience*.[55]

> Hegel had no doubt a tone of one who irritatingly gives out empty promises, but in a portrait of him as an old man, I imagine seeing exhaustion, the horror of being in the depths of things—of being God. Hegel, at the moment when the system closed, believed himself for

---

[54] See, e.g., G. Bataille, *IE*, 108–9; *OC*, 5.56.
[55] See G. Bataille, *IE*, 43; *OC*, 5.56.

two years to be going mad: perhaps he was afraid of accepting evil—which the system justifies and renders necessary; or perhaps linking the certainty of having attained Absolute Knowledge with the completion of history—with the passing of existence to the state of empty monotony—he saw himself, in a profound sense, becoming dead; perhaps even his various bouts of sadness took shape in the more profound horror of being God. It seems to me, however, that Hegel, shrinking back from the way of ecstasy (from the only direct resolution of anguish) *had* to take refuge in a sometimes effective (when he wrote or spoke), but essentially vain attempt at equilibrium and harmony with the existing, active, official world.[56]

The metaphysical concept of God is a modern derivative of the 'nothing' worshiped by negative theology. The Other, the Unspeakable, the Transcendent are the result of the attempt to reduce God to a "way of speaking" (Nancy),[57] to include Him in human language and relate Him to knowledge. For Bataille, Hegel's concept of the Spirit is the last, definitive variation in this series of reductions. It is definitive not because it is better than all the preceding or succeeding variations, but because it unintentionally recognizes its own bankruptcy. After Hegel, theology can only be atheology: no way of speaking about God can take itself seriously as speech, as Logos, once it realizes that it irrevocably leads to the loss of its own object—in silence: "We try to place ourselves in the presence of God, but God alive within us demands at once that we die; we only know how to grasp this by killing."[58] Does this recognition mean that 'God' is the resistance to objectivization? It seems as if Bataille concludes that the only object left to theology is the moment when people experience the limit, the borderline, or the "separating line" (Nancy's *"partage"*), as the central moment in this resistance. But how does this experience relate to the "God within us" of which Bataille speaks? Who is this anti-God? In "The Torment" he adopts a position on this question in which he, more explicitly and consistently than we have thus far seen, tries to surpass the level of critique of all concepts of God. Before I turn to this, I would first like to summarize and evaluate the view of the death of God presented so far in this chapter.

[56] G. Bataille, *IE*, 109–10; *OC*, 5.128–29.
[57] See the quotation cited above from Nancy, *Des lieux divins*, 40.
[58] G. Bataille, *IE*, 88; *OC*, 5.104.

The Death of God as the End of Every Completion: Modernity's Fear

At the sacred outer limit, people experience the violation of what Bataille calls the "homogeneous order." It is the moment when so-called normal, instrumental existence is interrupted by the heterogeneous, the extreme, the exceptional, when structuring laws are no longer self-evident, but refer to some exterior 'space': a moral and existential 'no-man's-land' where everything is at risk and only the experience of the finiteness of any law remains. In this space, people have to assume responsibility for instrumental life and at the same time "expiate" it, to use Bataille's vocabulary: they must discover new forms of instrumentality, formulate new laws, while maintaining sensitivity to and respect for its incomplete, finite, and vulnerable character. Instrumentality is unavoidable and human; its claims to totality and universality, to "wishing oneself to be everything" (xxxii), are translated into the illusion that life can become perfectly completed, in a final Law. This divine Law would raise existence above itself in a last, comprehensive provision of meaning and values.

But the moment when the exceptional is met is equally unavoidable. This moment, which Bataille puts in the center of his analysis of sacrality, is not an 'alternative' to completion but only unearths the outer limits of this movement toward completion, this totalitarian tendency that characterizes instrumental life, disrupting the illusion. At the outer limit we see revealed the insignificance of this "entirety." The desired Infinity is recognized as an infinite *finiteness*: the End (of history, of human purpose), the Object of instrumentality must be continually reformulated, rediscovered, and 'completed,' and this in a space that cannot be reduced to the logic of the End: in the space of the extreme that overwhelms every law, washing it away like a sand castle destroyed by the onrushing waves. The end of the Hegelian history of the Spirit becomes an infinite end, an end without end—a comedy. Totality becomes (in a variation on Levinas) infinity: it is confronted with its *own* infinity, its own endlessness. The history of meaning becomes an endless procession of meanings, and is thus faced with its own meaninglessness, as a woodland path (in a variation on Heidegger's "*Holzweg*") slowly disappears to reappear unexpectedly elsewhere only to disappear again. The experience that is the object of Bataille's atheology is oriented toward this confrontation, this outer limit between infinity and the finite.

> Anyone wanting slyly to avoid suffering, identifies with the entirety of the universe, judges each thing as if he were it. In the same way, he imagines, at bottom, that he will never die. We receive these hazy illusions like a narcotic necessary to bear life. But what happens to us when, disintoxicated, we learn what we are? Lost among babblers in a night in which we can only hate the appearance of light which comes from babbling. The self-acknowledged suffering of the disintoxicated is the subject of this book.[59]

While people formerly linked the sacred outer limit to the image and experience of God, and while the relationship with God that people sought and experienced as a vivid force filled a whole domain within social life, modernity denies this outer limit, excludes it, thereby denying the God that was its incarnation. When sacrality, its moments, its working, can nevertheless break through this denial, it does not find a new divine revelation, but only the emptiness of finiteness where "the impossible prevails" (33). God has disappeared, the outer limit is empty, and since then God is an "impossible" God. The outer limit is empty: this means that it is no longer the place or the position in culture where the human eye catches a glimpse of the divine world, of God. The outer limit is no longer the medium that brings the community of people in contact with the One that transcends this limit. Insofar as God made this sacred limit habitable and open to experience by His (and not humanity's) inhabiting it, this outer limit becomes uninhabitable once modern people have killed God.

The denial of the outer limit is in a certain sense unavoidable, but for Bataille it is also fatal. If God can no longer function as a necessary complement to instrumental life, as *something facing* that is both foreign and familiar, if, in other words, the relationship between sacrality and rationality is disturbed and finally abandoned, then the experience of the outer limit, divested of all images of God and the harmony they bring about, can only produce an experience of *fear*. It is the experience of 'nothingness' that becomes manifest when facing the outer limit: a nothingness that invites people to

---

[59] G. Bataille, *IE*, xxxii; *OC*, 5.10.

surrender to the simple nakedness and finiteness of their own existence.[60] This fear is fear of the "absence of God"—the end of every
completion, of divine harmony. It is the fear that sovereignty has
become nothing, that the place of a sovereign completion of existence has become empty, and that neither humanity nor God can be
realized as image, as last evidence. Sovereignty cannot be realized
and the fear of this fact is for Bataille determinative for the 'modern
condition.' We are left with a broken sovereignty leading only to the
experience of the pure outer limit, an outer limit without horizon,
without exterior. Modernity has excluded the exterior; the result is
that it can only 'interiorize' the outer limit, feel it in itself: this is
probably the meaning (or at least one of the meanings) of the 'inner
experience' that Bataille holds forth.

The fear of the outer limit is both unbearable and inescapable:
when it, in its turn, is denied and people keep believing in the End,
in sovereignty as completion, the catastrophe approaches that Bataille observes: World War II, against which his atheological summa
is both reaction and answer. The critical tendency of his philosophy
of culture can be summarized as follows: in a modernity that stub-
bornly continues to strive for a sovereign completion and tries to
eliminate the sovereignty of the outer limit (sovereignty as outer
limit), people are merely the "pinnacle of a disaster."[61]

---

[60] A radical plea for a philosophy of finiteness in the sense outlined here can be
found in two studies by Jean-Luc Nancy, *L'expérience de la liberté* (Paris: Galilée,
1988; English trans., *The Experience of Freedom* [Stanford, Calif.: Stanford University Press, 1994]); and *Une pensée finie* (Paris: Galilée, 1990). Geen Eng. vert. I
think the first book is, in part, a further development of what Bataille wanted to
discuss in *Inner Experience*, although it contains few direct references to Bataille.
Nancy's attempt to consider freedom a *surrender* that introduces the limits of instrumentality, of an existence oriented toward infinity, touches on the orientation
of Bataille's atheology as I have interpreted it in this study. The author formulates
the task of such a philosophy, in which experiences of freedom and finiteness are
related and are interpreted as a break with instrumentality (productivity, producing
existence), as follows: "Dès que l'existence n'est plus produite, ni déduite, mais
simplement posée (cette simplicité affole toute notre pensée), et dès qu'elle est
abandonnée à cette position en même temps que par elle, il faut penser la liberté
de cet abandon" (*L'expérience de la liberté*, 31). In *Une pensée finie*, Nancy collects
a compendium of texts that demonstrate how he arrived, in the 1980s, at this philosophy of finiteness. He enters a discussion mainly with Bataille (55–106) and to a
lesser extent with Blanchot, whom I believe he uses as keys to reach a new understanding of Kant, Hegel, and Heidegger, leading to a reevaluation, a new relationship to these 'modern classics.'

[61] G. Bataille, *Guilty*, 7; OC, 5.241.

It seemed to me there were two terms to human thought: God and the awareness of God's absence. But since God's just a confusion of the SACRED (a religious aspect) and REASON (an instrumental aspect [*l'utilitaire*]), the only place for him is a world where confusion of the instrumental and the sacred becomes a basis for reassurance. God terrifies when He's no longer the same as reason (Pascal and Kierkegaard). But if He's not the same as reason, I'm confronted with God's absence. And this absence is confused with the last stage of the world, which no longer has anything instrumental about it. . . . So the question is still outstanding: . . . *fear . . . yes, fear, that only boundless thought can reach* . . . fear, yes, but what *of . . . ?* The answer fills the universe and the universe in me: ". . . very clearly NOTHING. . . ."[62]

The God of "The Torment": Part Two

God is no longer the incarnation of the sacred outer limit; He is no longer the complement to instrumentality (which Bataille calls "utility"), which leads the instrumental order to Completion, conferring on it the sovereign glow of the universal, inviolable Law of existence. The exterior is empty and can *as* exterior no longer exist. It can no longer be represented in the sovereign God, and thus be intrinsically linked with the 'inner,' with the homogeneous order of instrumental life; via this link the 'inner' would raise itself and penetrate its negation, reaching an Absolute, its Completion. Sovereignty can no longer be personified or *reified* (made into a thing)—that is, the outer limit of instrumentality can no longer in any way be instrumentalized. According to Bataille, neither the unknown God of the mystics, nor the spiritualization of this unknown by metaphysics can take seriously the fear of this "nothing."

The task of modernity is the recognition of this fear. With this recognition, people become aware that God can only make Himself present as the Absent One in the margins of modern culture, without His being trapped in a dialectic of inner and exterior, without His making Himself visible or revealing Himself. This impossible God is no longer the exterior Completion and the hidden meaning of human existence, He is no longer the Transcendent Other. On

---

[62] G. Bataille, *Guilty*, 6; OC, 5.240. See, on Bataille's view of the 'nothingness of sovereignty,' the chapter by Marin Terpstra and Theo de Wit, who, however, in their conclusion state that this view would be a form of nihilism.

the contrary, after the unveiling of His sovereignty, He has come so near that we cannot see Him. It is this absent/close God that Bataille has act so puzzlingly in "The Torment."

It is a God who is met only in excess, in the exceptional, in the margin of instrumental life—without people knowing who or what they are meeting. He asserts Himself only as the Inhuman, the Unendurable: an earthy God, uglier, more desperate, and more lonely than humanity (see IE, 34). He is a naked presence, divested of pride, divested of subjectivity. He is a counterpoint, a dissenting voice who shows people their insufficiency as in a broken mirror and addresses them: Listen to me, look at yourself, this is what you are, you are not "everything." The confrontation with this God occurs in the border areas of instrumental existence that Bataille wanted to study in his work: for instance, eroticism, poetry, insanity, or revolution.

Only in such a confrontation can "supplication" find an unexpected meaning, as the expression of faith without hope, a hope without faith.

> Meaning of supplication. I express it thus, in the form of a prayer: "O God our father, You who, in a night of despair, crucified Your son, who, in this night of butchery, as agony became *impossible*—to the point of distraction—became the *Impossible* Yourself and felt *impossibility* right to the point of horror—God of despair, give me that heart, Your heart, which fails, which exceeds all limits and tolerates no longer that You should be!"[63]

This supplication says only: God, I do not know You, yet I cannot deny You. The God who can no longer be raised to the transcendence of Absolute Exteriority has become overly proximate.[64] He is too

---

[63] G. Bataille, *IE*, 35; OC, 5.47–48.

[64] Cf. with Levinas in *De Dieu qui vient à l'idée* (Paris: Vrin, 1982; English trans., *Of God Who Comes to Mind* [Stanford, Calif.: Stanford University Press, 1998]), who sees the relationship to God as a nearness that exceeds every fusionlike or complementary relationship. This nearness moves people to the outer limit of life where it is lived "without a reason for being" ("*sans raison d'être*"). Both Bataille and Levinas see in this outer limit the source of life and the point where it is always renewed after an interruption; but where Levinas speaks of the Good that reveals itself at this outer limit, in this nearness, Bataille speaks only of the extreme possible: the excess that in his eyes precedes ("meilleur que" in Levinas's words) every determination of good and evil. But it is doubtful whether Levinas's concept of 'le bien' is a moral or an ethical qualification. If the Good shows itself in a life lived without a reason for being, is it not a preethical (or metaethical or even postethical) notion? "Proximité de Dieu où se dessine, dans son irréductibilité au savoir, la

close to be seen, too present to become a presence, as lovers can look
too closely in one another's eyes: suddenly they no longer recognize
the other's face and they stare in the emptiness of an eye in which
the other becomes a blind, anonymous absence.[65]

> Prayer to put me to bed: "God who sees my efforts, give me the night
> of your blind man's eyes."
> Provoked, God replies; I become strained to the point of collapse and
> I see him; then I forget. As much disorder as in a dream.[66]

If the preceding analyses are correct, then I think that Nancy's
presentation closely agrees with the God to which Bataille so unexpectedly gives a role in "The Torment." Without directly citing Bataille, he gives an accurate description of the problem treated in the
fragments of "The Torment," and so reaches an atheological way of
speaking about God. If God is the Absent One, if His place is only
the place of the excess in which nothing counts and all is at risk,

---

socialité, *meilleure que* la fusion et que l'achèvement de l'être dans la conscience de
soi, proximité où, dans ce 'meilleur que', le *bien* se met seulement à signifier. Proximité qui déjà à la pure durée, à la patience de vivre, confère un sens, sens de la
vie purement vécue sans raison d'être, rationalité plus ancienne que la révélation de
l'être" (184).

[65] In this sense God is nameless, He has become *a* god. He lacks the capital letter
that distinguishes the proper name from other words. This is no longer the exalted
symbol of the Nameless or the Unmentionable, that as a final 'super-essence' (as
criticized by Derrida) surpasses all names. Bataille's God is the one Nancy refers to
as "le défaut d'un nom" (*Des lieux divins*, 10). He is the simple *failure* of a name,
and in a certain sense is always a blasphemy: the three letters g, o, d become an
empty space and everyone can use them. There is no permanent owner of this
'name,' neither as person or as idea. Everyone can speak these letters, as in the
expression 'My God,' or in Edwarda's words, "I am God" (*Madame Edwarda, OC*,
3.20). And everyone who speaks them necessarily curses, for this god is himself a
curse against God, a 'vain use of God's name,' as one of the Ten Commandments
in Exodus 20.7 forbids. Face to face with the God of "The Torment" people relate
to the one who may have no name and who is addressed as 'my' God. Is the exple-
tive 'My God!' not always an expression of surprise, of disbelief, of embarrassment?
A supplication—empty, because it lacks an addressee? " 'Mon Dieu' signifie: ici,
maintenant, j'entre en rapport singulier avec le défaut d'un nom singulier" (Nancy,
Des lieux divins, 10). Still, as Nancy suggests, the *rapport* with this nameless and as
such nonsingular God is an extremely singular event; in losing His name, God
reaches a most radical singularity, which 'is' only or 'acts' only in rapport with humans. Bataille would doubtlessly affirm this complex paradox. See, for further treatment of this paradox, J. Derrida, *Sauf le nom (Post-Scriptum)*, in *On the Name*, trans
J. Leavey Jr. (Stanford, Calif.: Stanford University Press, 1995), 35–85.

[66] G. Bataille, *IE*, 41; *OC*, 5.53–54.

then we may as well forget God and address Him as 'not-God' or 'no-God':

> No God: it would be or will be so, and this outside all relationship to atheism—at least with the metaphysical atheism that, as a dependent of theism, wants to put something new in the place of the denied or absent god. No god: that could mean: God's place set wide open, vacant, abandoned, the divine infinitely burst apart and dispersed. But it would also mean that the figure of God is so close that we can no longer see Him. Not because He has disappeared from our interior, but because He, in approaching us, continually disappears and again approaches and with His disappearance has caused our entire interior, our entire subjectivity to disappear. He must be so close that He is no more, neither for us, nor in us. He must be the absolute proximate to us—simultaneously frightening and glorious—the nearness of a naked presence, divested of every subjectivity.[67]

Humans as the Place of the God: Bataille versus Nancy?

In *Des lieux divins*, from which the preceding quotation comes, Nancy analyzes the moment of excess, of the exceptional, as the moment when people exceed themselves. For a moment, they are no longer 'people' but, at the outer limit, they become "the place of the god" ("*le lieu du dieu*").[68] Bataille introduces this "place" as the place of *supplication*, not of *knowing*. It is the place in between God and people, not of the divinization of people; or put differently, the place of sacrifice, not of identification and fusion. Edwarda's words ("I am God") are so insane because they are not an expression of ascertainment, but can only be understood as a supplication: God, let me be impossible, as You are impossible, "God, give me that heart, Your heart, which fails . . ." (35).

Nancy localizes this place in Isis's supplication to Osiris, the invisible god that Plutarch describes as the god of the dead, as the *dead* god: a god between the gods and people: "Come . . . I do not see you, and yet my heart presses against you and my eyes desire you. . . . The gods and the people turn their faces toward you and cry together."[69] If this impossible sentence, "I am God," only refers to a

---

[67] J.-L. Nancy, *Des lieux divins*, 33 (author's translation).
[68] Ibid., 46 (author's translation).
[69] Ibid., 42 (author's translation).

place, a space, an outer limit, and not to a new idea of God that would lead to a divinization, if Bataille's supplication exists only in begging for this space, for approaching this empty place, and not for God, who then is the God mentioned in the sentence? Who is met in the excess, when God and people risk losing themselves? How do we keep this "who" outside the logic of subjectivity? In an indirect discussion with Bataille, Nancy addresses this question and thus puts in relief the ambivalence of his own position.

On the one hand, he correctly avoids taking literally the meaning of the sentence that is found in several places in Bataille's work besides the story of *Madame Edwarda*. He refers to the movement, the "compulsion," that lies beneath the three words. "I am God" is not an assertion like any other, but an *exodus* from the inhabitable world in which God and people are defined positions that complement and elevate one another.

> "This God who inspires us from behind his clouds is insane. I know him, I am him."[70] These expressions find their value less in what they say (clear, evident, surprising, and deadly) than in the compulsion with which they are borne, and through which, in their turn, they bear me: in an experience of infinite fear and of infinite joy. In other words: in the experience that God is always outside himself, is outside God, that he is never what he himself would like. . . . It is this compulsion— which is not insane, which is something else than insanity—that we must name as the opposite of atheism. In God the links with God are repeatedly severed: this compulsion is divine beyond every divinity.[71]

While Nancy takes seriously the supplication contained in Edwarda's words, he balks in a following passage at the real meaning of these words. Suddenly Nancy no longer interprets "I am God" as a compulsion, a desire, but as a trap for the old way of speaking about God as about a subject:

> "I am God": perhaps it is impossible to avoid this answer, when the question "What is God?" presupposes that God is a Subject. This presupposition is always present—and we must take the risk (like Hölderlin wanted) of not giving any meaning at all to the word God, and of seeing it solely as the proper name of an unknown.[72]

---

[70] Here Nancy cites from *Le petit*, in *OC*, 3.39 (author's translation).
[71] J.-L. Nancy, *Des lieux divins*, 43 (author's translation).
[72] Ibid. (author's translation).

But Bataille's speaking about God as met in *Inner Experience* and especially in "The Torment" intends to leave the word 'God' without meaning. It cannot even be the name of someone or something unknown, but functions simply as an *unknown name:* a name that no one 'bears,' and that is met in the excess; "*Je suis Dieu*" is not, as Nancy suggests, an answer to the question of the 'who,' 'what,' and 'how' of God, but a disguised question, in the form of a supplication. It is not a matter of a new subject-position, a new variation of the onto-theology that Nancy repeatedly criticizes; Edwarda's words are the epigram above the inner experience in which all is at risk: 'I,' 'am' ('to be,' 'being'), and 'God.'

Nancy's description of humans as "the place of the god" leads him to depict what occurs in this place as a denudation ("*dénudement*") and a being destitute ("*dénuement*"). It is the place of a "surrender without shadow or protection" where God strips people, leaving them naked: "God drives people outside themselves."[73] This expulsion is at the same time the compulsion, the movement expressed in Edwarda's words.

But a few lines further on Nancy again balks at this 'localization' described meticulously in "The Torment" and relocates "the place of the god" back in the long ago past.

> [T]he whole experience of the temple and the altar penetrates the obscene experience. Indicating and naming God in the heat of love and in the bordello, as Bataille did, that is to continue to succumb to the modern temptation. The altars and temples—I repeat—have been abandoned.[74]

And yet, Bataille starts with this experience of the empty temple, but, however diffuse his use of the word 'God' may be, he avoids reassigning this empty space to God. This would be to give too great an honor to his atheology and to divest it of its hesitation. Only a suspicion rules his texts: the suspicion that in the excess, which Bataille repeatedly (perhaps this is the limitation of his work) recognizes in the "heat of love, of the bordello," people experience that they are without God. God's place is the place of nakedness, of 'being without God.'

---

[73] Ibid., 46 (author's translation).
[74] Ibid., 47 (author's translation).

The bordellos of our time are not the new temples, the beds in their rooms are not the new altars of an age-old religious activity. Nor can they monopolize the excess: it is everywhere. The sacred outer limit runs straight through Western culture and cannot be isolated in bordellos, nor in art, literature, or rebellion. But if these marginal areas are the places that have become impossible for people, then we have no other choice but to explore them as *"lieux divins,"* to visit and then to abandon them. Both Bataille and Nancy take the 'risk' of pointing to these places and doing justice to the emptiness of our temples. This observation shows clearly that Nancy's discussion with Bataille is less a rational, pragmatic debate than an emotional meeting, caught between recognition and rejection. It may well be that every confrontation with Bataille's atheology ultimately bears this characteristic.

> Divine places, without gods, without any god, surround us everywhere. They offer themselves and are open to our arrival and departure or for our presence, as a promise free for our visit. They are free to be visited by those who are not or are no longer humans, but who simply are there, in these places: we ourselves, alone, in a meeting with what we are not, and what the gods, for their part, have never been.[75]

God the Other, the Hidden, the Infinite, the Unknown—or even God the Nothing—are all attempts to fill the sacred emptiness. In the name of the sacred, Bataille questions every speaking about God. His criticism—that is, the *crisis* he observes and tries to analyze— touches on the critical questions Nancy poses to modern French theology, referring to the work of Jean-Luc Marion, who has tried since the 1970s to develop a modern negative theology in the border area of philosophy and theology, a "theology of distance."[76] Are we speaking of God when we speak of the Other? Does not this Other (person) run over into the Other (thing), that is, the failure of *our* language, the insufficiency of our reason, in short, the whole intriguing outer limit of thought that Marion so eloquently calls *"l'écart divin"* or *"la distance divine"*? Do we not need another way of speaking about God? Nancy suggests,

---

[75] Ibid., 50 (author's translation).
[76] On this, see Marion's own article and in particular that by Victor Kal elsewhere in this volume.

. . . in order to speak of God, we must speak of something else than the Other, the Hidden or the Hiding and His infinite distance. If we do not understand this, we remain stuck in the endless posttheology of a transcendence that continually turns into an immanence. . . . By baptizing our chasms 'God,' we create at least two errors, or two incoherences: we fill our chasms by giving them a bottom, and we misuse God's name by making it the name of a thing, of a *'quelque chose.'*[77]

8.3. POSTSCRIPT

The God of "The Torment" is too close to be God. If we still demand of Him that He be God and reveal Himself as such, we do nothing other than form an image of Him on which we can rely. When people are satisfied with this image and opt for this satisfaction, they and God have left the outer limit. The emptiness in which both were lost is again filled and the fear is quashed. The gift that brought each of them to this outer limit and which befell them there as a promise, the gift of loss,[78] is perhaps too vulnerable to be received. How can we envision a *receiving* that does not immediately become a *claiming*? How can the gift be kept free of the logic of 'the proper' and of property? The true gift in which the giver and receiver, God and person, lose themselves without *something* being exchanged always remains a promise. The gift of loss is timeless.[79] It can only 'occur' by opening an empty place where it *is* nothing, but always *will be*. From this nothingness it derives its sovereignty which cannot bear the "intoxications"[80] of instrumental life.

---

[77] J.-L. Nancy, *Des lieux divins*, 5 (author's translation).

[78] Cf. Rebecca Comay in "Gifts without Presents: Economies of 'Experience' in Bataille and Heidegger" (*Yale French Studies* 78 [1990]: 66–89): "Sacred experience never presupposes an original plenitude to be reestablished" (83). The experience is sacred insofar as it is no longer grounded on "the certitude of feeling nor the plenitude of sensation" (84), which, according to the author, Walter Benjamin is to have criticized correctly when he contrasted '*Erfahrung*' to '*Erlebnis*'. Bataille's 'expérience' (Benjamin's '*Erfahrung*') is not tolerated by and does not tolerate "the industrial era"; it is "taken up or overwritten by the circuit of productivity and exchange" (85). It can only exist as an "experience of loss."

[79] Cf. J. Derrida, "Folie de la raison économique: Un don sans présent," in *Donner le temps* (Paris: Galilée, 1991).

[80] G. Bataille, *IE*, xxxii; *OC*, 5.10.

The empty place where Bataille seeks modern sovereignty is like an interval between 'the proper' and 'the strange,' between 'being' and 'not-being': an interval between people and God where people are no longer people and the gods are no longer gods. This place is unbearable, no one can remain there, but when despite themselves people suddenly enter there, they discover that instrumental life can achieve everything but ultimately is left with nothing.

> We would really like to live as if death no longer existed, as if we could reduce the world to purposeful work and rest. We have departed from poetry, its congealed violence disturbs us.[81]

In writing *Inner Experience* Bataille has tried to contribute to a resistance against this reduction: by making sovereignty's empty space present in himself and in his readers as a "fear ruling, in a hidden way, within us like an unceasing stomachache."[82] For this he needed the poetry that he both distrusted and admired: he concluded his book with it.

GOD
With warm hands
I die you die
where is he
where am I
without laughter
I am dead
dead and dead
in the pitch-black night
arrow shot
at him.[83]

---

[81] G. Bataille, "Le sacré au vingtième siècle," in *OC*, 8.189 (author's translation).
[82] Ibid. (author's translation).
[83] G. Bataille, *IE*, 165; *OC*, 5.189.

Chapter 10

Is Adorno's Philosophy a Negative Theology?

Gerrit Steunebrink

1. Introduction

CAN ADORNO'S PHILOSOPHY, which he himself called a 'negative dia-lectic,' be understood as a form of negative theology? Is his philoso-phy an expression of modern religiosity? Or do we, in asserting this, walk into the same trap as do so many modern theologians and phi-losophers, for whom a denial of God is so unbearable that they use the term 'negative theology' to secretly transform a denial of God into His confirmation? Adorno was aware of this danger when he said of some unnamed theologians that they took advantage of a moment of doubt in the views of unbelievers to discover confirmation of God's existence: "they have gradually come to intone their Te Deum wherever God is denied, because at least his name is mentioned."[1]

It is undeniable that there are religious or theological themes in Adorno's work. He speaks of them openly. But we may ask, does perhaps Adorno's use of religious and/or theological themes contra-dict the intention of theology in general and of negative theology in particular?

To explain my conception of negative theology, I will give a brief preview of my interpretation of Adorno as it will be developed fur-ther in this chapter.

Negative Theology and Theodicy

Negative theology speaks of God in a negative way: God surpasses all finitude. This negation is not absolute because it expresses God's

---

[1] T. W. Adorno, *Negative Dialectics*, trans. E. B. Ashton (London: Routledge & Kegan Paul, 1990), 372; hereafter cited as *ND*.

eminent nonworldly, nonhuman positiveness and aims at a critical purification of human and world-oriented speaking about God.

Because God surpasses the world, He is not merely 'total Otherness' compared to the world. God is the pinnacle of identity, completely identical with Himself. To the extent that the world demonstrates identity with itself, it demonstrates identity with this final Identity, God. Only as complete identity is God the world's 'Other,' because the world is only an imperfect identity with itself and is thus non-God. God surpasses the contrast of identity and otherness by being Absolute Identity. Nicholas of Cusa speaks of God as 'non aliud,' not other.[2] A radical negative theology can even have monistic tendencies that identify God and the world instead of stressing the dualism between them. Negative theology presupposes the structure of identity that Adorno so passionately rejects in the critique of Hegel present in all his works.

Otherness, or 'transcendence,' in Adorno is not the divine transcendence that surpasses all what is worldly, something that lies at the source of the world. Otherness is the denial of this world in the name of a better world. The existing world cannot, as it were, be God's world. Adorno puts it paradoxically: "This is why one who believes in God cannot believe in God" (ND, 104). Adorno says this to a world that knew Auschwitz, a world in which human reality revealed its true face. After Auschwitz every confirmation of God should be withdrawn, especially by those who believe in Him. Adorno does not claim to be a believer, but he asks every believer to think about what he or she makes of God in calling Him the creator of the world (and thus of Auschwitz).

In his negative God-talk, which certainly resembles the language of negative theology, he reflects an ethical experience of the absence of a God *who should have been there*, and who is thus not totally absent. We sometimes speak of this experience, in our time inseparably linked to Auschwitz, as 'the presence of the Absent.'

Adorno's negative utterances about God have to do with the problem of *theodicy*. This problem confronts him and us with the question: Can this world be God's world? This world or another world? That is the question that interferes in our God-talk. A confusion

---

[2] Nicholas of Cusa, *Tetralogus de non aliud*, in *Opera omnia* (Hamburg: Felix Meiner, 1952).

about transcendence is the result. This confusion is the cradle of Adorno's concept of *utopia*. It is questionable indeed whether we may equate Adorno's concept of 'transcendence' with God. What we need first is a closer look at his concept of utopia.

'Otherness' as Utopia

Utopia is the object of hope in another, future world, but not in a naive way. For Adorno, utopia is both a historical-ontological category and a practical and even epistemological category. As such it is for him the ultimate goal of all human activity and knowledge.

Utopia must be the fulfillment of this world and at the same time radically different from it and in this sense transcendent. Utopia is the denial of the existing world. Referring to the Jewish prohibition of graven images, Adorno says that its reality can never be positively described. The way Adorno uses this prohibition to describe the other 'world' shows that he has difficulty distinguishing between an 'other' world (utopia) and God as Otherness or Difference from all possible worldly relationships. In Adorno, the meaning of 'otherness' floats somewhere in-between.

Transcendence is conceived as a fulfillment of immanence that does not completely coincide with it: as a new society, a new nature. In this sense Adorno's question to Goethe is essentially addressed to himself, and the interpretation of Hegel hidden in it is Adorno's Marxist interpretation. He wonders, after quoting the famous line "Die Botschaft hör ich wohl, allein mir fehlt der Glaube" (I hear the message, yet I lack the faith), whether in *Faust* transcendence may be a symbol for something else, whether its last word is another symbol ("nur ein Gleichnis," only a parable) and whether transcendence is secularized, in a more-or-less Hegelian fashion, into a picture of a totality of fulfilled immanence (ND, 400). Is this fulfilled immanence, this new society and new nature, possible? Is it not, we may ask, the ideal 'impossible' world, in which *human finitude* is denied? What does this new society and new nature, this utopia, have to do with negative theology? Let us start with the question: What is the historical background of Adorno's thought?

Adorno and Kant

Historically Adorno's concept of utopia has its origin in a very peculiar, Marxist interpretation of Kant. Adorno's interpretation of Kant, the first great critical Enlightenment thinker, shows that Otherness or utopia does not refer to God, but to 'another world'; this will make the notion of 'finitude' problematic for Adorno. Kant discusses the necessity of faith in a new, just, and happy world, called the 'highest good' or the 'best of all worlds,' as a reward for human moral striving. Of course, the making of this new world presupposes, according to Kant, the existence of God. In his own philosophy, despite his constant conversation with Kant, Adorno neglects the crucial Kantian distinction between, on the one hand, God as the highest original Good, and, on the other hand, the highest derived good, this best of all worlds, that is, the ideal and happy relationship among people and between human beings and nature as the fulfillment of human moral aspiration. For Kant, this best of all worlds is a reward for human moral aspiration, and a world that only God can bring about, because people cannot control the natural circumstances that are needed for the realization of happiness. By means of these postulates of God and of a better world, Kant is able to situate the moral duty to struggle endlessly for improvement in the context of an ultimately meaningful relationship between freedom and nature. The struggle for becoming worthy of happiness is not void. This trust prevents human aspiration from becoming Sisyphean. Humankind is not faced with a task before which it can only throw up its hands in despair, namely, having to produce ideal reality by our own strength.

Adorno's utopia is the highest derived good, the ideal world, and not the highest original good. His view of utopia is the result of a specific Marxist interpretation of Kant. Adorno's question whether transcendence is itself a reality or a symbol for 'fulfilled immanence' is the exact expression of his Marxist misunderstanding of the Kantian distinction between the highest good in its primary and secondary senses. Adorno becomes entangled in problems Kant sought to avoid with the postulate of God. Fulfilled reality becomes for Adorno a human task. Humankind is kept in a double bind. It should perform a task a finite being cannot perform nor may not perform. It is in this situation that human finitude succumbs as meaningful reality. The permanently unfulfilled, ever repeated struggle for improvement in a world that cannot be made ideal cannot, it seems to me, be regarded as a positive, meaningful task. The result of Adorno's position is despair at the meaning of morality.

The Mystery of Finitude

Insofar as Adorno neglects in a Marxist way this basic Kantian distinction, his utopia can be considered to be a Kingdom of God without God, a messianic situation without a Messiah. Utopia is the longing of all human beings and the ultimate goal of all their endeavors. But insofar as utopia transcends the human ability to think it and make it, it must be *given* to humankind. But in Adorno there is no divine Giver.

What is the relevance of this problem for negative theology? The language of negative theology in Adorno's philosophy is a sign of the fact that after his 'secularization' of Kant he could not, and in fact did not want to, get rid of the religious dimension. But how do we interpret this religous dimension? The experiences of negativity, of the 'presence of the Absent,' that Adorno discusses precede the nomenclature of 'negative theology.' The experience of indefinite transcendence as 'there must be something else' points to the question of finitude that has not found its true place. Perhaps it is not infinity that is the real mystery, but finitude itself!

We hope to show that Adorno's philosophy reveals an acute problem with finitude: he cannot allow any form of graduality, of never-ending improvement, and of an acceptance of what is present. We will explain the historical background of this situation. To do this, we have to scrutinize his 'nihilism,' his "belief in nothingness," to reach a definition of his 'negative philosophy.' Comparison of Adorno and Kant can provide an insight into the actuality of Adorno's articulation of the religious problems of modern consciousness.

2. Adorno's View of Kant's Metaphysical Ideas

In Adorno's work we repeatedly meet metaphysical ideas such as 'God' and 'the immortality of the soul.' For him, they have a utopian function in relation to a third metaphysical idea, 'the world.'

In the last chapter of *Negative Dialectics*, we find the historical situation that is the context in which, and the reason why, these must lead Adorno to a dialectic of despair. This chapter contains meditations on the possibility of metaphysics after Auschwitz.

Adorno's paradoxical position is twofold and antithetical: metaphysical ideals *may not be thought*, for then they would be posed positively; thus they would come within the grasp of dictatorial conceptual thinking and become part of 'the existing,' the factual, that metaphysical ideas are supposed to surpass. Yet these ideas *must be thought* because, if we abandon them, we accept an existing reality that has the last word.

In an essay on the composer Schoenberg, there seems at first sight to be a pronouncement of negative theology. In commenting on the theme of Schoenberg's *Moses and Aaron* (Moses' inability to name God), Adorno says of this theme: "The absolute remains beyond the reach of finite beings. If they call it by name, because they should, they betray it. If they keep silent about it, they succumb to their impotence and sin against what is no less than their task: to speak of it. They fail because they lack the ability to do what is demanded of them."[3]

Speaking about the unconditional is a task for a mortal, and at the same time is blasphemous. Schoenberg had earlier put this insight to music in Opus 22, which is based on a text from Rilke's *Stundenbuch* (*Book of Hours*): "All who attempt to find you, tempt you. And those who find you, bind you to image and gesture."[4]

Adorno's own dicta on the absolute and transcendent often sound like these lines from Rilke that apparently speak of God. Yet Adorno's concern is different, since what he calls the 'absolute' or the 'transcendent' is not God.

We can demonstrate this ambiguity in his interpretation of Kant. In his lecture notes, published under the title *Philosophische Terminologie* (Philosophical Terminology), Adorno tells why in his view Kant, after all his criticism of the proofs of God's existence, still maintained his belief in God: "The only and strongest support for Kant's position on the existence of God is, in my view, his argument

---

[3] Translation by author. The quotation is from T. Adorno, "Sakrales fragment," in *Quasi una fantasia*, in *Gesammelte Schriften* (Frankfurt am Main: Suhrkamp, 1970–1986), 16.307: "Das Absolute entziehe sich den endlichen Wesen. Wo sie es nennen wollen, weil sie es müssen, würden sie es verraten. Schwiegen sie jedoch davon, so beruhigten sie sich bei ihrer Ohnmacht und frevelten an dem nicht minder ihnen Auferlegten, einmal es zu sagen. Sie verzagen weil sie zu dem nicht ausreichen, was zu versuchen sie gleichwohl gehalten sind."

[4] R. M. Rilke, *Selected Works*, trans. J. B. Leishman (London: Hogarth Press, 1976), 2.5.

in his *Critique of Practical Reason,* according to which injustice and suffering are so endless in the world that the idea of a world without, as the simple say, some justice to make up for it and without its guarantor, God, would be too terrible to put into words."[5]

In this passage, while explaining Kant to his students, Adorno interprets Kant correctly. He respects the Kantian distinction between the highest derived good, a future world of justice, and the highest original good, its guarantor, God. But in his own philosophizing about these ideas of Kant he deliberately blurs these distinctions. There we find utopia, humanity, eternal peace, that is, a series of social ideas, called the transcendent. Of course, this is inspired by Marxism. This Marxist interpretation tries to find its foundation in Kant by considering the ideals of Kant's political philosophy of history, such as eternal peace for humanity, as the transcendent and the absolute. In this way of interpreting Kant's postulates as the ideal of humanity that has to realize itself by itself we find Adorno's passage from Kant to Hegel to Marx.

The Ontological Proof of God

We observe this passage in Adorno's treatment of the ontological proof of God. Here we find conjoined, in typically Adornian (and for me problematical) manner, the theoretical and the practical-ethical aspects of thinking about utopia. He does so in relation to the idea of God. Adorno writes of Kant: "He held on to the metaphysical ideas, and yet he forbade jumping from thoughts of the absolute which might one day be realized, like eternal peace, to the conclusion that therefore the absolute exists. His philosophy—as probably every other, by the way—circles about the ontological argument for God's existence" (*ND,* 385).

In this quotation Adorno links Kantian interest in metaphysical ideas with the practical and political idea of eternal peace. This gives

---

[5] Translation by author. *Philosophische Terminologie* (Frankfurt am Main: Suhrkamp, 1973–1974), 1.111: "Ich selber halte für den einzigen und stärksten Anhalt dazu, wie die Kantische Stellung zu der Existenz Gottes gewesen ist, sein Argument in der *Kritik der praktischen Vernunft*; das Unrecht und das Leiden in der Welt seien so unendlich, daß der Gedanke an die Welt ohne den an eine, wie man so schlicht und bürgerlich sagt, ausgleichende Gerechtigkeit und an deren Garanten, nämlich Gott, etwas zu Grauenhaftes wäre, um vorgestellt werden zu können."

the absolute the character of something that must be realized. But just as eternal peace is not realized, Adorno thinks we may not say of the absolute that it 'is.' In order to solve this predicament, Adorno smuggles Hegelian elements into Kant's way of thinking. Hegel sees the absolute in terms of self-realization. Adorno thinks of this absolute as something immanent and practical: the realization of eternal peace.

For Adorno, every philosophy, including Kant's philosophy, in hoping that even the most despairing idea may somehow touch reality, circles around the ontological proof of God.[6] That is why Adorno thinks Hegel's attempt to revive the ontological proof of God is not a question of obscurantism. Adorno's interpretation of Hegel's criticism of Kant sheds light on God's and/or utopia's immanence and transcendence: "The stringency of Hegel's attempt to salvage the ontological proof of God may be doubted. But its motivation was not the desire to darken reason, but, on the contrary, the utopian hope that the blockade, the 'limits of the possibility of experiencing,' will not have the last word."[7] Trying to prove God's existence is the expression of a utopian hope to surpass present experience and 'the existing reality' to which this experience is linked.

Adorno thought Kant blockaded the realization of utopia in his theory of the limits of experience: "What Kant saw, in terms of content, as the goal of reason, the creation of humankind, utopia, is hindered by the form of his thought, epistemology. It does not permit reason to go beyond the realm of experience, which, in the mechanism of mere material and invariant categories, shrinks to what has always already existed."[8]

In his interpretation of Kant, Adorno strangely mixes theoretical and practical reason: in Kant's epistemology the world is what always was, the existing. This mix hinders the coming of the new, of hu-

---

[6] See "Anmerkungen zum philosophischen Denken," in *Stichworte*, in *Gesammelte Schriften*, 10.2.606.

[7] Translation by author. See "Aspekte," in *Drei Studien zu Hege*, in *Gesammelte Schriften*, 5.286: "Die Stringenz von Hegel's Versuch der Rettung des ontologischen Gottesbeweises gegen Kant mag bezweifelt werden. Aber was ihn dazu bewog, war nicht der Wille zur Verdunkelung der Vernunft, sonder im Gegenteil, die utopische Hoffnung, daß der Block, die 'Grenzen der Möglichkeit der Erfahrung,' nicht das letzte sei."

[8] Adorno, *Notes to Literature*, 2 vols., trans. S. W. Nicolson (New York: Columbia University Press, 1991), 1.21.

manity's utopia, although this ideal is supposed to be the mainspring of Kant's own philosophy. This brings Adorno to formulate Kant's position as follows: "If one chose to reformulate Kant's question, one could ask today: *How is anything new possible at all?*"[9]

God, utopia, the new, and realized humankind are all figures in Adorno's interpretation of Kant that take the place of transcendence. Hegel is introduced to help rethink the relationship of the absolute to the immanent: "As soon as I speak, I postulate, as one could say, and Hegel has said so, at the same time the whole or the absolute. Because I copostulate it, I also say that it exists. One can thus not so radically distinguish between the utopia to which thinking as reason feels attracted and the reality in which we exist as it is posited in Kantian argumentation."[10]

God as regulative idea is the utopia of thinking. But God *as* utopia is presupposed in all thinking, and this utopia is not so radically separated from the existing world as Kant's epistemology leads us to suspect.

According to Adorno, Hegel has to pay a price. When utopia is not separated from the existing, it, the absolute, loses its transcendence. The absolute becomes a totality where there is no longer any transcendence. Now Adorno's terminology changes. He speaks of the nonidentical, the nonunderstandable, of whatever it is that escapes totalizing thinking. "In spite of and, so to speak, absorbing the Kantian critique, the ontological argument for the existence of God was resurrected in Hegelian dialectics. In vain, however. In Hegel's consistent resolution of nonidentity into pure identity, the concept comes to be the guarantor of the nonconceptual. Transcendence, captured by the immanence of human spirit, is at the same time turned into the totality of the Spirit and abolished altogether"(*ND*, 402).

---

[9] Translation by author. See "Veblens Angriff auf die Kultur," in *Prismen*, in *Gesammelte Schriften*, 10.1.72–97: "Wollte man die kantische Frage umformulieren, sie könnte heute wohl lauten: wie ist ein Neues überhaupt möglich?" (95). English edition in *Prisms*, trans. S. Weber and Sh. Weber (Cambridge, Mass.: MIT Press, 1983).

[10] *Philosophische Terminologie*, 1.114: "Schon indem ich spreche, setze ich, könnte man sagen, und Hegel hat das gesagt, das Ganze oder das Absolute mit, und indem ich es mitsetze, sage ich auch bereits, daß es sei. Es ließe also zwischen der Utopie, zu der das Denken sich gedrängt fühlt als Begriff, und der Wirklichkeit in der wir existieren, gar nicht so radikal sich scheiden, wie es in der kantischen Argumentation vorliegt."

Hegel is simultaneously complimented for removing the radical separation between the existing world and utopia, which lifts utopia out of the sphere of pure impossibility, and accused of abolishing utopia's transcendent character. Kant's case is the opposite. He is accused of thinking experience and the existing world in such a way that thinking of and realizing utopia become impossible. But Adorno compliments him for leaving utopia in this transcendence. Adorno now links the accusation and the compliment in an interpretation of Kant's philosophy as the *"unthinkability of despair"* ("die Unausdenkbarkeit der Verzweiflung"): "The secret of his [Kant's] philosophy is the unthinkability of despair. Constrained by the convergence of all thought in something absolute, he did not leave it at the absolute line between absoluteness and existence; but he was no less constrained to draw that line. He held on to the metaphysical ideas" (*ND*, 385). Kant is thus in the same double bind as Schoenberg and Rilke. But Kant's despair is not fed by God's unnameable sublimity but by injustice, suffering, and death in the world, in other words, by the experience of the 'presence of the Absent.' The relationship between the factual world and the ideal world is central.

We will now examine this complex field of tension between Kant, Hegel, and Adorno by using Adorno's interpretation of the 'postulate of immortality.'

Adorno's View of Kant's Postulate of Immortality

Here is Adorno on immortality as a postulate of practical reason:

> That the ground of the Kantian rescuing urge lives far deeper than just in the pious wish to have, amid nominalism and against it, some of the traditional ideas in hand—this is attested by the construction of immortality as a postulate of practical reason. The postulate condemns the intolerability of existant things and confirms the spirit of its recognition. That no reforms within the world sufficed to do justice to the dead, that none of them touched upon the wrong of death—this is what moves Kantian reason to hope against reason. [Then follows the words with which the previous passage began:] The secret of his philosophy is the unthinkability of despair." (*ND*, 385)

The postulates of practical reason must be thought theoretically because of the unbearableness of the existing world. The thinking of these postulates confirms the Spirit's transcendence insofar as it knows the existing is unbearable. In Kant these postulates include the soul's immortality, reward in the form of a perfect relationship of the soul to nature, and the God who can create this relationship.

According to Adorno, we must think the postulate of the soul's immortality because the existing world is characterized by injustice to the dead that cannot be removed by any inner worldly improvement. Injustice to the dead in the existing world points to something above this existing world. Adorno, without differentiating, calls what surpasses the existing world 'other' or 'transcendent.'

Transcendence is then "to have all thoughts converge upon the concept of something that would differ from the unspeakable world that is" (ND, 403). In this regard transcendence is a "situation of the world" since the hope for transcendence relies on "the experience that if thought is not decapitated it will flow into transcendence down to the idea of a world that would not only abolish existant suffering but revoke the suffering that is irrevocably past" (ND, 403).[11]

Transcendence is thus a situation in which the world is so totally different that even the irrevocable can be revoked. Adorno's concept of transcendence conceals the essential distinction between the primary highest good, God, and its highest derived good, another situation for the world. This lets him avoid the question of whether utopia, the true relationship between one person and another, and between people and nature, is really the absolute and transcendent or still something finite. This concealment is ultimately calamitous for his view of human activity.

Adorno's notion of transcendence stops at the compensation of all suffering, the elimination of existing suffering, and the revocation of irrevocably past suffering. Transcendence as a recompensed world is easily understood from Kant's postulate of the soul's immortality and eternal happiness. But Kant calls the recompensed world the best of all worlds and then distinguishes this best world as highest derived good from the primary highest good, God.

Because Kant makes this distinction and because he sees the notion of 'compensation' as a postulate of practical reason and not as

---

[11] The translation "idea of a world" is not quite adequate here. The German text (Negative Dialektik, in Gesammelte Schriften, 6.395) "Verfassung einer Welt" should be translated as "condition of a world" or "constitution of a world."

an idea of theoretical reason, the postulate of the soul's immortality functions differently in Kant than in Adorno. The latter puts the metaphysical ideas in a theoretical perspective, even when in Kant they take the form of practical postulates. He thinks of them theoretically-metaphysically as surpassing the existing, the sensible world, and not practically, in terms of being realized in the existing world. Adorno's idea of utopia is an uncritical identification of a metaphysical idea in theoretical perspective and a practical postulate. Therefore he can say, as we have seen, that Kant's epistemology blockades the idea of utopia, utopia now being formulated practically as realization of humanity.

Adorno can thus develop the practical theme of utopia into a fear of betraying the transcendent. If we could know it and try to realize it, then we would draw it in the sphere of the existing world and betray it. If we do not think it, then we have no perspective above the existing world.

But in the *Critique of Practical Reason* Kant thinks the relationship between the sensible, the existing reality, and the intelligible the other way around. Seen practically-ethically, thus in terms of Adorno's utopia, the relationship between the idea and the given or the sensible must be regarded from the point of view of a free will that must persevere and be realized in the sensible world. The human task is to allow the moral law to penetrate reality as far as possible. That is the realization of the highest derived good. For Kant, the world is not the unspeakably existing reality ("das unsäglich Seiende") that must be surpassed, but the reality that must be increasingly saturated with moral intelligibility. Because people are never morally perfect (i.e., holy), this ideal can only be understood as an infinite task, a *progressus ad infinitum*. The postulates of practical reason support this task and give content to the ideas of theoretical reason. To guarantee this peculiar future dimension of ethical action, Kant postulates the soul's immortality, by which he merely means that there is no end to the aspiration for perfection, which is not an impossible but a possible and meaningful task.

Thus, the postulates of the greatest happiness and of the highest derived good function analogously. For people, being happy means that their nature corresponds to their goodwill so that their spiritual and physical sides are in full agreement. The unity of the two is the 'best world.' But because they never control the external factors of nature, people can never realize this unity. They can strive to be *worthy* of happiness, but they can never *create* happiness.

To realize this unity, it is necessary to postulate a cause for nature that has complete power over nature and that itself has a moral causality. This cause is God who judges people morally and who can intervene in nature to bring about for each person the correct relationship to nature. When happiness is postulated, its cause, God, must also be postulated as the cause of nature: "Therefore, the supreme cause of nature, insofar as it must be presupposed for the highest good, is a being which is the cause (and consequently the author) of nature through understanding and will, that is, God. As a consequence, the postulate of the possibility of a highest derived good (the best world) is at the same time the postulate of the reality of a highest original good, namely the existence of God."[12]

The purpose of these postulates in Kant is to support action here and now. They do not express the 'unthinkability of despair' about how to surpass the unspeakably existing reality, but call upon people to act in this reality and stimulate an increasing innerworldly improvement. They support this action in the face of imperfection. The fulfillment that these postulates of hope promise to human action is the ability to act here and now in a meaningful way that is never finished and that always remains imperfect. To act is always a duty and always remains morally meaningful; it is always good to be good. To use Adorno's term, the attitude of practical reason is *"Vernunft als Verhalten"* (rationality as behavior).

In the context of Kant's philosophy, these postulates also say that it is senseless for people to try to realize the perfect world, since this is beyond their power. People cannot and need not realize that world. Utopia is not a task of human action. Utopia, the best world, is a gift, for which a giver must be postulated.

Because Adorno makes no distinction between the best world and a divine Giver, he makes realizing perfect reality a direct task of human action that humans cannot realize. He puts ethics in an embarrassing situation that Kant meticulously tried to avoid: *morality*

---

[12] I. Kant, *Critique of Practical Reason*, ed. L. W. Beck (Chicago: University of Chicago Press, 1949), 228. Cf. Jan Plat, "De ethiek van Kant in de kritische werken," in *Beschouwingen over de ethiek van Kant* (Nijmegen: Catholic University Press, 1983), 49ff.

becomes impossible in the existing world and unnecessary in the future world.

In Adorno we find this position in an allusion to Brecht: "The trouble is not that free men do radical evil, as evil is done beyond all measure conceivable to Kant; the trouble is that as yet there is no world in which—there are flashes of this in his work—men would no longer need to be evil"(*ND*, 218). But do we have to, as it were, act evilly in this evil world to reach a world where this is no longer necessary? Thanks to his doctrine of postulates, Kant can say that this situation cannot exist. It is always good to be good in a world that, never completely good, is always improvable. So, with his doctrine of postulates, Kant upholds a moral world by protecting it against counterproductive activist exaggeration.

The postulates of practical reason take human finitude into consideration. This prohibits demanding rational transparency of people who never have a completely pure intention nor control over all elements. In this situation morality is upheld by conscience that lets me feel whether I act in accordance with my best intentions. Having a conscience is a sign of the continuous distance between norm and fact, and is therefore an expression of human finitude. But Adorno criticizes conscience exactly on this point. Psychoanalytically, he sees conscience as a socially formed 'superego' no longer necessary in a true society.

According to Adorno, it is not sufficient for the relationship between conscience and the ego to be made conscious, as it is in Kant. Adorno argues that it must be eliminated, for the irresistibility of conscience lies in being unaware of it: "But this will not do, for, as in the case of the archaic taboos, the irresistibility that Kant found in the compulsion of conscience lies in such a turn to unconsciousness. If a state of universally rational actuality were conceivable, no superego would come into being" (*ND*, 273). For Adorno, criticism of the superego must lead to a criticism of society. Conscience might still have a social critical function insofar as conscience as representative of universality can recognize and surpass a given particular society. But in a free society conscience is no longer necessary: "Conscience is the mark of shame of an unfree society" (*ND*, 275). Reason's ideal is, according to Adorno, one of transparency, the elimination of the distance between conscience and deed. Then we could speak of a world where it is no longer necessary to be moral. Adorno applies this ideal of transparency to nature. He hopes that nature, now 'silent,' will one day have a transparency and a unity comparable to the ideal unity that Kant articulates in his description of the moral person as "intelligible character": "Nature, once equipped with meaning, substitutes itself for the possibility that was the aim of the intelligible characters' construction" (*ND*, 296). Kant would say of this transparency that people can never realize it in real existence because it contradicts human finitude.

Adorno divides the finite reality of human action, embodied in the idea of the world's amelioration and people's permanent aspiration for perfection, between an unintelligible reality, the unspeakably existing reality, and utopia, a contrast human activity cannot span and before which it fails. The idea of the 'unthinkability of despair' is the result of this division. In thinking and acting from a utopian perspective people should emerge from and above the existing world instead of digging themselves deeper into it.

We could mutatis mutandis apply to Adorno the criticism Richard Schaeffler once directed toward Bloch, that whoever allows the postulates of practical reason to function as ideas of theoretical reason ends up with a theory "that puts the antirational world on trial."[13] That world is a world that must be left to reach true freedom and true reality: "Open Sesame, I want to get out."[14] In his philosophy of history Adorno is doing the opposite, but with the same result.

3. PROGRESS AND REDEMPTION

We find Adorno's critique of the idea that utopia can be produced by human effort stressed in his essay on progress. He puts human history between the concepts 'progress' and 'redemption,' where progress marks the immanence of utopia in history and redemption its transcendence above history.

Humanity is the goal of progress. Yet, as long as there is no humanity, there is no progress. Rather, progress is the opening of a perspective for the redemption of a humanity faced with the threat of

---

[13] R. Schaeffler, *Religionsphilosophie* (Freiburg/Munich: Karl Alber Verlag, 1983), 228: "des Gerichts über die widervernünftige Welt."

[14] Adorno, *Einleitung zum 'Positivismusstreit' in der deutschen Soziologie*, in *Gesammelte Schriften*, 8.280: "Sesam öffne dich—ich möchte hinaus."

defeat: "No progress can be conceived as if a humanity already existed that could move forward. Rather, this progress would be the
creation of this humanity, a perspective that opens when faced with
its disappearance."[15] There is no ready-made, forward-moving humanity. Adorno consciously avoids any thought of a potentially present humanity that can develop into a true humanity. Adorno echoes
Walter Benjamin in saying that even when humanity during its history grows in skill and knowledge, this progress is not the same as
the progress of humanity.

Adorno also imitates Benjamin in introducing the concept of redemption and seeking to link it to Augustine. Adorno wants to save
the notion from the Enlightenment's secular view of history while
applying its original force in a new, but equally secular way. What
Adorno finds attractive in the idea of redemption is the transcendence of the redeemed state when compared to all human making,
which protects this state from the danger of succumbing to the evil
immanence of existing reality. This transcendent status is the redeemed humanity that as redeemed can move forward. Adorno says
that if we put existing humanity in the place of this not yet existing
humanity, history immediately becomes a history of salvation. According to Adorno, this is what happened in all theories of progress,
including those of Hegel and Marx. Augustine did not have this view
of progress.

> In Augustine's view of the City of God the idea of progress in history
> is linked with Christ's redemption as the historically successful re-
> demption. Only a redeemed humanity can be considered a humanity
> that, after the decision, can progress because of the grace conferred
> on it, in the continuum of time to the heavenly Kingdom. Perhaps it
> was the fate of later thinking on progress to adopt an immanent teleol-
> ogy and the concept of humanity as the subject of every progress,
> while Christian soteriology faded into the speculations of the philoso-
> phy of history. The idea of progress became included in the earthly
> state, its Augustinian opposite.[16]

---

[15] Translation by author. Adorno, "Fortschritt," in Stichworte, in Gesammelte Schriften, 10.2.619: "Kein Fortschritt ist derart zu unterstellen, als wäre die Menschheit
überhaupt schon und könne deshalb fortschreiten. Vielmehr wäre er erst ihre Her-
stellung, deren Perspektive angesichts der Auflöschung sich öffnet."

[16] Translation by author. "Fortschritt," 620: "In der augustinischen civitas dei ist
sie gebunden an die Erlösung durch Christus, als an die geschichtlich gelungene;
nur eine bereits erlöste Menschheit kann betrachtet werden, als bewege sie sich,

Adorno is inspired by the term 'redemption,' but does not use it to formulate a positive view of history. The relationship between historical progress, the human technical ideal, and the transcendent goal is not articulated positively. Consistent with his own style, Adorno sees the relationship between them negatively as a 'neither-nor.' History as we know it *neither* results in this goal *nor* is it completely and without mediation free from it. But Adorno does not positively formulate the specific nature and possibility of this mediation.

From Augustine he learns that 'progress,' 'redemption,' and 'history' are closely linked, but not subsumed in one another. Progress is tied to history's temporality. This is a blessing, since it says that history can end. With this Adorno protests against Heidegger's interpretation of history and time. History as progress in time says that there is a goal above history. But the realization of this goal may not be seen as the result of a transcendent 'intervention': this would condemn the structure of temporality to meaninglessness. Nor may the goal be placed in history, since history as we know it hinders real progress instead of realizing it. "Were progress, like redemption, to be seen as a transcendent intervention, it would lose with its temporal dimension every concrete meaning and would evaporate into unhistorical theology. But if progress is mediated by history, then history risks being divinized and what impedes progress risks being considered progress."[17]

History as we know it is not a history of progress, but a blockade of (real) progress. Adorno literally refuses to recognize present humanity positively as a real human potential and as the beginning of the true humanity that still has to be developed. Were this the case, the 'earthly state' would then be the beginning of the heavenly city.

---

nachdem die Entscheidung fiel, vermöge der Gnade, die ihr zuteil wurde, im Kontinuum der Zeit auf das himmlische Reich zu. Vielleicht wäre es das Verhängnis des späteren Denkens über den Fortschritt, daß es die immanente Teleologie und die Konzeption der Menschheit als des Subjekts allen Fortschritts übernahm, während die christliche Soteriologie in den geschichtsphilosophischen Spekulationen verblasste. Dadurch ist die Idee des Fortschritts aufgegangen in der civitas terrena, ihrem Augustinischen Widerpart."

[17] Translation by author. "Fortschritt," 621: "Wird Fortschritt gleichgesetzt der Erlösung als dem transzendenten Eingriff, so büßt er mit der Zeitdimension, jede faßliche Bedeutung ein und verflüchtigt sich in geschichtslose Theologie. Wird er aber in der Geschichte mediatisiert, so droht deren Vergötzung und, in der Reflexion des Begriffs wie in der Realität, der Widersinn, das sei bereits Fortschritt, was ihn inhibiert."

According to Adorno, the Enlightenment, including Kant's duality, put 'progress toward humanity' in the hands of existing 'earthly' humanity that must progress according to its own nature. "Even according to the dualistic Kant, it must advance according to its own principle, its 'nature.' But in such a conception of Enlightenment that puts progress toward humanity in the hands of humanity thus concretizing its idea as an idea to be realized lurks the danger of a conformistic affirmation of what merely is."[18] This is a radical dictum on Adorno's part!

His reference to Kant lets us guess why Adorno takes this position. Interpreting the realization of true or redeemed humanity as a task for existing humanity implies that existing humanity contains in its nature the possibility of realizing true humanity and thus to a certain extent already 'is' humanity instead of being on the way to it. This positive view of actual but finite humaneness is too much for Adorno. As a consequence of his negative view of humanity, the concept of progress loses its sense, for it presupposes a gradual improvement of something real.

His reference to Kant is highly relevant. He alludes to Kant's essay "Idea of a Universal Cosmopolital History." Kant hopes that not only nonhuman nature but all of human nature demonstrates something of a divine purpose to be fulfilled in the future, that is, that humanity can develop and reach its goal on earth. Kant wonders whether it can be meaningful to praise God's glory in irrational non-human nature while human history "is a ceaseless denial of it, whose sight forces us to look away in abhorrence, bringing us to the point where we, despairing of any fully rational intention in history, can only hope to find it in another world?"[19] This moral purpose is thus, for Kant, expressly immanent to human development, and cannot

---

[18] Translation by author. "Fortschritt," 621: "Sie soll, auch beim dualistischen Kant, nach ihrem eigenen Prinzip, ihrer 'Natur' fortschreiten. In solcher Aufklärung aber, die überhaupt erst den Fortschritt zur Menschheit in deren Händen legt und damit seine Idee als zu verwirklichende konkretisiert, lauert die konformistische Bestätigung dessen, was bloß ist."

[19] Translation by author. I. Kant, "Idee zu einer Geschichte in Weltbürgerlicher Absicht" (Idea of a Universal Cosmopolitan History) in Akademie-Ausgabe, 8.30: "ein unaufhörlicher Einwurf dagegen bleiben soll, dessen Anblick uns nötigt unsere Augen von ihm mit Unwillen wegzuwenden und, indem wir verzweifeln jemals darin eine vollendete vernünftige Absicht anzutreffen, uns dahin bringt, sie nur in einen anderen Welt zu hoffen?"

coincide with the goal of the postulates of practical reason. The ideal society is a goal of human action and human history, but the perfect relation between morality and happiness is definitely not a direct task of human action, because its realization surpasses the possibilities of human nature and can only be realized in another world. As we already said, this realization belongs to God. The postulate of God prevents human striving for being worthy of happiness from being Sisyphean. Even in history Kant acknowledges people are too imperfect to be turned into perfection, but this insight does not lead him to despair. Kant can live with the idea of neverending striving for perfection, whereas Adorno cannot!

Contrary to Kant's intention, Adorno makes the historical goal of moral improvement and the realization of true humanity into something that transcends human action, while Kant sees it as the germ that lies in nature and that must come to full development through antagonisms. But Kant does not expect the same thing from this development that Adorno expects from it. Kant does not speak about redemption, does not expect to be redeemed from historical conditions within history. He does not expect to realize the heaven of the postulates of practical reason on earth.

By making true humanity a goal that transcends human action, by speaking about redemption in a philosophy of history, Adorno posits two worlds and puts human endeavor in a double bind again. Humanity should realize what it is not allowed to realize at the same time. 'Humanity' as a work in progress is not acceptable for Adorno. Adorno cannot but get into trouble with the idea of progress itself. There are two types of progress and, again, this raises the problem of the relation between them. There is an innerworldly progress of technology, and a progress that transcends it. The end of the story is the vanishing of progress itself!

Innerworldly, technical progress, as a history of domination, leads to the other type of progress, although it may not be subsumed in it: "For this reason, innerworldly progress is the opposite of the other, although it is open to the latter's possibility, however powerless it is to draw it into its own law."[20]

---

[20] Translation by author. "Fortschritt," 632: "Darum ist der innerweltlichen Fortschritt, Widersacher des anderen, zugleich auch offen auf dessen Möglichkeit, wie wenig immer er dieser in sein eigenes Gesetz hineinzuschlingen vermag."

True progress consists in being liberated from an atmosphere of domination: "Progress means leaving the doom, including progress's own doom which is nature itself, through people acknowledging their own belonging to nature and putting an end to their own subjugation of nature, allowing the blind natural condition to continue. In this sense, you could say that progress occurs where it ends."[21]

Here we face the same problem as in Adorno's ethics. Where progress is necessary, it is not possible; where it is possible, it is no longer necessary. The problem that Adorno mentions, but never deals with, is finitude. How to understand this situation?

4. THE DIALECTIC OF THE TECHNICAL IDEAL

We can understand Adorno's thinking best from the Marxism he, following Benjamin, opposed: dialectical materialism as the scientific philosophy of the labor movement. Both criticized this philosophy as a glorification of technological progress that would automatically bring with it the realization of true humanity. Both wondered whether the technical ideal does not stand in the way of realizing utopia.

Their philosophy is a critique of the vulgar Marxist notion that utopia can be manufactured technically. At the same time they criticize the ideal of conceptual thinking that lies at the basis of the technological ideal. They try to formulate a metaphysics that surpasses human concepts and technology, and at the same time they do not want to lose its social basis. Metaphysics is legitimate, but only in a social context.

Benjamin therefore developed the strategy of interpreting metaphysical and theological ideas in a social way and social ideals in a theological way. From this point of view we can understand Adorno's strategy better.

Like Benjamin, he uses religious-sounding, messianic themes like redemption to protect the idea of progress against the banality of

---

[21] Translation by author. "Fortschritt," 625: "Fortschritt heißt: aus dem Bann heraustreten, auch aus dem des Fortschritts, der selber Natur ist, indem die Menschheit ihrer eigenen Naturwüchsigkeit innewird und der Herrschaft Einhalt gebietet, die sie über die Natur ausübt und durch welche sich die Natur fortsetzt. Insofern ließe sich sagen, der Fortschritt ereigne sich dort wo er endet."

total technical fabrication. Humanity is thought as a transcendent reality. It is something greater than the sum of our acts and in a certain sense it begins where our activity ends and acknowledges its relativity. He shows the theological background and content of the idea of progress without becoming a theologian himself. From the opposite direction he tries to stress the social and humane aspect of the postulates of practical reason, that is, the perfect relation between morality and happiness and the ideal of a new nature. Adorno wants to show to the Marxist labor movement that the realization of the social paradise neither eliminates death nor provides any compensation for the suffering of past generations. Therefore Adorno is compelled to say that no innerworldly improvement compensates for the injustice of death. By formulating the human desire for this compensation and at the same time by relativizing the technical ideal, Adorno's idea of utopia surpasses the ideal of a social paradise. The longing for this new world, a new fulfilled immanence as the hidden impetus of all ethical endeavors, is stressed without reflecting the necessity of a transcendent creator as a condition of its possibility. The result is ambiguous. By refusing to reflect explicitly on finitude as a mark of every human situation, now or in paradise, Adorno leaves humanity split up between a factual absurd world and an impossible coming world. Human activity, as I stated earlier, is kept in a double bind. This problem manifests itself explicitly when Adorno is dealing with the main theme of his philosophy: the relation between human activity and *receptivity*. He reflects on this theme within the theological framework of nature and grace.

5. Nature and Grace

Adorno formulates the idea that innerworldly progress is open to a transcendent goal without either being reduced to the other in an essay on the cultural sociologist Veblen, where he writes: "There is no happiness which does not promise the fulfillment of a socially formed wish, nor is there any happiness that does not promise otherness in this fulfillment."[22] Every happiness must fulfill a specific,

---

[22] Translation by author. Adorno, "Veblens Angriff auf die Kultur," 87: "Kein Glück, das nicht dem gesellschaftlich konstituierten Wunsch Erfüllung verhieße, aber auch keines, das nicht in dieser Erfüllung das Andere verspräche. Die abstrakte Utopie, die darüber sich täuscht, wird zur Sabotage am Glück und spielt dem in die Hände, was sie negiert."

social need if utopia is not to remain completely abstract, but eventually this happiness must transcend this context.

Adorno does not want to declare all human effort superfluous. He finds inspiration in the closing verses of Goethe's *Faust*: "He who makes an effort, striving, we can redeem." It is the task of humanity to try to reach the absolute in this 'Faustian' manner, although it cannot do so by itself. Only an exterior moment that shatters the guilt that this struggle causes, an act of grace, can bring about utopia.[23] Adorno uses Faust to liken the relationship between factuality and utopia to one between nature and grace. He is interested in terms like 'redemption' and 'grace' because they refer to a moment of exteriority.[24] This act of grace implies a critique of all human aspiration and fabrication. In an article on Goethe's *Iphigenia*, Adorno discusses hope. In Goethe, hope is not a human feeling but a star rising before humanity. Adorno says of this star shining upon us, "Hope puts a halt to the making and producing without which it does not exist."[25] In Adorno, the origin and the object of hope remain unclear. The same is true for the exact relation between activity and receptivity. We are left with a redeemed humanity without a Redeemer, a messianistic situation without a Messiah, and grace without a Giver of grace.

6. AUSCHWITZ, NIHILISM, AND UNBELIEVING

Now we can examine the negative terminology Adorno uses to describe the Auschwitz experience before moving on to a final comparison of his thought with 'negative theology.'

Despair about the world is the experience of Auschwitz. This experience is formulated in religious terminology that refers to the 'presence of the Absent.' In fact we are confronted with the mystery of theodicy. Adorno is very allergic to positively turning the experience of despair into the experience of something that would escape in despair. Those who, correctly, cannot endure the fall of the metaphysical ideas tend, according to Adorno, to this positive turn: "The

---

[23] Adorno, "On the Final Scene of *Faust*," in *Notes to Literature*, 2.118.

[24] See *Philosophische Terminologie*, 2.287–88.

[25] Adorno, "On the Classicism of Goethe's Iphigenie," in *Notes to Literature*, 2.109.

secret but wrong conclusion is that despair of the world, a despair that is true and based on facts, and that is neither esthetic *Weltschmerz* nor a false and reprehensible consciousness, would already guarantee the existence of the hopeless though existence at large has become a universal guilt context" (*ND*, 372).

He continues with a tirade against the positive religions that in their cries of joy over the unbelievers' despair have done theology the greatest damage. He does not mention any names, but we can imagine that the positive religions, according to Adorno, adopt an attitude toward unbelievers like "We still have God." Then follows the sentence we cited at the beginning of this chapter: "They have gradually come to intone their Te Deum wherever God is denied, because at least His name is mentioned" (*ND*, 372).

Every theological category becomes insanity in the light of Auschwitz, not only that of Providence—"that the finite world of infinite agony is surrounded by a divine plan"—but even the category of the paradox, theology's last bastion, becomes for everyone "insanity" or "public libel" (*ND*, 373). Here Adorno has come in conflict with the Kantian view of history as revelation of Providence.

For someone who tries to see something positive even in the despair of Auschwitz, even if he or she be a survivor, is accused of "trench religion" ("*Schützgraben-religion*"). Yet Adorno does not advocate total, radical despair. He starts from the 'unthinkability of despair.' Absolute despair is philosophically impossible because it enjoins a position where Auschwitz is confirmed absolutely. Only in absolute despair, without any transcending perspective, would Auschwitz have really won. This insight is apparent in Adorno's judgment of the terms 'nihilism' and 'unbelieving' as expressions of the experience of Auschwitz.

Adorno opposes a nihilism that abstractly says that everything is nothing. The word 'nothing' is here as empty as the word 'to be.' Wanting nothingness, as Nietzsche occasionally suggests, is for Adorno a ludicrous form of pride, as if society could succeed in destroying the earth. Likewise, Adorno opposes the term 'unbelieving,' which Schiller uses: "With believing in nothingness, we can mean scarcely more than nothingness itself; by virtue of its own meaning, the 'something' which, legitimately or not, we mean by the word 'believing' is not nothing. Faith in nothingness would be as insipid as would faith in being. It would be a palliative of the mind proudly content to see through the whole swindle" (*ND*, 379). In this context Adorno also speaks of mysticism, "that [which] finds the negated something even in nothingness, in the medieval *nihil privativum*" (*ND*, 380). But even this thinking of the 'nothing,' although according to Adorno it is no nihilism, is no solution for the problem of despair: "The medieval *nihil privativum* in which the concept of nothingness is recognized as the negation of something rather than as autosemantical is as superior to the diligent 'overcoming' as the image of Nirvana, of nothingness as something" (*ND*, 380). It may appear that there is something of negative theology in this combination of mysticism and 'nihil privativum,' but what Adorno says is that the 'nihil privativum' and the positive nothing of nirvana are both trickery. The same is true for the question of whether it is better that there be nothing at all than something: a general answer is impossible. "For a man in a concentration camp it would be better not to have been born—if one who escaped in time is permitted to venture any judgment about this. And yet the lighting up of an eye, indeed the feeble tail-wagging of a dog one gave a tidbit it promptly forgets, would make the ideal of nothingness evaporate" (*ND*, 380). After positing that it would have been better for a concentration camp victim never to have been born, Adorno says that the ideal of nothingness evaporates before the least of positive experiences. It is not possible to think of nothing as pure nothing, for it is conquered by the simplest positive experience.

Ultimately Adorno reaches a nihilism that he can appreciate positively: nihilism as criticism of the existing world. In this view one can never be enough of a nihilist. Samuel Beckett, in Adorno's view, sees things correctly: "What is, Beckett says, is like a concentration camp. At one time he speaks of a lifelong death penalty. The only dawning hope is that there will be nothing anymore. This, too, he rejects. From the fissure of inconsistency that comes about in this fashion, the image world of nothingness as something emerges to stabilize his poetry" (*ND*, 380). Without preaching nothingness, but also without making any positive reference to something above it, just by putting meaninglessness in place of action, Beckett silently says: "there must be something else." In this way Beckett can give a "positive" shape to nothingness (*ND*, 380–81).[26] It is this nihilism

---

[26] See the essay on Beckett's *End of the Game* in *Notes to Literature* 2.

of Beckett's with which Adorno agrees: "This kind of nihilism implies the opposite of identification with the nothing. The created world is for him, as it were, gnostic, the radically evil and its denial is the possibility of another, not yet existing world" (ND, 381).

Here we see that Adorno articulates his experience of Auschwitz completely within the concept of transcendence that we already know. It is another, not yet existing world, that contrasts with the created, radically evil world. Because the created world is the radically evil world, Adorno can say, as we already saw, that one who believes in God cannot believe in God. This world cannot be God's world, but the word 'God' only means there must be something else—God, a better world?[27]

There really is Spleen and *Weltschmerz* in Adorno's philosophy. But because he has not reflected explicitly on this topic, I would state that his religious terminology refers not to negative theology, but to a dimension of religious consciousness that precedes this and other theological explanations.

7. NEGATIVE THEOLOGY: FINDING A PASSAGE

Adorno's analysis of nihilism shows that the despair of Auschwitz is described within the framework of a two-worlds' doctrine. In the previous pages we showed that his theory has a basis in a special 'Marxist' utopian interpretation of Kant's postulates of practical reason. Not God was thought but only the best world. This idea of a just world transcending the evil world got mixed up with the social and political idea of humanity. In this two-worlds' doctrine the negativity and the positiveness that together shape the finite world are contrasted as opposites: evil reality versus the ideal utopian possibility. The association of different experiences—the mystical experience of the unnameable God, the ethical experience of God's absence in evil, and the avoidance of thematizing and thus accepting finitude—leads to a special contemporary kind of religious experience of 'otherness.' That one experience can hide behind the other belongs to the religious consciousness of our times. Theodicy, the

---

[27] See G. Steunebrink, *Kunst, utopie en werkelijkheid* (Tilburg: Tilburg University Press, 1991), 367.

impossibility of believing in God because of the suffering in this impossible finite world, and negative theology as the expression of God's unsurpassible sublimity that can even mean that the finite world is absorbed in God's infinity, can come together in a special combination precisely because one neglects to think finitude. Therefore we can say: Not God is the real mystery, but finitude.

Various names are possible for Adorno's negative philosophy. Given the tension between utopia and reality, or between possibility and reality, Adorno's philosophy belongs to what Hegel calls an 'unhappy consciousness.'[28] Adorno's philosophy can be further interpreted in line with Hegel's 'God is dead philosophy' because in his philosophy reality, in the sense of the brute factuality of nature and human circumstances, is no longer recognizable as a (in principle) rational reality in which people can rationally realize themselves.[29] At the same time it becomes clear that Auschwitz shattered the Enlightenment idea that a rational world is also a moral world. But even Adorno cannot and will not maintain that everything is 'nothing.' This 'not nothing' is expressed in the idea of another possible world that has no positive association with the existing world while never becoming an experience of a 'finite here and now,' of a unity of possibility and reality, of something positive, however humble and finite it may be. This becomes apparent in ethical decisions: present obligations are not always the ideal, but they do have an 'all or nothing' dimension that gives them an atmosphere of absoluteness in finitude. For Adorno, the world is neither meaningless reality nor ideal utopia. He does not articulate his own positive experiences, the upward glance that, in his view, evaporates the ideal of the nothing, as a victory, however fragile, over the nothing, and thus as a positive reality with an absolute character. In this he differs from Levinas, for whom fragile finitude does have an infinite character. Adorno never expressly elaborates on the dictum "Auschwitz never again" that implies a certain positive experience.

In this sense Adorno's philosophy still resembles Max Scheler's 'belief in nothingness,' a concept at the limit of religiosity. According

---

[28] See Hent de Vries, *Theologie im Pianissimo. Zur Aktualität der Denkfiguren Adornos und Levinas* (Kampen: Kok, 1989), 158.

[29] G. Steunebrink, "Kunst en reflexiviteit: Kant, Hegel en Adorno," in *Reflexiviteit en Metafysica, Feestbundel voor Jan Hollak*, University of Amsterdam Philosophical Series (Delft: Eburon, 1987), 157ff.

to Scheler, the religious dimension is inevitable. When it is denied, it still manifests itself as the absolutizing of something finite. Eventually this absolutizing leads to despair. Seen from this point of view, Adorno's philosophy contains an absolute dimension and in this sense it is religious. But this absolute dimension is identified with a finite reality which in its turn becomes absolutized. Evidence is Adorno's idea of utopia. When this absolutizing is abandoned, the absolute dimension either appears to contain 'nothing' or risks a new absolutism.[30] So a good society can be the absolute, or a new form of nature, or art. All this jumping back and forth only leads Adorno to the realization that it cannot all be 'nothing.' He does not find a way through, a passage from finitude to infinity, because he finds no positive moment in finitude, no absolute moment that points to its source, the absolute. This pointing to a source is the basis of classical negative theology. According to this theology, the source that supports the finite surpasses finitude maximally and thus cannot be put into human words. Adorno's contribution consists in pushing his idea of utopia, of a perfect world, so far that the sense of philosophically reflecting on the idea of God becomes finally obvious. In the idea of utopia human finitude is crushed under the unbearable pressure of absoluteness. Only in making the absolute absolute can humanity's own finite reality be seen as a meaningful reality. This is the successful passage through finitude that present-day religious consciousness finds so difficult to make. The association in Adorno's philosophy of, on the one hand, a refusal to find a passage through finitude with, on the other hand, 'God's unnameableness' and the experience of 'the presence of the Absent' apparent in the dictum "There must be something else" is an adequate expression of the many difficulties felt by modern religious consciousness.

---

[30] Cf. Max Scheler, *Vom Ewigen im Menschen* (Bern: Franke Verlag, 1968), 261–64.

Chapter 11

"No Spiritual Investment in the World As It Is"

JACOB TAUBES'S NEGATIVE POLITICAL THEOLOGY

Marin Terpstra and Theo de Wit

1. Introduction: What Is (Negative) Political Theology?

THE EXPRESSION 'negative political theology' was probably first used in discussions in the early 1980s organized by the group 'Religions-theorie und Politische Theologie' in Germany. Texts presented at this congress were later published in three volumes.[1] In the first volume Reinhart Maurer distinguishes between positive and negative political theology; under adherents of the second he mentions Augustine, Luther, Hobbes, and Hegel. According to Maurer, negative political theology, by "agreeing with Augustine's interpretation of Christianity, disputes the legitimacy of a positive political theology . . . insofar as the latter supports a specific policy to the point of absolutizing its goals."[2]

As a twentieth-century proponent of a negative political theology the Jewish philosopher Jacob Taubes (who died in 1987) is deserving

---

[1] Jacob Taubes, ed., *Religionstheorie und Politische Theologie*, Vol. 1: *Der Fürst dieser Welt. Carl Schmitt und die Folgen*; Vol. 2: *Gnosis und Politik*; and Vol. 3: *Theokratie* (Munich: Wilhelm Fink, 1983–1987).

[2] R. Maurer, "Chiliasmus und Gesellschaftsreligion. Thesen zur politischen Theologie," in J. Taubes, ed., *Der Fürst dieser Welt*, 1.117–35, 117. All translations by the authors, except where noted otherwise.

of mention.[3] In a posthumously published book[4] containing several of Taubes's lectures on Paul's epistle to the Romans, the editors explicitly mention the concept when characterizing Taubes's work. Taubes generally[5] spoke of 'political theology'; the addition of 'negative' relates to his own attitude within political theology.

Before examining the issues concerning this unique term and its relation to negative theology in contemporary philosophy, let us first address some elementary questions. What is political theology?[6] To what does the 'negative' in Taubes's case refer?

In Greek and Roman antiquity, 'political theology' referred to one of three *genera theologiae*. In his *De Civitate Dei* Augustine refers to a no-longer-extant text by Terentius Varro (116–127 B.C.) in which

---

[3] Jacob Taubes (1923–1987) was born in Vienna to an old rabbinical family. He studied philosophy and history in Basel and Zurich and, from 1949 to 1965, taught Judaism, religious science, and the philosophy of religion in the United States at Harvard, Princeton, and Columbia Universities. From 1965 until his death he held the chair of Judaism and hermeneutics at the Free University of Berlin.

[4] Jacob Taubes, *Die politische Theologie des Paulus: Vorträge, gehalten an den Forschungsstätte der evangelischen Studiengemeinschaft in Heidelberg, 23–27. Februar 1987* (Munich: Wilhelm Fink, 1993). Earlier he published *Abendländische Eschatologie* (1947; 2d ed., Munich: Matthes und Seitz, 1991) and *Ad Carl Schmitt: Gegenstrebige Fügung* (Berlin: Merve, 1987). For Taubes's articles, we refer to "Bibliografie Jacob Taubes" included in N. Bolz and W. Hübener, eds., *Spiegel und Gleichnis: Festschrift für Jacob Taubes* (Würzburg: Königshausen & Neumann, 1983), 423–26. Recently a new collection of Taubes's articles was published under the title *Vom Kult zur Kultur: Bausteine zu einer Kritik der historischen Vernunft: Gesammelte Aufsätze zur Religions- und Geistesgeschichte*, eds. Aleida Assmann, Jan Assmann, Wolf-Daniel Hartwich, and Winfried Menninghaus (Munich: Wilhelm Fink, 1996). Of particular interest are the "Introduction" and a text by Taubes dating from 1955, "Theologie und politische Theorie."

[5] In their "Nachwort" (Taubes, *Die politische Theologie des Paulus*, 143–81) the editors Wolf-Daniel Hartwich, Aleida Assmann, and Jan Assmann provide a summary of Taubes's unpublished last lecture delivered in Berlin in 1986 and entitled "Zur politischen Theologie des Paulus: Von Polis zu Ecclesia (nur für Fortgeschrittene)." Here Taubes expressly uses the term 'negative political theology' to characterize Paul's theology: "Taubes betrachtet die Funktion der paulinischen Gesetzeskritik als negative politische Theologie" (151, 152).

[6] For an excellent introduction to the field of political theology, see J. Assmann, *Politische Theologie zwischen Ägypten und Israel* (Munich: Carl Friedrich von Siemens Stiftung, 1992). For the history of the concept, see E. Feil, "Von der 'politischen Theologie' zur 'Theologie der Revolution'?," in E. Feil and R. Weith, eds., *Diskussion zur 'Theologie der Revolution'* (Munich: Kaiser, 1969), 110–32. For the variants of political theology, depending on the systematic context, see E.-W. Böckenförde, "Politische Theorie und politische Theologie," in Taubes, ed., *Der Fürst dieser Welt*, 16–25.

the author distinguished between the 'mythical' or narrative theology of poets, the 'natural' theology of philosophers, and the 'political' theology (*theologia politike; theologia civilis*) that citizens and priests of the *polis* were supposed to know and follow.[7] This political theology was an essential element of life in the ancient polis, which was also a cultic community. The polis constituted itself in public via cult, sacrifice rituals, and ceremonies. Political theology thus relates to the *deum colere kata ta nomina*, the correct and public interaction with the gods, and as such it is part of the polis's political identity and continuity.

Since Augustine's eschatological criticism of Varro, Christian theologians and philosophers have argued that Christian faith excludes this kind of political theology. But this argument only raises the question of the relationship between faith and the world, between church and state (or political power), it does not answer it. In the last century, the theologian Erik Peterson has argued that Christian eschatology and its Trinitarian doctrine makes of every political theology a theologically illegitimate and thus 'pagan' venture.[8] For Peterson, political theology as a heterodox project emerges where the strict separation between state and church, between the political and the theological, is ruptured.[9] The clearest, and also most scandalous, form of political theology is, in this perspective, the theological justification of a specific political regime. For Peterson, Bishop Eusebius is an excellent example of this *scandalum:* early in the fourth century he theologically defended the link between the church and the Roman Empire.

---

[7] Augustine, *De Civitate Dei*, 6.5, cited in E. Feil, "Von der 'politischen Theologie,'" 115.

[8] E. Peterson, "Der Monotheismus als politisches Problem," in *Theologische Traktate* (1935; Munich: Kösel, 1951), 45–147.

[9] In his answer to Peterson, written 35 years later, Carl Schmitt (1888–1985) correctly pointed out the blind spot in Peterson's argument: Peterson *presupposes* that the institutional separation between church and state, between the theological and the political, is the 'normal situation.' But the crisis in German evangelical theology "entstand daraus, daß die (aus Mittelalter und Reformation überkommenen) institutionellen Sicherungen, die bisher die zwei Reiche und Bereiche der Augustinischen Lehre getragen hatten und deren Kooperation und gegenseitige Anerkennung die Unterscheidung von Civitas Dei und Civitas Terrena—Religion und Politik, Jenseits und Diesseits—bisher überhaupt erst konkret ermöglicht hatte, 1918 für den deutschen Protestantismus entfielen . . . "; see C. Schmitt, *Politische Theologie II. Die Legende von der Erledigung jeder Politischen Theologie* (Berlin:

Peterson's treatise from 1935, which culminates in a rejection of every political theology, is itself a highly political intervention, for it was indirectly[10] aimed against the political theology of the *Deutsche Christen* who offered theological support to Hitler's regime.[11] It is therefore indisputable today that Peterson's *Der Monotheismus als politisches Problem* should itself be considered an eminent example of political theology.[12] The meaning Taubes gives to 'political theology' is broader and corresponds more closely to the way J. B. Metz introduced the term into theology in the 1960s.[13] In this broader

---

Duncker und Humblot, 1970), 18. Peterson denies that (re)drawing the borders between politics and religion is the best definition of 'political theology.'

[10] The tract was *directly* aimed at Carl Schmitt's *Politische Theologie: Vier Kapitel zur Lehre von der Souveränität* (1922, 1934; Berlin: Duncker en Humblot, 1979). In the last footnote to this essay Peterson writes: "The concept 'political theology' was, as far as I know, introduced by Carl Schmitt, in *Politische Theologie*, Munich 1922. His short presentations from that period were not systematic. We have tried here using a concrete example to demonstrate the impossibility of a 'political theology' " (Peterson, "Der Monotheismus," 147).

[11] See E. L. Fellechner, "Zur biographischen und theologischen Entwicklung Petersons bis 1935: Eine Skizze," in A. Schindler, ed., *Der Monotheismus als politisches Problem? Erik Peterson und die Kritik der politischen Theologie* (Gütersloh: Mohn, 1978), 76–120. For information on three Protestant theologians who provided theological material for Nazi ideology, see R. P. Ericksen, *Theologians under Hitler: Gerhard Kittel, Paul Althaus, and Emanuel Hirsch* (New Haven, Conn.: Yale University Press, 1985).

[12] A. Schindler tests and convincingly rejects Peterson's systematic-theological and historical thesis in his book cited above. See also P. Koslowski, "Politischer Monotheismus oder Trinitätslehre," in Taubes, ed., *Der Fürst dieser Welt*, 26–44.

[13] Metz understands his own political theological project "negatively as a critical correction to the extreme tendency toward privatization in contemporary theology, and positively as the attempt to formulate the eschatological message under present-day social conditions"; see J. B. Metz, *Zur Theologie der Welt* (Mainz and Munich: Matthias Grünewald/Chr. Kaiser, 1968), 99. See also Metz, *Glaube in Geschichte und Gesellschaft* (Mainz: Matthias Grünewald, 1977). Metz opposes the privatization and *Verbürgerlichung* given in the Christian religion. These are only legitimate when, following Protestantism and Hegel, we accept E. W. Böckenförde's choice in favor of Metz's second possibility, that of a positive political/eschatological theology: "Ist der christliche Glaube seiner inneren Struktur nach eine Religion wie andere Religionen auch und ist deshalb seine gültige Erscheinungsform die des öffentlichen (Polis-)Kults, oder transzendiert der christliche Glaube die bisherigen Religionen, liegt seine Wirksamkeit und Verwirklichung gerade darin, die Sakralformen der Religion und die öffentliche Kult-Herrschaft abzubauen und die Menschen zur vernunftbestimmmten, *weltlichen* Ordnung der Welt, zum Selbstbewußtsein ihrer Freiheit zu führen?"; see Böckenförde, "Die Entstehung des Staates als Vorgang der Säkularisation," in *Staat - Gesellschaft - Freiheit: Studien zur Staatstheorie und zum Verfassungsrecht* (1967; Frankfurt am Main: Suhrkamp, 1972), 42–64, 58. On this point Metz agrees with Schmitt, who cites this passage in his *Politische*

sense, every conscious use of speech about God in a political context is political theology. Thus, according to Taubes, when Paul sent a letter to the Christians in the capital of the Roman Empire in which he expressly put this community of Christians in an antagonistic position toward both Jews (a *religio licita*, a tolerated religion, in the Roman Empire) and Roman law (a man condemned and crucified by this law is proclaimed son of God and *imperator*), Paul's action can be explained as nothing other than as political theology. 'Politics' here encompasses all that has to do with worldly power in either a positive or a negative sense. Moreover, that Christians are in conflict with others in this world is, in itself, a political fact.

But Taubes also makes a clear distinction between a theological intervention in a political context such as Paul's and a theological justification of a particular political regime. The addition of 'negative' refers to this difference, which Taubes tries to discover in Paul's Epistle to the Romans. Negative political theology is thus a position *within* political theology, not a rejection or *Erledigung* (Peterson) of political theology in an attempt to return to a "pure theology."[14] But, according to Taubes, Paul's political theological intervention was not directed toward establishing a different political system or replacing a political regime through political revolution. His effort opened a more radical possibility: a theological *delegitimation* of all political power as a *political* attitude.[15]

When the theologian Karl Barth, whom Taubes regularly cites in his book on Paul, argues that recognizing God's "wholly otherness" prohibits either the theological legitimation of existing powers or

---

Theologie II, and calls Böckenförde's question "inevitable," but the alternative too limitedly formulated (50).

[14] Carl Schmitt's conclusion about Peterson's rejection of all political theology is that "Peterson glaubte, der Krise [i.e., the crisis of Protestant theology after World War I in Germany] durch die Rückkehr zu einem problemlosen Dogmatismus entgangen zu sein und die krisenfeste Reinheit des rein Theologischen zurückgefunden zu haben"; see *Politische Theologie II*, 85.

[15] The editors of Taubes's lectures on Paul put it this way: "Gegen eine Politik, die die römische Herrschaft als Schutzmacht der eigenen nationalen Traditionen (*patrioi nomoi; mos majorum*) anerkennt und diese als *religio licita* in ihr imperiales Konzept eingemeindet, macht Paulus seine negative politische Theologie geltend, die die rahmende weltliche Ordnungsmacht selbst aus den Angeln hebt. Sie untergräbt die Funktion des Gesetzes als Ordnungsmacht, sei es im Rahmen einer Herrschaft-, Kirchen- oder Naturordnung"; see Hartwich, Assmann, and Assmann, "Nachwort," to J. Taubes, *Die politische Theologie des Paulus*, 152.

their overthrow in the name of a theologically "true" order, Taubes does not contradict him. But Taubes puts more penetratingly than Barth the question of what this recognition means as *political* attitude in a world marked by political contradictions and political struggle. The reference to God as the *Ganz Andere* (wholly Other) remains a gesture in this world. Its political implications cannot be avoided. More strongly, Taubes formulates this responsibility by citing Paul's revolutionary task. But, as noted, this task cannot be executed and brought to perfection by establishing a perfect secular power, for this would then coincide with the world as *immanence*. Taubes's alternative is an apocalyptic political attitude marked by detachment from every existing order and the messianic expectation of the revolutionary interruption of history.[16] This is what Taubes, using Walter Benjamin's term, calls "nihilism as global policy."[17]

For Taubes, political theology is unavoidable and the separation between God and the world as Barth radically depicts it in his *Epistle to the Romans* (1922) is itself a theological intervention with an intense political impact. Barth's purpose was the destruction of the political-theological complex summarized by the term *Kulturprotestantismus*.[18] Generally Taubes refuses to understand the results of

---

[16] Besides Paul (see further on), Taubes relies here on the Talmudic commentary to Ex. 32 (b.Berachot 32a), which treats the difference between the divine and the human oath: "Spricht Moshe: Gedenke doch deiner Knechte Abraham, Jizchak und Jacob, denen du bei dir geschworen hast. Warum 'bei dir'? Rabbi Eliezer sagte: Folgendes sprach Moshe vor dem heiligen, gebenedeiet sei er: Herr der Welt! Hättest du ihnen bei Himmel und Erde geschworen, so könnte ich sagen: Wie Himmel und Erde einst aufhören werden, so kann auch dein Schwur aufhören." Taubes comments on this passage: "Sie sehen also: für Himmel und Erde als Permanenz ist da nix drin. Auch das rabbinische Denken ist profunde apokalyptisch. Es kann eben ein neuer Himmel, eine neue Erde geben, daß ist kein Problem. *Ich bin da nicht so festgelegt auf diese Erde*"; see Taubes, *Die politische Theologie des Paulus*, 46 (italics ours). And further on Taubes writes: "Der ganze Text macht nur Sinn vor der Erfahrung, dass es Vernichtung gibt" (47). Taubes also gives a contemporary example of the detachment referred to: pious Jews who prayed, fasted, and studied Torah on the day Israel became independent: "Ich hab' das mal mitgemacht; während das ganze Land jubelte und Preisungen in den Synagogen stattfanden, wie das an einem nationalen Unabhängigkeitstag so üblich ist, fastet eine respektable Gruppe und liest den Fastenabschnitt. Das ist ein Anti-Symbol, dessen Juden noch heute fähig sind! (Das werden Sie sicher nicht in der Jüdischen Zeitung erfahren)" (44).

[17] Taubes, *Die politische Theologie des Paulus*, 2.3: "Nihilismus als Weltpolitik und ästhetisierter Messianismus: Walter Benjamin und Theodor W. Adorno," 97–105.

[18] On Barth's purpose here, see D. Schellong, "Jenseits von politischer Theologie und unpolitischer Theologie. Zum Ansatz der 'dialektischen Theologie,'" in Taubes, ed., *Der Fürst dieser Welt*, 292–315.

spiritual life (such as theological concepts) only as harmless meta-phors. He wants to make explicit the 'political potential' of these theological metaphors; in Taubes's words, "all the Christian concepts I know are intensely political, explosive concepts, or become that at a certain moment."[19] For this reason Taubes took Carl Schmitt's side in the debate between himself, the jurist Schmitt, and the philoso-pher and 'metaphorologist' Hans Blumenberg on the (il)legitimacy of the concept 'secularization.'[20] It is interesting that here Schmitt chose as his motto Rimbaud's words, "Le combat spirituel est aussi brutal que la bataille d'homme" (Spiritual conflict is as cruel as human battle).[21]

We can call Taubes's paradoxical attitude—that, from a theologi-cal perspective, there is no legitimate political order, and that this idea must be at the center of political life—a 'negative political the-ology,' but it may just as well be characterized as a 'negative messian-ism' and thus as a standpoint in the philosophy of history. He focuses on more than just the traditional political-theological question of the relationship between the gods/God and the political order/politi-cal power. He also, and even primarily, studies the relationship be-tween world history and the Messiah. Here Taubes can only speak negatively of the Messiah as a *rupture* in history.

In this chapter we will attempt to clarify and interpret Taubes's political-theological position as sketched above. Taubes's view, in particular the concept 'negative political theology,' can only be un-derstood when we take into consideration the complex relationship

---

[19] Taubes, *Die politische Theologie des Paulus*, 95–99. See also his *Ad Carl Schmitt*, 62–63: "Eine religiöse Debatte über die Trinität klingt theologisch, wenn man aber in Konstantinopel auf die Straße geht und kämpft um die Formel, so oder so ist es dann politisch."

[20] Taubes, *Die Politische Theologie des Paulus*, 95. See Hans Blumenberg, *Die Le-gitimität der Neuzeit* (Frankfurt am Main: Suhrkamp, 1966), and Schmitt's com-mentary at the end of his *Politische Theologie II*, 109–26. Blumenberg answered this commentary in Hans Blumenberg, *Die Legitimität der Neuzeit*, Erneuerte Ausgabe (Frankfurt am Main: Suhrkamp, 1988), chap. 1:VIII: "Politische Theologie I und II," 99–113. For more information on this discussion, see the articles by W. Hübe-ner, "Carl Schmitt und Hans Blumenberg oder über Kette und Schuss in der histori-schen Textur der Moderne," and O. Marquard, "Politischer Polytheismus—auch eine politische Theologie," in Taubes, ed., *Der Fürst dieser Welt*.

[21] See Carl Schmitt, "Die geschichtliche Struktur des heutigen Welt-Gegensatzes von Ost und West: Bemerkungen zu Ernst Jüngers Schrift 'Der gordische Knoten,'" in A. Mohler, ed., *Freundschaftliche Begegnungen: Festschrift für Ernst Jünger zum 60. Geburtstag* (Frankfurt am Main: Vittorio Klostermann, 1955), 135–67; 146.

between his thinking and that of Carl Schmitt, the Roman Catholic specialist in constitutional law who introduced the concept 'political theology' into twentieth-century political thought.[22] Schmitt has been called the 'sphinx of German jurisprudence.' From many of his dicta, it is evident that Taubes was fascinated by this jurist's work and person. Yet his own view, summarized in the concept 'negative political theology,' seems on some crucial points to contradict, even to answer polemically, Schmitt's political theology.

For this reason we will start our exposition with a sketch of the meeting between these two thinkers, which Taubes described several times (Section 2).[23] Then we will interpret Taubes's reading of Paul's epistle to the Romans using Schmitt's key political-theological concept of "exception" (*Ausnahme*), in which Taubes was greatly interested, and its constitutional derivative, the "exceptional situation" (*Ausnahmezustand*). According to Taubes, Paul's polemical attitude toward Rome and Jerusalem should be understood as the existential experience of a revolutionary reversal. As such it marks the start of a messianic tradition that continues into the twentieth century and that can be identified as negative political theology (Section 3). After completing this reconstruction, we will try to determine the characteristics of Taubes's messianic political attitude, both in opposition to other variants of political theology, such as a 'positive political theology' and a 'negative revolutionary political theology,' and in opposition to the *tradition* of negative theology in general. Here we will also draw on some of Taubes's older texts (Section 4).

2. Jacob Taubes and Carl Schmitt: An Encounter

Undoubtedly, the encounter between Jacob Taubes and Carl Schmitt is one of the most intriguing stories in postwar intellectual

---

[22] See in particular Carl Schmitt, *Politische Theologie*. For a concise introduction to Schmitt's political-theological views, see H. Meier, "Was ist Politische Theologie?," in Assmann, *Politische Theologie zwischen Ägypten und* Israel, 17–19.

[23] See Taubes, *Ad Carl Schmitt* and "Anhang. Die Geschichte Jacob Taubes-Carl Schmitt," in *Die politische Theologie des Paulus*, 132–42. References to Schmitt in Taubes are found as early as the 1950s. See, e.g., Taubes, "Four Ages of Reason," *Archiv für Rechts- und Sozialphilosophie* 42 (1956): 1–14, 6, and "Kultur und Ideologie," in T. W. Adorno, ed., *Spätkapitalismus oder Industriegesellschaft?* (Stuttgart: Ferdinand Enke, 1969), 117–38, 121, and 130.

history. "We knew that we strongly opposed one another, but we understood one another very well," writes Taubes about his discussions with Schmitt.[24] A world historical, theological, and cultural doom does seem to hang above their encounter. Regarding the world historical doom, the Jewish Taubes and the Roman Catholic jurist Schmitt were political enemies.[25] From 1933 onward, Schmitt was not only closely linked to a regime whose goal was the elimination of all Jews, he wrote texts in this period that contain virulently anti-Semitic statements.[26] Nothing would have been easier and more obvious than for Taubes to do as many do today and declare Schmitt a Nazi ideologue and an author who may only be cited with contempt.[27] It was theological doom: political theology in postwar Germany was long a contaminated notion, not in the least because of the success enjoyed by Peterson's farewell to all political theology, which was directed against Schmitt.[28]

---

[24] Taubes, *Die politische Theologie des Paulus*, 96. He continues: "Wir wußten eines: daß wir auf derselben Ebene reden. Und das war eine sehr seltene Sache."

[25] Schmitt, in his *Der Begriff des Politischen* (1932; Berlin: Duncker und Humblot, 1963) describes the distinction between friend and enemy as criterium for politics: "Die spezifisch politische Unterscheidung, auf welche sich die politische Handlungen und Motive zurückführen lassen, ist die Unterscheidung von *Freund* und *Feind*" (26).

[26] One example is Schmitt's lecture given on 4 October 1936 at a congress organized by the Reichsgruppe Hochschullehrer in the NS-Rechtswahrersbund on "Die deutsche Rechtswissenschaft im Kampf gegen den jüdischen Geist," in which he spoke, among other things, about the Jews' 'parasitären, taktischen und händlerischen' spirit. It was published with other lectures in *Das Judentum in der Rechtswissenschaft* (Berlin: Deutscher Recht-Verlag, 1936). During this same congress Schmitt also said that a "jüdische Autor" has "für uns keine Autorität, auch keine 'rein wissenschaftliche' Autorität" (29–30). This statement is particularly amazing when we know that in 1930 Schmitt had praised the "unabhängige Geist" of the Jewish constitutional expert and publicist Hugo Preuss in his *Hugo Preuss. Sein Staatsbegriff und seine Stellung in der deutschen Staatslehre* (Tübingen: Mohr, 1930). For more on this, see B. Rüthers, *Carl Schmitt im Dritten Reich*, 2nd erweiterte Ausgabe (Munich: Beck, 1990).

[27] A recent example is R. J. Siebert, "From Conservative to Critical Political Theology," in A. J. Reimer, ed., *The Influence of the Frankfurt School on Contemporary Theology: Critical Theory and the Future of Religion*, Toronto Studies in Theology 64 (Lewiston/Queenston/Lampeter: Mellen, 1992), 147–219.

[28] J. B. Metz underwent the same experience in the 1960s when he reintroduced the term to refer to his own theology. One of Metz's first critics was the political scientist H. Maier, who took amiss what he considered to be Metz's unconcerned use of the term and said the concept was historically overburdened and theologically inappropriate. In so doing he referred to Schmitt's commitment to National Socialism and cited E. Peterson. See H. Maier, "Politische Theologie? Einwände eines

Another hindrance to the meeting was Taubes's association with the 'leftist' Frankfurter Schule (Frankfurt school), which considered the 'rightist' Schmitt in particular as one of the forerunners of Nazism. But 'left' and 'right' are not categories native to a creative thinker like Taubes. Taubes illustrates how questionable this division was when applied to intellectual life during the Weimar Republic by pointing to Walter Benjamin, another member of the Frankfurter Schule, with whom he felt a strong affinity. He recalls a letter Benjamin sent Schmitt in 1930—a period in which the Weimar Republic already was in crisis—which Adorno initially kept hidden.[29] In this letter Benjamin wrote that his own study of baroque tragedy[30] was in both method and content influenced by Schmitt's books.[31]

Taubes's own thesis, that Benjamin took Schmitt's side in the 'struggle against historicism,'[32] helps clarify Taubes's own interest in the constitutional jurist and situates his unique interpretation of Paul's Epistle to the Romans. Benjamin's antihistoricism is best represented in his famous theses on the philosophy of history, "Über den Begriff der Geschichte."[33] For our study, we are mainly interested in Benjamin's critical thoughts regarding the following three historicist views: (1) in his attempts to 'empathize with' an earlier historical period, the historiographer should try to forget all he knows about later historical developments, (2) history is the narrative of a continuous chain of causes and results, and (3) history is the harbinger of the future.

Laien," in H. Peukert, ed., *Diskussion zur 'politischen Theologie'* (Munich and Mainz: Grünewald, 1969), 1–25.

[29] The letter is missing from the two-volume edition of Benjamin's *Briefe*, eds. G. Scholem and T. W. Adorno (Frankfurt am Main: Suhrkamp, 1966). It is included in W. Benjamin, *Gesammelte Schriften* (Frankfurt am Main: Suhrkamp, 1980), 1.3.887. See also S. Weber, "Taking Exception to Decision: Walter Benjamin and Carl Schmitt," in H. Kunneman and H. de Vries, eds., *Enlightments: Encounters between Critical Theory and Contemporary French Thought* (Kampen: Kok, 1993), 141–61, 141ff.

[30] W. Benjamin, *Ursprung des deutschen Trauerspiels* (Frankfurt am Main: Suhrkamp, 1963). As Benjamin writes in the "Introduction," this book was "Entworfen 1916, Verfasst 1925," and published complete and for the first time in 1928.

[31] He mentions in particular Schmitt's *Politische Theologie* and his *Die Diktatur. Von den Anfängen des modernen Souveränitätsgedankens bis zum proletarischen Klassenkampf* (Munich and Leipzig: Duncker und Humblot, 1921).

[32] Taubes, *Ad Carl Schmitt*, 26.

[33] W. Benjamin, "Theses on the Philosophy of History," in *Illuminations*, ed. and with an "Introduction" by Hannah Arendt (New York: Harcourt, Brace & World, 1968), 255–66.

Regarding the first view we must, according to Benjamin, wonder *with whom* this apparently disinterested historiographer is to 'empathize.' Benjamin fears that the answer must be history's winners. The (historical materialistic) historiographer whom Benjamin prefers has the gift "of fanning the spark of hope in the past." A first condition for this is an awareness that "even the dead will not be safe from the enemy if he wins"; put differently, the dominant historiography is the story the winners tell about themselves.[34] This leads Benjamin to turn against the whole historical method of empathy.[35] He argues that this method fails when faced with the need to master the "true picture of the past" that always "flits by" *in the present.*

Against the second view—the core of historicism—Benjamin recalls the historical experience of revolution, especially the revolutionary consciousness of disrupting history's continuity. Historiography should not be concerned with displaying transitions or filling in a homogeneous and empty agenda with masses of facts; instead history should focus on the moments when time stops. Benjamin relates these moments, constituting the present (*Jetztzeit*), the time when "a revolutionary chance in the fight for the oppressed past" presents itself, to the intervention of the messianic in history.

Benjamin meets the third view—belief in progress—primarily in social-democratic theory and practice. Humanity's progress (*Fortschritt*) is conceived as a gradual progression (*Fortgang*) of history through a homogeneous and empty time. "Every day our cause becomes clearer and people get smarter," read Benjamin in the social-democrat Josef Dietzgen.[36] To dispute this view, he not only introduces the revolutionary *Jetztzeit*, he also recalls the Jewish attitude to the past. Both are interdependent. For the Jews, only the past can be an object of knowledge. This 'knowledge' does not refer to the scientific kind of knowledge that detects causal relationships, but to a remembering and commemorating events in prayer and in teaching the Torah. Whoever pauses before the victims of past history cannot

---

[34] Benjamin, "Theses," 257. That Taubes had this awareness is evident from his protest against the later honor paid to the rebels in the Warsaw ghetto, and the denigration of those "led like sheep to the slaughter"; see Taubes, *Die politische Theologie des Paulus*, 41.

[35] Benjamin seeks the origin of the idea of empathy (*Einfühlung*) in the theological concept *acedia*, the 'slowness of heart,' which, according to medieval theologians, was the basis of melancholy. See Benjamin, *Ursprung*, 134ff.

[36] Cited by Benjamin, "Theses," 262.

regard the future as simply the continuation of past and present, nor as the magical something sought from soothsayers. The future is taboo as the object of knowledge: for Jews, "every second of time was the strait gate through which the Messiah might enter."[37]

The core characteristic of Benjamin's antihistoricism is sensitivity to the exceptional and the extreme. This historical sensitivity to the exceptional presents history as the arena in which victims are *distinguished* from victors (a separation or distinction that the victors soon forget or that they see as transitory); it sees pauses in time as moments of *decision* and reversal in which the causal chain is interrupted; finally, it is linked to the expectation of the end of time with the intervention of the Messiah arriving from the 'nothing' of the future.

Taubes also meets a great sensitivity for the exceptional and the extreme in Schmitt, especially in his *Politische Theologie*. The passages that Taubes cites from this juridical work in his book on Paul all have to do with the importance Schmitt gives in his juridical teaching to the 'exceptional' and the 'state of emergency.'[38] In this text interest in the exceptional is accompanied by arguments against the rationalistic and positivist legal doctrine (e.g., in H. Kelsen and G. Anschütz) present in Germany in the 1920s, rather than against historicism. Just as Benjamin's *Jetztzeit* interrupts the historicist 'progression' of history, Schmitt's "force of real life" present in the *Ausnahme* (exception) of juridical rules shatters the "repetitious, fixated automatism" of the legal system. That is why the exception is, for Schmitt, "more interesting than the normal case. The normal case proves nothing, the exception demonstrates everything; it not only confirms the rule, it keeps it alive."[39] Taubes starts his discussion

---

[37] The full quotation reads: "The soothsayers who found out from time what it had in store did not experience time as either homogeneous or empty. Anyone who keeps this in mind will perhaps get an idea of how past times were experienced in remembrance—namely, in just the same way. We know that the Jews were prohibited from investigating the future. The Torah and the prayers instruct them in remembrance, however. This stripped the future of its magic, to which all those succumb who turn to the soothsayers for enlightenment. This does not imply, however, that for the Jews the future turned into homogeneous, empty time. For every second of time was the strait gate through which the Messiah might enter"; Benjamin, "Theses," 266.

[38] Taubes, *Die politische Theologie des Paulus*, 89ff.

[39] Schmitt, *Politische Theologie*, 22, cited by Taubes, *Die politische Theologie des Paulus*, 90.

on Schmitt by recalling the famous definition of sovereignty with
which *Politische Theologie* opens: "Souverän ist, wer über den Ausnahmezustand entscheidet" (Sovereign is he who decides on the exception).[40]

Taubes's comment on this definition shows that he read it in the
context of the philosophy of history: "This has been written by a
jurist, not a theologian, but *this is not praise of secularization*, it is a
disclosure."[41] The definition discloses the bigotry and the limitation
of a secularized rationalistic legal system cut off from the existential
possibility of the *Ausnahme*.[42] It is this possibility—and here Taubes
agrees with Schmitt—that gives permanent relevance to the political
theological question (the question of how the "sacred and profane
orders" relate[43]).

Shortly before his death Taubes admitted that reading Schmitt's
Politische Theologie was a "turning point in my years of study." But
he also noted, "Yet in every one of Carl Schmitt's words I found
something alien to me, a fear and anxiety of the storm that was
imminent in the secularized messianic arrow of Marxism."[44] We will
see shortly that Taubes, like Benjamin,[45] provides a radically different

---

[40] Schmitt, *Politische Theologie*, 11; Taubes, *Die politische Theologie des Paulus*,
89.

[41] Taubes, *Die politische Theologie des Paulus*, 89 (italics ours).

[42] This quotation from *Politische Theologie*, which Taubes places after Schmitt's
definition of sovereignty, is as follows: "Es wäre konsequenter Rationalismus, zu
sagen, daß die Ausnahme nichts beweist und nur der Normale Gegenstand wissen-
schaftlichen Interesses sein kann. Die Ausnahme verwirrt die Einheit und Ordnung
des rationalistischen Schemas. In der positiven Staatslehre begegnet man öfters
einem ähnlichen Argument. So antwortet Anschütz auf die Frage, wie bei nicht
vorhandenem Etatsgesetz zu verfahren ist, das sei überhaupt keine Rechtsfrage. Es
liegt hier nicht sowohl eine Lücke im Gesetz, das heißt im Verfassungstekst, als
vielmehr eine Lücke im Recht vor, welche durch keinerlei rechtswissenschaftliche
Begriffsoperationen ausgefüllt werden kann. Das Staatsrecht hört hier auf" (*Politische Theologie*, 21–22).

[43] Taubes, *Ad Carl Schmitt*, 28.

[44] Taubes, *Ad Carl Schmitt*, 10 and 15.

[45] S. Weber subtly showed that Benjamin, citing Schmitt's teaching on sover-
eignty in his *Ursprung des deutschen Trauerspiels*, gives this teaching a radical new
meaning. Schmitt starts from the thesis that "Alle prägnante Begriffe der modernen
Staatslehre . . . säkularisierte theologische Begriffe (sind)" (*Politische Theologie*, 49).
He thinks of theological and modern political concepts in terms of analogy (e.g.,
"Der Ausnahmezustand hat für die Jurisprudenz eine analoge Bedeutung wie das
Wunder für die Theologie") and ultimately of structural identity, such that the
'sovereign' for him transcends the state as God transcends creation. However, for
Benjamin, the transcendent position of the sovereign is abrogated in seventeenth-

answer to Schmitt's political theological problem in his interpretation of Paul's Epistle to the Romans.

The story of Taubes's *personal* encounter with Schmitt begins in 1952. In that year Taubes wrote a letter from Jerusalem to Armin Mohler,[46] a classmate from Zurich who was then Ernst Jünger's secretary. In this letter he informs Mohler that the question of why Schmitt and Heidegger became involved in National Socialism still fascinated him. Where, Taubes wondered, lay Nazism's "attraction" for these thinkers whom he considered "*the* intellectual force, that stood head and shoulders above all the intellectuals' scribbling"?[47] In the same letter he tells Mohler of a striking occurrence that took place in Jerusalem a few years earlier, in 1948. While looking for Schmitt's main work, the *Verfassungslehre*, Taubes learned that the Ministry of Justice had just requested the book. They wanted to consult it while preparing the Israeli constitution. It is understandable that Taubes was 'baffled,'[48] for this meant that the main work of an individual branded the "Nazi's top jurist" was now being used to compose the Israeli constitution!

Jünger—as Taubes learned afterward—passed the letter on to Schmitt, who circulated it among his friends with the comment, "Letter from a Jewish intellectual who understands me better than any of my followers." From that time on Schmitt sent Taubes copies of all his books, with inscribed dedications. While Taubes did not respond to these overtures, neither did he send the books back. In 1967 Taubes began to reconsider his refusal to have any direct contact with the jurist. When the Hegel specialist Alexandre Kojève told

---

century German baroque tragedy: the sovereign becomes a creature like any other. *Distance* from God is characteristic of the baroque sovereign. This does not imply the elimination of all transcendence, but the radical *separation* between immanence and transcendence, between *Diesseits* and *Jenseits*. According to Weber, "What the Baroque rejects is any admission of the *limitation of immanence* and does so by emptying transcendence of all possible representable content. Far from doing away with transcendence, however, such emptying only endows it with an all the more powerful force: that of the vacuum, of the absolute and unbounded other, which, since it is no longer representable, is also no longer localisable out there or as a beyond. The otherness that is no longer allowed to remain transcendent therefore reappears this side of the horizon, represented as a cataract, abyss or fall. Or, even more radically, such transcendence will be represented by, and as, *allegory*"; see Weber, "Taking Exception to Decision," 153–54.

[46] The letter is included in Taubes, *Ad Carl Schmitt*, 31–35.

[47] Taubes, *Die politische Theologie des Paulus*, 134.

[48] Taubes, *Die politische Theologie des Paulus*, 134.

him, after a lecture in Berlin, that he planned to go to Plettenberg, where Schmitt lived, Taubes's surprised glance was answered with, "Mit wem sonst ist in Deutschland zu reden?" (With whom else could one speak in Germany?). Hans Blumenberg also tried to convince Taubes to meet Schmitt.[49] But it was not until 1979 that Taubes broke his self-imposed ban and finally wrote to Schmitt. The latter then phoned him and invited him to come to Plettenberg: "I read and reread your letter. I am not in good health, I do not know how long I have to live. Come right away."[50] And so it happened. At Schmitt's suggestion the discussion treated primarily chapters 9–11 of Paul's Epistle to the Romans. On what Taubes had to say, Schmitt is to have commented, "Bevor Sie sterben, sagen Sie das einigen" (Before you die, tell these things to a few others).

Typical of Taubes's contact with Schmitt is the way he defended the latter in a dispute with the German political scientist Kurt Sontheimer that took place in Paris in 1986. Here Sontheimer took the usual German position of linking all of Schmitt's thinking with National Socialist crimes. Taubes refused to join the camp of those who either judge or condemn,[51] and chose instead to try to understand.[52] Taubes rejected every form of abstract normativism, that is, issuing judgmental dicta about history instead of first examining and understanding what actually happened. Like Schmitt, he distrusted every 'pure' (reine) theory, every theory that denies its link to historical reality. To deny historical, and thus finite, human reality is to ignore the truth that we must always judge within a given situation.[53]

---

[49] "Hören Sie doch endlich auf mit dieser tribunalistischen Einstellung?," wrote Blumenberg to Taubes, who then thought: "Hör, mal, Jacob, du bist nicht der Richter, gerade als Jude bist du nicht der Richter, denn du mußt doch zugeben, wenn du was gelernt hat, dann hast du was von Schmitt gelernt" (Taubes, Die politische Theologie des Paulus, 137).

[50] According to Taubes's account, in Taubes, Die politische Theologie des Paulus, 10.

[51] Taubes, Ad Carl Schmitt, 46: "Konträr zu dem, was viele tun, bringt mich das in die Lage, mich des Urteils zu enthalten. Über viele Dinge zögere ich den Stab zu brechen, weil wir als Juden in all den unaussprechlichen Grauen, das geschehen ist, vor einem bewahrt geblieben sind, nämlich mitzumachen."

[52] Taubes, Ad Carl Schmitt, 47: "Die Frage ist nun, was ist der Nationalsozialismus, daß er Leute wie Heidegger und Schmitt anziehen kann."

[53] Taubes, Ad Carl Schmitt, 56–57 and 62. Here Taubes defends Schmitt's 'decisionism,' which Sontheimer had branded an immoral position. In doing so, said Taubes, Sontheimer had "etwas grundlegend Menschliches vergessen, daß der

But their paths diverge at the crucial point of the answer to the political theological question. While, for Schmitt, law, state, and sovereignty ultimately derive their legitimacy from their analogy to theological concepts,[54] so that the "sovereign, who decides the exceptional situation" restores not only the existing order but also God's creation, Taubes insists on the unbridgeable *difference* between the profane and the sacred orders and refuses every *'spiritual investment'* in the existing. This opens a chasm between the "apocalyptist of the contra-revolution" and the "apocalyptist from below,"[55] which Taubes describes as follows:

> The jurist must legitimate the world as it is. This is inherent in the whole education and in the whole image of the legal profession. He is a clerk. He does not consider it his task to create justice but to interpret law. Schmitt was interested in only one thing: the party, chaos must not emerge, the state must continue. At whatever price. . . .

Mensch, was immer er tut und sagt, es in der Zeit tut. . . . das Problem der Zeit ist ein moralisches Problem, und Dezisionismus heißt zu sagen, es geht nicht unendlich lange."

[54] Schmitt believes (1) that the possibility of an 'exception,' in law the exceptional situation, is the political theological problem par excellence, and (2) that modernity is completing the turn toward immanence which implies that there are no longer any exceptions or 'miracles.' Taubes agrees with both presuppositions. "Wir sind immer beim selben Problem . . . Die Frage ist, ob man die Ausnahme für möglich hält" (Taubes, *Die politische Theologie des Paulus*, 118). And: "Die Moderne ist ein immanenter Kosmos" (117). However, Taubes and Schmitt have different views of the 'miracle' that they believe possible even in modernity. For Schmitt the miracle—and the continuity of the political-theological tradition—is an unexpected return of the 'transcendent' sovereign (in an extreme case, a dictator) who unravels 'from above' what disturbs social order. This theological 'spiritual investment' in the existing world is unthinkable for Taubes because he looks at history from the victims' point of view. His thought is a commemoration. For the oppressed, the victims of history, the *Ausnahmezustand* is part of daily experience, is the 'normal situation.' For them the 'miracle' (the *liberation* from the 'normal situation') is the real *Ausnahmezustand*. Taubes thus underwrites Benjamin's eighth historical-philosophical thesis which adopts but radically redefines Schmitt's key term. "The tradition of the oppressed teaches us that the 'state of emergency' in which we live is not the exception but the rule. We must attain to a conception of history that is in keeping with this insight. Then we shall clearly realize that it is our task to bring about a real state of emergency, and this will improve our position in the struggle against Fascism" (Benjamin, "Theses," 259). Taubes cites and agrees with this passage in *Ad Carl Schmitt*, 28.

[55] These are the terms Taubes uses to describe, respectively, Schmitt and himself in *Ad Carl Schmitt*.

Later he called this the kat-echon:[56] the restrainer, who oppresses the
chaos emerging from below. . . . This is not my worldview, this is not
my experience. As apocalyptist I can imagine that the world will be
destroyed. *I have no spiritual investment in the world as it is.*[57]

The difference between the two thinkers cannot be put more co-
gently. Each understands what is at risk: worldly power and order are
unstable, they are continually threatened. The extreme case, even
the very worst case, is always possible. But while Schmitt, "from
above," descries chaos and (theologically speaking) the Antichrist,
Taubes, "from below," refuses any theological engagement with
worldly powers and sees the revolutionary potential of a *negative
theological* tradition initiated by Paul. This is evident in his explanation of Paul's fundamental existential experience, which (using
Schmitt's term) we will call the messianic experience of the "exceptional situation."[58]

---

[56] Schmitt refers in various places in his work to the 'κατέχον' mentioned in 2
Thess. 2: 6–8. There Paul writes about what is to be expected before Christ's return,
about the time of the Antichrist: "And now you know that which restraineth [καὶ
νῦν τὸ κατέχον οἴδατε] , to the end that he may be revealed in his own season.
For the mystery of lawlessness doth already work: only there is one that restraineth
[ὁ κατέχων] now, until he he be taken out of the way. And then shall be revealed the
lawless one whom the Lord Jesus shall slay with the breath of his mouth, and bring
to nought by the manifestation of his coming." In his posthumous *Glossarium.
Aufzeichnungen der Jahre 1947–1951* (Berlin: Dunker und Humblot, 1991), Schmitt
writes: "Ich glaube an den κατέχον; es ist für mich die einzige Möglichkeit, als
Christ Geschichte zu verstehen und sinnvoll zu finden" (63). What this means for
him is explained in his *Der Nomos der Erde* (Berlin: Dunker und Humblot, 1950):
"In der konkreten Ortung auf Rom, nicht in Normen und allgemeinen Ideen, liegt
die Kontinuität, die das mittelalterliche Völkerrecht mit dem Römischen Reich ver-
bindet. Diesem christlichen Reich ist es wesentlich, das es kein ewiges Reich ist,
sondern sein eigenes Ende und das Ende des gegenwärtigen Äon im Auge behält
und trotzdem einer geschichtlichen Kontinuität fähig ist. Der entscheidende ge-
schichtsmächtige Begriff seiner Kontinuität ist der des Aufhalters, des κατέχον.
'Reich' bedeutet hier *die geschichtliche Macht, die das erscheinen des Antichrist und
das Ende des gegenwärtigen Äon aufzuhalten vermag*" (29, italics ours). For Schmitt,
medieval imperialism, including the Crusades and the Inquisition, is theologically
legitimate: it is the God-given duty to use earthly power to impede the 'Antichrist.'
See further: L. Berthold, "Wer hält zur Zeit den Satan auf? —Zur Selbstglossierung
Carl Schmitts," *Leviathan* 21 (1994): 285–99. Since both Schmitt and Taubes call
on Paul for their respective versions of 'political theology' and of 'negative political
theology,' we must note that the decisive divergence takes place in Paul.

[57] Taubes, *Die politische Theologie des Paulus*, 139.

[58] As the reader will understand, this is a metaphorical use of Schmitt's legal
category *Ausnahmezustand*.

3. The Messianic Experience of the Exceptional Situation

Paul, the convert, faces a double justification problem, one continually present in the epistle to the Romans.[59] Paul must justify his activity, the establishment of a new people of God, against the background of his own history. Taubes underlines the dramatic character of Paul's undertaking.[60] He must also justify himself before the Christians as spiritual leader. After all, Paul is not one of the original apostles. His conversion represents a break with the religion of his father and ancestors, perhaps even a break with the covenant God made with his chosen people, but it also represents the foundation of a new covenant whose meaning is by no means obvious.[61]

Paul's problem has several aspects. The justification of the new community presupposes *removing legitimacy* from the old community by abrogating the old covenant between God and the Jewish people. The justification of the new community is a claim to power that reacts polemically against the existing community: the Jewish community and the political order of the Roman Empire. Finally, those moving from one community to the other do not have a basis to justify this move. There is no third community, no *tertium comparationis*, that itself justifies the change. Paul is in what we might call a 'justification vacuum' where the traditional source of justification is destroyed and the new one is still in the design stage. The *negativity* or destruction of the existing legitimacy is an essential moment in the experience of someone making this change. Taubes sees in this experience of negativity the continuity between Paul and the Jewish tradition.[62]

---

[59] Taubes refers here particularly to Rom. 8, which should be read from the premise, "Paulus steht unter Anklage" (Taubes, *Die politische Theologie des Paulus*, 40).

[60] Taubes, *Die politische Theologie des Paulus*, 42: "Es steht an für Paulus *die Gründung und Legitimierung eines neuen Gottesvolkes*. Das kommt ihnen nach zweitausend Jahren Christentum nicht sehr dramatisch vor. Es ist aber der dramatischste Vorgang, den man sich vorstellen kann in einer jüdischen Seele. Die Basis einer solchen Vorstellung ist doch, daß die ὀργή θεοῦ, der Zorn Gottes, das Volk vertilgen will, weil es gesündigt hat, weil es abtrünnig geworden ist."

[61] Taubes notes twice (*Die politische Theologie des Paulus*, 33–34, 56–57) and expressly that the term 'Christian' does not occur in the Epistle to the Romans.

[62] This is apparent from the conclusions Taubes draws from his interpretation of the Talmud tract b. Berachot 32a: "Der ganze Text macht nur Sinn vor der Erfahrung, daß es Vernichtung gibt." See also note 16.

Paul's experience is that the new community arose from nothing. At the moment when legitimacy passes from an old community to a new one, justification is strictly speaking not possible. There is only a decision forced by a fait accompli: in this case, Jesus who is called the Messiah. The old community does not permit such a decision— for the old community, it is excluded or forbidden. In the new community it is no longer a *decision*, but a *conclusion*, the starting point of all justification. The justification of the decision comes from elsewhere, but this 'elsewhere' is not a positive, tangible ground for justification.

For Taubes, bringing forward the experience of revolution that Paul undergoes and narrates in his text (esp. in Rom. 9–13) has a clearly subversive meaning—at least when regarded from the viewpoint of established Christian tradition. Early in his book on Paul, Taubes asserts that Paul had so far been given no place in Jewish religious history.[63] Incorrectly so, he wants to show, for the way Paul depicts his struggle with the revolution cannot be separated from, and is even a part of, the Jewish tradition. Seen in this manner, Paul is no longer one of the authorities who confers legitimacy on Christianity. Taubes is less interested in Paul's claim to power or its continuation in Christianity than in the Pauline *experience* that accompanied the change.

This experience can first be described with the paradoxical circle of the "self-authorizing authority."[64] Paul's "transfiguration

---

[63] Taubes, *Die politische Theologie des Paulus*, 15.

[64] This paradox is met repeatedly in texts by Jacques Derrida and other deconstructivists. See how Derrida, in a text devoted to Walter Benjamin, describes the so-called revolutionary situation: "Here we are dealing with a *double bind* or a contradiction that can be schematized as follows. On the one hand, it appears *easier* to criticize the violence that founds since it cannot be justified by any preexisting legality and so appears savage. But on the other hand, and this reversal is the whole point of this reflection, it is *more difficult*, more illegitimate to criticize this same violence since one cannot summon it to appear before the institution of any preexisting law: it does not recognize existing law in the moment that it founds another"; see. J. Derrida, "Force of Law: The 'Mystical Foundation of Authority,' " *Cardoso Law Review* 11, nos. 5–6 (1990): 920–1038, 1001. On this paradox and its relation to (dis)continuity in Roman Catholic tradition, see J. Caputo, "Deconstruction and Catholicism: Advocating Discontinuity and Bedeviling the Tradition," in J. Wissink, ed., *(Dis)continuity and (De)construction* (Kampen: Kok, 1995), 12–34; and T. W. A. de Wit, "Katholicisme, deconstructie en democratie," in E. Borgman, B. van Dijk, and T. Salemink, eds., *Katholieken in de moderne tijd* (Zoetermeer: De Horstink, 1995), 195–217.

of"[65] the people of God and the admission of nonbelievers occurs "in great sorrow and unceasing pain of heart" (Rom. 9.2). For Taubes, Paul is aware that in providing a foundation for this transfiguration (Taubes points out that Rom. 9 is overloaded with citations from the Old Testament), he is *establishing* a new people of God, and this establishing action cannot be legitimized.

Second, Taubes speaks about Paul in terms of a "messianic concentration on the paradoxical."[66] Paul polemically contrasts obedience to laws to "obedience to faith" (Rom. 1.5) in a crucified man proclaimed Messiah. Taubes invites us to realize that this means a complete reversal of the values in Roman and Jewish thinking: "excluded from the community, he hangs there as one cursed. In the evening he must be removed from his cross lest the earth be contaminated."[67]

Finally, such a faith that contradicts all evidence betrays not only a political 'nihilism,' a readiness to reverse dominant values completely, but also a nihilistic view of the world as nature and as creation. Here Taubes refers to the Pauline view of creation in Rom. 8. In his own German translation, this reads: "Denn der Nichtigkeit wurde allem Gescheffenen unterworfen . . ." (For the creation was subjected to futility . . . ; Rom. 8.20) and "Denn wir wissen, daß alles geschaffene insgesamt seufzt und sich schmerzlich ängstigt bis jetzt" (For we know that the whole creation groans and suffers the pains of childbirth together until now; Rom. 8.22).

When Taubes now calls himself a "Paulist,"[68] this does not mean he is declaring an adherence to the founder of Christianity (a title he tends to give to Paul rather than to Jesus). It means that he is identifying himself with the Pauline political theological attitude. In other words, he does not consider himself bound by the conclusion produced by Paul's decision (the positiveness of Christianity and even of Christian 'culture'), but opens anew the messianic possibility of the 'exception.' For this reason he does not correct later messianic expectations, such as Benjamin's, with the assertion that the Messiah has already come. Taubes does not adhere to the Christian faith.

---

[65] Taubes, *Die politische Theologie des Paulus*, 59.
[66] Taubes, *Die politische Theologie des Paulus*, 21.
[67] Taubes, *Die politische Theologie des Paulus*, 21, 38.
[68] Taubes, *Die politische Theologie des Paulus*, 183.

It is thus understandable that Taubes, in his reading, gives Paul's text a much broader interpretation. He thinks the Pauline experience can be detected in many moments in history. This experience is itself a 'tradition,' an undercurrent that continually undermines dominant thinking. The dominant thinking is always the victors' thinking, the thinking in terms of decisions already made, of the normality of 'immanence,' and not thinking in terms of the experience of the messianic 'exception.' Taubes's historical reconstruction of the Pauline experience, for him a specifically Jewish experience, links a whole series of experiences that form one front against 'immanence thinking.' On one side Taubes points to an analogy with Moses' position when he was confronted with the threatened execution of God's warning that He would destroy the Jewish people when they turned to sin (Ex. 32.19). Moses defended the possibility of a new covenant that would not necessarily abrogate the old, but would reveal the radical contingency of forms of dominance and their religious sanctioning.[69] In the second part of his book on Paul Taubes discusses the influence of Paul's text. He points to thinkers such as Søren Kierkegaard, Karl Barth, and Walter Benjamin as those who represent modern "transfigurations of the messianic."

Based on these aspects of his thought, we can now describe Taubes's negative theological project in greater detail.

---

[69] The question recurs in the later Middle Ages in the context of the interpretation of the covenant between people and God: Does God have obligations toward people who fulfill their obligations? The distinction here is between the *potentia Dei ordinata*, in which God can create an order in which He assumes obligations, and the *potentia Dei absoluta*, in which God can abrogate every order. In the latter case we recognize the subversive aspect to which Taubes continually refers. Many Christians in the late Middle Ages and during the Reformation were also aware of it. See esp. Stephen Ozment, *Mysticism and Dissent: Religious Ideology and Social Protest in the Sixteenth Century* (New Haven, Conn.: Yale University Press, 1973). Regarding the distinction, see F. Oakley, "Pierre d'Ailly and the Absolute Power of God: Another Note on the Theology of Nominalism," *Harvard Theological Review* 56 (1963): 59–73; F. Oakley, "Jacobean Political Theology: The Absolute and Ordinary Powers of the King," *Journal of the History of Ideas* 29 (1968): 323–96; H. A. Oberman, *The Harvest of Medieval Theology* (Grand Rapids, Mich.: Eerdmans, 1967); and W. J. Courtenay, *Covenant and Causality in Medieval Thought* (London: Variorum Reprints, 1984).

4. Messianism as Negative Political Theology

Messianism is a belief in liberation[70] that can only, in Taubes's view, come from elsewhere.[71] But this faith is a faith for people living in this world. In this world, they turn to something that is not of this world. They are part of a kingdom, are even obedient to the ruler of a kingdom, that has nothing to do with secular political entities and rulers. Whoever belongs to this kingdom is at least a foreigner in this world. Obedience to the foreign kingdom may or may not conflict with obedience owed to secular kingdoms and rulers. For Taubes, this is the first and ever-renewed task of political theology: *separating the spiritual from the secular claims and powers.*[72]

This definition of the meaning of the term 'political theology' is noteworthy because it makes us think first of the *link between* both powers. A positive (or 'right-leaning') political theology would provide a spiritual justification for secular power, while a negative (revolutionary, critical, or 'left-leaning') political theology would undermine a spiritual justification of secular power.

As we saw, the position Taubes presents in his book on Paul does not coincide with a theological or messianic justification of subversive or revolutionary activities. It cannot be denied that Taubes (imi-

---

[70] Hartwich, Assmann and Assmann, "Nachwort" to *Die politische Theologie des Paulus*, 144–45. Taubes definitely reads Paul in the light of the Jewish (collective) experience. One result of this is that concepts such as liberation, law, and faith are defined differently than in the dominant Christian interpretation of Paul (e.g., Luther's faith instead of good works). For Taubes, 'faith' is the collective "paradoxical experience of salvation amid the catastrophic dimension of history" (144); the concept loses its individualistic, Protestant associations.

[71] This explains Taubes's positive view of Benjamin (esp. his *Theologisch-Politisches Fragment*, in *Schriften*, 1.511–13) and Karl Barth, and his polemical attitude toward German idealism and the 'Goethe-Religion': "Benjamin ist von Karl-Barthscher Härte. Da ist nichts vom Immanenten. Von daher kommt man zu nichts. Die Fallbrücke ist von der anderen Seite" (*Die politische Theologie des Paulus*, 105).

[72] "Ohne diese Unterscheidung," wrote Taubes in a letter dated 18 September 1979 to Carl Schmitt (included in *Ad Carl Schmitt*, 42), "sind wir ausgeliefert an die Throne und Gewalten die in einem 'monistischen' Kosmos kein Jenseits mehr kennen. Die Grenzziehung zwischen geistlich und weltlich mag strittig sein und ist immer neu zu ziehen (ein immerwährendes Geschäft der politischen Theologie), aber fällt diese Scheidung dahin, dann geht uns der (abendländische) Atem aus, auch dem Thomas Hobbes, der wie immer *power ecclesiastical and civil* unterscheidet." On Taubes's appreciation of Hobbes, see also his "Statt einer Einleitung: Leviathan als sterblicher Gott. Zur Aktualität von Thomas Hobbes," in Taubes, ed., *Der Fürst dieser Welt*, 9–15.

tating Benjamin) was decidedly sympathetic toward the oppressed and the struggle against oppression that leads to the undermining of worldly powers. It is also clear that his reason for speaking of political theology in relation to Paul lies in the latter's polemical position against Jerusalem and Rome, a position of whose political ramifications Paul himself was well aware. Taubes's point, however, is that while, to be sure, messianic expectations remove legitimacy from political powers, they can never *justify* revolutionary activities. Put differently, fostering messianic expectations ultimately implies expecting nothing of the world as it is. Messianic faith (Taubes uses the word *'pistis'*[73]) is a kind of obedience in which on God's authority, or at His order, someone does or accepts something that conflicts with all that is natural (all that is customary or is *known: gnosis*). Faith is a readiness to abandon all if that is desired. This is the ultimate meaning of "no spiritual investment in the world as it is." For Taubes, Kierkegaard's interpretation of Abraham's willingness to sacrifice his son, Isaac, at God's command is paradigmatic of pistis, the faith that dissolves all natural ties.[74] Differing from Kierkegaard, however, Taubes does not understand the "paradox of faith" as a private relationship to the Absolute; he regards it from the perspective of the collective experience (of suffering) in (Jewish) history.

A 'revolutionary' negative political theology, a theological justification of the negation of political power, is easily suspected of being a twisted form of positive political theology. Taubes was also subject to this accusation.[75] The unavoidable intermixture of spiritual and

---

[73] See also Taubes's older text, where he discusses in more detail the difference between *pistis* and *gnosis*, "The Realm of Paradox," *Review of Metaphysics* 7 (1953–1954): 482–91.

[74] On Kierkegaard's interpretation of Abraham's obedience, see also J. Derrida, "Donner la mort," in J.-M. Rabaté and M. Wetzel, eds., *L'éthique du don: Jacques Derrida et la pensée du don* (Paris: Transition, 1992), 11–108, 56ff.

[75] See O. Marquard, "Aufgeklärter Polytheismus—auch eine politische Theologie?," in Taubes, ed., *Der Fürst dieser Welt*, 77–84. According to Marquard, political theology today is a secularized Christian eschatology appearing in the form of a revolutionary philosophy of history. His examples are Löwith and particularly Taubes's *Abendländische Eschatologie*. This modern form proves, for him, that political theology need not exist only as a theological apology for political power but can also occur as an attack on an existing order. In this case it is a 'futurist conformism'—an apology for *future* political powers (78): "Die revolutionäre Geschichtsphilosophie ist die mißlungene Säkularisierung der biblischen Eschatologie und darum 'politische Theologie'" (80). The *Neuzeit* is thus a rejection of every eschatology. It addresses the *potentia Dei absoluta*, because this—in nominalistic theology—is no

secular matters and duties in this world (in Scholastic terms, the problem of *res mixtae*) requires an investigation of the problem of political theology. Taubes's position is thus complex. Its complexity is expressed in his refusal on principle to distinguish between the true Messiah and pseudomessiahs.[76]

Messianic expectation accepts the Messiah's absolute transcendence, implying that people cannot decide who or what will fulfill this expectation. This explains Taubes's impassioned interest in a thinker such as Schmitt, whose specific political and ideological choices he will have to reject. This interest in a blacklisted author like Schmitt bears witness to an attitude little concerned with the ideological divisions and the political-ethical structures of "the world as it is." Both positive and negative 'revolutionary' political theologies permit a theological justification of a political act in this world. Taubes separates himself from these positions when they become gnosis, a knowledge-based *apology* for the exercise or overthrow of power. He opts for still another negative political theology, one that does not automatically imply a political theological justification of subversion and revolution. Taubes's position is now that only a political theology tied to the "paradox of faith" (messianic logic) can be preserved from becoming secularized and from being an apology, since it relies on a covenant with the absolutely Transcendent. The Law, the source of obligation, is not of this world, and thus the obligation cannot be fulfilled in this world.

The core of this thesis is already present in texts that Taubes wrote in the 1950s, even though he did not use the term 'political theology' at that time. In his article published in 1953 on the "paradox of faith," he distinguishes radically between "pistic" and "gnostic" in-

---

longer a guarantee, but is a possible destroyer, of the world. The legitimacy of the world (of immanence) must be defended before this God (81). According to Marquard, the text as occasion for reading and explanation must replace the absolute text just as the many histories and narratives must replace the one authorized (by political power or revolution) version of history. This is the source of Marquard's postmodern "praise of polytheism." See also Taubes's answer, "Zur Konjunktur des Polytheismus," in K. H. Bohrer, ed., *Mythos und Moderne* (Frankfurt am Main: Suhrkamp, 1983), 457–70.

[76] Taubes, *Die politische Theologie des Paulus*, 20: "Die Literatur ist da schnell bei der Hand, von Pseudo-Messiassen zu sprechen. Ich halte das für einen absoluten Blödsinn, wir sind nicht berufen, in der Geschichte zu sagen, was pseudo ist und was nicht. Menschen haben es geglaubt, das ist unser Problem, und wir müssen es verstehen lernen."

terpretations of religious experience, between "revelation religions" and "enlightenment religions."[77] Besides Paul, he mentions Augustine, Luther, Kant, Kierkegaard, and Karl Barth as representatives of the "pistic" interpretation. Typical of the second tradition is, according to Taubes, the attempt to integrate the "paradox of faith" into the realm of gnosis where it can, in principle, be neutralized. Paul's "foolishness of the cross," Luther's *sola fide*, or Kierkegaard's "leap over the abyss" are generalized as a 'way' and a 'method.' Faith as *para-doxa* again becomes *doxa*:

> The paradox of faith implies a *sola fide* which can never be turned into a general and universal method. But theology is stronger than faith! It turns even the paradox of faith into a method relating the way of paradox to the classical ways of theology, the method of negation and analogy. The paradox of faith is thereby taken out of its context, its energy diffused and its motif turned into a general argument for apologetic theology.[78]

This integration of the paradox, according to Taubes, is just what marks the classic tradition of negative theology. Between Paul and negative theology (via Clement of Alexandria, Dionysius the Areopagite, and Eckhart) there is not continuity but a break caused by the influence of gnosticism and Neoplatonism on Christian theology. In the *via negativa et analogia*, the paradox of faith—faith in the crucified as Messiah—becomes a universal method expanded toward God or the divine in general instead of only toward the *deus revelatus*.[79]

Here we see that Taubes's interest in Paul is linked to an extremely critical attitude toward Christian thinking and the dominant Chris-

---

[77] Taubes, "The Realm of Paradox," 482; see also his "Notes on an Ontological Interpretation of Theology," *Review of Metaphysics* 2, no. 8 (1949): 97–104, "Virtue and Faith: A Study of Terminology in Western Ethics," *Philosophy East and West* 7 (1957): 27–32, and "Von Fall zu Fall: Erkenntnistheoretische Reflexion zur Geschichte vom Sündenfall," in *Text und Applikation. Poetik und Hermeneutik* 9 (Munich: Fink, 1981), 111–16.

[78] Taubes, "The Realm of Paradox," 482.

[79] For Paul, in contrast, it was not so much a question of God as of Jesus: "God is never a question for Paul; only Jesus as the Messiah is a 'paradox' for him" ("The Realm of Paradox," 490). And "if such considerations are taken seriously it is impossible to confuse Eckhart's gnostic division between *deitas* and *deus* with Luther's pistic division between *deus absconditus* (the God of wrath and justice) and *deus revelatus* (God in Christ)" ("The Realm of Paradox," 487).

tian theological tradition, including that of negative theology. Those who succeeded Paul immediately repressed his scandalous eschatological faith, that is, neutralized it through interpretations.[80] Taubes's reading of Paul is directed against the apologetic use that post-Pauline Christianity made of Paul's text. He wants to show that Paul does not legitimate anything, but rather undermines the legitimation of *all* secular claims to power—even that of the spiritual powers, the *potestates spirituales*.

While emphasizing the discontinuity between Paul and the dominant Chistian tradition, Taubes tries to strengthen the continuity between Paul's faith and the Jewish community. As we saw, Taubes compares Paul's struggle in Rom. 9 with that of Moses in Ex. 32: Paul "faced the same problem as Moses."[81] The starting point is the idea that rejecting God's Law by worshiping a golden calf and rejecting Christ as the Messiah both provoke God's anger. According to this logic, the stubborn people in Exodus will be destroyed and Moses, because of his loyalty, will be spared. But Moses shatters this logic of justice and prefers—as replacement—to take death upon himself: "Yet now, if thou wilt forgive their sin—; and if not, blot me, I pray thee, out of thy book which thou hast written" (Ex. 32.32). As one chosen, Moses puts his trust in God's mercy. It is presupposed here that "the righteous, who incarnates an attribute of God, can influence divine will with his prayer."[82] But God's righteousness requires from the pardoned sinner a symbolic penalty that keeps the memory of the sin alive. Taubes interprets Yom Kippur, the Jewish Day of Atonement on which promises and oaths can be undone,[83]

---

[80] "A critical study of basic Christian concepts reveals that already one generation after Paul the original eschatological meaning of the basic concepts of Paul's theology had fallen into oblivion" (Taubes, "The Realm of Paradox," 488).

[81] Taubes, *Die politische Theologie des Paulus*, 54.

[82] Hartwich, Assmann and Assmann, "Nachwort," to *Die politische Theologie des Paulus*, 158.

[83] "Von den Gemeinden Jemens bis zu den Gemeinden Polens intonieren die Juden diese Formeln in derselben Tonfolge, die in der *Jewish Encyclopaedia* mit angegeben ist: 'Alle Gelöbnisse, Verzichtungen, Schwüre, Bannformeln oder Versagungen, Büssungen oder als solche geltende Ausdrücke, durch die wir uns etwas geloben, bekräftigen, uns verpflichten oder uns versagen, von diesem bis zum nächsten zum Guten uns eingehenden Versöhnungstage, bereuen wir hierdurch, daß sie alle aufgelöst, erlassen und vergeben seien, null und nichtig, ohne Geltung und Bestand. Unsere Gelöbnisse sind keine Gelöbnisse, unsere Versagungen sind keine Versagungen, und unsere Schwüre sind keine Schwüre' " (Taubes, *Die politische Theologie des Paulus*, 49).

as the ritualization of the controversy between God and Moses, a repetition of the "primeval scene" where God changed his mind about destroying the people of Israel.[84]

Like Moses, Paul is at a "zero-point" in Israel's relationship to God, and like Moses, he stands at this point and asks to be cursed: "For I could wish that I myself were accursed and separated [ἀνάθεμα]from Christ for my brethren's sake, my kinsmen according to the flesh: who are Israelites" (Rom. 9.3). For Taubes, this is not mere rhetoric but instead an honest expression of Paul's "dismay that the people of God were no longer the people of God."[85] Paul identifies himself with Moses (by taking on the role of scapegoat, or *anathema*), but he wants to surpass Moses by turning to the Gentiles. In this way Paul construes both continuity (like Moses, Paul is concerned with saving Israel) and discontinuity (in his 'pneumatic' surpassing of the ethnic limits of the people of God) with the Jewish tradition.

This ambivalent structure of paradoxical continuity ('paradoxical' because of the recurring experience of the "zero-point," the "suspension of all operative relations"[86]) and discontintuity is also present in Rom. 11.28: "As touching the gospel, they are enemies for your sake; but as touching the election, they are beloved for the Father's sake." How catastrophic, according to Taubes, abandoning Paul's ambivalence is, is apparent from his dispute with Schmitt on this passage and from his reference to Marcion and the tradition he initiated.

In his discussions with the author of *Der Begriff des Politischen* and the 'friend/enemy criterium of politics' that it develops regarding Rom. 9–11, Taubes confronted Schmitt with the fact that he, like the Christian church after the year 70, had missed the dialectic that moved Paul in Rom.11:28. In the Germany of the 1930s, what Schmitt adopted was "not a text, but a tradition, namely, the popular tradition of ecclesiastical anti-Semitism which he, uninhibited, then provided with a racist theo-zoology in the period 1933–1936."[87] Here, too, Taubes, like Benjamin, protests against a history written by victors, in this case the Christians, who drew a sharp, and then

---

[84] Taubes, *Die politische Theologie des Paulus*, 67, 159.

[85] Taubes, *Die politische Theologie des Paulus*, 55.

[86] Hartwich, Assmann and Assmann, "Nachwort," to *Die politische Theologie des Paulus*, 159.

[87] Taubes, *Die politische Theologie des Paulus*, 72.

(in Schmitt's sense) political, demarcation line between Judaism and Christianity. But Paul remained united with the Jewish people; immediately following Rom.11.28 we read, "For the gifts and calling of God are without repentance."

We wish here to go into somewhat greater detail regarding Taubes's interest in Marcion. The second volume of his lectures, devoted to how Paul was received, opens with a chapter on Marcion and his gnostic interpretation of Paul. The point of this interpretation was that the Father of Jesus Christ could not be the same as the Old Testament Creator of heaven and earth, *Creator coeli et terrae*. For Marcion, the God of the Old Testament becomes first suspect, then superfluous. He is marked by demonic traits: He is righteous, powerful, and angry; as Creator-God He is responsible for all the evil in the world. But the God of Jesus Christ is the Redeemer-God, a truly transcendent God, and compared to the Creator-God, *Deus alienus*. Marcion thus considers Christians—those who have accepted the gift of the gospel—as "strangers in this world" liberated by an alien God from the prison of the Creator, the *cellula creatoris*. He reduces the canon to the Gospel According to Luke and Paul's Epistles (purified of all Old Testament elements).

It is clear that Marcion abandons Paul's ambivalence, the continuity and discontinuity of the New and Old Testaments, linked to the equally ambivalent dialectic of God's anger and His mercy (as Taubes shows in his discussion of the Yom Kippur ritual) in favor of the gospel's complete 'alterity.' As we know, the later, dominant reception of Paul, as represented by the official Church, preserved the unity (*concordia*) of the Old and New Testaments, and to further this, developed the allegorical interpretation of the Old Testament.

For Taubes, Marcion is not simply a heterodox figure in the history of Christianity, nor is Taubes concerned with any—easily provided—proof that Marcion deviates from Paul. His thesis is that there remains in Christianity a latent Marcionism that has been revived in modernity. For this reason he seeks the elements in Paul's text that permitted Marcion's gnostic interpretation.

He refers here to Paul's polemical reduction of Jesus' double commandment (to love God and one's neighbor) to one single commandment (Rom.13.8, "for he that loveth his neighbor has fulfilled the law"), and to his fear of being separated from God's love (Rom.

8.39). Taubes suspects that, for Paul, God's love, without Christ, is "very far away."[88] Decisive, however, is the following consideration:

> Creation plays no role in the New Testament. . . . It is only concerned with redemption. . . . The connection between creation and redemption is thin, very thin. It can break. That is Marcion, there the connection is broken. He reads—and he can read—that the Father of Jesus Christ is *not* the Creator of heaven and earth.[89]

Taubes then refers to moments in modern Christianity where the Pauline thread between creation and redemption, between Old and New Testaments, becomes thinner (as with Luther[90] and in deism[91]) until it snaps: in the liberal theologian Adolf von Harnack, who openly argued in his major study on Marcion (1921) for casting off the Old Testament.[92] Taubes considered this rejection the extreme consequence of a liberal and 'inwardly'-oriented Protestantism. Taubes emphasizes that even this last, the individualization of faith, was present in Marcion. While, for Paul, love still meant that "the center lies not in myself" but refers to the community (the people of God, the body of Christ), for the gnostic Marcion "each one is perfect in himself"; as believing subject, the individual stands immediately before a transcendent God.[93] Harnack reassessed the gnostic Marcion because of his "modernity," because his faith was already "completely un-Jewish and un-Greek."[94] Harnack's gospel "turns in-

---

[88] Taubes, *Die politische Theologie des Paulus*, 80.

[89] Taubes, *Die politische Theologie des Paulus*, 83.

[90] For Luther, "gibt es Stellen, die vom Haß gegen Gott sprechen, wirklicher Haß, wenn nicht in Christus" (Taubes, *Die politische Theologie des Paulus*, 81).

[91] "Deismus bedeutet radikale Kritik des Alten Testaments mit genau denselben Argumenten. . . . Die Argumente sind immer die Gegenüberstellung von Gerechtigkeit und Liebe" (Taubes, *Die politische Theologie des Paulus*, 85).

[92] A. von Harnack, *Marcion: das Evangelium vom fremden Gott* (1921; Darmstadt: Wissenschaftliche Buchgesellschaft, 1985). Taubes cites Harnack's main thesis: "Die These, die im folgenden begründet werden soll, lautet: das Alte Testament im zweiten Jahrhundert zu verwerfen, war ein Fehler, den die grosse Kirche mit recht abgelehnt hat. Es im sechzehnten Jahrhundert beizubehalten, war ein Schicksal, dem sich die Reformation noch nicht zu entziehen vermochte. Es aber seit dem neunzehnten Jahrhundert als kanonische Urkunde im Protestantismus noch zu konservieren, ist die Folge einer religiösen und kirchlichen Lähmung" (Taubes, *Die politische Theologie des Paulus*, 84).

[93] Hartwich, Assmann and Assmann, *Die politische Theologie des Paulus*, 78, and the "Nachwort," 166.

[94] Harnack, *Marcion*, 225.

ward and sacrifices history. History has no salvation and salvation has no history."[95]

Yet Taubes does not forget to explain the context in which Harnack's political theological work was done.[96] In 1933 German liberal Protestantism could "not pass the test. Why should it be concerned with the Old Testament stories of shepherds, did they really have to teach their children the story of Jacob, such a particularly sly person? What good would this do them? They would do better to learn the German sagas and the pure love of Jesus Christ!"[97] This was roughly the attitude in German liberal Protestantism on the eve of the rise of Nazism. Taubes does not mean to suggest that Harnack was anti-Semitic.[98] His Marcionism was not the motor of the anti-Semitic seduction, but the "secret" of liberal Protestantism's weakness at the moment it was tested.

Like Marcion, secular twentieth-century Protestantism, which Harnack had developed into a general *Religionsphilosophie*, could not maintain the Pauline, ambivalent, and paradoxical tension between creation and redemption, between 'world' and 'grace,' and between history and the messianic. It is this tension that characterizes Taubes's negative political theology.

CONCLUSION: A THEOLOGICAL REBELLION AGAINST THE SELF-EMPOWERMENT OF SECULAR POWER

Taubes was not a theologian. His interest in religious traditions,[99] and in Paul's Epistle to the Romans in particular, is not primarily religious, but political-philosophical. The opposition of pistis to gno-

---

[95] J. Taubes, "Das stählerne Gehäuse und der Exodus daraus oder der Streit um Marcion, einst und heute," in Taubes, ed., *Gnosis und Politik* (Munich: Fink, 1984), 9–15; 13.

[96] Taubes also cites Martin Buber's commentary: "Harnack died in 1930; three years later his idea, Marcion's idea, was put into practice, not with spiritual means, but with violence and terror." Taubes notes that "the connection between gnosis and politics could not have been portrayed more drastically" (Taubes, "Das stählerne Gehäuse," 12).

[97] Taubes, *Die politische Theologie des Paulus*, 85.

[98] Taubes, "Das stählerne Gehäuse," 12: "Harnack [war] keineswegs 'Antisemit,' vielmehr Repräsentant eines breiten Liberalismus."

[99] Taubes was the editor of three volumes under the general title *Religionstheorie und Politische Theologie*. See n. 1 above.

sis plays a decisive role. Knowledge (gnosis) implies an orientation toward and a "spiritual investment" in the world, in "Alles, was der Fall ist,"[100] while faith, as a paradoxical given, is open to what is not—what "is not" in the sense that objective reality "is."[101] Faith thus has to do with something that can be expected; in this sense it relates *negatively* to the existing world.

Taubes's negative theology—which, as we explained it, differs greatly from what is traditionally known as the method of negative theology—is *political* because he expressly does not see this interpretation of the spiritual domain (as opposite of the secular domain) as a call to withdraw from the world (as it is). Responding to the call of the nonsecular is itself a historical and political act: it is a protest against any attempt to establish a closed worldview. Belief in the Messiah's return has the concrete political meaning of an expectation that history is not finished, but awaits or is open to an intervention from outside, an intervention that cannot possibly be manipulated from within this world.

Taubes's thinking remains unclear on the point of the political implications of a messianic or theological negativity. It is certain that Taubes opposes both an individualistic, interiorizing explanation of Paul (paradigm: Marcion) and an institutionalizing and juridical explanation (paradigm: Schmitt). Somewhere between the inwardness of the individual completely closed off from intercourse[102] and the visible power of a church as incarnation of salvation[103] lies the collec-

---

[100] Taubes cites Wittgenstein's famous saying with which he starts his *Tractatus logico-philosophicus*, "Die Welt ist Alles, was der Fall ist," but adds, "ein Satz, der positivistisch und theologisch zumal klingt und klingen soll" (Taubes, "Das stählerne Gehäuse," 13–14).

[101] Taubes, "Notes on an Ontological Interpretation of Theology," 102–3: "in the realm of the 'is'-assertion, there is no place for God. With an 'is'-assertion, an object is referred to and described. The sum of 'is'-assertions constitutes science. What is not an object is not knowable, cannot enter the realm of knowledge, and must be declared by science as null. But 'God is not' is also the assertion of theology. For theology has always denied that God is an object and agrees in this with atheism, and with science grounded on atheism."

[102] In both the social and the sexual sense of intercourse. Taubes recalls that Marcion's church was a church for ascetics whose first commandment was celibacy and, in the case of already existing marriages, abstinence: "Der Gedanke zu Ende gedacht heißt ja: die Welt auszuhungern, indem ihr der Same entzogen wird. Es ist eine das Weltende praktizierende und exekutierende Kirche" (Taubes, *Die politische Theologie des Paulus*, 82).

[103] Symbolic is the title of Schmitt's article "Die Sichtbarkeit der Kirche: Eine scholastische Erwägung," in *Summa. Eine Vierteljahrschrift* 2 (1917): 71–80.

tivity that Taubes calls the *ecclesia*, or body of Christ. It is also clear that this collectivity continues the Jewish tradition, or even incarnates the (paradoxical) continuation of this tradition. The difference is only that it is not limited to an ethnic group, but is universal. Finally, this *ecclesia* publicly withdraws from secular authority and even challenges it, since it makes the same claims to power as did the Roman Empire. The problem remains, however, of how this collectivity can withdraw from every political form. Is there a space between private inwardness and public power? Or better, can one conquer this space without becoming a visible power (political opposition or revolutionary party)?

Here we should make a comparison with a thinker from a totally different background: Georges Bataille. In his work, too, we find the idea of a community (*"communauté"*) that frees individuals from their individuality and inwardness without seeking to become a political power (*"pouvoir"*). It is a community that arises from or is founded by the surpassing of individuality. For Bataille, this surpassing (*"transgression"*) is not, however, nourished by messianism. Rather, it expresses the heterogeneity of transcendence, of *"sovereignty,"* in Bataille's terminology.[104] "Notes on an Ontological Interpretation of Theology," Taubes's 1949 article on the "ontological foundation" of theology,[105] runs in many ways parallel to Bataille's text on sovereignty. Both are attempts to depict the problem of the heterogenity of transcendence and to find a language that will remove from the realm of "objectivity" and reduce to nothing (i.e., not "something") the "object" of theology (*"Atheology"* in Bataille), namely, God or sovereignty. But Taubes's messianism, and thus his *ecclesia*, remain explicitly linked with the Jewish and Christian traditions and is articulated within them.

---

[104] Georges Bataille, "La souveraineté" (1953), in *Oeuvres complètes* (Paris: Gallimard, 1976), 8.243–456 .

[105] See above. In this article Taubes concludes, "Theology and atheism reveal God as the nothing. . . . If God creates out of nothing, he must be related to this nothing. But how can he be 'related' to the nothing if God is God? Only if the 'relation' between God and the nothing is one of identity, if *deus* and *nihil* are identical. Then *creatio ex nihilo* means *creation ex deo*. But if *creatio ex nihilo a deo* means *creatio ex nihilo a nihilo*, what can be the sense of *creatio*? Is not *ex nihilo fit ens creatum* contradictory to *ex nihilo nihil fit*? This contradiction is resolved in the coincidence of *deus* and *nihil*. If *deus* and *nihil* are identical, then *creatio ex nihilo* and *ex nihilo nihil fit* coincide. *Creatio* means then the shattering of the nothing into the many of the something" (Taubes, "Notes," 104).

We must also localize both texts in the debate on the legitimacy of modern politics, which presents itself as an immanent legitimacy: secular (worldly) power can only be legitimized in and by the world. This doubtlessly frees the way toward the self-empowerment of secular power and the fulfillment of secularization.[106] The last moment in the process of secularization, which is justified in an immanency thinking, is the appropriation of the *future* by secular powers.

It seems as if this is the reason for Taubes's attempt to rewrite the history of Western culture. Appropriating the future implies a secularization of the *eschaton,* a secularization of eschatology. This is foreseen in the secularization of utopia, the attempts to realize paradise or the Kingdom of God on earth. The attempt to rule and dominate tomorrow and the day after, leaving the creation of the future in human hands, deprives the spiritual powers of their last domain. The reference to an eternal life of salvation or damnation loses its power, care for one's own life before an inevitable death makes its claim gains ground.

Georges Bataille suspected that the ultimate form of eschatology could only lie in the *moment* itself, made completely free from the past and future, presenting itself as independent before all what could occur. Here Bataille introduces a completely nihilistic eschatology.[107] In their sovereignty—at the moment of surrender—people deliver themselves to "nothing," or else they deliver themselves completely to all that can occur. They give up every expectation or goal that could come after this moment. They deliver themselves to the possibility of their own destruction.

Here Bataille, with his atheology, diverges radically from the negative messianism in Benjamin's historical philosophical theses and from Taubes's interpretation of Paul. For them, people have no say in the coming of the Messiah. The only thing they can do is be prepared at every moment. This does imply a nihilistic attitude

---

[106] This is also the most important point for Carl Schmitt in his reaction to Hans Blumenberg's *Die Legitimität der Neuzeit.* To Blumenberg's thesis ("Die Erkenntnis bedarf keiner Rechtfertigung, sie rechtfertigt sich selbst; sie verdankt sich nicht Gott, hat nichts mehr von Erleuchtung und gnädigem Teilhabenlassen, sondern ruht in ihrer eigenen Evidenz, der sich Gott und Mensch nicht entziehen können," 395), Schmitt answers, "Das ist es. Der Autismus ist der Argumentation immanent. Ihre Immanenz, die sich polemisch gegen eine theologische Transzendenz richtet, ist nichts anderes als Selbstermächtigung" (Schmitt, *Politische Theologie II,* 114).

[107] See Bataille, esp. the first part of "La souveraineté."

toward the world (and its politics), a complete detachment from and a refusal to invest in the world, but the expectation itself is by no means nihilistic. Benjamin and Taubes expect the Messiah who, before all else, will bring *justice* to history's victims. In Bataille, disillusionment has reached the spiritual domain: one can expect nothing. Sovereignty consists only in subjecting oneself to nothing, not putting the *moment* in the service of anyone or anything whatever. Every positive moral or religious evaluation of this nothing is, for him, a breach of principle.

In this context, sovereignty becomes completely meaningless. It seems to be the negative counterweight to modernity and its absolute understanding of the world, according to which every act is directed toward a useful purpose. Modernity finds its completion in what we can call *the dictatorship of the agenda,* an element that is both cultural and political. The future is filled in and planned; the present consists of performing certain tasks at given moments. The dictatorship of the agenda could be called the perfect "spiritual investment in this world": the whole person is devoted to secular matters. The only defense against such a dictatorship is an aesthetic or theological rebellion.

For Taubes, an aesthetic rebellion is unsatisfactory since it can only understand the messianic moment as simulation, as is the case with Adorno.[108] Benjamin, by contrast, in the *Theologische-politische Fragment*, treats the Messiah as a person, not as any aesthetic representation of it. Only a theological rebellion remains. In this chapter we wanted to show that such a theological rebellion must necessarily be both *political* and *negative.* A political-theological rebellion is needed because we are people who live and struggle in this world; a negative theology is needed to escape the trap of absolutizing the world "as it is."

---

[108] Taubes, *Die politische Theologie des Paulus,* 103.

Chapter 12

The Author's Silence

TRANSCENDENCE AND REPRESENTATION IN MIKHAIL BAKHTIN

Anton Simons

1. Mikhail Bakhtin's Dialogism

THE FOLLOWING PAGES are devoted to the ideas of the Russian thinker Mikhail Mikhailovich Bakhtin (1895–1975). I intend to draw attention to the concept of silence that lies hidden in his ideas on language and to the silence in Bakhtin's own speaking that illuminates something about that speaking.

From the start this silence seems to contradict the colorful image that many have formed of Bakhtin. At one moment he seems to move strictly within the limits of linguistic and literary science, at another he seems to use literature to address philosophical, theological, and sociological themes. In doing so he addresses his themes from several different perspectives. Sometimes Bakhtin appears to be a Marxist, sometimes a hermeneuticist, a phenomenologist, a religious humanist, and/or a semioticist. But under this variety a constant interest is tangible, one that can be called *dialogism*. It focuses on a communication that does not take place according to prescribed patterns, but continually arises as something new and unrepeatable. The 'dialogue' (on which more later) can be situated in the tension that exists between language's possibilities and its insufficiencies. In Bakhtin this insufficiency lies hidden in the rules of language: the dialogue occurs *within* language, but the rules of language are not enough by themselves to explain dialogue completely. What occurs in our speaking is different from, and less transparent than, the rules of speech. The meaning and value of something is not given, but is created each time anew at the moment of dialogue.

The originality of Bakhtin's dialogism can be measured against the dramatic context in which it arose. Russia in the period in which he lived (1895–1975) was marked by a series of dramatic events: the Russian Revolution, civil war, the Stalinist terror, World War II, and the post-Stalinist thaw. Bakhtin was educated in various schools and universities in prerevolutionary Russia. His family moved repeatedly to different parts of the Russian Empire, so that Bakhtin in his youth lived successively in Orel, Vilnius, Odessa, and Leningrad. During and after the Russian Revolution he was the center of a group of friends who participated in deep philosophical and theological discussions. In 1929 he published his now famous study on Dostoevsky. In that same year, a conflict with the government led to a six-year-long banishment to Kazakhstan. Later, while still in that province, he prepared a thesis on Rabelais's work and popular culture. In the same period Bakhtin was appointed lecturer at the Pedagogical Institute in Saransk (Mordovia). But he had to wait until 1963 before he saw his work in print. Only then did Bakhtin enjoy in Moscow a certain fame as an independent and charismatic thinker. Thanks to the many translations of and commentaries on his work published since 1963, interest in Bakhtin's thought continues to grow outside Russia. Yet the meaning of his work remains a subject of discussion.

This uncertainty probably has to do with Bakhtin himself and his relationship to his historical period. In his work he does not thematize the events of his time directly, which makes it difficult to include him in a class of people with those who either did or did not adhere to Stalinism. Furthermore, he exerted little effort in trying to mold his work into a theoretical whole. Every researcher is therefore faced with the task of creating his own image of Bakhtin to illuminate the originality of his dialogism.

The image of Bakhtin that I create here comes from the linguistic philosophical notion of dialogism and the cultural, philosophical, and theological foundation of that notion. The last may seem strange when applied to a thinker who did not make theology an obvious central focus of his work. But Bakhtin's hidden religious philosophical opinions are revealed when we examine his work against the background of religious themes and obsessions in his cultural context: in the revival, fed by Orthodoxy, of an interest in philosophy of religion, and in the postrevolutionary ambiguous relationship of cultural and political movements to religion.

In the post-1905 cultural climate, after Russia lost its war against Japan, there was a lively interest in religious philosophical questions. Nicolay Berdyaev, Sergey Bulgakov, and Semyon Frank joined several others in a common publication *(Vekhi,* 'signposts'[1]) to turn against direct intellectual engagement in the communist revolution and to plead for a renewal of Orthodox religious traditions. This was the start of a revival of ideas originally promoted in the nineteenth century by authors such as Khomyakov, Dostoevsky, and Solovyov concerning the spiritual and political path Russia should follow within (or outside) European culture. The period of publications and heated debates that followed is known as the 'religious renaissance' or the 'silver age.' Although the Bolshevik Revolution put an end to this religious renaissance, the debates it fostered continued in the years after the revolution when Bakhtin was developing his dialogism. Bakhtin took part in these debates and kept in contact with various, mostly underground, religious groups, among which were the avidly monarchistic and chauvinistic Brotherhood of Saint Seraphim but also the ecumenical Voskresenie that pursued a synthesis of Christianity and Marxism.

It would be too simple to see the whole of postrevolutionary culture as the victory of atheism over an increasingly oppressed religiosity. Evidence points more toward a return of the sacral to Russian culture. First we could refer to the artistic avant-garde and literary sciences after 1915. These movements are called symbolism, futurism, and formalism, and are represented by names such as Mayakovsky, Khlebnikov, Akhmatova, Blok, Shklovsky, and Eikhenbaum. At first glance, their links with religion seem less obvious. These movements were not interested in a revival of religious culture in any institutionalized form. Indeed, this was often categorically rejected. Nevertheless, we observe in the images of the avant-garde world many symbols that refer to religious and mystical traditions. The mystery play *Victory on the Sun* by Khlebnikov, Kruchyonnykh, and Malevich portrayed the 'murder of the sun' followed by a mystical

---

[1] *Wegzeichen. Zur Krise der russischen Intelligenz,* trans. K. Schlögel (Frankfurt am Main: Eichborn Verlag, 1990).

night. Then followed the artificial sun of a new culture and a new technical world. Alexandr Blok's poem *The Twelve* has the revolution face and defeat the myth of holy Russia, but the revolution is fostered by twelve revolutionaries led by Jesus Christ.

The most contradictory, yet most dramatic, return of the religious takes place in Bolshevism itself. It is false to reduce Bolshevism to a radical ideological atheism. Although its propaganda forcefully promoted atheism, and Stalin's regime fanatically repressed all forms of religion, Stalinist culture cannot be seen as anything else than a catalyst of (quasi-)religious feelings and symbols. It is no accident that the writer Maxim Gorky was given the task, in 1932, of presiding over the commission that would design socialist realism. Gorky proclaimed the revolution's need to link Marxist culture to religious symbols. He saw the socialist collective as 'god builders' who through their collectivity could develop superhuman abilities for creativity. Here he laid the ideological foundation for Stalinism's enormous cultural and technological delusions of grandeur.

Thus Bakhtin's work was created in a contradictory world that wanted to settle scores with traditional religion, but that also wanted to shape this settlement by calling on sacral and religious symbols. Bakhtin tried in several ways to develop a relationship to this culture, and in so doing, regularly if not always expressly, sought association with religious and theological traditions, specifically the mystical traditions that affirmed the inability to give God a name. A negative theology in this sense was an important element in the cultural foundation of Bakhtin's work, serving then as an inspiration for creating his dialogism and today as a key to interpreting it. Besides being a linguistic philosophical idea, this dialogism also belongs to the philosophy of religion, to the theory of art, and to political culture.

I will discuss Bakhtin's view of dialogue in four separate sections. Using several of his early texts, I will first outline his view of artistic creativity (Section 2). Then I will use his study of Dostoevsky to show how this activity focused on dialogue (Section 3). My third step is the confirmation, found in Bakhtin's later work, of his explicit return to negative theology (Section 4). Finally, I seek to clarify Bakhtin's cultural political position in his book on Rabelais and its connection to negative theology (Section 5).

2. Transcendence and Grace

Bakhtin's early texts, posthumously distributed under the publisher's titles *Towards a Philosophy of the Act*[2] and *Author and Hero in Aesthetic Activity*,[3] are an ambitious and incomplete attempt at creating a practical philosophy in which creative human activity is intended to stand central. For Bakhtin, this was to provide the answer to the spiritual impoverishment of modern culture, whose orientation is overly dependent on theories and concepts such that it risks losing contact with real life. Because concepts are always general, they can never coincide with life, which is always singular and unique. Bakhtin did believe that people could, through their activity, forge a unique connection between concepts and life. A moral revitalization of culture can only be based on this kind of activity, a unique moral deed, and not on general norms or theories. Bakhtin posited that theories or norms could only provide an imaginary alibi for moral activity.

Bakhtin planned to develop this as a starting point for various forms of activity: aesthetic, political, and religious. But we only have the text *Towards a Philosophy of the Act*, in which Bakhtin lays a philosophical foundation for moral deeds, and *Author and Hero in Aesthetic Activity*, in which he discusses the creative activity of the author of a literary work. From these texts, and from diverse scattered comments, we can form a picture of Bakhtin's religious philosophical position. These diverse comments confirm the impression derived from biographical data that Bakhtin was a believer who, in the tradition of the religious renaissance, wanted to link a comprehensive view of modern culture to the Christian tradition.

Here I will leave aside the complicated question of Bakhtin's religious and philosophical sources (which would be a study in itself) and move directly to a characterization of his religious philosophical

---

[2] M. M. Bakhtin, "K filosofii postupka," in *Filosofiya i sotsiologiya nauky i tekhniki—Ezhegodnik, 1984–1985* (Moscow: Labirint, 1986), 82–160; translated into English as *Toward a Philosophy of the Act*, trans. V. Liapunov (Austin: University of Texas Press, 1993).

[3] M. M. Bakhtin, "Avtor i geroj v èstetitcheskoy deyatel'nosti," in *Estetika slovesnogo tvorchestva* (Moscow: Iskusstvo,1979), 7–187; translated into English as "Author and Hero in Aesthetic Activity," in *Art and Answerability: Early Philosophical Essays*, trans. V. Liapunov (Austin: University of Texas Press, 1990), 4–256; hereafter cited as AA.

position. In his early work it is characterized by two basic moments: a radical *critique of immanence*, the critique of the view in which God is reduced to something in our world, and a *pneumatology*, the idea that God is present in our world as Spirit, through and in which the creation of literary works is possible. It is obvious that both moments are in a high mutual tension. This tension is amplified by their apparent reliance on two different Christian traditions.

Bakhtin's *critique of immanence* is related to the mystical traditions in which it is only possible to meet God when every representation of His essence or substance is abandoned. We see this same critique of immanence in Dionysius the Areopagite and the theology of the Cappadocians, in particular that of Gregory of Nyssa. Besides the significance of the latter for Orthodox spirituality, it is also important that Gregory linked this criticism of the representation of God to the possibility of a moral relationship to Him. Gregory makes an important distinction between God's essence (*ousia*) and His energy (*energeia*). We are destined to share in divine life, but this is a sharing in God's energy, in His activity, and not in His essence. This link between God's inscrutability and the call to share in His energy agrees with Bakhtin's early 'metaphysics.' Bakhtin speaks of Being and of a unique, unrepeatable event, which we cannot fixate in a general concept, but in which we can nevertheless participate through activity. God's inscrutability implies the absolute responsibility of acting people. This activity, be it founding a social order or creating a work of art, cannot be grounded in God's essence, because there is no general norm or general concept that allows this.

What we could call Bakhtin's *pneumatology* is a view of God's presence in the world. This moment is more strongly represented in Bakhtin's work than is his critique of immanence, and sometimes pushes the latter completely into the background. Bakhtin's explicit references to Christian tradition always involve figures who are not easily associated with a critique of immanence: Bernard of Clairvaux, Francis of Assisi, Giotto, and Dante. Specifically, Bakhtin quotes Bernard's commentaries on the biblical Song of Songs in a positive sense. In his view they point to God's loving grace, which permits a reevaluation of my self and even of my body. God's presence in the world consists, for Bakhtin, primarily in His love of the other, which in its turn makes possible my love for the other. A person's creative activity is a creating in God's Spirit. Unique to Bakhtin's pneumatological moment is not only the relationship to the other made possible by God's relationship to us, but also a clear emphasis on God's grace and love for us, at the expense of his justice and severity. It is therefore not surprising that Bakhtin tends to link God's creation to aesthetic, artistic activity rather than to ethical activity. The latter is much more 'negative': to act ethically we must refuse something in this world if we are to change it, whereas to act aesthetically implies a positive, active evaluation of what exists through which the existing reality can change.

Both fundamental moments of this religious philosophical view can be found in Bakhtin's study of how an author creates literary forms: *Author and Hero in Aesthetic Activity*. Here Bakhtin posits that the creation of a literary work implies the author's transcendence.[4] In the line of the tradition of Dionysius and others sketched above, the work should be seen as the author's activity, but the author being transcendent to his work, we cannot deduce from it the author's identity or convictions. The second basic moment comes in view when Bakhtin develops further the nature of this creative activity as the author's loving grace toward the work's protagonist, its 'hero.' The author makes of the hero an image, which reveals the hero to us as a living person. Let us follow Bakhtin as he develops these two moments.

The author's transcendence relates to his or her relationship to the hero. According to Bakhtin, we only have a work of art when the author's position is clearly different from the hero's, and when the distance between both positions is productive in the work of art. Bakhtin calls this distance "*vnenakhodimost'*," which I will translate as *ectopy*,[5] outsideness, exteriority, 'finding oneself outside.' Bakhtin himself explains this term: "The productiveness of the event of a life does not consist in the merging of all into one. On the contrary, it

---

[4] Bakhtin does not use here the word '*transcendent*,' but '*transgredientnyi*' ('transgredient,' surpassing). The reason for this could be that he wanted to distinguish the author's transcendence from God's. The author's transcendence takes place here and now, while God's presupposes a responsibility to Him, and thus a distance between the reality and the ideal. I choose the word 'transcendent' because the word 'transgredient' is unknown in English.

[5] I borrow this term from the French translation of "Author and Hero" (M. Bakhtin, *Esthétique de la création verbale*, trans. A. Aucouturier [Paris: Gallimard, 1984], 36). 'Ectopy' is an adaptation, not a direct translation, of the French '*exotopie*.' An English equivalent would be 'outsideness.'

consists in fully exploiting the privilege of one's own unique place outside other human beings" (AA, 88).

The ectopic tension between the author and the hero is a prerequisite for a meaningful literary production. Bakhtin uses the tragedy of Oedipus to demonstrate this. Compared to the hero Oedipus, the author and the audience have an *overabundance* of knowledge; they sense that the man Oedipus killed and the woman he wed could be important people. They therefore maintain a distance from Oedipus necessary for him to appear as a complete person. "Having merged with Oedipus, having lost my own place *outside* him, I cease to enrich the event of his life by providing a new, creative standpoint, a standpoint inaccessible to Oedipus himself from his own unique place. In other words, I cease to enrich the event of his life as an author/contemplator" (AA, 71).

The ectopic principle is a hierarchical principle because adopting a given position, here the author's position, presupposes an overabundance of knowledge on his part and an overview above the other. Only the author can fuse the hero's different characteristics into one image and present him as a whole. The hero cannot do this. At the same time this hierarchical tension leans toward a solution because gradually more knowledge is included in the hero's image. At the end of Sophocles' drama Oedipus also knows what the author/audience already knew, that he killed his father and married his mother. But it is obvious that the hero will never be completely equal to the author. As observers and readers we can adopt the author's perspective and interpret the drama in ever new ways. In this sense Freud is as much an author of the Oedipus drama as is Sophocles.

The ectopic distance does not lead to neutrality, nor to detachment. It implies that the hero is presented from the author's changing perspective, or, in general anthropological terms, that the other's relation to me always bears an emotional charge. The author continually rearranges the separate words and movements into a new whole. The author shows each time 'who' the hero is and what he thinks of him. Everything he says about the hero is emotionally charged.

From the perspective of the author's transcendence, Bakhtin reaches a vision of the author's presence in his work. This is possible because the hero relates the way the author thinks of him and presents him to his self-experience. The hero includes this evaluation in

his own view of himself. Alone he cannot stand back from himself,
but he can, to a certain extent, see himself as the author sees him.
The author's activity is not only an activity of the self toward the
other but also permits the self's experience of itself, the "I-for-myself."

Bakhtin ascribes this step to Christianity. For Bakhtin, Christianity is a crossroad in the history of ethics and aesthetics because it
includes the relationship to the other in people's relationship to
themselves. He clarifies this view of Christianity by contrasting
Christianity to two other traditions: Judaism and (the non-Christian
variation of) Neoplatonism. According to Bakhtin, the ethics of Neoplatonism are founded completely on the relationship to the self:

> Neoplatonism is the purest and the most consistently prosecuted axio-
> logical comprehension of man and the world on the basis of pure self-
> experience: the universe, God, other people—all are no more than *I-
> for-myself*. Their own judgment about themselves is the most compe-
> tent and the final judgment. The other has no voice here. As for the
> fact that they are also an *I-for-the-other*, it is fortuitous and unessential
> and engenders no valuation that is new in principle. (AA, 55)

According to Bakhtin, Christianity borrows the role of the other
in self-experience from Judaism. Moreover both Christianity and Judaism link the relationship to the other to a valuation of the body.
Although Bakhtin does not develop this idea further, we can sub-
scribe to his judgment, although we must add that Judaism values
the body differently in the 'sanctification' made possible by the gift
of the Law. For Bakhtin, the Law hardly plays a role: he primarily
emphasizes that the Jewish prohibition of images had an inhibiting
effect on an aesthetic, imaginative relationship to the body. This
step is of decisive importance not only for Bakhtin's theories of religion and of aesthetic representation but also for the rest of his work.
God's transcendence could have resulted in a reflection on ethical
activity and the relationship to the Law. Instead of this, Bakhtin
chooses to concentrate more on aesthetics, the relationship to the
other in artistic representation.

In Bakhtin's thinking, Christianity permits this aesthetic relationship because it sees God's presence in this world as a loving activity
toward the other, in which His visibility and corporality is affirmed.
The author can aesthetically and lovingly depict the hero because

God has done and will do so to others: Christ, the Church, the people of God. The author can create because and insofar as he does so "in the Spirit." But Bakhtin adds to this that the Spirit cannot be thought of as completely present in myself: "The Spirit, however, does not exist yet; everything is yet-to-be for the Spirit,[6] whereas everything that already exists is, for the Spirit, something that *has* already existed" (AA, 206). Bakhtin clings to God's transcendence in His presence in the world.

Is Bakhtin not asking for the impossible here? He reaches the conclusion that the author is unknowable from the literary work but at the same time does nothing else but create images. We may wonder whether the author can recognize himself in his own work. According to Bakhtin, the author cannot oversee the process of creation from within: "An author creates, but he sees his own creating only in the object to which he is giving form, that is, he sees only the emerging product of creation" (AA, 6). The "I-for-myself" experience is only possible through the eyes of the other, based on the category "the-other-for-me." For Bakhtin, this other is in the last instance the highest Other, that is, God. His presence in the world as Spirit permits a relationship with Him in a special *responsibility* that is distinct from the responsibility for individual creativity. In the last instance, this ethical creativity is based on a special responsibility to God: "This specialization of answerability, however, can be founded only upon a deep trust in the highest level of authority that blesses a culture— upon trust, that is, in the fact that there is another—the highest Other—who answers for my own special answerability, and trust in the fact that I do not act in an axiological void" (AA, 206).

3. THE INFINITY OF DIALOGUE IN DOSTOEVSKY

Problems of Dostoevsky's Poetics (1929)[7] appeared a few years after *Author and Hero*. Bakhtin describes Dostoevsky as the creator of a

---

[6] "dlya nego vsë predstoit eschchë"; see M. M. Bakhtin, *Estetika slovesnogo tvorchestva* (Moscow: Iskusstvo, 1979), 179. 'Predstoyat' means to lie ahead, be in prospect, be coming. The spirit is thus in the immediate future.

[7] M. M. Bakhtin, *Problemy tvortsjestva Dostoevskogo* [Problems of Dostoevsky's work] (Leningrad: Priboj, 1929); a thorough revision of this book appeared many years later as *Problemy poètiki Dostoevskogo* [Problems of Dostoevsky's poetics] (Moscow: Sovetskij Pisatel, 1963). It is available in English translation as *Problems*

completely new novel genre, the 'polyphonic' novel. By this he means a novel in which "a *plurality of consciousnesses, with equal rights and each with its own world*, combine but are not merged in the unity of the event" (*PDP*, 6). In a monophonic novel the hero is the object of the *author's* word, in the polyphonic novel he is the subject of *his own* word. Thus we could say that the polyphonic novel presents the hero's emancipation from the author. In certain senses, Dostoevsky's polyphonic novel is a reversal of the more traditional relationship as Bakhtin described it in *Author and Hero*. Bakhtin speaks of this reversal as a 'Copernican revolution,' the discovery that the earth revolves around the sun and not vice versa. In the history of the novel, Dostoevsky is credited by Bakhtin with bringing about a similar revolution by making the hero and not the author the center of the literary universe.

In *Dostoevsky's Poetics* Bakhtin hardly addresses the theological consequences of this literary revolution. Using the theological schema of *Author and Hero*, however, we can delineate the tension between transcendence and representation in the Dostoevsky study.

In his book on Dostoevsky, Bakhtin himself points to the shift in his aesthetics away from the traditional, monophonic novel, a shift that alters several insights from *Author and Hero*. The author's transcendence, his 'being-outside-himself,' remains undiminished in the Dostoevsky book, but it is no longer realized by supplying information from above. The author's activity shifts from content to form; its new purpose is to make possible and to confront other contents: the hero's ideas. Bakhtin describes this shift by using several constructive principles. According to him, the author in Dostoevsky's novels normally does not speak of the hero when he is absent. The author limits himself to the absolutely essential surplus information. He makes every effort to let the hero participate in the information available about him. The author gives him the chance to react to this information, and to refute all the images of the hero that the author suggests. Bakhtin calls this the "hero's rebellion," and illustrates it with Makar Devushin, the hero in Dostoevsky's first novel, *Poor Folk*, who feels deeply offended when he reads Gogol's short

---

of *Dostoevsky's Poetics*, trans. C. Emerson (Minneapolis: University of Minnesota Press, 1984); hereafter cited as *PDP*. Since in this article the history of ideas is less important, I take the liberty of disregarding the difference between the two editions and refer to both as *Problems of Dostoevsky's Poetics*.

novel *The Overcoat*. At that moment Dostoevsky's hero discovers that his life is only a copy of that of Akaky Akakievich, the hero of Gogol's novel. The author holds up a mirror before the hero and allows him to react to the image, and to try to refute it.

Because Bakhtin describes the polyphonic novel via a 'poetics' consisting of principles that determine the polyphonic form, the problem arises of the limitation of the author's transcendence through the laws of his own creation. It seems as if Bakhtin, after having rejected the link between the process of creation and the Law, reconsiders his decision. The hierarchical difference between author and hero found in *Author and Hero* is eliminated to make room for a logical, polyphonic space in which there is no transcendence.

But this would only be the case were the polyphonic novel to coincide with the principles of its construction. In reality, we must interpret Bakhtin's poetics in the framework of his view of aesthetic activity. He is not concerned with formulating technical rules for modern literature, but with showing that here there are new possibilities for representation that radicalize rather than limit transcendence. The problem to which Bakhtin finds an answer in the polyphonic novel is how it is possible to have a representation in which the other is not imprisoned in the image. The judgment on the other must be so expressed that the other is not reduced to a thing or a collection of characteristics, but can share in the transcendent truth that the author gives him. To this end the hero is himself given the ability to speak: "Dostoevsky's hero is not an objectified image but an autonomous discourse, *pure voice*, we do not see him, we hear him" (*PDP*, 53). Sharing in the transcendent truth becomes possible by letting the other speak without turning him into an object. This means speaking *with* him. Bakhtin thinks a nonobjectivizing relationship to the other is possible in *dialogue*.

What does Bakhtin mean by 'dialogue'? Not a specific linguistic form. The genre of dialogue can conceal a completely monophonic content. Nor does Bakhtin mean a situation in which various speakers alternate and patiently allow one another to speak. This situation lacks the real, meaningful confrontation that turns a conversation into a unique event. To avoid confusion with other forms of dialogue, Bakhtin prefers to speak about Dostoevsky in terms of the "great dialogue." This always occurs between various fully fledged, *unadul-*

terated consciousnesses, between the various characters in the novel. It is a confrontation in which the characters' voices participate in one unique event. Bakhtin addresses the dialogue on a level that is radically different from the everyday, practical conversation in which dialogue is an instrument of practical ends. He reverses the relationship of means to ends by declaring dialogue the goal of everyday activity.

He does not hesitate to approach great dialogue in religious and metaphysical terms. One such term is "infinity," which Bakhtin says can be applied to dialogue in various ways. First, by "infinity of dialogue" Bakhtin means the inability to end the dialogue. Dialogue implies that an irreducible difference between the voices continues to exist. This difference is not something negative, as is a conversation or last imperfection. Dialogue, the lack of a definitive last word, is itself "the last word." Bakhtin links dialogue to a "catharsis." In contrast to the catharsis in tragedy, dialogue opens us to the last word as something yet unspoken, but as always in the future: "Nothing conclusive has yet taken place in the world, the ultimate word of the world and about the world has not yet been spoken, the world is open and free, everything is still in the future and will always be in the future" (*PDP*, 166).

Furthermore, with "infinity" Bakhtin refers to the dialogue's situation. In Dostoevsky, dialogue takes place in moments where everyday events are interrupted, in an 'extraordinary' or 'borderline' situation. Dostoevsky exerts every effort to reach a derailment: occasional meetings on staircases, parties that turn scandalous, nervous breakdowns, and so on. There thus arises a situation outside space and time, a situation of "infinity" in which a *decisive* dialogue occurs among the characters. As one example Bakhtin mentions the meeting between Shatov and Stavrogin in *The Possessed*, in which Shatov bears the weight of the dialogue: "we are two *beings*, and have come together *in infinity* . . . for the *last time in the world*. Drop your tone, and speak like a *human being!* Speak, if only for once in your life, with the voice of a man."[8]

Finally, with the predicate "eternity" Bakhtin raises dialogue to a divine level: "At the level of his religious-utopian world view Dostoevsky carries dialogue into eternity, conceiving it as eternal co-

---

[8] F. Dostoevsky, *The Possessed*, Part 2, Chapter 1; cited by Bakhtin in *PDP*, 177.

rejoicing, co-admiration, concord" (*PDP*, 252). It may be surprising that here Bakhtin agrees with Dostoevsky's occasionally dubious religious convictions. This is more comprehensible when we realize that Bakhtin highly values the difference between Dostoevsky's two roles of journalist and writer. The journalist is associated with an extreme monophonic view of the Russian people's destiny to save Europe, whereas the writer is the creator of an artistic, logical space in which dialogue is possible.

What is the content of this "codivinization of the self," of this dialogue from a religious perspective? As in *Author and Hero*, God is present as Spirit *in whom* the author creates, but is not Himself presented in the work. What happens when God is present in the novel? Dostoevsky presented this possibility in the well-known story of the Grand Inquisitor in *The Brothers Karamazov*. In that story Christ returns to earth during the Spanish Inquisition. He appears before the Grand Inquisitor who, as we know, asks Christ if he would also be prepared to sacrifice human life to save other lives. Christ remains silent, and kisses the Inquisitor on the forehead. In a notebook, Dostoevsky explains that he wants to make this silent Christ the criterion for his own activity: Dostoevsky, says Bakhtin, "prefers to remain with the mistake but with Christ, that is, without truth in the theoretical sense of the word, without truth-as-formula, truth-as-proposition" (*PDP*, 98).

With *Dostoevsky's Poetics* Bakhtin accentuates the relationship between transcendence and representation. God's transcendence demands that the author accept absolute responsibility to represent the other in such a way that he is not imprisoned in the image. The polyphonic novel is one way to do this, because the technical literary means Dostoevsky devised are used to make possible a dialogue, that is, a communication in which the truth is spoken in such a way that it is not fixed in an image but continues to transcend the image.

4. The Author's Silence

Among some notes from Bakhtin's later years we find again an affirmation of the reader's inability to imagine the author:

> The problem of the image of the author. The primary (not created) and secondary author (the image of the author created by the primary

author). The primary—*natura non creata quae creat* (not created nature that creates); the secondary author—*natura creata quae non creat*
(created nature that does not create). The image of the hero—*natura
creata quae non creat.* The primary author cannot be an image. He
eludes any figurative representation. When we try to imagine the primary author figuratively, we ourselves are creating his image, that is,
we ourselves become the primary author of the image. The creating
image (i.e., the primary author) can never enter into any image that
he has created. The word of the primary author cannot be *his own*
word. It must be consecrated by something higher and impersonal (by
scientific argument, experiment, objective data, inspiration, intuition,
authority, and so forth). The primary author, if he expresses a direct
word, cannot simply be a *writer.* One can tell nothing from the face of
a writer (the writer is transformed into a commentator, a moralist, a
scholar, and so forth). Therefore, the primary author clothes himself
in *silence.* But this silence can assume various forms of expression,
various forms of reduced laughter (irony), allegory and so forth.[9]

What is most striking here is the difference between uncreated creating nature and created uncreating nature, which Bakhtin borrows
from Johannes Scotus Erigena, the ninth-century philosopher who
translated works by Dionysius the Areopagite and Gregory of Nyssa.
With this treatment of authorship, Bakhtin explicitly joins the tradition of negative theology.

The quotation can be read as an explanation of Dostoevsky's
search and of the author's transcendence. It is, however, formulated
in the telegraphic style characteristic of Bakhtin and thus requires
some explanation. Bakhtin bases the difference between the primary
author and secondary authors on their role in the representation.
The *secondary author* is not the author who—for example, as narrator or chronicler—plays a role in the literary work, but the one who
answers to what Wayne Booth calls the *implied author,* the individuality of the author indicated by the work, the sum of the choices that
as author he makes in the story.[10] The implied author makes his
choices known in the work. Just like the narrator, the chronicler, or
the hero, he belongs to the level of the immanence of the repre-

---

[9] M. Bakhtin, *Speech Genres and Other Late Essays,* trans. V. H. McGee (Austin:
University of Texas Press, 1986), 148; hereafter cited as SG.
[10] Cf. Wayne Booth, *The Rhetoric of Fiction* (Harmondsworth, U.K.: Penguin
Books, 1987), 71–76.

sented. In contrast, Bakhtin's *primary author* is not discernible in the represented, he is the unique spatiotemporal position who as creator of the work stands outside it. He is presupposed in the work, but is never reduced to it and cannot be deduced from it. Nor does he coincide with the biographical figure who can be described in a historical, psychological, or literary narrative: when we describe him, the author changes into the *hero* of another story. In that case, says Bakhtin, *we* become the primary authors of this story. Bakhtin drives this transcendence home when he distinguishes the primary author from the "I": "I myself can only be a character and not the primary author" (SG, 149). This problem of recognition is linked with what we noted in *Author and Hero*: How can the author himself be recognized in his work? There Bakhtin referred us to the author's responsibility to God. But here he says nothing about God, not, in all likelihood, because he lost his faith, but because the only way we can think about God is as primary author. Transcendence removes the primary author from every identification and every representation, into a *silence* in which he is wrapped and to which he tries to give expression.

This silence must not be seen as the opposite of speech. The primary author's silence is to be interpreted as an attempt to express his own word, a word that, as long as it is not found, can only be expressed in silence.

We may well wonder, what is the point of problematizing the author's image? For an answer we must consult the context of the passage cited above. Bakhtin speaks there of a "search for one's own [authorial] voice" (SD, 147) and of "my own word." His question is how people in our time can speak their "own word." Paradoxically, this presupposes that they must leave their own word "with which nothing essential can be said" (SG, 149). When I recognize myself in my own words, I recognize myself as character, not as primary author. Therefore, the search for my own words presupposes that I become the author of myself as character. In other words, this "I" is not given but has to be sought in the activity of representation. As we saw, this leads to a logic of transcendence and representation which, in the Dostoevsky study, results in dialogue, in sharing the absence of the last truth that is experienced in catharsis as an ever-*future* truth. Dostoevsky developed a literary form to represent this event: the polyphonic novel.

Bakhtin lists other directions in which a way can be sought to give expression to silence. First is the word that is removed from daily life, "the word of the idiot, the holy fool, the insane, the child, the dying person, and sometimes women. Delirium, intuition (inspiration), unconsciousness, alogicality (alogism), involuntary behavior, epilepsy, and so forth" (SG, 148). Besides these are modern forms of literature such as a montage of documents and the literature of the absurd, the inspiration for popular tales and biblical quotations (in this context Bakhtin mentions Tolstoy). And finally, "Another route would be to cause the world to begin speaking and to listen to the word of the world itself (Heidegger)" (SG, 149). Bakhtin thus believes transcendence is present in the heart of our time's search, even when the novel is abandoned as exclusive form.

What exactly is the connection between this silence and the modern period? What is relevant about Bakhtin redefinition of authorship? Bakhtin hardly gives any direct answer to this question, but from mostly marginal comments we can reconstruct his view. The author's silence is related to the loss of authority that is the root of the modern period. Previously, it was possible to speak with one's own voice because the other who made our self-appreciation possible was incarnated in stable institutions with moral authority. Authorship rested tacitly on the moral *authority* of these institutions. Since these institutions have lost their authority, the ability to speak individually with authority is no longer something to be taken for granted. In complete agreement with a strong antilegalistic tradition in Russian philosophy, Bakhtin sees nothing to be gained by the restoration of official institutions. These no longer have any innate moral authority, nor can they compel it. The individual is left with only a search for ways to find his or her own word.

It is consistent with this view that Bakhtin does not want to imprison this search in modern institutions, including science and literature. In the 1930s he witnessed how Stalinism used institutions to impose extreme terror from outside on all. His interest shifted from literary forms to the collective forces of culture, which could reform violence *from within*. This interest culminates in Bakhtin's magisterial study of Rabelais and his world. This book contains, in hidden terms, a cultural political position that reveals a new aspect of the relationship between transcendence and representation.

5. Bakhtin's Silence

Bakhtin presents his book *Rabelais and His World*[11] as a prehistory of socialist realism in which the materialistic imagery of the carnival serves as the most important source of inspiration for Rabelais's works. According to Bakhtin, it is essential that the carnival be a work of art played out in life itself. With this he wished to demonstrate that not literature alone as an institution but culture as a whole knows exceptional situations (feasts) in which it is confronted with a world outside itself against which it cannot protect itself. Bakhtin considered popular culture as a "collective body" that, like every body, has a vital relationship with the world outside and with other bodies. The carnival represents culture's open dimension in the central position given to festivities in the body's exchange with the outer world (drinking, gluttony, sexual contact).

Moreover, it is important that the exceptional situation of the feast occurs in culture's *representation* of itself. Modern culture, too, knows many moments—for example, national feasts, commemorations, or moments in political theaters varying from elections to show trials—in which it presents itself in its full glory to its participants. These situations can always become a problem for power when people no longer recognize themselves in this representation. The feast is therefore the wager of a political struggle between official authorities who consider the feast a formal sanction of the existing order and others who experience the feast as a different possibility for culture itself. This risk, however, cannot be avoided because the feast functions as a 'release' in the social order itself.

Bakhtin's analysis of culture in his *Rabelais* can be read as a critique of socialist realism. This was in essence an aesthetic of the *heroistic*. That means first of all that people who performed superhuman feats—pilots, athletes, war heroes, and so on—were heaped with praise and held up as examples for everyone. Beside them, the everyday people—the worker, the mother—were also seen as heroes. This means that in representation the human was transcended in the direction of the superhuman. Bakhtin's contribution consists in

---

[11] M. Bakhtin, *Tvorchestvo Fransua Rable i narodnaya kul'tura srednevekov'ya i Renessansa* (Moscow: Chudozhestvennaya Literatura, 1965); translated into English as *Rabelais and His World*, trans. H. Iswolsky (Bloomington: Indiana University Press, 1984); hereafter cited as *RW*.

showing that this representation goes back to Rabelais's grotesque *comic* realism, which lies at the origin of socialist realism. Characteristic of this form of realism is its ability to so emphasize the lowest dimensions of the praised that they can be accepted with laughter, for example, in the carnival custom where the king is removed in an insulting ritual and is replaced by the first schlemiel to cross the road. Comic realism works via a logic of *reversal*, but then in a different direction from socialist realism: in the representation, grotesque realism 'transcends' the praised in a downward direction. Where socialist realism reflects matters on a very exalted plane, it misinterprets the revolution which began by tearing down the statues of the czar. Where socialist realism saw transcendence exclusively in terms of an exaltation, Bakhtin showed that the way up and the way down coincide.

In this coincidence we recognize a Christian awareness that is visible in negative theology. Although Bakhtin in his *Rabelais* disagrees with the hierarchy concept of Dionysius the Areopagite (RW, 400–401), we can see a similarity between Bakhtin's grotesque realism and the way Dionysius sees people passing along the mystical path: beside a way up (*'epagogē'*) which the soul follows by standing back from creation, there is also the way down of God's turning toward creation (*'epistrophē'*). We cannot imagine Christianity without the notion of an intermixing and reversal of exaltation and humiliation. The birth of the Savior in a manger, and his insulting death on the cross, which indicates both shame and exaltation, have not only provoked doctrinal problems, but, if we believe Erich Auerbach, also have had important results for representation: "In antique theory, the sublime and elevated style was called *sermo gravis* or *sublimis*; the low style was *sermo remissus* or *humilis*; the two had to be kept strictly separated. In the world of Christianity, on the other hand, the two are merged, especially in Christ's Incarnation and Passion, which realize and combine *sublimitas* and *humilitas* in overwhelming measure."[12] Bakhtin makes clear with his carnivalesque variation of this scheme that in the very representation lies enclosed the possibility of its transcendence because the representation aims at an exalta-

---

[12] Erich Auerbach, *Mimesis: The Representation of Reality in Western Literature*, trans. H. R. Trask (Princeton, N.J.: Princeton University Press, 1971), 151. German original published in 1946.

tion of the existing and this exaltation is only possible when the humiliation is part of the deal. The transcendent cannot be limited to an exalted representation, and can only be approached when this representation is abandoned, when it is humiliated.

We must not view this humiliation too optimistically. Although, consistent with socialist realism, Bakhtin tends to encase the carnival in exalted words, violence was not absent. He cites from Rabelais wars caused by stolen bread, the carnival custom wherein people strike one another, complex fractures as a result of the fights, and the dismemberment of those who refuse to participate in the carnival. Bakhtin accepts that "the author's silence" is expressed in violent images because this violence is sublimated to a comic image.

But here Bakhtin arrives at a contradiction. For him, the sublimation of violence in a comic representation means in the last instance an exaltation. Of this we must say that it also, according to the ambivalent logic of the grotesque, is never without its opposite, the humiliation of violence in the still worse violence of terror. Bakhtin must represent the carnivalesque humiliation as an extremely optimistic "liturgical"[13] event. In reality, Stalinist culture knew an extremely violent carnival. Beside the celebration of heroism, there was a simultaneous, continuous unmasking and punishing of the heroes. They too were tossed before the public in show trials. Here we see the extent to which the representation, even in its continuous self-transcendence, including dialogue, can be a part of violence, and degenerate into terror, totally arbitrary violence. The author Bakhtin had to keep silent on this violence if he wanted to be heard at all in a Stalinistic culture.

We may think of this silence as naiveté, but this is contradicted by Bakhtin's experience with banishment, and by the starvation and death of his friends. We could, with some commentators, see this silence as an error, an anarchistic mistake in a predominantly Christian-humanistic life, but this is contradicted by Bakhtin's later attempts to link the carnival to Dostoevsky's poetics. We must ask

---

[13] Cf. Mikhail K. Ryklin, "Bodies of Terror: Theses Toward a Logic of Violence," *New Literary History* 24 (1993): 51–74: "[T]he text has a liturgical sound that is constantly being borne up: in the text the folk perpetually celebrate a Mass of its own blessedness, righteousness, unerringness. In this sacralized atmosphere, words become ultimate values and cease to signify things that can be seen, things that have a smell, things that act on us independently of their liturgical meaning" (52).

whether Bakhtin's silence on violence did not mean that he, in one way or another, allowed for a connection, had to allow for a connection, between transcendence, representation, and violence? This seems unfitting for the philosopher who saw representation as a deed of grace, of loving acceptance of human activity. But, in reality, violence cannot be held at bay. Because the author, in Bakhtin's view, rejects an appeal to strict justification, he shares in the violence, in the same sense as the silent Christ shares in the violence of the Grand Inquisitor.

Bakhtin's relationship with negative theology can show that the first steps of a reflection on violence are present in his philosophy. Negative philosophy summons us to share in God's activity but tells us that He surpasses the image that we have of Him. His unrepresentability can console us or give us hope, but it can also become violent when God's transcendence appears in the derailment of the familiar. The Bakhtinian dialogue takes place in the violence of this derailment, and does not eliminate this violence. It is an expression of the silence, and leaves the last word to the future.

Chapter 13

On Faith and the Experience of Transcendence

AN EXISTENTIAL REFLECTION ON NEGATIVE THEOLOGY

Paul Moyaert

1. INTRODUCTION

THERE ARE AT LEAST two perspectives from which one can approach negative theology.

The *first perspective* remains within the framework of traditional speculative inquiry. Can we orient our language about God in such a way that it perfectly satisfies the minimal demand imposed on it by our preconception of God? In other words, is it possible to find and use words, concepts, and predicates applicable exclusively to God such that they truly respect God's alterity, His absolute otherness? A *similar* problem arises when we wish to orient our language or judgment in a way so as to perfectly fit something like the radically singular—something that in its singularity is so unique that it neither can nor should be compared with anything else.[1] Is it ever possible for us to have contact with the unique (e.g., a person, an event) without that very contact threatening its singularity? On the one hand, the *unique* is that which is totally singular, something of which there exists only one; and yet on the other hand, as soon as we begin to delineate and describe this so-called incomparable singularity, we inevitably compare it with other things. While what is absolutely unique lies outside of every context or framework of meaning, de-

---

[1] Examples of this effort appear in the work of Jacques Derrida and Jean-François Lyotard.

scribing it always involves inserting it into such a context or framework. Because words are by definition general, it is unavoidable that the totally singular is linked to a general scheme and framework, so that its exceptional character is in danger of being lost. Speech that tries to preserve the unique in its uniqueness is, if not impossible, at least paradoxical. This is also true of speech about the 'other' in its radical otherness, and of speech about a secret one does not wish to reveal.

With respect to *negative theology*, this difficulty can be developed further. Beginning from the idea that God is radically different and thus beyond comparison, we can no longer apply to Him the words, concepts, and dialectical oppositions that we use to determine and describe beings in the world. In the case of God, we find that the customary meaning of all our words and concepts has already been eliminated before we use them. According to negative theologians, in order to respect this fact, speech about God can consist only in the patient exercise of an endless chain of negations: we neither can nor may speak of God's 'essence'; we cannot say that God 'is' or 'is not.' God is neither multiplicity nor unity, and so forth.

Natural or rational theology will object to negative theology by arguing that although God is radically different, this does not mean that we can negate every possible attribute in the same way. For, after all, saying that God is neither good nor evil could lead to the unacceptable conclusion that God is *morally indifferent*. Natural theology's task is to convince negative theology that, taking everything else into account, at the very least God's goodness (justice, wisdom, etc.) is beyond human measure. It seems more correct to say that God is infinitely good than to say that He is morally indifferent, even if we do not know exactly what we mean by 'goodness.'

Well then, if negative theology accepts this reasoning, *then* it becomes particularly difficult to also claim that God's goodness has nothing in common with what the term 'good' seems to mean for us. To deny this common meaning would be to deny that we know what we mean when we apply it to God in the first place. The same problem arises when we speak of the desire for a totally different or new form of rationality. To claim to understand a rationality totally different from what one has always understood by 'rationality' would be a contradiction. In this sense, a rationality that is totally different cannot even be called a rationality. If we nonetheless persist in doing so, then we no longer know what we are saying. It is in this line that natural theology defends the necessity and possibility of a doctrine of *analogy*, however deficient it may have to be.

From a *second perspective*, negative theology can be discussed in the context of *negative experiences*. Negative theology is then seen as a description of a specific dramatic experience of God's transcendence—that is to say, the experience of God's *absence*. This raises the question of what it means to continue to believe, against all else—without the mediating intervention of signs—in the goodness of God's creation. In this chapter, I will approach negative theology solely from this second perspective. I will begin by analyzing *basic trust* (Section 2), then describe what it means to trust a *person* (Section 3), and finally show how negative theology discusses a generally human *experience:* one that is recognizable as such, even for a nonreligious community (Section 4).

2. Faith As Basic Trust

Life is borne by a fundamental trust preceding every personal volition and not dependent on any rational justification. Human existence is anchored in a primordial trust neither in need of nor in search of grounds. Through this faith, which in the strict sense is not an act of any autonomous 'I,' the world in which we live always appears clothed with a certain evidence. We do not begin as if seeking justification for what we do. The *experience of alienation* or of a more radical confusion is possible only against the already pliant background of minimal familiarity with the world. Because of this self-evidence, what we do happens automatically, as if simply evident, such that the I-subject is freed of itself as burden: 'It' happens, automatically and despite me. This fundamental trust does not imply or correspond to any specific or explicit consciousness. Instead, *we stand in it;* we live from a trust that supports us.

This basic trust does not originate in some primal experience, where it would somehow show itself to consciousness for the first time. It has always been ours, from a past that has never been 'now' and can therefore never be recovered. We notice this trust only when it wavers or is shaken. We thus become aware of this natural self-evidence implicity supporting us *only when it is no longer self-evident*, when it is on the verge of no longer supporting us, or no longer permitting us to begin again. Only someone who loses this basic trust truly experiences and understands that it is something we must have in order to live.

Just as it cannot be said that I decide autonomously for life, so likewise it cannot be said that I can decide and exercise control over this trust. Rather, it is this *trust* that can abandon or fall away from *me*, so that it is no longer given to me to believe in the possibility of continued faith. The initiative does not lie with the 'I.' A confrontation with the potential fragility of trust leads to an awareness of the fact that this natural acceptance is in a certain sense not so natural after all—not so natural and thus in no way an objective characteristic of being. It is rather a 'gift': trust gives us the ability to involve ourselves in life and in the other. But, paradoxically, the gift only appears as gift when it begins to *withdraw*. It is misleading to say that we are attached to life because being is itself good. For us to experience being (life, creation) as good, it must first have already been given to us to do so. The natural light in which things appear to us is marked by something else, by the light of a more original gift over which the 'I' has no control. For the same sort of reason, it is also misleading to say that I, by my own power, affirm life. Every such personal affirmation depends first on a primordial '*Bejahung*' (a yes-saying) that has already occurred in me, preceding every personal initiative.

For those who lose this basic trust, nothing is self-evident anymore. Everything becomes alien and alienating, as occurs in schizophrenic delusion or paranoid suspicion. The isolated person is left to his or her own devices, no longer able to participate in life or in the intersubjective exchange of meaning. She is so alone that she tries, albeit in vain, without a foundation in anything else—ex nihilo—to create a framework or order in which it is still possible to live. Only those who are borne up by basic trust are *liberated* from themselves. They can participate in a shared framework of meaning: whatever they do derives its meaning from the self-evidence of the framework. The framework itself need not be created.

3. TRUST IN A PERSON

Likewise, trust in a person (e.g., in his honesty, love, goodness, etc.) cannot be grounded in objective reasons and facts; it has no objective foundation in being. Trust is necessary already *before* it is possible to trust someone. One way of demonstrating this is as follows.

First, suppose that I do not trust Person X. Regardless of any arguments and evidence this person may give me, unless there is already in place the openness of trust, I can in principle keep repeating "I know what you say is true, but still. . . ." Without that trust, everything the other person says or does is ambiguous. Someone who, in spite of everything else, nonetheless keeps responding "I know it, but still . . ." is not reasoning illogically; he or she is not drawing a false conclusion from correct premises. It is true that we will consider such a person 'unreasonable,' but what we mean by that is that he or she displays the symptoms of paranoid suspicion. The other person cannot demonstrate why she can be trusted. I have only her word for it. Trust, then, is an affectively laden event: if the other person does not inspire my trust from the start —if she has not always inspired my trust—then nothing will convince me to offer it. Distrust cannot be taken away by purely rational arguments or by objective facts that are in principle available and knowable to all.

In some circumstances it can be meaningful to question the basis of my trust in someone. Especially in practical matters, it would be unwise for me to trust just anyone. One way to justify my trust would be to say that I have known Person Y for a long time and am familiar with aspects of her character (I can point to her high degree of constancy, perhaps, or to her honest face). Someone else can tell me that these reasons are not good enough, and that I am therefore making a mistake. This might lead me to revise or to reshape my judgment. In this way, it can be said that trust is dependent on a knowledge (i.e., knowledge that 'this' or 'that' is the case) that can be corrected.

But this form of justification is also misleading, since it can give the impression that trust follows automatically from *knowing* that something is the case. It is indeed unwise to board a plane if we know that it can crash at any minute. But the objective information that the chance of a crash is negligible does not automatically produce the trust necessary for me to board a plane. Knowing certain facts, possibilities, qualities, and characteristics is, as such, not necessarily enough to inspire trust in someone or something. Someone else can know the same things on which I supposedly base my trust, and yet say, "I know, but still. . . ."[2]

Second, the fact that one is, for example, prepared to give and to receive signs of trust or acceptance is possible only because the 'underlying' trust had been restored or had not quite disappeared. A renewed exchange or acceptance of signs 'inspiring confidence' is itself a sign of mutual trust. Such a remnant of trust is presupposed even when I personally say to the other, "I don't trust you." Or, again, seeking cause for hope is *itself* a sign that not all is despair. *Hope* must exist for one to ask for signs supporting hope.[3]

In giving oneself and the other person reasons for trust, in justifying faith, the *groundlessness of faith* remains somewhat hidden. Some may say—incorrectly—that a rational justification is needed in order to place limits on the purely subjective arbitrariness of faith (or love). Here, rationalization rather fulfills a psychological function, keeping the groundlessness of faith *at a distance.*

While we may have good reason not to doubt someone's honesty and love, this does not imply an objective guarantee or certainty. We cannot predict how someone will act in the future. Every act of trust involves some degree of risk. Ironclad justification is no longer a matter of trust. Trust and rational justification are in this sense mutually exclusive. Trusting someone therefore means entrusting oneself to another person *whom one does not know.* To be sure, one's trust can be firm, but this is not the same thing as certainty. Trust and certainty are mutually exclusive. When I say, "I *am certain* you'll follow me," I look upon the other person, though perhaps indirectly, as if he or she were a machine or a robot that will continue to follow, or even pursue, me. Certainty rules out the possibility of the other person acting unpredictably. Such certainty is insensitive to the tension

---

[2] Something similar can be said of love. Even though I (later) give reasons why I love Person Y, this does not necessarily mean that I will love someone else who answers to the same description. It is precisely because there can be no definitive justification of love that love can address the other's absoluteness. A love that can be justified is thus *finite,* which is to say, not unconditional.

[3] Something similar can be seen in the case of *supplication* (prayer for grace). Grace already exists in the prayer, or *in the ability to even ask for grace.*

with a *transcendent* future or a *discontinuous* time. However, when instead I say, "I *trust* that you will follow me," I imply that I am not certain, and thus assume responsibility for my vulnerability and dependence. I relate to the other person as to a transcendent future that can interrupt and disturb my desires and expectations.

Faith accompanies the hope that something will be the case. It also expresses an implicit fear. Hope will inevitably shape certain expectations and expressions, even though it cannot give them definitive content. Hope is an orientation toward a future without genuine or ultimate content: it maintains a minimal distance or discrepancy with regard to the facts and events that contradict expectations. *It shatters the atemporal eternity of the present.*

At the same time, trust provides us with a certain naturalness and confidence in the face of the tension arising from the threat of a transcendent future. It is both an acknowledgment and a coming to terms with uncertainty. In trust, we recognize the real possibility of numerous threats, but at the same time we do not 'take them seriously.' They do not become obsessive thoughts fully possessing the mind. 'It' will turn out all right, even—and especially—when we cannot imagine how it will happen. That the 'I' is liberated from itself means that I will not have to do it; 'it' will take care of itself, apart from me.

Given this analysis, we can now understand why, according to Kierkegaard, faith is cut off from every objective order of being and that, before every possible foundation, it implies a discontinuous *leap*. It cannot be deduced from something else, and is not a form of uncertain knowledge to be improved or eliminated by more information. For someone without this trust, that leap can be experienced only as flinging oneself—and losing oneself—in an *abyss*. This is not so for those borne up by trust. For then it is a leap always performed, as it were, naturally. Faith cannot be founded on anything else. This is why it is *faith*.

4. Faith and the Painful Experience of Transcendence

Trust cannot be founded on anything else. However, this does not prevent people from desiring to support it, even if it is also true that this very desire presupposes that the heart is *already* 'illumined,' or

inspired, to either ask for signs (of hope) or to find them in something else (of course, there are indeed signs that can change someone's opinion, moving them to trust).

Because neither basic trust nor faith in life or a particular person
depend on rational justification or an objective grounds, they are in
that sense invulnerable to external events that contradict them. This
is not to say that trust and faith are completely invulnerable. Faith
and love can be so strongly contradicted that we lose them. A trust
that is completely invulnerable is not trust at all. In this regard, we
could speak of a nonsymmetrical exchange or dependence between
trust and the signs that confirm, support, or contradict it. While it
is difficult to think that faith and love will remain insensitive to
contradiction or that hope can never give way to doubt and despair,
it is also true that hope sometimes perseveres seemingly without
end, even without the tangible support of visible signs.

Someone who, in the face of all else to the contrary, nonetheless
continues to believe in the other, does this not because she has good
reasons to do so, or because she simply opts for this faith. This is not
a question of any alleged virile heroism. Such a person does not
continue to believe in someone else, or love him or her, because she
knows that this faith and love are, in the end, still for some reason
justifiable. Rather, faith itself supplies the necessary justification.
Even though it may well be true that life itself is impossible without
an unsupported faith, this insight is not enough to move a person to
continue believing. We do not *choose* for life. Those of us who, despite all else, can—or, better, may—continue to believe gain no personal merit for this. We *receive* faith, and must therefore speak of it
as a gift: *grace*.

As an orientation toward a future that cannot be internalized,
faith takes the shape of a *perseverance in* or a *toleration of* what might
be called the *transcendence of the other*. By 'experience of transcendence' we mean the experience in which we are confronted by a
world that contradicts our desires, and by an other who is not an
extension of the images we may have of him or her. Here, it is a
matter of experiences in which we are struck by discrepancy (contradiction) between something 'for me' and something 'in itself,' with
the latter signifying an otherness beyond, or despite, my images and
expectations. The world pursues its own course without me; it does
not take me into consideration. What breaks through, interrupting

this course, is not itself a course, is not itself a source of supplementary enrichment. The experience of transcendence is in essence linked to *negative* existential experiences.

From this perspective, one must also speak of the experience of God's transcendence within the framework of religious belief. The idea that God is more than I can imagine, that He infinitely surpasses my capacity to imagine, is sometimes unjustly linked to an experience of an inexhaustible richness in meaning: God's goodness, it is then said, is infinitely richer than we can imagine. In contrast with this, I consider an experience of God's transcendence to test the belief in His goodness, such that in this world and in this life—at their very limit—we no longer see, possess, or receive any sign that could support that belief, and such that even the recollection of earlier signs disappears. God's transcendence is manifest in the *suspension* of any sign of His goodness, which is to say in His radical absence. When every link between this world and God's goodness falls away, when that goodness is nowhere visible or when it is no longer mediated in any way, then faith can be nothing other than a suffering of God's transcendence. The faith that then sometimes perseveres is a faith that no longer has any sign to rely on. It is faith feeling its way in the darkness. At such a moment, faith is revealed in all its purity.

We call such a faith 'simple' faith, or a 'pure, naked' faith—a faith that, as John of the Cross said, is a faith purified of every image that could nourish it. From the perspective of natural reason, such a faith can only be foolishness, just as common sense says that it is equally foolish to keep loving someone without being able to give a reason for it. This is a faith that saves some people from despair even while they are in despair.[4]

---

[4] Does this describe 'authentic' faith, or 'true' faith? We can no longer say even this. We can only hope that it will be seldom or never that we need the grace of pure faith without signs or support—in despair—and that there will always turn up one or another sign on which our trust might find support. My analysis is intended only to show that the *existential logic* of religious faith is, at least in a certain sense, comparable to belief or trust in another person or in the world. The description of this latter trust should, in principle and apart from any religious context, be recognizable to everyone.

EPILOGUE

Ilse N. Bulhof

THIS EPILOGUE DOES NOT pretend to sketch an outline of the body of a book, or to indicate how individual contributions cohere, or to explain what the point of it all is, let alone pronounce a last word on the matter discussed.[1] It is an afterthought, a gesture of farewell or letting go, to a common project that brought the authors of the book together but that now, having been preserved in writing, begins a life of its own. At this point I would like to offer the reader some personal reflections.

What do these studies show us, and how do they stimulate thought? Do they confirm the editors' thesis put forward in the Introduction that echoes of negative theology can be heard in the specific embarrassment we experience in speaking of God? The answer cannot be a straight yes or a straight no. I will begin with a few observations.

A first observation is that throughout history, from classical antiquity to our own time, negative theology has made its appearance in many shapes. There is no one original negative theology of which all later shapes are mere variations. Put differently, there is no yardstick to categorize these shapes as more or less faithful to a one-and-only 'pure' negative theology. This absence of an original negative theology makes room for the interplay of what the editors sometimes tentatively call 'shapes' of negative theology. In this interplay the various negative theologies can be appreciated for their specific qualities.

A second observation concerns the division between the cultural climate of antiquity and the Middle Ages, on the one hand, and that of modern times, on the other. In classical and medieval times life

---

[1] The editors' Introduction can be considered a partial attempt to meet this task.

was lived in an unquestioned trust in the goodness of Being, of God, or of the Supra Being beyond words and thoughts. In our time, however, this trust has vanished. Trust in Being, in the world, in creation, it is felt, has turned out to be misplaced. Nietzsche's thought was inspired to a great extent by his keen awareness of the cruelty of life, a cruelty he no longer wanted to obfuscate by reconciliatory metaphysical theories. Every philosophy and theology in our time has to come to terms with this discomfiture of metaphysics, often referred to as "the death of God."

This leads to a third observation. Philosophers and theologians have come to realize that there has always been a people for whom this trust in the world was simply impossible: the Jews. Their hope against hope was oriented toward an unfathomable source not of this world: the Old Testament Yahweh. We are now learning from the painful Jewish experience of homelessness and persecution, and from the impressive way so many Jews have stuck to their faith despite everything they have suffered for remaining true to it, how to lament without falling into despair.

Can we state that the God of metaphysics, the traditional God of our culture who used to be present in the world, is no more? The momentous change implied in this question can, as these studies show, be experienced very differently.

Initially, the question can be experienced as an opportunity, exemplified by Moyaert: an opportunity that may be painful, even cruel, to 'purify' Christian faith, realizing that God is beyond all computing and faith is groundless.

Second, it can be an occasion to think through again that same Christian faith, weeding out past errors, rediscovering the forgotten but profound truth of Dionysius the Areopagite, Anselm, and even Thomas Aquinas: that God is a Transcendence surpassing all understanding and turning human wisdom into foolishness. In doing so, the role of Christ may be rediscovered as our only hope of experiencing God's love, as the only one who can bring us in touch with the Father (this experience I find in Marion on Anselm; see also Kal's reflections on Marion in this volume).

Furthermore, God's absence might be experienced as a chance to doubt, probe, question, and explore the very notions of Being, Highest Being, God, and Super-Essence, those metaphysical notions on which our culture is founded. For example, God may be absent, but not in the sense of being somewhere 'beyond,' or in being withdrawn into Himself in order to let us be. The experience of God's absence may merely concern our human *idea* of what Being and non-Being are. The realization that the death of God concerns only the death of the concepts and images of God, but not the death of God Himself, shows affinity with negative theology as we know it from the Neoplatonic and Christian past. Today, it leads to a search for new languages for addressing the divine while bowing before God's incomprehensible transcendence and screaming *de profundis*, "God!" in our anguish. Are the tentative languages tried out by contemporary philosophers such as Nietzsche (de Schutter), Bataille (ten Kate), and Derrida (de Vries, Bulhof, Sneller) indeed echoes of negative theology? Does a long-hidden undercurrent of that ancient tradition surface in their thought? I will discuss these questions below.

In some authors in this book (Steunebrink in discussion with Adorno) attempts to approach the question of God in such desperate terms arouse mixed feelings: irritation at all this gloom, or even indignation. They react to so-called postmodern attempts to find a new language for the divine by reconfirming a more traditional form of Christian faith and philosophy, returning to the tools of metaphysical thought—be it only in a Kantian, postulated form.

Most remarkable is the way Jewish thinkers succeed in experiencing the absence of God in a spirit of nonexpectation toward life in the world, that, however, does not make worldly activity useless (as explained by Terpstra and de Wit in their discussion of Taubes).

The possibility remains that the silence forced upon us by a radically transcendent God leads to complicity with the forces of evil (Simons on Bakhtin), which is a warning against an easy enthusiasm for silence and mysticism.

In the studies collected here, Nietzsche, Bataille, and Derrida emerge as truly creative—maybe even 'religious'—thinkers attempting to forge new forms of 'God talk.' If echoes of negative theology can be heard in contemporary philosophy, it is certainly also in their work. But the negative theology echoed is definitely not negative theology in its traditional Christian sense, tied as the latter was to a curious mixture of Neoplatonism and belief in revelation through Christ. The divine adumbrated here is nontheistic and radically beyond, without being far away. If we agree with Derrida that traditional Christianity has no monopoly on God, we may discern a form of negative theology in the thought of these modern philosophers: because traditional Christian negative theology itself might be but an echo of this Beyond that is totally Other.

Looking more closely at these contemporary authors, we may state that the parallels between Nietzsche and Eckhart are most surprising, as is Nietzsche's vision of Jesus and Zarathustra as fools, true children of God. De Schutter's contribution is more than a promising interpretation of Nietzsche. It suggests that an outsider like Nietzsche may put traditional Christian faith in a new perspective. Bataille and Derrida think through the experience of the death of God as they found it in Nietzsche. Together they open up an abyss in modern culture that simultaneously marks the impossibility of morality and religion and the possibility of their reappearance in radically new forms. The sustained ambivalence in the experience of God's death shows that these thinkers are not mere nihilists, despite Terpstra's and de Wit's criticism of Bataille. In the writings of Nietzsche, Bataille, and Derrida one meets an aporetic way of speaking about God in which God in one and the same movement appears and disappears, 'lives' and 'dies.' Such speaking about God has a clearly iconoclastic effect, but for that very reason it testifies to unsuspected ethical and religious possibilities. Bataille's prayers to an "impossible" God, as ten Kate shows, are a remarkable example of this. So is Derrida's later work. In particular, in his most recent publications, as Sneller points out, Derrida echoes negative theology in a way that, *mirabile dictu*, recalls Barth, and is at the same time critical of Christian negative theology. Striking is the emphasis on the importance of performance in the contributions by de Vries and Bulhof on Derrida: a performance that seems to parallel the transformation of the believers that Blans points to in his presentation of John of the Cross.

In the interplay between these various shapes of negative theology there is a tension between those inspired by Greek and Christian philosophy, including their negative theological forms—let us call them 'Athens' and 'Rome'—and inspired by Jewish thought—let us call them "Jerusalem." This is the tension between, on the one hand, thinking in terms of a (hidden) divine *presence* and of the world's ultimate sacrality, and, on the other hand, thinking in terms of divine *absence* and of the world's profoundly secular nature. We might

ask in passing, does this volume not lack a type of thinking connected to another religious capital with great negative theological
potential: Mecca?

Taken together, the contributions assembled here testify to a
changing relationship between philosophy and religion. After centuries of antagonism between philosophers and theologians, we see in
these studies the beginning of a tentative and remarkable rapproche-
ment. Religion, it seems, is no longer taboo for philosophers, including those who find themselves at the far end of 'Christian
philosophy.' After all, the traditional existential themes ignored by
many modern philosophers—the divine, trust, faith, finitude, death,
evil, forgiveness, grace, and so on—have been guarded in Christian
faith. These topics arise anew today in philosophy, where they are
being studied in a concrete, radical way in philosophies of culture,
rather than in metaphysics. Openness to God's mystery, or at least
interest in and fascination with a mysterious alterity, characterize all
of the thinkers who have made their appearance in this study. The
latter are beginning to realize that discursive thought, 'thinking
about,' is always a perhaps provisional, inadequate but at the same
time inevitable response to this mystery.

While this book was taking shape, the editors became increasingly
aware of its 'blank spots,' if I may call them that: spaces that are
empty but should not be. A women's perspective is altogether absent. Jewish thought remains underrepresented. Islamic and Asian
traditions are not even mentioned. Understandable as these blank
spots might be from a practical perspective—that is, the background
and scope of a book issuing from a research group rooted in a Western philosophical tradition—they are shortcomings nevertheless.

The editors can only hope that this book will stimulate further
explorations in this field, and that in particular it may help widen its
circle of participants, both inside and outside the confines of the
Western tradition. The presentation of these studies to an English-
speaking public is itself an extension of its readership. Will it also
stimulate the specific widening envisioned here, toward the participation of feminist Jewish, Islamic, and Asian thinkers and culture?

As we all know, such widening is not an easy matter: it requires
from all participants a certain detachment from cherished beliefs—
and not in the last place the typically cherished modern beliefs in
progress, instrumental reason, and the centrality of humankind in

the cosmos. It is therefore hardly surprising that at first glance only radical fundamentalists in Christianity and Islam seem to question these pillars of modern Western culture. The quiet voices of scholars also questioning modernity while rejecting a simple return to the past are easily lost in the tumult. Perhaps the attitude of rebellion described by Terpstra and de Wit in characterizing Taubes's "negative political theology" could provide the frame of mind that would make this cosmopolitan interplay possible.

BIBLIOGRAPHY

1. History of Negative Theology: Medieval Sources (Editions Used in This Volume)

Angelus Silesius. *The Cherubinic Wanderer*. Translated by M. Shrady. New York: Paulist Press, 1986.

Anselm of Canterbury. *Opera omnia*. Edited by F. S. Schmitt. Edinburgh/Rome: Thomas Nelson, 1938–1961. See especially the *Proslogion* and the *Monologion*.

———. *Works*. Edited and translated by Jasper Hopkins and Herbert Richardson. Toronto/New York: Edwin Mellen, 1974.

Augustine. *Confessiones*. Translated by W. Wats. Cambridge, Mass.: Harvard University Press, 1996.

———. *De doctrina christiana*. Latin/English edition, edited and translated by R. P. H. Green. Oxford, U.K.: Clarendon Press, 1995.

———. *De ordine*. Latin/French edition, edited and translated by J. Doignon. Paris: Études Augustiniennes, 1997. See especially part 2, 16.44.

———. *De Trinitate*. Latin edition by W. J. Mountain. Turnhout: Brepols, 1968.

Boethius. *Consolatio philosophiae*. Latin/German edition, edited and translated by Ernst Gegenschatz and Olof Gigon. Munich: Artemis, 1990.

Cusa, Nicholas of. *Tetralogus de non aliud*. In *Opera omnia*. Hamburg: Meiner, 1952

———. *De Visione Dei*. In *Philosophisch-Theologische Schriften*, vol. 3. Edited by L. Gabriel. Vienna: Herder, 1967.

Damascius Diadochus. *Damascii Philosophi Platoni Quaestiones de Primis Principiis*. Edited by J. Kopp. Frankfurt am Main: Broenner, 1826.

Dionysius the Areopagite. *The Divine Names and The Mystical Theology*. Translated by C. E. Rolt. London: SPCK, 1977.

Eckhart. *Sermons and Treatises.* 2 vols. Edited and translated by M. O. C. Walsh. Longmead, U.K.: Element, 1989.

———. *Meister Eckharts Predigten.* 3 vols. Edited by J. Quint. Stuttgart: Kohlhammer, 1936.

John of the Cross. *The Complete Works of Saint John of the Cross, Doctor of the Church.* Edited by P. Silvero de Santa Teresa and E. Allison Pres. London: Burns & Oates, 1943.

———. *Mystieke Werken.* Ghent, Belgium: Carmelitana, 1980.

Migne, J. P. *Patrologia Graeca.* Paris: Garnier, 1844–1864. See especially volume 3 (works of Dionysius the Areopagite), volume 12–13 (works of Origen), volume 37 (works of Gregory of Nazianzus), and volume 44 (works of Gregory of Nyssa).

———. *Patrologia Latina.* Paris: Garnier, 1844–1864. See especially volume 25 (*De moribus Manichaeorum* of Augustine), vol. 32 (*Confessiones* of Augustine), volume 34 (*De doctrina christiana* of Augustine), vol. 38 (Sermons of Augustine), volume 42 (*De duabus animabus contra Manichaeos* and *De natura boni contra Manichaeos* of Augustine), and volume 183 (works of Bernard of Clairvaux).

Thomas Aquinas. *Summa Theologiae.* London: Blackfriars and Eyre & Spottisville/New York: McGraw-Hill, 1964–1975.

2. WORKS AND ARTICLES RELEVANT TO THE HISTORY OF NEGATIVE THEOLOGY (EXPLICIT AS WELL AS IMPLICIT)

Alquié, F. *L'argument ontologique chez Saint Anselme. Les critiques de Gaunilon et Saint Thomas d'Aquin.* Diplôme d'Études supérieures directed by Étienne Gilson, May 1929.

Bouillard, H. "Le preuve de Dieu dans le *Proslogion* et son interprétation par K. Barth. In *Spicilegium Beccense,* vol. 1. Paris: Vrin, 1959.

Burrell, D. *Aquinas: God and Action.* London: Routledge & Kegan Paul, 1979.

———. *Knowing the Unknowable God: Ibn-Sina, Maimonides, Aquinas.* Notre Dame, Ind.: University of Notre Dame Press, 1986.

Carabine, D. *The Unknown God: Negative Theology in the Platonic Tradition: From Plato to Eriugena.* Leuven: Peeters Press, 1995.

Carré, Meyrick H. *Realists and Nominalists.* Oxford, U.K.: Oxford University Press, 1961. Originally published in 1946.

Certeau, Michel de. *La fable mystique*, Vol. 1: XVIe–XVIIe siècle. Paris: Gallimard, 1982. English ed., *The Mystic Fable*. Translated by M. B. Smith. Chicago: University of Chicago Press, 1992.

Chatillon, J. "De Guillaume d'Auxerre à Saint Thomas d'Aquin: L'argument de Saint Anselme chez les premiers scolastiques du XIIème siècle." In *Spicilegium Beccense*, vol. 1. Paris: Vrin, 1959.

Copleston, F. *A History of Philosophy*. London: Burns, Oates & Washbourne, 1948. See especially volume 2, part 1: *Augustine to Bonaventure*, volume 2, part 2: *Albert the Great to Duns Scotus*, and volume 3: *Late Medieval and Renaissance Philosophy*.

Corbin, M. "Cela dont plus grand ne puisse être pensé." *Anselm Studies* 1 (1983).

———. *Le chemin de la théologie chez Thomas d'Aquin*. Paris: Beauchesne, 1974.

———. "Introduction au *Proslogion*." In *L'oeuvre de Anselme de Cantorbéry*. Paris: Cerf, 1986.

Courtenay, W. J. *Covenant and Causality in Medieval Thought*. London: Variorum Reprints, 1984.

Dalferth, I. U. "Fides quaerens intellectum: Theologie als Kunst der Argumentation in Anselms *Proslogion*." *Zeitschrift für Theologie und Kirche* 81 (1984).

Daniels, A. "Quellenbeiträge und Untersuchungen zur Geschichte der Gottesbeweise im dreizehnten Jahrhundert, mit besonderer Berücksichtigung des Arguments im *Proslogion* des heiligen Anselm." *Beiträge zur Geschichte der Philosophie des Mittelalters* 8, nos.1–2 (Münster, 1909).

Dupré, Louis. *The Deeper Life: An Introduction to Christian Mysticism*. New York: Crossroad, 1983.

Eijnden, J. v.d. "Sacris sollemniis: Inleidende beschouwingen." In *De gelovige Thomas: Beschouwingen over de Hymna Sacris Sollemniis van Thomas van Aquino*, edited by J. v.d. Eijnden. Baarn: Ambo, 1986.

Evans, G. R. *A Concordance to the Works of St. Anselm*. Millwood, N.Y.: Kraus, 1984.

Festugière, A. J. *Le dieu inconnu et la gnose*, vol. 4 of *La révélation d'Hermès Trismégiste*. Paris: Gabalda, 1953.

Gilson, Étienne. *Études médiévales*. Paris: Vrin, 1983.

———. "Sens et nature de l'argument de Saint Anselme." *Archives d'Histoire doctrinale et littéraire du Moyen Age* 9 (1934): 26ff.

Harnack, A. von. *Marcion. Das Evangelium vom fremden Gott.* Darmstadt: Wissenschaftliche Buchgesellschaft, 1985. Originally published in 1921.

Hochstaffl, J. *Negative Theologie. Ein Versuch zur Vermittlung des patristischen Begriffs.* Munich: Kösel-Verlag, 1976.

Ivánka, E. Von. *Plato Christianus. Übernahme und Umgestaltung des Platonismus durch die Väter.* Einsiedeln: Johannes Verlag, 1964.

Kohlenberger, M. *Similitudo und Ratio. Überlegungen zur Methode bei Anselm von Canterbury.* Bonn: Grundmann und Bouvier, 1972.

Koyré, Alexandre. *L'idée de Dieu dans la philosophie de Saint Anselme.* Paris: Vrin, 1984. Originally published in 1923.

Lossky, V. *The Mystical Theology of the Eastern Church.* Cambridge, U.K.: Cambridge University Press, 1957.

Lubac, Henri de. " 'Seigneur, je cherche ton visage': Sur le chapitre XIVe du *Proslogion* de Saint Anselme." *Archives de Philosophie* 39, no. 2 (1976).

————. "Sur le chapitre XIVe du *Proslogion.*" In *Spicilegium Beccense,* vol. 1. Paris: Vrin, 1959.

Mortley, Raoul. *The Way of Negation: Christian and Greek,* vol. 2 of *From Word to Silence.* Bonn: Hanstein, 1986.

Naulin, P. "Réflexions sur la portée de la preuve ontologique chez Anselme de Cantorbéry." *Revue de Métaphysique et de Morale* (1969).

Oakley, F. "Jacobean Political Theology: The Absolute and Ordinary Powers of the King." *Journal of the History of Ideas* 29 (1968): 323–46.

————. "Pierre d'Ailly and the Absolute Power of God: Another Note on the Theology of Nominalism." *Harvard Theological Review* 56 (1963): 59–73.

Oberman, Heiko. *The Harvest of Medieval Theology: Gabriel Biel and Late Medieval Nominalism.* Grand Rapids, Mich.: Eerdmans, 1976.

Ozment, Stephen. *Mysticism and Dissent: Religious Ideology and Social Protest in the Sixteenth Century.* New Haven, Conn.: Yale University Press, 1973.

O'Meara, John D. *Eriugena.* Oxford, U.K.: Clarendon Press, 1988.

Paliard, J. "Prière et dialectique. Méditation sur le Proslogion de Saint Anselme." *Dieu vivant* 6 (1946).

Plantinga, Alvin. *The Ontological Argument: From Anselm to Contemporary Philosophers*. Garden City, N.Y.: Anchor, 1965.

Rahner, Karl. "Fragen zur Unbegreiflichkeit Gottes nach Thomas von Aquin." In *Schriften zur Theologie* 12, 306–319. Zurich/Einsiedeln/Cologne: Benziger Verlag, 1975.

Rappe, Sara. *Reading Neoplatonism: Non-discursive Thinking in the Text of Plotinus, Proclus, and Damascius*. Cambridge, U.K.: Cambridge University Press, 2000.

Roques, R. *L'univers dionysien*. Paris: Aubier, 1954.

Semmelroth, O. "Die Theologia des Pseudo-Dionysius Areopagita." *Scholastik* 27 (1952):1–343.

Tonnard, F. "Caractères augustiniens de la méthode philosophique de Saint Anselme." In *Spicilegium Beccense*, vol. 1. Paris: Vrin: 1959.

Turner, D. *The Darkness of God: Negativity in Christian Mysticism*. Cambridge, U.K.: Cambridge University Press, 1997.

Valkenberg, W. *Did Not Our Hearts Burn? Place and Function of Holy Scripture in the Theology of St. Thomas Aquinas*. Utrecht: Thomas Institute, 1990.

Vanneste, J. *Le mystère de Dieu. Essai sur la structure rationelle de la doctrine mystique du pseudo-Denys l'Areopagite*. Paris: Desclée de Brouwer, 1959.

Vedder, B. "De metafoor van de vruchtbaarheid." In *Vruchtbaar woord. Wijsgerige beschouwingen bij een theologische tekst van Thomas van Aquino, Summa contra Gentiles IV, 11*, edited by J. A. Aertsen. Leuven: Leuven University Press, 1990.

Vignaux, P. "Structure et sens du *Monologion*." *Revue des sciences philosophiques et théologiques* 31 (1947).

Viola, C.-É. "Journées internationales anselmiennes." *Archives de Philosophie* 35 (1972).

Vuillemin, J. *Le Dieu d'Anselme et les apparences de la raison*. Paris: Aubier et Montaigne, 1971.

Weinberg, Julius R. *A Short History of Medieval Philosophy*. Princeton, N.J.: Princeton University Press, 1964. See especially 46–57 (on Dionysius Areopagita and others).

Wissink, Jozef. "Aquinas: The Theologian of Negative Theology. A Reading of *Summa Theologiae* I, Quest. 14–16." *Jaarboek van het Thomas-Instituut te Utrecht* 13 (1993): 15–83.

3. Works and Articles by the Authors Treated in
Particular in This Volume

Adorno, Theodor. *Drei Studien zu Hegel.* In *Gesammelte Schriften,*
vol. 5. Frankfurt am Main: Suhrkamp, 1970–1986. This volume
includes "Aspekte."

———. *Einleitung zum "Positivismusstreit" in der deutschen Soziologie.* In *Gesammelte Schriften,* vol. 8. Frankfurt am Main: Suhrkamp, 1970–1986.

———. *Negative Dialectics.* Translated by E. B. Ashton. New York:
Seabury Press, 1973. Republished, London: Routledge & Kegan
Paul, 1990. Originally published in German in 1966 as *Negative
Dialektik.* In *Gesammelte Schriften,* vol. 6. Frankfurt am Main:
Suhrkamp, 1970–1986.

———. *Notes to Literature.* 2 vols. Translated by S .W. Nicolson.
New York: Columbia University Press, 1991. Volume 2 includes
"On the Final Scene of *Faust*" and "On the Classicism of
Goethe's *Iphigenie.*"

———. *Philosophische Terminologie.* Frankfurt am Main: Suhrkamp,
1973–1974.

———. *Prisms.* Translated by S. Weber and S. Weber. Cambridge,
Mass.: MIT Press, 1983. This volume includes "Veblen's Attack on
Culture." Originally published in German in 1977.

———. *Quasi una fantasia.* In *Gesammelte Schriften,* vol. 16. Frankfurt am Main: Suhrkamp, 1970–1986. This volume includes "Sakrales Fragment."

———. *Stichworte.* In *Gesammelte Schriften,* vol. 10.2. Frankfurt am
Main: Suhrkamp, 1970–1986. This volume includes "Anmerkungen zum philosophischen Denken" and "Fortschritt."

Bakhtin, Mikhail. *Art and Answerability: Early Philosophical Essays.*
Translated by V. Liapunov. Austin: University of Texas Press, 1990.
This volume includes "Author and Hero in Aesthetic Activity,"
4–256. French edition, *Esthétique de la création verbale.* Translated
by A. Aucouturier. Paris: Gallimard, 1984.

———. *Problems of Dostoevsky's Poetics.* Translated by C. Emerson.
Minneapolis: University of Minnesota Press, 1984.

———. *Rabelais and His World.* Translated by H. Iswolsky. Bloomington/Indianapolis: Indiana University Press, 1984.

————. *Speech Genres and Other Late Essays.* Translated by V. H. McGee. Austin: University of Texas Press, 1986.

————. *Toward a Philosophy of the Act.* Translated by V. Liapunov. Austin: University of Texas Press, 1993.

Barth, Karl. *Fides quaerens intellectum. Anselms Beweis der Existenz Gottes.* Munich: Kaiser, 1931.

————. *Kirchliche Dogmatik.* Zurich: EVZ-Verlag, 1932–1967. English edition, *Church Dogmatics.* Edited by G. W. Bromley and T. F. Torrance. Edinburgh: Clark, 1936ff.

————. *Der Römerbrief.* Munich: Kaiser, 1924. Second rewritten edition first published in 1922. English edition, *The Epistle to the Romans.* Translated by E. C. Hoskins. Oxford, U.K.: Oxford University Press, 1968.

Bataille, Georges. *The Absence of Myth: Writings on Surrealism.* Edited and translated by M. Richardson. New York: Verso, 1994.

————. *The Accursed Share: An Essay on General Economy.* Vol. 1: *Consumption*; vol. 2: *The History of Eroticism*; vol. 3: *Sovereignty.* Translated by R. Hurley. New York: Zone Books, 1988–1991. Originally published in French, *La part maudite* (1949), *Histoire de l'érotisme* (1951; only in *Oeuvres complètes*, vol. 8), *La souveraineté* (1953; only in *Oeuvres complètes*, vol. 8).

————. *The Bataille Reader.* Edited by F. Botting and S. Wilson. Oxford, U.K.: Blackwell, 1997.

————. *Eroticism.* Translated by M. Dalwood. San Francisco: City Light Books, 1986. Originally published in French in 1957.

————. *Essential Writings.* Edited and translated by M. Richardson. London: Sage, 1998.

————. *The Impossible.* Translated by R. Hurley. San Francisco: City Light Books, 1991. Originally published in French in 1962.

————. *Literature and Evil.* Translated by A. Hamilton. New York: Marion Boyars, 1990. Originally published in French in 1957.

————. *My Mother, Madame Edwarda, The Dead Man.* Translated by A. Wainhouse. New York: Marion Boyars, 1989. Originally published in French in 1966, 1941, and 1967, respectively.

————. "Le sacré au vingtième siècle." In *Oeuvres complètes*, vol. 8, 474–80.

————. *La somme athéologique.* Vols. 5 and 6 of *Oeuvres complètes.* Paris: Gallimard, 1970–1988. This "summa" is made up by four books that appeared separately:

L'expérience intérieure. Paris: Gallimard, 1943. In *Oeuvres complètes,* vol. 5, 7–189. English edition, *Inner Experience.* Translated by L. A. Boldt. Albany: State University of New York Press, 1988.

Méthode de méditation. Paris: Gallimard, 1947. In *Oeuvres complètes,* vol. 5, 191–228.

Le coupable. Paris: Gallimard, 1944. In *Oeuvres complètes,* vol. 5, 235–391. English edition, *Guilty.* Translated by B. Boone. Venice, Calif.: Lapis Press, 1988.

Sur Nietzsche. Volonté de chance. Paris: Gallimard, 1945. In *Oeuvres complètes,* vol. 6, 7–207. English edition, *On Nietzsche.* Translated by B. Boone. New York: Paragon Books, 1994. First edition 1992.

———. *Story of the Eye.* Translated by J. Neugroschal. New York: Marion Boyars, 1979. Originally published in French in 1928.

———. *Theory of Religion.* Translated by R. Hurley. New York: Zone Books, 1989. Originally published in French in 1948.

———. *Visions of Excess: Selected Writings, 1927–1939.* Edited by A. Stoekl. Minneapolis: University of Minnesota Press, 1985.

Derrida, Jacques. *Adieu. A Emmanuel Levinas.* Paris: Galilée, 1997.

———, and Pierre-Jean Labarrière. *Altérités.* Paris: Osiris, 1986.

———. *Aporias.* Translated by T. Dutoit. Stanford, Calif.: Stanford University Press, 1993. Originally published in French in 1993.

———. "At This Very Moment in This Work Here I Am." In *Re-reading Levinas,* edited by R. Bernasconi and S. Critchley, 11–48. Originally published in French, in *Psyché,* 1987.

———. "Avances." Introduction to Serge Margel, *Le Tombeau du dieu artisan: Sur Platon,* 11–43. Paris: Minuit, 1995.

———. *Circumfession: Fifty-nine Periods and Periphrases.* In Geoffrey Bennington and Jacques Derrida, *Jacques Derrida.* Chicago: University of Chicago Press, 1993. Originally published in French in 1991.

———. *A Derrida Reader: Between the Blinds.* Edited by P. Kamuf. New York: Columbia University Press, 1991.

———. "Faith and Knowledge: The Two Sources of 'Religion' within the Mere Limits of Reason." In *Religion,* translated by S. Weber, edited by J. Derrida and G. Vattimo, 1–78. Stanford, Calif.: Stanford University Press, 1998. Originally published in French in 1996.

———. "Force of Law: The 'Mystical Foundation of Authority.'" *Cardozo Law Review* 11, nos. 5–6 (1990): 920–1001. Translated by

M. Quaintance. Originally published in French as *Force de loi. Le "fondement mystique de l'autorité."* Paris: Galilée, 1994.

———. *The Gift of Death.* Translated by D. Wills. Chicago: University of Chicago Press, 1995. Originally published as "Donner la mort," in *L'Éthique du don. Jacques Derrida et la pensée du don,* edited by J.-M. Rabaté and M. Wetzel, 11–108. Paris: Transition, 1992.

———. *Given Time, 1: Counterfeit Money.* Translated by P. Kamuf. Chicago: University of Chicago Press, 1991. Originally published as *Donner le temps.* Paris: Galilée, 1991. See especially chapter 2: "Folie de la raison économique. Un don sans présent."

———. *Margins of Philosophy.* Translated by A. Bass. Chicago: University of Chicago Press, 1982. Originally published in French in 1967. See especially the essays "Différance" and "White Mythology."

———. *Of Grammatology.* Translated by G. C. Spivak. Baltimore: Johns Hopkins University Press, 1974. Originally published in French in 1967.

———. *Of Spirit: Heidegger and the Question.* Translated by G. Bennington and R. Bowlby. Chicago: University of Chicago Press, 1989. Originally published in French in 1987.

———. *On the Name.* Edited by T. Dutoit. Stanford, Calif.: Stanford University Press, 1995. This volume includes *Sauf le Nom (Post-Scriptum),* translated by J. Leavey, 33–85, originally published in French in 1993; and *Khôra,* translated by I. McLeod, 87–127, originally published in French in 1987.

———. "On a Newly Arisen Apocalyptic Tone in Philosophy." In *Raising the Tone of Philosophy: Late Essays by Immanuel Kant, Transformative Critique by Jacques Derrida,* edited by P. Fenves, 117–71. Baltimore: Johns Hopkins University Press, 1993. Originally published in French in 1983.

———. *Parages.* Paris: Galilée, 1986. (On M. Blanchot.)

———. "Passions: 'An Oblique Offering.'" In *Derrida: A Critical Reader,* edited by D. Wood, 5–35. Oxford, U.K.: Blackwell, 1992. Later published as *Passions.* Paris: Galilée, 1993.

———. *Positions.* Translated by A. Bass. London: Athlone, 1981. Originally published in French in 1972.

———. *Psyché: Invention de l'autre.* Paris: Galilée, 1987. This volume includes

"Psyché, Invention de l'autre," 11–61. English translation by C. Porter, in *Reading de Man Reading*, edited by L. Waters and W. Godzich, 25–65. Minneapolis: University of Minnesota Press, 1991.

"Des tours de Babel," 203–35. English translation in *Difference in Translation*, edited by J. F. Graham, 165–207. Ithaca, N.Y.: Cornell University Press, 1985.

"Comment ne pas parler. Dénégations," 535–95. English translation, "How to Avoid Speaking: Denials," by K. Frieden. In Coward and Foshay, eds. *Derrida and Negative Theology*, and in Budick and Iser, eds. *Languages of the Unsayable* (see below).

"Nombre de oui," 639–50. English Translation as "A Number of Yes," by B. Holmes. *Qui Parle* 2 (1988): 120–33.

―――. "Shibboleth: For Paul Celan." In *Word Traces: Readings of Paul Celan*, edited by A. Fioretos, 3–71. Baltimore: Johns Hopkins University Press, 1994. Originally published in French in 1986.

―――. "Le siècle et le pardon." Interview in *Le Monde des Débats*, December 1999, 10–17.

―――. *Specters of Marx: The State of the Debt, the Work of Mourning, and the New International*. Translated by D. Allison. Evanston, Ill.: Northwestern University Press, 1973. Originally published in French in 1993.

―――. *Speech and Phenomena, and Other Essays on Husserl's Theory of the Signs*. Translated by D. B. Allison. Evanston, Ill.: Northwestern University Press, 1973. This volume also includes the essay "Différance" (see above). Originally published in French as *La voix et le phénomène*, 1967.

―――. *Spurs: Nietzsche's Styles*. Translated by B. Harlow. Chicago: University of Chicago Press, 1979. Originally published in French in 1976.

―――. *Le toucher. Jean-Luc Nancy*. Paris: Galilée, 2000.

―――. *Ulysse gramophone. Deux mots pour Joyce*. Paris: Galilée, 1987. English translation as "Two Words for Joyce," by G. Bennington, in *Post-Structuralist Joyce: Essays from the French*, edited by D. Attridge and D. Ferrer, 145–159. Cambridge, U.K.: Cambridge University Press, 1984.

―――. *Writing and Difference*. Translated by A. Bass. Chicago: University of Chicago Press, 1978. Originally published in French in 1967. This volume includes Derrida's essay on Levinas, "Violence and Metaphysics," 79–153.

Heidegger, Martin. *Beiträge zur Philosophie*, vol. 65 of the *Gesamtausgabe*. Frankfurt am Main: Klostermann, 1989.

———. *Holzwege*. Frankfurt am Main: Klostermann, 1950. See especially "Nietzsches Wort: Gott ist tot," 193–247.

———. *Identität und Differenz*. Pfullingen: Neske, 1957. See especially "Die Onto-Theo-Logische Verfassung der Metaphysik," 35–73. English edition, *Identity and Difference*, translated by J. Stambaugh. New York: Harper & Row, 1974.

———. *Mein bisheriger Weg* (1937–1938). In *Gesamtausgabe*, vol. 66. Frankfurt am Main : Klostermann, 1976ff.

———. *The Principle of Reason*. Bloomington/Indianapolis: Indiana University Press, 1991.

———. *Sein und Zeit*. Tübingen: Niemeyer, 1986. Originally published in 1927.

———. Seminar of Zurich 1951 on a "Theology without Being." Edited by F. Fédier and D. Saatdjian. *Poésie* 13 (1980).

———. *Wegmarken*. Frankfurt am Main: Klostermann, 1978. This volume includes "Brief über den Humanismus."

Levinas, Emmanuel. *L'au-delà du verset*. Paris: Minuit, 1982. English edition, *Beyond the Verse: Talmudic Readings and Lectures*, translated by G. D. Mole. Bloomington/Indianapolis: Indiana University Press, 1994.

———. *Autrement qu'être ou au-delà de l'essence*. The Hague, The Netherlands: Nijhoff, 1974. English edition, *Otherwise Than Being or Beyond Essence*, translated by A. Lingis. The Hague, The Netherlands: Nijhoff/Dordrecht, The Netherlands: Kluwer, 1981.

———. *Basic Philosophical Writings*. Edited by A. Peperzak. Bloomington/Indianapolis: Indiana University Press, 1996.

———. *De Dieu qui vient à l'idée*. Paris: Vrin, 1982. English edition, *Of God Who Comes to Mind*, translated by B. Bergol. Stanford, Calif.: Stanford University Press, 1998.

———. *Dieu, la mort et le temps*. Paris: Grasset, 1993.

———. *Difficult Freedom: Essays on Judaism*. Translated by S. Hand. Baltimore: Johns Hopkins University Press, 1990. Originally published in French in 1963 and 1976 (rev. ed.).

———. *Du sacré au saint*. Paris: Minuit, 1977.

——— and others. *Emmanuel Levinas*. Edited by C. Chalier and M. Abensour. Paris: L'Herne, 1991

———. *Entre Nous: On Thinking-of-the-Other*. Translated by M. B.

Smith and B. Harshav. London: Athlone, 1998. Originally published in 1991.

———— and others. *L'éthique comme première philosophie*. Colloque de Cerisy-la-Salle 1986. Edited by J. Greisch and J. Rolland. Paris: Cerf, 1993. English edition, *Ethics as First Philosophy: The Significance of Emmanuel Levinas for Philosophy, Literature, and Religion*, edited by A. Peperzak. London: Routledge, 1995. This volume includes Hent de Vries. "Adieu, à dieu, a-dieu," 211–20.

————. *Existence and Existants*. Translated by A. Lingis. The Hague, The Netherlands: Nijhoff, 1978. Originally published in 1946.

————. *Outside the Subject*. Translated by M. B. Smith. Stanford, Calif.: Stanford University Press, 1994. Originally published in 1987.

————. "Pensée et prédication." In *The Self and the Other: The "Crisis of Man."* Analecta Husserliana. Edited by A.-T. Tymieniecka. Dordrecht, The Netherlands: D. Reidel, 1977.

————. *Totalité et Infini. Essai sur l'extériorité*. The Hague, The Netherlands: Nijhoff, 1961. English edition, *Totality and Infinity: An Essay on Exteriority*. Trans. A. Lingis. Pittsburgh: Duquesne University Press, 1969.

Marion, Jean-Luc. *Cartesian Questions: Method and Metaphysics*. Chicago: University of Chicago Press, 1999. Originally published in French in 1996.

————. *La croisée du visible*. Paris: Presses Universitaires de France, 1996.

————. "De connaître à aimer. L'éblouissement." *Communio* 3 (1978). Later republished as "L'évidence et l'éblouissement," in *Prolégomènes à la charité* (see below).

————. "De 'la mort de Dieu' aux noms divins: L'itinéraire de la métaphysique." In *L'être et Dieu*. Preface by Henri-Bernard Vergote. Paris: Cerf, 1986.

————. "La double idolâtrie. Remarques sur la différence ontologique et la pensée de Dieu." In *Heidegger et la question de Dieu*, edited by Kearney and O'Leary (see below).

————. *Étant donné—Essai d'une phénoménologie de la donation*. Paris: Presses Universitaires de France, 1997.

————. "Fragments sur l'idole et l'icône." *Revue de Métaphysique et de Morale* 84 (1979).

————. *God without Being: Hors-Texte*. Translated by T. A. Carlson, with a preface by D. Tracy. Chicago: University of Chicago Press, 1991. Originally published in French in 1981.

———. *L'idole et la distance. Cinq études*. Paris: Grasset, 1977.

———. "L'intentionnalité de l'amour." In *Les cahiers de la nuit surveillée* 3, "Emmanuel Levinas." Paris: Verdier, 1984. Later republished in *Prolégomènes à la charité* (see below).

———. *On Descartes' Metaphysical Prism: The Constitution and the Limits of Onto-Theo-logy in Cartesian Thought*. Translated by J.-L. Kosky. Chicago: University of Chicago Press, 1999. Originally published in French in 1986.

———. *Prolégomènes à la charité*. Paris: Éditions de la Différence, 1986.

———. *Reduction and Givenness: Investigations of Husserl, Heidegger, and Phenomenology*. Translated by T. A. Carlson. Evanston, Ill.: Northwestern University Press, 1998. Originally published in French in 1989.

———. "Réponses à quelques questions." *Revue de Métaphysique et de Morale* 96, no. 1 (1991): 65–76.

———. *Sur la théologie blanche de Descartes*. Paris: Presses Universitaires de France, 1981.

———. *Sur l'ontologie grise de Descartes*. Paris: Vrin, 1981. Originally published in 1975.

———. "Die Strenge der Liebe." In *Gott nennen. Phänomenologische Zugänge*, edited by B. Casper. Freiburg/Munich: Alber, 1981.

Nancy, Jean-Luc. "La déconstruction du christianisme." *Les études philosophiques* 4 (1998): 503–19.

———. *Être singulier pluriel*. Paris: Galilée, 1996.

———. *The Experience of Freedom*. Stanford, Calif.: Stanford University Press, 1994. Originally published in French in 1988.

———. *Hegel. L'inquiétude du négatif*. Paris: Hachette, 1997.

———. *The Inoperative Community*. Translated by P. Connor, L. Garbus, M. Holland, and S. Sawhney. Edited by P. Connor. Minneapolis: University of Minnesota Press, 1991. Originally published in French in 1986.

———. *Des lieux divins*. Mauvezin: T.E.R., 1987. English translation "Of Divine Places," by M. Holland. In *The Inoperative Community*, 110–50 (see above).

———. *Une pensée finie*. Paris: Galilée, 1990.

Nietzsche, Friedrich. *Beyond Good and Evil: Prelude to a Philosophy of the Future*. Translated by R. J. Hollingdale. Harmondsworth, U.K.: Penguin, 1975. Originally published in German in 1886.

―――. *Daybreak*. Translated by R. J. Hollingdale. Cambridge, U.K.: Cambridge University Press, 1982. Originally published in German in 1881.

―――. *Ecce Homo*. Translated by R. J. Hollingdale. Harmondsworth, U.K.: Penguin, 1980. Originally published in German in 1888.

―――. *The Gay Science*. Translated by W. Kaufmann. New York: Vintage, 1974. Originally published in German in 1882.

―――. *Human, All Too Human: A Book for Free Spirits*. Translated by M. Faber. Lincoln: University of Nebraska Press, 1984. Originally published in German in 1878.

―――. *Kritische Gesamtausgabe*. Edited by G. Colli and M. Montinari. New York/Berlin: De Gruyter, 1967ff.

―――. "On Truth and Lies in a Nonmoral Sense." In *Philosophy and Truth: Selections from Nietzsche's Notebooks of the Early 1870's*, edited by David Breazeale, 79–197. New Brunswick, N.J.: Humanities Press, 1979.

―――. *Thus Spoke Zarathustra: A Book for Everyone and Noone*. Translated by R. J. Hollingdale. Harmondsworth, U.K.: Penguin, 1975. Originally published in German in 1885.

―――. *"Twilight of the Idols" and "The Anti-Christ."* Translated by R. J. Hollingdale. Harmondsworth, U.K.: Penguin, 1972. Originally published in German in 1888.

―――. *The Will to Power*. Translated by W. Kaufmann and R. J. Hollingdale. New York: Vintage, 1968. Originally published in German in 1888.

Schmitt, Carl. *Die Diktatur. Von den Anfängen des modernen Souveränitätsgedankens bis zum proletarischen Klassenkampf*. Munich/Leipzig: Duncker & Humblot, 1921.

―――. "Die geschichtliche Struktur der heutigen Welt-Gegensatzes von Ost und West: Bemerkungen zu Ernst Jüngers Schrift 'Der gordische Knoten.' " In *Freundschaftliche Begegnungen. Festschrift für Ernst Jünger zum 60. Geburtstag*, edited by A. Mohler, 135–67. Frankfurt am Main: Klostermann, 1955.

―――. *Glossarium. Aufzeichnungen der Jahre 1947–1951*. Berlin: Duncker & Humblot, 1991.

―――. *Hugo Preuss. Sein Staatsbegriff und seine Stellung in der deutschen Staatslehre*. Tübingen: Mohr, 1930.

————. *Der Nomos der Erde*. Berlin: Duncker & Humblot, 1950.

————. *Politische Theologie. Vier Kapitel zur Lehre von der Souveränität*. Berlin: Duncker & Humblot, 1979. Originally published in 1922 and 1934.

————. *Politische Theologie II: Die Legende von der Erledigung jeder Politischen Theologie*. Berlin: Duncker & Humblot, 1970.

————. "Die Sichtbarkeit der Kirche: Eine scholastische Erwägung." *Summa. Eine Vierteljahrschrift* 2 (1917): 71–80.

Taubes, Jacob. *Abendländische Eschatologie*. Munich: Matthes & Seitz, 1991. Originally published in 1947.

————. *Ad Carl Schmitt: Gegenstrebige Fügung*. Berlin: Merve, 1987.

————. "Four Ages of Reason." *Archiv für Rechts- und Sozialphilosophie* 42 (1956): 1–14.

————. "Kultur und Ideologie." In *Spätkapitalismus oder Industriegesellschaft?*, edited by T. W. Adorno, 117–38. Stuttgart: Ferd. Enke, 1969.

————. "Notes on an Ontological Interpretation of Theology." *Review of Metaphysics* 2 (1949): 97–104.

————. *Die politische Theologie des Paulus. Vorträge, gehalten an den Forschungsstätte der evangelischen Studiengemeinschaft in Heidelberg* (February 23–27, 1987). Munich: Fink, 1993. This volume includes "Nachwort," by the editors, A. Assmann, J. Assman, and W.-D. Hartwich.

————. "The Realm of Paradox." *Review of Metaphysics* 7 (1953–1954): 482–91.

————, ed. *Religionstheorie und Politische Theologie*: Vol. 1, *Der Fürst dieser Welt. Carl Schmitt und die Folgen*; Vol. 2, *Gnosis und Politik*; Vol. 3, *Theokratie*. Munich: Fink, 1983–1987. Volume 1 includes "Statt einer Einleitung: Leviathan als sterblicher Gott. Zur Aktualität von Thomas Hobbes," 9–15. Volume 2 includes "Das Stählerne Gehäuse und der Exodus daraus oder der Streit um Marcion, einst und heute," 9–15.

————. "Virtue and Faith: A Study of Terminology in Western Ethics." *Philosophy East and West* 7 (1957): 27–32.

————. "Vom Adverb 'nichts' zum Substantiv das 'Nichts.' Überlegungen zu Heideggers Frage nach dem Nichts." In *Positionen der Negativität*, vol. 6 of *Poetik und Hermeneutik*, edited by H. Weinrich, 141–53. Munich: Fink, 1975.

————. *Vom Kult zu Kultur: Bausteine zu einer Kritik der historischen*

Vernunft. Gesammelte Aufsätze zur Religions- und Geistesge-schichte. Edited by A. Assmann, J. Assmann, W.-D. Hartwich, and W. Menninghaus. Munich: Fink, 1996. This volume includes "Theologie und politische Theorie" (1955).

————. "Von Fall zu Fall. Erkenntnistheoretische Reflexion zur Geschichte vom Sündenfall." In *Text und Applikation. Poetik und Hermeneutik*, vol. 9, 111–16. Munich: Fink, 1981.

————. "Zur Konjunktur des Polytheismus." In *Mythos und Moderne*, edited by K. H. Bohrer, 457–70. Frankfurt am Main: Suhrkamp, 1983.

4. PRESENCE OF NEGATIVE THEOLOGY IN (POST)MODERN
CULTURE AND THOUGHT

Balthasar, Hans Urs von. *Fächer der Style,* vol. 2 of *Herrlichkeit.* Einsiedeln: Johannes Verlag, 1962.

————. "Kénose." In *Dictionnaire de spritualité ascétique et mystique.* Paris: Beauchesne, 1974.

————. "Negative Theologie." In *Theologik*, vol. 2, 80–112. Einsiedeln: Johannes Verlag, 1985.

Budick, S., and W. Iser, eds. *Languages of the Unsayable: The Play of Negativity in Literary Theory.* New York: Columbia University Press, 1989. This volume includes J. Derrida, "How to Avoid Speaking: Denials," 3–70.

Buning, Marius. Review of recent publications on negative theology and philosophy. *Literature and Theology: An International Journal of Theory, Criticism, and Culture* 9, no. 1 (1995): 99–103.

Caputo, John D. "Mysticism and Transgression: Derrida and Meister Eckhart." In *Derrida and Deconstruction*, edited by H. J. Silverman. New York: Routledge, 1989.

Chrétien, Jean-Louis. *L'appel et la réponse.* Paris: Minuit, 1992.

————. "La réserve de l'être." In *Martin Heidegger*, edited by M. Chrétien, 233–60. Paris: L'Herne, 1983.

————. *Lueur du secret.* Paris: L'Herne, 1985.

————. *La voix nue. Phénoménologie de la promesse.* Paris: Minuit, 1990.

Coward, H., and T. Foshay, eds. *Derrida and Negative Theology.* Albany: State University of New York Press, 1992. This volume in-

cludes J. Derrida, "Aporias, Ways, and Voices (Post-Scriptum),"
283–323, and "How to Avoid Speaking: Denials," 25–72.

Guibal, F. "L'altérité de l'autre-autrement sur les traces de Jacques
Derrida." In *Altérités. J. Derrida et Pierre-Jean Labarrière*. Paris:
Osiris, 1986.

Jüngel, E. *Gott als Geheimnis der Welt*. Tübingen: J. C. B. Mohr (P.
Siebeck), 1977.

Law, David R. *Kierkegaard as Negative Theologian*. Oxford, U.K.:
Clarendon Press, 1994.

Rikhof, H. "Negative Theology." In *(Dis)continuity and (De)con-
struction: Reflections on the Meaning of the Past in Crisis Situations*, edited by J. Wissink, 154–71. Kampen, The Netherlands:
Kok, 1995.

Scharlemann, Robert P., ed. *Negation and Theology*. Charlottesville:
University Press of Virginia, 1992. See especially David E. Klemm,
"Open Secrets: Derrida and Negative Theology," 8–24.

Sells, Michael A. *Mystical Languages of Unsaying*. Chicago: University of Chicago Press, 1994.

Sneller, Rico. *Het Woord is schrift geworden. Derrida en de negatieve
theologie* (The Word has become Scripture: Derrida and negative
theology). Kampen, The Netherlands: Kok Agora, 1998.

Theunissen, Michael. *Negative Theologie der Zeit*. Frankfurt am
Main: Suhrkamp, 1991.

Weinrich, Harald, ed. *Positionen der Negativität*, vol. 6 of *Poetik und
Hermeneutik*. Munich: Fink, 1975.

5. General and Specific Philosophical and Theological Works
and Articles on the Relation of Religion and (Post)Modernity

Adriaanse, H. *Vom Christentum aus. Aufsätze und Vorträge zur Religionsphilosophie*. Kampen, The Netherlands: Kok Pharos, 1995

Agamben, G. *Homo sacer. Le pouvoir souverain et la vie nue*. Paris:
Seuil, 1997. Originally published in 1995.

Ahmed, A. S. *Postmodernity and Islam: Predicament and Promise*.
London: Routledge, 1992.

Alan, G. A. *Postmodern Philosophical Theology: The Barthian and
Heideggerian Origins of the Hermeneutic Dimension in the Con-*

temporary American Religious Thought of M. C. Taylor and J. D. Caputo. Ann Arbor, Mich.: U.M.I., 1991.

Altizer, Thomas, ed. *Towards a New Christianity: Readings in the Death of God Theology.* New York: Harcourt, Brace & World, 1967.

Andrews, Isolde. *Deconstructing Barth: A Study of the Complementary Methods in Karl Barth and Jacques Derrida.* Frankfurt: Lang, 1996.

Asad, Talal. *Genealogies of Religion: Discipline and Reason in Christianity and Islam.* Baltimore: Johns Hopkins University Press, 1993.

Assmann, J. *Politische Theologie zwischen Ägypten und Israel.* Munich: Carl Friedrich von Siemens Stiftung, 1992.

Bailey Gill, Carolyn, ed. *Bataille: Writing the Sacred.* New York: Routledge, 1995. Includes an English bibliography.

Bailly, Christoph. *Adieu. Essai sur la mort des dieux.* La Tour d'Aigues: L'Aube, 1993.

Benjamin, Walter. "Theologisch-Politisches Fragment." In *Schriften,* vol. 1, 511–13. Frankfurt am Main: Suhrkamp, 1955.

Benveniste, Émile. *Vocabulaire des institutions indo-européennes.* See especially volume 2: *Pouvoir, droit, religion.* Paris: Minuit, 1969. English edition, *Indo-European Language and Society,* translated by E. Palmer. Coral Gables, Fla.: University of Miami Press, 1973.

Bergson, Henri. *Les deux sources de la morale et la religion.* Paris: Presses Universitaires de France, 1951. Originally published in 1932.

Berry, Philippa, and Andrew Wernick, eds. *Shadow of Spirit: Postmodernism and Religion.* London: Routledge, 1992.

Berthold, L. "Wer Hält zur Zeit den Satan auf?—Zur Selbstglossierung Carl Schmitts." *Leviathan* 21 (1994): 285–99.

Blanchot, Maurice. "Du côté de Nietzsche." In *La part du feu,* 278–89. Paris: Gallimard, 1949:

———. *L'écriture du désastre.* Paris: Gallimard, 1980.

Bloch, Ernst. *Atheism in Christianity: The Religion of the Exodus and the Kingdom.* New York: Herder & Herder, 1972. Originally published in German in 1968.

Blumenberg, Hans. *Die Legitimität der Neuzeit.* Rev. ed. Frankfurt am Main: Suhrkamp, 1988 See especially the chapter on Carl

Schmitt: "Politische Theologie I und II." Originally published in 1966.

———. *Die Lesbarkeit der Welt*. Frankfurt am Main: Suhrkamp, 1981.

Böckenförde, E.-W. *Staat—Gesellschaft—Freiheit. Studien zur Staatstheorie und zum Verfassungsrecht*. Frankfurt am Main: Suhrkamp, 1972. Originally published in 1967. This volume includes "Die Entstehung des Staates als Vorgang der Säkularisation," 42–64.

———. "Politische Theorie und politische Theologie." In *Der Fürst dieser Welt*, edited by J. Taubes, 16–25. Munich: Fink, 1983.

Boer, Theo de. *De god van de filosofen en de god van Pascal. Op het grensgebied van filosofie en theologie*. Zoetermeer: Meinema, 1989.

Bolz, N., and W. Hübener, eds. *Spiegel und Gleichnis. Festschrift für Jacob Taubes*. Würzburg: Königshausen & Neumann, 1983. Includes a bibliography.

Brkic, Pero. *Martin Heidegger und die Theologie. Ein Thema in driefacher Fragestellung*. Mainz: Grünewald, 1994.

Caputo, John D. "Deconstruction and Catholicism: Advocating Discontinuity and Bedeviling the Tradition." In *(Dis)continuity and (De)construction: Reflections on the Meaning of the Past in Crisis Situations*, edited by J. Wissink, 12–34. Kampen, The Netherlands: Kok, 1995.

———. *Heidegger and Aquinas: An Essay on Overcoming Metaphysics*. New York: Fordham University Press, 1982.

———. *The Prayers and Tears of Jacques Derrida: Religion without Religion*. Bloomington/Indianapolis: Indiana University Press, 1997. Includes a select bibliography on Derrida and religion.

———. *Radical Hermeneutics: Repetition, Deconstruction, and the Hermeneutic Project*. Bloomington/Indianapolis: Indiana University Press, 1987.

Carr, Karen L. *The Banalization of Nihilism: Twentieth-Century Responses to Meaninglessness*. New York: State University of New York Press, 1992.

Certeau, Michel de. "The Fiction of History: The Writing of *Moïse et le monothéisme*." In *The Writing of History*, translated by T. Conley, 308–54. New York: Columbia University Press, 1988.

Chatelion-Counet, Patrick. *Over God zwijgen. Postmodern bijbel-*

lezen. Zoetermeer, The Netherlands: Meinema, 1998. Includes a bibliography on spirituality and postmodernity.

————. *De Sarcofaag van het Woord. Postmoderniteit, deconstructie en het Johannesevangelie.* Kampen, The Netherlands: Kok, 1995.

Ciapalo, R. T., ed. *Postmodernism and Christian Philosophy.* Mishawaka, Ind.: American Maritain Association, 1997.

Colpe, C. *Die Diskussion um das "Heilige."* Darmstadt: Wissenschaftliche Buchgesellschaft, 1977.

Cupitt, Don. *After God: The Future of Religion.* London: Phoenix, 1998. Originally published in 1997.

Dastur, Françoise. "Heidegger et la théologie."*Revue philosophique de Louvain* 2, no. 3 (1994): 226–45.

Delumeau, Jean. *La peur en occident.* Paris: Fayard, 1978.

Dufrenne, Mikel. "Pour une philosophie non-théologique." In *Le poétique,* 7–57. Paris: Presses Universitaires de France, 1973. Originally published in 1963.

Dupré, Louis. *The Other Dimension: A Search for the Meaning of Religious Attitudes.* New York: Doubleday, 1972.

————. *Passage to Modernity: An Essay in the Hermeneutics of Nature and Culture.* New Haven, Conn.: Yale University Press, 1993.

Ericksen, P. *Theologians under Hitler: Gerhard Kittel, Paul Althaus, and Emanuel Hirsch.* New Haven, Conn.: Yale University Press, 1985.

Feil, E. "Von 'der politischen Theologie' zur 'Theologie der Revolution'?" In *Diskussion zur "Theologie der Revolution,"* edited by E. Feil and R. Weith, 110–32. Munich: Kaiser, 1969.

Fellechner, E. L. "Zur biographischen und theologischen Entwicklung Petersons bis 1935. Eine Skizze." In *Der Monotheismus als politisches Problem? Erik Peterson und die Kritik der politischen Theologie,* edited by A. Schindler, 76–120. Gütersloh: Mohn, 1978.

Figuier, R., ed. *Dieux en sociétés. Le religieux et le politique,* vol. 127 of *Autrement* (series "Mutations"), February 1992.

Ford, David F. "Hosting a Dialogue: Jüngel and Levinas on God, Self, and Language." In *The Possibilities of Theology,* edited by J. Webster, 23–59. Edinburgh: Clark, 1994.

————, ed. *The Modern Theologians: An Introduction to Christian Theology in the 20th Century.* 2nd rev. ed. Oxford, U.K.: Blackwell, 1997. See especially Graham Ward, "Postmodern Theology," 585–601.

Gadamer, H.-G. "Martin Heidegger und die Marburger Theologie." In *Heidegger. Perspektiven zur Deutung seines Werkes*, edited by O. Pöggeler. Königstein: Athenäum Verlag, 1984.

Gasché, Rodolphe. *Inventions of Difference: On Jacques Derrida.* Cambridge, Mass.: Harvard University Press, 1994. See especially "The Eclipse of Difference," 82–106, and "God, for Example," 150–70.

Gauchet, Marcel. *Le désenchantement du monde. Une histoire politique de la religion.* Paris: Gallimard, 1985.

Gellner, Ernest. *Postmodernism, Reason, and Religion.* New York: Routledge, 1992.

Gisel, Pierre, and Patrick Evrard, eds. *La théologie en postmodernité.* Geneva: Labor et Fides, 1996. Includes an elaborate "Essai bibliographique," 429–76; see especially the sections "Théologies et religions en postmodernité" and "Critique biblique," 450–58, and the sections "Derrida, déconstruction et théologie ou religion" and "Déconstruction et critique biblique," 466–76.

Goud, Johan. *Levinas en Barth. Een godsdienstwijsgerige en ethische vergelijking.* Amsterdam: Rodopi, 1984.

Griffin, David Ray. *God and Religion in the Postmodern World: Essays in Postmodern Theology.* Albany: State University of New York Press, 1989.

Halbertal, Moshe, and Avishai Margalit. *Idolatry.* Translated by N. Goldblum. Cambridge, Mass.: Harvard University Press, 1992.

Handelman, Susan. *Fragments of Redemption.* Bloomington/Indianapolis: Indiana University Press, 1991.

———. "Jacques Derrida and the Heretic Hermeneutics." In *Displacement: Derrida and After*, edited by M. Krupnick, 98–129. Bloomington/Indianapolis: Indiana University Press, 1983.

———. *The Slayers of Moses: The Emergence of Rabbinic Interpretation in Modern Literary Theory.* Albany: State University of New York Press, 1982.

Hart, Kevin. *The Trespass of the Sign: Deconstruction, Theology, and Philosophy.* Cambridge, U.K.: Cambridge University Press, 1989 (revised New York: Fordham University Press, 2000).

Heyde, Ludwig. *The Weight of Finitude: On the Philosophical Question of God.* Translated by A. Harmsen and W. Desmond. Albany: State University of New York Press, 1999. Originally published in Dutch in 1994.

————. *De maat van de mens. Over autonomie, transcendentie en sterfelijkheid*. Amsterdam: Boom, 2000.

Hofmannsthal, Hugo von. *The Lord Chandos Letter*. Translated by R. Stockman. Vermont: University Press of New England, 1986.

Houdijk, R. "De mens onttroond? Het postmoderne denken en de theologie." *Tijdschrift voor Theologie* 30 (1990): 276–96.

Hübener, W. "Carl Schmitt und Hans Blumenberg oder über Kette und Schuss in der historischen Textur der Moderne." In *Der Fürst dieser Welt*, edited by J. Taubes, 57–76. Munich: Fink, 1983.

Huxley, Francis. *The Way of the Sacred*. London: Bloomsbury Books, 1989.

Ingraffia, Brian D. *Postmodern Theory and Biblical Theology: Vanquishing God's Shadow*. Cambridge, U.K.: Cambridge University Press, 1995.

Janicaud, Dominique. *Le tournant théologique de la phénoménologie française*. Combas: Éditions de l'Éclat, 1991. English translation, *Phenomenology and the Theological Turn: The French Debate*, translated by Bernard Prusak, New York: Fordham University Press, 2000.

Jespers, F. P. M. "Sporen van Derrida bij de Noordamerikaanse theologen." *Tijdschrift voor Theologie* 30 (1990): 173–83.

Kal, Victor. "Deernis en toewijding. Ethiek en religieuze cultuur bij Emmanuel Levinas." *De Uil van Minerva* 7 (1991).

Kant, Immanuel. *Die Religion innerhalb der Grenzen der blossen Vernunft*, vol. 7 of *Werke in zehn Bänden*. Edited by W. Weischedel. Darmstadt: Wissenschaftliche Buchgesellschaft, 1983. English edition, *Religion within the Boundaries of Mere Reason*, translated by G. di Giovanni. In the *Cambridge Edition of the Works of Immanuel Kant*, edited by P. Gruyer and A. W. Wood. Cambridge, U.K.: Cambridge University Press, 1996.

Kate, Laurens ten. *De lege plaats. Revoltes tegen het instrumentele leven in Bataille's atheologie* (The empty place: Revolts against instrumental life in Bataille's atheology). Kampen, The Netherlands: Kok Agora, 1994.

————. "Randgänge der Theologie: Prolegomena einer 'Theologie der Differenz' im Ausgang von Derrida und Barth." *Zeitschrift für dialektische Theologie* 14, no. 1 (1998): 9–31.

Kearney, R., and J. S. O'Leary, eds. *Heidegger et la question de Dieu*. Paris: Grasset, 1980.

Kellendonk, Frans. *Mystiek lichaam. Een geschiedenis.* In *Het complete werk,* 291–451. Amsterdam: Meulenhoff, 1992.

Kemp, Peter. "L'éthique au lendemain des victoires des athéismes. Réflexions sur la philosophie de Jacques Derrida." *Revue de théologie et de philosophie* 111 (1979): 105–21.

Klemm, David E. "Towards a Rhetoric of Postmodern Theology through Barth and Heidegger." *Journal of the American Academy of Religion* 55, no. 3 (1987): 443–69.

Klimek, Nicolaus. *Der Begriff "Mystik" in der Theologie Karl Barths.* Paderborn: Bonifatius, 1990.

Kooi, C. van der. *De denkweg van de jonge Karl Barth. Een analyse van de ontwikkeling van zijn theologie in de jaren 1909–1927 in het licht van de vraag naar de geloofsverantwoording.* Amsterdam: V.U. Press, 1985.

Korsch, D. "Die Moderne als Krise. Zum theologischen Begriffs einer geschichtsphilosophischer Kategorie." *Zeitschrift für dialektische Theologie* 11, no. 1 (1995): 43–59.

———. "Postmoderne Theologie? Ein aktueller Blick auf die *Kirchliche Dogmatik* Karl Barths." *Zeitschrift für dialektische Theologie* 4, no. 2 (1989): 241–58.

Koslowski, Peter, Robert Spaemann, and Reinhard Low, eds. *Diskussion über Kirche und Moderne. Moderne oder Postmoderne?* Weinheim: VCH Verlagsgesellschaft, 1986.

Kristeva, Julia. *Au commencement était l'amour. Psychanalyse et foi.* Paris: Hachette, 1985.

Kuitert, Harry M. *De mensvormigheid Gods. Een dogmatisch-hermeneutische studie over de antropomorfismen van de Heilige Schrift.* Kampen, The Netherlands: Kok, 1969.

Lacan, Jacques. *Le séminaire. Livre VII: L'éthique de la psychanalyse.* Edited by J.-A. Miller. Paris: Seuil, 1986. See especially chapter 13: "La mort de dieu."

Leiris, Michel. "Le sacré dans la vie quotidienne." In *Le collège de sociologie (1937–1939),* edited by D. Hollier. Paris: Gallimard, 1979.

Lowe, Walter. *Theology and Difference: The Wound of Reason.* Bloomington: Indiana University Press, 1993.

Löwith, Karl. *Meaning in History: The Theological Implications of the Philosophy of History.* Chicago: University of Chicago Press, 1949.

Maggie Kim, C. W., S. M. St. Ville, and S. M. Simonaitis, eds. *Trans-*

figurations: Theology and the French Feminists. Minneapolis: Fortress, 1993.

Marquard, O. "Politischer Polytheismus—auch eine politische Theologie." In *Der Fürst dieser Welt*, edited by J. Taubes, 77–84. Munich: Fink, 1983.

Maurer, R. "Chiliasmus und Gesellschaftsreligion. Thesen zur politischen Theologie." In *Der Fürst dieser Welt*, edited by J. Taubes, 117–35. Munich: Fink, 1983.

Mauthner, Fritz. *Der Atheismus und seine Geschichte im Abendlande.* 4 vols. Stuttgart/Berlin: Deutsche Verlags-Anstalt, 1922.

Meier, H. "Politische Theologie? Einwände eines Laien." In *Diskussion zur "politischen Theologie,"* edited by H. Peukert, 1–25. Munich/Mainz: Grünewald, 1969.

———. "Was ist Politische Theologie?" In *Politische Theologie zwischen Ägypten und Israel*, edited by J. Assmann, 7–19. Munich: Carl Friedrich von Siemens Stiftung, 1992.

Metz, J. B. *Glaube in Geschichte und Gesellschaft.* Mainz: Grünewald, 1977.

———. *Zur Theologie der Welt.* Mainz/Munich: Grünewald and Kaiser, 1968.

Millbank, John. *Theology and Social Theory: Beyond Secular Reason.* Oxford, U.K.: Blackwell, 1990.

Miskotte, Kornelis Heiko. *Wenn die Götter schweigen. Vom Sinn des Alten Testaments.* Translated by H. Stoevesandt. Munich: Kaiser, 1966. Originally published in Dutch in 1956.

Moore, Stephen D. *Poststructuralism and the New Testament: Derrida and Foucault at the Foot of the Cross.* Minneapolis: Fortress, 1994.

Moyaert, Paul. *De mateloosheid van het christendom. Over naastenliefde, betekenisincarnatie en mystieke liefde.* Nijmegen: SUN, 1999.

Nault, François. *Derrida et la théologie: Dire Dieu après la déconstruction.* (Montreal: Médiaspaul and Paris: Cerf, 2000).

Ochs, Robert. *Verschwendung. Die Theologie im Gespräch mit Georges Bataille.* Frankfurt am Main: Lang, 1995.

Otto, Rudolph. *Das Heilige. Über das Irrationale in der Idee des Göttlichen und sein Verhältnis zum Rationalen.* Munich: Beck, 1997. Originally published in 1917. English edition, *The Idea of the Holy: An Inquiry into the Non-Rational Factor in the Idea of the Divine and Its Relation to the Rational*, translated by J. W. Harvey. Oxford, U.K.: Oxford University Press, 1958.

Overbeck, Franz. *Christentum und Kultur. Gedanken und Anmerkungen zur modernen Theologie.* Edited by A. Bernouilli, 1919. Reprint, Darmstadt, The Netherlands: Wissenschaftliche Buchgesellschaft, 1973.

Patoka, Jan. *Heretical Essays in the Philosophy of History.* Translated by E. Kohák, edited by J. Dodd. Chicago: Open Court, 1996. Originally published in Czech in 1975.

Peterson, E. "Der Monotheismus als politisches Problem." In *Theologische Traktate.* Munich: Kösel, 1951. Originally published in 1935.

Robinson, J. M., and J. B. Cobb. *The Late Heidegger and Theology.* New York: Harper & Row, 1963.

Robinson, John A. T. *Honest to God.* London: SCM Press, 1963.

Rosenzweig, Franz. *The Star of Redemption.* London: Routledge & Kegan Paul, 1970. Originally published in German in 1921.

Schaeffler, R. *Religionsphilosophie.* Freiburg/Munich: Alber, 1983.

Scharlemann, Robert P. "The No to Nothing and the Nothing to Know: Barth and Tillich, and the Possibility of a Theological Science." *Journal of the American Academy of Religion* 55 (1987): 57–72.

———. *Theology at the End of the Century: A Dialogue on the Postmodern.* Charlottesville: University of Virginia Press, 1989.

Scheler, Max. *Vom Ewigen Im Menschen.* Bern: Franke Verlag, 1968. Originally published in 1921.

Schelling, F. W. *Philosophie der Offenbarung*, vol. 13 of *Sämtliche Werke.* Stuttgart/Hamburg: Cotta, 1856–1861.

Schellong, D. "Jenseits von politischer Theologie und unpolitischer Theologie. Zum Ansatz der 'dialektischen Theologie.'" In *Der Fürst dieser Welt*, edited by J. Taubes, 292–315. Munich: Fink, 1983.

Scheltens, D. "Middeleeuwse illuminatieleer en het denken van Heidegger." *Tijdschrift voor Filosofie* 21 (1969): 416–40.

Siebert, R. J. "From Conservative to Critical Political Theology." In *The Influence of the Frankfurt School on Contemporary Theology: Critical Theory and the Future of Religion*, Toronto Studies in Theology 64, edited by A. J. Reimer, 147–219. Lewiston/Queenston/Lampeter: Mellen, 1992.

Smith, Jonathan Z. "A Matter of Class: Taxonomies of Religion." *Harvard Theological Review* 89, no. 4 (1996): 387–403.

Smith, Steven C. *The Argument to the Other: Reason beyond Reason in the Thought of Karl Barth and Emmanuel Levinas.* Chico, Calif.: Scholars Press, 1983.

————. *In the Margins of Deconstruction: Jewish Conceptions of Ethics in Emmanuel Levinas and Jacques Derrida.* Dordrecht, The Netherlands: Kluwer, 1998.

Sokolowski, R. *The God of Faith and Reason: Foundations of Christian Theology.* Notre Dame, Ind.: University of Notre Dame Press, 1982.

Sontag, Susan. *Tradities van het nieuwe, of: Moeten wij modern zijn?* (Traditions of the new, or: Must we be modern?). Huizinga Lecture for 1989. Amsterdam: Bert Bakker, 1990.

Stacy Johnson, William. *The Mystery of God: Karl Barth and the Postmodern Foundations of Theology.* Louisville, Kent.: Westminster J. Knox Press, 1997.

Taylor, Charles. *Sources of the Self: The Making of Modern Identity.* Cambridge, U.K.: Cambridge University Press, 1989.

Taylor, Mark C. *Deconstructing Theology.* New York: Crossroads, 1982.

————. *Erring: A Postmodern A/theology.* Chicago: University of Chicago Press, 1984.

————. *Nots.* Chicago: University of Chicago Press, 1993.

Tilley, Terrence W., and others. *Postmodern Theologies: The Challenge of Religious Diversity.* Maryknoll, N.Y.: Orbis Books, 1995.

Tillich, Paul. *Biblische Religion und die Frage nach dem Sein.* Stuttgart: Evangelisches Verlagswerk, 1956.

Valentin, J. *Atheismus in der Spur Gottes. Theologie nach J. Derrida.* Mainz: Grünewald, 1997.

Vries, Hent de. *Philosophy and the Turn to Religion.* Baltimore: Johns Hopkins University Press, 1999.

————. "Le schibboleth de l'éthique. Derrida avec Celan." In *L'éthique du don. Jacques Derrida et la pensée du don*, Colloque de Royaumont, December 1990, edited by J.-M. Rabaté and M. Wetzel, 212–38. Paris: Métailié-Transition, 1992.

————. *Theologie im pianissimo. Zwischen Rationalität und Dekonstruktion. Zur Aktualität der Denkfiguren Adornos und Levinas.* Kampen, The Netherlands: Kok, 1989.

Vroom, H. M. *Religions and the Truth: Philosophical Reflections and Perspectives.* Translated by J. W. Rebel. Grand Rapids, Mich.: Eerdmans, 1989. Originally published in Dutch in 1988.

Wallace, M. I., ed. *Refiguring the Sacred: Religion, Narrative, and Imagination.* Minneapolis: Fortress, 1995.

Ward, Graham. *Barth, Derrida, and the Language of Theology.* Cambridge, U.K.: Cambridge University Press, 1995.

―――, ed. *The Postmodern God: A Theological Reader.* Oxford, U.K.: Blackwell, 1997.

―――. "Theology and the Crisis of Representation." In *Literature and Theology at Century's End,* edited by G. Salyer and R. Detweiler, 131–58. Atlanta: Scholars Press, 1995.

Webb, Stephen H. *The Gifting God: A Trinitarian Ethics of Excess.* Oxford, U.K.: Oxford University Press, 1996.

―――. *Re-figuring Theology: The Rhetoric of Karl Barth.* Albany: State University of New York Press, 1991.

Weischedel, Wilhelm. *Der Gott der Philosophen. Grundlegung einer philosophischen Theologie im Zeitalter des Nihilismus.* Darmstadt, The Netherlands: Wissenschaftliche Buchgesellschaft, 1983.

Westphal, M. "Nietzsche as Theological Resource." *Modern Theology* 13, no. 2 (1997): 213–26.

Winquist, Charles E. *Desiring Theology.* Chicago: University of Chicago Press, 1995.

―――. *Epiphanies of Darkness: Deconstruction and Theology.* Chicago: University of Chicago Press, 1986.

Wissink, Jozef. "Providentie, predestinatie en praktijk." In *De praktische Thomas. Thomas van Aquino; de consequenties van zijn theologie voor hedendaags gedrag.* KTUU series *Theologie en samenleving* 10. Hilversum: Gooi en Sticht, 1987.

Wit, Han de. *Contemplatieve psychologie.* Kampen, The Netherlands: Kok, 1987.

Wit, Theo de. "Katholicisme, deconstructie en democratie." In *Katholieken in de moderne tijd,* edited by E. Borgman, B. van Dijk, and T. Salemink, 195–217. Zoetermeer: De Horstink, 1995.

Wyschogrod, Edith. *Saints and Postmodernism: Revisioning Moral Philosophy.* Chicago: University of Chicago Press, 190.

Zarader, Marlène. *La dette impensée: Heidegger et l'héritage hébraïque.* Paris: Seuil, 1990.

6. OTHER WORKS AND ARTICLES OF RELEVANCE

Arendt, Hannah. *The Human Condition*. Chicago: University of Chicago Press, 1958.

Auerbach, Erich. *Mimesis: The Representation of Reality in Western Literature*. Translated by H. R. Trask. Princeton, N.J.: Princeton University Press, 1971. Originally published in German in 1946.

Auster, Paul. *Moon Palace*. Boston: Faber & Faber, 1987.

Benjamin, Walter. *Briefe*. Edited by G. Scholem and T. W. Adorno. Frankfurt am Main: Suhrkamp, 1966.

―――. *Gesammelte Schriften*. Frankfurt am Main: Suhrkamp, 1972–1989.

―――. "Theses on the Philosophy of History." In *Illuminations*, edited and with an introduction by H. Arendt, 255–66. New York: Harcourt, Brace & World, 1968. Originally published in German in *Schriften*, vol. 1.2, 693–704. Frankfurt am Main: Suhrkamp, 1955.

―――. *Ursprung des deutschen Trauerspiels*. Frankfurt am Main: Suhrkamp, 1963. Originally published in 1928.

Berdyaev, N., and others. *Wegzeichen. Zur Krise der russischen Intelligenz*. Translated by K. Schlögel. Frankfurt am Main: Eichborn Verlag, 1990. Originally published in Russian.

Bernasconi, Robert, and David Wood, eds. *Derrida and Différance*. Evanston, Ill.: Northwestern University Press, 1988. Includes an interview with Derrida, 71–83.

Berns, Egide. "Derrida's huishouding." *Algemeen Nederlands Tijdschrift voor Wijsbegeerte* (1990): 269–81.

Biser, Eugen, and others. *Nietzsche aujourd'hui:* Vol. 1: *Intensités;* Vol. 2: *Passions*. Paris: Union Générale d'Editions/"10/18," 1973.

Blanchot, Maurice. *Faux pas*. Paris: Gallimard, 1943.

Booth, Wayne. *The Rhetoric of Fiction*. Harmondsworth, U.K.: Penguin, 1987.

Bulhof, Ilse N. *The Language of Science: A Study of the Relationship between Literature and Science in the Perspective of a Hermeneutical Ontology, with a Case Study of Darwin's "The Origin of Species."* Leiden, The Netherlands: Brill, 1992.

―――. *Van inhoud naar houding. Een nieuwe visie op filosoferen in een pluralistische cultuur*. Kampen, The Netherlands: Kok Agora, 1995.

Cahen, Didier. "Entretien avec Jacques Derrida." *Digraphe* 42 (1987): 14–27.

Caputo, John D, ed.. *Deconstruction in a Nutshell: A Conversation with Jacques Derrida*. New York: Fordham University Press, 1997.

Celan, Paul. *Lichtzwang*. Frankfurt am Main: Suhrkamp, 1997. Originally published in 1970.

———. *Die Niemandsrose*. Frankfurt am Main: Suhrkamp, 1996. Originally published in 1963.

Cicero. *De natura deorum*. Latin/English edition, translated by H. Rackham. Cambridge, Mass.: Harvard University Press, 1979.

Comay, Rebecca. "Gifts without Presents: Economies of 'Experience' in Bataille and Heidegger." *Yale French Studies* 78 (1990): 66–89.

Courtine, Jean-François. *Suarez et le système de la métaphysique*. Paris: Presses Universitaires de France, 1990.

Creech, J. P. Kamuf, and J. Todd, eds. "Deconstruction in America: An Interview with Jacques Derrida." *Critical Exchange* 17 (Winter 1985): 1–33.

Delacampagne, Christian. Introduction to "Philosophies." In *Entretiens avec "Le Monde,"* vol. 1, 78–90. Paris: Éditions de la Découverte, 1984–1985.

Deleuze, Gilles. *Nietzsche and Philosophy*. London: Athlone, 1986. Originally published in French in 1967.

Descartes, René. *Discours de la méthode*. Edited by É. Gilson. Paris: Vrin, 1976.

———. *Meditationes de cognitione, veritate, et ideis*. Edited by C. J. Gerhardt. In *Die philosophischen Schriften*, vol. 4. Hildesheim: Olms, 1978.

———. *Oeuvres*. Edited by Adam-Tannery, revised by P. Costabel and B. Rochot. Paris: Vrin, 1966ff.

Dews, Peter. *Logics of Disintegration: Poststructuralist Thought and the Claims of Critical Theory*. London: Verso, 1987.

Donato, E., and R. Macksey, eds. *The Structuralist Controversy: The Languages of Criticism and the Sciences of Man*. Baltimore: Johns Hopkins University Press, 1972.

Eco, Umberto. *The Name of the Rose*. Translated by W. Weaver. London: Picador, 1983.

Erasmus of Rotterdam. *In Praise of Folly*. Translated by R. H. Hudson. Princeton, N.J.: Princeton University Press, 1941.

Foucault, Michel. *The Order of Things: An Archeology of Human Sciences.* New York: Vintage, 1994. Originally published in French in 1966.

———. "A Preface to Transgression." In *Language, Counter-Memory, Practice: Selected Essays and Interviews,* edited by D. F. Bouchard, translated by D. F. Bouchard and S. Simon, 19–52. Ithaca, N.Y.: Cornell University Press, 1977. Originally published in French in 1963. Later published in *Dits et écrits,* vol. 1, 233–50. Paris: Gallimard, 1994.

———. "The Thought from Outside." Translated by B. Massumi. In *Foucault, Blanchot,* 9–58. New York: Zone Books, 1987. Originally published as "La pensée du Dehors," in *Critique* 229 (1966): 523–46.

Frank, Manfred. "Kleiner (Tübinger) Programmentwurf." In *Frankfurter Rundschau,* March 5, 1988.

———. *Was ist Neostrukturalismus?* Frankfurt am Main: Suhrkamp, 1984.

Gasché, Rodolphe. *The Tain of the Mirror: Derrida and the Philosophy of Reflection.* Cambridge, Mass.: Harvard University Press, 1986.

Habermas, Jürgen. *Die philosophische Diskurs der Moderne.* Frankfurt am Main: Suhrkamp, 1985. English edition, *Philosophical Discourse of Modernity.* Oxford, U.K.: Blackwell, 1988.

Hamann, J. G. "Konxompax." Edited by J. Nadler. In *Sämtliche Werke,* vol. 3. Vienna: Herder, 1950.

Harvey, Irene E. *Derrida an the Economy of Différance.* Bloomington/Indianapolis: Indiana University Press, 1986.

Hegel, G. W. F. *Vorlesungen über die Geschichte der Philosophie.* In *Vorlesungen. Ausgewählte Nachschriften und Manuskripte,* edited by P. Garniron and W. Jaeschke. Hamburg: Meiner, 1983ff.

———. *Vorlesungen über die Geschichte der Philosophie.* In *Werke,* von 1832–1835. Rev. edition by E. Moldenhauer and K. Markus Michel. Frankfurt am Main: Suhrkamp, 1971.

Huizinga, Johan. *The Waning of the Middle Ages.* London: Edwin Arnold, 1976. Originally published in Dutch in 1919.

———. *Erasmus.* In *Verzamelde Werken,* vol. 6, 3–194. Haarlem: Tjeenk Willink, 1950.

Husserl, Edmund. *L'origine de la géometrie.* Translated by J. Derrida. Paris: P.U.F., 1974. Originally published in 1962.

IJsseling, Samuel. *Mimesis. Over schijn en zijn.* Baarn, The Netherlands: Ambo, 1990.

Jabès, Edmond. *The Book of Questions.* Middletown, Conn.: Wesleyan University Press, 1983. Originally published in French in 1963–1965.

Jacobi, Friedrich Heinrich. *The Main Philosophical Writings and the Novel "Allwill."* Translated from German by G. di Giovanni. Montreal: McGill-Queen's University Press, 1994.

Jay, Martin. *Downcast Eyes: The Denigration of Vision in Twentieth-Century Thought.* Berkeley/Los Angeles: University of California Press, 1993.

Kant, Immanuel. *Critique of Practical Reason.* Edited by L. W. Beck. Chicago: University of Chicago Press, 1949.

———. *Critique of Pure Reason.* Edited by P. Guyer and A. W. Wood. Cambridge, U.K.: Cambridge University Press, 1998.

———. "Idee zu einer Geschichte in weltbürgerlicher Absicht." In *Akademie-Ausgabe,* vol. 8.

———. *Prolegomena zu einer jeden künftigen Metaphysik, die als Wissenschaft wird auftreten können.* Edited by K. Vorländer. Hamburg: Meiner Verlag, 1993. Originally published in 1783. English edition, *Prolegomena to Any Future Metaphysics That Will Be Able to Come Forward as Science.* Translated by G. Hatfield. Cambridge, U.K.: Cambridge University Press, 1997.

Kearney, Richard. *Dialogues with Contemporary Thinkers: The Phenomenological Heritage.* Manchester, U.K.: Manchester University Press, 1984.

Kofman, Sarah. *Explosion.* Paris: Galilée, 1993.

Lacoue-Labarthe, P. *Le sujet de la philosophie.* Paris: Aubier-Flammarion, 1979.

Laruelle, F. *Les philosophes de la différence. Introduction critique.* Paris: Presses Universitaires de France, 1986.

Lyotard, Jean-François. *Le différend.* Paris: Minuit, 1983. English edition, *The Differend: Phrases in Dispute.* Translated by G. Van Den Abbeele. Minneapolis: University of Minnesota Press, 1988.

———. *L'inhumain. Causeries sur le temps.* Paris: Galilée, 1988. English edition, *The Inhumane: Reflections on Time.* Translated by R. Bowlby. Stanford, Calif.: Stanford University Press, 1991.

MacIntyre, A. *Three Rival Versions of Moral Enquiry.* London: Duckworth, 1990.

Malebranche, Nicolas. *Entretiens sur la métaphysique et la religion*, vol. 12 of *Oeuvres complètes*. Edited by André Robinet. Paris: Vrin, 1965.

―――. *Recherche de la vérité*, vol. 2 of *Oeuvres complètes*. Edited by André Robinet and Geneviève Rodis-Lewis. Paris: Vrin, 1972.

Marquet, J.-F. *Singularité et événement*. Grenoble: Millon, 1995.

Mortley, Raoul. *French Philosophers in Conversation*. London: Routledge, 1991.

Pascal, Blaise. "Le mémorial." In *Oeuvres complètes*, edited by L. Lafuma, with an introduction by H. Gouhier. Paris: Seuil, 1963.

Petersen, P. *Geschichte der aristotelischen Philosophie im protestantischen Deutschland*. Stuttgart: Friedrich Fromann, 1962. Originally published in 1921.

Plat, Jan. "De ethiek van Kant in de kritische werken." In *Beschouwingen over de ethiek van Kant*. Nijmegen: Nijmegen University Press, 1983.

Plato. *Timaeus, Critias, Cleitophon, Menexenus, Epistles*. Greek/English translation by R. G. Bury. Cambridge, Mass.: Harvard University Press/London: Heinemann, 1967.

Rawie, Jean-Pierre. *Woelig stof*. Amsterdam: Bert Bakker, 1989.

Ricoeur, Paul. *Oneself as Another*. Translated by K. Bramley. Chicago: University of Chicago Press, 1992. Originally published in French in 1990.

Rilke, Rainer Maria. *Selected Works*. Translated by J. B. Leishman. London: Hogarth Press, 1976.

Rüthers, B. *Carl Schmitt im Dritten Reich*. 2nd rev. ed. Munich: Beck, 1990.

Ryklin, Mikhail K. "Bodies of Terror: Theses toward a Logic of Violence." *New Literary History* 24 (1993): 51–74.

Saussure, Ferdinand de. *Course in General Linguistics*. Edited by C. Bally and A. Sechehaye. Translated by R. Harris. La Salle, Ind.: Open Court, 1986.

Schelling, F. W. *Zur Geschichte der neueren Philosophie*, vol. 10 of *Sämtliche Werke*. Stuttgart/Hamburg: Cotta, 1856–1861.

Sloterdijk, Peter. *Critique of Cynical Reason*. London: Verso, 1988. Originally published in German in 1983.

―――. *Das Judentum in der Rechtswissenschaft*. Berlin: Deutscher Recht-Verlag, 1936.

Spinoza, Baruch de. *Ethica*. In *Opera*. Edited by G. Gawlick, F. Niewöhner, and K. Blumenstock. Darmstadt, The Netherlands: Wissenschaftliche Buchgesellschaft, 1989.

Steiner, George. *Real Presences: Is There Anything in What We Say?* Boston: Faber & Faber, 1989.

Steunebrink, Gerrit. "Kunst en reflexiviteit: Kant, Hegel en Adorno." In *Reflexiviteit en Metafysica. Feestbundel voor Jan Hollack.* Delft, The Netherlands: Eburon, 1987.

———. *Kunst, utopie en werkelijkheid.* Tilburg: Tilburg University Press, 1991.

Stoekl, Allan, ed. *Yale French Studies* 78 (1990), "On Bataille."

Surya, Michel. *Georges Bataille. La mort à l'oeuvre* (Biography). Paris: Gallimard, 1992. Originally published in 1987.

Tilliette, X. *L'absolu de la philosophie: Essais sur Schelling.* Paris: Presses Universitaires de France, 1987.

———. "Argument ontologique et ontothéologique. Notes conjointes. Schelling et l'argument ontologique."*Archives de Philosophie* 26, no. 1 (1963).

Velthoven, T. van. "Teken, waarheid, macht." In *De intersubjectiviteit van het zijn.* Kampen, The Netherlands: Kok Agora, 1988.

Visker, Rudi. *Truth and Singularity: Taking Foucault into Phenomenology.* Dordrecht, The Netherlands: Kluwer, 1999.

Vollrath, E. "Die Gliederung der Metaphysik in eine *Metaphysica generalis* und eine *Metaphysica specialis.*" *Zeitschrift für philosophische Forschung* 16, no. 2 (1962).

Vroman, Leo. *262 gedichten.* Amsterdam: Querido, 1974.

———. *God en Godin.* Amsterdam: Querido, 1967.

Warin, F. *Nietzsche et Bataille.* Paris: Presses Universitaires de France, 1994.

Weber, S. "Taking Exception to Decision: Walter Benjamin and Carl Schmitt." In *Enlightenments: Encounters between Critical Theory and Contemporary French Thought,* edited by H. Kunneman and H. de Vries, 141–61. Kampen, The Netherlands: Kok Agora, 1993.

Wittgenstein, Ludwig. *Tractatus Logico-Philosophicus.* Translated by C. K. Ogden. London: Routledge & Kegan Paul, 1955. Originally published in 1920.

Wundt. M. *Die deutsche Schulmetaphysik des 17. Jahrhunderts.* Tübingen: J. C. B. Mohr (Siebeck), 1939.

INDEX OF NAMES AND TITLES

GENERAL INDEX

ABOUT THE AUTHORS

Bert Blans received his doctorate from the University of Leuven, Belgium, in 1975; his dissertation was entitled *De taal in de filosofie van Schelling* (Language in Schelling's philosophy). Today he is a professor of philosophy appointed by the Radboud Foundation at the University of Wageningen, The Netherlands; his inaugural lecture bore the title "De natuur van de aandacht" (The nature of attention; Wageningen University Press, 1991). He is also a university instructor in the Philosophy Department of the Catholic Theological University in Utrecht, and in the Faculty of Theology of the University of Utrecht. His areas of research include hermeneutics, metaphysics, and the philosophy of religion. He has published on Derrida ("Hermeneutiek en deconstructie" [Hermeneutics and deconstruction]), in Theo de Boer and others, *Hermeneutiek. Filosofische grondslagen voor mens- en cultuurwetenschappen* (Amsterdam: Boom, 1988). In 1996 he published, in cooperation with Susanne Lijmbach, *Heidegger en de wereld van het dier* (Heidegger and the world of the animal; Assen: Van Gorcum).

Ilse N. Bulhof was, until her retirement in 1997, a professor of philosophy appointed by the Radboud Foundation at the University of Leiden and also senior university instructor in the Philosophy Department of the Catholic Theological University of Utrecht, and in the Faculty of Theology of the University of Utrecht. She has published books on Nietzsche, Dilthey, and Freud and on the philosophy of science (*The Language of Science: A Study of the Relationship between Literature and Science in the Perspective of a Hermeneutical Ontology. With a Case Study of Darwin's "The Origin of Species"*; Leiden: Brill, 1992). In her research into the possibilities and limits of scientific texts, she is oriented toward a hermeneutical ontology ("Metaphors and Praxis: Reading the Book of Nature, Creating New Worlds, and the Ethical Implications of Knowledge," in *Revue Belge de Philologie et d'Histoire* 68 [1990]). In 1995 she published *Van* *inhoud naar houding. Een nieuwe visie op filosoferen in een pluralistische cultuur* (From content to attitude: A new view of philosophy in a pluralistic culture; Kampen: Kok Agora). At present her primary area of interest is the relation between philosophy and (Western and non-Western) spirituality.

Victor Kal is senior university instructor in philosophy at the Faculty of Theology at the University of Amsterdam. He is the author of *On Intuition and Discursive Reasoning in Aristotle* (Leiden: Brill, 1988). He has published on Kierkegaard and Derrida, and recently on Rosenzweig and Levinas (*Levinas en Rosenzweig. De filosofie en de terugkeer tot de religie* [Levinas and Rosenzweig: Philosophy and the turn to religion]; Zoetermeer: Meinema, 1999). At present he is researching the relationship between rationality and revelation.

Laurens ten Kate holds degrees in theology and philosophy. His dissertation on Bataille's atheology was entitled *De lege plaats. Revoltes tegen het instrumentele leven in Batailles atheologie* (The empty place: Revolts against instrumental life in Bataille's atheology; Kampen: Kok Agora, 1994, summary in French), and was presented to the Catholic Theological University, Utrecht, where he taught for several years. He publishes regularly on the meaning of Bataille's work for modern philosophy and theology. He has also published books and articles on Nietzsche, Foucault, Derrida, Blanchot, Nancy, Lyotard, and Ingeborg Bachmann. Today he is a senior researcher at the Theological University of Kampen, where he is preparing a book on Derrida and Barth concerning the (im)possibilities of a "theology of difference" (see also his "Randgänge der Theologie: Prolegomena einer 'Theologie der Differenz' im Ausgang von Derrida und Barth," in *Zeitschrift für dialektische Theologie* 14, no. 1 [1998]). In the field of political philosophy, especially the critique of modern subjectivity, he published recently "Solidair tegen wil en dank: Singulariteit, pluraliteit en de crisis van het subject" (Unwilling solidarity: Singularity, plurality, and the crisis of the subject), in Theo de Wit and Henk Manschot, eds., *Solidariteit. Filosofische kritiek, ethiek en politiek* (Solidarity: Philosophical critique, ethics, and politics; Amsterdam: Boom, 1999). Besides his university work, he is an editor of philosophy books for the general/academic publishing house Boom, Amsterdam.

Jean-Luc Marion is professor at the Université Paris IV and visiting professor at the University of Chicago. In addition, he is general editor of the series "Épiméthée" published by the Presses Universitaires de France. His most important works include *L'idole et la distance. Cinq études* (Paris: Grasset, 1977; a translation is forthcoming from Fordham University Press), *God without Being: Hors-Texte* (Chicago: University of Chicago Press, 1991; 2nd ed., 1995), *Reduction and Givenness: Investigations of Husserl, Heidegger, and Phenomenology* (Evanston, Ill.: Northwestern University Press, 1998), and *Étant donné: Essai d'une phénoménologie de la donation* (Paris: P.U.F., 1997). In addition he publishes on Descartes, Husserl, and Heidegger. In 1992 he received the Grand Prix de Philosophie de l'Académie Française for his life's work.

Paul Moyaert is a professor of philosophy at the Higher Institute of Philosophy of the Catholic University of Leuven; he is also a member of the Belgian School for Psychoanalysis. His publications most relevant to the theme of this volume include *Mystiek en liefde* [with J. Walgrave] (Mysticism and love; Leuven: Peeters Press/Leuven University Press, 1988), "Theologie, antropologie en theodicee" (Theology, anthropology, and theodicy; in *Wijsgerig perspectief* 30 [1989]), *Ethiek en sublimatie* (Ethics and sublimation; Nijmegen: SUN, 1994), and *De mateloosheid van het christendom. Over naastenliefde, betekenisincarnatie en mystieke liefde* (The excessiveness of Christianity: On the love of one's neighbor, the incarnation of meaning, and mystic love; Nijmegen: SUN, 1998).

Dirk de Schutter holds a doctorate from the Higher Institute of Philosophy of the Catholic University of Leuven. He is a professor of English and philosophy at EHSAL (Brussels). In English, he has published articles on Heidegger, Lacan, Paul de Man, Nicholas Mosley, and John Banville. In Dutch, he has published a collection of essays on the philosophy of art and literature, *De plek van afscheid. Opstellen over kunst* (A place of parting: Essays on art; Kapellen: Pelckmans, 1994), in which he addresses Kant, Hölderlin, Rilke, and Derrida; and an introduction to and translation from French of Derrida's "Violence and Metaphysics" (*Geweld en metafysica* [Kampen/Kapellen: Kok Agora/Pelckmans, 1996]). He also coedited *In het licht van de letter. Zes oefeningen in deconstructie* (Six exercises in deconstruction; Leuven: Peeters, 1988), and was editor-in-chief of the journal *Tmesis*. With Remi Peeters he recently translated Hannah Arendt's essays on political philosophy as *Politiek in donkere tijden. Essays over vrijheid en vriendschap* (On politics in dark times: Essays on freedom and friendship; Boom: Amsterdam, 1999).

Anton Simons holds degrees in theology and philosophy. His dissertation, presented to the Catholic Theological University of Utrecht, was entitled *Carnaval en terreur. De ethische betekenis van Bachtins Rable* (Carnival and terror: The ethical meaning of Bakhtin's "Rable"; diss., Utrecht, 1996, summary in English). He is the author of an introduction to Bakhtin's work, *Het groteske van de taal. Over het werk van Michail Bachtin* (Grotesque language: On Bakhtin's work; Amsterdam: SUA, 1990). Today he is a senior researcher in the Philosophy Department of the University of Nijmegen, where he participates in an international research program on the Russian thinker Solovyov.

Rico Sneller holds degrees in theology and philosophy. In 1998 he presented his dissertation to the Catholic Theological University of Utrecht: *Het Woord is schrift geworden. Derrida en negatieve theologie* (The Word has become Scripture: Derrida on negative theology; Kampen: Kok Agora, 1998, with a summary in English). He translated and wrote an introduction to Derrida's "How to Avoid Speaking: Denials" (*Hoe niet te spreken*; Kampen: Kok Agora/Kapellen: Pelckmans, 1997) and *Sauf le Nom (Post-Scriptum)* (*'God' Anonymus*; Kampen: Kok Agora/Kapellen: Pelckmans, 1998). Today he is a university instructor in the Philosophy Department of the Catholic Theological University of Utrecht.

Gerrit Steunebrink teaches philosophy of religion and philosophy of culture in the Philosophy Department of the Catholic University of Nijmegen. He publishes on topics from the fields of philosophy of religion, metaphysics, esthetics, and multiculturalism. His works on Adorno include his dissertation, *Kunst, utopie en werkelijkheid. Adorno's esthetica en metafysica tegen de achtergrond van Kant en Hegel* (Art, utopia, and reality: Adorno's esthetics and metaphysics against the background of Kant and Hegel; Tilburg: Tilburg University Press, 1991), and "Ars imitatur naturam. Über ein traditionelles

Motiv in Adornos Ästhetik" (Art Imitates Nature: On a traditional motif in Adorno's esthetics), in H.-D. Klein and J. Reikerstorfer, eds., *Philosophia perennis. Erich Heintel zum 80. Geburtstag* (Frankfurt am Main: Lang, 1993).

Marin Terpstra received his doctoral degree in 1990 from the University of Nijmegen for a study of Spinoza's political philosophy entitled *De wending naar de politiek. Een studie over het gebruik van de begrippen "potentia" en "potestas" door Spinoza in het licht van de verhouding tussen ontologie en politieke theorie* (Spinoza's turn toward politics: A study of the concepts 'potentia' and 'potestas' as used by Spinoza, viewed in the light of the relation between ontology and political theory; diss. Nijmegen, 1990, summary in English). Currently, he is a university instructor in the Department of Social and Political Philosophy at the Catholic University of Nijmegen. He has published studies of Hobbes, Bataille, Schmitt, and Spinoza. He is now studying the philosophy of management sciences, and has recently published *Maakbaarheid en beleid. Inleiding tot de filosofie van bestuur en beleid* (Management and the making of the world: An introduction to the management sciences; Nijmegen: SUN, 1998). With Theo de Wit, he is cofounder of *Res Mixtae*, an international research group on political theology. (www.baserv.uci.kun.nl/marinter/resmixtae/docuwebstekken.html).

Hent de Vries received his doctoral degree from the University of Leiden in 1989 for his dissertation entitled *Theologie in pianissimo: zwischen Rationalität und Dekonstruktion. Zur Aktualität der Denkfiguren Adornos und Levinas* (Theology in pianissimo: Between rationality and deconstruction: On the topicality of the concepts of thought in Adorno and Levinas; Kampen: Kok, 1989; an English translation is forthcoming). He has taught at Loyola University (Evanston, Illinois), and is now a professor of philosophy (specializing in metaphysics and its history) in the Department of Philosophy at the University of Amsterdam and chair of the board of the Amsterdam School for Cultural Analysis, Theory, and Interpretation (ASCA). Together with Harry Kunneman, he is coeditor of two volumes of essays, one on the concept of Enlightenment and the other concerning the debate between critical theory and recent French thought. He has just published *Philosophy and the Turn to Religion*

(Baltimore: Johns Hopkins University Press, 1999), a study of the work of Derrida and other contemporary French thinkers. With Samuel Weber, he coedited *Violence, Identity, and Self-Determination* (Stanford University Press, 1997); and with Mieke Bal, he coedits the series *Cultural Memory in the Present* (Stanford University Press). In 2001 his *Horror religiosus* will appear (Johns Hopkins University Press), as well as *Religion and Media*, coedited with Samuel Weber (Stanford University Press).

Jozef Wissink received his doctoral degree in 1984 from the Catholic Theological University of Utrecht. His dissertation bore the title *De inzet van de theologie. Een onderzoek naar de motieven en de geldigheid van Karl Barths strijd tegen de natuurlijke theologie* (A study of the motivations and validity of Karl Barth's criticism of natural theology; Amersfoort: De Horstink, 1984). He is a professor of systematic theology appointed by the Radboud Foundation at the University of Groningen; his inaugural lecture was entitled "Te mooi om onwaar te zijn" (Too beautiful to be untrue; Vught: Radboud Foundation, 1993). He is also a university instructor in the Systematic Theology Department of the Catholic Theological University of Utrecht. He edited *The Eternity of the World* (Leiden: Brill, 1990) and, with Theo Zweerman, coedited *Ruimte van de geest* (The space of the spirit; Kampen: Kok, 1989). At present he is researching the themes of knowledge, will, and ability in Thomas.

Theo de Wit received his doctoral degree in 1992 from the Catholic Theological University of Utrecht. His dissertation bore the title *De onontkoombaarheid van de politiek. De soevereine vijand in de politieke filosofie van Carl Schmitt* (The inevitability of politics: The sovereign enemy in the political philosophy of Carl Schmitt; Ubbergen: Pomppers, 1992, summary in German). He now teaches political philosophy and philosophy of culture in the Philosophy Department of the Catholic Theological University of Utrecht. He has published on Hobbes, Weber, Derrida, Benjamin, Finkielkraut, and Bataille. Today his main fields of research are the demystification of the world and the question of tolerance and autonomy. With Henk Manschot, he coedited *Solidariteit. Filosofische kritiek, ethiek en politiek* (Solidarity: Philosophical critique, ethics, and politics; Amsterdam: Boom, 1999). With Marin Terpstra, he is cofounder of *Res Mixtae*, an international research group on political theology.